CLYMER® MANUALS

YAMAHA

GRIZZLY 660 • 2002-2008

More information available at Clymer.com
Phone: 805-498-6703

Haynes Publishing Group
Sparkford Nr Yeovil
Somerset BA22 7JJ England

Haynes North America, Inc
859 Lawrence Drive
Newbury Park
California 91320 USA

ISBN 10: 1-59969-305-4
ISBN-13: 978-1-59969-305-7
Library of Congress: 2009935571

Author: *Jay Bogart*
Technical Illustrations: *Mitzi McCarthy*
Cover: *Mark Clifford Photography, Los Angeles, California (www.markclifford.com)*
Motorcycle courtesy Simi Valley Cycles, Simi Valley, CA

Printed in Malaysia

M285-2, 4U1, 16-312 **ABCDEFGHIJKLMNOPQR**

Chapter One
General Information 1

Chapter Two
Troubleshooting 2

Chapter Three
Lubrication, Maintenance and Tune-up 3

Chapter Four
Engine Top End 4

Chapter Five
Engine Lower End 5

Chapter Six
Clutch and Sheaves 6

Chapter Seven
Transmission and Shift Mechanisms 7

Chapter Eight
Fuel System 8

Chapter Nine
Electrical System 9

Chapter Ten
Cooling System 10

Chapter Eleven
Front Suspension and Steering 11

Chapter Twelve
Front Axles and Differential 12

Chapter Thirteen
Rear Suspension 13

Chapter Fourteen
Rear Axles and Final Drive 14

Chapter Fifteen
Brakes 15

Chapter Sixteen
Body 16

Index 17

Wiring Diagrams 18

Common spark plug conditions

NORMAL

Symptoms: Brown to grayish-tan color and slight electrode wear. Correct heat range for engine and operating conditions.
Recommendation: When new spark plugs are installed, replace with plugs of the same heat range.

WORN

Symptoms: Rounded electrodes with a small amount of deposits on the firing end. Normal color. Causes hard starting in damp or cold weather and poor fuel economy.
Recommendation: Plugs have been left in the engine too long. Replace with new plugs of the same heat range. Follow the recommended maintenance schedule.

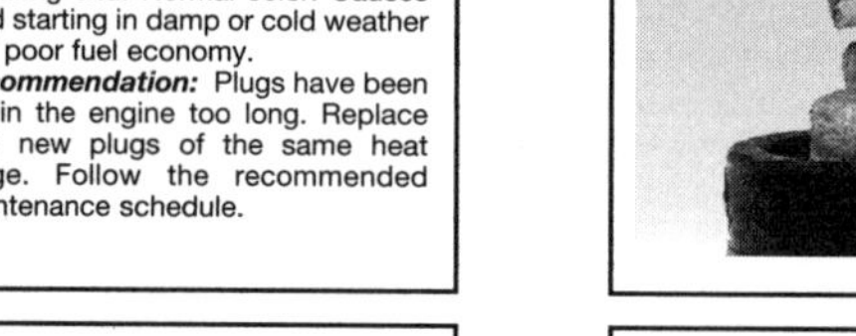

CARBON DEPOSITS

Symptoms: Dry sooty deposits indicate a rich mixture or weak ignition. Causes misfiring, hard starting and hesitation.
Recommendation: Make sure the plug has the correct heat range. Check for a clogged air filter or problem in the fuel system or engine management system. Also check for ignition system problems.

ASH DEPOSITS

Symptoms: Light brown deposits encrusted on the side or center electrodes or both. Derived from oil and/or fuel additives. Excessive amounts may mask the spark, causing misfiring and hesitation during acceleration.
Recommendation: If excessive deposits accumulate over a short time or low mileage, install new valve guide seals to prevent seepage of oil into the combustion chambers. Also try changing gasoline brands.

OIL DEPOSITS

Symptoms: Oily coating caused by poor oil control. Oil is leaking past worn valve guides or piston rings into the combustion chamber. Causes hard starting, misfiring and hesitation.
Recommendation: Correct the mechanical condition with necessary repairs and install new plugs.

GAP BRIDGING

Symptoms: Combustion deposits lodge between the electrodes. Heavy deposits accumulate and bridge the electrode gap. The plug ceases to fire, resulting in a dead cylinder.
Recommendation: Locate the faulty plug and remove the deposits from between the electrodes.

TOO HOT

Symptoms: Blistered, white insulator, eroded electrode and absence of deposits. Results in shortened plug life.
Recommendation: Check for the correct plug heat range, over-advanced ignition timing, lean fuel mixture, intake manifold vacuum leaks, sticking valves and insufficient engine cooling.

PREIGNITION

Symptoms: Melted electrodes. Insulators are white, but may be dirty due to misfiring or flying debris in the combustion chamber. Can lead to engine damage.
Recommendation: Check for the correct plug heat range, over-advanced ignition timing, lean fuel mixture, insufficient engine cooling and lack of lubrication.

HIGH SPEED GLAZING

Symptoms: Insulator has yellowish, glazed appearance. Indicates that combustion chamber temperatures have risen suddenly during hard acceleration. Normal deposits melt to form a conductive coating. Causes misfiring at high speeds.
Recommendation: Install new plugs. Consider using a colder plug if driving habits warrant.

DETONATION

Symptoms: Insulators may be cracked or chipped. Improper gap setting techniques can also result in a fractured insulator tip. Can lead to piston damage.
Recommendation: Make sure the fuel anti-knock values meet engine requirements. Use care when setting the gaps on new plugs. Avoid lugging the engine.

MECHANICAL DAMAGE

Symptoms: May be caused by a foreign object in the combustion chamber or the piston striking an incorrect reach (too long) plug. Causes a dead cylinder and could result in piston damage.
Recommendation: Repair the mechanical damage. Remove the foreign object from the engine and/or install the correct reach plug.

CONTENTS

QUICK REFERENCE DATA . . . . **IX**

CHAPTER ONE
GENERAL INFORMATION **1**

Manual organization
Warnings, cautions and notes
Safety
Serial numbers
Fasteners
Shop supplies
Tools
Measuring tools
Electrical system fundamentals
Service methods
Storage
Specifications

CHAPTER TWO
TROUBLESHOOTING **28**

Water damage
Starting the engine
Engine spark test
Electrical testing
Engine starting system
Engine performance
Engine noise
Frame noise
Leakdown test
Transmission
Axles, differential and final drive units
Drive shafts and middle gear unit
Brake system
Steering and handling

CHAPTER THREE
LUBRICATION, MAINTENANCE AND TUNE-UP . . . 41

Pre-ride inspection
Engine break-in
Battery
Engine oil and filter
Final drive
Front differential
Air filter
Front drive shaft lubrication
Rear suspension pivot lubrication
Control cable lubrication
Fastener inspection
Speed limiter adjustment
Axle boot inspection
Drain inspection
Cooling system
Exhaust system
Fuel system
Drive belt inspection
Control cable adjustment
Brake system
Tire inspection
Tune-up
Valve clearance
Carburetor adjustment
Ignition timing
Compression test
Spark plug
Specifications

CHAPTER FOUR
ENGINE TOP END . . . 67

Exhaust system
Cylinder head cover
Camshaft and cam chain tensioner
Cylinder head
Valves
Cylinder
Piston and piston rings
Specifications

CHAPTER FIVE
ENGINE LOWER END . . . 95

Engine
Recoil starter
Balancer and oil pump gears
Cam chain and rear guide
Crankcase
Crankcase seal replacement
Crankcase bearing replacement
Engine balancer
Oil pump
Crankshaft
Middle gear assembly
Middle gear assembly shim and lash adjustment
Specifications

CHAPTER SIX
CLUTCH AND SHEAVES . . . 126

Drive belt cover
Outer bearing housing
Drive belt inspection and replacement
Primary and secondary sheaves
Right crankcase cover
Clutch
Specifications

CHAPTER SEVEN
TRANSMISSION AND SHIFT MECHANISMS . . . 139

Select lever assembly
Select lever cable replacement
External shift mechanism
Transmission
Shift drum and forks
Specifications

CHAPTER EIGHT
FUEL SYSTEM 151

Carburetor
Fuel valve
Throttle cable replacement
Specifications

CHAPTER NINE
ELECTRICAL SYSTEM. 165

Electrical component replacement
Ignition and charging system operation
Alternator cover
Stator and pickup coil
Rotor, starter clutch and starter gears
Starter
Starting system switches
Ignition system
Charging system
Fan system
Coolant temperature warning system
Four-wheel drive relays and gear motor
Indicator circuits
Switches
Headlights
Taillight
Specifications

CHAPTER TEN
COOLING SYSTEM. 185

Cooling system safety
Radiator and fan
Fan sending unit
Coolant temperature sending unit
Thermostat
Water pump
Specifications

CHAPTER ELEVEN
FRONT SUSPENSION AND STEERING 193

Front wheel
Front hub
Tie rods
Steering knuckle
Control arms
Shock absorbers
Steering shaft
Handlebar
Tires
Wheel runout
Specifications

CHAPTER TWELVE
FRONT AXLES AND DIFFERENTIAL 212

Front axles
Differential
Front drive shaft
Specifications

CHAPTER THIRTEEN
REAR SUSPENSION 228

Rear wheel
Rear hub
Rear knuckle
Stabilizer
Control arms
Shock absorbers
Specifications

CHAPTER FOURTEEN
REAR AXLES AND FINAL DRIVE 237

Rear axles
Final drive unit
Specifications

CHAPTER FIFTEEN
BRAKES 253

Brake operation
Brake service
Front brake pads
Front brake caliper
Front master cylinder
Rear brake pads
Rear brake caliper
Rear master cylinder
Left hand brake cable replacement
Brake system draining
Brake system bleeding
Brake disc
Specifications

CHAPTER SIXTEEN
BODY 279

Body panel fasteners
Seat
Fuel tank side panels
Fuel tank cover and fuel tank
Engine side cover and side panel
Front carrier
Front fender hood
Front bumper and skid plate
Front grille and lights
Front fender assembly
Rear carrier and fender panel
Rear fender
Footrest panels
Center and rear skid plates

INDEX 289

WIRING DIAGRAMS 295

QUICK REFERENCE DATA

ATV INFORMATION

MODEL:______________________________ YEAR:______________

VIN NUMBER:______________________________

ENGINE SERIAL NUMBER:______________________________

CARBURETOR SERIAL NUMBER OR I.D. MARK:______________________________

TIRE AND WHEEL SPECIFICATIONS

Tires	
Type	Tubeless radial
Sizes	
Front	AT25 × 8-12 Dunlop KT131
Rear	AT25 × 10-12 Dunlop KT135
Tire pressure (cold)	
Front	
Standard	35 kPa (5.1 psi)
Minimum	32 kPa (4.6 psi)
Maximum	38 kPa (5.5 psi)
Rear	
Standard	30 kPa (4.4 psi)
Minimum	27 kPa (3.9 psi)
Maximum	33 kPa (4.8 psi)
Bead seating pressure	250 kPa (36.3 psi) maximum
Tire wear limit	3 mm (0.12 in.)
Wheels	
Size	
Front	12 × 6.0 AT
Rear	12 × 7.5 AT
Runout (radial and lateral)	2 mm (0.08 in.)

LUBRICANT RECOMMENDATIONS AND CAPACITIES

Air filter	Foam air filter oil
Brake fluid	DOT 4
Control cables	Cable lube
Cooling system	
Capacity	
Radiator	0.78 L (0.82 U.S. qt.)
Reserve tank	0.3 L (0.32 U.S. qt.)
Total (including engine passages)	1.8 L (1.9 U.S. qt.)
Coolant	
Type	Ethylene glycol antifreeze containing anti-corrosion inhibitors for aluminum engines
Mixture ratio	50:50 antifreeze:distilled water
Fuel	
Type	Unleaded gasoline
Octane rating (minimum)	86 (R+M/2) or 91 RON
Tank capacity	
Main	20 liters (5.3 U.S. gal.)
Reserve	3.5 liters (0.92 U.S. gal.)

(continued)

LUBRICANT RECOMMENDATIONS AND CAPACITIES (continued)

Oil	
Differential	Hypoid gear oil
Grade	API-rated GL 4
Viscosity	SAE 80
Capacity	
Change	0.28 L (0.30 U.S. qt.)
Total	0.33 L (0.35 U.S. qt.)
Engine	Four-stroke engine oil
Grade	API-rated SG
Viscosity	
Below 0° C (30° F)	SAE 5W-30
0°-35° C (30°-100° F)	SAE 10W-30
5°-45° C (40°-120° F)	SAE 20W-40
Capacity	
Without filter change	1.9 L (2.0 U.S. qt.)
With filter change	2.0 L (2.1 U.S. qt.)
Total	2.2 L (2.3 U.S. qt.)
Final drive	Hypoid gear oil
Grade	API-rated GL 4
Viscosity	SAE 80
Capacity	
Change	0.25 L (0.26 U.S. qt.)
Total	0.30 L (0.32 U.S. qt.)

MAINTENANCE AND TUNE-UP SPECIFICATIONS

Battery	YTX20L-BS, 12 volt, 18 amp-hour
Brakes	
Brake pad lining minimum thickness	1.0 mm (0.040 in.)
Rear brake lever free play	0.5-2 mm (0.02-0.08 in.)
Rear brake pedal height	45 mm (1.8 in.)
Choke cable service limit	15 mm (0.6 in.) range from extreme right to extreme left
Compression	
Standard	1324 kPa (192 psi)
Minimum	1150 kPa (167 psi)
Maximum	1480 kPa (215 psi)
Cooling system pressure test (maximum)	137 kPa (20 psi)
Drive belt width	33.2 mm (1.31 in.)
Service limit	29.9 mm (1.18 in.)
Idle speed	1450-1550 rpm
Ignition timing*	12° BTDC at 1500 rpm
Intake vacuum	30.7-33.3 kPa (9.07-9.83 in. Hg)
Pilot mixture screw (initial setting)	2-1/2 turns out
Radiator cap relief pressure	93.3-122.7 kPa (13.5-17.8 psi)
Spark plug	
Type	NGK DPR8EA-9
Gap	0.8-0.9 mm (0.032-0.035 in.)
Speed limiter screw length (standard)	12 mm (0.47 in.)
Throttle lever free play	3-5 mm (0.12-0.20 in.)
Tire pressure (cold)	
Front	
Standard	35 kPa (5.1 psi)
Minimum	32 kPa (4.6 psi)
Maximum	38 kPa (5.5 psi)
Rear	
Standard	30 kPa (4.4 psi)
Minimum	27 kPa (3.9 psi)
Maximum	33 kPa (4.8 psi)
Toe-in	0-10 mm (0-0.40 in.)
Wear limit	3 mm (0.12 in.)

(continued)

MAINTENANCE AND TUNE-UP SPECIFICATIONS (continued)

Valve clearance (cold)	
Intake	0.10-0.15 mm (0.004-0.006 in.)
Exhaust	0.15-0.20 mm (0.006-0.008 in.)
Wheel runout (radial and lateral)	2 mm (0.08 in.)
*Not adjustable.	

MAINTENANCE TORQUE SPECIFICATIONS

	N•m	in.-lb.	ft.-lb.
Coolant drain plug	10	89	–
Crankcase oil drain plug	30	–	22
Differential			
Oil drain plug	10	89	–
Oil fill plug	23	–	17
Final drive oil drain/fill plugs	23	–	17
Oil filter cartridge	17	–	13
Oil gallery bolt	7	62	–
Recoil starter housing bolts	14	–	10
Spark plugs	18	–	13
Valve adjuster locknuts	14	–	10
Valve cover bolts			
Exhaust	12	106	–
Intake	10	89	–

CHAPTER ONE

GENERAL INFORMATION

This detailed and comprehensive manual covers the 2002-2009 Yamaha Grizzly ATV.

MANUAL ORGANIZATION

A shop manual is a tool and as in all Clymer manuals, the text provides complete information on maintenance, tune-up, repair and overhaul. Hundreds of original photographs and illustrations created during a complete disassembly of the ATV guide the reader through every job.

All procedures are in step-by-step form and designed for the reader who may be working on the machine for the first time. The chapters are thumb-tabbed for easy reference. Main topic headings are listed in the table of contents and the index.

Frequently used specifications from individual chapters are summarized in the *Quick Reference Data* section at the front of the manual.

During some of the procedures there are references to headings in other chapters or sections of the manual. When a specific heading is called out in a step it will be *italicized.* If a subheading is indicated as being "in this section," it is located under the same main topic heading. For example, the subheading *Handling Gasoline Safely* is located under the main heading *Safety*.

This chapter provides general information on shop safety, tool use, service fundamentals and shop supplies. **Tables 1-6** at the end of the chapter, provide the following:

1. ATV dimensions and weight.
2. Conversion formulas.
3. Technical abbreviations.
4. Metric tap and drill sizes.
5. Metric, decimal and fractional equivalents.
6. Torque recommendations.

Chapter Two provides methods for quick and accurate diagnosis of problems. Troubleshooting procedures present typical symptoms and logical methods to pinpoint and repair the problem.

Chapter Three explains routine maintenance and recommended tune-up procedures.

Subsequent chapters describe specific systems such as engine, transmission, clutch, drive system, fuel and exhaust systems, suspension and brakes. Metric and U.S. standard specifications are located at the end of each applicable chapter.

WARNINGS, CAUTIONS AND NOTES

The terms, WARNING, CAUTION and NOTE each have specific meanings in this manual.

A WARNING emphasizes areas where injury or even death could result from negligence. Mechanical damage may also occur. WARNINGS *are to be taken seriously*.

A CAUTION emphasizes areas where equipment damage could result. Disregarding a CAUTION could cause permanent mechanical damage, though injury is unlikely.

A NOTE provides additional information to make a step or procedure easier or clearer. Disregarding a NOTE could cause inconvenience but most likely would not cause equipment damage or personal injury.

SAFETY

Follow these guidelines and practice common sense to safely service the machine.

1. Do not operate the machine in an enclosed area. The exhaust gasses contain carbon monoxide, an odorless, colorless, and tasteless poisonous gas. Carbon monoxide levels build quickly in small enclosed areas and can cause unconsciousness and death in a short time. Properly ventilate the work area, or operate the machine outside.
2. *Never* use gasoline or any extremely flammable liquid to clean parts. Refer to *Cleaning Parts* and *Handling Gasoline Safely* in this section.
3. *Never* smoke or use a torch in the vicinity of flammable liquids, such as gasoline or cleaning solvent.
4. If welding or brazing on the machine, move the fuel tank a safe distance away from the work area.
5. Do not remove the radiator cap or cooling system hoses while the engine is hot. The cooling system is pressurized, and high-temperature coolant can cause injury.
6. Dispose of and store coolant in a safe manner. Do not allow children or pets access to open containers of coolant. Animals are attracted to antifreeze.
7. Avoid contact with engine oil and other chemicals. Most are known carcinogens. Wash your hands thoroughly after coming in contact with engine oil. If possible, wear a pair of disposable gloves.
8. Use the correct type and size of tools to avoid damaging fasteners.
9. Keep tools clean and in good condition. Replace or repair worn or damaged equipment.
10. When loosening a tight fastener, be careful not to let the tool slip.
11. When replacing fasteners, check that the new fasteners are of the same size and strength as the original ones.
12. Keep the work area clean and organized.
13. Wear eye protection *anytime* eye injury is possible. This includes procedures involving drilling, grinding, hammering, compressed air and chemicals.
14. Wear the correct clothing for the job. Tie up or cover long hair so it cannot get caught in moving equipment.
15. Do not carry sharp tools in clothing pockets.

16. Always have an approved fire extinguisher available. Check that it is rated for gasoline (Class B) and electrical (Class C) fires.
17. Do not use compressed air to clean clothes, the machine or the work area. Debris may be blown into the eyes or skin. *Never* direct compressed air at yourself or others. Do not allow children to use or play with any compressed air equipment.
18. When using compressed air to dry rotating parts, hold the part so it cannot rotate. Do not allow the force of the air to spin the part. The air jet is capable of rotating parts at extreme speed. The part may be damaged or disintegrate, causing serious injury.
19. Do not inhale the dust created by brake pad and clutch wear. In most cases these particles contain asbestos. In addition, some types of insulating materials and gaskets may contain asbestos. Inhaling asbestos particles is dangerous.
20. Never work on the machine while someone is working under it.
21. When placing the machine on a stand, check that it is secure.

Handling Gasoline Safely

Gasoline is a volatile, flammable liquid and is one of the most dangerous materials in the shop. Keep in mind that when working on a machine, gasoline is always present in the fuel tank, fuel line and carburetor. To avoid an accident when working around the fuel system, carefully observe the following precautions:

1. *Never* use gasoline to clean parts. See *Cleaning Parts* in this section.
2. When working on the fuel system, work outside or in a well-ventilated area.
3. Do not add fuel to the fuel tank or service the fuel system while the machine is near open flames, sparks or where someone is smoking. Gasoline vapor is heavier than air; it collects in low areas and is more easily ignited than liquid gasoline.

4. Allow the engine to cool completely before working on any fuel system component.
5. Do not store gasoline in glass containers. If the glass breaks, a serious explosion or fire may occur.
6. Immediately wipe up spilled gasoline. Store the contaminated shop cloths in a metal container with a lid until they can be properly disposed, or place them outside in a safe place for the fuel to evaporate.
7. Do not pour water onto a gasoline fire. Water spreads the fire and makes it more difficult to put out. Use a class B, BC or ABC fire extinguisher to extinguish the fire.
8. Always turn off the engine before refueling. Avoid spilling fuel onto the engine or exhaust system. Do not overfill the fuel tank. Leave air space at the top of the tank to allow room for the fuel to expand due to temperature fluctuations.

Cleaning Parts

Cleaning parts is one of the more time-consuming jobs performed in the home shop. There are many types of chemical cleaners and solvents available for shop use. Most are poisonous and extremely flammable. To prevent chemical exposure, vapor buildup, fire and serious injury, observe each product warning label and note the following:

1. Read and observe the entire product label before using any chemical. Always know what type of chemical is being used and whether it is poisonous and/or flammable.
2. Do not use more than one type of cleaning solvent at a time. If mixing chemicals is called for, measure the proper amounts according to the manufacturer.
3. Work in a well-ventilated area.
4. Wear chemical-resistant gloves.
5. Wear safety glasses.
6. Wear a vapor respirator when necessary.
7. Wash hands and arms thoroughly after cleaning parts.
8. Keep chemical products away from children and pets.
9. Thoroughly clean all oil, grease and cleaner residue from any part that must be heated.
10. Use a nylon brush when cleaning parts. Wire brushes may cause a spark.
11. When using a parts washer, only use the solvent recommended by the manufacturer. Check that the parts washer is equipped with a metal lid that will lower in case of fire.

Warning Labels

The manufacturer's labels contain important safety, operating, servicing, transporting and storage instructions. Refer to the owner's manual for the description and location of labels. Order replacement labels from the manufacturer if they are missing or damaged.

SERIAL NUMBERS

A serial number is stamped on the frame and a label is affixed to the frame, under the seat. Record these numbers in the *Quick Reference Data* section at the front of the manual. Have these numbers available when ordering parts.

The vehicle identification number (VIN) is stamped on the front left frame near the air duct drain (**Figure 1**).

The vehicle model label is on the frame under the seat (**Figure 2**).

FASTENERS

WARNING
Do not install fasteners with a strength classification lower than what was originally installed by the manufacturer. Doing so may cause equipment failure and/or damage.

CAUTION
To ensure that fastener threads are not mismatched or become cross-threaded, start all fasteners by hand. If a fastener is hard to start or turn, determine the cause before tightening with a wrench.

Threaded Fasteners

Threaded fasteners secure most of the components on the machine. Most are tightened by turning them clockwise (right-hand threads). If the normal rotation of the component being tightened would loosen the fastener, it may have left-hand threads. If a left-hand threaded fastener is used, it is noted in the text.

Two dimensions are required to match the thread size of the fastener: the number of threads in a given distance and the outside diameter of the threads.

Two systems are currently used to specify threaded fastener dimensions: the U.S. Standard system and the metric system (**Figure 3**). Pay particular attention when working with unidentified fasteners; mismatching thread types can damage threads.

The length (L) (**Figure 4**), diameter (D) and pitch, or distance between thread crests (T), classify metric screws and bolts. A typical bolt may be identified by the numbers, 8—1.25 × 130. This indicates the bolt has a diameter of 8 mm, the distance between thread crests is 1.25 mm and the length is 130 mm. Always measure bolt length as shown by L (**Figure 4**) to avoid purchasing replacements of the wrong length.

The numbers located on the top of the fastener (**Figure 4**) indicate the strength of metric screws and bolts. The higher the number, the stronger the fastener. Unnumbered fasteners are the weakest.

Many screws, bolts and studs are combined with nuts to secure particular components. To indicate the size of a nut, manufacturers specify the internal diameter and the thread pitch.

The measurement across two flats on a nut or bolt is the wrench size.

Torque Specifications

The materials used in the manufacture of the machine may be subjected to uneven stresses if the fasteners of the various subassemblies are not installed and tightened correctly. Fasteners that are improperly installed or that work loose can cause extensive damage. It is essential to use an accurate torque wrench, described in this chapter, with the torque specifications in this manual.

Specifications for torque are provided in Newton-meters (N•m), foot-pounds (ft.-lb.) and inch-pounds (in.-lb.). Refer to the torque specifications at the end of each applicable chapter for specific fastener applications. If a fastener is not listed, refer to **Table 6** at the end of this chapter for torque recommendations based on fastener size.

Self-Locking Fasteners

Several types of bolts, screws and nuts incorporate a system that creates interference between the two fasteners. Interference is achieved in various ways. The most common type is the nylon insert nut and a dry adhesive coating on the threads of a bolt.

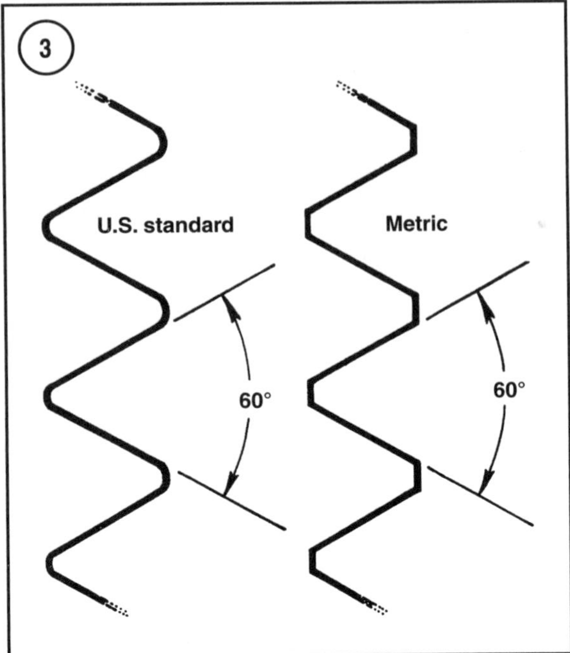

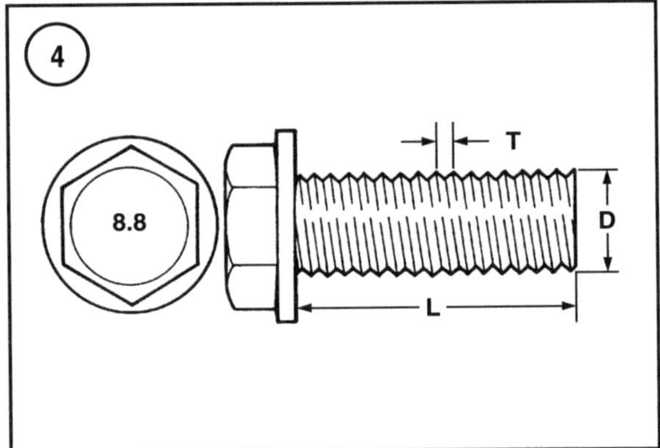

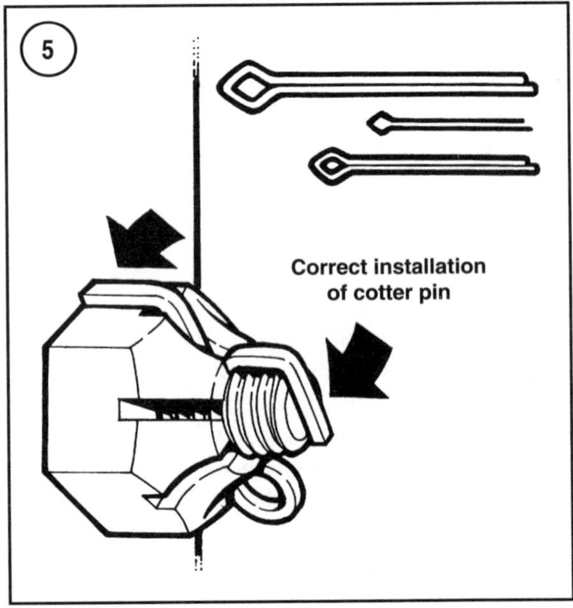

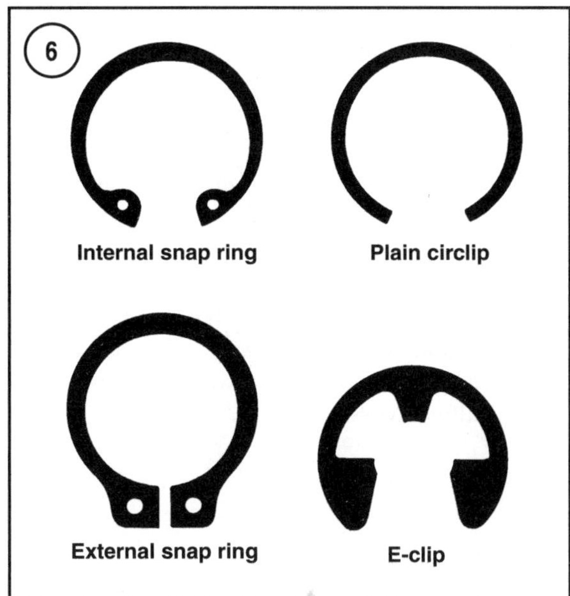

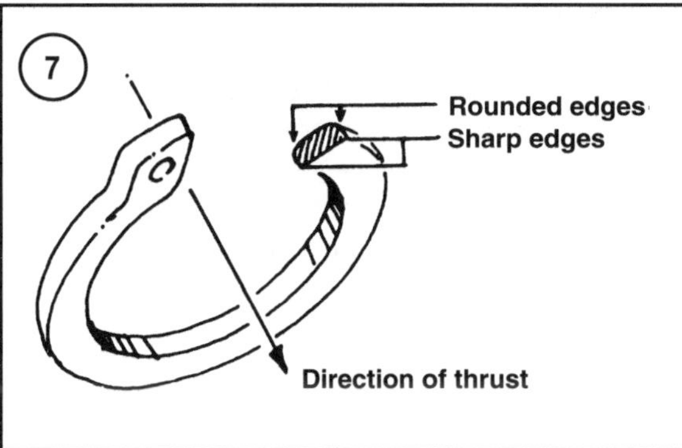

Self-locking fasteners offer greater holding strength than standard fasteners, which improves their resistance to vibration. Most self-locking fasteners cannot be reused. The materials used to form the lock become distorted after the initial installation and removal. It is a good practice to replace self-locking fasteners after their removal. Do not replace self-locking fasteners with standard fasteners.

Washers

There are two basic types of washers: flat washers and lockwashers. Flat washers are simple discs with a hole to fit a screw or bolt. Lockwashers are used to prevent a fastener from working loose. Washers can be used as spacers and seals, or to help distribute fastener load and to prevent the fastener from damaging the component.

As with fasteners, when replacing washers check that the replacement washers are of the same design and quality.

Cotter Pins

A cotter pin is a split metal pin inserted into a hole or slot to prevent a fastener from loosening. In certain applications, such as the rear axle on an ATV or motorcycle, the fastener must be secured in this way. For these applications, a cotter pin and castellated (slotted) nut is used.

To use a cotter pin, first make sure the diameter is correct for the hole in the fastener. After correctly tightening the fastener and aligning the holes, insert the cotter pin through the hole and bend the ends over the fastener as shown in **Figure 5**. Unless instructed to do so, never loosen a torqued fastener to align the holes. If the holes do not align, tighten the fastener just enough to achieve alignment.

Cotter pins are available in various diameters and lengths. Measure length from the bottom of the head to the tip of the shortest pin.

Snap Rings and E-clips

Snap rings (**Figure 6**) are circular metal retaining clips. They are required to secure parts and gears in place on parts such as shafts, pins or rods. External type snap rings are used to retain items on shafts. Internal type snap rings secure parts within housing bores. In some applications, in addition to securing the component(s), snap rings of varying thickness also determine end play. These are usually called selective snap rings.

Two basic types of snap rings are used: stamped and machined snap rings. Stamped snap rings (**Figure 7**) are manufactured with a sharp edge and a round edge. When installing a stamped snap ring in a thrust application, install the sharp edge facing away from the part producing the thrust. Machined snap rings can be installed in either direction, since both faces have sharp edges.

E-clips are used in some applications. Remove E-clips with a flat blade screwdriver by prying between the shaft and E-clip. To install an E-clip, center it over the shaft groove and push or tap it into place.

Observe the following when installing snap rings:

1. Remove and install snap rings with snap ring pliers.
2. In some applications, it may be necessary to replace snap rings after removing them.
3. Compress or expand snap rings only enough to install them. If overly expanded, they lose their retaining ability.
4. After installing a snap ring, check that it seats completely.
5. Wear eye protection when removing and installing snap rings.

SHOP SUPPLIES

The following section describes typical shop supplies. Make sure to follow the manufacturer's recommendations for lubricant types.

Recycling

Do-it-yourself maintenance and repair come with a responsibility to properly dispose of vehicle and shop waste products. These include: engine and transmission oils, oil filters, coolant (a petroleum product), hydraulic fluids, batteries and any cleaning chemicals. Many local and regional organizations provide collection centers for these waste products.

Lubricants and Fluids

Engine oils

Engine oil for four-stroke ATV or motorcycle engines is classified by two standards: the American Petroleum Institute (API) service classification and the Society of Automotive Engineers (SAE) viscosity rating. Some oils may also have passed the T903 Standard for friction, performed by the Japanese Automobile Standards Organization (JASO). These standards are indicated on the oil container label.

Two letters indicate the API service classification. The service classification indicates that the oil meets specific lubrication standards. The first letter in the classification *S* indicates that the oil is for gasoline engines. The second letter indicates the standard the oil satisfies.

If an oil meets the JASO standards for four-stroke ATV and motorcycle engines, there will be a registration number and certification rating on the container. The certifications are MA (high friction applications) and MB (low friction applications).

Always use an oil with a classification recommended by the manufacturer. Using an oil with a classification different than that recommended may cause engine damage.

The SAE viscosity rating is an indication of the oil's ability to lubricate and circulate at specific temperatures. The index number also indicates the oil's viscosity. The higher the index number, the higher the viscosity of the oil. The SAE viscosity rating for a single-grade oil is indicated by a single number (SAE 30 for example). The index numbers for a multigrade oil will indicate a range (SAE 10W-40, for example). The *W* (for winter) after the first number indicates the low-temperature viscosity.

The engine requires a multigrade oil with an SAE rating of 20W-40. Other grades are acceptable for lower temperatures. The API service classification should be SG or higher.

Greases

Grease is lubricating oil with thickening agents added to it. The National Lubricating Grease Institute (NLGI) grades grease. Grades range from No. 000 to No. 6, with No. 6 being the thickest. Typical multipurpose grease is NLGI No. 2. For specific applications, manufacturers may recommend water-resistant type grease or one with an additive such as molybdenum disulfide (MoS_2).

Gear oil

Gear oil is used in transmissions and drive axles. As with engine oils, gear oils receive a service classification and viscosity rating from the American Petroleum Institute (API). Follow the manufacturer's recommendations when choosing gear oil. Most manufacturers recommend gear oil that meets the GL-5 hypoid gear oil standard.

The differential and final drive unit require hypoid gear oil. This type of lubricant is capable of lubricating under extreme pressure conditions

Air filter oil

Filter oil is specifically designed for foam air filters. The oil is blended with additives making it easy to pour and apply evenly to the filter. Some filter oils include additives that evaporate quickly, making the filter oil very tacky. This allows the oil to remain suspended within the foam pores, trapping dirt and preventing it from being drawn into the engine.

Do not use engine oil as a substitute for foam filter oil. Engine oils will not remain in the filter. Instead, they will be drawn into the engine, leaving the filter ineffective.

Use a good-quality lithium-based grease to lubricate components requiring grease. Some components require the extreme-pressure qualities of molybdenum disulfide grease or the protective qualities of waterproof grease. Grease components frequently to purge water and grit from them and to extend their service life.

Control cable lubricant

Use lithium grease to lubricate the control cable pivots. Lubricate the cable with light oil or a commercial cable lubricant.

Brake fluid

WARNING
Never put a mineral-based (petroleum) oil into the brake system. Mineral oil will cause rubber parts in the system to swell and break apart, causing brake failure.

Brake fluid is a hydraulic fluid that transmits hydraulic pressure (force) to the wheel brakes. Brake fluid is classified by the Department of Transportation (DOT). This classification appears on the fluid container.

Each type of brake fluid has its own definite characteristics. Do not mix different types of brake fluid. Silicone-based fluid is not compatible with other fluids or in systems for which it was not designed. Mixing silicone fluid with other fluids may cause brake system failure. When adding brake fluid, *only* use the fluid recommended by the manufacturer.

Brake fluid will damage any plastic, painted or plated surface it contacts. Use extreme care when working with brake fluid and remove any spills immediately with soap and water.

Hydraulic brake systems require clean and moisture-free brake fluid. Never reuse brake fluid. Keep containers and reservoirs tightly sealed.

Coolant

Coolant is a mixture of water and antifreeze used to dissipate engine heat. Ethylene glycol is the most common form of antifreeze. Check the manufacturer's recommendations when selecting an antifreeze; most require one specifically designed for aluminum engines. These types of antifreezes have additives that inhibit corrosion.

Only mix distilled water with antifreeze. Impurities in tap water may damage internal cooling system passages.

Cleaners, Degreasers and Solvents

Many chemicals are available to remove oil, grease and other residue from the machine.

Before using cleaning solvents, consider how they will be used and disposed of, particularly if they are not water-soluble. Local ordinances may require special procedures for the disposal of many types of cleaning chemicals. Refer to *Safety* in this chapter.

Use brake parts cleaner to clean brake components wherever contact with petroleum-based products will damage seals. Brake parts cleaner leaves no residue. Use electrical contact cleaner to clean electrical connections and components without leaving any residue. Carburetor cleaner is a strong solvent used to remove fuel deposits and varnish from fuel system components. Use this cleaner carefully, as it may damage some finishes.

Generally, degreasers are strong cleaners used to remove heavy accumulations of grease from engine and frame components.

Most solvents are designed to be used in a parts washing cabinet for individual component cleaning. For safety, use only nonflammable or high flash-point solvents.

Gasket Sealant

Sealant is used in combination with a gasket or seal. Follow the manufacturer's recommendation when using a sealant. Use extreme care when choosing a sealant other than the type recommended. Choose sealant based on its resistance to heat, various fluids and its sealing capabilities.

A common sealant is RTV, or room temperature vulcanizing sealant. This sealant cures at room temperature over a specific time period. This allows the repositioning of components without damaging gaskets.

Moisture in the air causes the RTV sealant to cure. Always install the tube cap after applying RTV sealant. RTV sealant has a limited shelf life and will not cure properly if the shelf life has expired. Keep partial tubes sealed and discard them if they have surpassed the expiration date.

Applying RTV sealant

Clean all gasket residue from the mating surfaces. Remove all gasket material from the blind threaded holes to prevent inaccurate bolt torque. Spray the mating surfaces with aerosol parts cleaner and then wipe with a lint-free cloth. The area must be clean for the sealant to adhere.

Apply RTV sealant in a continuous bead 2-3 mm (0.08-0.12 in.) thick. Circle all the fastener holes unless otherwise specified. Do not allow any sealant to enter these holes. Assemble and tighten the fasteners to the specified torque within the time frame recommended by the RTV sealant manufacturer.

Gasket Remover

Aerosol gasket remover can help remove stubborn gaskets. This product can speed up the removal process and prevent damage to the mating surface that may be caused by using a scraping tool. Most of these types of products are very caustic. Follow the manufacturer's instructions for use carefully.

Threadlocking Compound

CAUTION
Threadlocking compounds damage most plastics. Use caution when using these products in areas where there are plastic components.

Threadlocking compound is a fluid applied to the threads of fasteners. After tightening the fastener, the fluid sets and becomes a solid filler between the threads. This makes it difficult for the fastener to work loose from vibration or heat expansion and contraction. Some threadlocking compounds also provide a seal against fluid leaks.

Before applying threadlocking compound, remove any old compound from both thread areas and clean them with aerosol parts cleaner. Use the compound sparingly. Excess fluid can run into adjoining parts.

Threadlocking compounds are available in a wide range of compounds for various strength, temperature and repair applications. Follow the manufacturer's recommendations regarding compound selection.

TOOLS

Most of the procedures in this manual can be carried out with simple hand tools and test equipment. Always use the correct tools for the job at hand. Keep tools organized and clean. Store them in a tool chest with related tools organized together.

Quality tools are essential. The best are constructed of high-strength alloy steel. These tools are light, easy to use and resistant to wear. Their working surface is devoid of sharp edges and is carefully polished. They have an easy-to-clean finish and are comfortable to use. Quality tools are a good investment.

Some of the procedures in this manual specify special tools. In many cases the tool is illustrated in use. Home mechanics with a large tool kit may be able to use a suitable substitute or fabricate a suitable replacement. However, in some cases, the specialized equipment or expertise may make it impractical for the home mechanic to attempt the procedure. When necessary, such operations come with the recommendation to have a dealership or specialist perform the task. It may be less expensive to have a professional perform these jobs, especially when considering the cost of equipment.

The manufacturer's part number is provided for many of the tools mentioned in this manual. These part numbers are correct at the time of first edition publication. The publisher cannot guarantee the part numbers or tools listed in this manual will be available in the future.

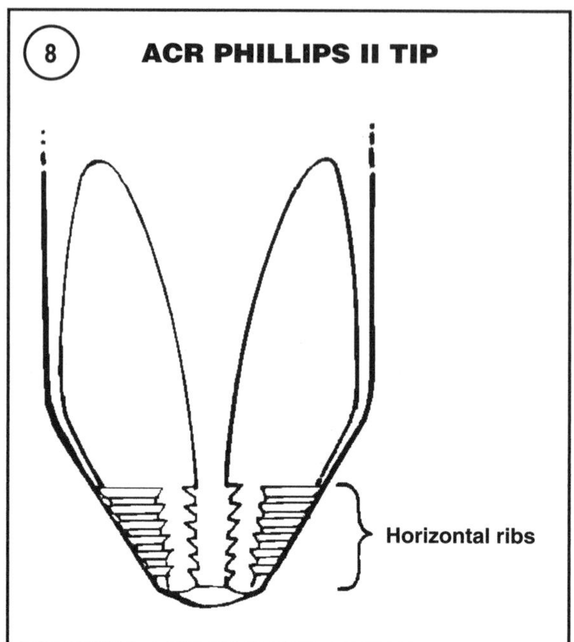

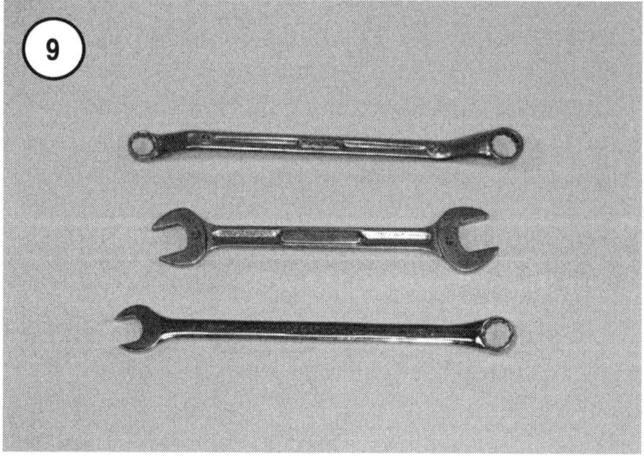

When purchasing tools to perform the procedures covered in this manual, consider the tool's potential frequency of use. If a tool kit is just now being started, consider purchasing a basic tool set from a quality tool supplier. These sets are available in many tool combinations and offer substantial savings when compared to individually purchased tools. As work experience grows and tasks become more complicated, specialized tools can be added.

Screwdrivers

The two basic screwdriver types are the slotted tip (flat blade) and the Phillips tip. These are available in sets that often include an assortment of tip sizes and shaft lengths.

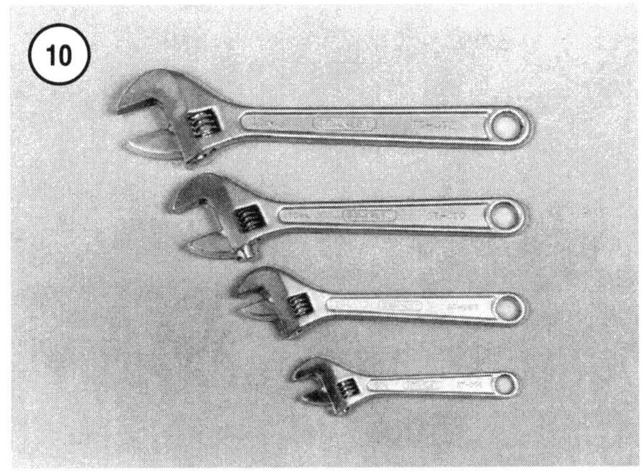

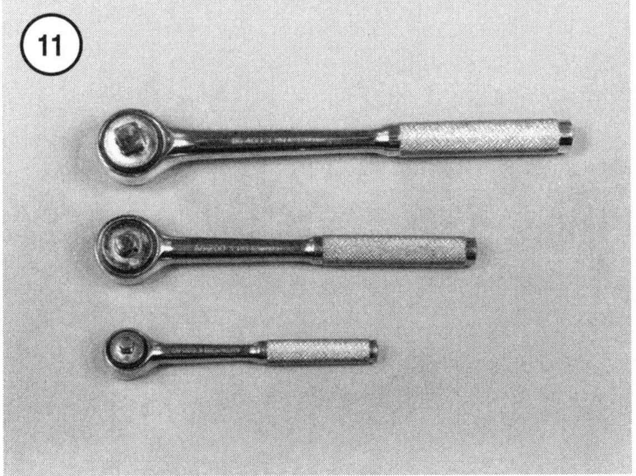

As with all tools, use a screwdriver designed for the job. Check that the size of the tip conforms to the size and shape of the fastener. Use them only for driving screws. Never use a screwdriver for prying or chiseling metal. Repair or replace worn or damaged screwdrivers. A worn tip may damage the fastener, making it difficult to remove.

Poor quality or damaged Phillips screwdrivers can back out (camout) and round over the screw head. In addition, weak or soft screw materials can make removal difficult.

An effective screwdriver to use on Phillips screws is an ACR Phillips II screwdriver. Anticamout ribs (ACR) on the driving faces or flutes of the screwdriver's tip (**Figure 8**) improve the driver-to-fastener grip. ACR Phillips II screwdrivers are designed to be used with ACR Phillips II screws, but they work well on all common Phillips screws. ACR Phillips II screwdrivers are available in different tip sizes and with interchangeable bits to fit screwdriver holders.

Another way to prevent camout and to increase the grip of a Phillips screwdriver is to apply valve grinding compound or Permatex Screw & Socket Gripper onto the screwdriver tip. After loosening or tightening the screw, clean the screw recess.

Wrenches

Box-end, open-end and combination wrenches (**Figure 9**) are available in a variety of types and sizes.

The number stamped on the wrench refers to the distance between the areas where the wrench grips the fastener. This size must match the size of the fastener head.

The box-end wrench grips the fastener on all sides. This reduces the chance of the tool slipping. The box-end wrench is designed with either a 6- or 12-point opening. For stubborn or damaged fasteners, the 6-point provides superior holding ability by contacting the fastener across a wider area at all six edges. For general use, the 12-point works well. It allows the wrench to be removed and reinstalled without moving the handle over such a wide arc.

An open-end wrench is fast and works best in areas with limited access. It contacts the fastener at only two points, and is subject to slipping under heavy force, or if the tool or fastener is worn. A box-end wrench is preferred in most instances, especially when breaking loose and applying the final tightness to a fastener.

The combination wrench has a box-end on one end, and an open-end on the other. This combination makes it a very convenient tool.

Adjustable Wrenches

An adjustable wrench or Crescent wrench (**Figure 10**) can fit nearly any nut or bolt head that has clear access around its perimeter. Adjustable wrenches are best used as a backup wrench to keep a large nut or bolt from turning while the other end is being loosened or tightened with a box-end or socket wrench.

Adjustable wrenches contact the fastener at only two points. Since one jaw is adjustable and may become loose, this makes them more likely to slip off the fastener. To minimize slipping, check that the fixed jaw of the wrench is the one transmitting the force.

Socket Wrenches, Ratchets and Handles

WARNING

Do not use hand sockets with air or impact tools, as they may shatter and cause injury. Always wear eye protection when using impact or air tools.

Sockets that attach to a ratchet handle (**Figure 11**) are available with 6-point (A, **Figure 12**) or 12-point (B) openings and different drive sizes. The drive size indicates the size of the square hole that accepts the ratchet handle. The number stamped on the socket is the size of the work area and must match the fastener head.

As with wrenches, a 6-point socket provides superior holding ability, while a 12-point socket needs to be moved only half as far to reposition it on the fastener.

Sockets are designated for either hand or impact use. Impact sockets are made of thicker material for more durability. Compare the size and wall thickness of a 19-mm hand socket (A, **Figure 13**) and the 19-mm impact socket (B). Use impact sockets when using an impact driver or air tools. Use hand sockets with hand-driven attachments.

Various handles are available for sockets. Use the speed handle for fast operation. Flexible ratchet heads in varying lengths allow the socket to be turned with varying force, and at odd angles. Extension bars allow the socket setup to reach difficult areas. The ratchet is the most versatile. It allows the user to install or remove the nut without removing the socket.

Sockets combined with any number of drivers make them the fastest, safest and most convenient tool for fastener removal and installation.

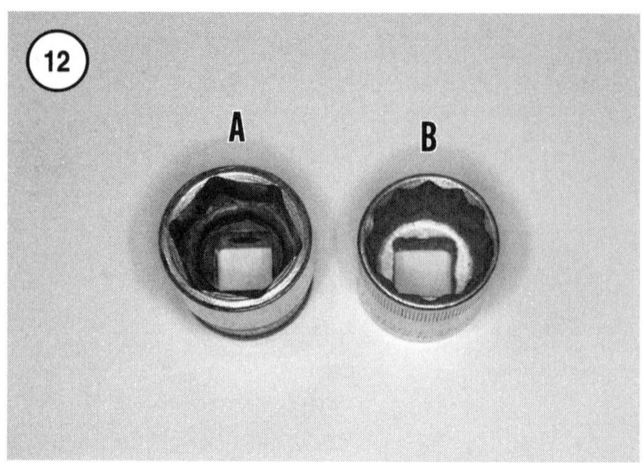

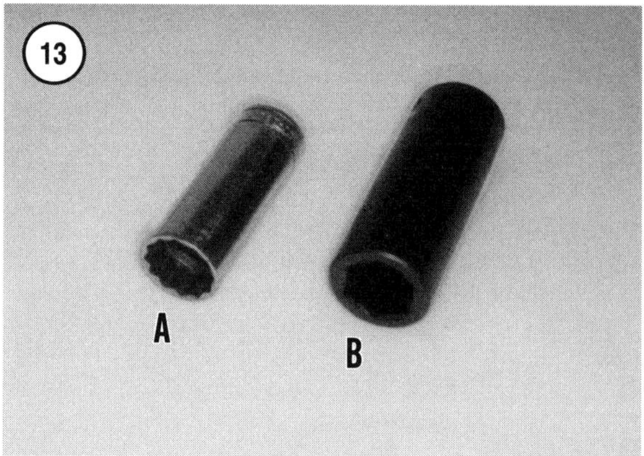

Impact Driver

WARNING
Do not use hand sockets with air or impact tools as they may shatter and cause injury. Always wear eye protection when using impact or air tools.

An impact driver provides extra force for removing fasteners, by converting the impact of a hammer into a turning motion. This makes it possible to remove stubborn fasteners without damaging them. Impact drivers and interchangeable bits (**Figure 14**) are available from most tool suppliers. When using a socket with an impact driver check that the socket is designed for impact use. Refer to *Socket Wrenches, Ratchets and Handles* in this section.

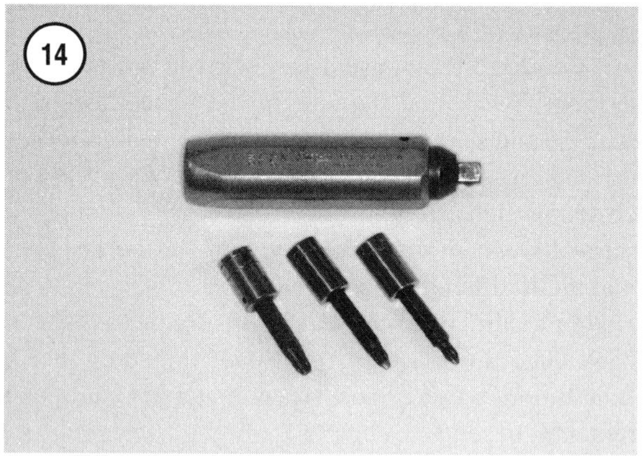

Allen Wrenches

Use Allen or setscrew wrenches (**Figure 15**) on fasteners with hexagonal recesses in the fastener head. These wrenches are available in L-shaped bar, socket and T-handle types. A metric set is required when working on most machines. Allen bolts are sometimes called socket bolts.

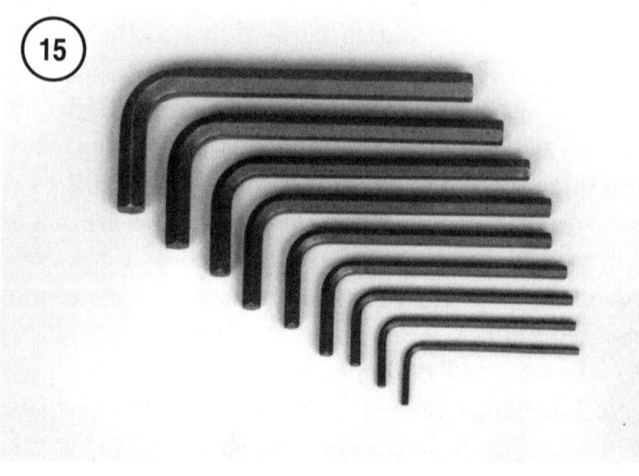

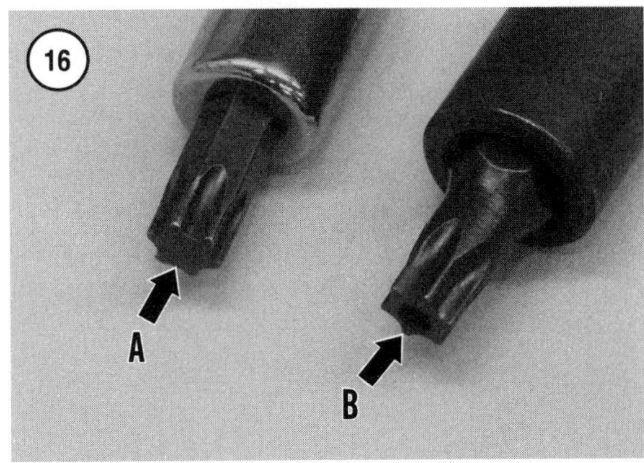

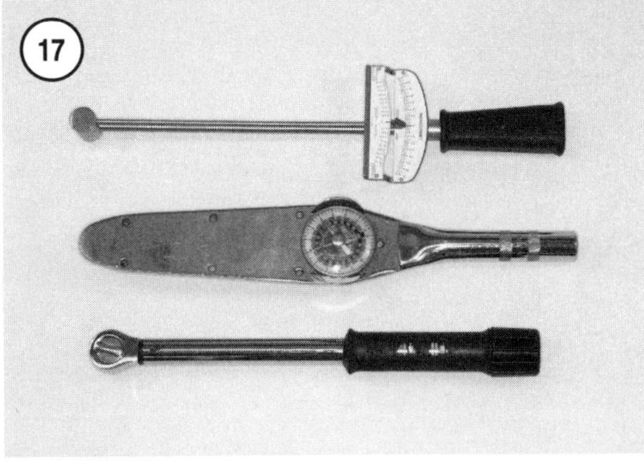

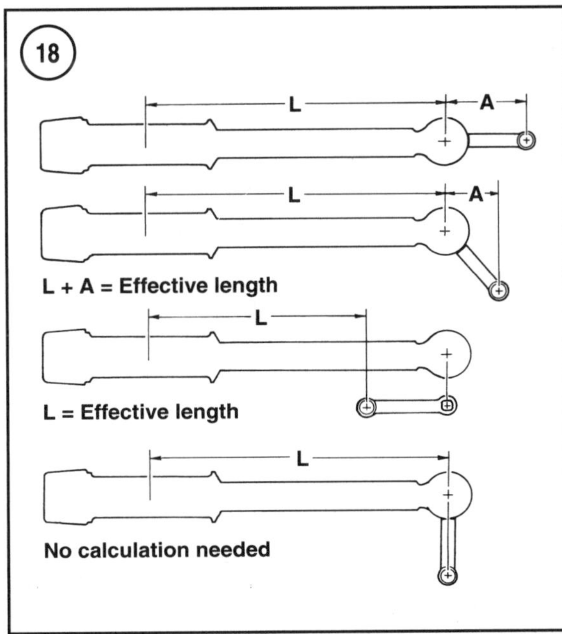

Torx Fasteners

A Torx fastener is a 6-point star-shaped pattern (A, **Figure 16**). Torx fasteners are identified with a T and then a number to indicate their size: T25, for example. Torx drivers are available in L-shaped bars, sockets and T-handles. Tamper-resistant Torx fasteners are also used and have a round shaft in the center of the fastener head. Tamper-resistant Torx fasteners require a Torx bit with a hole in the center of the bit (B, **Figure 16**) to accommodate the shaft of the fastener.

Torque Wrenches

Use a torque wrench with a socket, torque adapter or similar extension to tighten a fastener to a measured torque. Torque wrenches come in several drive sizes (1/4, 3/8, 1/2 and 3/4 in.) and have various methods of reading the torque value. The drive size indicates the size of the square drive that accepts the socket, adapter or extension. Common types of torque wrenches are the deflecting beam, dial indicator and audible click (**Figure 17**).

When choosing a torque wrench, consider the torque range, drive size and accuracy. The torque specifications in this manual provide an indication of the range required.

A torque wrench is a precision tool that must be properly cared for to remain accurate. Store torque wrenches in cases or separate padded drawers within a toolbox. Follow the manufacturer's instructions for their care and calibration.

Torque Adapters

Torque adapters or extensions extend or reduce the reach of a torque wrench. In many cases, the torque adapter is used to tighten a fastener that cannot be reached due to the size of the torque wrench head, drive, and socket. If a torque adapter changes the effective lever length (**Figure 18**), the torque reading on the wrench will not equal the actual torque applied to the fastener. It is necessary to recalibrate the torque setting on the wrench to compensate for the change of lever length. When using a torque adapter at a right angle to the drive head, calibration is not required, since the effective length has not changed.

To recalculate a torque reading when using a torque adapter, use the following formula, and refer to **Figure 18**.

$$TW = \frac{TA \times L}{L + A}$$

TW is the torque setting or dial reading on the wrench.

TA is the torque specification and the actual amount of torque that will be applied to the fastener.

A is the amount that the adapter increases (or in some cases reduces) the effective lever length as measured along the centerline of the torque wrench.

L is the lever length of the wrench as measured from the center of the drive to the center of the grip.

The effective length of the torque wrench measured along the centerline of the torque wrench is the sum of L and A.

Example:

TA = 20 ft.-lb.

A = 3 in.

L = 14 in.

$$TW = \frac{20 \times 14}{14 + 3} = \frac{280}{17} = 16.5 \text{ ft. lb.}$$

In this example, the torque wrench would be set to the recalculated torque value (TW = 16.5 ft.-lb.). When using a beam-type wrench, tighten the fastener until the pointer aligns with 16.5 ft.-lb. In this example, although the torque wrench is preset to 16.5 ft.-lb., the actual torque is 20 ft.-lb.

Pliers

Pliers come in a wide range of types and sizes. Pliers are useful for holding, cutting, bending, and crimping. Do not use them to turn fasteners. **Figure 19** and **Figure 20** both show several types of useful pliers. Each design has a specialized function. Slip-joint pliers are general purpose pliers used for gripping and bending. Diagonal cutting pliers are needed to cut wire and can be used to remove cotter pins. Needlenose pliers are used to hold or bend small objects. Locking pliers (**Figure 20**), sometimes called Vise Grips, are used to hold objects very tightly. They have many uses ranging from holding two parts together, to gripping the end of a broken stud. Use caution when using locking pliers, as the sharp jaws will damage the objects they hold.

Snap Ring Pliers

Snap ring pliers (**Figure 21**) are specialized pliers with tips that fit into the ends of snap rings to remove and install them.

Snap rings pliers are available with a fixed action (either internal or external) or convertible (one tool works on both internal and external snap rings). They may have fixed tips or interchangeable ones of various sizes and angles. For general use, select a convertible-type plier with interchangeable tips.

WARNING

Snap rings can spring from the pliers during removal or installation. Also, the snap ring plier tips may break. Always wear eye protection when using snap ring pliers.

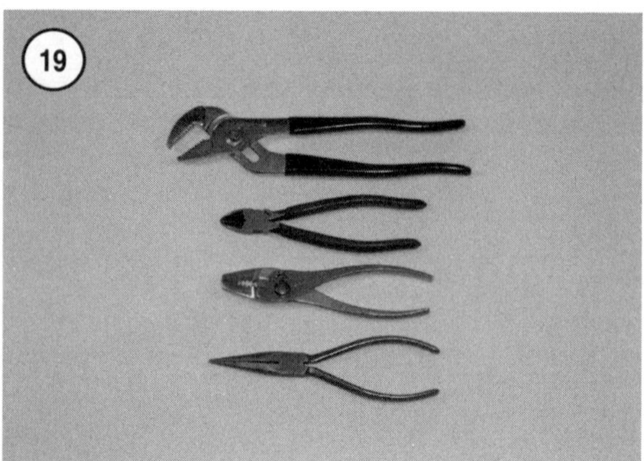

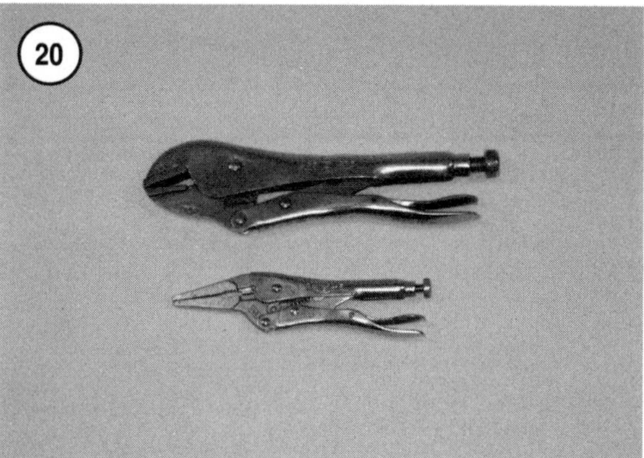

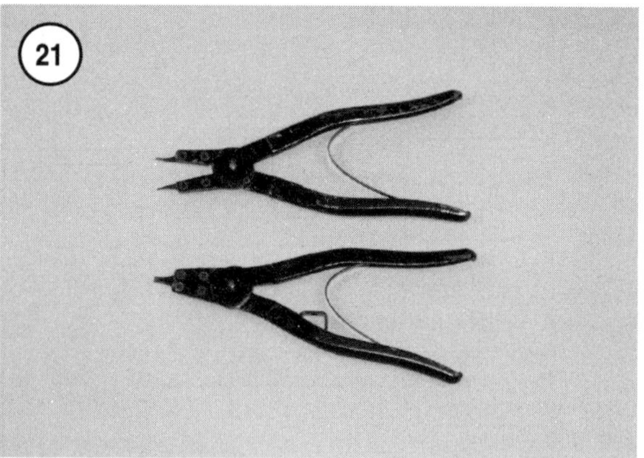

Hammers

Various types of hammers are available to fit a number of applications. Use a ball-peen hammer to strike another tool, such as a punch or chisel. Soft-faced hammers are required when a metal object must be struck without damaging it. *Never* use a metal-faced hammer on engine and suspension components, as damage will occur in most cases.

Always wear eye protection when using hammers. Check that the hammer face is in good condition and the handle is not cracked. Select the correct hammer for the job and make sure that it strikes the object

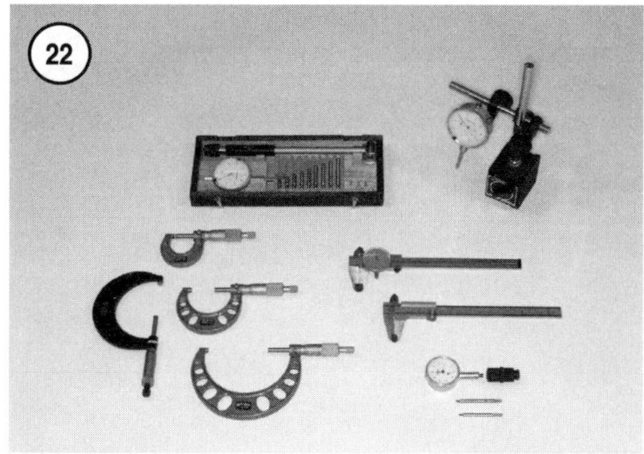

22

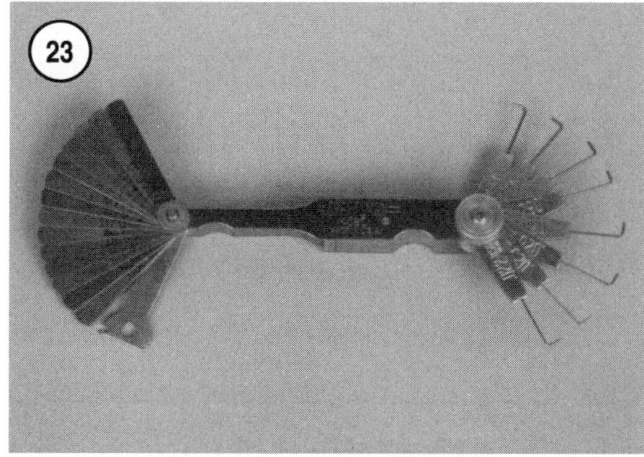

23

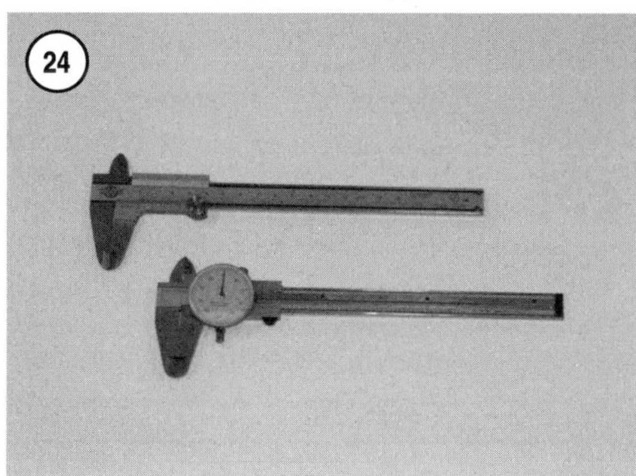

24

squarely. Do not use the handle or the side of the hammer to strike an object.

MEASURING TOOLS

The ability to accurately measure components is required to perform many of the procedures described in this manual. Accurate measurements are essential in determining which components require replacement or further service.

Each type of measuring instrument (**Figure 22**) is designed to measure a dimension with a certain degree of accuracy and within a certain range. Always use a measuring tool that is designed for the task.

As with all tools, measuring tools provide the best results if cared for properly. Improper use can damage the tool and cause inaccurate results. If any measurement is questionable, verify the measurement using another tool. A standard gauge is usually provided with measuring tools to check accuracy and calibrate the tool if necessary.

Precision measurements can vary according to the experience of the person performing the procedure. Accurate results are only possible if the mechanic possesses a feel for using the tool. Heavy-handed use of measuring tools produces less accurate results. Hold the tool gently with the fingertips to easily feel the point at which the tool contacts the object. This feel for the equipment produces more accurate measurements and reduces the risk of damaging the tool or component. Refer to the following sections for specific measuring tools.

Feeler Gauge

Use a feeler or thickness gauge (**Figure 23**) for measuring the distance between two surfaces.

A feeler gauge set consists of an assortment of steel strips of graduated thickness. Each blade is marked with its thickness. Blades can be of various lengths and angles for different procedures.

A common use for a feeler gauge is to measure valve clearance. Wire (round) type gauges are used to measure spark plug gap.

Calipers

Use calipers (**Figure 24**) to determine inside, outside and depth measurements. Although not as precise as a micrometer, they allow reasonable precision, typically to within 0.05 mm (0.001 in.). Most calipers have a range up to 150 mm (6 in.).

Calipers are available in dial, vernier or digital versions. Dial calipers have a dial readout that provides convenient reading. Vernier calipers have marked scales that must be compared to determine the measurement. The digital caliper uses an LCD to show the measurement.

Properly maintain the measuring surfaces of the caliper. There must not be any dirt or burrs between the tool and the object being measured. Never force the caliper closed around an object; close the caliper around the highest point so it can be removed with a slight drag. Some calipers require calibration. Always refer to the manufacturer's instructions when using a new or unfamiliar caliper.

To read a vernier caliper, refer to **Figure 25**. The fixed scale is marked in 1-mm increments. Ten individual lines on the fixed scale equal 1 cm. The movable scale is marked in 0.05 mm (hundredth) increments. To obtain a reading, establish the first number by the location of the 0 line on the movable scale in relation to the first line to the left on the fixed scale. In this example, the number is 10 mm. To determine the next number, note which of the lines on the movable scale align with a mark on the fixed scale. A number of lines will appear close, but only one will align exactly. In this case, 0.50 mm is the reading to add to the first number. The result of adding 10 mm and 0.50 mm is a measurement of 10.50 mm.

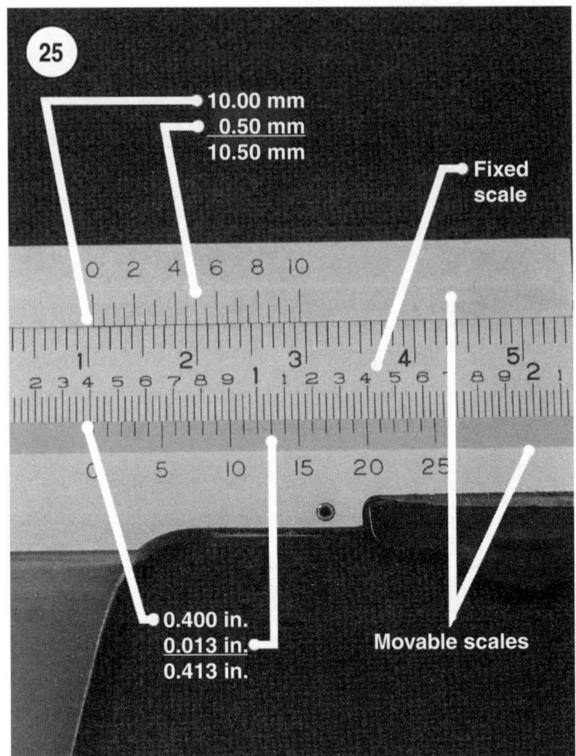

Micrometers

A micrometer (**Figure 26**) is an instrument designed for linear measurement using the decimal divisions of the inch or meter. While there are many types and styles of micrometers, most of the procedures in this manual call for an outside micrometer. The outside micrometer is used to measure the outside diameter of cylindrical forms and the thickness of materials.

A micrometer's size indicates the minimum and maximum size of a part that it can measure. The usual sizes (**Figure 27**) are 0-25 mm (0-1 in.), 25-50 mm (1-2 in.), 50-75 mm (2-3 in.) and 75-100 mm (3-4 in.).

Micrometers that cover a wider range of measurement are available. These use a large frame with interchangeable anvils of various lengths. This type of micrometer offers a cost savings; however, its overall size may make it less convenient.

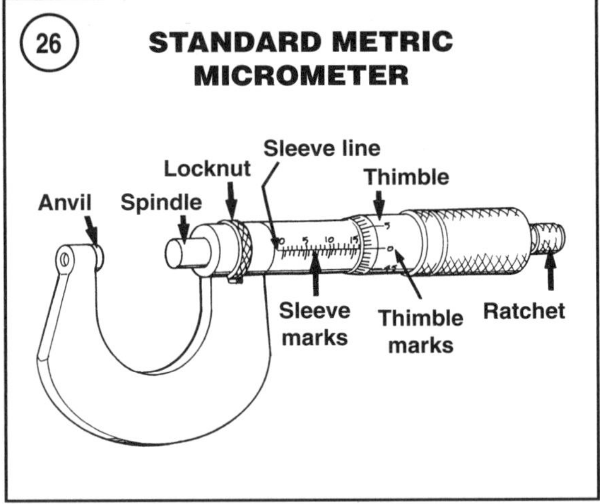

Adjustment

Before using a micrometer, check its adjustment as follows:

1. Clean the anvil and spindle faces.

2A. To check a 0-1 in. or 0-25 mm micrometer:

a. Turn the thimble until the spindle contacts the anvil. If the micrometer has a ratchet stop, use it to ensure that the proper amount of pressure is applied.
b. If the adjustment is correct, the 0 mark on the thimble will align exactly with the 0 mark on the sleeve line. If the marks do not align, the micrometer is out of adjustment.
c. Follow the manufacturer's instructions to adjust the micrometer.

2B. To check a micrometer larger than 1 in. or 25 mm, use the standard gauge supplied by the manufacturer. A standard gauge is a steel block, disc or rod that is machined to an exact size.

a. Place the standard gauge between the spindle and anvil, and measure its outside diameter or length. If the micrometer has a ratchet stop, use it to ensure that the proper amount of pressure is applied.
b. If the adjustment is correct, the 0 mark on the thimble will align exactly with the 0 mark on the sleeve line. If the marks do not align, the micrometer is out of adjustment.

27

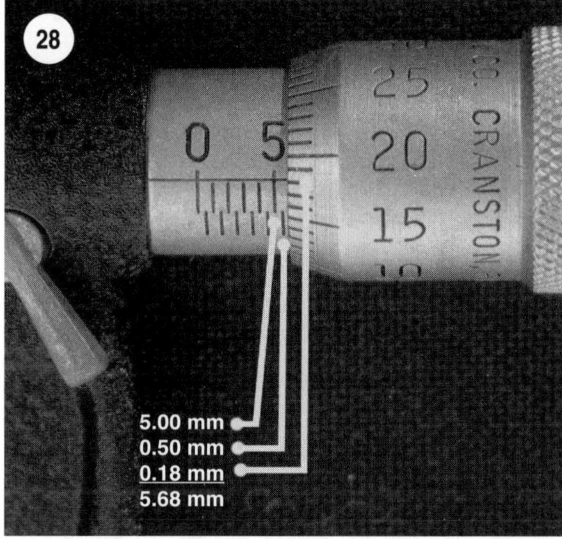

28

c. Follow the manufacturer's instructions to adjust the micrometer.

Care

Micrometers are precision instruments. They must be used and maintained with great care. Note the following:

1. Store micrometers in protective cases or separate padded drawers in a toolbox.
2. When in storage, make sure the spindle and anvil faces do not contact each other or another object. If they do, temperature changes and corrosion may damage the contact faces.
3. Do not clean a micrometer with compressed air. Dirt forced into the tool causes wear.
4. Lubricate micrometers to prevent corrosion.

Reading

The standard metric micrometer (**Figure 26**) is accurate to one one-hundredth of a millimeter (0.01 mm). The sleeve line is graduated in millimeter and half millimeter increments. The marks on the upper half of the sleeve line equal 1.00 mm. Every fifth mark above the sleeve line is identified with a number. The number sequence depends on the size of the micrometer. A 0-25 mm micrometer, for example, will have sleeve marks numbered 0 through 25 in 5 mm increments. This numbering sequence continues with larger micrometers. On all metric micrometers, each mark on the lower half of the sleeve equals 0.50 mm.

The tapered end of the thimble has fifty lines marked around it. Each mark equals 0.01 mm.

One complete turn of the thimble aligns its 0 mark with the first line on the lower half of the sleeve line or 0.50 mm.

When reading a metric micrometer, add the number of millimeters and half-millimeters on the sleeve line to the number of one one-hundredth millimeters on the thimble. Perform the following steps while referring to **Figure 28**.

1. Make sure the measuring surfaces of the micrometer and component are clean.
2. Close the micrometer around the highest point so it can be removed with a slight drag.
3. Read the upper half of the sleeve line and count the number of lines visible. Each upper line equals 1 mm.
4. See if the half-millimeter line is visible on the lower sleeve line. If so, add 0.50 to the reading in Step 1.
5. Read the thimble mark that aligns with the sleeve line. Each thimble mark equals 0.01 mm.
6. If a thimble mark does not align exactly with the sleeve line, estimate the amount between the lines, or use a metric vernier micrometer.
7. Add the readings from Steps 3-6.

Telescoping and Small Bore Gauges

Use telescoping gauges (**Figure 29**) and small bore gauges (**Figure 30**) to measure bores. Neither gauge has a scale for direct readings. Use an outside micrometer to determine the reading.

To use a telescoping gauge, select the correct size gauge for the bore. Compress the movable post and carefully insert the gauge into the bore. Carefully move the gauge in the bore to check that it is centered. Tighten the knurled end of the gauge to hold the movable post in position. Remove the gauge and measure the length of the posts. Telescoping gauges are typically used to measure cylinder bores.

To use a small bore gauge, select the correct size gauge for the bore. Carefully insert the gauge into the bore. Tighten the knurled end of the gauge to carefully expand the gauge fingers to the limit within the bore. Do not overtighten the gauge, as there is no built-in release. Excessive tightening can damage the bore surface and damage the tool. Remove the gauge and measure the outside dimension (**Figure 31**). Small bore gauges are typically used to measure valve guides.

Dial Indicator

A dial indicator (A, **Figure 32**) is a gauge with a dial face and needle used to measure variations in dimensions and movements. A typical use for a dial indicator is measuring brake rotor runout.

Dial indicators are available in various ranges and graduations and with three basic types of mounting bases: magnetic (B, **Figure 32**), clamp, or screw-in stud. When purchasing a dial indicator, select the magnetic stand type with a continuous dial.

Cylinder Bore Gauge

A cylinder bore gauge is similar to a dial indicator. The gauge set shown in **Figure 33** consists of a dial indicator, handle, and different length adapters (anvils) to fit the gauge to various bore sizes. The bore gauge is used to measure bore size, taper and out-of-round. When using a bore gauge, follow the manufacturer's instructions.

Compression Gauge

A compression gauge (**Figure 34**) measures combustion chamber (cylinder) pressure, usually in psi or kg/cm^2. The gauge adapter is either inserted or screwed into the spark plug hole to obtain the reading. Disable the engine so it does not start and hold the throttle in the wide-open position when performing a compression test. An engine that does not have adequate compression cannot be properly tuned. See Chapter Three.

Multimeter

A multimeter (**Figure 35**) is an essential tool for electrical system diagnosis. The voltage function indicates the voltage applied or available to various electrical components. The ohmmeter function tests circuits for continuity, or lack of continuity, and measures the resistance of a circuit.

Some manufacturer's specifications for electrical components are based on results using a specific test

29

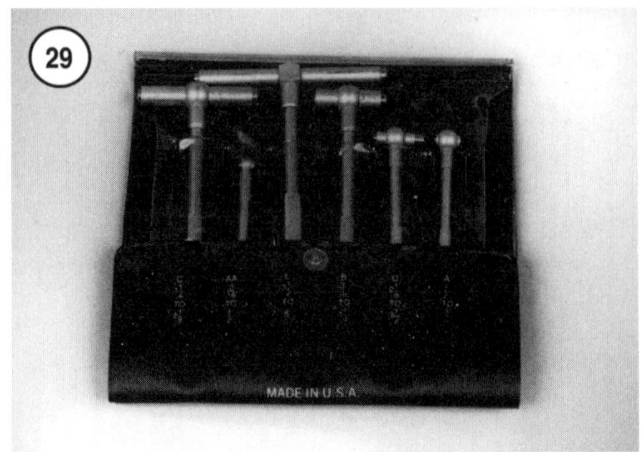

30

31

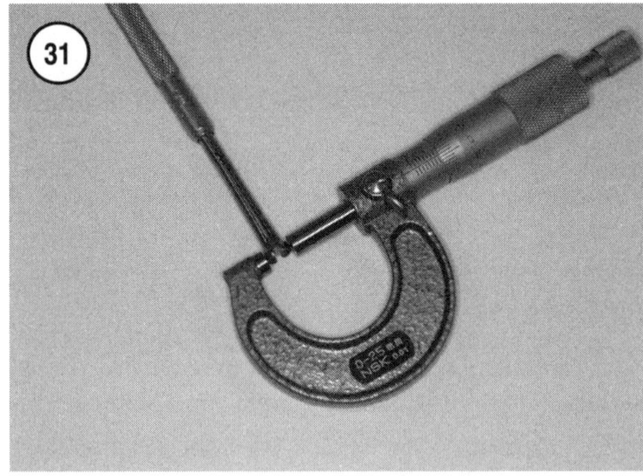

meter. Results may vary if using a meter not recommended by the manufacturer. Such requirements are noted when applicable.

Each time an analog ohmmeter is used or if the scale is changed, the ohmmeter must be calibrated following the manufacturer's instructions.

ELECTRICAL SYSTEM FUNDAMENTALS

An understanding of electrical fundamentals is necessary to perform diagnostic tests.

32

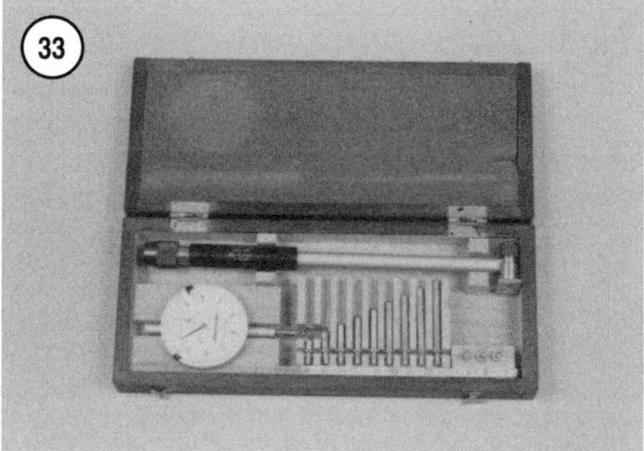

33

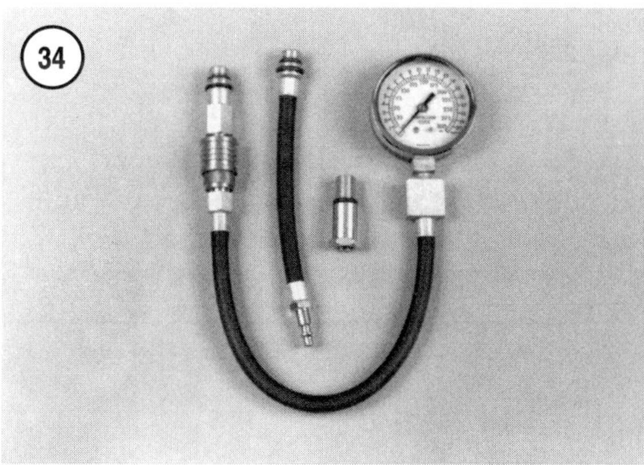

34

35

Voltage

Voltage is the electrical potential or pressure in an electrical circuit and is expressed in volts. The more pressure (voltage) in a circuit, the more work that can be performed.

Direct current (DC) voltage means the electricity flows in one direction. All circuits powered by a battery are DC circuits.

Alternating current (AC) means that the electricity flows in one direction momentarily, then switches to the opposite direction. Alternator output is an example of AC voltage. This voltage must be changed or rectified to direct current to operate in a battery powered system.

Resistance

Resistance is the opposition to the flow of electricity within a circuit or component and is measured in ohms. Resistance causes a reduction in available current and voltage.

Resistance is measured in a inactive circuit with an ohmmeter. The ohmmeter sends a small amount of current into the circuit and measures how difficult it is to push the current through the circuit.

An ohmmeter, though useful, is not always a good indicator of a circuit's actual ability under operating conditions. This is due to the low voltage (6-9 volts) that the meter uses to test the circuit. The voltage in an ignition coil secondary winding can be several thousand volts. Such high voltage can cause the coil to malfunction, even though it tests acceptable during a resistance test.

Resistance generally increases with temperature. Perform all testing with the component or circuit at room temperature. Resistance tests performed at high temperatures may indicate high resistance readings and cause the unnecessary replacement of a component.

Amperage

Amperage is the unit of measure for the amount of current within a circuit. Current is the actual flow of electricity. The higher the current, the more work that can be performed up to a given point. If the current flow exceeds the circuit or component capacity, the system will be damaged.

SERVICE METHODS

Most of the procedures in this manual can be performed by anyone reasonably competent with tools.

However, consider personal capabilities carefully before attempting any operation involving major disassembly of the engine.

1. Front, in this manual, refers to the front of the machine. The front of any component is the end closest to the front of the machine. The left and right sides refer to the position of the parts as viewed by the rider sitting on the seat facing forward.
2. Whenever servicing an engine or suspension component, secure the machine in a safe manner.
3. Tag all similar parts for location and mark all mating parts for position. Record the number and thickness of any shims while removing them. Identify parts by placing them in sealed and labeled plastic bags.
4. Tag disconnected wires and connectors with masking tape and a marking pen.
5. Protect finished surfaces from physical damage or corrosion. Keep gasoline and other chemicals off painted surfaces.
6. Use penetrating oil on frozen or tight bolts. Avoid using heat where possible. Heat can warp, melt or affect the temper of parts. Heat also damages the finish of paint and plastics.
7. When a part is a press-fit or requires a special tool for removal, the information or type of tool is identified in the text. Otherwise, if a part is difficult to remove or install, determine the cause before proceeding.
8. Cover all openings to prevent objects or debris from falling into the engine.
9. Read each procedure thoroughly and compare the illustrations to the actual components before starting the procedure. Perform the procedure in sequence.
10. Recommendations are occasionally made to refer service to a dealership or specialist. In these cases, the work can be performed more economically by the specialist than by the home mechanic.
11. The term replace means to discard a defective part and replace it with a new part. Overhaul means to remove, disassemble, inspect, measure, repair and/or replace parts as required to recondition an assembly.
12. Some operations require a hydraulic press. If a press is not available, have these operations performed by a shop equipped with the necessary equipment. Do not use makeshift equipment that may damage the machine.

CAUTION

Do not direct high-pressure water at steering bearings, carburetor hoses, wheel bearings, suspension and electrical components, or O-ring drive chains. The water will force the grease out of the bearings and possibly damage the seals.

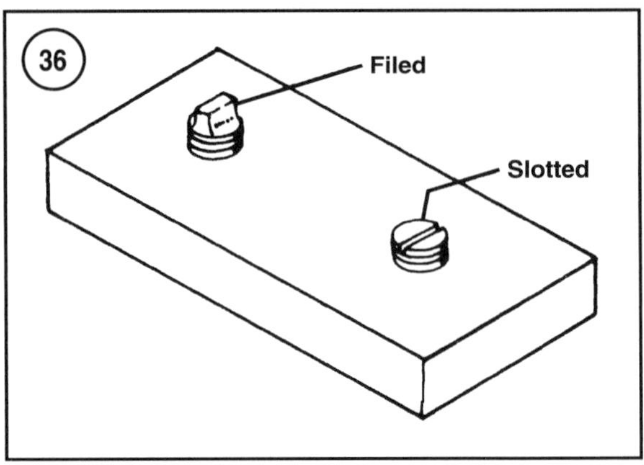

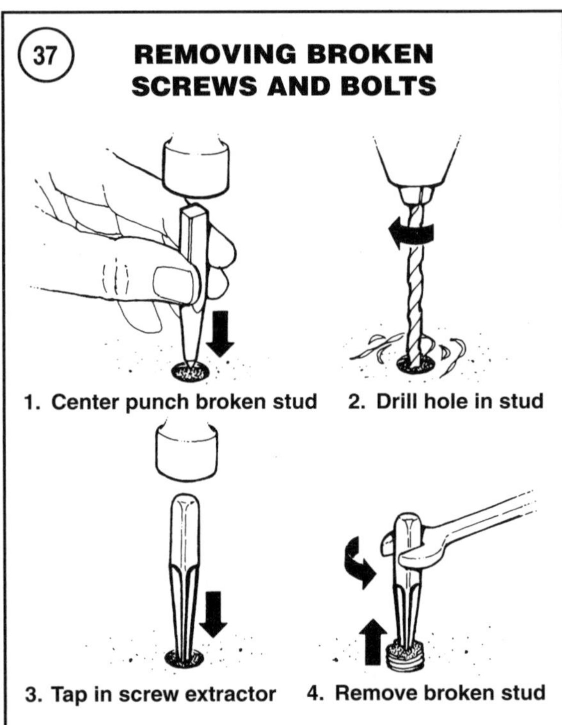

13. Repairs are much faster and easier if the machine is clean before starting work. Degrease the machine with a commercial degreaser; follow the directions on the container for the best results. Clean all parts with cleaning solvent while removing them.
14. If special tools are required, have them available before starting the procedure. When special tools are required, they will be described in the procedure.
15. Make diagrams of similar-appearing parts. For instance, crankcase bolts are often not the same lengths. Do not rely on memory alone. It is possible that carefully laid out parts will become disturbed, making it difficult to reassemble the components correctly without a diagram.

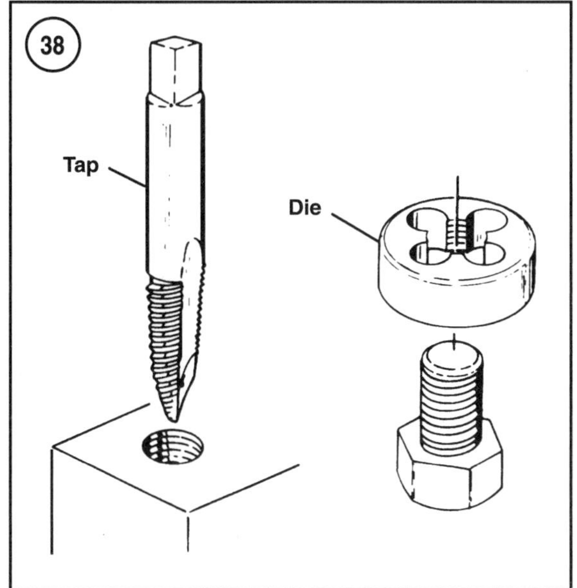

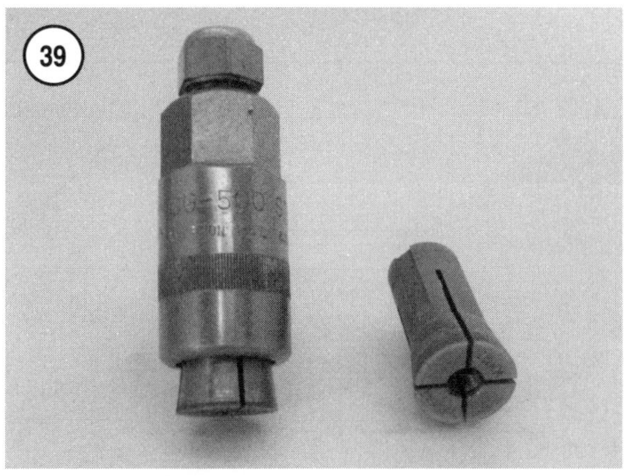

16. Check that all shims and washers are reinstalled in the same location and position.
17. Whenever rotating parts contact a stationary part, look for a shim or washer.
18. Use new gaskets if there is any doubt about the condition of old ones.
19. If self-locking fasteners are used, replace them. Do not install standard fasteners in place of self-locking ones.
20. Use grease to hold small parts in place if they tend to fall out during assembly. Do not apply grease to electrical or brake components.

Removing Frozen Fasteners

If a fastener cannot be removed, several methods may be used to loosen it. First, apply a penetrating oil such as Liquid Wrench or WD-40. Apply it liberally and let it penetrate for 10-15 minutes. Strike the fastener several times with a small hammer. Do not hit it so hard as to cause damage. Reapply the penetrating oil if necessary.

For frozen screws, apply penetrating oil as described, then insert a screwdriver in the slot and strike the top of the screwdriver with a hammer. This loosens the rust so the screw can be backed out. If the screw head is too damaged to use this method, grip the head with locking pliers and twist the screw out.

Avoid applying heat unless specifically instructed, as it may melt, warp or remove the temper from parts.

Removing Broken Fasteners

If the head breaks off a screw or bolt, several methods are available for removing the remaining portion. If a large portion of the remainder projects out, try gripping it with locking pliers. If the projecting portion is too small, file it to fit a wrench or cut a slot in it to fit a screwdriver (**Figure 36**).

If the head breaks off flush, use a screw extractor. To do this, center punch the remaining portion of the screw or bolt. Drill a small hole in the screw and tap the extractor into the hole. Back the screw out with a wrench on the extractor (**Figure 37**).

Repairing Damaged Threads

Occasionally, threads are stripped through carelessness or impact damage. Often the threads can be repaired by using a tap (for internal threads) or die (for external threads) on the threads (**Figure 38**). To clean or repair spark plug threads, use a spark plug tap.

If an internal thread is damaged, it may be necessary to install a Helicoil or some other type of thread insert. Follow the manufacturer's instructions when installing their insert.

If it is necessary to drill and tap a hole, refer to **Table 4** for metric tap and drill sizes.

Stud Removal/Installation

A stud removal tool is available from most tool suppliers. This tool makes the removal and installation of studs easier. If one is not available, thread two nuts onto the stud and tighten them against each other. Remove the stud by turning the lower nut (**Figure 39**).

1. Measure the height of the stud above the surface.
2. Thread the stud removal tool onto the stud and tighten it, or thread two nuts onto the stud.
3. Remove the stud by turning the stud remover or the lower nut.

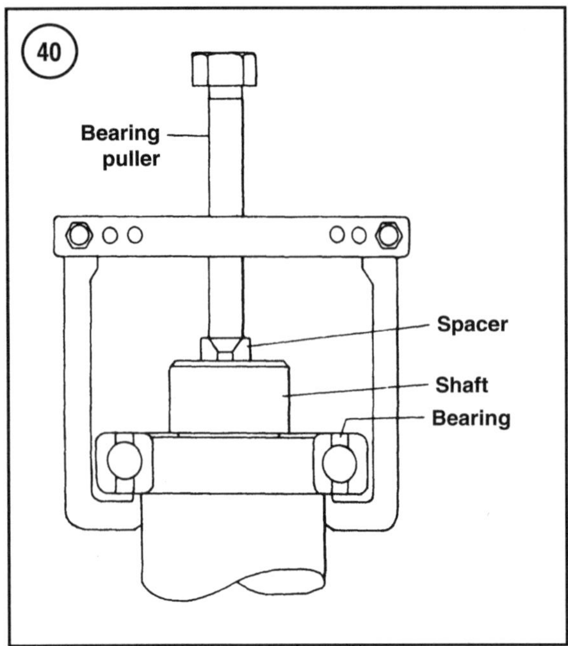

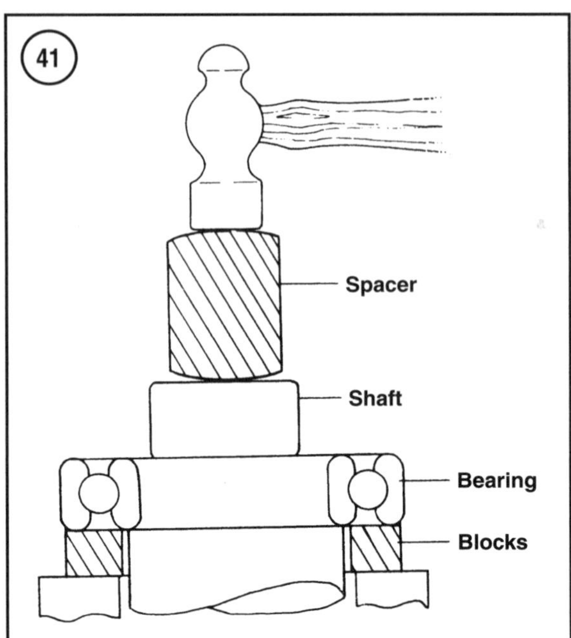

4. Remove any threadlocking compound from the threaded hole. Clean the threads with an aerosol parts cleaner.
5. Install the stud removal tool onto the new stud or thread two nuts onto the stud.
6. Apply threadlocking compound to the threads of the stud.
7. Install the stud and tighten with the stud removal tool or the top nut.
8. Install the stud to the height noted in Step 1 or its torque specification.
9. Remove the stud removal tool or the two nuts.

Removing Hoses

When removing stubborn hoses, do not exert excessive force on the hose or fitting. Remove the hose clamp and carefully insert a small screwdriver or pick tool between the fitting and hose. Apply a spray lubricant under the hose and carefully twist the hose off the fitting. Clean the fitting of any corrosion or rubber hose material with a wire brush. Clean the inside of the hose thoroughly. Do not use any lubricant when installing the hose (new or old). The lubricant may cause the hose to come off the fitting, even with the clamp secure.

Bearings

Bearings are used in the engine and transmission assembly to reduce power loss, heat and noise resulting from friction. Because bearings are precision parts, they must be maintained by proper lubrication and maintenance. If a bearing is damaged, replace it immediately. When installing a new bearing, take care to prevent damaging the part. Many bearing replacement procedures are included in the individual chapters where applicable; however, use the following as a guideline. Unless otherwise specified, install bearings with the manufacturer's mark or number facing outward.

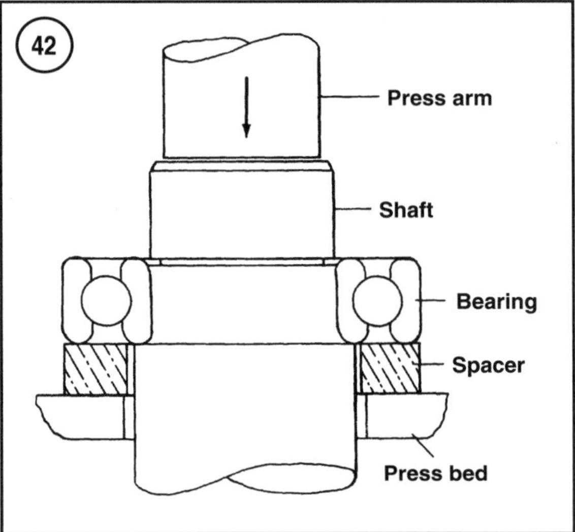

Removal

While bearings are normally removed only when damaged, there may be times when it is necessary to remove a bearing that is in good condition. However,

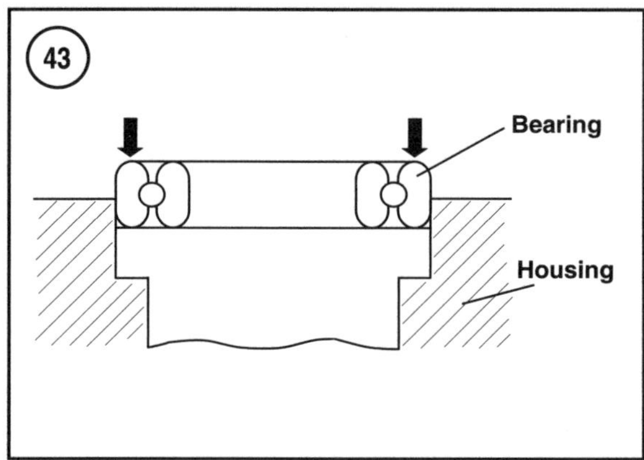

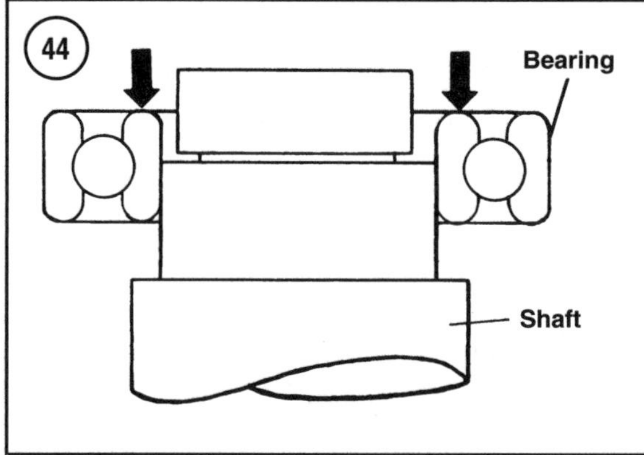

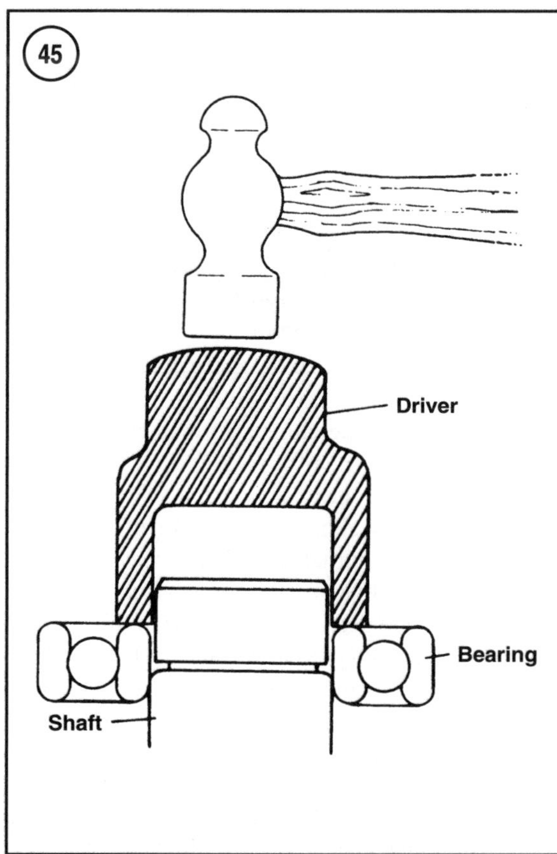

improper bearing removal will damage the bearing and maybe the shaft or case half. Note the following when removing bearings.

1. When using a puller to remove a bearing from a shaft, be careful not to damage the shaft. Always place a piece of metal between the end of the shaft and the puller screw. In addition, place the puller arms next to the inner bearing race. See **Figure 40**.
2. When using a hammer to remove a bearing from a shaft, do not strike the hammer directly against the shaft. Instead, use a brass or aluminum spacer between the hammer and shaft (**Figure 41**) and make sure to support both bearing races with wooden blocks, as shown.
3. The ideal method of bearing removal is with a hydraulic press. Note the following when using a press:
   a. Always support the inner and outer bearing races with a suitable size wooden or aluminum ring (**Figure 42**). If only the outer race is supported, pressure applied against the balls and/or the inner race will damage them.
   b. Always check that the press arm (**Figure 42**) aligns with the center of the shaft. If the arm is not centered, it may damage the bearing and/or shaft.
   c. The moment the shaft is free of the bearing, it will drop to the floor. Secure or hold the shaft to prevent it from falling.

Installation

1. When installing a bearing in a housing, apply pressure to the *outer* bearing race (**Figure 43**). When installing a bearing on a shaft, apply pressure to the *inner* bearing race (**Figure 44**).
2. When installing a bearing as described in Step 1, some type of driver is required. Never strike the bearing directly with a hammer or the bearing will be damaged. When installing a bearing, use a length of pipe or a driver with a diameter that matches the bearing race. **Figure 45** shows the correct way to use a driver and hammer to install a bearing.
3. Step 1 describes how to install a bearing in a case or over a shaft. However, when installing a bearing over a shaft and into a housing at the same time, a tight fit will be required for both outer and inner bearing races. In this situation, install a spacer under the driver tool so that pressure is applied evenly across both races (**Figure 46**). If the outer race is not supported, the balls will push against the outer bearing race and damage it.

Interference fit

1. Follow this procedure when installing a bearing over a shaft. When a tight fit is required, the bearing inside diameter will be smaller than the shaft. In this case, driving the bearing onto the shaft using normal methods may cause bearing damage. Instead, heat the bearing before installation. Note the following:
   a. Secure the shaft so it is ready for bearing installation.
   b. Clean all residues from the bearing surface of the shaft. Remove burrs with a file or sandpaper.
   c. Fill a suitable container with clean mineral oil. Place a thermometer rated above 248° F (120° C) in the oil. Support the thermometer so it does not rest on the bottom or side of the container.
   d. Remove the bearing from its wrapper and secure it with a piece of heavy wire bent to hold it in the container. Hang the bearing so it does not touch the bottom or sides.
   e. Turn the heat on and monitor the thermometer. When the oil temperature rises to approximately 248° F (120° C), remove the bearing and quickly install it. If necessary, place a socket on the inner bearing race and tap the bearing into place. As the bearing chills, it will tighten on the shaft so installation must be done quickly. Check that the bearing is installed completely.
2. Follow this step when installing a bearing in a housing. Bearings are generally installed in a housing with a slight interference fit. Driving the bearing into the housing using normal methods may damage the housing or cause bearing damage. Instead, heat the housing before installing the bearing. Note the following:
   a. Wash the housing thoroughly with detergent and water. Rinse and rewash the housing as required to remove all traces of oil and other chemical deposits.

CAUTION
Do not heat the housing or bearing with a propane or acetylene torch. The direct heat will destroy the case hardening of the bearing and will likely warp the housing. Cases that are made of magnesium alloy can ignite.

   b. Heat the housing to approximately 212° F (100° C) in an oven, or use a heat gun to warm the immediate area around the bearing bore. An easy way to check that it is at the proper temperature is to place drops of water on the housing; if they sizzle and evaporate immediately, the temperature is correct. Heat only one housing at a time.
   c. Handle the heated housing with insulated gloves or welding gloves. Do not place the housing on burnable surfaces.
   d. Hold the housing with the bearing side down and tap the bearing out. Repeat for all bearings in the housing. Remove and install the bearings with a suitable-size socket and extension used as a driver.
   e. Before heating the bearing housing, place the new bearing in a freezer if possible. Chilling a bearing slightly reduces its outside diameter while the heated bearing housing assembly

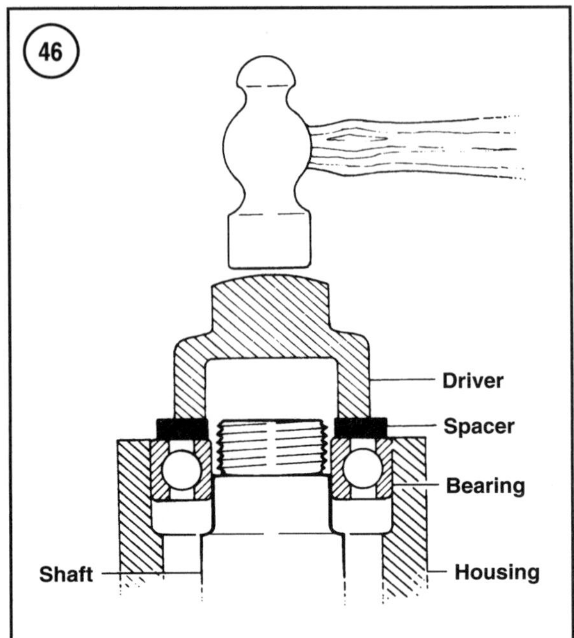

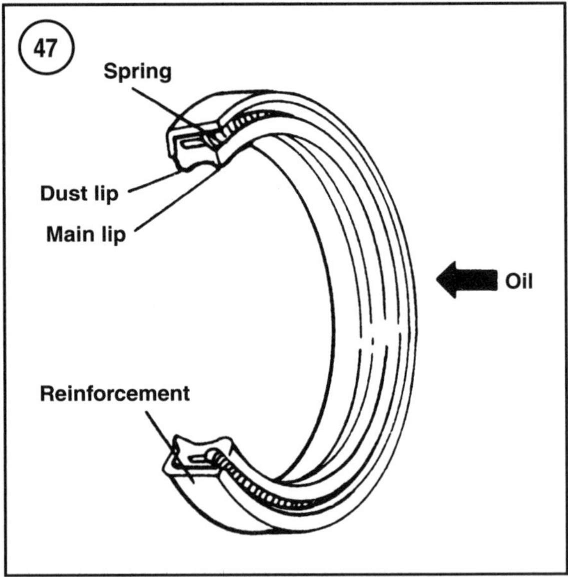

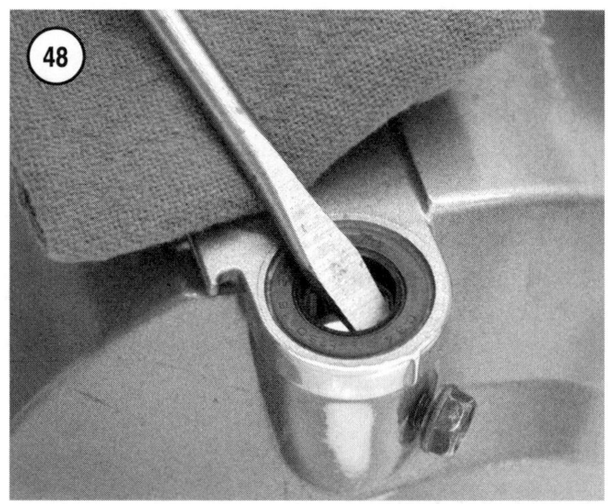

48

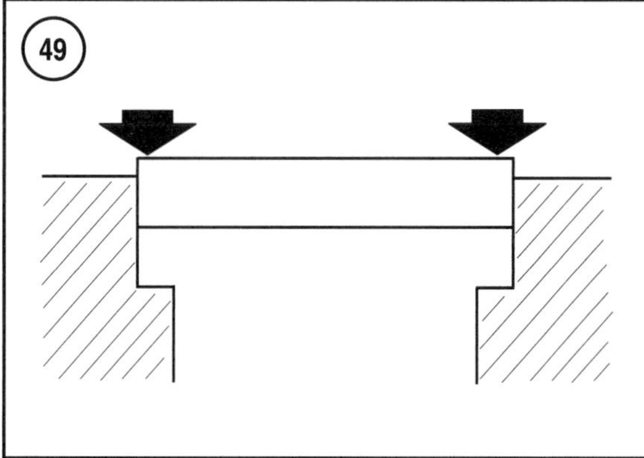

49

is slightly larger due to heat expansion. This makes bearing installation easier.

f. While the housing is still hot, install the new bearing(s) into the housing. Install the bearings by hand, if possible. If necessary, lightly tap the bearing(s) into the housing with a socket placed on the outer bearing race (**Figure 43**). Do not install new bearings by driving on the inner bearing race. Install the bearing(s) until it seats completely.

Seal Replacement

Seals (**Figure 47**) contain oil, water, grease or combustion gasses in a housing or shaft. Improper removal of a seal can damage the housing or shaft. Improper installation of the seal can damage the seal. Note the following:

1. Prying is generally the easiest and most effective method of removing a seal from a housing. However, always place a shop cloth under the pry tool (**Figure 48**) to prevent damage to the housing.
2. Pack the appropriate grease in the seal lips before installing the seal.
3. In most cases, install seals with the manufacturer's numbers or marks facing out.
4. Install seals with a socket placed on the outside of the seal as shown in **Figure 49**. Drive the seal squarely into the housing. Drive the seal until it is flush or driven to the specified depth. Never install a seal by hitting the top of it with a hammer.

1

STORAGE

Several months of non-use can cause a general deterioration of the machine. This is especially true in areas of extreme temperature variations. This deterioration can be minimized with careful preparation for storage. A properly stored machine will be much easier to return to service.

Storage Area Selection

When selecting a storage area, consider the following:

1. The storage area must be dry. A heated area is best, but not necessary. It should be insulated to minimize extreme temperature variation.
2. If the building has large window areas, cover them to keep sunlight off the machine.
3. Avoid areas close to saltwater, corrosive chemicals or emissions.
4. Consider the risk of fire, theft or vandalism. Check with an insurer regarding machine coverage while in storage.

Preparing the Machine for Storage

The amount of preparation a machine should undergo before storage depends on the expected length of non-use, storage area conditions and personal preference. Consider the following list the minimum requirements:

1. Wash the machine. Remove all dirt, mud and debris, particularly in fender wells and skid plates.
2. Check the cooling system for proper level and mix ratio.
3. Start the engine and allow it to reach operating temperature. Drain the engine oil regardless of the riding time since the last service. Fill the engine with the recommended type of oil.
4. Drain all fuel from the fuel tank. Run the engine until all fuel is consumed from the lines and carburetor.
5. Remove the spark plug and pour a teaspoon (15-20 mL) of engine oil into the cylinder. Place a shop cloth over the opening and slowly turn the engine over to distribute the oil. Reinstall the spark plug.

6. Remove the battery. Store the battery in a cool, dry location. Charge the battery monthly.
7. Cover the exhaust and intake openings.
8. Apply a commercial protectant to the plastic and rubber components. Follow the manufacturer's instructions for each type of product being used.
9. If possible, place the machine on stands so the tires are off the ground.
10. Cover the machine with a drop cloth or similar cover. Avoid using plastic covers because these trap moisture and create corrosion.

Returning the Machine to Service

The amount of service required to return a machine to operating condition depends on the length of non-use and storage conditions. Follow the above procedure and install/check each area that was prepared at the time of storage. Check air pressure in the tires and adjust as needed. Also check that the brakes, throttle and engine stop switch work properly before operating the machine. Refer to the maintenance and lubrication schedule in Chapter Three and determine which areas require additional service.

Table 1 GENERAL DIMENSIONS AND WEIGHT

	mm	in.
Ground clearance	275	10.8
Minimum turning radius	3200	126
Overall length	2085	82.01
Overall width	1150	45.3
Overall height	1210	47.6
Seat height	880	34.7
Wheelbase	1275	50.2
Weight		
Dry	272 kg	600 lb.
With oil, water and full fuel tank	290 kg	639 lb.

Table 2 CONVERSION FORMULAS

Multiply:	By:	To get the equivalent of:
Length		
Inches	25.4	Millimeter
Inches	2.54	Centimeter
Miles	1.609	Kilometer
Feet	0.3048	Meter
Millimeter	0.03937	Inches
Centimeter	0.3937	Inches
Kilometer	0.6214	Mile
Meter	3.281	Feet
Fluid volume		
U.S. quarts	0.9463	Liters
U.S. gallons	3.785	Liters
U.S. ounces	29.573529	Milliliters
Liters	0.2641721	U.S. gallons
Liters	1.0566882	U.S. quarts
Liters	33.814023	U.S. ounces
Milliliters	0.033814	U.S. ounces
Milliliters	1.0	Cubic centimeters
Milliliters	0.001	Liters
Torque		
Foot-pounds	1.3558	Newton-meters
Foot-pounds	0.138255	Meters-kilograms
Inch-pounds	0.11299	Newton-meters
Newton-meters	0.7375622	Foot-pounds
Newton-meters	8.8507	Inch-pounds
Meters-kilograms	7.2330139	Foot-pounds
Volume		
Cubic inches	16.387064	Cubic centimeters

(continued)

Table 2 CONVERSION FORMULAS (continued)

Multiply:	By:	To get the equivalent of:
Volume (continued)		
Cubic centimeters	0.0610237	Cubic inches
Temperature		
Fahrenheit	(°F – 32) × 0.556	Centigrade
Centigrade	(°C × 1.8) + 32	Fahrenheit
Weight		
Ounces	28.3495	Grams
Pounds	0.4535924	Kilograms
Grams	0.035274	Ounces
Kilograms	2.2046224	Pounds
Pressure		
Pounds per square inch	0.070307	Kilograms per square centimeter
Kilograms per square centimeter	14.223343	Pounds per square inch
Kilopascals	0.1450	Pounds per square inch
Pounds per square inch	6.895	Kilopascals
Speed		
Miles per hour	1.609344	Kilometers per hour
Kilometers per hour	0.6213712	Miles per hour

Table 3 TECHNICAL ABBREVIATIONS

A	Ampere
AC	Alternating current
A.h.	Ampere hour
C	Celsius
cc	Cubic centimeter
CDI	Capacitor discharge ignition
cm	Centimeter
cu. in.	Cubic inch and cubic inches
cyl.	Cylinder
DC	Direct current
F	Fahrenheit
fl. oz.	Fluid ounces
ft.	Foot
ft.-lb.	Foot-pounds
gal.	Gallon and gallons
hp	Horsepower
Hz	Hertz
in.	Inch and inches
in.-lb.	Inch-pounds
in. Hg	Inches of mercury
kg	Kilogram
kg/cm^2	Kilogram per square centimeter
kgm	Kilogram meter
km	Kilometer
km/h	Kilometer per hour
kPa	Kilopascals
kW	Kilowatt
L	Liter and liters
L/m	Liters per minute
lb.	Pound and pounds
m	Meter
mL	Milliliter
mm	Millimeter
MPa	Megapascal
N	Newton
N•m	Newton meter
oz.	Ounce and ounces
p	Pascal
psi	Pounds per square inch

(continued)

Table 3 TECHNICAL ABBREVIATIONS (continued)

pt.	Pint and pints
qt.	Quart and quarts
rpm	Revolution per minute
TDC	Top dead center
V	Volt
VAC	Alternating current voltage
VDC	Direct current voltage
W	Watt

Table 4 METRIC TAP AND DRILL SIZES

Metric size	Drill equivalent	Decimal fraction	Nearest fraction
3 × 0.50	No. 39	0.0995	3/32
3 × 0.60	3/32	0.0937	3/32
4 × 0.70	No. 30	0.1285	1/8
4 × 0.75	1/8	0.125	1/8
5 × 0.80	No. 19	0.166	11/64
5 × 0.90	No. 20	0.161	5/32
6 × 1.00	No. 9	0.196	13/64
7 × 1.00	16/64	0.234	15/64
8 × 1.00	J	0.277	9/32
8 × 1.25	17/64	0.265	17/64
9 × 1.00	5/16	0.3125	5/16
9 × 1.25	5/16	0.3125	5/16
10 × 1.25	11/32	0.3437	11/32
10 × 1.50	R	0.339	11/32
11 × 1.50	3/8	0.375	3/8
12 × 1.50	13/32	0.406	13/32
12 × 1.75	13/32	0.406	13/32

Table 5 METRIC, DECIMAL AND FRACTIONAL EQUIVALENTS

mm	in.	Nearest fraction	mm	in.	Nearest fraction
1	0.0394	1/32	26	1.0236	1 1/32
2	0.0787	3/32	27	1.0630	1 1/16
3	0.1181	1/8	28	1.1024	1 3/32
4	0.1575	5/32	29	1.1417	1 5/32
5	0.1969	3/16	30	1.1811	1 3/16
6	0.2362	1/4	31	1.2205	1 7/32
7	0.2756	9/32	32	1.2598	1 1/4
8	0.3150	5/16	33	1.2992	1 5/16
9	0.3543	11/32	34	1.3386	1 11/32
10	0.3937	13/32	35	1.3780	1 3/8
11	0.4331	7/16	36	1.4173	1 13/32
12	0.4724	15/32	37	1.4567	1 15/32
13	0.5118	1/2	38	1.4961	1 1/2
14	0.5512	9/16	39	1.5354	1 17/32
15	0.5906	19/32	40	1.5748	1 9/16
16	0.6299	5/8	41	1.6142	1 5/8
17	0.6693	21/32	42	1.6535	1 21/32
18	0.7087	23/32	43	1.6929	1 11/16
19	0.7480	3/4	44	1.7323	1 23/32
20	0.7874	25/32	45	1.7717	1 25/32
21	0.8268	13/16	46	1.8110	1 13/16
22	0.8661	7/8	47	1.8504	1 27/32
23	0.9055	29/32	48	1.8898	1 7/8
24	0.9449	15/16	49	1.9291	1 15/16
25	0.9843	31/32	50	1.9685	1 31/32

Table 6 TORQUE RECOMMENDATIONS*

Thread diameter	N•m	in.-lb.	ft.-lb.
5 mm			
Bolt and nut	5	44	–
Screw	4	35	–
6 mm			
Bolt and nut	10	88	–
Screw	9	80	–
6 mm flange bolt and nut	12	106	–
6 mm bolt with 8 mm head	9	80	–
8 mm			
Bolt and nut	22	–	16
Flange bolt and nut	27	–	20
10 mm			
Bolt and nut	35	–	26
Flange bolt and nut	40	–	30
12 mm			
Bolt and nut	55	–	40.5

*Torque recommendations for fasteners without a specification. Refer to the torque specification table at the end of each applicable chapter for specific applications.

CHAPTER TWO

TROUBLESHOOTING

Diagnosing problems, either mechanical or electrical, is easier if the three fundamental operating requirements are kept in mind. These are: correct air/fuel mixture, adequate compression and properly timed spark. If one of these is not correct, the engine will not run, or will run poorly. The first steps are:

1. Define the symptom(s) of the problem.
2. Determine which area(s) could exhibit the symptom(s).
3. Test and analyze the suspect area(s).
4. Isolate the problem.

Being quick to assume a particular area is at fault can lead to increased problems, lost time and unnecessary parts replacement.

Always start with the simple and obvious checks when troubleshooting. These checks include: engine stop switch operation, fuel level, fuel valve position and spark plug cap tightness.

WATER DAMAGE

If the ATV is regularly operated in very wet conditions, the brakes, cables, wheel bearings, engine oil and differential oil need to be serviced more often than specified. In addition, corrosion may increase the likelihood of electrical problems.

CAUTION

If the engine oil is contaminated with water, it will foam and/or have a whitish appearance. Frequently, this will be evident by foam on the inside of the fill cap. Oil diluted with water will not lubricate properly.

Change the oil, and if necessary, run the engine until it reaches operating temperature, and repeat the process until all contaminates are removed.

CAUTION

If the ATV has been completely submerged, there is a chance that the cylinder is filled with water. Water does not compress, thus attempting to start the engine before pumpking the water out can create hydraulic lock and result in engine damage.

If the ATV has been completely submerged and will no longer run, perform the following:

1. Drain the fuel tank.
2. Clean the carburetor (Chapter Eight).
3. Drain and replace the engine oil (Chapter Three).
4. Remove the spark plug, and crank the engine over to remove water from the cylinder.
5. Drain the air filter housing (Chapter Three). Clean the air filter housing, cover and inspection cup.
6. Clean or replace the air filter (Chapter Three).
7. Lubricate the cables (Chapter Three).
8. Clean the brakes and check brake fluid for contamination.

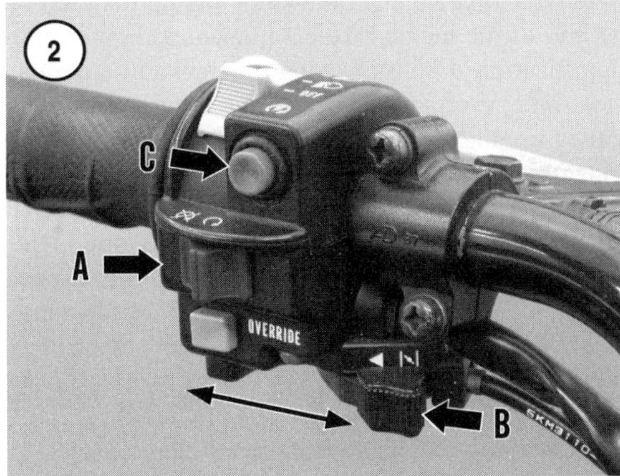

STARTING THE ENGINE

Before starting the engine, always perform a pre-ride inspection of the machine, as described in Chapter Three.

Starting Interlock Switches

Besides the engine stop switch, safety switches prevent the engine from starting if certain conditions are not met. Note the following:

1. The engine will start if the transmission is in neutral. This closes the neutral safety switch.
2. The engine will start if the transmission is in park. This closes the rear brake safety switch.
3. The engine will start if the transmission is in gear and the rear brake lever is pulled. This closes the rear brake safety switch.

Starting a Cold Engine

1. Shift the transmission into park.
2. Turn on the fuel valve (**Figure 1**). An arrow on the fuel valve points to the lever position.
3. Check that the engine stop switch (A, **Figure 2**) is in the run position.
4. Fully open the choke lever (B, **Figure 2**) to the left to richen the air/fuel mixture.
5. Turn on the ignition switch.
6. Check that the park indicator light comes on.
7. Press the starter button (C, **Figure 2**) while keeping the throttle closed.
8. When the engine starts, keep the engine speed slightly above an idle and gradually move the choke lever to the closed position. The choke should be completely off after 30 seconds. In extremely cold weather, the choke may be required for a longer period. Allow the engine to warm up until it responds smoothly.

CAUTION

Do not race the engine during the warm-up period. Excessive wear and potential engine damage can occur when the engine is not at operating temperature.

Starting a Warm or Hot Engine

1. Shift the transmission into park.
2. Turn on the fuel valve (**Figure 1**). An arrow on the fuel valve points to the lever position.
3. Check that the engine stop switch (A, **Figure 2**) is in the run position.
4. Turn on the ignition switch.
5. Check that the park indicator light comes on.
6. Slightly open the throttle and press the starter button (C, **Figure 2**).

Engine Is Flooded

If the engine fails to start after several tries (particularly if the choke has been used), it is probably flooded. This occurs when too much fuel is drawn into the engine and the spark plug fails to ignite the air/fuel mixture. The smell of gasoline is often evident whenever the engine is flooded. If there are no obvious signs of fuel overflow from the carburetor, attempt to start the engine by fully opening the throttle (no choke) and operating the starter. If the engine starts, keep the engine running at a fast idle until it has burned the excess fuel from the engine.

If the engine does not start, perform the following troubleshooting steps before making other checks.

1. Make sure the choke lever is fully closed.
2. Look for gasoline overflowing from the carburetor or overflow hose. If gasoline is evident, the float in the carburetor bowl is stuck or adjusted too high. Remove and repair the float assembly (Chapter Eight).
3. Check the air filter for excessive buildup.

4. Remove the spark plug and dry the electrodes. Reinstall the plug and attempt to start the engine as described above.
5. Perform an engine spark test.

ENGINE SPARK TEST

An engine spark test indicates whether the ignition system is providing power to the spark plug. It is a quick way to determine if a problem is in the electrical system or fuel system.

CAUTION
When performing this test, the spark plug lead must be grounded before cranking the engine. If it is not, it is possible to damage the CDI circuitry.

1. Remove the spark plug. Inspect the spark plug by comparing its condition to the plugs shown in Chapter Three.
2. Connect the spark plug lead to the spark plug, or to a spark tester (**Figure 3**).
3. Ground the plug/tester to bare metal on the engine (**Figure 4**). Position the plug/tester so the firing end is visible.
4. Crank the engine and observe the spark. A fat, blue spark should appear at the firing end. The spark should fire consistently as the engine is cranked.
5. If the spark appears weak, or fires inconsistently, check the following areas for the possible cause:
   a. Battery voltage too low.
   b. Fouled/improperly gapped spark plug.
   c. Damaged/shorted spark plug lead and cap.
   d. Loose connection in ignition system.
   e. Damaged coil.
   f. Damaged ignition switch.
   g. Dirty/shorted engine stop switch or safety interlock switch.
   h. Damaged pickup coil.
   i. Damaged CDI unit.

ELECTRICAL TESTING

WARNING
High voltage may be present during electrical testing. Do not hold wires or components while cranking the engine or when it is running.

This section describes electrical troubleshooting and the use of test equipment.

Never assume anything and do not overlook the obvious, such as a blown fuse or an electrical connector that has separated. Test the simplest and most obvious items first and try to make tests at easily accessible points on the ATV. Make sure to troubleshoot systematically. Refer to the color wiring diagram at the end of the manual for component and connector identification. Use the wiring diagram to determine how the circuit should work by tracing the current paths from the power source through the circuit components to ground. Also check any circuits that share the same fuse, ground or switch. If the other circuits work properly and the shared wiring is good, the cause must be in the wiring used only by the suspect circuit. If all related circuits are faulty at the same time, the probable cause is a poor ground connection or a blown fuse(s).

Refer to Chapter Nine for specific starting, ignition, charging and fan system procedures. Refer to *Engine Starting System* in this chapter for starting system troubleshooting.

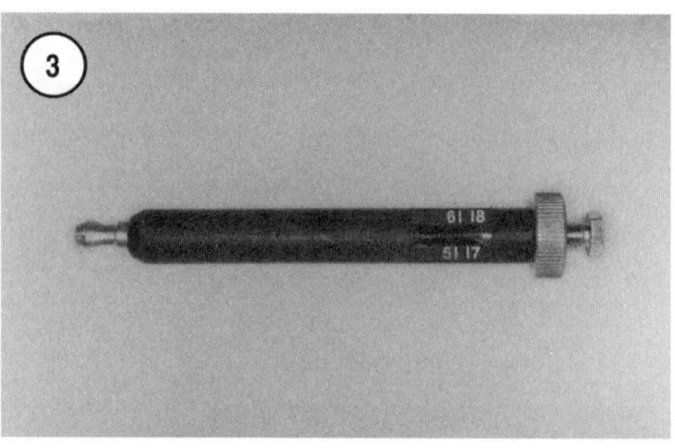

Preliminary Checks and Precautions

Before starting any electrical troubleshooting, perform the following:
1. Inspect the fuse for the suspected circuit, and replace it if blown.
2. Inspect the battery (Chapter Three). Make sure it is fully charged and the battery leads are clean and securely attached to the battery terminals.
3. Electrical connectors are often the cause of electrical system problems. Inspect the connectors as follows:
   a. Disconnect each electrical connector in the suspect circuit and make sure there are no bent terminals in the electrical connector(s). A bent terminal will not connect to its mate, causing an open circuit.
   b. Make sure the terminals are pushed all the way into the connector. If not, carefully push them in with a narrow blade screwdriver.
   c. Check the wires where they attach to the terminals for damage.
   d. Make sure each terminal is clean and free of corrosion. Clean them, if necessary, and pack the connectors with dielectric grease.

e. Push the connector halves together. Make sure the connectors are fully engaged and locked together.

f. Never pull the wires when disconnecting a connector. Pull only on the connector housing.

4. Never use a self-powered test light on circuits that contain solid-state devices. The solid-state devices may be damaged.

5. Never disconnect electrical connectors with the ignition on, or with the engine running or cranking.

6. When performing peak voltage tests make sure the connections are secure. Use caution when high voltage is present.

Intermittent Problems

Problems that do not occur all the time can be difficult to isolate during testing. For example, when a problem only occurs when the ATV is ridden over rough roads (vibration) or in wet conditions (water penetration). Note the following:

1. Vibration. This is a common problem with loose or damaged electrical connectors.

NOTE
An analog ohmmeter is useful when making this type of test. Slight needle movements are visibly apparent, which indicate a loose connection.

a. Perform a continuity test as described in the appropriate service procedure or under Continuity Test in this section.

b. Lightly pull or wiggle the connectors while repeating the test. Do the same when checking the wiring harness and individual components, especially where the wires enter a housing or connector.

c. A change in meter readings indicates a poor connection. Find and repair the problem or replace the part. Check for wires with cracked or broken insulation.

2. Heat. This is a common problem with connectors or joints that have loose or poor connections. As these connections heat up, the connection or joint expands and separates, causing an open circuit. Other heat related problems occur when a component starts to fail as it heats up.

a. Troubleshoot the problem to isolate the circuit.

CAUTION
A heat gun will quickly raise the temperature of the component being tested. Do not apply heat directly to the component or use heat in excess of 140° F (60° C) on any electrical component.

b. To check a connector, perform a continuity test as described in the appropriate service procedure or under Continuity Test in this section. Then repeat the test while heating the connector with a heat gun. If the meter reading was normal (continuity) when the connector was cold, and then fluctuated or read infinity when heat was applied, the connection is bad.

c. To check a component, allow the engine to cool, and then start and run the engine. Note operational differences when the engine is cold and hot.

d. If the engine will not start, isolate and remove the suspect component. Test it at room temperature and again after heating it with a heat gun. A change in meter readings indicates a temperature problem.

3. Water. When the problem occurs when riding in wet conditions or in areas with high humidity, start and run the engine in a dry area. Then, with the engine running, spray water onto the suspected component/circuit. Water-related problems often stop after the component heats up and dries.

Test Light or Voltmeter

Use a test light to check for voltage in a circuit. Attach one lead to ground and the other lead to various points along the circuit. It does not make a difference which test lead is attached to ground. The bulb lights when voltage is present.

Use a voltmeter in the same manner as the test light to find out if voltage is present in any given circuit. The voltmeter, unlike the test light, also indicates how much voltage is present at each test point.

Voltage test

Unless otherwise specified, make all voltage tests with the electrical connectors still connected. Insert the test leads into the backside of the connector and make sure the test lead touches the electrical terminal within the connector housing. If the test lead only touches the wire insulation, it will cause a false reading. Always check both sides of the connector because one side may be loose or corroded, thus preventing electrical flow through the connector. This type of test can be performed with a test light or a voltmeter.

1. Attach the voltmeter negative test lead to a confirmed ground location. If possible, use the battery ground connection. Make sure the ground is not insulated.
2. Attach the voltmeter positive test lead to the point to be tested.
3. Turn the ignition switch on. If using a test light, the test light will come on if voltage is present. If using a voltmeter, note the voltage reading. The reading should be within 1 volt of battery voltage. If the voltage is less there is a problem in the circuit.

Voltage drop test

The wires, cables, connectors and switches in the electrical circuit are designed to carry current with low resistance. This ensures current can flow through the circuit with a minimum loss of voltage. Voltage drop indicates where there is resistance in a circuit. A higher-than-normal amount of resistance in a circuit decreases the flow of current and causes the voltage to drop between the source and destination in the circuit.

Because resistance causes voltage to drop, a voltmeter is used to measure voltage drop when current is running through the circuit. If the circuit has no resistance, there is no voltage drop so the voltmeter indicates 0 volts. The greater the resistance in a circuit, the greater the voltage drop reading.

To perform a voltage drop:

1. Connect the positive meter test lead to the electrical source (where electricity is coming from).
2. Connect the voltmeter negative test lead to the electrical load (where the electricity is going). Refer to **Figure 5**.
3. If necessary, activate the component(s) in the circuit.
4. Read the voltage drop (difference in voltage between the source and destination) on the voltmeter. Note the following:
   a. The voltmeter should indicate 0 volts. If there is a drop of 1 volt or more, there is a problem within the circuit. A voltage drop reading of 12 volts indicates an open in the circuit.
   b. A voltage drop of 1 or more volts indicates that a circuit has excessive resistance. For example, consider a starting problem where the battery is fully charged but the starter turns over slowly. Voltage drop would be the difference in the voltage at the battery (source) and the voltage at the starter (destination) as the engine is being started (current is flowing through the battery cables). A corroded battery cable would cause a high voltage drop (high resistance) and slow engine cranking.
   c. Common sources of voltage drop are loose or contaminated connectors and poor ground connections.

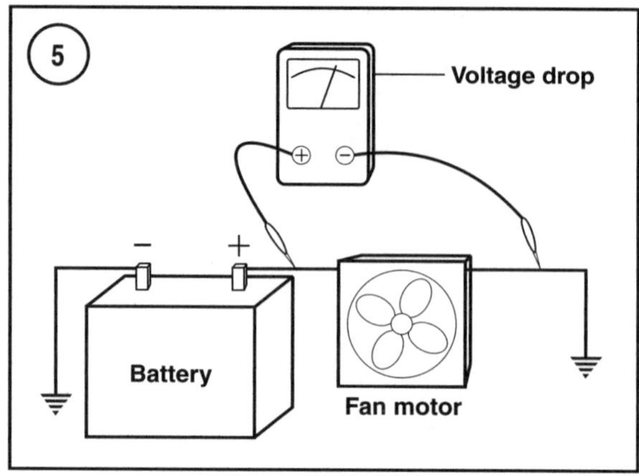

Testing for a short with a voltmeter

A test light may also be used.

1. Remove the blown fuse from the fuse panel.
2. Connect the voltmeter across the fuse terminals in the fuse panel. Turn the ignition switch on and check for battery voltage.
3. With the voltmeter attached to the fuse terminals, wiggle the wiring harness relating to the suspect circuit at approximately 15.2 cm (6 in.) intervals. Start next to the fuse panel and work systematically away from the panel. Note the voltmeter reading while progressing along the harness.
4. If the voltmeter reading changes (test light blinks), there is a short-to-ground at that point in the harness.

Peak voltage testing

Peak voltage tests check the voltage output of the ignition coil, ignition pulse generator and exciter coil at cranking speed. Refer to Chapter Nine.

Ammeter

Use an ammeter to measure the flow of current (amps) in a circuit (**Figure 6**). When connected in series in a circuit, the ammeter determines if current is flowing through the circuit and if that current flow

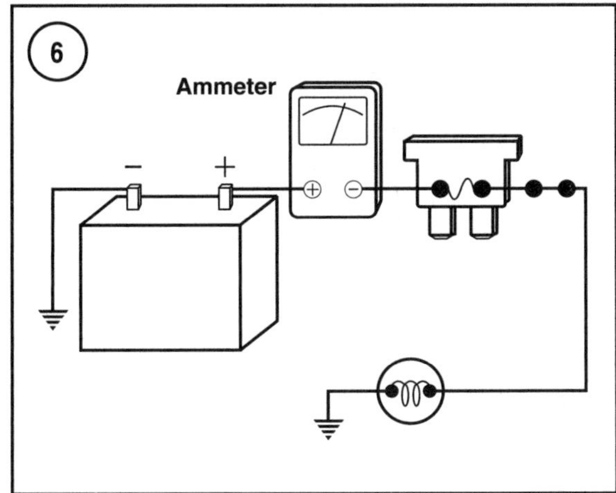

is excessive because of a short in the circuit. Current flow is often referred to as current draw. Comparing actual current draw in the circuit or component to current draw specification (if specified by the manufacturer) provides useful diagnostic information.

Self-Powered Test Light

A self-powered test light can be constructed from a 12-volt light bulb, a pair of test leads and a 12-volt battery. When the test leads are touched together the light bulb should go on.

Use a self-powered test light as follows:

1. Touch the test leads together to make sure the light bulb goes on. If not, correct the problem.
2. Disconnect the ATV's battery or remove the fuse(s) that protects the circuit to be tested. Do not connect a self-powered test light to a circuit that has power applied to it.
3. Select two points within the circuit where there should be continuity.
4. Attach one lead of the test light to each point.
5. If there is continuity, the test light bulb will come on.
6. If there is no continuity, the test light bulb will not come on, indicating an open circuit or a break in the wire.

Ohmmeter

CAUTION

To prevent damage to the ohmmeter, never connect it to a circuit that has power applied to it. Always disconnect the battery negative lead (Chapter Three) before using an ohmmeter.

Use an ohmmeter to measure the resistance (in ohms) to current flow in a circuit or component. Ohmmeters may be analog type (needle scale) or digital type (LCD or LED readout). Both types of ohmmeters have a switch that allows the user to select different ranges of resistance for accurate readings. The analog ohmmeter also has a set-adjust control which is used to zero or calibrate the meter (digital ohmmeters do not require calibration). Refer to the ohmmeter's instructions to determine the correct scale setting.

2

Use an ohmmeter by connecting its test leads to the circuit or component to be tested. If an analog meter is used, it first must be calibrated by touching the test leads together and turning the set-adjust knob until the meter needle reads zero. When the leads are uncrossed, the needle should move to the other end of the scale, indicating infinite resistance. During a continuity test, a reading of infinite resistance indicates there is an open in the circuit or component. A reading of zero indicates continuity; that is, there is no measurable resistance in the circuit or component. A measured reading indicates the actual resistance to current flow that is present in that circuit. Even though resistance is present, the circuit has continuity.

Continuity test

Perform a continuity test to determine the integrity of a circuit, wire or component. A circuit has continuity if it forms a complete circuit; that is, if there are no opens in either the electrical wires or components within the circuit. A circuit with an open, on the other hand, has no continuity. This type of test can be performed with a self-powered test light or an ohmmeter. An ohmmeter gives the best results.

1. Disconnect the negative battery cable (Chapter Three) or disconnect the test circuit/component from its power source.
2. Attach one test lead (test light or ohmmeter) to one end of the part of the circuit to be tested.
3. Attach the other test lead to the other end of the part or the circuit to be tested.
4. The self-powered test light comes on if there is continuity. An ohmmeter reads 0 or low resistance if there is continuity. A reading of infinite resistance indicates no continuity; the circuit is open.
5. If testing a component, note the resistance and compare this to the specification if available.

Testing for short with an ohmmeter

An analog ohmmeter or one with an audible continuity indicator works best for short testing. A self-powered test light may also be used.

1. Disconnect the negative battery cable (Chapter Three).

2. If necessary, remove the blown fuse from the fuse panel.
3. Connect one test lead of the ohmmeter to the load side (battery side) of the fuse terminal in the fuse panel.
4. Connect the other test lead to a confirmed ground location. Make sure the ground is not insulated. If possible, use the battery ground connection.
5. Wiggle the wiring harness relating to the suspect circuit at approximately 15.2 cm (6 in.) intervals. Watch the ohmmeter while progressing along the harness.
6. If the ohmmeter needle moves or the ohmmeter beeps, there is a short-to-ground at that point in the harness.

Jumper Wire

Use a jumper wire to bypass a potential problem and isolate it to a particular point in a circuit. If a faulty circuit works properly with a jumper wire installed, an open exists between the two jumped points in the circuit.

To troubleshoot with a jumper wire, first use the wire to determine if the problem is on the ground side or the load side of a device. Verify the ground by connecting the jumper wire between the device and a good ground. If the device comes on, the problem is the connection between the device and ground. If the device does not come on with the wire installed, the device's connection to ground is good, so the problem is between the device and the power source. To isolate the problem, connect the wire between the battery and the device. If it comes on, the problem is between these two points. Next, connect the wire between the battery and the fuse side of the switch. If the device comes on, the switch is good. By successively moving the wire from one point to another, the problem can be isolated to a particular place in the circuit. Note the following when using a jumper wire:

1. Make sure the wire gauge (thickness) is the same as that used in the circuit being tested. Smaller gauge wire rapidly overheats and could melt.
2. Make sure the jumper wire has insulated alligator clips. This prevents accidental grounding (sparks) or possible shock. Install an inline fuse/fuse holder in the jumper wire.
3. A jumper wire is a temporary test measure. Do not leave a jumper wire installed as a permanent solution. This creates a fire hazard.
4. Never use a jumper wire across any load (a component that is connected and turned on). This would cause a direct short and blow the fuse(s).

ENGINE STARTING SYSTEM

Starter Does Not Operate

If the starter does not operate after making the following checks, refer to the *Starter Operational Test* and *Starting System Switches* in Chapter Nine for testing the individual components in the starting system.

1. Engine stop switch in off position.
2. Blown fuse.
3. Weak or discharged battery.
4. Damaged neutral safety switch.
5. Damaged rear brake safety switch.

Starter Turns Slowly

1. Weak battery.
2. Poorly connected/corroded battery terminals and cables.
3. Poorly connected/corroded starter cable.
4. Worn or damaged starter.

Starter Turns but Does Not Crank Engine

1. Worn or damaged starter clutch.
2. Damaged starter motor shaft or starter gears.

ENGINE PERFORMANCE

If the engine does not operate at peak performance, refer to the following for possible causes.

Engine Does Not Start or Starts and Dies

Fuel system

1. Fuel valve off or clogged vent hose.
2. Fuel tank near empty.
3. Improper operation of choke or choke stuck open.
4. Idle speed too low.
5. Engine flooded.
6. Contaminated fuel.
7. Clogged fuel valve, fuel line or carburetor.
8. Clogged air filter.
9. Pilot mixture screw misadjusted.
10. Float valve clogged or sticking.
11. Improper float adjustment.
12. Air leaks at intake duct.
13 Clogged muffler.

Ignition system

1. Weak battery.
2. Loose, fouled or improperly gapped spark plug.

3. Damaged/shorted spark plug lead and cap.
4. Dirty/shorted engine stop switch.
5. Loose connection in ignition system.
6. Damaged neutral safety switch.
7. Damaged rear brake safety switch.
8. Damaged ignition switch.
9. Damaged coil.
10. Damaged rotor rotation direction sensing coil.
11. Damaged ignition pickup coil.
12. Damaged CDI unit.
13. Broken or bent rotor Woodruff key.

Engine

1. Compression release malfunctioning.
2. Improper valve clearance.
3. Leaking cylinder head gasket.
4. Stuck/seized valve.
5. Worn piston and/or cylinder.

Poor Idle and Low Speed Performance

Fuel system

1. Fuel valve off or clogged vent hose.
2. Improper operation of choke or choke stuck open.
3. Idle speed too low.
4. Engine flooded.
5. Contaminated fuel.
6. Clogged fuel valve, fuel line or carburetor.
7. Clogged air filter.
8. Pilot mixture screw misadjusted.
9. Float valve clogged or sticking.
10. Improper float adjustment.
11. Air leaks at intake duct.
12. Loose carburetor diaphragm cover.
13. Torn or damaged slide diaphragm.
14. Dragging carburetor slide.
15. Clogged muffler.

Ignition system

1. Loose, fouled or improperly gapped spark plug.
2. Damaged/shorted spark plug lead and cap.
3. Loose connection in ignition system.
4. Damaged coil.
5. Damaged ignition switch.
6. Dirty/shorted engine stop switch.
7. Damaged ignition pickup coil.
8. Damaged CDI unit.
9. Broken or bent rotor Woodruff key.

Engine

1. Compression release malfunctioning.
2. Improper valve clearance.
3. Leaking cylinder head gasket.
4. Low compression.
5. Improper valve/camshaft timing.

Engine Lacks Power and Acceleration

Fuel system

1. Improper operation of choke or stuck choke plunger.
2. Contaminated fuel.
3. Clogged fuel valve, fuel line or carburetor jets.
4. Clogged air filter.
5. Float valve clogged or sticking.
6. Improper float adjustment.
7. Air leaks at intake duct.
8. Improper clip position on jet needle.
9. Loose carburetor diaphragm cover.
10. Torn or damaged slide diaphragm.
11. Dragging carburetor slide.
12. Main jet or needle jet clogged.
13. Clogged muffler.

Ignition system

1. Loose, fouled or improperly gapped spark plug.
2. Damaged/shorted spark plug lead and cap.
3. Loose connection in ignition system.
4. Damaged coil.
5. Damaged ignition switch.
6. Dirty/shorted engine stop switch.
7. Damaged ignition pickup coil.
8. Damaged CDI unit.

Engine

1. Compression release malfunctioning.
2. Improper valve clearance.
3. Low compression.
4. Improper valve/camshaft timing.
5. Excessive amount of oil in engine.

Brakes and wheels

1. Brake pads dragging on brake disc.
2. Worn/seized wheel bearings.

Clutch and sheaves

1. Drive belt slipping, worn or damaged.
2. Primary sheave pulley cam and weights jammed or damaged.
3. Sliding sheave(s) dragging or damaged.
4. Clutch shoes jammed or worn.

Poor High Speed Performance

Fuel system

1. Improper operation of choke or stuck choke plunger.
2. Contaminated fuel.
3. Clogged fuel valve, fuel line or carburetor jets.
4. Clogged air filter.
5. Float valve clogged or sticking.
6. Improper float adjustment.
7. Air leaks at intake duct.
8. Loose carburetor diaphragm cover.
9. Torn or damaged slide diaphragm.
10. Dragging carburetor slide.
11. Main jet or needle jet clogged.
12. Worn needle and jet.
13. Clogged muffler.

Ignition system

1. Damaged ignition pickup coil.
2. Damaged CDI unit.

Engine

1. Weak/broken valve spring(s).
2. Improper valve clearance.
3. Low compression.
4. Improper valve/camshaft timing.
5. Excessive amount of oil in engine.

Engine Backfires

1. Pilot mixture screw adjusted too lean.
2. Air leaks into exhaust system.
3. Inoperative air cut-off valve (backfiring during deceleration).
4. Damaged ignition pickup coil.

Engine Overheats

Engine overheating can occur at slow speed during severe off-road riding conditions. Even though the fan turns on, excessive heat buildup can cause the engine to overheat.

Cooling system

1. Coolant level low.
2. Water in system; no coolant mix.
3. Air in system.
4. Radiator clogged.
5. Radiator cap damaged.
6. Thermostat damaged.
7. Fan sending unit faulty.

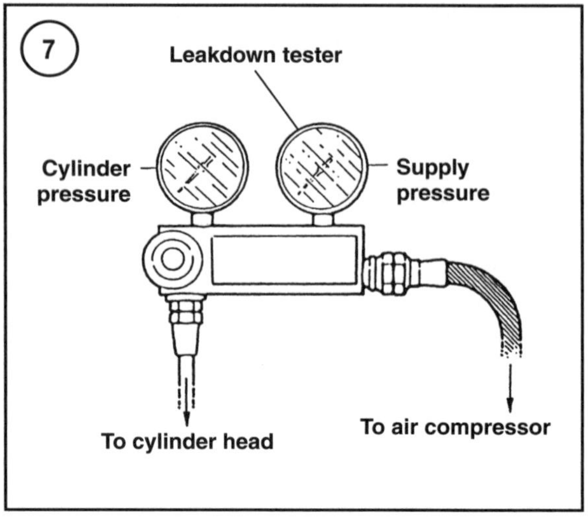

8. Fan shaft seized.
9. Water pump impeller loose.
10. Water pump impeller damaged.
11. Coolant temperature sending unit faulty.
12. Coolant temperature warning light faulty.

Engine

1. Excessive idling.
2. Insufficient oil level or viscosity.
3. Incorrect spark plug heat range.
4. Clogged crankcase oil strainer or oil filter.
5. Damaged oil pump.
6. Excessive carbon buildup on piston/cylinder head.

Brakes and wheels

1. Brake pads dragging on brake disc.
2. Worn/seized wheel bearings.

Fuel system (lean fuel mixture)

1. Air leaks at intake duct.
2. Wrong pilot or main jet for altitude.
3. Clogged carburetor jets.
4. Float level too low.

Ignition

1. Improper spark plug heat range.
2. Damaged ignition pickup coil.

ENGINE NOISE

Noise is often the first indicator that something is wrong with the engine. In many cases, damage can be avoided or minimized if the rider immediately stops the machine and diagnoses the source of the noise. Anytime engine noise is ignored, even when the machine seems to be running correctly, the rider risks causing more damage.

Pinging During Acceleration

1. Poor quality or contaminated fuel.
2. Lean fuel mixture.
3. Excessive carbon buildup in combustion chamber.
4. Damaged ignition pickup coil.

Knocks, Ticks or Rattles

Engine top end

1. Incorrect valve clearance.
2. Broken or weak valve spring.
3. Damaged compression release.
4. Loose cam chain/damaged tensioner.
5. Worn piston pin or piston pin bore.
6. Worn connecting rod small end.
7. Worn piston, rings and/or cylinder.

Engine lower end

1. Worn or loose clutch and sheave components.
2. Worn connecting rod bearing.
3. Worn crankshaft bearings.
4. Worn balancer bearings.
5. Worn transmission bearings.
6. Worn or damaged transmission gears.

FRAME NOISE

Noises from the frame or suspension are usually caused by loose, worn or damaged parts. Check for the following:

1. Loose exhaust system.
2. Loose/missing body fasteners.
3. Loose skid plate.
4. Loose shock absorber.
5. Loose engine mounting bolts.
6. Brake pads dragging on brake disc.
7. Loose wheel lug nuts.
8. Worn/seized wheel bearings.

LEAKDOWN TEST

The condition of the piston rings and valves can be checked with a leakdown tester. With all valves in the closed position, the tester is screwed into the spark plug hole and air pressure is applied to the combustion chamber. The gauge on the tester is then observed to determine the leak rate from the combustion chamber. An air compressor is required to use the leakdown tester (**Figure 7**).

1. Start the engine and allow it to warm up.
2. Shut off the engine and remove the carburetor and exhaust pipe.
3. Remove the spark plug.
4. Set the piston to TDC on the compression stroke.
5. Install the leakdown tester following the manufacturer's instructions. The tester must not leak around the spark plug threads.
6. When pressure is applied to the cylinder, make sure the engine remains at TDC.
7. While the cylinder is under pressure, listen for air leaking at the following areas.
   a. A leak at the exhaust port indicates leaking exhaust valves.
   b. A leak at the intake port indicates leaking intake valves.
   c. A leak at the crankcase breather indicates leaking piston rings.
8. A cylinder with a leak rate of 5 percent or less is ideal. Inspect a cylinder with a leak rate over 10 percent to determine the cause and repair it.

TRANSMISSION

If problems with the transmission are suspected, evaluate all variables and always start with the easiest checks before disassembling the engine. If the transmission exhibits abnormal noise or operation, drain the engine oil and check it for contamination or metal particles. Examine a small quantity of oil under bright light. If a metallic cast or pieces of metal are seen, there is excessive wear and/or part failure.

Difficult Shifting Into/Out of Park or Reverse

1. Incorrect select lever cable adjustment.
2. Broken select lever cable.

Difficult Shifting To All Positions

Select lever

1. Incorrect select lever rod adjustment.
2. Bent select lever rod.
3. Worn shift arm on select lever rod.

External shift mechanism

1. Loose, jammed or damaged shift levers.
2. Broken shift lever return spring.

Shift drum and shift forks

1. Worn shift drum grooves and guide pins.
2. Broken shift drum spring.
3. Worn/bent shift forks.
4. Bent shift fork shaft.

Gears Do Not Stay Engaged

Select lever

1. Incorrect select lever rod adjustment.
2. Bent select lever rod.
3. Worn shift arm on select lever rod.

Shift drum and shift forks

1. Worn shift drum grooves and guide pins.
2. Broken shift drum spring.
3. Worn/bent shift forks.
4. Bent shift fork shaft.
5. Improper return of stopper lever.

Transmission

1. Worn gear dogs and mating recesses.
2. Worn gear grooves for shift forks.
3. Worn/damaged shaft snap rings, washers or bushings.

AXLES, DIFFERENTIAL AND FINAL DRIVE UNIT

Problems with the axles, differential and final drive unit are often accompanied by noise. If damage to one of these areas is suspected, try to isolate where the sound originates. Turn the axles and feel the exterior of the differential and final drive unit. Excessive wear can often be felt through the parts. Also, immediately after operating the machine, feel the components for excessive heat, particularly around the axle and drive shaft bearings.

Symptoms of Damage

The following are likely symptoms of damage to the axles, differential or final drive unit.

1. Excessive play in axle.
2. Axle binding and vibration.
3. Locked axle.
4. A low-pitch rumble or high-pitch whine when the machine is in motion.
5. A delayed knock or metallic sound that quickly follows acceleration or deceleration.

Possible Causes of Damage

The following are possible causes of damage to the axles, differential or final drive unit.

1. Worn or damaged CV joints.
2. Bent axle.
3. Seized or damaged wheel bearing.
4. Seized or damaged differential/final drive unit bearing.
5. Broken or damaged teeth in differential/final drive unit.
6. Improper gear lash in differential/final drive unit.
7. Debris lodged between differential/final drive unit parts.

DRIVE SHAFTS AND MIDDLE GEAR UNIT

Problems with the drive shafts and middle gear components are difficult to diagnose without removing and inspecting the parts. Always try to isolate where the sound originates before assuming the drive shafts or middle gear components are damaged. Inspect the axles, differential and final drive unit before disassembling the drive shafts and middle gear unit.

Symptoms of Damage

The following are likely symptoms of damage to the drive shaft and/or middle gear components.

1. A low-pitch rumble or high-pitch whine when the machine is in motion.
2. A delayed knock or metallic sound that quickly follows acceleration or deceleration.
3. Binding or erratic machine movement, accompanied by inconsistent engine speed.
4. Locked drive shafts, with no power going to either axle.

Possible Causes of Damage

The following are possible causes of damage to the drive shaft and/or middle gear components.

1. Stripped or slipping drive shaft splines and couplers.
2. Bent drive shaft.
3. Seized or damaged middle gear unit bearing.
4. Broken or damaged teeth in middle gear unit.
5. Improper gear lash in middle gear unit.
6. Debris lodged between middle gear unit parts.

BRAKE SYSTEM

The brake system is critical to riding performance and safety. Inspect the brakes frequently and replace worn or damaged parts immediately. The brake system requires DOT 4 brake fluid. Always use new fluid from a sealed container. Refer to the troubleshooting checks in **Figure 8** to isolate the brake problems.

When checking brake pad wear, make sure the pads in each caliper squarely contact the disc. Uneven pad wear on one side of the disc can indicate a warped or bent disc, damaged caliper or pad pins.

STEERING AND HANDLING

Correct poor steering and handling immediately. Check the following areas:

Excessive handlebar vibration

1. Incorrect tire pressure.
2. Loose wheel lug nuts.
3. Damaged wheel (excessive runout).
4. Bent tie rod.
5. Incorrect toe-in.
6. Loose or damaged handlebar clamps.
7. Loose steering shaft nut or bearings.
8. Worn or damaged front wheel bearings.
9. Bent or loose axle.
10. Damaged steering knuckle.

Handlebar is hard to turn

1. Tire pressure too low.
2. Incorrect cable routing.
3. Steering shaft too tight.
4. Steering shaft bent.
5. Seized or damaged steering shaft bearing.

Handlebar pulls to one side

1. Uneven tire pressure.
2. Bent tie rod.
3. Dragging brake.
4. Mismatched tire sizes.

Frame vibration

1. Loose wheel lug nuts.
2. Bent suspension components.
3. Bent frame.
4. Worn or missing suspension bushings.
5. Loose engine mounts.
6. Loose shock absorber.

Suspension too soft

1. Low tire pressure.
2. Weak shock absorber spring.
3. Leaking shock absorber.
4. Improper shock absorber settings.

Suspension too hard

1. High tire pressure.
2. Bent shock absorber shaft.
3. Improper shock absorber settings.

Figure 8 is on the following page.

8

BRAKE TROUBLESHOOTING

Disc brake fluid leaks	Check: • Loose or damaged line fittings • Worn caliper piston seals • Scored caliper piston or bore • Loose banjo bolts • Damaged brake line washers • Leaking master cylinder diaphragm • Leaking master cylinder secondary seal • Cracked master cylinder housing • Incorrect brake fluid level • Loose or damaged master cylinder
Brake overheating	Check: • Warped brake disc • Incorrect brake fluid • Caliper piston and/or brake pads hanging up • Riding brakes during riding
Brake chatter	Check: • Warped brake disc • Incorrect caliper alignment • Loose caliper mounting bolts • Loose front axle nut and/or clamps • Worn wheel bearings • Damaged hub • Restricted brake line • Contaminated brake pads
Brake locking	Check: • Incorrect brake fluid • Plugged passages in master cylinder • Caliper piston and/or brake pads hanging up • Warped brake disc
Insufficient brakes	Check: • Air in brake lines • Worn brake pads • Low brake fluid • Incorrect brake fluid • Worn brake disc • Worn caliper piston seals • Glazed brake pads • Leaking primary cup seal in master cylinder • Contaminated brake pads and/or disc
Brake squeal	Check: • Contaminated brake pads and/or disc • Dust or dirt collected behind brake pads • Loose parts

CHAPTER THREE

3

LUBRICATION, MAINTENANCE AND TUNE-UP

This chapter provides maintenance procedures. Refer to **Tables 1-4** at the end of the chapter.

Refer to *Shop Supplies* in Chapter One for general fluid information.

PRE-RIDE INSPECTION

Perform the following checks before riding the machine. Perform these checks when the engine is *cold*. Check the following:

1. Fuel line and fittings.
2. Fuel level.
3. Engine oil level.
4. Coolant level.
5. Throttle operation and free play.
6. Brake operation, fluid level and lever/pedal free play.
7. Engine stop switch.
8. Lights.
9. Air filter.
10. Air filter drain.
11. Drive belt case drain.
12. Drive belt cooling duct drain.
13. Select lever box drain.
14. Steering operation.
15. Tire condition and air pressure.
16. Wheel condition and lugnut tightness.
17. Axle boot condition.
18. Suspension.
19. Exhaust system.
20. Fasteners.

ENGINE BREAK-IN

The performance and service life of a new or reconditioned engine depends greatly on a careful and sensible break-in. Observe the following:

1. Fill the engine with the correct amount and weight of engine oil.
2. Fill the cooling system with the recommended coolant.
3. Install a new spark plug.
4. Make sure the air filter is clean.
5. For the first 10 hours of operation, use no more than one-half throttle. Vary the speed as much as possible within this throttle range. Avoid running the machine at a steady speed. Avoid hard acceleration. After every hour of operation, allow the engine to cool for 10 minutes.
6. For the next 10 hours of operation, use no more than three-fourths throttle. Vary the speed as much as possible within this throttle range. Hard acceleration within this range is permissible.
7. At the end of the break-in period, perform the 20-hour service items in **Table 1**.

BATTERY

The original equipment battery is a 12-volt, 18-amp-hour, maintenance-free type.

If necessary, refer to *Charging System* in Chapter Nine for additional battery and charging system tests.

Removal and Installation

1. Remove the seat (Chapter Sixteen).
2. Remove the battery holder and cover (**Figure 1**).
3. Disconnect the negative battery cable (A, **Figure 2**).
4. Remove the insulator cover from the positive cable (B, **Figure 2**). Then remove the cable from the battery.
5. Remove the battery. Then clean and check the components for damage.
6. Reverse this procedure to install the battery. Note the following:
   a. Make sure the battery terminals face the front of the machine.
   b. To prevent corrosion, apply a thin coat of dielectric grease to the battery terminals and cable ends.
   c. Tighten the cables firmly. Do not apply excessive force.

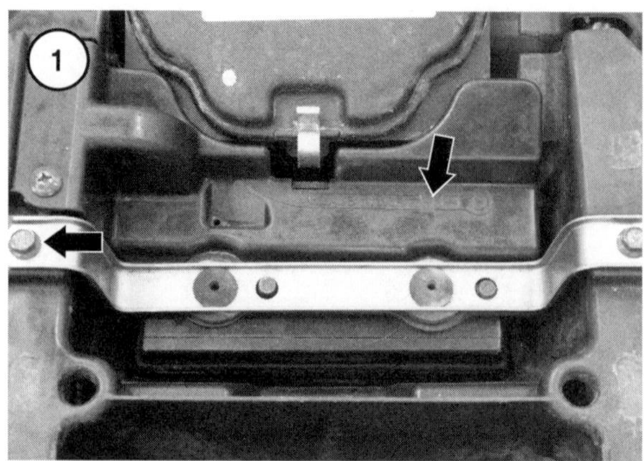

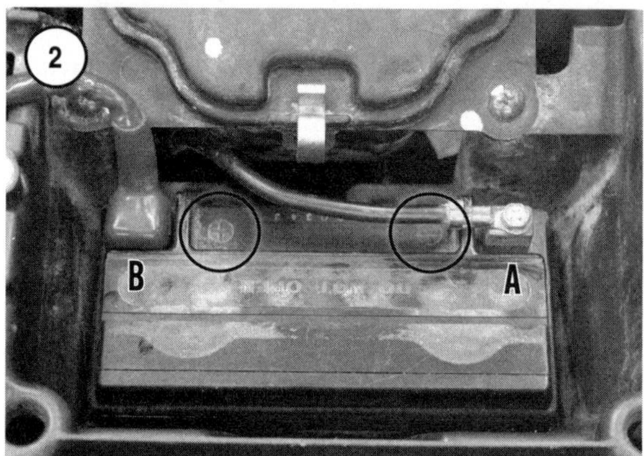

Voltage Testing

For a maintenance-free battery (original equipment), check the unloaded voltage using a voltmeter. An unloaded test will indicate the state of charge. If necessary, refer to Chapter Nine and load test the battery.

1. Disconnect the battery cables.
2. Connect a voltmeter to the negative and positive terminals as shown in **Figure 3**.
3. Measure the voltage.
   a. A fully charged battery will have a minimum of 12.8 volts.
   b. A battery that is approximately 75 percent charged will have a minimum of 12.5 volts.
   c. A battery that is approximately 50 percent charged will have a minimum of 12.0 volts.

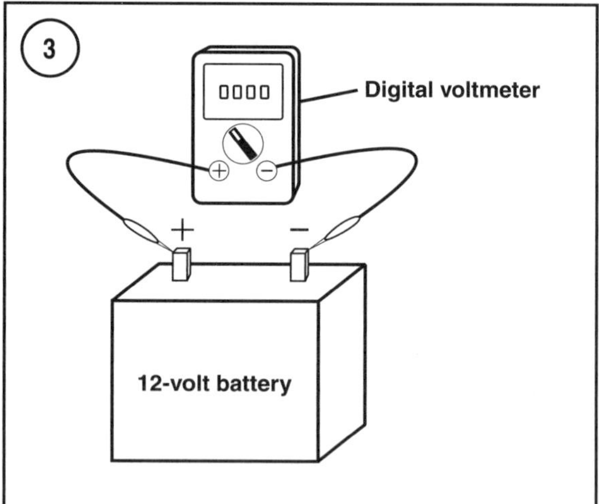

Charging

When recharging the battery, do not use a charger that is rated higher than 1.8 amps output. An excessive charge rate will overheat the battery and damage the plates.

Charge the battery regularly if the ATV is not used for extended periods.

CAUTION
To prevent possible electrical system damage, always remove the cables from the battery before charging.

1. Remove the battery as described in this section.
2. Connect the positive and negative leads of the charger to the positive and negative terminals on the battery.
3. Set the charger to 12 volts. If the charger has a variable charge rate, select a low setting. Using a 1 amp,

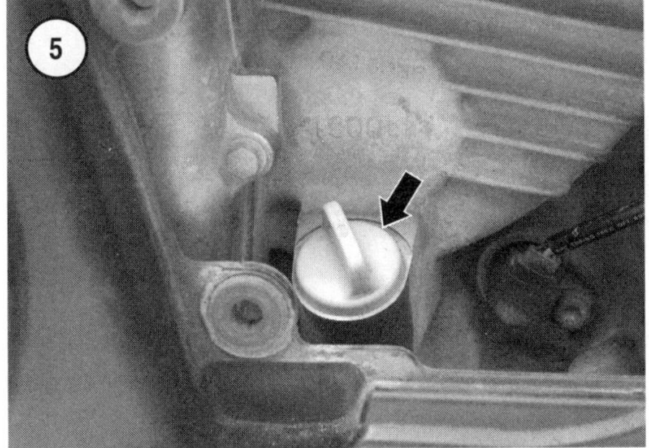

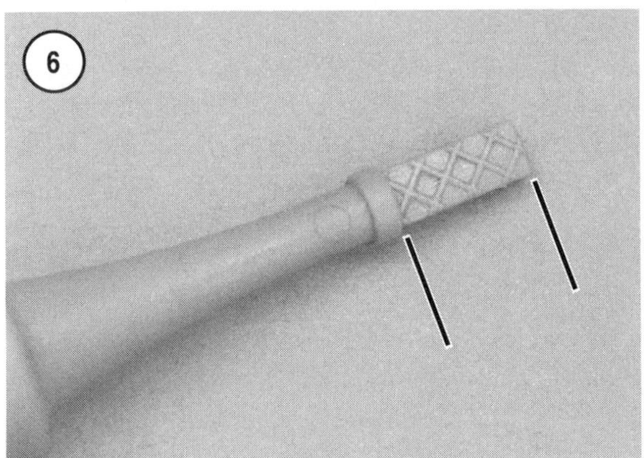

constant-current charger, the suggested charge rates for a maintenance-free battery are:

a. 75 percent charge: 1 amp for 3-6 hours.
b. 50 percent charge: 1 amp for 5-11 hours.

4. Turn on the charger and charge the battery for the specified time.
5. After the battery is charged, turn off the charger and remove the leads from the terminals. Allow the battery to stabilize for at least 30 minutes.
6. Check battery voltage as described in this section. If the battery voltage does not remain stable for at least one hour, or continues to be undercharged, replace the battery.

ENGINE OIL AND FILTER

Oil Level Check

Check and replenish the oil level at the dipstick, which is located behind the side panel (**Figure 4**) on the engine side cover. Check the oil after the engine has been warmed up and then allowed to stand for a few minutes. To check the oil:

1. Park the machine on level ground.
2. Remove the side panel (Chapter Sixteen).
3. Remove the dipstick (**Figure 5**) and wipe it clean.
4. Insert the dipstick into the crankcase, but *do not* screw it in.
5. Remove the dipstick and check the oil level. The oil level should be between the upper and lower level marks (**Figure 6**).
6. If the oil level is too low, add the appropriate amount of oil to bring the level to the upper mark. Add oil in small quantities and check the level often. Do not overfill the engine.
7. Screw the dipstick into place. If oil is evident around the top of the dipstick, replace the dipstick O-ring.

Oil and Filter Change

WARNING
Prolonged contact with used engine oil may cause skin cancer. Minimize contact with the engine oil.

Change the oil and filter at the intervals in **Table 1**. If the machine is used in extreme conditions (hot, cold, wet or dusty) change the oil more often and use the oil recommended in **Table 2**. Always change the oil when the engine is warm. Contaminants will remain suspended in the oil, and it will drain more completely. To change the oil:

1. Park the machine on level ground.
2. Remove the seat, left fuel tank side panel and engine side cover (Chapter Sixteen).
3. Wipe the area around the dipstick (**Figure 5**), then loosen it.
4. Drain the oil from the crankcase as follows:
   a. Place a drain pan below the crankcase drain plug (**Figure 7**). The drain plug is shown with the skid plate removed. A hole is provided in the skid plate to access the plug.
   b. Remove the drain plug and drain the oil from the engine.
5. Replace the oil filter as follows:
   a. Unscrew the oil filter from the engine (**Figure 8**). If necessary, use a small oil filter wrench (Yamaha part No. YU-38411).

b. Wipe clean the mounting threads and filter contact area (**Figure 9**).
c. Apply clean engine oil to the filter O-ring (**Figure 10**).
d. Install and tighten the oil filter to 17 N•m (13 ft.-lb.).

6. Install a new washer on the crankcase drain plug. If oil is evident around the dipstick, replace the dipstick O-ring.
7. Wipe dirt and oil from around the crankcase drain plug hole, then install and tighten the drain plug to 30 N•m (22 ft.-lb.).
8. Fill the crankcase with engine oil. Install and tighten the dipstick. Refer to **Table 2** for the required amount and type of engine oil.
9. Start and warm the engine for a few minutes.
10. Stop the engine and check the engine oil level as described in this section.
11. Check for leaks.
12. Install the bodywork.
13. Dispose of the filter and used engine oil in an environmentally safe manner.
14. If the ATV has been submerged or if low oil pressure is suspected, loosen the oil gallery bolt (**Figure 11**) and perform the following:

a. Start the engine and allow it to idle.
b. Oil should seep from the bolt within one minute. If not, stop the engine immediately and check the oil filter, oil pump and oil passages.

FINAL DRIVE

Oil Level Check

Check the oil level in the final drive at the oil level check bolt (A, **Figure 12**). Replenish the oil level at the fill plug (B, **Figure 12**). Both are located at the left side of the final drive case. To check the oil level:

1. Park the machine on level ground.
2. Loosen the check bolt. Then momentarily remove the bolt.

a. If oil flows from the hole, the oil level is adequate. Tighten the check bolt securely.
b. If oil does not flow from the hole, the oil level is too low. Proceed to Step 3 to adjust the oil level.

CAUTION
If water flows from the check bolt hole, change the final drive oil. Damage can occur if water remains in the final drive unit. Water-diluted oil will appear cream-colored.

3. Adjust the oil level in the final drive unit as follows:

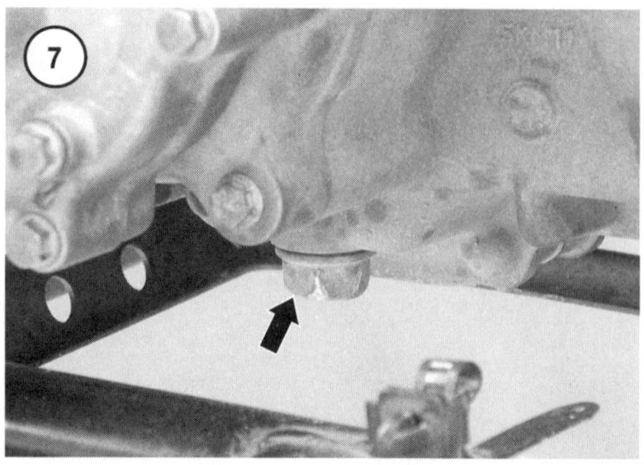
7

8

9

10

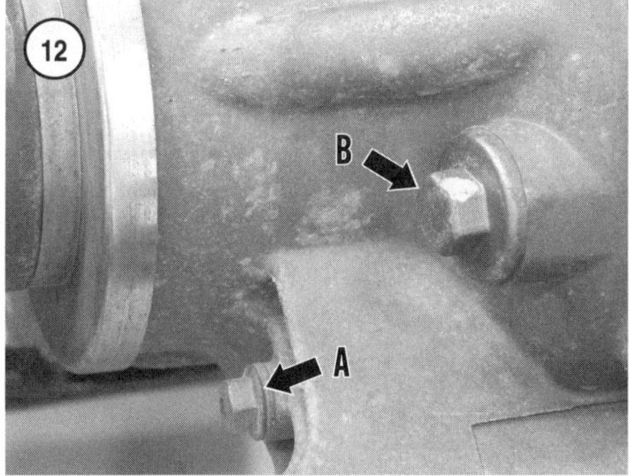

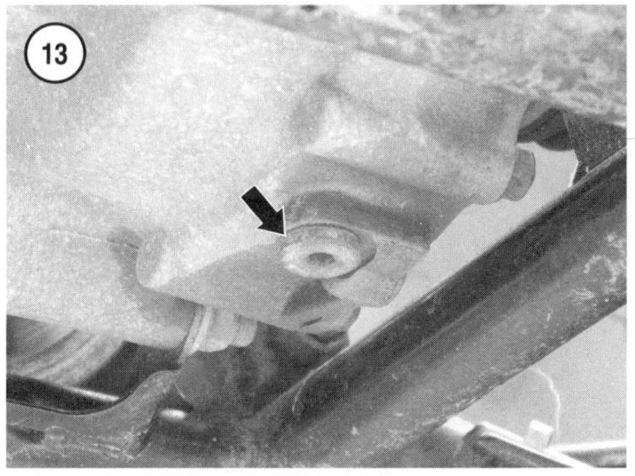

a. Wipe the area around the fill plug (B, **Figure 12**). Then remove the plug.
b. Inspect the inside of the final drive. If rust, dirt or moisture is evident, then the vent hose or the seals leak. If contamination is evident, determine where the leak is occurring and then change the oil.
c. Add hypoid gear oil until oil flow is visible at the check bolt hole. Use the appropriate hypoid gear oil as recommended in **Table 2**.
d. Install and tighten the check bolt securely.
e. If necessary, replace the washer on the fill plug, then install and tighten the fill plug to 23 N•m (17 ft.-lb.).

Oil Change

WARNING
Prolonged contact with used gear oil may cause skin cancer. Minimize contact with gear oil.

Change the final drive oil at the interval recommended in **Table 1**. Use the appropriate hypoid gear oil and amount as recommended in **Table 2**. Always change the oil when the machine is warm. Contaminants will remain suspended in the oil, and it will drain more completely. To change the oil:

1. Park the machine on level ground.
2. Wipe the area around the fill plug, then loosen the plug (B, **Figure 12**).
3. Drain the oil from the final drive unit as follows:
   a. Place a drain pan below the drain plug (**Figure 13**). The drain plug is shown here with the skid plate removed. A hole is provided in the skid plate to provide access to the plug.
   b. Remove the drain plug and allow the oil to drain from the case. If rust, dirt or moisture is evident, then the vent hose or the seals leak. Water-diluted oil will appear cream colored. If contamination is evident, determine where the leak is occurring before proceeding.
   c. Clean the plug. If necessary, replace the washer.
   d. Wipe dirt and oil from around the drain hole, then install the drain plug.
   e. Tighten the drain plug to 23 N•m (17 ft.-lb.).
4. Fill the final drive unit as follows:
   a. Remove the fill plug and clean all dirt and oil from the plug. If necessary, replace the washer on the plug.
   b. Refer to **Table 2** for the recommended amount and type of hypoid gear oil.
   c. Fill the final drive unit with gear oil.
5. Check the oil level as described in this section.

FRONT DIFFERENTIAL

Oil Level Check

Check and replenish the oil level at the fill plug (**Figure 14**) located on the right side of the differential case. To check the oil level:

1. Park the machine on level ground.
2. Wipe the area around the fill plug. Then remove the plug.

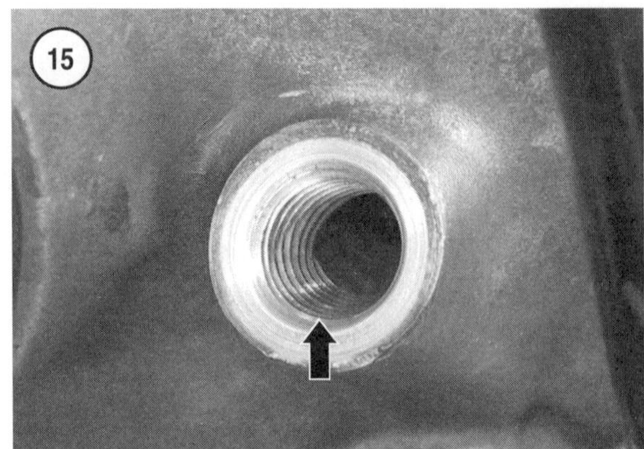

3. The oil level should be to the bottom edge of the filler plug hole (**Figure 15**). If rust, dirt or moisture is evident, then the vent hose or the seals leak. Water-diluted oil will appear cream-colored. If contamination is evident, determine where the leak is occurring and then change the oil.
4. If necessary, add hypoid gear oil to achieve the proper level. Use the appropriate hypoid gear oil for the differential as recommended in **Table 2**.
5. Clean the plug. If necessary, replace the washer on the plug.
6. Install and tighten the fill plug to 23 N•m (17 ft.-lb.).

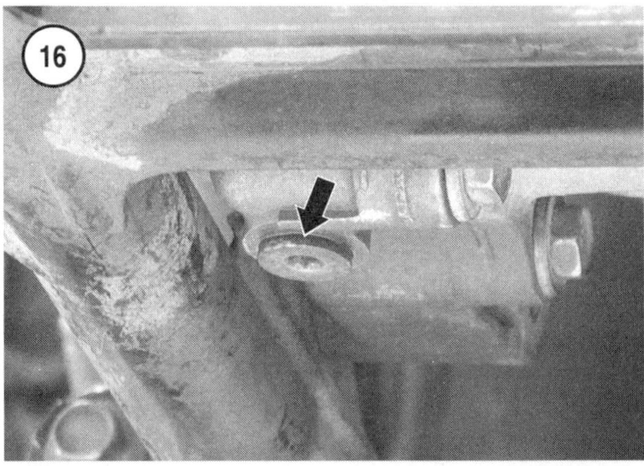

Oil Change

WARNING
Prolonged contact with used gear oil may cause skin cancer. Minimize contact with the gear oil.

Change the differential oil at the interval recommended in **Table 1**. Use the appropriate hypoid gear oil and amount recommended in **Table 2**. Always change the oil when the machine is warm. Contaminants will remain suspended in the oil, and it will drain more completely. To change the oil:

1. Park the machine on level ground.
2. Wipe the area around the fill plug. Then loosen the plug (**Figure 14**).
3. Drain the oil from the differential as follows:
   a. Place a drain pan below the drain plug (**Figure 16**). The drain plug is shown with the skid plate removed. A hole is provided in the skid plate to access the plug.
   b. Remove the drain plug and drain the oil from the case. If rust, dirt or moisture is evident, then the vent hose or the seals leak. Water-diluted oil will appear cream-colored. If contamination is evident, determine where the leak is occurring before proceeding.

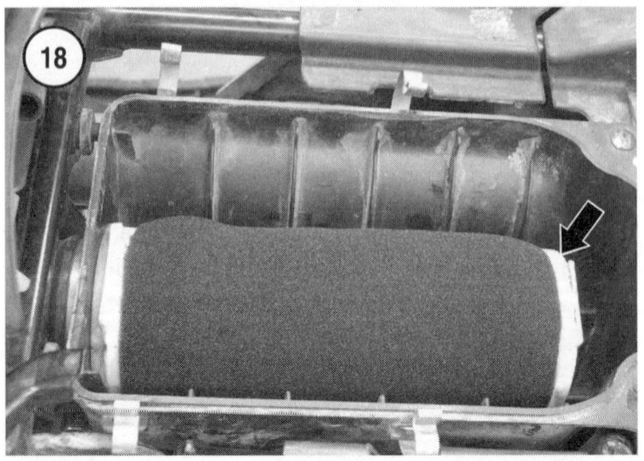

19

20

21

22

c. Clean the plug. If necessary, replace the washer.
d. Wipe dirt and oil from around the drain plug hole. Then install the drain plug.
e. Install and tighten the drain plug to 10 N•m (89 in.-lb.).

4. Fill the differential as follows:
   a. Remove the fill plug and clean all dirt and oil from the plug. If necessary, replace the washer on the plug.
   b. Refer to **Table 2** for the recommended amount and type of hypoid gear oil.
   c. Fill the differential with gear oil. The oil level should be to the bottom edge of the filler plug hole (**Figure 15**).
   d. Install and tighten the fill plug to 23 N•m (17 ft.-lb.).

AIR FILTER

Cleaning and Lubrication

CAUTION
Use oil specifically formulated for foam filters. This type of oil stays adhered to the foam and traps dust effectively.

The engine is equipped with a reusable foam air filter. Do not operate the engine without the air filter and cover, or with a damaged air filter.

1. Remove the seat (Chapter Sixteen).
2. Remove the retainer clips (**Figure 17**) from the air filter cover.
3. Remove the cover from the air filter housing and disconnect the breather hose at the front of the cover.
4. Lift out the air filter assembly (**Figure 18**).
5. Rotate and remove the end cap (**Figure 19**). Then remove the air filter from the frame (**Figure 20**).
6. Wash all parts in solvent (kerosene), a commercial filter cleaner, or hot, soapy water.
   a. *Squeeze* the cleaner from the filter. Do not wring the filter, as tearing may occur.
   b. Shake off any particles that may remain on the filter.
   c. Allow the filter to dry completely.
7. Apply filter oil to the filter, while squeezing the filter so the oil is distributed evenly. Squeeze out the excess oil. When performing this step, handle the filter with disposable gloves, or put the filter in a plastic bag. Also, oil the seal on the frame.
8. Install the frame into the filter, seating the filter against the front of the frame.
9. Install and lock the end cap to the frame (**Figure 21**).
10. Clean the air filter housing and cover.

11. Remove and clean the inspection cup (**Figure 22**) on the bottom of the air filter housing. Regularly inspect the cup for water, dirt and other contaminants. When contaminants are evident, inspect and clean the air filter and housing regardless of when they were last serviced.
12. Seat the filter assembly into the air filter housing. The square edge of the frame seal must face up. Make sure the cap tabs are seated and the filter is tight against the front of the housing.
13. Connect the breather hose to the cover, then seat the cover into place. Seat the notch in the cover (**Figure 23**) with the end of the filter.
14. Install the seat.

FRONT DRIVE SHAFT LUBRICATION

On 2002 models, the U-joint at each end of the front drive shaft is equipped with a grease fitting. Lubricate the U-joints with lithium-based grease at the intervals recommended in **Table 1**.

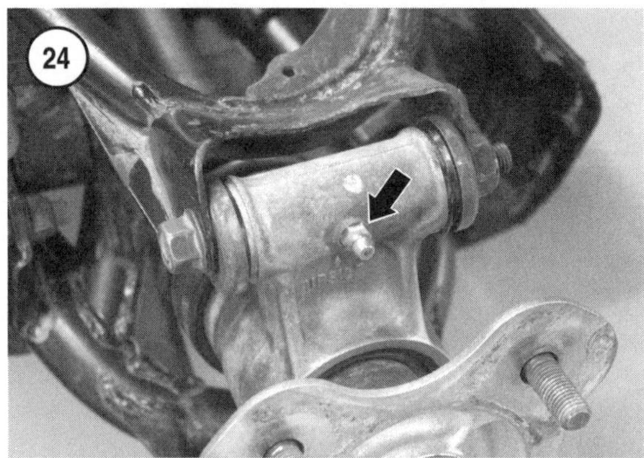

REAR SUSPENSION PIVOT LUBRICATION

The rear suspension knuckle pivots are equipped with a grease fitting at the top and bottom of the knuckle (**Figure 24**). Access to the fittings is possible through the holes in the wheel (**Figure 25**). Lubricate the upper and lower pivots with lithium-based grease at the intervals recommended in **Table 1**.

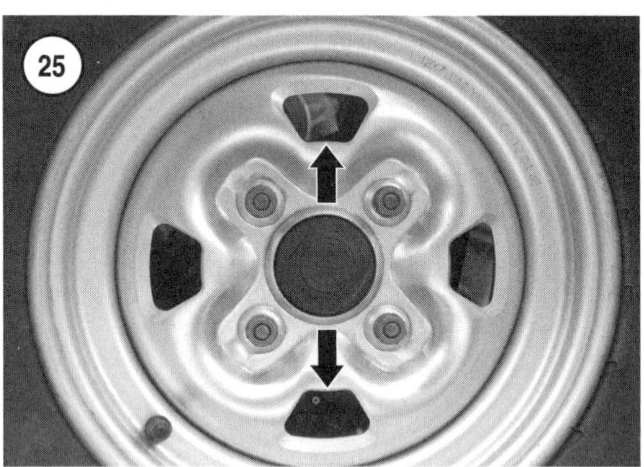

CONTROL CABLE LUBRICATION

If there is binding or drag in a cable, this can indicate a lack of cable lubrication or worn parts. Lubricate the control cable pivots with grease. Inspect the cables and lubricate them with light oil or an aerosol cable lubricant and attachment (**Figure 26**) at the intervals recommended in **Table 1**. If the cable continues to operate poorly after lubrication, disconnect the cable at both ends and check for binding or drag. Replace the cable, if necessary.

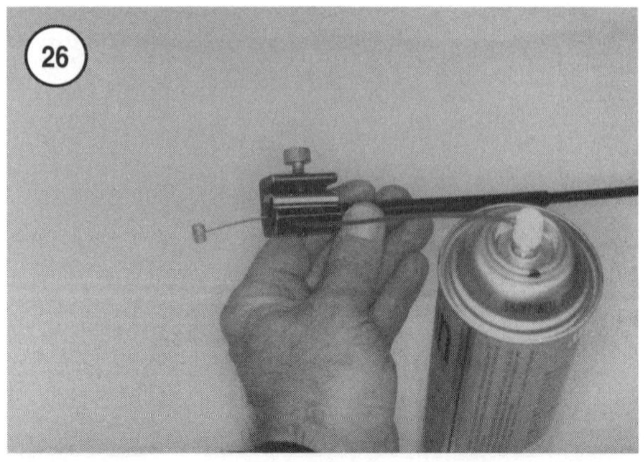

FASTENER INSPECTION

Inspect all fasteners on the machine for tightness and condition at the intervals recommended in **Table 1**.

1. Tighten fasteners to the torque specifications. Refer to **Table 6** in Chapter One if a torque value is not specified.
2. Make sure all cotter pins are secure and undamaged.

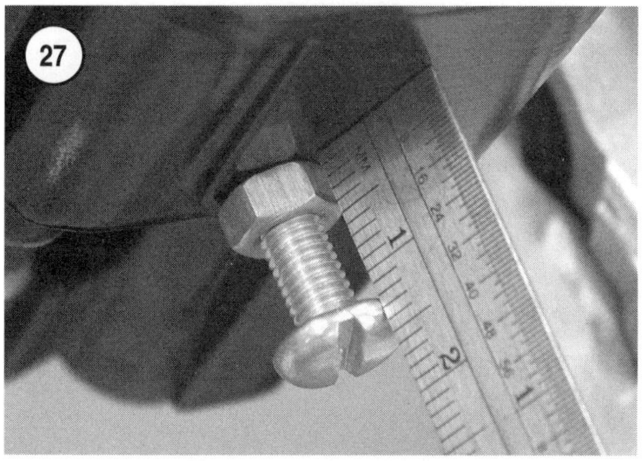

3. Check that tie straps, used to secure cables and electrical wiring, are not broken or missing.

SPEED LIMITER ADJUSTMENT

Use the speed limiter screw to restrict the travel of the throttle lever and set maximum engine speed for less experienced riders.

The limiter is also useful during the engine break-in period. Refer to **Table 1** for recommended service intervals.

To adjust the speed limiter:

1. At the throttle housing, measure the distance from the housing to the screw head (**Figure 27**). Maximum distance should not exceed 12 mm (0.47 in.).
2. If necessary, loosen the locknut and screw the adjuster to the desired position. Tighten the locknut.

AXLE BOOT INSPECTION

The axle boots (A, **Figure 28**) and clamps (B) must be in good condition to prevent the entry of dirt and moisture into the CV joints. Failure to replace damaged boots and loose/missing clamps can cause rapid wear of the CV joints, requiring replacement.

DRAIN INSPECTION

Inspect the drains whenever the machine has been operated in wet conditions, particularly deep water.

Air filter housing

Access the air filter housing drain (**Figure 22**) through the right rear wheel well. Remove the inspection cup and drain water and other contaminants from the housing. Also inspect the air filter and housing.

Select lever box

Remove the seat and left fuel tank side panel to access the select lever box drain (**Figure 29**). Remove the inspection cup and drain water and other contaminants from the select lever box.

Drive belt case

The drive belt drain is located on the right side of the engine at the bottom of the drive belt cover (**Figure 30**). Pull the tethered plug and drain water and other contaminants from the cover.

Drive belt cooling duct

The drive belt drain is located on the left side of the engine (**Figure 31**). Access the drain through the left front wheel well. Remove the inspection cup and drain water and other contaminants from the duct.

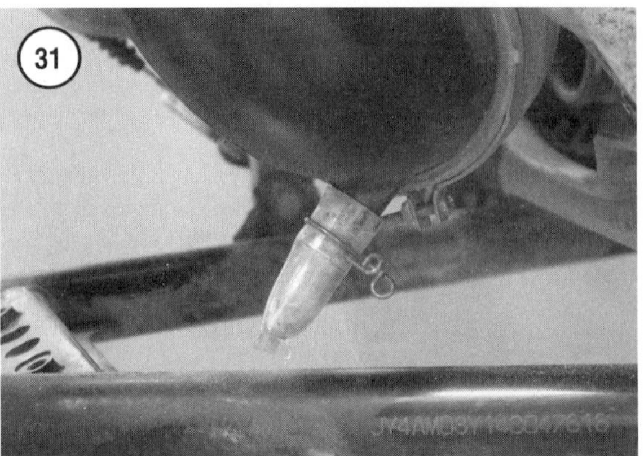

COOLING SYSTEM

WARNING
Inspect the cooling system when the engine and coolant are cold. Severe injury could occur if the system is checked while hot. If the radiator cap must be removed while the coolant is still warm, cover the cap with a towel and open it slowly. Do not remove the cap until all pressure is relieved.

CAUTION
Do not allow coolant to contact painted surfaces. If contact does occur, immediately wash the surface with water.

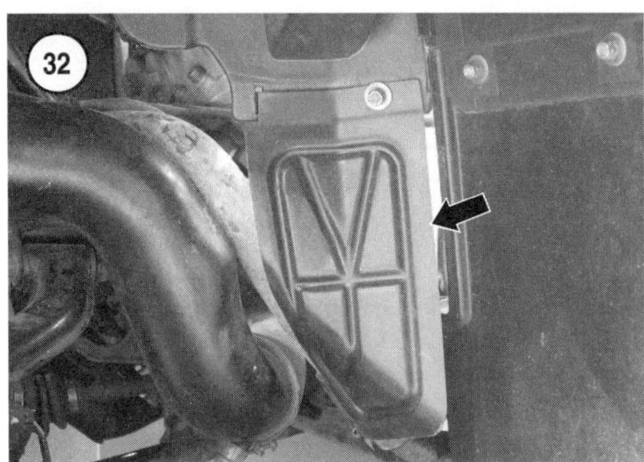

Coolant Level Inspection

Refer to **Table 2** for the recommended coolant type and mixing ratio. To inspect the coolant level:

1. Park the machine on level ground.
2. Remove the reserve tank inspection cover (**Figure 32**) in the left front wheel well.
3. Visually check the coolant level. The level should be between the low and full marks embossed on the tank (**Figure 33**).
4. If the level is low, remove the seat and left fuel tank side panel (Chapter Sixteen) so the coolant reserve tank can be filled. Remove the cap from the tank and add coolant. Do not allow the tank level to fall below the low mark.
5. Make the following checks as necessary:
   a. Check the hoses for damage at the top and bottom of the tank.
   b. If the reserve tank is empty, remove the front fender. Then check the level in the radiator. The coolant level should be at the bottom of the filler neck (**Figure 34**). If the coolant level is below the filler neck, add coolant mixture to raise the level.
   c. Install the radiator cap and start the engine. Inspect for leaks at all hoses and fittings. Check for leaks in the drain hose in the bottom of the water pump (A, **Figure 35**). If coolant is evident, this indicates the water pump mechanical seal is leaking. If engine oil is evident, the oil seal in the water pump is leaking. Refer to

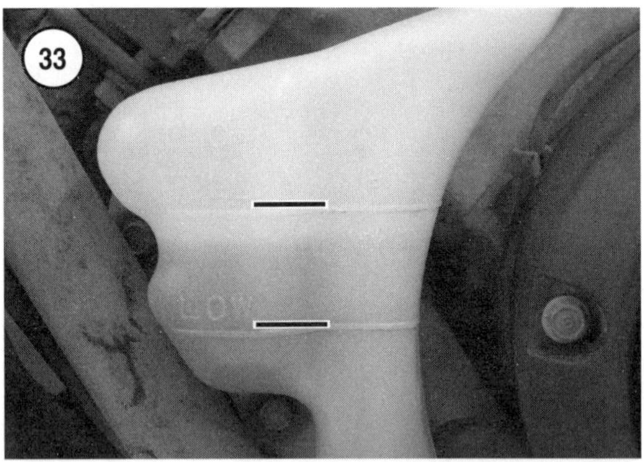

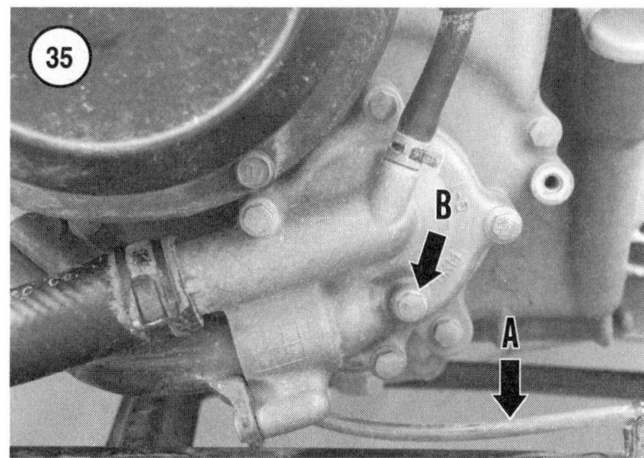

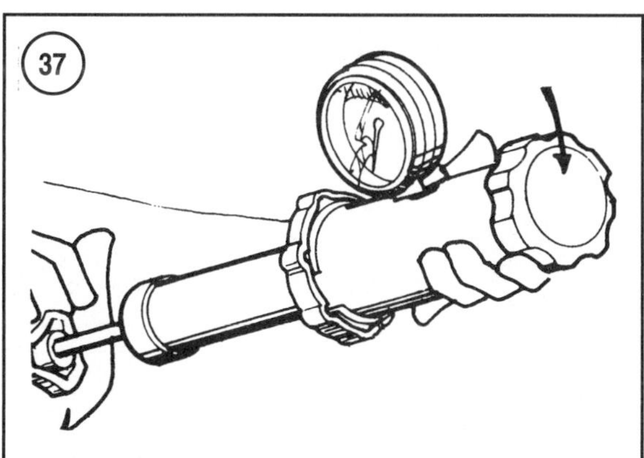

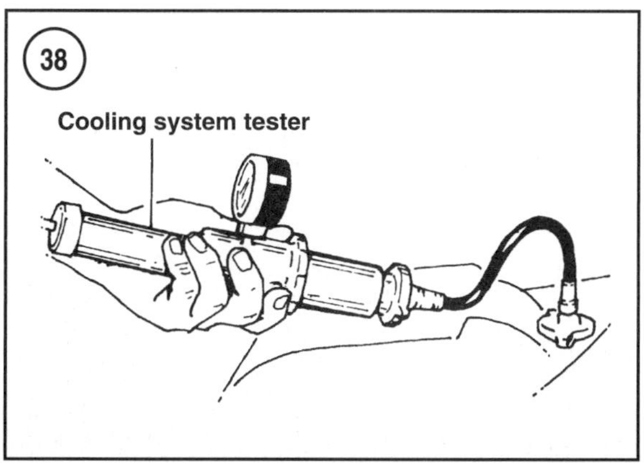

Chapter Ten to replace the seals.

5. Install the bodywork.

Cooling System Inspection

Check the condition of the cooling system whenever the coolant is changed, or whenever the front fender is removed. Immediately inspect the cooling if overheating occurs.

1. Remove the front fender (Chapter Sixteen).
2. Remove the radiator cap and make the following checks. Replace the cap if any damage is evident. Refer to **Figure 36**.
   a. Rubber seals (A). Check for cracks, compression and pliability.
   b. Relief valve (B). Check for damage and seizure.
   c. Radiator neck (C). Check for dents and distortion. The surfaces must be smooth and dent-free so the cap can seal and hold pressure. Repair or replace the radiator if the radiator neck is damaged.
3. Check the cap relief pressure. Wet the seal on the radiator cap, then attach the cap to a tester (**Figure 37**). Apply pressure to the cap. Relief pressure for the cap is 93.3-122.7 kPa (13.5-17.8 psi).
   a. If the gauge holds pressure up to the relief pressure range, the cap is in good condition.
   b. If the gauge does not hold pressure, or the relief pressure is too high or low, replace the cap.
4. Check that the radiator is filled to the bottom of the filler neck (**Figure 34**). Attach the tester to the radiator (**Figure 38**), then pump the tester to 137 kPa (20 psi).

CAUTION
Do not exceed 137 kPa (20 psi). Excessive pressure can damage the cooling system components.

   a. If the gauge holds the required pressure, the cooling system is in good condition.
   b. If the gauge does not hold the required pressure, check for leaks at the radiator and all fittings. If the pressure lowers and then stabilizes, check for swollen radiator hoses. Replace or repair the cooling system components so it maintains the test pressure.
5. Install the bodywork.

Coolant Draining and Replacement

To drain or replace the coolant:

1. Park the machine on level ground.
2. Remove the front fender assembly and coolant reservoir cover (Chapter Sixteen).

3

3. Remove the lower hose from the reserve coolant tank (**Figure 39**). Then drain and rinse the tank. Install the lower hose onto the tank.
4. To minimize cleanup of coolant from spills, place a folded cardboard trough under the coolant drain plug (B, **Figure 35**). The trough should extend across the footrest panel and drain into a pan placed below the trough.
5. Remove the drain plug from the water pump.
6. As coolant begins to drain from the engine, loosen the radiator cap (**Figure 40**) so the flow from the engine increases. Be ready to reposition the drain pan.
7. Flush the cooling system with clean water. Check that all water drains from the system. Applying *light* air pressure to the radiator can aid in purging the water passages.
8. Inspect the condition of:
   a. Radiator hoses. Check for soft spots, leaks, cracks and loose clamps.
   b. Radiator core. Check for leaks, debris and the tightness of the mounting bolts.
   c. Radiator fan. Check for damaged fan blades and tight wiring connections.
9. Install a new washer on the coolant drain plug. Then install and tighten the plug to 10 N•m (89 in.-lb.).
10. Refill the radiator with the coolant mixture and quantity specified in **Table 2**.
   a. Refill the radiator as the coolant level goes down.
   b. When the coolant level no longer goes down, fill the radiator to the bottom of the filler neck (**Figure 34**). Install the radiator cap.
   c. Fill the reserve tank to the full mark.
11. Start the engine and allow the coolant to circulate for a few minutes. Shut off the engine and do the following:
   a. Remove the radiator cap and check the coolant level. If necessary, add coolant to bring the level to the bottom of the filler neck.
   b. Install the radiator cap.
12. Start the engine and allow it to reach operating temperature. Shut off the engine and do the following:
   a. Check for leaks at the drain plug, hoses and reserve tank.
   b. Check the level in the reserve tank. If necessary, fill the reserve tank to the full mark.
13. Rinse the frame and engine where coolant was splashed.
14. Install the bodywork.
15. Dispose of the used coolant in an environmentally safe manner.

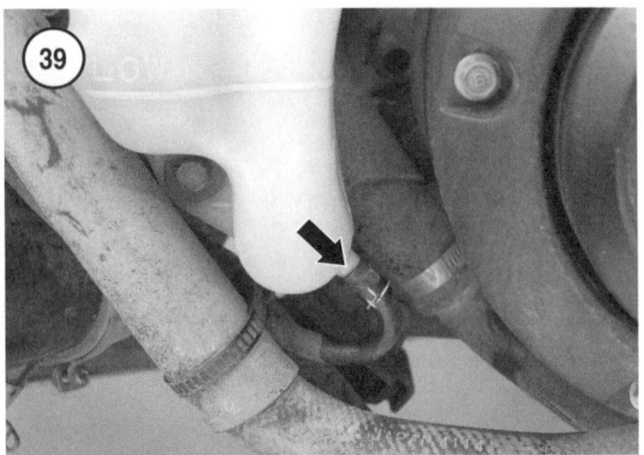

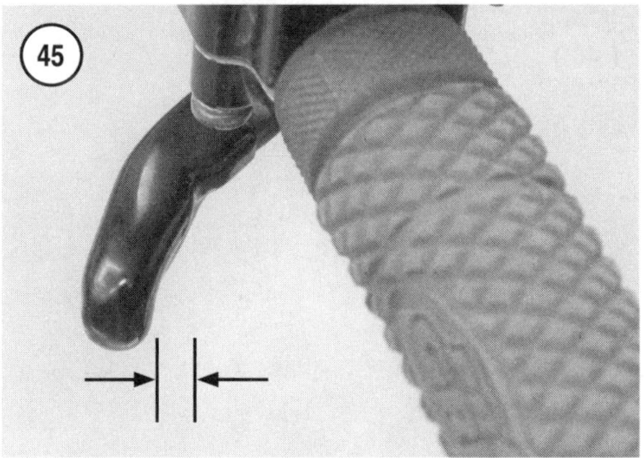

EXHAUST SYSTEM

Muffler Cleaning

WARNING
Do not spray solvents or other combustible liquids into the muffler. An explosion and/or fire could occur if solvents are present in the exhaust system during engine operation.

1. Park the machine in an open area, away from combustible materials.
2. Remove the retaining bolts (**Figure 41**) and baffle.
3. Clean the baffle with a wire brush.
4. Clean excessive buildup from the interior of the muffler.
5. Start the engine, then raise and lower the engine speed to purge the buildup from the muffler. If necessary, tap the muffler with a rubber mallet to dislodge additional buildup.
6. When all of the loose carbon particles are purged, stop the engine and allow the muffler to cool.
7. Install the baffle and bolt it into place.

3

FUEL SYSTEM

Carburetor Float Chamber Drain

WARNING
Do not attempt to drain the float chamber while the engine is hot or running.

Drain the float chamber by loosening the drain screw (**Figure 42**) and draining the fuel out the float chamber hose.

DRIVE BELT INSPECTION

Inspect and measure the drive belt as follows:
1. Remove the drive belt cover (Chapter Six).

NOTE
When measuring and inspecting the belt, it is not necessary to remove the belt from the sheaves.

2. Measure the width of the drive belt (**Figure 43**). Refer to **Table 3** for specifications.
3. Inspect the belt (**Figure 44**) for wear, cracks, contamination or damaged teeth.
4. If the belt is in good condition, install the cover. If the drive belt is damaged, replace it as described in Chapter Six.

CONTROL CABLE ADJUSTMENT

Throttle Cable

To achieve accurate cable adjustment, the cable must not bind or drag. Make sure the engine idle speed is correct before adjusting the cable. If necessary, refer to Chapter Eight for throttle cable replacement.
1. Measure the amount of free play at the throttle lever end (**Figure 45**). Free play should be 3-5 mm (0.12-0.2 in.). If free play is incorrect, adjust the cable as described in the following step(s).

2. Loosen the locknut (A, **Figure 46**) and turn the cable adjuster (B) to increase/decrease play in the cable and lever. Note the following:
   a. If correct play can be achieved, and the adjuster is close to the middle of its range of travel, tighten the locknut. Adjustment is complete.
   b. If correct play cannot be achieved with the adjuster, or if the adjuster is fully screwed in or out, set the adjuster to the middle of its travel. Proceed to Step 3 to make the adjustment at the carburetor.
3. Adjust the cable at the carburetor as follows:
   a. Remove the seat and right fuel tank side panel (Chapter Sixteen).
   b. Loosen the locknut (A, **Figure 47**) and turn the cable adjuster (B) to increase/decrease play in the cable and lever.
   c. Tighten the locknut securely.
   d. If necessary, make fine adjustments at the handlebar (Step 2).
4. At engine startup, turn the handlebar from side to side as the engine idles. If engine speed varies, check for proper cable adjustment and cable routing.

Choke Cable

On 2003-on models, the choke cable is not adjustable and must be replaced if it is out of specification.

1. Remove the seat and left fuel tank side panel (Chapter Sixteen).
2. Remove the choke plunger from the carburetor (**Figure 48**).
3. Lay the cable and plunger assembly on a flat surface so it can be measured.
4. At the handlebar, move the choke lever to the left and right (**Figure 49**) to ensure the cable moves freely. If the cable binds, inspect the cable for damage and lack of lubrication. If necessary, replace the cable.
5. At the handlebar, move the choke lever *fully to the right*. In this position, the plunger should be extended. Measure the distance from the tip of the plunger to the edge of the housing (**Figure 50**). Record the measurement.
6. Move the choke lever *fully to the left*. In this position, the plunger should be retracted. Measure the distance from the tip of the plunger to the edge of the housing (**Figure 50**). Record the measurement.
7. The difference between the two measurements should be 15 mm (0.6 in.). On 2003-on models, replace the cable if it is out of specification. If necessary, adjust the cable on 2002 models as follows:
   a. Loosen the locknut (A, **Figure 50**) and turn the cable adjuster (B) to increase/decrease the length of the plunger stroke.

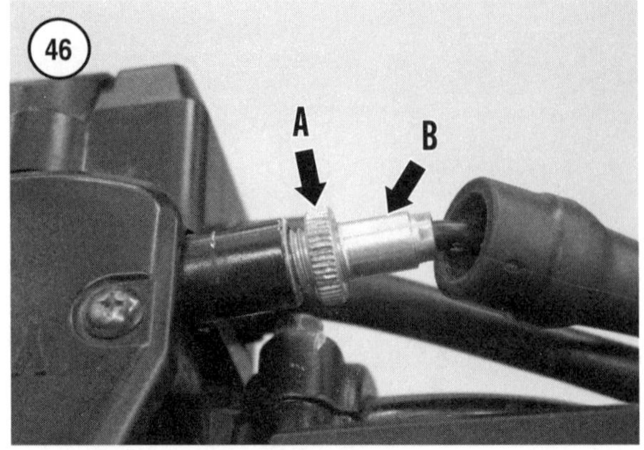

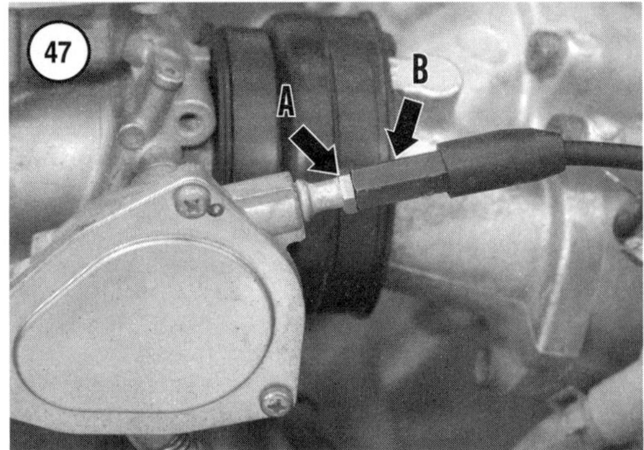

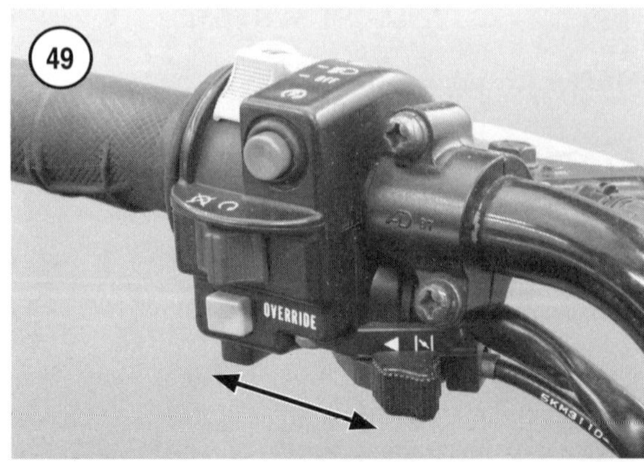

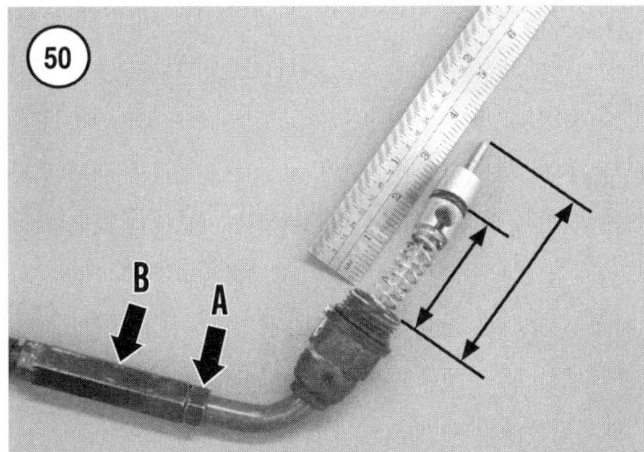

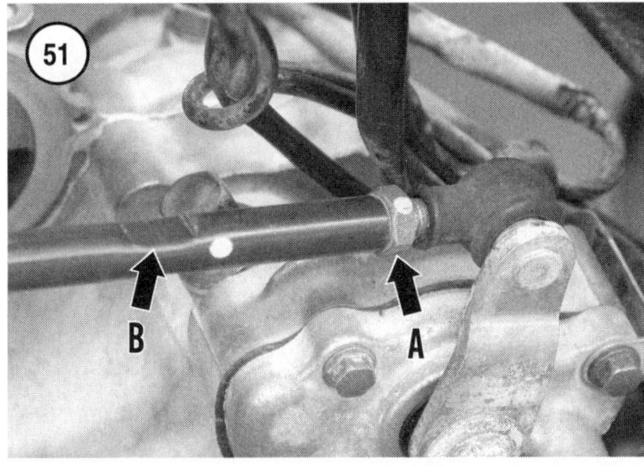

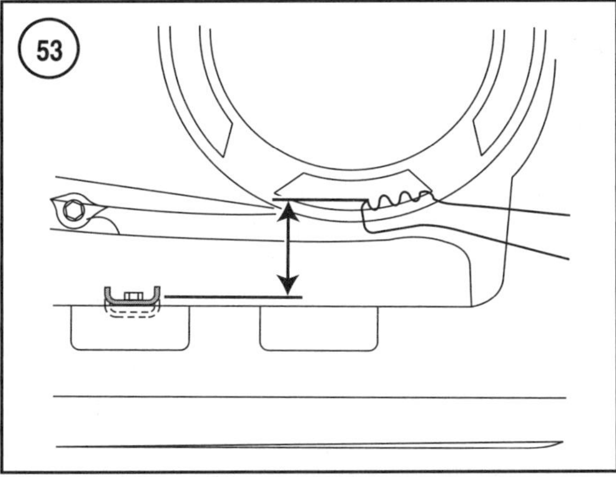

b. When adjustment is correct, tighten the locknut securely.

8. Route the cable to the carburetor and install the plunger.

9. Install the left fuel tank side panel and seat.

Select Lever Shift Rod

Adjust the select lever shift rod to ensure smooth, complete engagement and disengagement of the transmission.

1. Place the select lever in neutral.
2. Loosen the locknut (A, **Figure 51**) at each end of the shift rod.
3. Use a wrench to turn the shift rod at the flats (B, **Figure 51**) provided. Adjust the shift rod length until the shifting is smooth.
4. Tighten the locknuts to 15 N•m (11 ft.-lb.).

Select Lever Cable

Adjust the select lever cable to ensure proper engagement and lockout of the select lever. Adjust the select lever cable *after* adjusting the rear brake pedal and left hand lever. Adjust the brake pedal and lever as described in this chapter.

1. Place the select lever into neutral.
2. At the rear brake master cylinder, check for any play or tension in the select lever cable and spring (A, **Figure 52**). There should be no play or tension in the parts.
3. If necessary, loosen the cable locknuts (B, **Figure 52**) and adjust the cable so there is no play or tension. If additional adjustment is required, also use the cable housing adjuster (C, **Figure 52**). Check that all locknuts are tightened securely.
4. Test the adjustment of the select lever cable and brakes as described under *Brake System* in this chapter.

BRAKE SYSTEM

Rear Brake Pedal and Left Hand Brake Lever Adjustment

The rear brake can be actuated by the brake pedal, or by the left hand lever at the handlebar. Since the pedal and lever are individually connected to the rear master cylinder, it is necessary to adjust both parts when adjusting the rear brake.

1. Measure the distance from the top of the footpeg to the top of the rear brake pedal (**Figure 53**). The brake pedal should be positioned 45 mm (1.8 in.) above the footpeg. If the distance is incorrect, adjust the pedal as follows:

a. At the handlebar, loosen the brake cable locknut (A, **Figure 54**). Then fully turn in the adjuster (B).
b. Remove the rear brake master cylinder cover (**Figure 55**) located behind the right front wheel.

WARNING
The end of the pushrod should always be visible in the clevis. If the end of the pushrod is not visible, inspect the master cylinder and brake pedal for worn or damaged parts.

c. Loosen the locknut at the master cylinder pushrod (A, **Figure 56**). Then turn the adjuster (B) to increase/decrease pedal height. Correct pedal height should be achieved when the clearance (C, **Figure 56**), between the adjuster and locknut, is 5-6 mm (0.20-0.24 in.). Tighten the locknut when adjustment is correct.

2. Measure the clearance for the hand lever cable at A, **Figure 57** as follows:
   a. Make sure the clevis pin (B, **Figure 57**) is fully to the right in the slotted link.
   b. Loosen the locknut (C, **Figure 57**) and pull the brake outer cable up. The clearance should be 1 mm (0.04 in.). If necessary, turn the adjuster nut until the proper clearance is achieved.
   c. Hold the adjuster in place and tighten the locknut.
3. At the handlebar, turn out the cable adjuster (B, **Figure 54**) until the left brake lever free play (C) is 0.5-2 mm (0.02-0.08 in.). Tighten the locknut (A, **Figure 54**). If proper play cannot be achieved within the adjustment range, readjust the cable at the master cylinder to increase/decrease free play at the handlebar.
4. Adjust the select lever cable as described under *Control Cable Adjustment* in this chapter. Then test the brake and select lever adjustments in the following steps.
5. Place the machine in two-wheel drive and raise the rear wheels. Place the select lever into neutral. Turn the wheels and operate the brake pedal and brake lever.
   a. The rear wheels should lock when either the pedal or lever is fully applied. If the brake does not engage, or if brake performance is poor, recheck adjustments.
   b. The rear wheels should turn freely when the pedal and lever are disengaged. It is normal for the brake pads to lightly contact the brake disc(s) when the brake is disengaged. If excessive drag is evident, recheck adjustment.
6. Test the adjustment of the select lever cable. Verify the following:

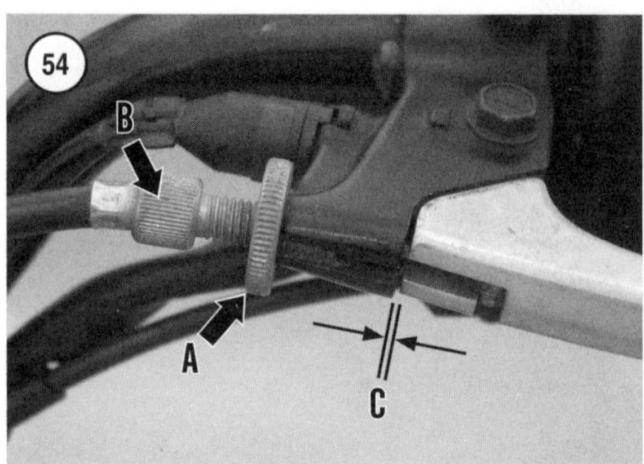

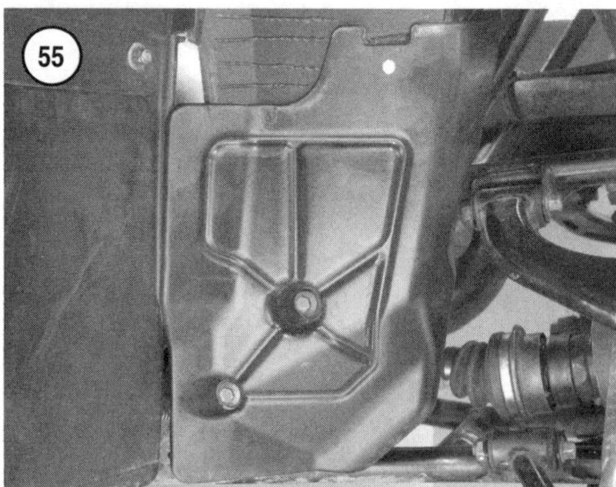

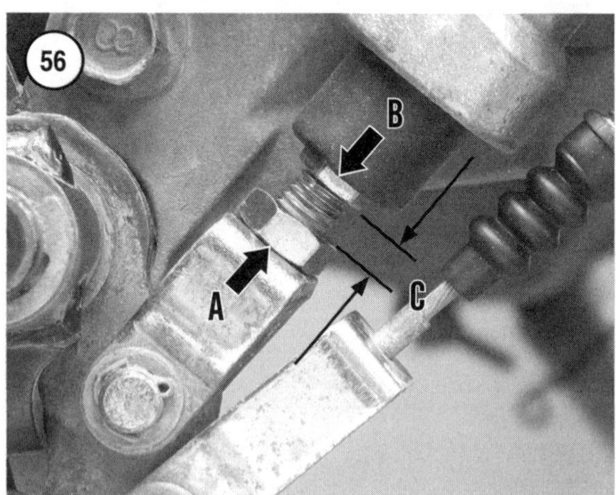

   a. When the rear brake is applied, the select lever *should* be able to shift from neutral to reverse, from reverse to neutral and from reverse to park.
   b. When the rear brake is disengaged, the select lever *should not* be able to shift from neutral to reverse, from reverse to neutral and from park to reverse.
   c. If the select lever fails any test, check cable condition and adjustment.

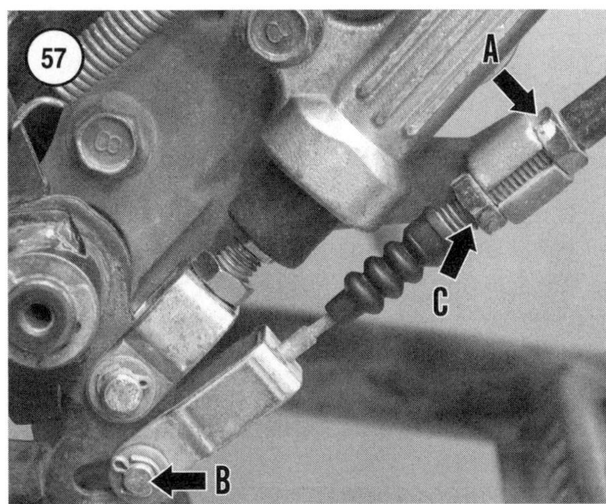

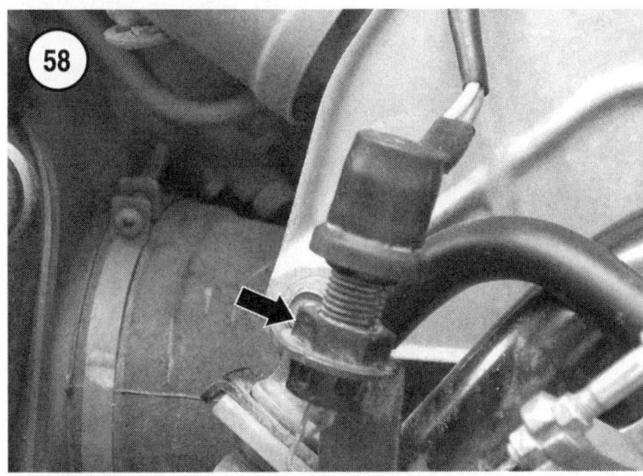

7. Check brake light operation. If necessary, adjust the switch as described in this section.
8. Install the rear brake master cylinder cover.

Rear Brake Light Switch Adjustment

The rear brake light should turn on whenever the brake pedal or left hand brake lever is slightly activated. The brake light switch is located above the brake pedal pivot and is attached by a spring. Check switch adjustment after the brake pedal and rear brake lever have been properly adjusted.

1. Remove the rear brake master cylinder cover (**Figure 55**), located behind the right front wheel.
2. Adjust the brake light switch position by turning the nut on the switch as follows:
   a. If the light comes on too late (too much pedal or lever travel), turn the switch adjustment nut (**Figure 58**) and *raise* the switch position.
   b. If the light comes on too early (too little pedal or lever travel), turn the switch adjustment nut and *lower* the switch position.

Right Hand Brake Lever Adjustment

There is no routine adjustment required for the right hand hydraulic brake lever. If the master cylinder is in good condition and properly bled, the right lever is automatically adjusted. If the front brakes drag, or front brake lever play is unacceptable, inspect the master cylinder and front brake calipers (Chapter Fifteen).

Brake Fluid Level Inspection

1. Park the machine on a level surface and position the handlebar so the front brake fluid reservoir is level.
2. Inspect the front reservoir as follows:
   a. The fluid level should be between the lower level mark and the top of the sight glass (**Figure 59**).
   b. If the fluid level is below the low mark, remove the reservoir cap and diaphragm, then add DOT 4 brake fluid. Install the diaphragm and cap. Note that the cap is not rectangular. Install the cap so the printing on the cap is readable from the rider's position.
   c. Check for master cylinder leaks and worn brake pads.
3. Inspect the rear reservoir as follows:
   a. Remove the rear brake master cylinder cover (**Figure 55**), located behind the right front wheel.
   b. The fluid level should be between the upper and lower level marks embossed on the reservoir (**Figure 60**).
   c. If the fluid level is below the low mark, remove the cap, diaphragm holder and diaphragm. Then add DOT 4 brake fluid.
   d. Replace the diaphragm, diaphragm holder and cap. Then install the cover.
   e. Check for master cylinder leaks and worn brake pads.

3

60

61

Brake Pad and Disc Inspection

Check the brake discs and pads regularly to make sure they are in good condition. During severe riding conditions, the scoring of a disc can occur rapidly if the brake pads are damaged or have debris lodged in the pad material. If damage is evident for any of the following inspections, refer to Chapter Fifteen for brake pad replacement, disc specifications and service limits.

To inspect the front brake pads and discs, the front wheels must be removed. A general inspection of the rear brake pads and disc can be performed by inspecting the parts from the left side of the machine. If wear or damage is evident, remove the left rear wheel to access the parts.

1. Visually inspect the front and rear discs for the following:
   a. Scoring. The disc should be smooth in the friction area. If disc scoring is evident, remove the caliper and inspect the surface of the pads.
   b. Runout. For a front disc, spin the disc and visually check for lateral movement of the disc. Runout should not be evident. For the rear disc, raise the rear wheels and put the select lever in neutral. Turn the rear wheels to turn the drive shaft and disc. If runout is obvious, refer to Chapter Fifteen.
   c. Disc thickness. If the disc(s) shows wear in the friction area, refer to Chapter Fifteen.
2. Inspect the brake pads. If the pads are less than 1 mm (0.04 in.) thick, or worn to/through the wear indicator grooves (**Figure 61**), replace the pads. Refer to Chapter Fifteen for pad replacement.

Shock Absorber Adjustment

The front and rear shock absorbers are adjustable to meet the riding conditions. Refer to *Shock Absorbers* in Chapter Eleven and Chapter Thirteen.

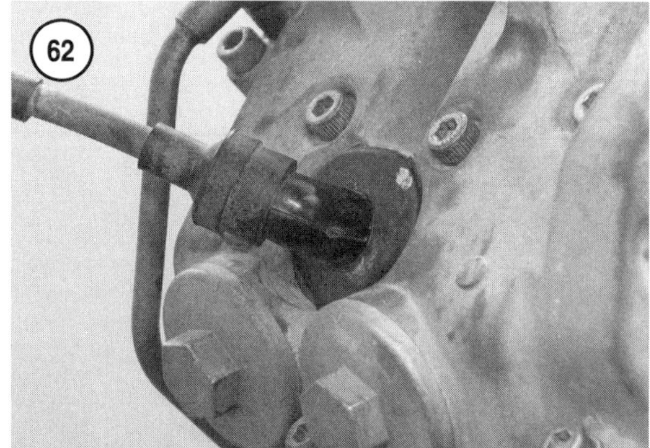

62

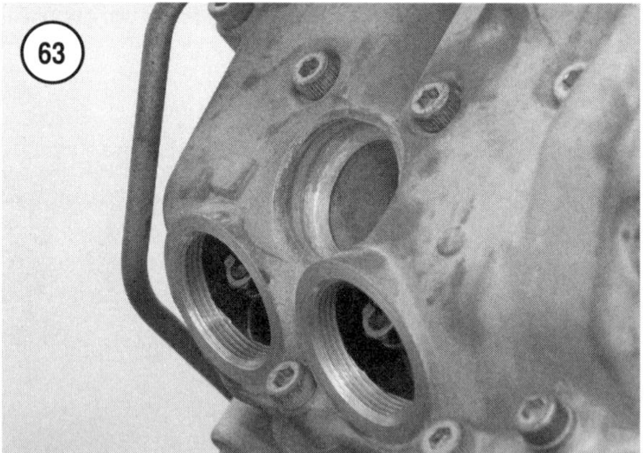

63

64

65

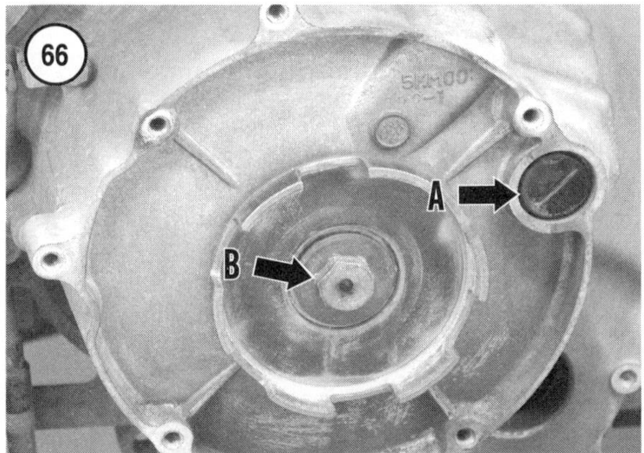

66

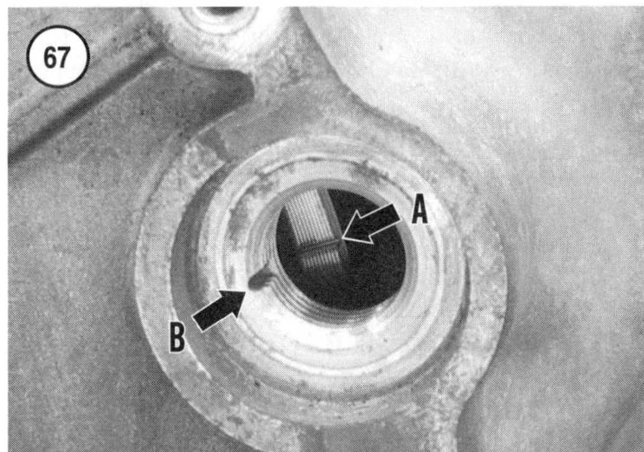

67

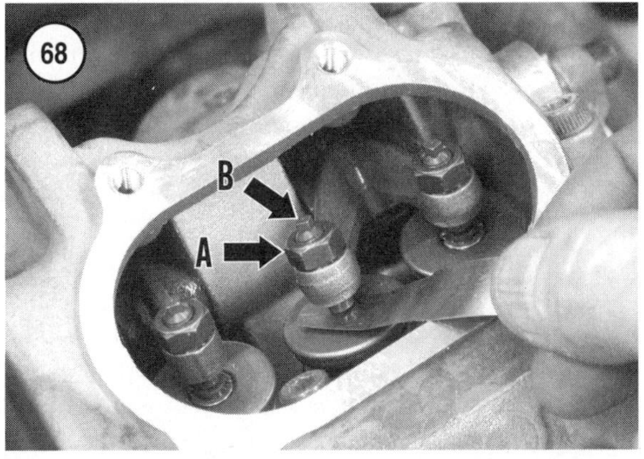

68

TIRE INSPECTION

Inflate the tires to meet the riding conditions. The standard air pressure recommendation is in **Table 3**. Slight over- or under-inflation is permissible if the riding conditions justify the change. However, do *not* exceed the inflation range embossed on the tire sidewall.

TUNE-UP

When performing a tune-up, service the following in order as described in this chapter:

1. Air filter.
2. Spark plug.
3. Compression test.
4. Valve clearance.
5. Carburetor.

VALVE CLEARANCE

Inspection/Adjustment

The engine uses three intake valves and two exhaust valves. The valves must be adjusted correctly so they will open and close completely during the combustion cycle. Valves that are out of adjustment can cause poor performance and engine damage. Check the valve clearance when the engine is cold.

1. Park the machine on level ground.
2. Remove the front fender, seat, engine side cover and fuel tank (Chapter Sixteen).
3. Remove the spark plug (**Figure 62**).
4. Remove the two exhaust valve covers (**Figure 63**).
5. Remove the intake valve cover (**Figure 64**).
6. Remove the recoil starter (**Figure 65**).
7. Remove the timing plug (A, **Figure 66**).
8. Set the engine at TDC as follows:
   a. Fit a socket onto the starter pulley bolt (B, **Figure 66**) and turn the crankshaft *counterclockwise* until the mark on the rotor (A, **Figure 67**) is aligned with the index mark in the timing hole (B).
   b. Verify the engine is at TDC by watching the tops of the intake and exhaust valve adjusters. If properly set, all adjusters will be up when the rotor mark aligns with the index mark. If the exhaust valve adjusters are down, rotate the crankshaft one full turn and realign the marks.
9. For each valve:
   a. Refer to **Table 3** for the correct valve clearance.
   b. Use a flat feeler gauge to determine the clearance between the top of the valve and adjuster (**Figure 68**). Clearance is correct if slight resistance is felt when the gauge is inserted and withdrawn.

10. If necessary, adjust the valve as follows:
 a. Loosen the locknut (A, **Figure 68**) and turn the adjuster (B) to achieve the correct clearance.
 b. Hold the adjuster and tighten the locknut to 14 N•m (10 ft.-lb.).
 c. Check the clearance. Readjust if necessary.
11. Repeat the procedure for the remaining valves.
12. Reverse this procedure and note the following:
 a. Install new, lubricated O-rings on the valve covers and timing hole plug.
 b. Install the spark plug. Tighten the spark plug to 18 N•m (13 ft.-lb.).
 c. Tighten the intake valve cover bolts to 10 N•m (89 in.-lb.).
 d. Tighten the exhaust valve covers to 12 N•m (106 in.-lb.).
 e. Apply threadlocking compound to the recoil starter housing bolts and tighten to 14 N•m (10 ft.-lb.).
13. Install the bodywork.

CARBURETOR ADJUSTMENT

Adjust the carburetor so the idle speed keeps the engine running but is also low enough to provide engine braking. Additionally, adjust the pilot mixture screw so throttle response is good from idle to about one-fourth throttle.

1. Remove the seat and fuel tank side panels (Chapter Sixteen).
2. Check the throttle cable for proper adjustment.
3. Check the air filter for cleanliness.
4. At the lower left side of the carburetor, set the pilot mixture screw (A, **Figure 69**) as follows:
 a. *Lightly* seat the screw. Turn the screw out 2 1/2 turns. This is an initial setting for adjustment.
 b. Start the engine and allow it to warm up.
 c. Set the engine idle speed to 1450-1550 rpm. Set the idle speed by turning the throttle stop screw (B, **Figure 69**). Raise and lower the engine speed a few times with the throttle to ensure that it returns to the set idle speed.
 d. Mark the position of the pilot air screw or adjustment tool. From its initial setting, turn the pilot air screw in and out in small increments to find the points where the engine speed begins to decrease. Set the pilot screw between the two points.
 e. Reset the idle speed as needed to bring it back within specification.
5. Test ride the machine and check throttle response. If throttle response is poor from an idle, adjust the pilot mixture screw out (richer) or in (leaner) by one-eighth turn increments until the engine accelerates smoothly.

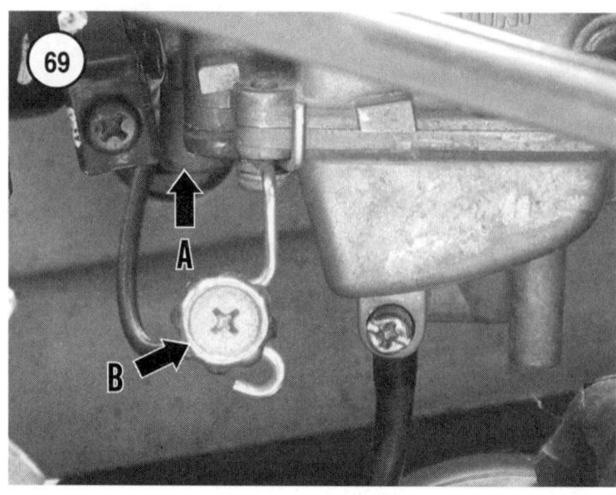

6. If necessary, adjust the throttle cable for proper play.

IGNITION TIMING

The ignition timing is controlled by the CDI unit. No adjustment is possible to the timing. Refer to *Ignition Timing Inspection* in Chapter Nine.

COMPRESSION TEST

A cylinder compression check can help verify the condition of the piston, rings and cylinder head assembly without disassembling the engine. By keeping a record of the compression reading at each tune-up, readings can be compared to determine if normal wear is occurring.

Refer to **Table 3** for the compression specifications.

1. Warm the engine to operating temperature.
2. Remove the spark plug. Insert the spark plug into the cap, then ground the plug to the cylinder to prevent possible damage to the CDI unit.
3. Thread a compression gauge into the spark plug hole. The gauge must fit airtight in the hole for an accurate reading. If necessary, use a gauge adapter (Yamaha part No. YU-33223-3).
4. Hold or secure the throttle fully open.
5. Operate the starter and turn the engine over until the highest gauge reading is achieved.
6. Record the reading. Compare the reading with previous readings, if available. Under normal operating conditions, compression will slowly lower from the original specification, due to wear of the piston rings and/or valve seats.
 a. If the reading is higher than normal, a damaged compression release mechanism could be the cause. Commonly, carbon buildup in the combustion chamber is another cause of high compression. This can cause high combustion

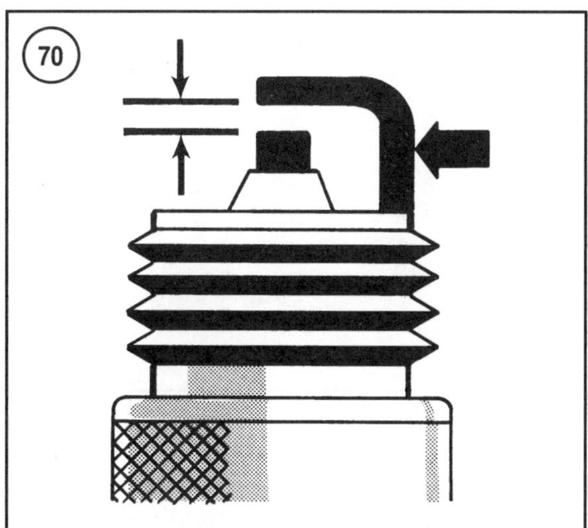

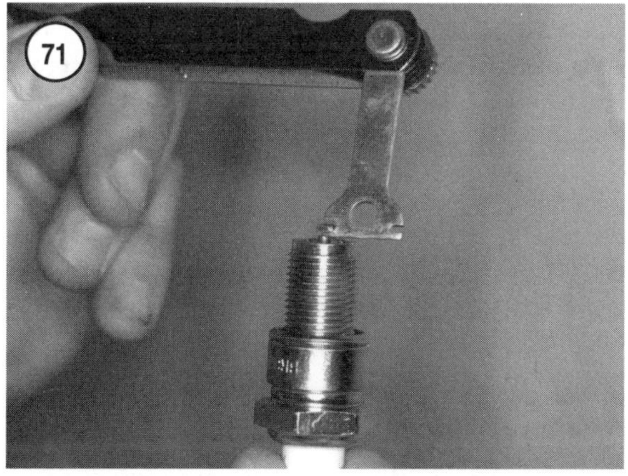

chamber temperatures and potential engine damage.

b. If the reading is lower than normal, worn piston rings, worn valves, a damaged piston, a leaking head gasket, or a combination of these could be the cause.

c. To help pinpoint the source, pour 15 cc (1/2 oz.) of four-stroke engine oil through the spark plug hole and into the cylinder. Turn the engine over to distribute the oil. Recheck compression. If compression increases, the piston rings are worn or damaged. If compression is the same, the piston, head gasket or valves are worn or damaged.

SPARK PLUG

Removal

1. Remove the seat and right fuel tank side panel (Chapter Sixteen).
2. Grasp the spark plug cap (**Figure 62**) and twist it loose from the spark plug.
3. Clean around the plug well with compressed air to prevent entry of debris.
4. Fit a spark plug wrench onto the spark plug. Then remove it by turning the wrench counterclockwise. If the plug is seized or drags during removal, stop and perform the following:
   a. Apply a penetrating lubricant and allow it to stand for 15 minutes.
   b. If the plug is completely seized, apply moderate pressure in both directions with the wrench. Only attempt to break the seal so lubricant can penetrate under the spark plug and into the threads. If this does not work, and the machine is still operable, install the spark plug cap and start the engine. Allow it to completely warm up. The heat of the engine may be enough to expand the parts and allow the plug to be removed easily.
   c. When a spark plug has been loosened, but drags excessively during its removal, apply penetrating lubricant around the spark plug threads. Turn the plug *in* (clockwise) to help distribute the lubricant onto the threads. Slowly remove the plug, working it in and out of the cylinder head as lubricant is added.
   d. Clean and true the threads with a spark plug thread-chaser. If excessively damaged, remove the cylinder head from the engine and install a thread repair insert.
5. Inspect the removed plug to determine if the engine is operating properly.
6. A spark plug in good condition that will be reused can be cleaned with electrical contact cleaner and a shop cloth. Do not use abrasives or wire brushes to clean the plug.

Gap and Installation

Proper adjustment of the electrode gap is important for reliable and consistent spark. Also, the proper preparation of the spark plug threads will ensure that the plug can be removed easily in the future, without damage to the cylinder head threads.

1. Refer to **Table 3** for the required spark plug gap.
2. Insert the correct size wire feeler gauge between the center electrode and the ground electrode.
3. Pull the gauge through the gap. If there is a slight drag, the setting is correct. If the gap is too large or small, adjust the gap by bending the ground electrode (**Figure 70**) to achieve the required gap. Use an adjusting tool (**Figure 71**) to bend the electrode. Do not pry the electrode with a screwdriver or other tool. Damage to the center electrode and insulator is possible.
4. Inspect the spark plug to ensure it is fitted with a crush washer.

5. Wipe a small amount of antiseize compound onto the spark plug threads. Do not allow the compound to get on the electrodes.
6. Finger-tighten the spark plug into the cylinder head. This ensures the plug is not cross-threading.
7. Tighten the spark plug to 18 N•m (13 ft.-lb.). If a torque wrench is not available, turn a new spark plug one-quarter to one-half turn farther once seated. Turn used spark plugs one-eighth to one-quarter turn farther once seated.
8. Press and twist the cap onto the spark plug. To help prevent water from migrating under the cap, wipe a small amount of dielectric grease around the interior of the cap before installing it.

Selection

CAUTION

The following paragraphs provide general information and operation fundamentals that apply to all spark plugs. However, before changing to an other-than-recommended plug, check with the plug manufacturer for specific part numbers and equivalents that apply to this machine. Poor performance or engine damage can occur by installing a spark plug that is not compatible with this engine.

Refer to **Table 3** for the recommended spark plug type.

Heat range

Spark plugs are available in several heat ranges to accommodate the load and performance demands put on the engine. The standard spark plug is usually a medium heat-range plug that operates well over a wide range of engine speeds. As long as engine speeds vary, these plugs will stay relatively clean and perform well.

If the engine is run in hot climates, at high speed or under heavy loads for prolonged periods, a spark plug with a colder heat range is recommended. A colder plug quickly transfers heat away from its firing tip to the cylinder head (**Figure 72**). This is accomplished by a short path up the ceramic insulator and into the body of the spark plug. By transferring heat quickly, the plug remains cool enough to avoid overheating and preignition problems. If the engine is run slowly for prolonged periods, this type of plug will foul and cause poor performance.

If the engine is run in cold climates or at slow speed for prolonged periods, a spark plug with a hotter heat range is recommended. A hotter plug slowly transfers heat away from its firing tip to the cylinder head. This is accomplished by a long path up the ceramic insulator and into the body of the spark plug (**Figure 72**). By transferring heat slowly, the plug remains hot enough to avoid fouling and buildup. If the engine is run in hot climates or fast for prolonged periods, this type of plug will overheat, cause preignition problems and possibly melt the electrode. Damage to the piston and cylinder assembly is possible.

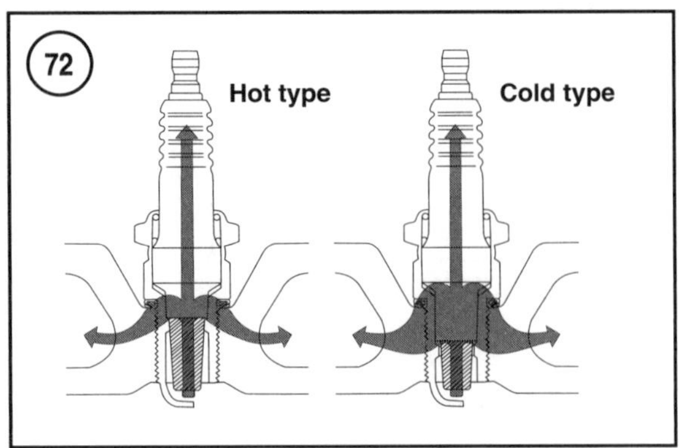

If choosing to change a spark plug to a different heat range, go one step hotter or colder from the recommended plug. Do not try to correct poor carburetor or ignition problems by using a different spark plug. This can only compound the existing problems and possibly lead to excessive engine damage.

Reach

Reach is the length of the threaded portion of the plug. Always use a spark plug that is the correct reach. Too short of a reach can lead to deposits or burning of the exposed threads in the cylinder head. Misfiring can also occur since the tip of the plug is shrouded and not exposed to the fuel mixture. If the reach is too long, the exposed plug threads can burn, causing preignition. It is possible the piston may contact the plug on the upstroke, causing excessive engine damage.

Reading/Inspection

The spark plug is an excellent indicator of how the engine is operating. A good way to diagnose and pinpoint problems or potential problems is to correctly evaluate the condition of the plug. The firing tip should be compared with the ones shown in **Figure 73**.

Normal

The plug has light tan or gray deposits on the tip. No erosion of the electrodes or abnormal gap is evi-

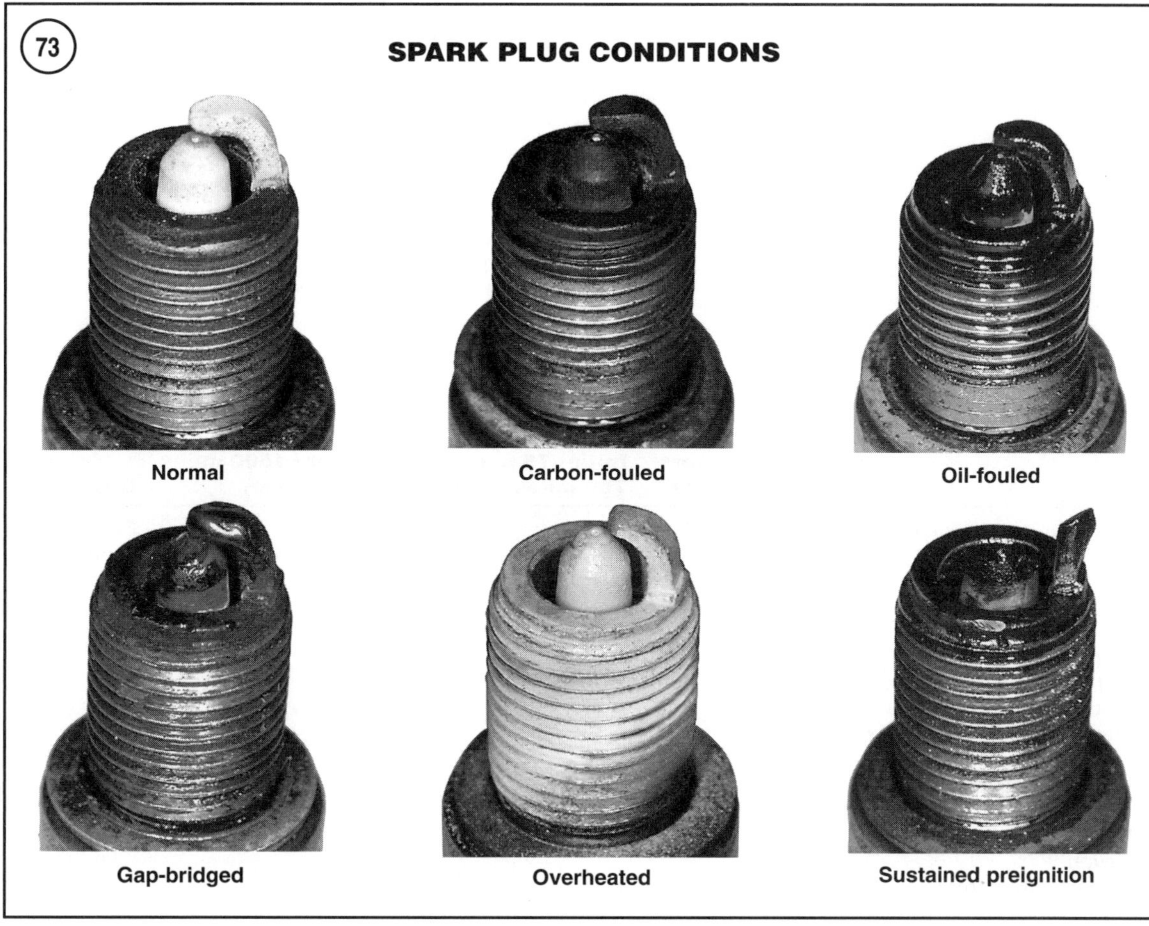

dent. This indicates an engine that has properly adjusted carburetion, ignition timing, and proper fuel. This heat range of the plug is appropriate for the conditions in which the engine has been operated. The plug can be cleaned and reused.

Carbon-fouled

The plug is black with a dry, sooty deposit on the entire plug surface. This dry, sooty deposit is conductive and can create electrical paths that bypass the electrode gap. This often causes misfiring of the plug.

1. Fuel mixture too rich.
2. Improperly adjusted choke.
3. Clogged air filter.
4. Spark plug range too cold.
5. Prolonged idling.
6. Faulty ignition component.
7. Poor compression.

Oil-fouled

The plug is wet with black, oily deposits on the electrodes and insulator. The electrodes do not show wear.

1. Incorrect carburetor jetting.
2. Prolonged idling or low idle speed.
3. Spark plug range too cold.
4. Worn valve guides.
5. Worn piston rings.
6. Ignition component failure.

Gap-bridged

The plug is clogged with deposits between the electrodes. The electrodes do not show wear.

1. Incorrect oil being used.
2. Incorrect fuel or fuel contamination.
3. Carbon deposits in combustion chamber.
4. High-speed operation after excessive idling.

Overheated

The plug is dry and the insulator has a white or light gray cast. The insulator may also appear blistered. The electrodes may have a bluish-burnt appearance.

1. Fuel mixture too lean.
2. Spark plug range too hot.
3. Air leak into intake system.

4. No crush washer on plug.
5. Plug improperly tightened.
6. Faulty ignition component.

Preignition

The plug electrodes are excessively eroded or melted. This condition can lead to engine damage.

1. Faulty ignition component.
2. Spark plug range too hot.
3. Air leak into intake system.
4. Carbon deposits in combustion chamber.

Worn out

The plug electrodes are rounded from normal combustion. There is no indication of abnormal combustion or engine conditions. Replace the plug.

Table 1 MAINTENANCE AND LUBRICATION SCHEDULE

	Initial 20 hours or 200 miles (320 km)	Initial 75 hours or 750 miles (1200 km)	Every 1500 miles (2400 km)	Other
Clean/replace air filter	x			Every 20-40 hours or as necessary
Inspect final drive oil level	x			
Inspect differential oil level	x			
Inspect coolant level	x	x	x	
Inspect/adjust speed limiter	x	x	x	
Inspect/adjust engine idle speed	x	x	x	
Inspect/adjust throttle lever	x	x	x	
Inspect/adjust front brake	x	x	x	
Inspect/adjust rear brake	x	x	x	
Inspect/adjust rear brake light switch	x	x	x	
Inspect/replace brake pads	x	x	x	
Inspect/replace spark plug	x	x	x	
Inspect/charge battery	x	x	x	
Inspect/lubricate cables	x	x	x	
Tighten all fittings and fasteners	x	x	x	
Change engine oil	x		x	
Replace engine oil filter	x		x	
Inspect/adjust valve clearance	x		x	
Inspect/replace V-belt	x		x	
Inspect/adjust select lever	x		x	
Inspect brake fluid level	x		x	
Inspect/adjust steering toe-in	x		x	
Inspect wheels and bearings	x		x	
Lubricate drive shaft U-joints			x	
Inspect front and rear axle boots	x			Every 3000 miles or 300 hours

(continued)

Table 1 MAINTENANCE AND LUBRICATION SCHEDULE (continued)

	Initial 20 hours or 200 miles (320 km)	Initial 75 hours or 750 miles (1200 km)	Every 1500 miles (2400 km)	Other
Lubricate rear suspension pivots			x	
Clean muffler			x	
Inspect/replace fuel hose			x	
Inspect stabilizer bushings			x	
Change coolant				Every two years
Change final drive oil				Every 3000 miles (4800 km)
Change differential oil				Every 3000 miles (4800 km)

Table 2 RECOMMENDED LUBRICANTS, FLUIDS AND CAPACITIES

Air filter	Foam air filter oil
Brake fluid	DOT 4
Control cables	Cable lube
Cooling system	
Capacity	
Radiator	0.78 L (0.82 U.S. qt.)
Reserve tank	0.3 L (0.32 U.S. qt.)
Total (including engine passages)	1.8 L (1.9 U.S. qt.)
Coolant	
Type	Ethylene glycol antifreeze containing anti-corrosion inhibitors for aluminum engines
Mixture ratio	50:50 (antifreeze:distilled water)
Fuel	
Type	Unleaded gasoline
Octane rating (minimum)	86 (R+M/2) or 91 RON
Tank capacity	
Main	20 liters (5.3 U.S. gal.)
Reserve	3.5 liters (0.92 U.S. gal.)
Oil	
Differential	Hypoid gear oil
Grade	API-rated GL 4
Viscosity	SAE 80
Capacity	
Change	0.28 L (0.30 U.S. qt.)
Total	0.33 L (0.35 U.S. qt.)
Engine	Four-stroke engine oil
Grade	API-rated SG
Viscosity	
Below 0° C (30° F)	SAE 5W-30
0°-35° C (30°-100° F)	SAE 10W-30
5°-45° C (40°-120° F)	SAE 20W-40
Capacity	
Without filter change	1.9 L (2.0 U.S. qt.)
With filter change	2.0 L (2.1 U.S. qt.)
Total	2.2 L (2.3 U.S. qt.)
Final drive	Hypoid gear oil
Grade	API-rated GL 4
Viscosity	SAE 80
Capacity	
Change	0.25 L (0.26 U.S. qt.)
Total	0.30 L (0.32 U.S. qt.)

Table 3 MAINTENANCE AND TUNE-UP SPECIFICATIONS

Battery	YTX20L-BS, 12 volt, 18 amp-hour
Brakes	
Brake pad lining minimum thickness	1.0 mm (0.040 in.)
Rear brake lever free play	0.5-2 mm (0.02-0.08 in.)
Rear brake pedal height	45 mm (1.8 in.)
Choke cable service limit	15 mm (0.6 in.) range from extreme right to extreme left
Compression	
Standard	1324 kPa (192 psi)
Minimum	1150 kPa (167 psi)
Maximum	1480 kPa (215 psi)
Cooling system test pressure (maximum)	137 kPa (20 psi)
Drive belt width	33.2 mm (1.31 in.)
Service limit	29.9 mm (1.18 in.)
Idle speed	1450-1550 rpm
Ignition timing*	12° BTDC at 1500 rpm
Intake vacuum	30.7-33.3 kPa (9.07-9.83 in. Hg)
Pilot mixture screw (initial setting)	2-1/2 turns out
Radiator cap relief pressure	93.3-122.7 kPa (13.5-17.8 psi)
Spark plug	
Type	NGK DPR8EA-9
Gap	0.8-0.9 mm (0.032-0.035 in.)
Speed limiter screw length (standard)	12 mm (0.47 in.)
Throttle lever free play	3-5 mm (0.12-0.20 in.)
Tire pressure (cold)	
Front	
Standard	35 kPa (5.1 psi)
Minimum	32 kPa (4.6 psi)
Maximum	38 kPa (5.5 psi)
Rear	
Standard	30 kPa (4.4 psi)
Minimum	27 kPa (3.9 psi)
Maximum	33 kPa (4.8 psi)
Toe-in	0-10 mm (0-0.40 in.)
Wear limit	3 mm (0.12 in.)
Valve clearance (cold)	
Intake	0.10-0.15 mm (0.004-0.006 in.)
Exhaust	0.15-0.20 mm (0.006-0.008 in.)
Wheel runout (radial and lateral)	2 mm (0.08 in.)

*Not adjustable.

Table 4 MAINTENANCE TORQUE SPECIFICATIONS

	N•m	in.-lb.	ft.-lb.
Coolant drain plug	10	89	–
Crankcase oil drain plug	30	–	22
Differential			
Oil drain plug	10	89	–
Oil fill plug	23	–	17
Final drive oil drain/fill plugs	23	–	17
Oil filter cartridge	17	–	13
Oil gallery bolt	7	62	–
Recoil starter housing bolts	14	–	10
Select lever shift rod locknut	15	–	11
Spark plugs	18	–	13
Valve adjuster locknuts	14	–	10
Valve cover bolts			
Exhaust	12	106	–
Intake	10	89	–

CHAPTER FOUR

ENGINE TOP END

This chapter covers the engine top end. This includes the exhaust system, cylinder head cover, cylinder head, camshaft, cam chain tensioner, valves, cylinder and piston. All the parts can be removed with the engine mounted in the frame.

Refer to the tables at the end of this chapter for specifications.

EXHAUST SYSTEM

Removal and Installation

Refer to **Figure 1**.

1. To remove the complete exhaust system, remove the seat, fuel tank side panels, fuel tank, fuel tank pan and front fender (Chapter Sixteen). If removing only the muffler, remove the seat and right fuel tank side panel, then proceed to Step 5.
2. Remove the air ducts, as necessary.
3. Remove the carburetor (Chapter Eight).
4. Remove the exhaust heat shield.
5. Remove the muffler as follows:
   a. Remove the bolt securing the muffler clamp to the exhaust pipe and the bolt securing the pipe to the exhaust pipe bracket.
   b. Remove the bolt securing the muffler, then pull the muffler and pipe from the frame.
6. Remove both exhaust pipes as follows:
   a. At the cylinder head, remove the exhaust pipe flange nuts. Apply penetrating oil as needed during removal.
   b. Remove the bolt securing the pipe to the exhaust pipe bracket.
   c. Pull the exhaust pipes out of the cylinder head and route the pipes out of the frame.
   d. Remove the gaskets from the exhaust ports.
7. Reverse these steps to install the system. Note the following:
   a. Clean the exhaust ports and install new exhaust pipe gaskets. If necessary, hold the gaskets in place with a small amount of antiseize compound.
   b. Apply antiseize compound to all threads.
   c. Install and align the entire exhaust system, with all fasteners finger-tight. Tighten the exhaust pipes squarely into the exhaust ports. Then tighten the remaining fasteners.
   d. Tighten the exhaust pipe flange-to-cylinder head nuts to 14 N•m (10 ft.-lb.).
   e. Tighten the exhaust pipe-to-exhaust pipe bracket bolt to 15 N•m (11 ft.-lb.).
   f. Tighten the exhaust heat shield bolts to 11 N•m (97 in.-lb.).
   g. Tighten the muffler-to-frame bolt to 20 N•m (15 ft.-lb.).
   h. Tighten the muffler clamp-to-exhaust pipe bolt to 20 N•m (15 ft.-lb.).

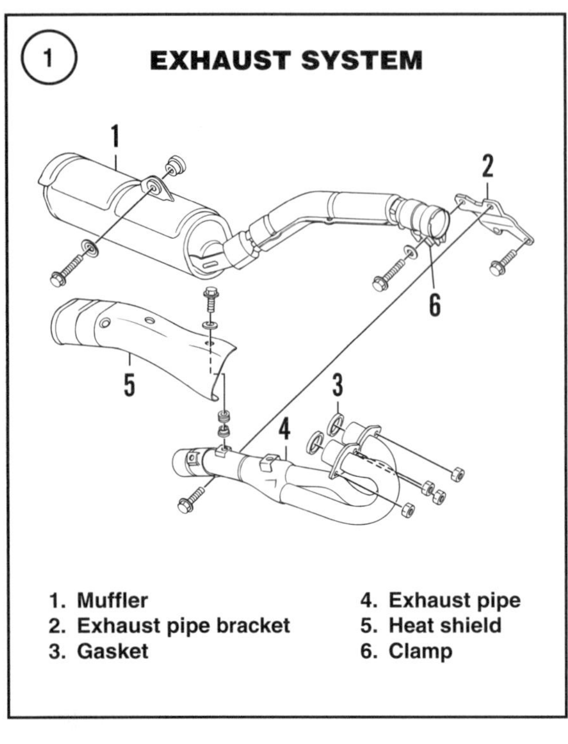

1. Muffler
2. Exhaust pipe bracket
3. Gasket
4. Exhaust pipe
5. Heat shield
6. Clamp

i. Tighten the muffler-to-exhaust pipe bracket bolt to 15 N•m (11 ft.-lb.).

CYLINDER HEAD COVER

Removal and Installation

1. Park the machine on level ground.
2. Remove the seat, fuel tank side panels, engine side cover, fuel tank and front fender (Chapter Sixteen).
3. Remove the select lever unit mounting bolts (**Figure 2**). Secure the unit away from the cylinder head. It is not necessary to disconnect the select lever rod.
4. Remove the exhaust valve covers (A, **Figure 3**), spark plug (B), upper oil pipe (C) and intake valve cover (D).
5. Remove the oil pressure check plate (**Figure 4**).
6. Remove the recoil starter (**Figure 5**).
7. Remove the timing plug (A, **Figure 6**).
8. Turn the starter pulley bolt (B, **Figure 6**) counterclockwise until the mark on the rotor (A, **Figure 7**) aligns with the index mark in the timing hole (B). The timing mark indicates the piston is at top dead center (TDC). To check that the piston is at TDC on the compression stroke, all valve adjusters should be up and there should be clearance between all valves and their rocker arms. If any of the valve adjusters are in the down position, turn the crankshaft counterclockwise one full revolution and realign the marks.
9. Loosen the cylinder head cover bolts. Work in a crossing pattern and loosen the bolts evenly in several passes.

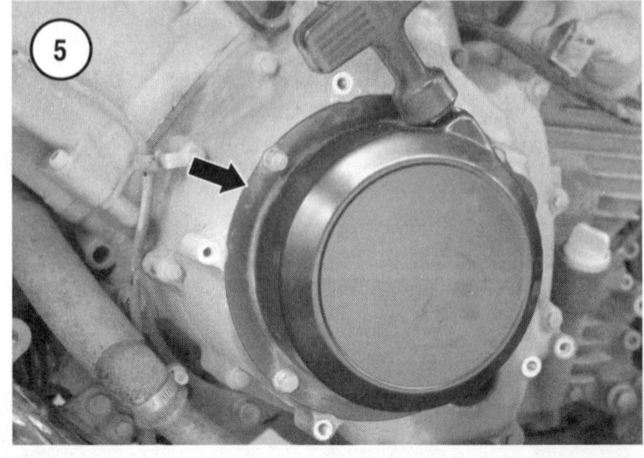

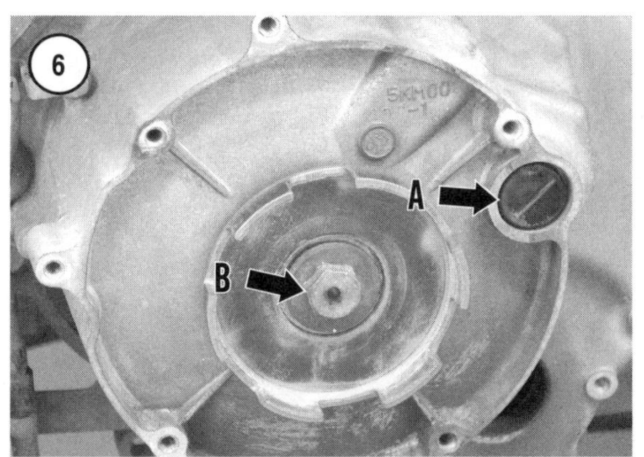

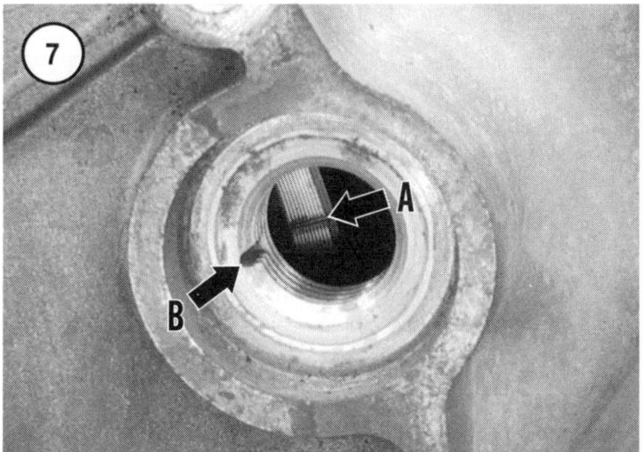

10. Loosen the cylinder head cover. The cover is sealed to the cylinder head with sealant. Pull up on the cover to break the seal between the parts. Do not pry on the sealing surfaces.

11. When the cylinder head cover is loose, slowly pull up on the cover and account for the two dowels (**Figure 8**) located in the bores at the left side.

  a. If the dowels are seated in the cylinder head, leave them in place until the cover is removed and the cam chain tunnel is stuffed with a shop cloth.

  b. If the dowels are in the cylinder head cover, grip the dowels and remove the cylinder head cover from the engine.

NOTE

*Verify the engine is at TDC by checking the position of the camshaft oil holes. If properly set, the oil holes will point up (***Figure 9***). If the holes point down, hold the camshaft in place and slowly rotate the crankshaft one full turn counterclockwise and realign the rotor and timing hole marks.*

12. Inspect the cylinder head cover assembly (**Figure 10**) as described in this section.

13. Reverse this procedure to install the cylinder head cover. Note the following:

  a. Make sure that the three bolt holes inline with the intake rocker shaft allow the bolts to pass through the cover. The shaft is notched to allow the bolts to lock the shaft into place. If necessary, align the shaft before applying sealant to the cover.

  b. Clean the mating surfaces on the cylinder head and cover. Apply Yamabond 1215 sealant (part No. 90890-85505) to all mating surfaces on the cylinder head. Do not over apply the sealant. Excess sealant can cause engine damage.

  c. Install the cylinder head, washers and bolts. Refer to **Figure 11** for head bolt lengths and their locations.

d. Tighten the cylinder head cover bolts. Work in a crossing pattern and tighten the bolts evenly in several passes. Tighten the bolts to 10 N•m (89 in.-lb.).
e. If necessary, refer to *Valve Clearance* in Chapter Three and adjust the valves.
f. Install new seal washers onto the oil pipe banjo bolts.
g. Install new, lubricated O-rings onto the valve covers, oil pressure check plate and the timing hole plug.
h. Tighten the exhaust valve covers to 12 N•m (106 in.-lb.).
i. Tighten the intake valve cover bolts to 10 N•m (89 in.-lb.).
j. Tighten the spark plug to 18 N•m (13 ft.-lb.).
k. Tighten the upper banjo bolt to 20 N•m (15 ft.-lb.).
l. Tighten the lower banjo bolt to 35 N•m (26 ft.-lb.).
m. Tighten the oil pressure check plate mounting bolt to 10 N•m (89 in.-lb.).
n. Tighten the shift lever unit mounting bolts to 25 N•m (18 ft.-lb.).

Inspection

Refer to **Figure 12**.

1. Clean the cylinder head cover in solvent and dry with compressed air. Remove sealant from the mating surfaces, threads and dowel bores. Sealant particles that remain on the cover can cause damage.
2. Visually inspect the inner and outer surfaces of the cover. Check for cracks, scoring or other damage around the bolt holes and on all mating surfaces.
3. Inspect the valve covers and bolts (**Figure 13**) for damage. Replace the O-ring on each cover.
4. Inspect the rocker contact pads, valve adjusters and camshaft bearing surfaces (**Figure 14**).
   a. If the pads or bearing surfaces are pitted or scored, inspect the camshaft for damage. Also, clean and inspect the oil pockets, below the camshaft lobes, for debris.
   b. The rockers should pivot freely on their shafts with no perceptible play.
   c. Replace adjusters and locknuts that are flared or worn.
   d. If the camshaft bearing surfaces are damaged, replace the cylinder head cover and cylinder head as a set.
5. If necessary, remove the rocker arms and shafts as follows:
   a. For the intake assembly, thread a cylinder head cover bolt into the end of the shaft. Pull the shaft and O-ring from the cover as shown in **Figure 15**.
   b. For the exhaust assemblies, remove the lockbolt from each shaft. The bolts are located by the rocker arms. Remove the cap covering the left exhaust shaft. Remove the shafts and O-rings with a cylinder head cover bolt.

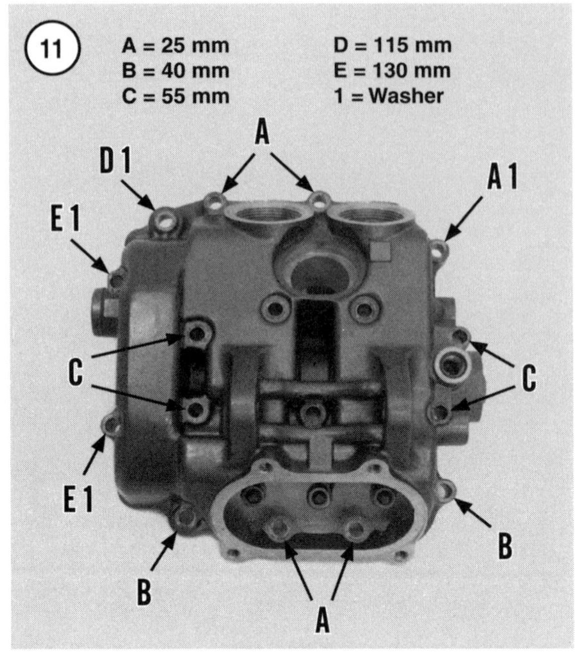

6. Inspect the rocker arm and shaft assemblies. Refer to **Table 2** for specifications.
   a. Inspect the rocker bores and oil holes for scoring, cracks, debris or other damage.
   b. Measure the inside diameter (A, **Figure 16**) of the rocker arm.
   c. Measure the outside diameter (B, **Figure 16**) of the rocker arm shaft, where it contacts the rocker arm.
   d. Inspect the wave washers and replace the shaft O-rings, where used.
7. Install the rocker arm and shaft assemblies into the cylinder head cover. Note the following:
   a. Lubricate new O-rings before installing the shafts.
   b. Install the shafts so the O-ring is to the outside of the cover. The left exhaust shaft does not use an O-ring.
   c. Install the intake rocker shaft with the shaft notches aligned with the three cylinder head cover bolt holes. The shaft is notched to allow the cover bolts to lock the shaft into place. Turn the shaft so the slot in the shaft is vertical and the bolts will pass through the cover (**Figure 17**).
   d. Tighten the exhaust shaft lockbolts to 10 N•m (89 in.-lb.). Install and tighten the left shaft's cap securely.

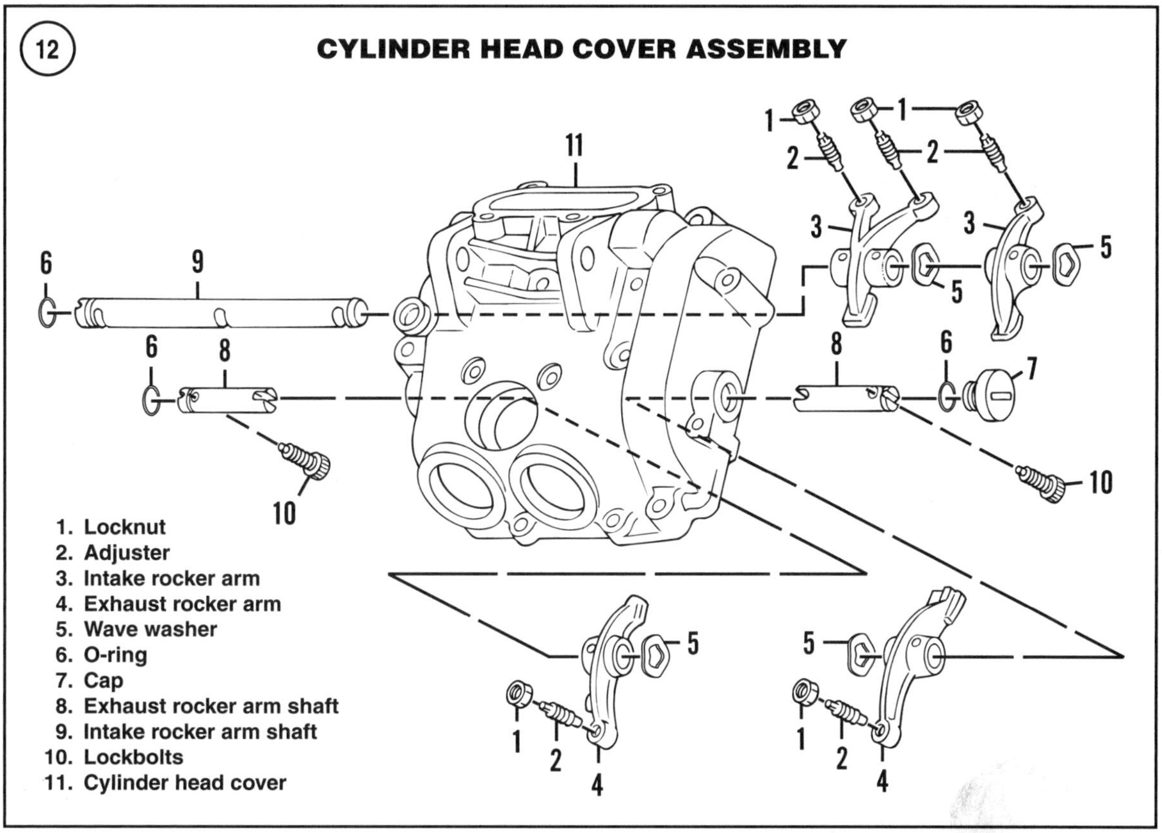

12

CYLINDER HEAD COVER ASSEMBLY

1. Locknut
2. Adjuster
3. Intake rocker arm
4. Exhaust rocker arm
5. Wave washer
6. O-ring
7. Cap
8. Exhaust rocker arm shaft
9. Intake rocker arm shaft
10. Lockbolts
11. Cylinder head cover

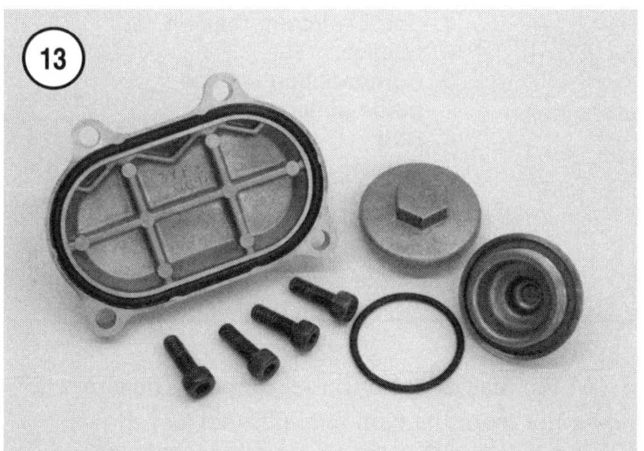
13

15

14

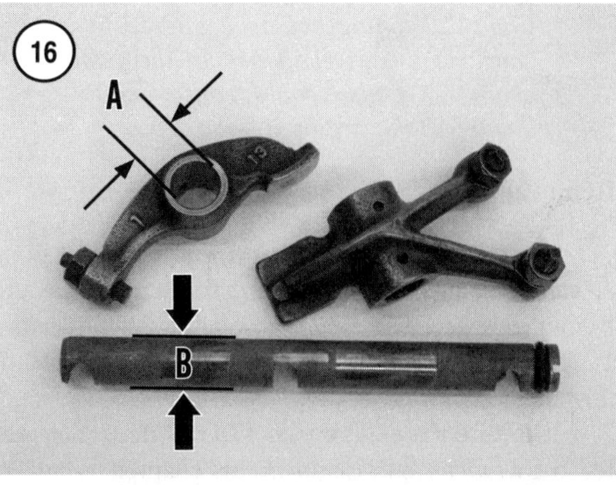

16

17

8. Install the cylinder head cover as described in this section.

CAMSHAFT AND CAM CHAIN TENSIONER

CAUTION

When working on the camshaft assembly, stuff the cam chain tunnel with a shop cloth to prevent the entry of parts and debris.

CAUTION

Anytime the tensioner mounting bolts are loosened, the tensioner must be completely removed and reset. Do not partially remove, then retighten the bolts. The one-way plunger will have extended and locked itself. Retightening the bolts will cause the cam chain and tensioner to be too tight, possibly causing engine damage if the engine is operated.

CAUTION

Do not turn the crankshaft after removing the tensioner from the engine. Camshaft timing could be altered because of the excess slack in the cam chain. This also could cause engine damage if the engine is operated.

Removal

The camshaft (**Figure 18**) and cam chain tensioner can be removed with the engine mounted in the frame.

1. Remove the cylinder head cover as described in this chapter.
2. Make sure the engine is at TDC. If necessary, refer to *Cylinder Head Cover* in this chapter.

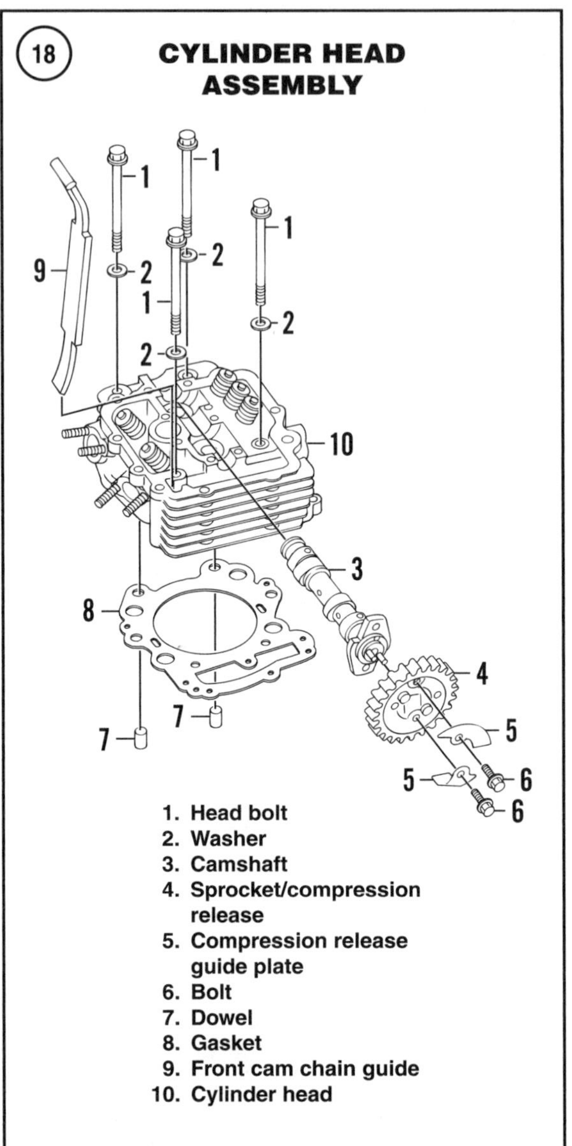

3. At the rear of the cylinder, remove the cam chain tensioner from the cam chain tunnel as follows:
   a. Remove the center bolt and washer (A, **Figure 19**).
   b. Remove the two mounting bolts (B, **Figure 19**). Then remove the tensioner and gasket.
4. Remove the camshaft sprocket as follows:
   a. Hold the crankshaft at TDC, then remove the bolt (A, **Figure 20**) and compression release guide plate.
   b. Rotate the crankshaft counterclockwise and remove the remaining bolt and guide plate. Have a length of wire at the work area to secure the cam chain after the sprocket is removed.
5. Remove the camshaft.
6. Remove the front cam chain guide.
7. Inspect the camshaft, compression release and cam chain tensioner as described in this section.

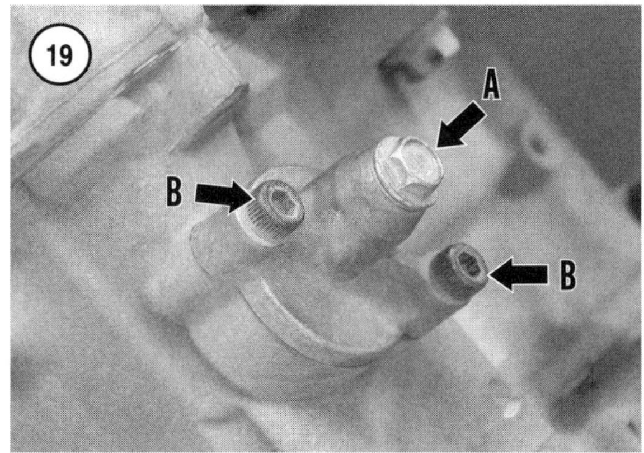

a. Reset the cam chain tensioner as described in the inspection procedure. The tensioner must be reset before installation.

b. If necessary, refer to Chapter Five for cam chain inspection. Although the chain cannot be removed from the engine, a partial inspection can be performed.

Installation

1. Prior to installing the camshaft and cam chain tensioner, note the following:
   a. Make sure that the cam chain tensioner is disassembled and reset, as described in the inspection procedure.
   b. Lubricate parts with engine oil during assembly.
2. Inspect the cylinder head and ensure that all surfaces are clean. Remove any shop cloths from the cam chain tunnel.
3. Make sure that the engine is at TDC and is held in this position. The engine must remain at TDC when installing and timing the camshaft.
4. Install the front cam chain guide.
5. Install the camshaft with the oil holes pointing up (**Figure 19**). This is the TDC position for the camshaft.
6. Identify the three alignment marks on the cam sprocket (**Figure 21**).
   a. When installed on the camshaft (**Figure 22**), the top mark must point up and be perpendicular to the cylinder head. This mark also aligns vertically with the mark on the end of the camshaft.
   b. The marks to the front and rear of the sprocket must be parallel with the top of the cylinder head.
7. Align and install the cam sprocket and compression release guide plates. Note the following:
   a. During installation, keep the front of the cam chain taut so there is no play in the chain when installing the sprocket.
   b. Check that the compression release levers engage with the pins on the camshaft (B, **Figure 20**).
   c. When turning the crankshaft to install the second sprocket bolt, turn the crankshaft counterclockwise (forward) to keep the front side of the cam chain taut.
   d. Tighten the sprocket bolts to 20 N•m (15 ft.-lb.).
8. Install the cam chain tensioner as follows:
   a. Make sure the tensioner is reset, as described in the inspection procedure.
   b. Inspect the housing and locate the UP mark.

   c. Install a new gasket, the housing and the mounting bolts. Tighten the bolts to 10 N•m (89 in.-lb.).
   d. Insert a small flat-blade screwdriver into the back of the tensioner and turn the adjuster (**Figure 23**) counterclockwise until the plunger is released. Install a new washer on the center bolt, then tighten the bolt to 7 N•m (62 in.-lb.).
9. With the engine at TDC, inspect the installation.
   a. The cam chain should be taut at the front and rear.
   b. The alignment marks on the sprocket must be parallel to the top of the cylinder head.
   c. Hold the camshaft in place and slowly rotate the crankshaft counterclockwise two full turns. Verify all alignments when the crankshaft is at the TDC mark.

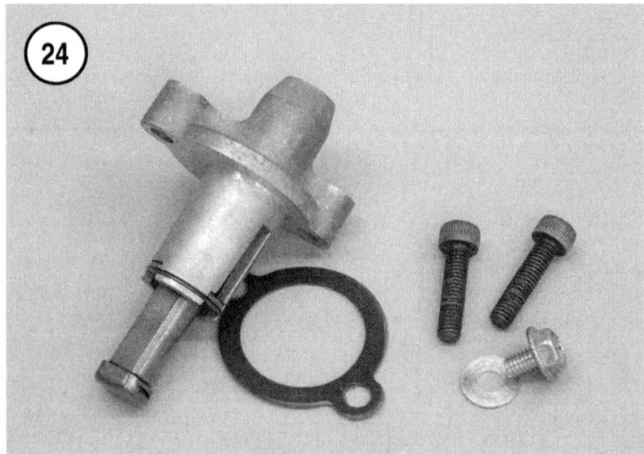

Inspection

Cam chain tensioner and front guide

The tensioner assembly is a spring-loaded, ratcheting-type tensioner. As the cam chain wears, the spring-loaded plunger extends and locks itself against the rear chain guide. The guide then pivots forward and retightens the chain.

1. Inspect the parts (**Figure 24**) for wear or damage. Install a new gasket and washer at installation.
2. Reset the plunger as follows:
   a. Insert a small flat-blade screwdriver into the back of the tensioner and turn the adjuster (**Figure 25**) clockwise until the plunger is fully retracted and locked. Lightly press in on the plunger while turning the adjuster. The plunger is under spring pressure and resistance should be felt as the screwdriver is turned. If the plunger does not fully retract, or does not stay locked in the tensioner housing, replace the tensioner.
   b. Do not install the center bolt until the tensioner housing has been mounted and the tensioner is released.
3. Inspect the front cam chain guide for wear or deterioration. The guide must be in good condition to minimize chain oscillation.

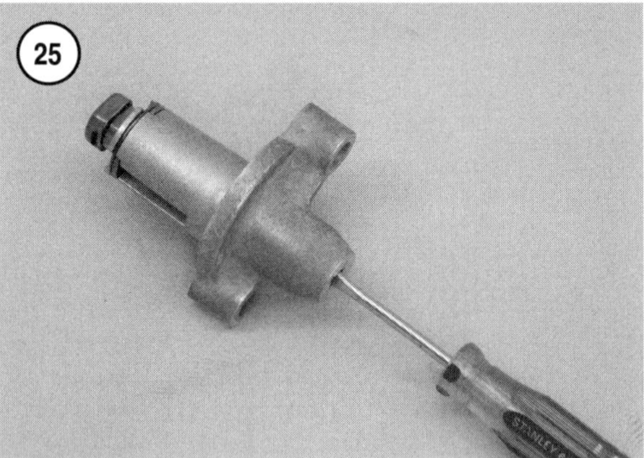

Camshaft sprocket and compression release

The compression release is located on the sprocket at the end of the camshaft. The release slightly opens the left exhaust valve during engine cranking. The resulting reduction in compression makes starting easier.

In operation, the notches in the spring-loaded release levers (A, **Figure 26**) are engaged with the

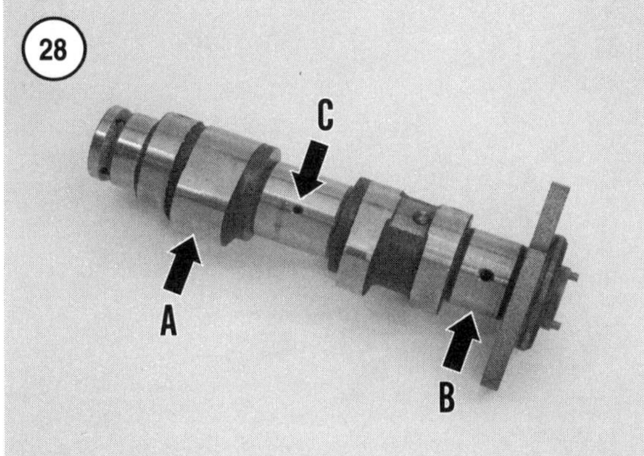

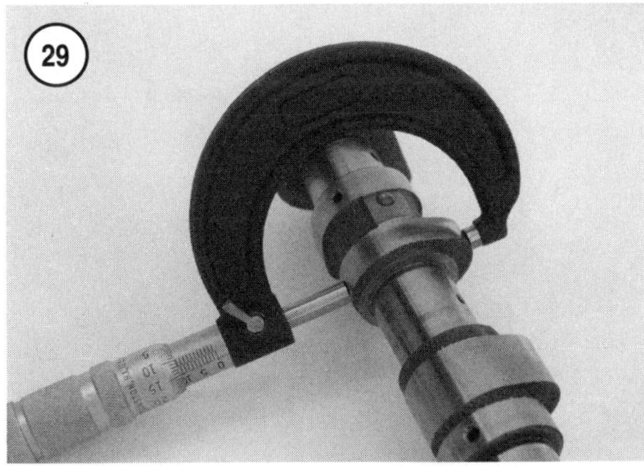

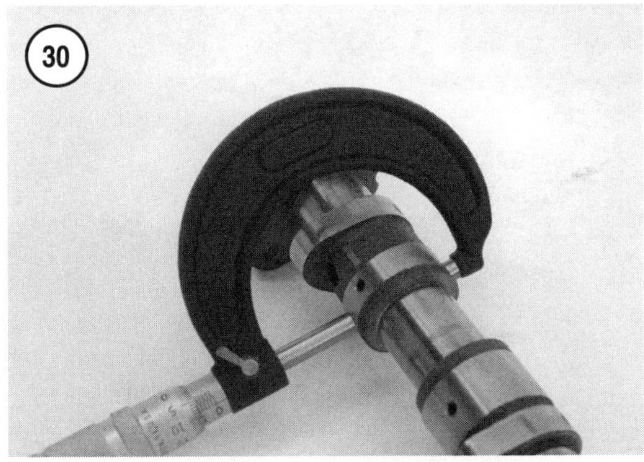

drum and pins (B) in the camshaft. The pivoting action of the drum raises and lowers the lifter (C, **Figure 26**). When the engine is off, the release levers are contracted and the lifter is raised. During startup, the left exhaust rocker arm contacts the lifter and slightly opens the exhaust valve. When startup occurs, centrifugal force pivots the release levers outward and the drum lowers the lifter.

1. Clean the sprocket and release mechanism.
2. Inspect the parts.
   a. Pivot each lever outward and check for smooth operation. When the lever is pivoted and released, the spring should fully retract the lever. Replace the spring if it is fatigued.
   b. Inspect the springs and pivots for buildup, binding or other damage.
   c. Check the fit of the guide plates on the release assembly. The levers should not drag on the guide plates.
   d. Inspect the shoulders (A, **Figure 27**) on the bolts. When installed, the bolts should fit in the sprocket with minimal play.
   e. Inspect the sprocket teeth (B, **Figure 27**) for wear or other damage. The profile of each tooth should be symmetrical. When mounted in the chain, maximum movement of the chain is one-fourth tooth. If the sprocket is worn, replace the cam sprocket and cam chain as a set and inspect the crankshaft sprocket and chain guides for wear or damage.
   f. Inspect the lifter (C, **Figure 26**), drum and pins (B) on the camshaft. The lifter should smoothly raise and lower as the drum is rotated.

Camshaft

In the following procedure, replace the camshaft if it is damaged, or not within specification. Refer to **Table 2** for specifications.

1. Clean the camshaft in solvent and dry with compressed air.
2. Inspect the camshaft lobes (A, **Figure 28**), journals (B) and oil holes (C).
   a. Check for pitting and scoring on the machined surfaces. If damage is evident, inspect the cylinder head, cylinder head cover and rocker arm assemblies for damage.
   b. Inspect the oil holes for dirt and debris.
3. Measure the camshaft with a micrometer.
   a. Measure the cam lobe heights (**Figure 29**).
   b. Measure the cam lobe widths (**Figure 30**).

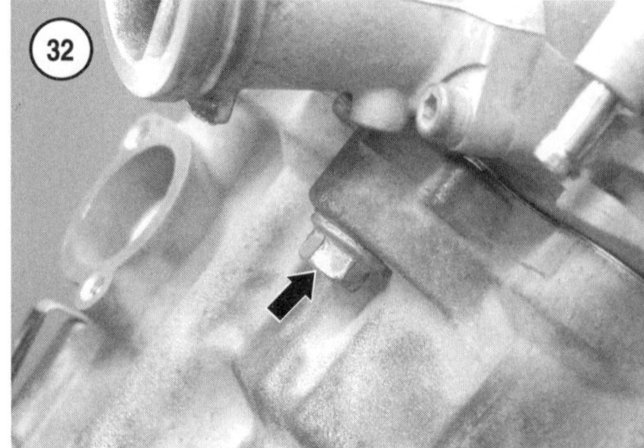

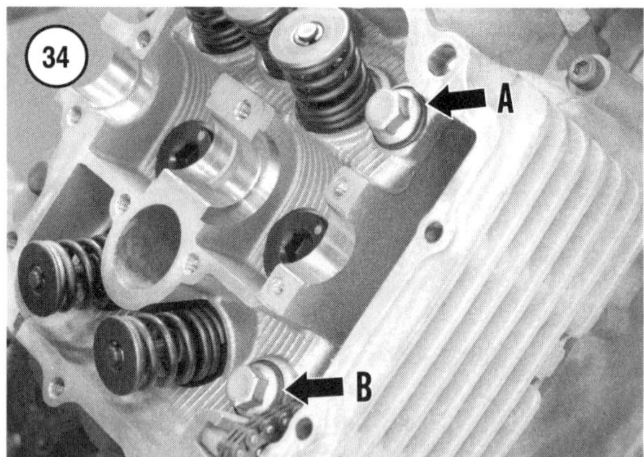

CYLINDER HEAD

Removal

The cylinder head can be removed with the engine mounted in the frame. Refer to **Figure 18**.

1. Drain the engine coolant (Chapter Three).
2. Remove the bypass hose and thermostat (Chapter Ten).
3. Remove the carburetor (Chapter Eight).
4. Disconnect the coolant temperature sending unit lead.
5. Remove the exhaust system as described in this chapter.
6. Remove the cylinder head cover, camshaft and cam chain tensioner as described in this chapter.
7. Loosen the cylinder head bolts in the following order. Make several passes and loosen each bolt a quarter-turn at a time until all bolts are loose.
   a. Left rear bolt (**Figure 31**).
   b. Right rear bolt (**Figure 32**).
   c. Front bolt (**Figure 33**).
   d. Head bolt (A, **Figure 34**).
   e. Head bolt (A, **Figure 35**).
   f. Head bolt (B, **Figure 34**).
   g. Head bolt (B, **Figure 35**).
8. Loosen the cylinder head by lightly tapping around its base with a soft mallet. Lift the head off the engine while routing the cam chain out of the head. Secure the chain so it does not fall into the engine.
9. Stuff shop cloths into the cam chain tunnel. Then remove the head gasket. Account for the two dowels located at the right side of the cylinder (**Figure 36**).
10. At the workbench, remove the carburetor intake duct and coolant temperature sending unit (**Figure 37**).
11. If necessary, remove and inspect the valve assembly as described in this chapter.
12. Wash all parts in solvent and dry with compressed air. Note the following:
    a. Remove all gasket residue from the cylinder head and cylinder. Do not scratch or gouge the surfaces.

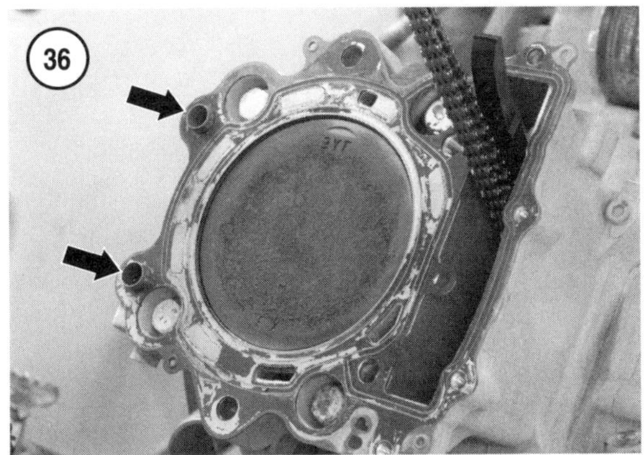

b. With the valves installed, remove all carbon deposits from the combustion chamber. Use solvent and a soft brush or hardwood scraper. Do not use sharp-edged tools that could scratch the valves or combustion chamber. If the piston crown is cleaned, keep solvent and carbon deposits out of the gap between the piston and cylinder.

c. After the head has been reconditioned, wash the entire assembly in hot, soapy water. This will remove any grit that is lodged in crevices and threads. Clean and chase all threads to ensure no grit remains.

d. Check all oil passages for debris.

e. Check all parts for wear or damage.

13. Inspect the cylinder head as described in this section.

Inspection

Anytime the cylinder head is removed, test the valves for leaks with solvent. Refer to *Valves* in this chapter.

1. Inspect the spark plug hole threads. If the threads are dirty or mildly damaged, use a spark plug thread tap to clean and straighten the threads. Lubricate the tap while cleaning the threads.
2. If the threads are galled, stripped or cross-threaded, the cylinder head should be fitted with a steel thread insert.
3. Clean the entire cylinder head assembly in fresh solvent.
4. Inspect the inside of the cylinder head.
   a. Look for cracks or damage in the spark plug hole (A, **Figure 38**), combustion chamber, water jackets (B) and exhaust ports (C).
   b. Inspect the exhaust studs (D, **Figure 38**) for damage or looseness.
5. Inspect the outside of the cylinder head.
   a. Look for cracks or damage on the casting and mating surfaces, as well as at the bolt holes (A, **Figure 39**).
   b. Inspect the camshaft bearing surfaces (B, **Figure 39**) for scoring or damage. If damaged, replace the cylinder head and cylinder head cover as a set.
   c. If cracks are evident anywhere in the cylinder head, take the head to a dealership or machine shop to see if the head can be repaired. If not, replace the head and cylinder head cover as a set.
6. Inspect the cylinder head for warp as follows:
   a. Lay a machinist's straightedge across the cylinder head (**Figure 40**).
   b. Try to insert a flat feeler gauge between the straightedge and the machined surface of the

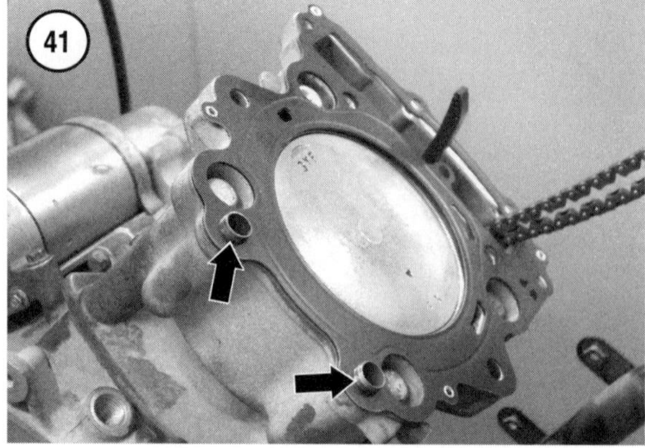

head. If clearance exists, record the maximum measurement.

c. Repeat substep a and substep b several times, laying the straightedge both across and diagonally on the head.

d. Compare the measurements to the warp service limit in **Table 2**. If the clearance is not within the service limit, take the cylinder head to a dealership or machine shop for further inspection and possible resurfacing.

7. Inspect the cylinder fasteners for damaged threads and heads. Replace fasteners that are rusted.

8. Inspect the carburetor intake duct for cracks and damage.

9. Assemble and install the cylinder head as described in this section.

Installation

Check that all gasket residue is removed from all mating surfaces. Refer to **Figure 18**.

1. Install the carburetor intake duct and coolant temperature sending unit (**Figure 37**).
   a. For the intake duct, install new, lubricated O-rings. Then tighten the mounting bolts to 10 N•m (89 in.-lb.).
   b. For the sending unit, apply sealant to the threads of the unit. Then tighten the unit to 8 N•m (71 in.-lb.).
2. Install the dowels and a new cylinder head gasket onto the cylinder (**Figure 41**).
3. Lower the cylinder head onto the engine, routing the cam chain through the head.
   a. Keep adequate tension on the cam chain so it does not bind at the crankshaft sprocket. Secure the cam chain when the cylinder head is seated.
   b. Avoid dislodging the dowels while positioning the head.
   c. Cover engine openings as needed.

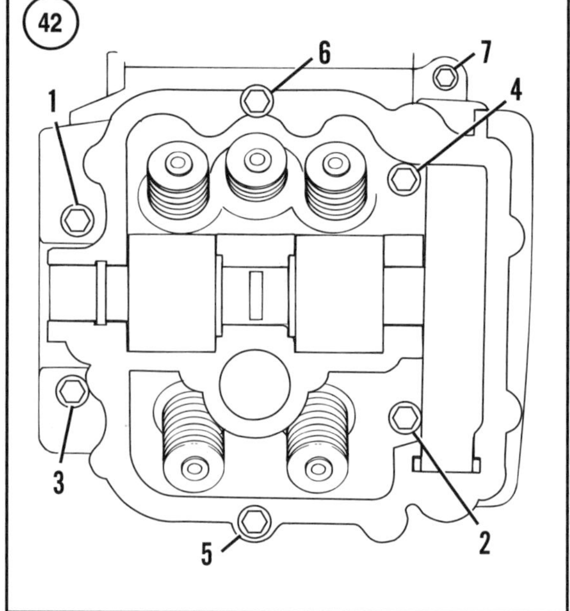

4. Install and tighten the cylinder head bolts. Note the following:
   a. Refer to the tightening sequence in **Figure 42**.
   b. Tighten the bolts in two passes. Tighten the 9-mm bolts equally in the first pass.
   c. On the second pass, tighten the 9-mm bolts (bolts 1-6) to 38 N•m (28 ft.-lb.).
   d. Tighten the 6-mm bolt (bolt 7) to 10 N•m (89 in.-lb.).
5. Install the camshaft, cam chain tensioner and cylinder head cover as described in this chapter.
6. Install the exhaust system as described in this chapter.
7. Connect the coolant temperature sending unit lead.
8. Install the carburetor (Chapter Eight).
9. Install the bypass hose and thermostat (Chapter Ten).
10. Fill the engine with coolant (Chapter Three).
11. Install a new spark plug (Chapter Three).

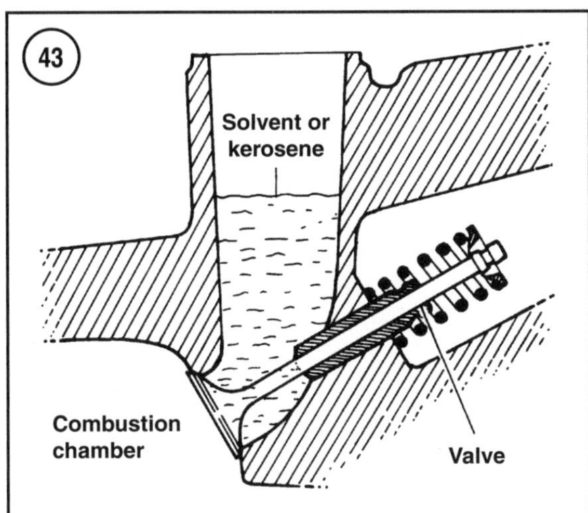

VALVES

Solvent Test

The solvent test can reveal if valves are fully seating, as well as expose undetected cracks in the cylinder head.

1. Remove the cylinder head as described in this chapter.
2. Make sure that the combustion chamber is dry and the valves are seated.

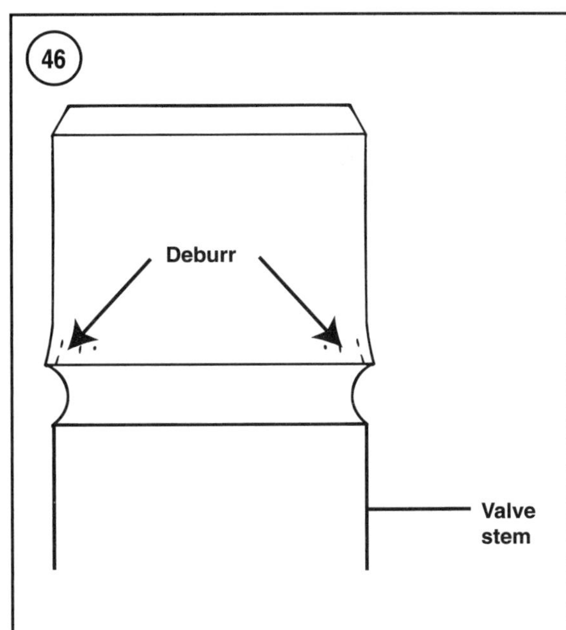

3. Support the cylinder head so the port faces up (**Figure 43**).
4. Pour solvent or kerosene into the port.
5. Inspect the combustion chamber for leaks around the valve.
6. Repeat Steps 3-5 for the other valves.
7. If leaks are evident, this can be caused by:
   a. A worn or damaged valve face.
   b. A worn or damaged valve seat (in the cylinder head).
   c. A bent valve stem.
   d. A crack in the combustion chamber.

Valve Removal

1. Perform the solvent test on the intake and exhaust valves as described in this section.
2. Install a valve spring compressor squarely over the valve head and the spring retainer (**Figure 44**).

CAUTION
Do not overtighten and compress the valve spring too far. This can cause loss of valve spring tension.

3. Tighten the compressor until the spring retainer no longer holds the valve keepers in position. Lift the keepers from the valve stem (**Figure 45**).
4. Slowly relieve the pressure on the valve spring and remove the compressor from the head.
5. Remove the spring retainer, valve spring, oil seal and lower spring seat.
6. Inspect the valve stem for sharp and flared metal (**Figure 46**) around the groove for the keepers. If necessary, deburr the valve stem before removing

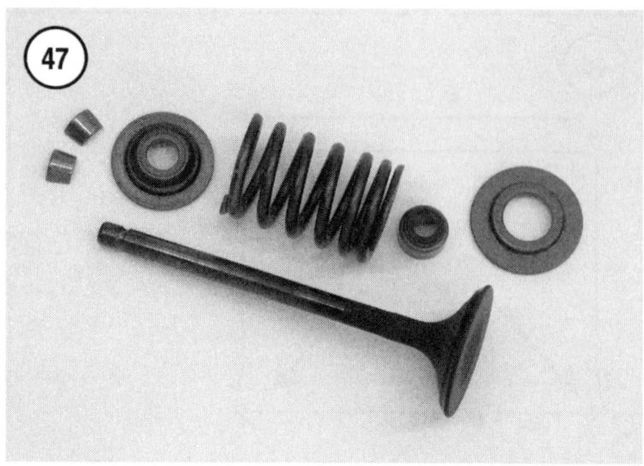

47

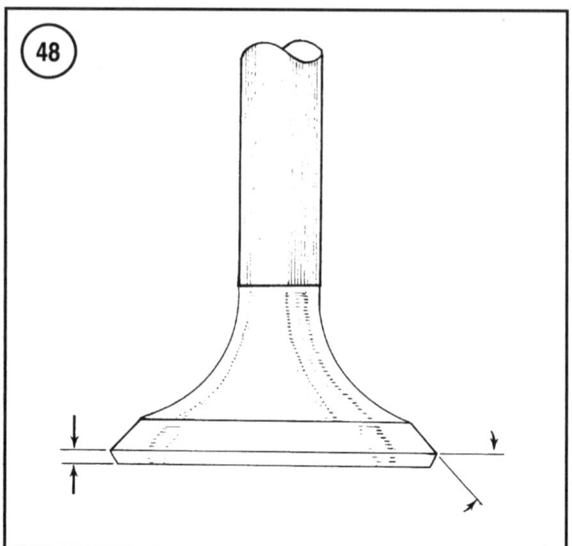

48

the valve from the head. Burrs on the valve stem can damage the valve guide.

7. Remove the valve from the cylinder head.
8. Store all components of each valve assembly together (**Figure 47**). Prevent parts from being intermixed.
9. Repeat this procedure for the remaining valves.
10. Inspect the components as described in this section.

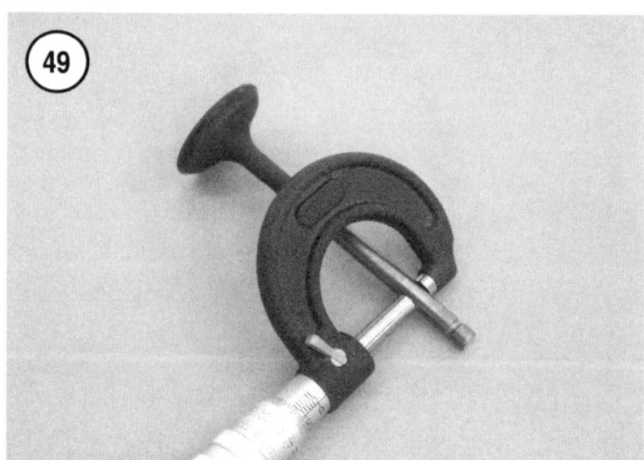

49

Valve Component Inspection

During the cleaning and inspection of the valve assemblies, do not intermix the parts. Work with one set of parts at a time, repeating the procedure until all parts are inspected. After inspecting each set of parts, return them to their storage container.

If valve service is required, refer the service to a machine shop.

Refer to **Table 2** for specifications.

1. Clean the valve assembly in solvent.

CAUTION

The valve seating surface is a critical surface and must not be damaged. Do not scrape the seating surface or place the valve where it could roll off the work surface.

2. Inspect the valve head as follows:
   a. Inspect the top and perimeter of each valve. Check for burning or other damage on the top and seating surface. Replace the valve if damage is evident. If the valve head appears uniform, with only minor wear, and if the other valve measurements are acceptable, the valve can be lapped (described in this section) and reused.
   b. Measure the margin (thickness) (**Figure 48**).
3. Inspect the valve stem as follows:
   a. Inspect the stem for wear and scoring. Also check the end of the valve stem for flare.

50

   b. Measure the valve stem diameter (**Figure 49**).
   c. Check the valve stem for runout. Place the valve in a V-block and measure runout with a dial indicator (**Figure 50**).

4A. With a small bore gauge and micrometer, inspect the valve guides as follows:

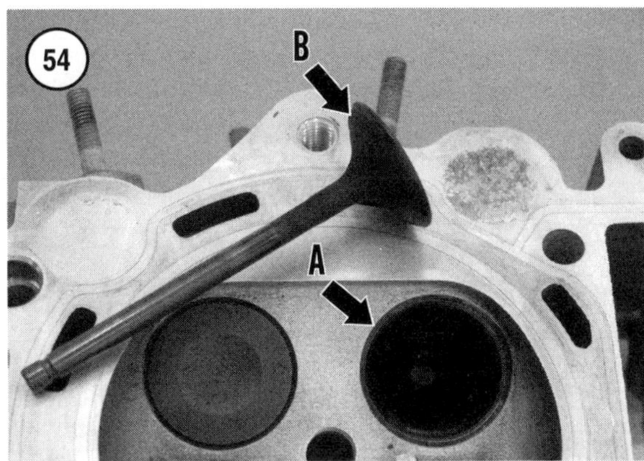

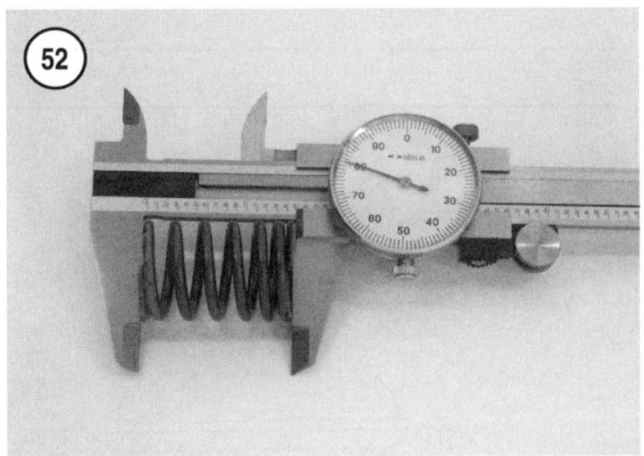

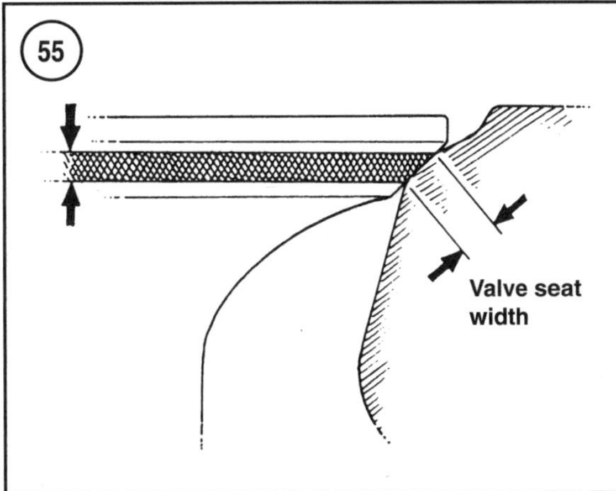

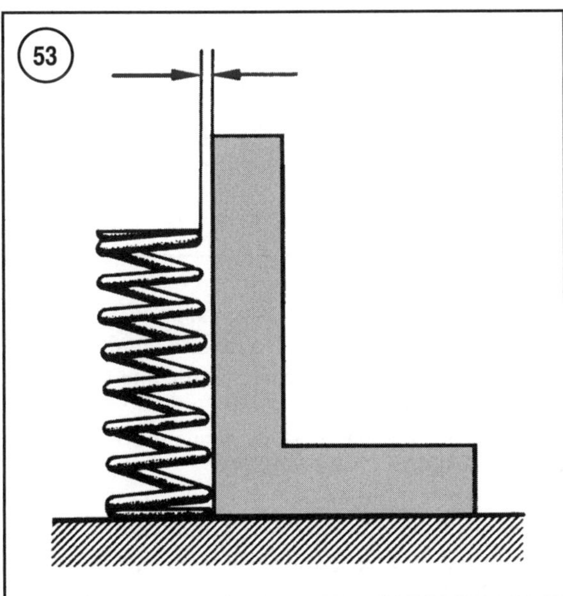

a. Clean the valve guides so they are free of all carbon and varnish. Use solvent and a stiff, narrow brush.
b. Measure each valve guide bore (**Figure 51**) at the top, center and bottom. Use a small bore gauge and micrometer to make the measurements.

4B. If a small bore gauge and micrometer are not available, inspect the valve guides as follows:

a. Insert the appropriate valve into its guide.
b. With the valve head off the seat, move the valve stem side to side in the valve guide. Move the valve in several directions, checking for obvious play. If movement is easily detected, the valve guide and/or valve is worn. Take the valves and cylinder head to a dealership and have the parts accurately measured to determine the extent of wear.

5. Check the valve springs as follows:
   a. Visually check the springs for damage.
   b. Measure the length of each valve spring (**Figure 52**).
   c. Measure the valve spring tilt (**Figure 53**).
6. Inspect the valve spring retainers, seats and keepers for wear or damage.
7. Inspect the valve seats (A, **Figure 54**) to determine if they must be reconditioned.
   a. Clean and dry the valve seats with contact cleaner.
   b. Coat the face (B, **Figure 54**) of the valve with machinist's marking fluid.
   c. Install the valve into the appropriate guide, then *lightly* tap the valve against the seat to

4

make a clear pattern on the cylinder head. Do not rotate the valve.

d. Remove the valve from the guide and measure the imprinted valve seat width (**Figure 55**) at several locations.

e. Clean all marking fluid from the valves and seats.

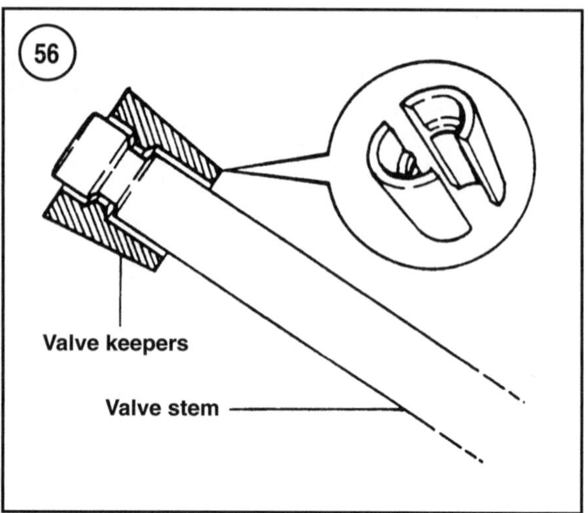

Valve Installation

Perform the following procedure for each set of valve components (**Figure 47**). All components should be clean and dry.

1. Coat the valve stem and interior of the oil seal with molybdenum disulfide grease.
2. Install the lower spring seat into the head. Install the seat so the perimeter rests on the head.
3. Install and seat a new oil seal onto the valve guide.
4. Insert the appropriate valve into the cylinder head. Rotate the valve stem as it enters and passes through the seal. Check that the seal remains seated. Then hold the valve in place.
5. Install the valve springs with the *small* coil pitch, facing down.
6. Install the spring retainer, fitting the center of the retainer into the spring.
7. Install a valve spring compressor over the valve assembly. Fit the tool squarely onto the valve spring retainer.

CAUTION
Do not overtighten and compress the valve springs too far. This can cause loss of valve spring tension.

8. Tighten the compressor until the spring retainer is compressed just far enough to install the valve keepers.
9. Insert the keepers around the groove in the valve stem (**Figure 45**).
10. Slowly relieve the pressure on the spring retainer. Then remove the compressor from the head.
11. Tap the end of the valve stem with a soft mallet to ensure that the keepers are fully seated in the valve stem groove (**Figure 56**).
12. After installing all valves, perform the *Solvent Test* as described in this section.
13. Install the cylinder head as described in this chapter.

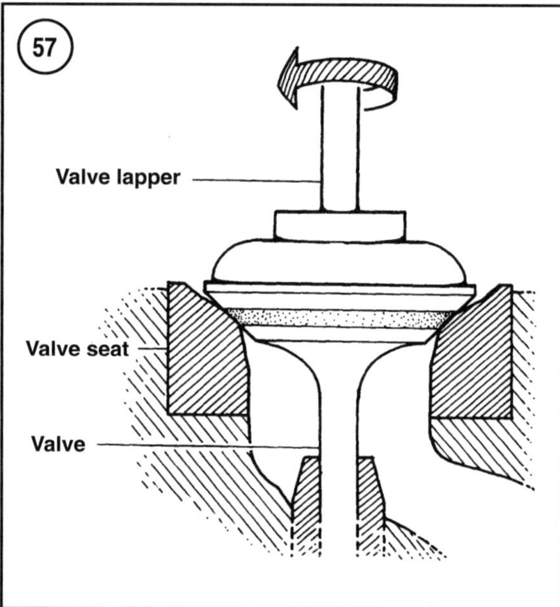

Valve Lapping

Valve lapping can restore the sealing between the valve seat and valve face contact area on parts that are within specification. Valves and valve seats that have been reconditioned also require lapping.

1. Lightly coat the valve face with fine-grade lapping compound.
2. Lubricate the valve stem, then insert the valve into the head.
3. Wet the suction cup on the lapping tool and press it onto the head of the valve (**Figure 57**).
4. Spin the tool back and forth between your hands to lap the valve to the seat. Every 5-10 seconds, rotate the valve 180° and continue to lap the valve into the seat.
5. Frequently inspect the valve seat. Stop lapping the valve when the valve seat is smooth, even and polished. Keep each lapped valve identified so it can be installed in the correct seat during assembly.
6. Clean the valves and cylinder head in solvent and remove all lapping compound. Any abrasive remain-

58

PISTON AND CYLINDER

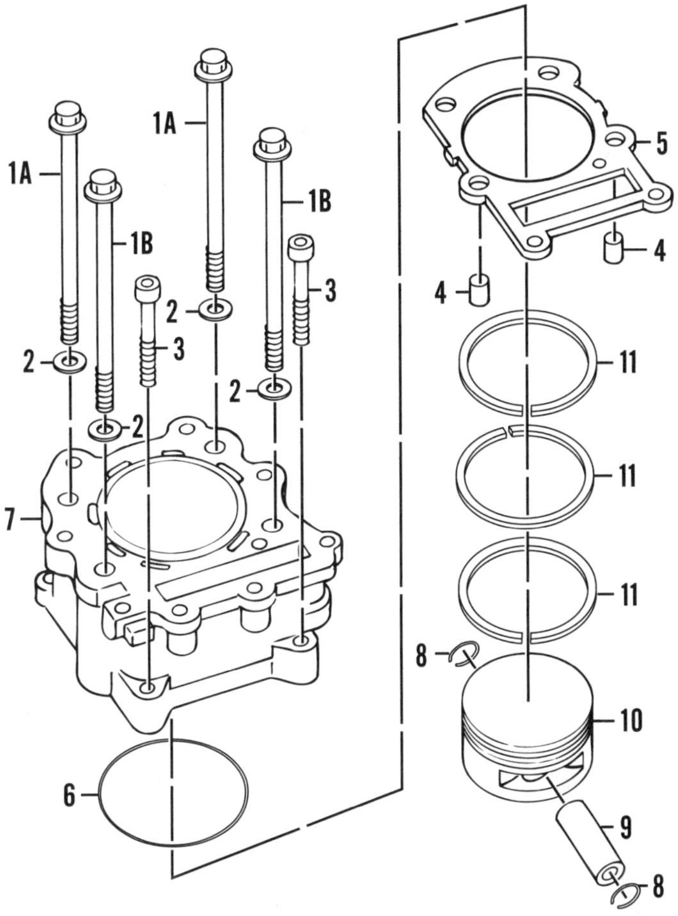

1A. 10-mm mounting bolt (short)
1B. 10-mm mounting bolt (long)
2. Washer
3. 6-mm mounting bolt
4. Dowel
5. Base gasket
6. O-ring
7. Cylinder
8. Circlip
9. Piston pin
10. Piston
11. Piston rings

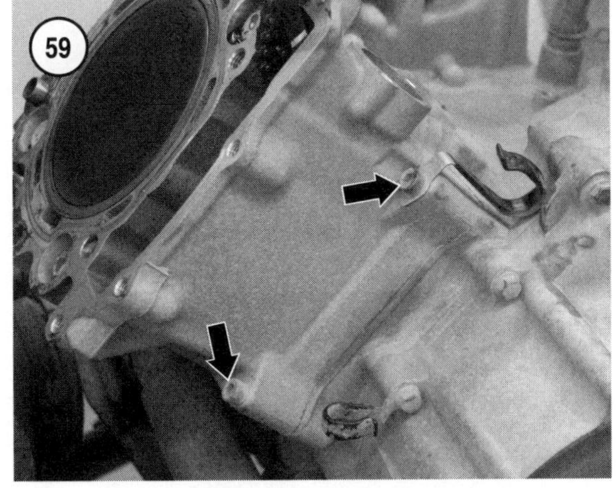

ing in the head will cause premature wear and damage other engine parts.

7. After installing the valves in the head, perform the *Solvent Test* described in this section. If leakage is evident, remove that valve and repeat the lapping process.

CYLINDER

Removal

The cylinder and piston can be removed with the engine mounted in the frame. Refer to **Figure 58**.

1. Remove the cylinder head as described in this chapter.
2. Remove the two cylinder mounting bolts (6 mm) and hose clamp at the left side of the cylinder (**Figure 59**).
3. Remove the four cylinder mounting bolts (10 mm) at the top of the cylinder (**Figure 60**). Loosen the bolts in several passes, working in a crossing pattern. Note that the left bolts are longer than the right bolts.
4. Loosen the cylinder by lightly tapping around the base with a soft mallet. If necessary, apply penetrating oil to the joint.
5. *Slowly* lift the cylinder from the crankcase.

60

61

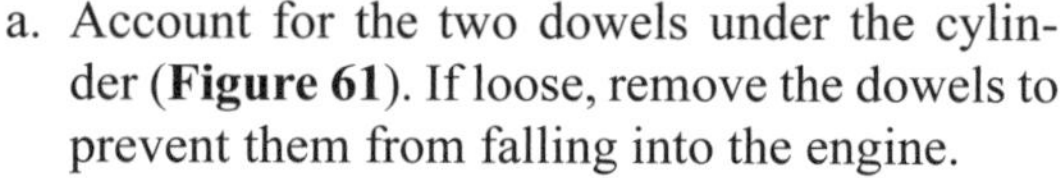

a. Account for the two dowels under the cylinder (**Figure 61**). If loose, remove the dowels to prevent them from falling into the engine.
b. Route and secure the cam chain out of the cylinder.

6. Remove the base gasket.
7. Stuff shop cloths into the cam chain tunnel and around the piston. Support the piston and rod so it does not contact the crankcase (**Figure 62**).
8. Remove the O-ring from the bottom of the cylinder (**Figure 63**).
9. Remove the water jacket inlet housing from the front of the cylinder (**Figure 64**).
10. Inspect the cylinder as described in this section.

62

Inspection

1. Remove all gasket residue from the top and bottom cylinder block surfaces.
2. Wash the cylinder in solvent and dry with compressed air.
3. Inspect the overall condition of the cylinder for wear or damage.
   a. Inspect the cylinder bore (A, **Figure 65**) for scoring or gouges. If damaged, bore the cylinder.
   b. Inspect the water jackets (B, **Figure 65**) for deposits.
   c. Inspect all threads (C, **Figure 65**) for condition and cleanliness.
4. Measure and check the cylinder for wear. Measure the inside diameter of the cylinder with a bore gauge or inside micrometer as follows:
   a. Measure the overall cylinder wear at three points along the bore axis (**Figure 66**). At each point, measure the cylinder front to back (measurement X) and side to side (measurement Y). Make the middle measurement 50 mm (2.0 in.) down from the top of the cylinder. Record the measurements for each location.
   b. To determine if the cylinder is within specification, find the average of the X and Y mea-

63

64

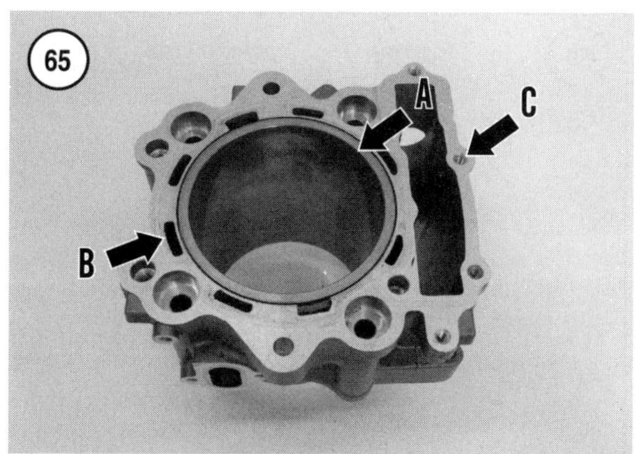

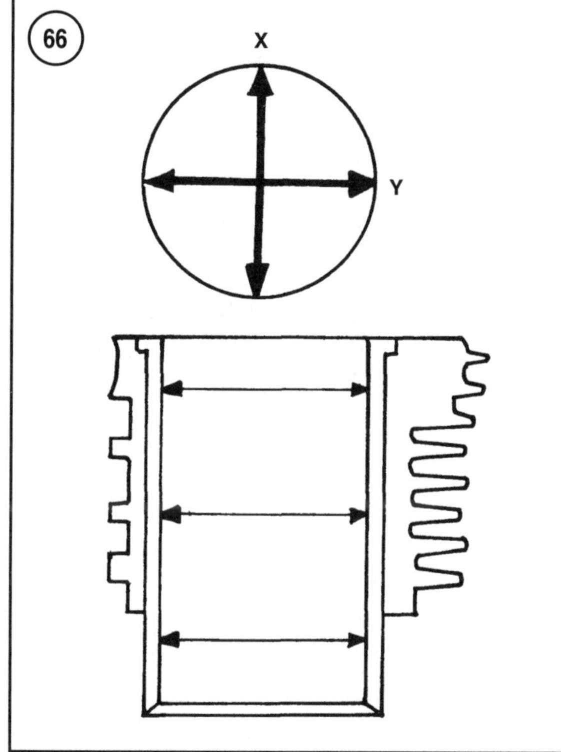

surements recorded at the *middle* position. Compare this averaged measurement to the specification and service limit in **Table 2**. If the cylinder bore is not within the service limit, bore and hone the cylinder.

5. If cylinder boring is necessary, take the cylinder to a machine shop. If the cylinder is to be overbored and fitted with the next size piston, have a new piston available so the cylinder can be bored and honed to the actual piston size.

6. Cylinder glaze appears as a hard, shiny surface. After deglazing, the crosshatching in the cylinder provides a uniform surface, capable of retaining oil and allowing the rings to seat by sealing them against the cylinder. If the cylinder is within all service limits, deglaze the cylinder with a 240-grit, silicone-carbide Flex-Hone tool (**Figure 67**) as follows:
   a. When deglazing the cylinder, apply plenty of honing lubricant to the hone and cylinder surface.
   b. Move the hone evenly and smoothly in an up-and-down motion for 30 seconds.
   c. The hone should continue to spin as it leaves the cylinder. Proper movement speed of the hone is achieved when a 45° crosshatch pattern is visible on the cylinder wall.

7. Thoroughly wash and scrub the cylinder in hot, soapy water after inspection and service, to remove all fine grit and material/residue left from machine operations. Check cleanliness by rubbing a clean, white cloth over the bore. No residue should be evident. When the cylinder is thoroughly clean and dry, immediately coat the cylinder bore with oil to prevent corrosion. Wrap the cylinder until engine reassembly.

8. Perform any service to the piston assembly before installing the cylinder.

Installation

Refer to **Figure 58**.

1. Make sure all gasket residue is removed from all mating surfaces.

2. Install the water jacket inlet housing at the front of the cylinder (**Figure 64**).
   a. Install a new, lubricated O-ring.
   b. Tighten the bolts to 10 N•m (89 in.-lb.).

3. Install the dowels and a new base gasket onto the crankcase (**Figure 68**).

4. Install a new, lubricated O-ring on the bottom of the cylinder (**Figure 63**)

5. Lubricate the following components with engine oil:
   a. Piston and rings.
   b. Piston pin and connecting rod.
   c. Cylinder bore.

6. Support the piston so the cylinder can be lowered into place.
7. Stagger the piston ring gaps on the piston as shown in **Figure 69**. Note that the top and second ring gaps are opposite one another, as well as the gaps in the oil ring rails.
8. Lower the cylinder onto the crankcase.
   a. Route the cam chain and guide through the chain tunnel. Secure the cam chain so it cannot fall into the engine.
   b. As the piston enters the cylinder, compress each ring so it can enter the cylinder. A ring compressor can also be used. When the bottom ring is in the cylinder, remove any holding fixture and shop cloths from the crankcase.
9. Install the four cylinder mounting bolts (10 mm) into the top of the cylinder.

CAUTION

The two long bolts must be installed onto the left side of the cylinder.

   a. Working in a crossing pattern, tighten the bolts equally in several passes.
   b. Tighten the bolts to 42 N•m (31 ft.-lb.).
10. Install the two cylinder mounting bolts (6 mm) at the left side of the cylinder. Install the clamp under the rear bolt. Tighten the bolts to 10 N•m (89 in.-lb.).
11. Install the cylinder head and cylinder head cover as described in this chapter.

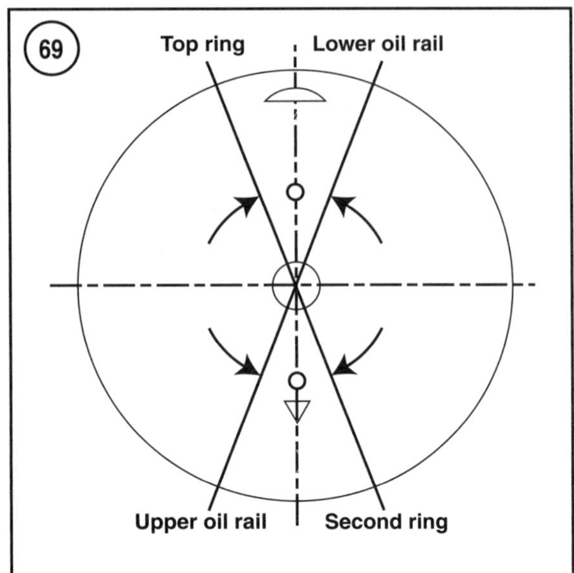

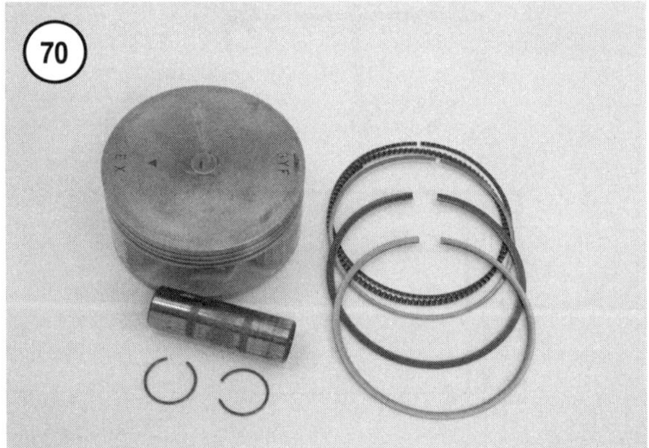

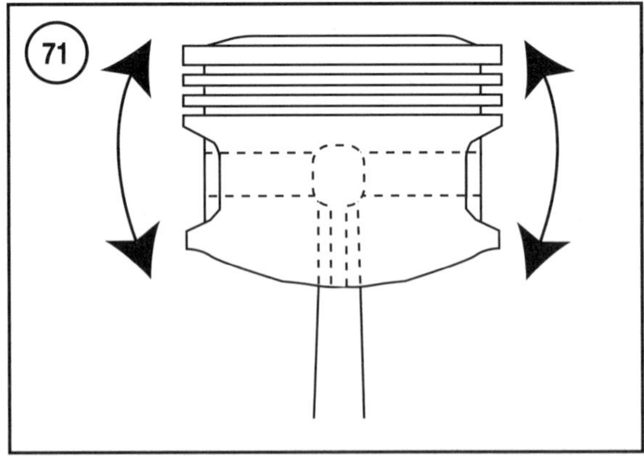

PISTON AND PISTON RINGS

The piston is made of aluminum alloy and fitted with three rings. The piston is held on the small end of the connecting rod by a chrome-plated, steel piston pin. The pin is a precision fit in the piston and rod, and is held in place by circlips.

While cleaning and measuring each component of the piston assembly (**Figure 70**), identify and record all measurements. Refer to the measurements when checking dimensions and wear limits.

Piston Removal

1. Remove the cylinder as described in this chapter.
2. Before removing the piston, check the piston and

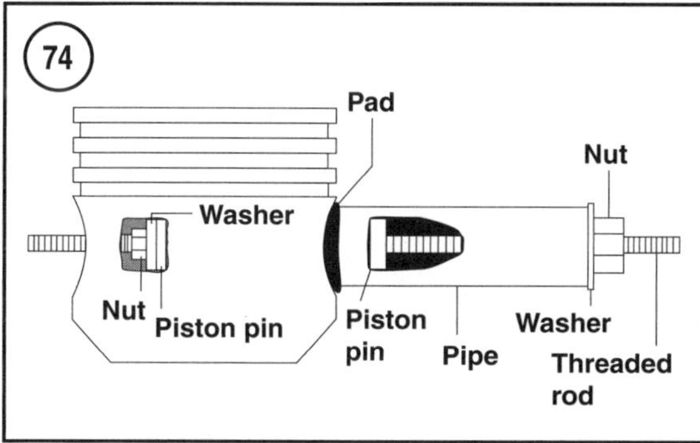

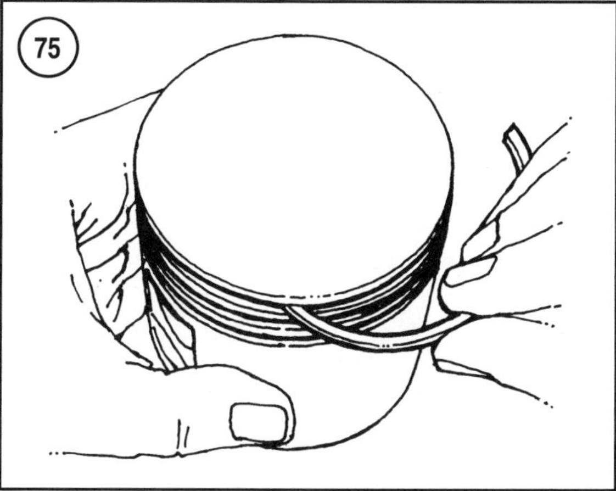

piston pin for obvious play. Hold the rod and try to tilt the piston side to side (**Figure 71**). If tilting (not sliding) motion is evident, there is wear on either the piston pin, pin bore or connecting rod. Wear could be on any combination of the three parts. Careful inspection is required to determine which parts require replacement.

3. Stuff shop cloths around the connecting rod and in the cam chain tunnel to prevent parts from entering the crankcase.
4. Rotate the ends of the circlips to the removal gaps. Then remove the circlips from the piston pin bore (**Figure 72**). Discard the circlips.

CAUTION
Do not drive the pin out with a hammer and drift. The piston and connecting rod assembly will likely be damaged.

5. Press the piston pin out of the piston by hand (**Figure 73**). If the pin is tight, a removal tool can be made as shown in **Figure 74**. The end of the padded pipe rests against the piston, not the piston pin. The hole in the pipe must be larger than the diameter of the piston pin. As the nut on the end of the rod is tightened, the nut and washer at the opposite end drive the piston pin into the pipe.
6. Lift the piston off the connecting rod.
7. Inspect the piston and piston pin as described in this section.

Piston Inspection

1. Remove the piston rings as described in this section.
2. Clean the piston.
   a. Clean the carbon from the piston crown. Use a soft scraper, brushes and solvent. Do not use tools that can gouge or scratch the surface. This type of damage can cause hot spots on the piston during engine operation.
   b. Clean the piston pin bore, ring grooves and piston skirt. Clean the ring grooves with a soft brush, or use a broken piston ring to remove carbon and oil residue (**Figure 75**). Mild galling or discoloration can be polished off the piston skirt with fine emery cloth and oil.
3. Inspect the piston. Replace the piston if damage is evident.
   a. Inspect the piston crown (A, **Figure 76**) for damage. If the piston is pitted, overheating is likely occurring. This can be caused by a lean fuel mixture and/or preignition.
   b. Inspect the ring grooves for (B, **Figure 76**) dents, nicks, cracks or other damage. The grooves should be square and uniform for the

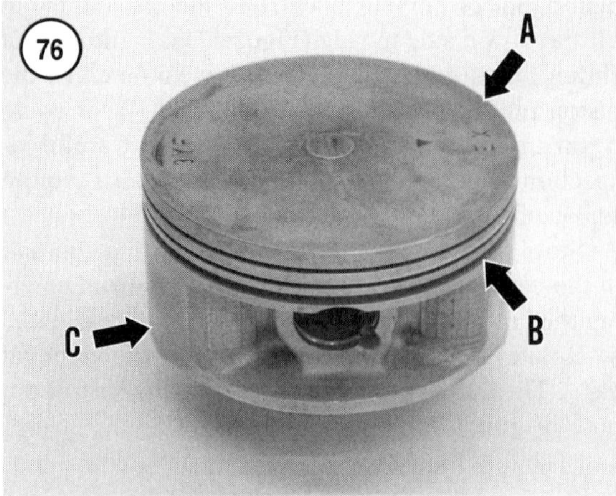

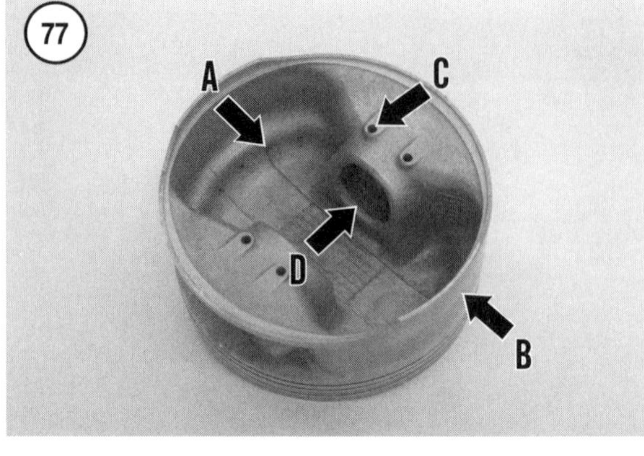

circumference of the piston. Particularly inspect the top compression ring groove. It is lubricated the least and is nearest the combustion temperatures. If the oil ring appears worn, or if the oil ring is difficult to remove, the piston has probably overheated and distorted.

c. Inspect the piston skirt (C, **Figure 76**). If the skirt shows signs excessive galling or partial seizure (bits of metal embedded in the skirt), replace the piston.
d. Inspect the interior of the piston. Check the crown (A, **Figure 77**), skirt (B) and bosses for cracks or other damage. Check the oil holes (C, **Figure 77**) and circlip grooves (D) for cleanliness and damage.
e. Inspect the pin bores for scoring (**Figure 78**), wear or discoloration from overheating.
f. Measure the inside diameter of the pin bores. Refer to **Table 2** for specifications.

4. Inspect the piston ring to ring groove clearance as described in *Piston Ring Inspection and Removal* in this section.

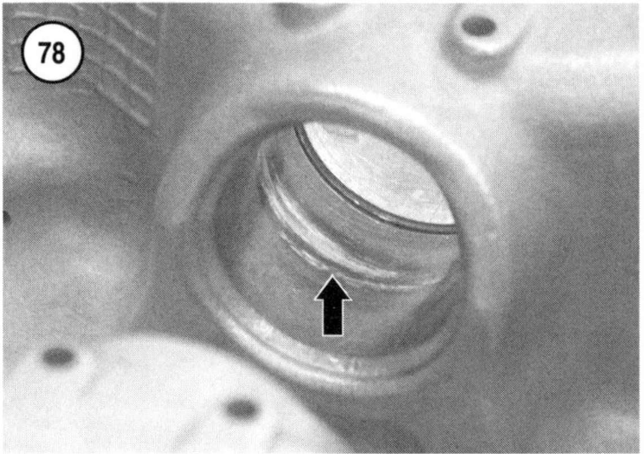

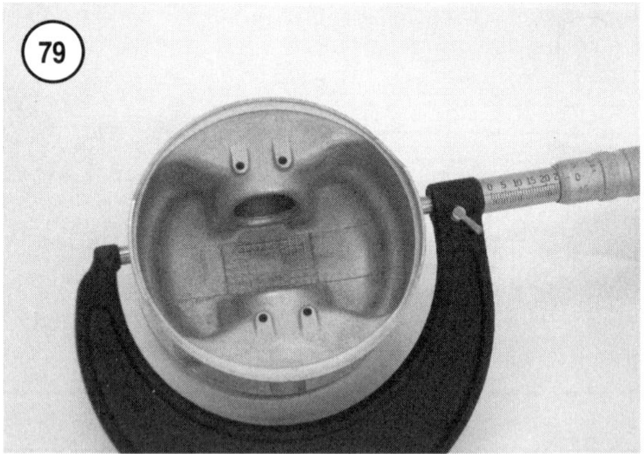

Piston-to-Cylinder Clearance Check

Calculate the clearance between the piston and cylinder to determine if the parts can be reused. If parts do not fall within specification, bore the cylinder oversize to match an oversize piston. Clean and dry the piston and cylinder before measuring.

1. Measure the outside diameter of the piston. Measure 5 mm (0.2 in.) from the bottom edge of the piston skirt and 90° to the direction of the piston pin (**Figure 79**). Record the measurement.
2. Determine clearance by subtracting the piston measurement from the averaged cylinder measurement. Refer to *Cylinder, Inspection* in this chapter. If the clearance exceeds the specifications in **Table 2**, the cylinder must be bored and fitted with an oversize piston.

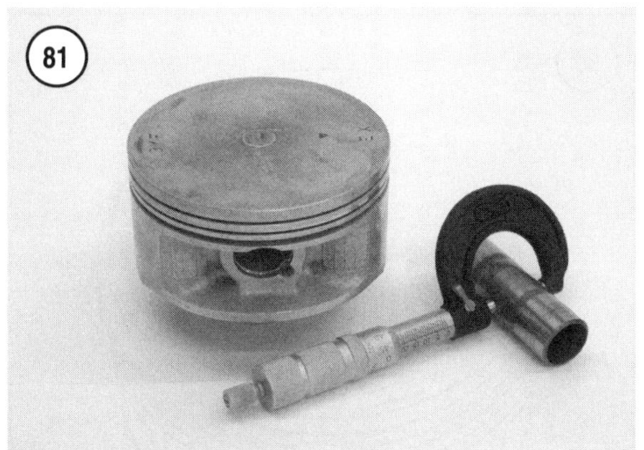
81

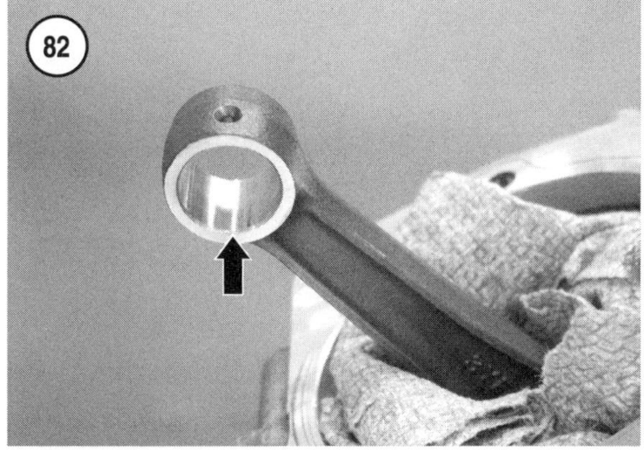
82

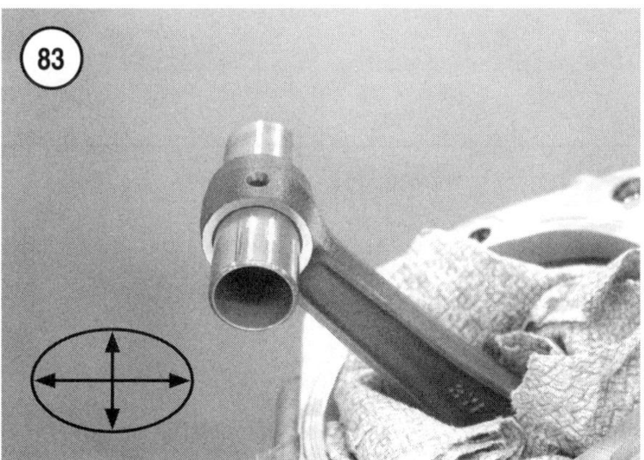
83

84

Piston Pin Inspection

Refer to **Table 2** for specifications.

1. Clean the piston pin.
2. Inspect the pin for chrome flaking, scoring (**Figure 80**), wear or discoloration from overheating.
3. Measure the outside diameter of the pin (**Figure 81**).
4. Determine the pin-to-pin bore clearance. Subtract the pin outside diameter from the pin bore inside diameter.
5. Inspect the bore in the small end of the connecting rod (**Figure 82**). Check for scoring, uneven wear, and discoloration from overheating.
6. Lubricate the piston pin and slide it into the connecting rod. Slowly rotate the pin and check for radial play (**Figure 83**). If play is detectable, one or both of the parts are worn. No specifications for the connecting rod bore are available. If the pin diameter is marginally within specification, check the fit of a new pin. If play still exists, replace the connecting rod.

4

Piston Ring Inspection and Removal

The piston is fitted with two compression rings and an oil control ring assembly. The oil ring assembly consists of two side rails and an expander ring.

Refer to **Table 2** for specifications.

1. Check the piston ring-to-ring groove clearance as follows:
    a. Clean the rings and grooves so accurate measurements can be made with a flat feeler gauge.
    b. Press the top ring into the piston groove.
    c. Insert a flat feeler gauge between the ring and groove (**Figure 84**). Record the measurement. Repeat this step at other points around the piston. Replace the rings if any measurement exceeds the service limit. If excessive clearance remains after installing new rings, replace the piston.
    d. Repeat substep b and substep c for the remaining rings.
2. Remove the top and second rings with a ring expander (**Figure 85**) or by hand (**Figure 86**).
    a. Spread the rings only enough to clear the piston.
    b. The top ring and oil ring rails are not marked. If the rings may possibly be reused, mark the top surface of the rings so they can be installed in their original direction. The second ring is marked with an *R* on its top surface (**Figure 87**).
3. Remove the oil ring assembly by first removing the top rail, followed by the bottom rail. Remove (by hand) the expander ring last.

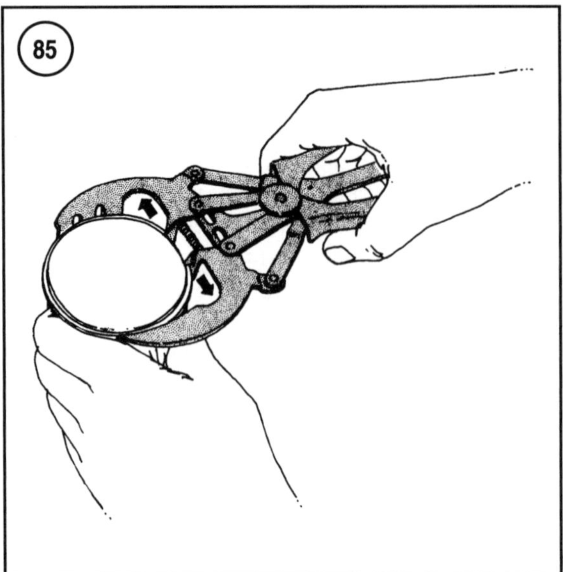

4. Clean and inspect the piston as described in this section.
5. Measure the height and width of the rings (**Figure 88**). Replace all the rings if any measurement exceeds the specifications.
6. Inspect the end gap of the rings as follows:
   a. Insert a ring into the bottom of the cylinder. Use the piston to square the ring to the cylinder wall. Push the ring 50 mm (2 in.) into the cylinder (**Figure 89**).
   b. Measure the end gap with a feeler gauge. For the oil control ring, measure only the rails.
   c. Replace all the rings if any measurement exceeds the service limit. Always replace rings as a set. If new rings are to be installed, gap the new rings after the cylinder has been serviced. If the new ring gap is too narrow, carefully widen the gap using a fine-cut file as shown in **Figure 90**. Work slow and measure often.
7. Roll each ring around its piston groove and check for binding or snags (**Figure 91**). Repair minor groove damage with a fine-cut file.

Piston Ring Installation

If new piston rings will be installed, hone the cylinder as described under *Cylinder, Inspection* in this chapter.

1. Make sure the piston and rings are clean and dry. When installing, spread the rings only enough to clear the piston.
2. Install the rings as follows:
   a. Install the oil ring expander into the bottom groove, followed by the bottom rail and top rail. The ends of the expander must *not* overlap. The rails can be installed in either position or direction for new rings. Install used rings in their original position.

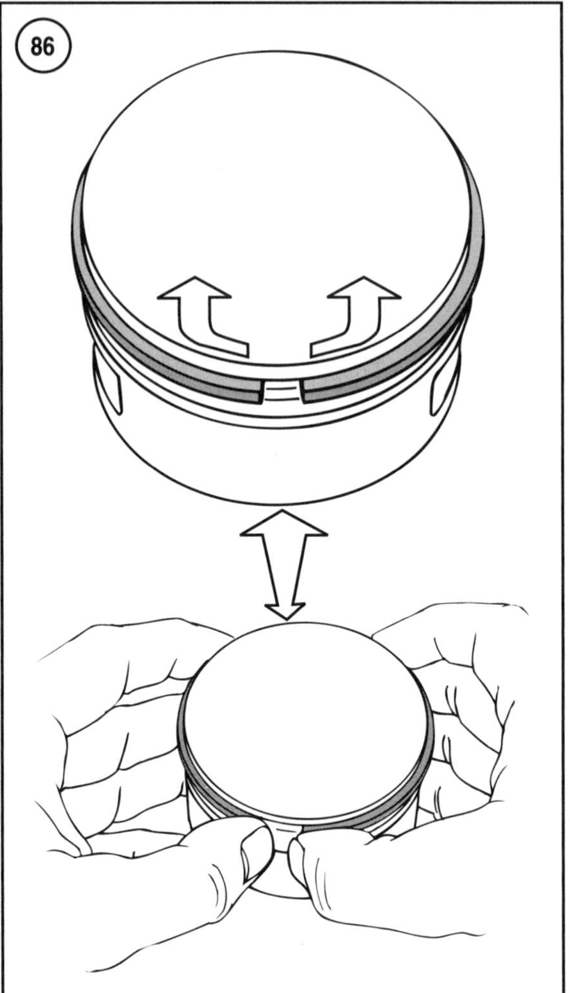

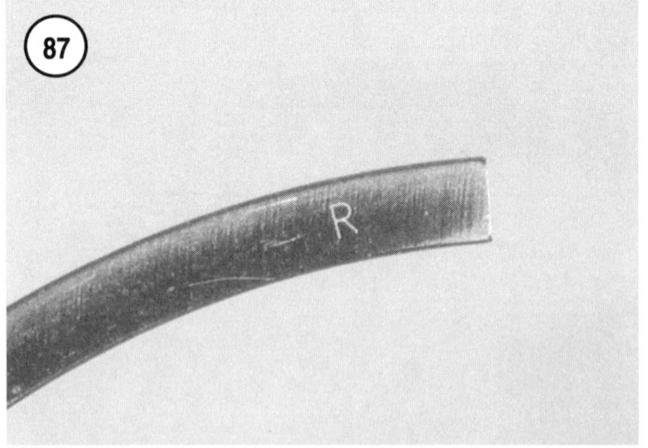

   b. Install the second ring. Check that the *R* mark faces up (**Figure 87**).
   c. Install the top ring. The ring can be installed in either direction for new rings. Install a used ring in its original direction.
3. Check that all rings rotate freely in their grooves.

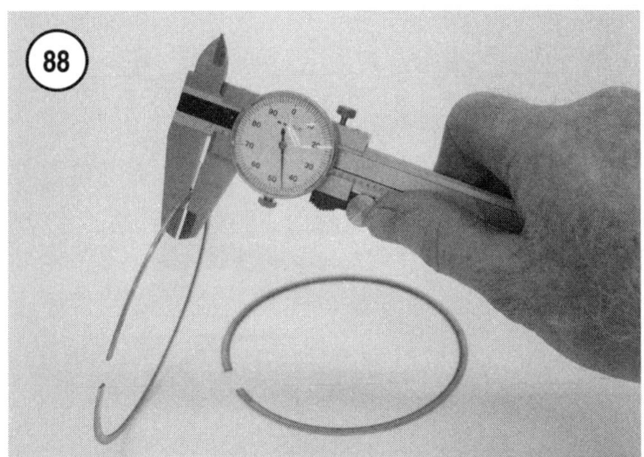

88

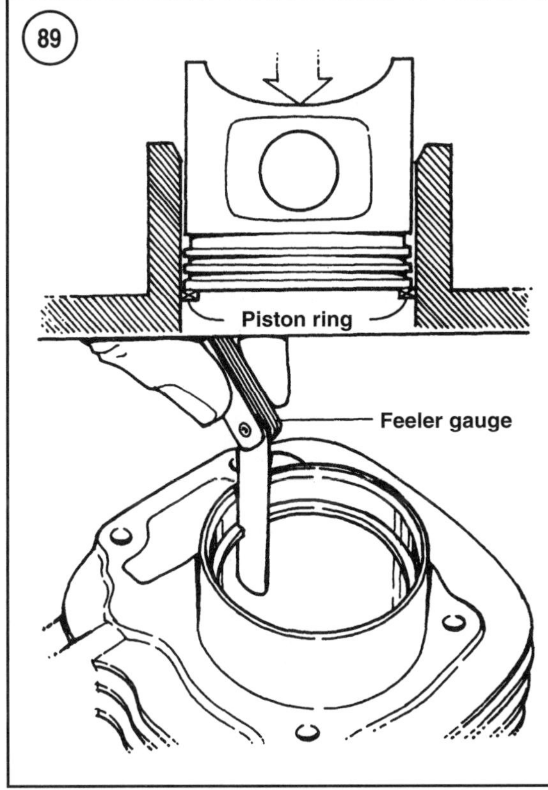

89

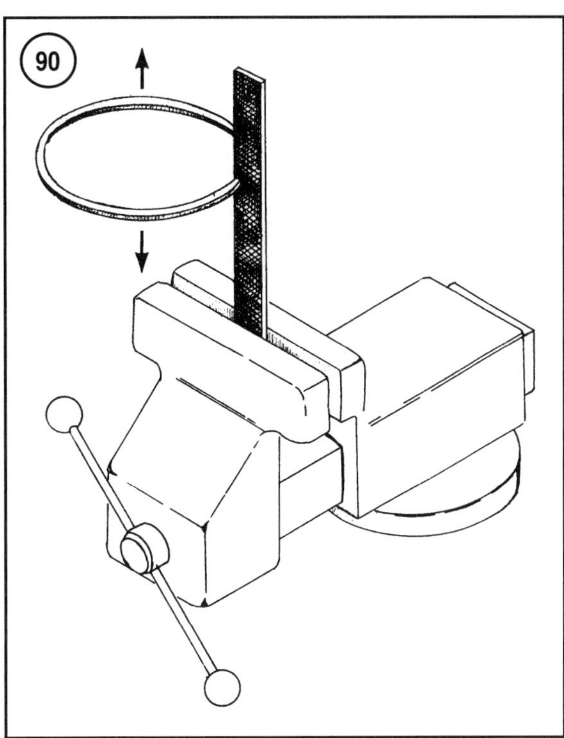

90

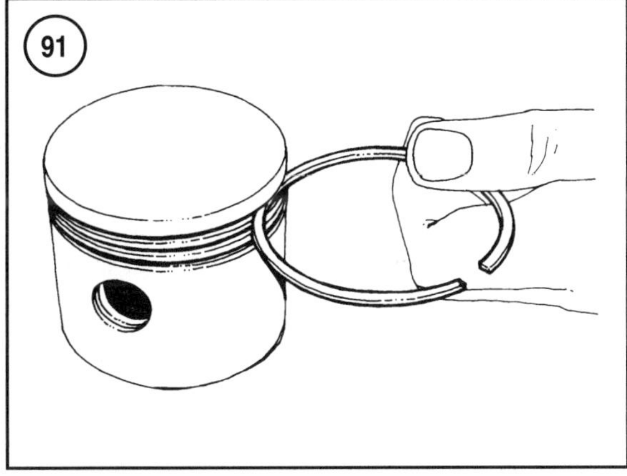

91

Piston Installation

1. Install the piston rings onto the piston as described in this section.
2. Check that all parts are clean and ready to be installed.

CAUTION
Never install used circlips. Engine damage could occur if a circlip fails. Circlips fatigue and distort when they are removed, even though they appear reusable.

3. Install a *new* circlip into one of the piston pin bosses. Rotate the ends of the circlip away from the gap.
4. Lubricate the following components with engine oil:
   a. Piston pin.
   b. Piston pin bores.
   c. Connecting rod bore.

CAUTION
The piston must be installed correctly. Failure to install the piston correctly can lead to excessive engine damage.

5. Start the piston pin into the open pin bore, then place the piston over the connecting rod. The arrow and letters *EX*, stamped on the piston crown (**Figure 92**), must point forward.
6. Align the piston with the rod, then slide the pin through the rod (**Figure 73**) and into the other piston bore.

4

7. Support the piston so it is stable. Stuff shop cloths into crankcase openings to prevent the remaining circlip from entering the engine if it slips and falls.
8. Install a *new* circlip into the remaining piston pin boss (**Figure 72**). Rotate the ends of the circlip away from the gap.
9. Stagger the piston ring gaps on the piston as shown in **Figure 69**. Note that the top and second ring gaps are opposite one another, as well as the gaps in the oil ring rails.
10. Install the cylinder as described in this chapter.
11. Refer to Chapter Three for engine break-in.

Table 1 GENERAL ENGINE SPECIFICATIONS

Engine type	Four-stroke single cylinder
Lubrication system	Forced pressure, wet sump
Valve system	Five valve, chain-driven SOHC
Cooling system	Liquid cooled
Engine displacement	660 cc (40.28 cu. in.)
Bore and stroke	100.0 × 84.0 mm (3.94 × 3.31 in.)
Compression ratio	9.1:1

Table 2 ENGINE TOP END SPECIFICATIONS

	New mm (in.)	Service limit mm (in.)
Camshaft		
Lobe height		
Intake	35.69-35.79 (1.4051-1.4091)	35.59 (1.4012)
Exhaust	36.50-36.60 (1.4370-1.4409)	36.40 (1.4331)
Lobe width		
Intake	30.06-30.16 (1.1835-1.1874)	29.96 (1.1795)
Exhaust	30.11-30.21 (1.1854-1.1894)	30.01 (1.1815)
Runout	–	0.03 (0.0012)
Cylinder compression		
Standard	1324 kPa (192 psi)	
Minimum	1150 kPa (167 psi)	
Maximum	1480 kPa (215 psi)	
Cylinder head warp limit	–	0.03 (0.0012)
Cylinder		
Inside diameter	100.005-100.055 (3.9372-3.9392)	100.10 (3.9410)
Measurement point from top of cylinder	50 (2.0)	
Piston		
Mark direction	Arrow pointing forward	
Outside diameter measurement point	2.5 (0.10) from bottom	–
Outside diameter	99.945-99.995 (3.9348-3.9368)	–
Pin bore inside diameter	22.004-22.015 (0.8663-0.8667)	22.045 (0.8679)
Pin bore offset (toward intake side)	1.0 (0.04)	–
Piston-to-cylinder clearance	0.05-0.07 (0.0020-0.0028)	0.15 (0.0059)
Piston pin outside diameter	21.991-22.0 (0.8658-0.8661)	21.971 (0.8650)
Piston pin-to-pin bore clearance	0.004-0.024 (0.00016-0.00095)	0.07 (0.0028)
Piston rings		
Top ring profile	Barrel	

(continued)

Table 2 ENGINE TOP END SPECIFICATIONS (continued)

	New mm (in.)	Service limit mm (in.)
Piston rings (continued)		
Top ring height and width	1.2 × 3.8 (0.0472 × 0.1496)	–
Top ring end gap	0.30-0.45 (0.0118-0.0177)	0.70 (0.0276)
Top ring-to-piston groove clearance	0.04-0.08 (0.0016-0.0032)	0.13 (0.0051)
Second ring profile	Taper	
Second ring height and width	1.2 × 4.0 (0.0472 × 0.1575)	–
Second ring end gap	0.30-0.45 (0.0118-0.0177)	0.80 (0.0315)
Second ring-to-piston groove clearance	0.03-0.07 (0.0012-0.0028)	0.13 (0.0051)
Oil ring height and width	2.5 × 3.4 (0.0984 × 0.1339)	–
Oil ring end gap	0.2-0.7 (0.0079-0.0276)	–
Oil ring-to-piston groove clearance	0.06-0.15 (0.0024-0.0059)	–
Top mark identification	R (second ring only)	
Rocker arm inside diameter	12.0-12.018 (0.4724-0.4732)	–
Rocker arm shaft outside diamter	11.976-11.991 (0.4715-0.4721)	–
Rocker arm-to-rocker arm shaft clearance	0.009-0.042 (0.0004-0.0017)	–
Valve clearance (cold)		
Intake	0.10-0.15 (0.004-0.006)	–
Exhaust	0.15-0.20 (0.006-0.008)	–
Valve dimensions		
Head diameter		
Intake	29.9-30.1 (1.1772-1.1850)	–
Exhaust	31.9-32.1 (1.2559-1.2638)	–
Face width		
Intake	2.25 (0.0886)	–
Exhaust	2.26 (0.0890)	–
Seat angle	45°	
Seat width	0.9-1.1 (0.0354-0.0433)	1.6 (0.0630)
Margin thickness	0.85-1.15 (0.0335-0.0453)	–
Stem outside diameter		
Intake	5.975-5.990 (0.2352-0.2358)	5.945 (0.2341)
Exhaust	5.960-5.975 (0.2347-0.2352)	5.930 (0.2335)
Stem runout	–	0.01 (0.0004)
Valve guide inside diameter	6.0-6.012 (0.2362-0.2367)	6.050 (0.2382)
Valve stem-to-guide clearance		
Intake	0.010-0.037 (0.0004-0.0015)	0.08 (0.0032)
Exhaust	0.025-0.052 (0.0010-0.0020)	0.10 (0.0039)
Valve spring		
Free length		
Intake	32.63 (1.29)	31.0 (1.22)
Exhaust	36.46 (1.44)	34.6 (1.36)
Set length (valve closed)		
Intake	27.5 (1.08)	–
Exhaust	31.0 (1.22)	–
Compressed pressure		
Intake	100-115.7 N (22.48-26.01 lbs.)	
Exhaust	120.6-138.3 N (27.11-31.09 lbs.)	
Tilt limit	–	1.6 (0.06)

4

Table 3 ENGINE TOP END TORQUE SPECIFICATIONS

	N•m	in.-lb.	ft.-lb.
Cam chain tensioner center bolt	7	62	–
Cam chain tensioner mounting bolts	10	89	–
Cam sprocket bolts	20	–	15
Carburetor intake duct bolts	10	89	–
Coolant temperature sending unit	8	71	–

(continued)

Table 3 ENGINE TOP END TORQUE SPECIFICATIONS (continued)

	N•m	in.-lb.	ft.-lb.
Cylinder head bolt (6 mm)	10	89	–
Cylinder head bolts (9 mm)	38	–	28
Cylinder head cover bolts	10	89	–
Cylinder mounting bolts (6 mm)	10	89	–
Cylinder mounting bolts (10 mm)	42	–	31
Exhaust heat shield bolts	11	97	–
Exhaust pipe-to-exhaust pipe bracket bolt	15	–	11
Exhaust pipe flange-to-cylinder head nuts	14	–	10
Exhaust rocker shaft lockbolt	10	89	–
Exhaust valve covers	12	106	–
Intake valve cover bolts	10	89	–
Muffler clamp-to-exhaust pipe bolt	20	–	15
Muffler-to-exhaust pipe bracket bolt	15	–	11
Muffler-to-frame bolt	20	–	15
Oil pressure check plate bolt	10	89	–
Select lever shift rod locknut	15	–	11
Select lever unit mounting bolt	25	–	18
Shift arm pivot bolt	14	–	10
Spark plug	18	–	13
Upper oil pipe			
Lower banjo bolt	35	–	26
Upper banjo bolt	20	–	15
Water jacket housing bolts	10	89	–

CHAPTER FIVE

ENGINE LOWER END

5

This chapter covers the engine lower end. This includes the recoil starter, balancer and oil pump gears, cam chain and rear guide, crankcase, balancer, oil pump, crankshaft and middle gear assembly. Some parts can be removed with the engine mounted in the frame, while access to other parts requires engine removal and crankcase separation.

Refer to **Tables 1-3** at the end of this chapter for specifications.

ENGINE

Depending on the planned level of engine disassembly, consider removing top end components, and those located in the crankcase covers, while the engine remains in the frame. Because the frame keeps the engine stabilized, fasteners are easier to remove if the engine is held steady. Also, if the actual engine problem is unknown, it may be discovered in another assembly other than the crankcase.

Removal and Installation

1. Park the machine on level ground.
2. If possible, perform a compression test (Chapter Three) and leakdown test (Chapter Two) before dismantling the engine.
3. Remove all bodywork and air ducts (Chapter Sixteen).
4. Drain the engine oil (Chapter Three).
5. Drain the engine coolant (Chapter Three).
6. Disconnect the coolant hoses at the engine.
7. Remove the water pump (Chapter Ten) if the cylinder assembly will not be removed prior to engine removal. Removing the pump provides needed clearance during engine removal.
8. Remove the carburetor (Chapter Eight).
9. Remove the exhaust system (Chapter Four).
10. Disconnect the select lever and shift rod (Chapter Seven).
11. Disconnect all electrical leads connected to the engine. Label each connector and note how it is routed.

NOTE

*In the following steps, the engine will be removed, without removing the final drive unit from the machine. This is possible when the cylinder assembly is removed, creating clearance above the crankcase (**Figure 1**). Assistance is required to raise the engine and disengage the parts. If assistance is not available, or if the cylinder assembly remains on the engine, removing the final drive unit and drive shaft is necessary. Refer to Chapter Fourteen.*

12. Inspect the engine and verify that it is ready for removal.
13. Note how the engine bolts are installed, and remove them as follows:

WARNING

Use a jack to support the engine as it is being prepared for removal. When removing the bolts, be aware that the engine may shift in the frame. Keep hands protected and check the stability of the engine after removing each set of bolts. Get assistance when removing the engine from the frame.

a. Remove the bolts from the rear mounting brackets (**Figure 2**). If the cylinder is mounted on the engine, remove the entire left bracket.
b. Remove the bolts from the front mounting brackets (**Figure 3**). If the cylinder is mounted on the engine, remove the entire left bracket and rubber damper.
c. Raise the engine and remove the front drive shaft, followed by the rear drive shaft.
d. Remove the engine from the frame.
e. Clean and inspect the frame. Check for cracks and damage, particularly at welds.

14. Reverse this procedure to install the engine. Note the following:
a. Install the rear drive shaft first, followed by the front drive shaft. Have assistance in handling and engaging the parts.
b. Install the engine mounting brackets (if removed), bolts and nuts. Finger-tighten all nuts before tightening. Follow the original direction of the bolts during installation.
c. Tighten the rubber damper (if removed) to the frame nuts to 42 N•m (31 ft.-lb.).
d. Tighten the large, rear engine mounting throughbolt to 56 N•m (41 ft.-lb.).
e. Tighten the small, rear engine mounting bolts to 10 N•m (89 in.-lb.).
f. Tighten the large, front engine mounting bolts to 33 N•m (24 ft.-lb.).
g. Tighten the small, front engine mounting bolts to 10 N•m (89 in.-lb.).
h. Carefully route electrical wires so they are not pinched or in contact with surfaces that get hot.
i. Apply dielectric grease to electrical connections before reconnecting.
j. If assemblies have been removed from the top end or crankcase covers, install those components. Refer to the appropriate chapters for inspection and installation procedures.
k. Fill the engine with engine oil (Chapter Three).
l. Fill the cooling system with coolant (Chapter Three).
m. Adjust the throttle cable (Chapter Three).
n. Start the engine and check for leaks.
o. Check throttle operation.
p. If the engine top-end has been rebuilt, perform a compression test. Record the result and compare it to future tests. Read the *Engine Break-In* procedure in Chapter Three.

1

2

3

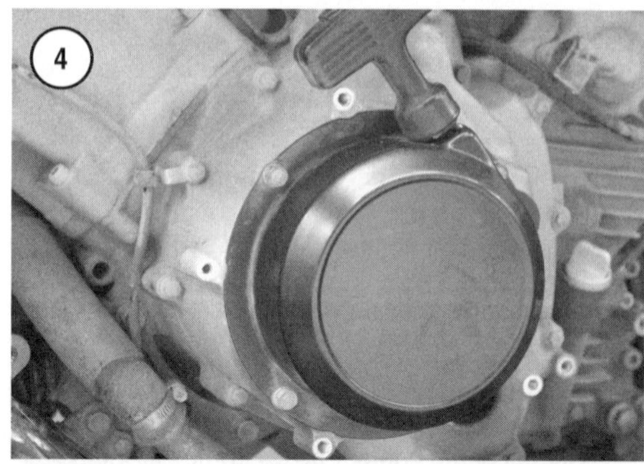
4

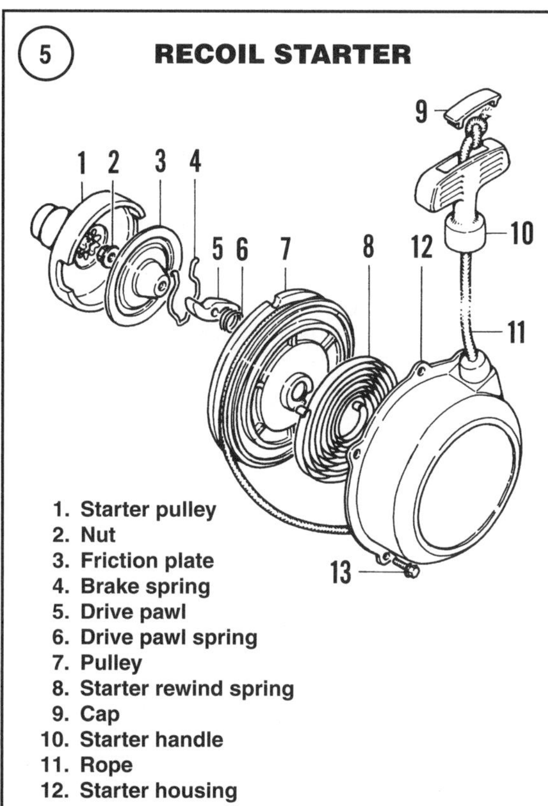

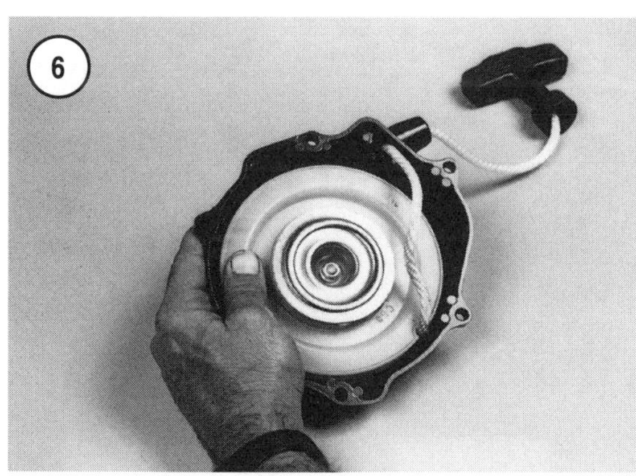

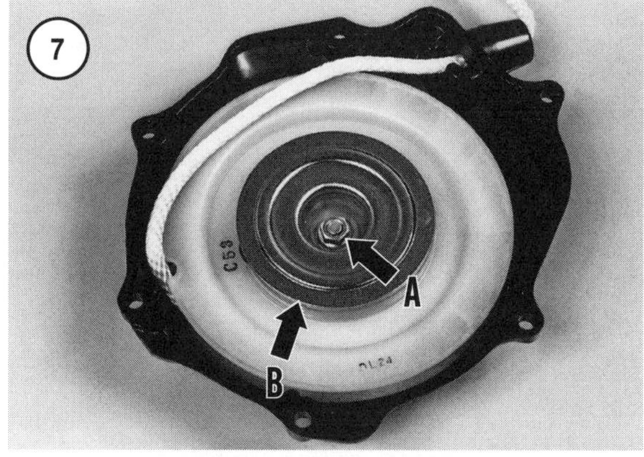

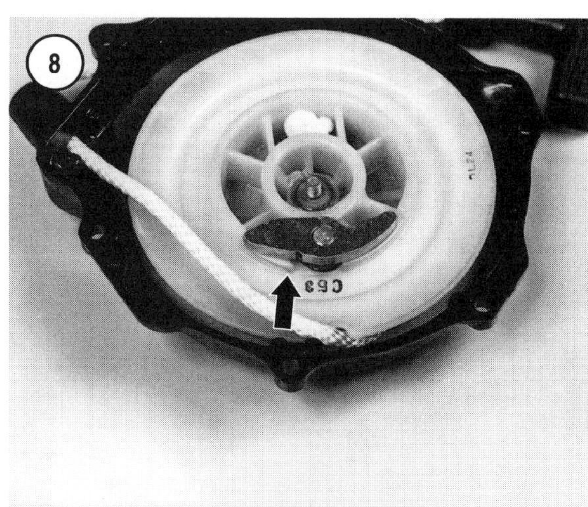

RECOIL STARTER

Starter Housing Removal and Installation

The recoil starter is located on the left side of the crankcase (**Figure 4**). Refer to **Figure 5**.

1. Remove the engine side cover (Chapter Sixteen).
2. Remove the bolts from the perimeter of the housing. Then remove the housing.
3. Clean the housing and starter pulley.
4. If necessary, repair the recoil starter as described in this section.
5. Install the housing and tighten the bolts to 14 N•m (10 ft.-lb.).

Recoil Starter Repair

WARNING
The recoil starter is under spring tension. Wear safety glasses when disassembling the starter.

1. Remove the starter housing as described in this section.
2. Disassemble the starter housing as follows:
   a. Pull the starter rope out of the housing and hold the pulley as shown in **Figure 6**. Route the rope through the notch in the pulley.
   b. Slowly relieve pressure on the pulley and allow the pulley to unwind.
   c. Pry the cap from the starter handle and untie the rope. Remove the handle.
   d. Remove the nut (A, **Figure 7**) and the friction plate (B).
   e. Remove the drive pawl (**Figure 8**) and drive pawl spring (**Figure 9**).
   f. Slowly raise the pulley and rope (**Figure 10**). Avoid dislodging the rewind spring below the pulley.

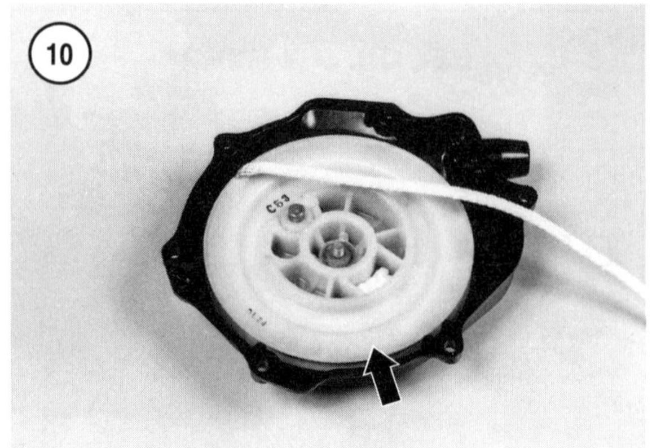

g. Remove the rewind spring by turning the housing over and tapping the outside of the housing to dislodge the spring.

3. Clean and inspect the parts for damage and wear.
   a. Check that both ends of the rewind spring are hook-shaped (**Figure 11**).
   b. If replacing the rope, use rope that is identical in diameter and strength. Heat the ends of the rope to prevent fraying. Insert the rope into the pulley and tie a knot that fits in the pulley (A, **Figure 12**).
4. Assemble the starter housing as follows:
   a. Wrap the rope onto the pulley clockwise. Make 4 1/2 turns, then pass the rope through the pulley notch (B, **Figure 12**). The rope must remain wound on the pulley throughout the assembly procedure.
   b. Lubricate the rewind spring and the housing cavity with waterproof grease.
   c. Hook the outer end of the spring (A, **Figure 13**) to the slot in the housing. Work clockwise and wind the spring into the housing so the inner hook is positioned as shown (B, **Figure 13**).
   d. Install the pulley into the housing, engaging the center hub with the inner end of the rewind spring. Keep the rope wound and locked in the pulley notch while engaging the parts.
   e. Turn the pulley clockwise to verify that the parts are engaged. Spring tension should be felt.
   f. Route the end of the rope through the housing (**Figure 14**).
   g. Insert the long end of the drive pawl spring into the pulley (**Figure 9**).
   h. Engage the drive pawl with the end of the drive pawl spring (**Figure 8**).
   i. Turn the drive pawl one turn counterclockwise. Then seat it into the pulley. This will preload the spring.
   j. Clip the brake spring onto the friction plate (**Figure 15**).

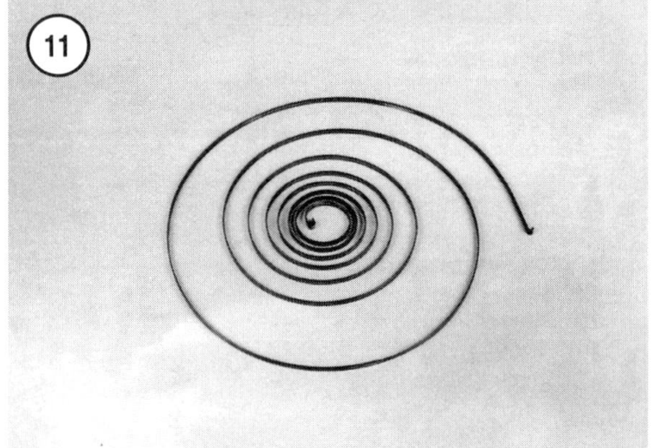

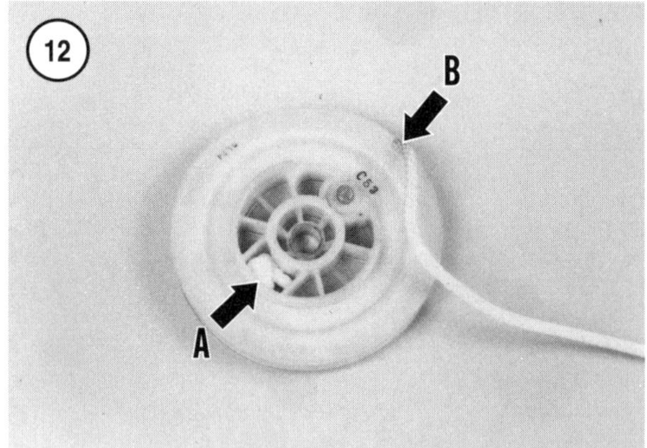

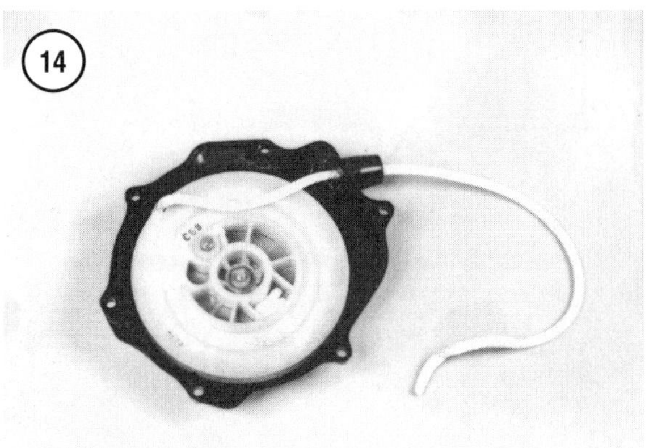

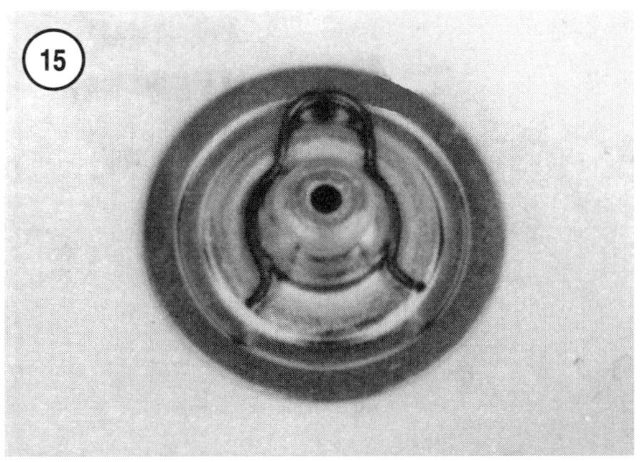

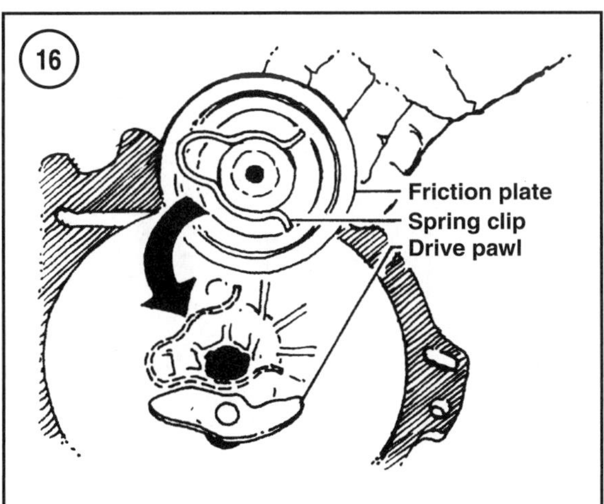

k. Seat the friction plate onto the housing assembly, positioning the parts as shown in **Figure 16**.

l. Install and tighten the retaining nut.

5. Preload the rewind spring as follows:

a. Grasp the rope at the pulley notch and turn the pulley three full turns clockwise. Hold the pulley in this position.

b. With the rope routed through the housing, tie a temporary knot on the outside of the housing to prevent the pulley from turning. Spring tension must be maintained until the handle is attached.

c. Attach the handle to the rope and install the cap on the handle.

d. Untie the temporary knot in the rope.

6. Pull the handle and make sure the rope fully rewinds and the drive pawl extends.

a. If the rope does not fully rewind, place the rope in the pulley notch (**Figure 6**) and turn the pulley one turn clockwise.

b. If the drive pawl does not extend, inspect the parts for damage or improper installation.

Starter Pulley
Removal, Inspection and Installation

1. Remove the recoil starter housing as described in this section.

2. To hold the starter pulley while loosening the bolt, place a pry bar or similar tool across the starter pulley (**Figure 17**). Brace the tool against the work surface.

3. Remove the bolt and washer, securing the starter pulley to the crankshaft.

a. Account for the O-ring in the starter drum (**Figure 18**).

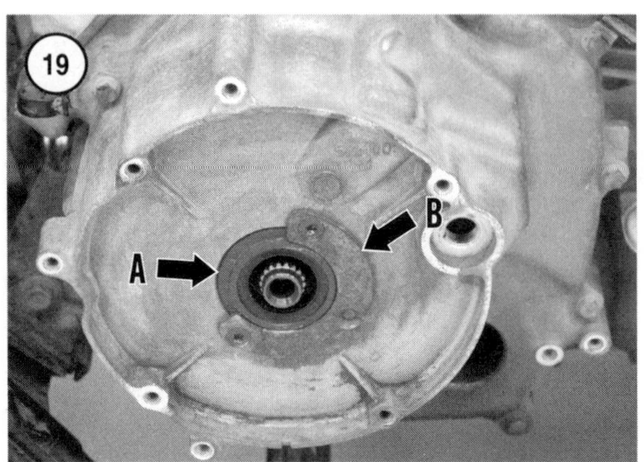

b. Inspect the starter pulley slots for damage. If necessary, file burrs from the slots. On the back of the pulley, if there is scoring or signs of heat damage on the pulley shaft, the bearing in the alternator cover is probably damaged.

c. If there is oil leaking at the seal in the alternator cover (A, **Figure 19**), the seal is damaged.

d. If necessary, replace the seal and bearing as described in this section.

4. Reverse this procedure to install the starter drum.
   a. Install a new, lubricated O-ring.
   b. Tighten the starter pulley bolt to 55 N•m (41 ft.-lb.).

Starter Pulley Seal and Bearing Replacement

1. Replace the seal as follows:
   a. Remove the retainer from the seal (B, **Figure 19**).
   b. Pry the seal from the bore. To ease removal, warm the seal with a heat gun.
   c. Inspect the bearing for seizure and damage. The bearing should turn smoothly. If necessary, replace the bearing.
   d. Lubricate the seal lips with grease. Then hand-fit the seal into the bore.
   e. Apply threadlocking compound to the retainer screws. Then install the retainer and tighten the retainer screws securely.
2. Replace the bearing as follows:
   a. Remove the alternator cover (Chapter Nine).
   b. Remove the retainer and seal as described in Step 1.
   c. Support the alternator cover in a press with the stator coils facing up. Support the cover close to the bearing bore.
   d. Place a driver on the bearing (**Figure 20**). Then drive the bearing from the bore.
   e. Clean the bearing bore. Then place the alternator cover in the press with the bore facing up.

f. Lubricate the new bearing with grease. Then fit the bearing squarely over the bore.
g. Press the bearing into place using a driver that fits on the outer bearing race.
h. Install the seal and retainer as described in Step 1.
i. Install the alternator cover (Chapter Nine).

BALANCER AND OIL PUMP GEARS

The engine balancer and oil pump are driven by a set of gears and a chain, behind the alternator cover.

Removal, Inspection and Installation

1. Remove the alternator cover, rotor, starter clutch (A, **Figure 21**) and starter idle gear assembly (B) as described in Chapter Nine.
2. Remove the balancer driven gear (A, **Figure 22**) and oil pump driven gear (B) as follows:
   a. Bend the lockwasher tab (A, **Figure 23**) away from the locknut.
   b. Lock the gears with a copper washer, or other soft metal. Place the washer above the meshed gears (B, **Figure 23**).
   c. Remove the locknut and lockwasher.
   d. Remove the snap ring on the oil pump driven gear (**Figure 24**).
   e. Slide the gears and chain off the shafts (**Figure 25**). Account for the key on the balancer driven gear shaft.

CAUTION
Do not rotate the crankshaft with the balancer drive gear removed. The balancer shaft weight will jam against the crankshaft unless it is moved to provide clearance.

3. Remove the balancer drive gear (C, **Figure 22**) as follows:
   a. Remove the snap ring (A, **Figure 26**) and plate (B).
   b. Place a plastic bag over the gear. Then pull the gear from the boss (**Figure 27**). The bag will catch any springs and pins that dislodge from the buffer boss.
   c. Pry and remove the springs and pins from the buffer boss (**Figure 28**).

CAUTION
Do not to remove the buffer boss. The boss is an interference fit on the crankshaft. If the boss is damaged, remove the crankshaft and have the boss replaced by a machine shop.

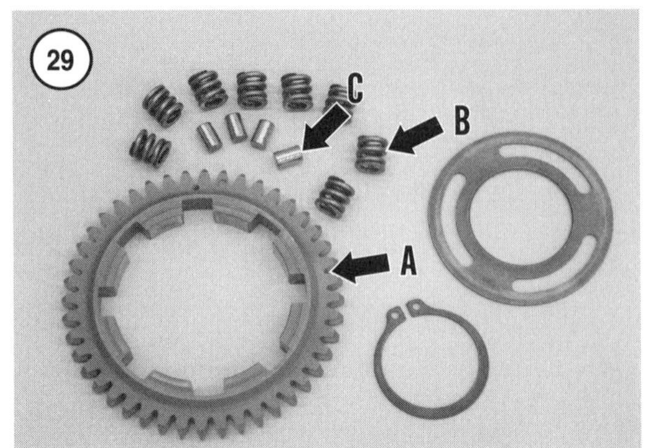

4. Inspect the parts. Replace any worn or damaged components.
   a. Clean the parts and shaft with solvent.
   b. Inspect the balancer drive gear assembly. Inspect the gear (A, **Figure 29**) for worn or broken teeth. Inspect the springs (B, **Figure 29**) and pins (C) for damage.
   c. Inspect the buffer boss (**Figure 30**) for damage.
   d. Inspect the balancer driven gear assembly (**Figure 31**). Inspect the gear for worn or broken teeth. Inspect the key and its fit in the balancer shaft. The key must not be distorted and should fit tightly in the shaft.
   e. Inspect the oil pump driven gear assembly (**Figure 32**). Inspect the chain and sprocket teeth for wear.
5. Install the balancer drive gear as follows:
   a. Install the pins and springs into the balancer driven gear. Alternate the pins in the springs (**Figure 33**). Use adjustable pliers to lightly compress the springs while inserting them into the gear.
   b. Align the marks on the buffer boss and balancer drive gear (**Figure 34**).
   c. Slowly and carefully press the gear and spring assemblies into the buffer boss. Work around the gear, pressing the springs into the boss until all parts are seated (**Figure 35**).
   d. Install the plate and a new snap ring (**Figure 26**). Install the snap ring with the sharp edge facing out.
6. Install the balancer driven gear and oil pump driven gear as follows:
   a. Apply molybdenum disulfide grease to the balancer shaft threads, balancer shaft and oil pump driveshaft.
   b. Fit the key into the balancer shaft.
   c. Assemble the chain and two gears.
   d. With the balancer driven gear assembly near the balancer drive gear, turn the crankshaft and

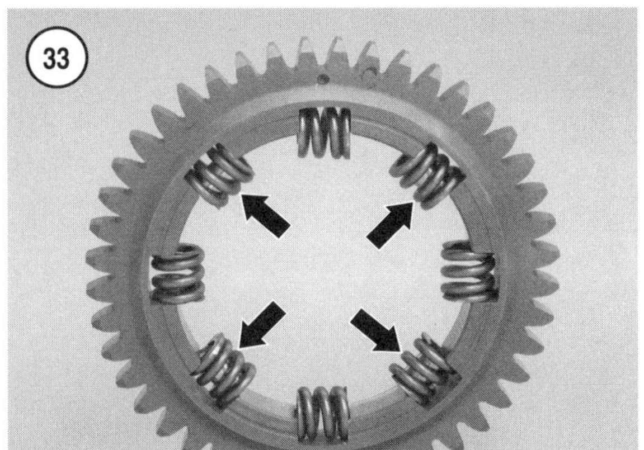

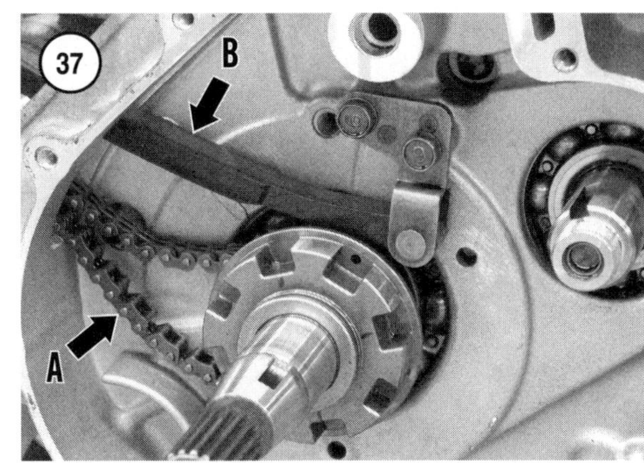

align the mark on the balancer drive gear with the mark on the balancer driven gear. Seat the balancer driven gear and oil pump driven gear when alignment is verified (**Figure 36**).

e. Install a new snap ring on the oil pump driveshaft with the sharp edge facing out.
f. Install a new lockwasher, engaging the tab with the slot in the gear.
g. Lock the gears with a copper washer, or other piece of soft metal. Place the washer below the meshed gears. Then install and tighten the locknut to 110 N•m (81 ft.-lb.).
h. Bend the lockwasher tab (A, **Figure 23**) against the the locknut.

CAM CHAIN AND REAR GUIDE

The cam chain (A, **Figure 37**) and rear guide (B) are behind the buffer boss, at the left side of the crankcase. The front guide can be removed with the cylinder head cover removed.

Removal, Inspection and Installation

1. Remove the camshaft. Then remove the cam chain from the camshaft sprocket (Chapter Four).
2. Remove the balancer drive gear as described in this chapter.
3. Remove the bolts securing the rear guide, then remove the guide and cam chain.
4. Inspect the cam chain and guide (**Figure 38**).
   a. Pull the chain tight and check for excessive play or binding between the links.
   b. Inspect the condition of the chain sprocket.
   c. Inspect the guide for wear and deterioration.
   d. If the chain or sprocket is worn or damaged, replace the parts as a set.
5. Reverse this procedure to install the cam chain and guide. Note the following:
   a. Apply threadlocking compound to the bolt threads.

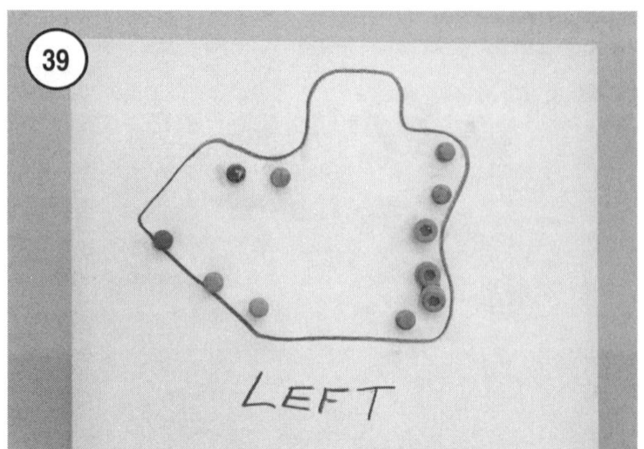

b. Tighten the rear guide bolts to 8 N•m (71 in.-lb.).

CRANKCASE

The following procedures detail the disassembly and reassembly of the crankcase. When the two halves of the crankcase are disassembled, the crankshaft, balancer, transmission, oil pump and middle gear assemblies can be removed for inspection and repair. All assemblies located in the crankcase covers must be removed before disassembling the crankcase. It is usually easier to remove these assemblies with the engine in the frame. The engine will remain steady during the disassembly process. After removing all assemblies from the exterior of the crankcase, remove the crankcase from the frame as described in this chapter.

The crankcase halves are made of cast aluminum alloy. Do not hammer or pry excessively on the cases. The cases will fracture or break. The cases are aligned at the joint by dowels, and joined with liquid sealant.

NOTE
The balancer, oil pump, oil pump relief valve and middle gear assembly can be removed from the left crankcase housing without disturbing other parts in the housing. If desired, after separating the cases, perform only the steps required to remove and install these part(s).

Disassembly

References to the *left* or *right* side of the engine refer to the side of the engine as it is mounted in the frame, not how it may be placed on the workbench. While removing components, keep the parts organized and clean. Leave the left case half facing up until the transmission assembly has been removed.

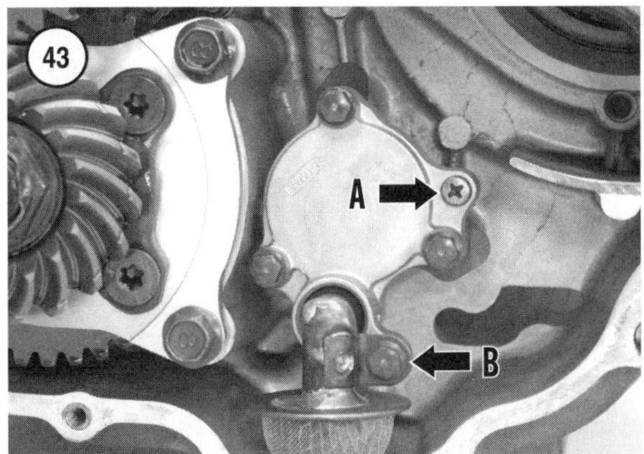

1. Make a drawing of the crankcase shape on a piece of cardboard. Punch holes in the cardboard at the bolt locations. As the bolts are removed from the crankcase, put each bolt in its respective hole in the template (**Figure 39**).
2. Loosen the crankcase bolts on both sides of the engine. Loosen each bolt one-fourth turn, working in a crossing pattern. Remove all bolts from the left crankcase. Then place the engine on wooden blocks with the right crankcase facing up. Remove the bolts from the right crankcase.
3. Separate the crankcase halves as follows:
   a. With the right side of the engine facing up, lightly and evenly pry between the case halves at the reinforced areas around the perimeter. Do not pry on gasket surfaces. Pry slowly and use only enough force to break the seal. If necessary, a heat gun can be used to soften the sealant, making separation easier.
   b. Evenly raise the right case half until it fully releases.
   c. Account for the two dowels between the case halves (**Figure 40**).
   d. Account for the washer on the transmission shaft in the left crankcase (**Figure 41**).
4. Remove the balancer (**Figure 42**). Refer to *Balancer and Oil Pump Gears* in this chapter for inspection.
5. Remove the oil pump and gasket. If the pump is going to be disassembled, loosen the rotor cover (A, **Figure 43**) screw and strainer bolt (B) before removing the mounting bolts. Refer to *Oil Pump* in this chapter for inspection and repair.
6. Remove the oil pump relief valve (**Figure 44**) by removing the bolts and retainer plate. Then pull the valve body from the crankcase. Refer to *Oil Pump* in this chapter to disassemble and inspect the valve.
7. Remove the left middle gear assembly (**Figure 45**). Remove the four bearing housing bolts. Then disengage the assembly from the transmission. Refer to *Middle Gear Assembly* in this chapter to inspect and repair the assembly.
8. Remove the transmission assembly from the crankcase as follows:
   a. Remove the washer (**Figure 46**) and gear from the end of the transmission shaft.
   b. Remove the shift drum stopper bolt (**Figure 47**), washer, spring and ball. Use a magnetic retrieval tool to remove the ball from the bore.
   c. Rotate the shift drum so the pin on the drum is positioned as shown in A, **Figure 48**. This positions the drum for removal.
   d. Lift all the shaft assemblies enough to prevent binding. Then disengage and remove the shift drum from the shift fork guide pins (B, **Figure 48**).

(47)

(48)

e. Again, lift all the shaft assemblies. Then disengage and remove the shift fork assembly (**Figure 49**).
f. Remove the input and output shaft assemblies together (**Figure 50**).
g. Remove the stopper shaft, washer, lever, spring and cam (**Figure 51**).

CAUTION
Take extreme care when removing, handling and storing the transmission. Wrap and store the assembly until it will be inspected. Do not expose the assembly to dirt or place it in an area where it could roll and fall to the floor.

h. Disassemble and inspect the transmission components (Chapter Seven).

9. If necessary, remove the crankshaft from the crankcase (**Figure 52**). Unless obviously damaged, the crankshaft does not have to be removed for most inspection procedures. Refer to *Crankshaft* in this chapter to remove/install and inspect the crankshaft.

10. In the right crankcase, remove the collars (**Figure 53**).

11. Remove the oil pipe and any switches that remain on the crankcases.

12. If necessary, remove the middle driven gear shaft assembly from the right crankcase (**Figure 54**). Unless obviously damaged, the assembly does not have to be removed for the inspection procedures. Refer to *Middle Gear Assembly* in this chapter to repair the shaft assembly.

13. Refer to *Inspection* in this section to verify crankcase condition.

(49)

(50)

(51)

Assembly

1. Note the following prior to beginning assembly:
   a. Leave the left case half facing up until the right case half is installed and secure.

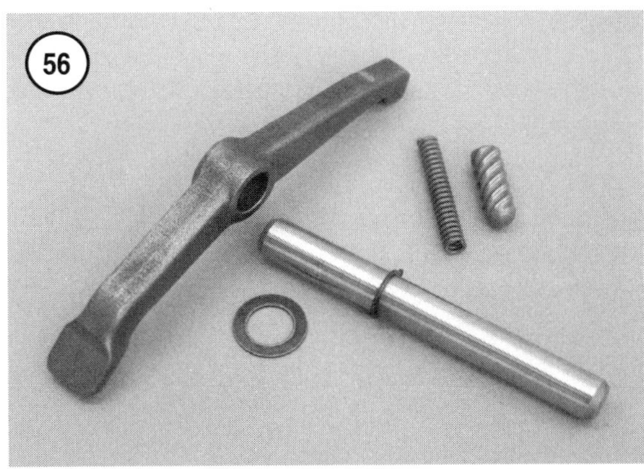

b. Check that all mating surfaces are smooth, clean and dry. Minor irregularities can be repaired with an oil stone. After thoroughly removing the old sealant, clean all mating surfaces with brake part cleaner. The new sealant will not adhere to oily surfaces.

c. Lubricate the connecting rod, bearings, transmission and middle gear assembly with engine oil. Wipe away excess oil that may drain toward the sealant when the case halves are assembled.

d. Lubricate the seal lip with grease.

2. If necessary, install the middle driven gear shaft assembly into the right crankcase (**Figure 54**). Refer to *Middle Gear Assembly* in this chapter to install the shaft assembly.

3. In the right crankcase, install the collars (**Figure 53**).

a. Install the large collar with the wide end (A, **Figure 55**) facing in and the small collar with the beveled edge (B) facing in.

b. Install a new, lubricated O-ring inside the small collar.

4. If necessary, install the crankshaft into the left crankcase (**Figure 52**). Refer to *Crankshaft* in this chapter to install the crankshaft.

5. Install the transmission assembly into the left crankcase as follows:

a. Install the spring, cam, lever, washer and stopper shaft (**Figure 56**). The wide end of the lever should contact the cam (**Figure 51**).

b. Install the input and output shaft assembly (**Figure 57**). Remove the loose washer and gear from the end of the output shaft. Then install the joined shafts into the crankcase (**Figure 50**).

c. Install the shift fork assembly (**Figure 58**). Lift the shaft assemblies and engage the shift forks with the appropriate gears (**Figure 49**).

d. Install the shift drum and shift drum stopper assembly (**Figure 59**). Lift all the shaft assemblies enough to prevent binding. Then engage

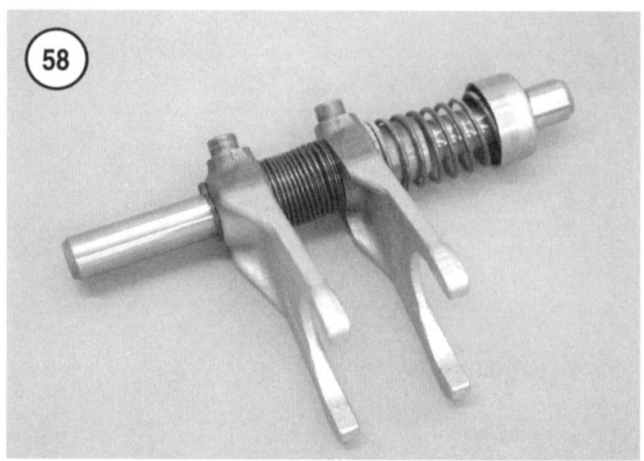

the shift fork guide pins (B, **Figure 48**) with the grooves in the shift drum. Note the position of the pin on the drum (A, **Figure 48**), when meshing the parts together. Install the ball, spring, washer and shift drum stopper bolt (**Figure 47**). Tighten the bolt to 18 N•m (13 ft.-lb.).

e. Install the loose gear and washer onto the end of the output shaft (**Figure 46**).
f. Check that all parts are engaged and seated.

6. Install the left middle gear assembly (**Figure 60**). Engage the driven gear with the transmission drive gear. Then tighten the bearing housing bolts (**Figure 61**) to 32 N•m (24 ft.-lb.).

7. Inspect the transmission for proper installation and shifting. The transmission can be checked by rotating the shift drum (A, **Figure 62**) to specific positions, then turning the transmission input shaft (B). As the shaft is turned, the rotation of the pinion gear (**Figure 61**) is observed. Make the following checks:

NOTE

*During the checks, keep pressure on the shift fork shaft (C, **Figure 62**) so the forks and gears accurately engage and disengage. Always turn the input shaft clockwise.*

a. Rotate the shift drum so the pin on the drum is at the 9 o'clock position (A, **Figure 62**). This is the *neutral* position. The pinion gear should freewheel and not be affected by the input shaft.
b. Rotate the shift drum clockwise so the pin on the drum is at the 11 o'clock position. This is the *reverse* position. The pinion gear should turn *counterclockwise* when the input shaft is turned.
c. Rotate the shift drum clockwise so the pin on the drum is at the 1 o'clock position. This is the *park* position. The pinion gear should be locked and not turn when the input shaft is turned.
d. Rotate the shift drum counterclockwise so the pin on the drum is at the 8 o'clock position. This is the *high gear* position. The pinion gear

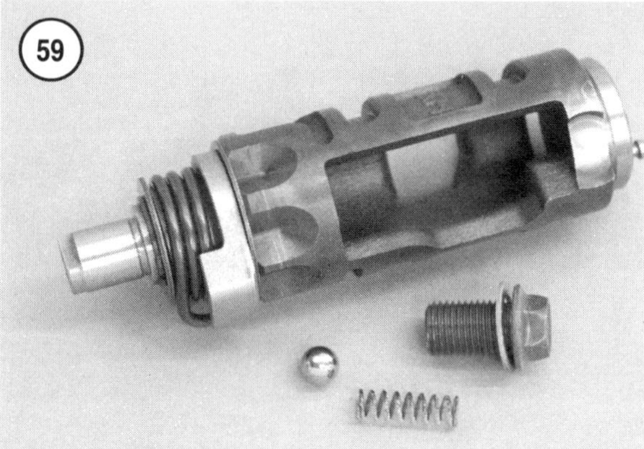

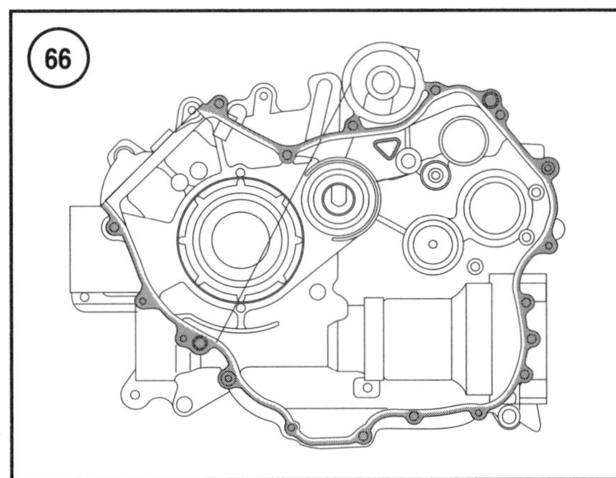

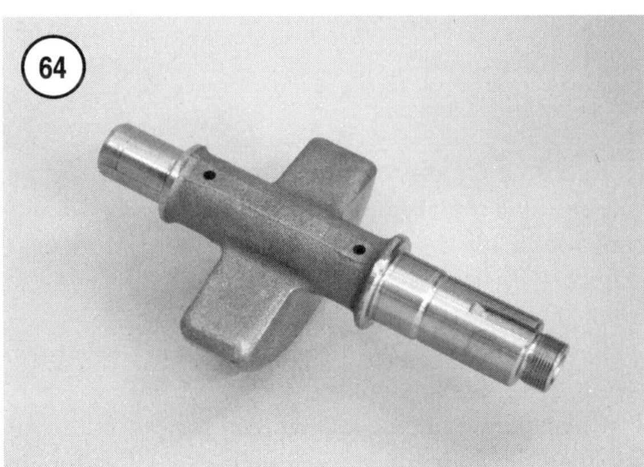

should turn *clockwise* when the input shaft is turned. The pinion gear should turn approximately 1 revolution for every 2 1/2 revolutions of the input shaft.

e. Rotate the shift drum counterclockwise so the pin on the drum is at the 6 o'clock position. This is the *low gear* position. The pinion gear should turn *clockwise* when the input shaft is turned. The pinion gear should turn approximately 1 revolution for every 4 revolutions of the input shaft.

f. Repeat the checks several times, then leave the transmission in the neutral position. If the transmission does not shift correctly, check assembly and installation of the parts. Do not continue engine assembly until the transmission shifts correctly.

8. Install the oil pump relief valve (**Figure 44**). Seat the valve into the crankcase. Then install the retainer plate and bolts.

   a. Apply threadlocking compound to the bolt threads.

   b. Tighten the bolts to 10 N•m (89 in.-lb.).

9. Install the oil pump (**Figure 63**).

   a. Install a new gasket.

   b. Apply threadlocking compound to the bolt threads.

   c. Tighten the bolts to 10 N•m (89 in.-lb.).

   d. After installation, check that the rotor cover screw and strainer bolt are tight (**Figure 43**).

10. Install the balancer (**Figure 64** and **Figure 42**).

11. Install the right crankcase onto the left crankcase as follows:

   a. Make sure all mating surfaces are clean and dry.

   b. If loose, install the two dowels in the left crankcase. Do not disturb the dowels if they are secure in the right crankcase (**Figure 65**).

   c. Apply liquid gasket sealant, such as Yamabond 1215 or Yamabond 4, to all mating surfaces (**Figure 66**). Apply the sealant around all bolt holes. Use enough sealant to fill voids and provide a continuous seal on the entire joint. Avoid excessive amounts of sealant.

d. Check that all shafts are aligned vertically. Then fit the right case half squarely onto the left case half.

e. If necessary, *tap* the right case half with a mallet to evenly seat the crankcase. Do not force the crankcase together. If the crankcase will not seat, a shaft is probably misaligned with its bore. Lift the case half and slightly move it side to side until the shaft(s) are properly aligned.

12. Remove the crankcase bolts from the templates and insert them into the appropriate holes. All bolts should protrude from the crankcase equally, before tightening. Finger-tighten the bolts.

13. Tighten the bolts equally in several passes and in a crossing pattern. Tighten the bolts to 10 N•m (89 in.-lb.).

14. Check that the collars on the crankshaft and transmission shaft are seated.

15. Pivot the balancer. Then rotate the crankshaft and check for smooth operation. If binding is evident, separate the case halves and correct the problem.

16. Rotate the transmission shaft and check for smooth operation. If binding or poor operation is evident, separate the case halves and correct the problem.

17. Allow the sealant to set for at least an hour before handling the crankcase. When the sealant is dry, use a razor blade to remove excess sealant from the cylinder seating surface.

18. Install the switches and oil pipe onto the crankcase.

19. The crankcase assembly is ready for installation into the frame. If desired, top end components and those located in the crankcase covers can be installed at this time. If the final drive unit was not removed for engine removal, install the crankcase assembly into the frame before installing the cylinder and top end.

Inspection

CAUTION

Before cleaning or inspecting the crankcase, record any middle gear assembly specifications marked on the parts remaining in the right crankcase. These numbers are required when shimming the middle gear assembly. Some numbers are engraved on the parts, while others are indicated with a marking pen. Often, these numbers are faint, and may be completely removed during cleaning.

1. Record the number at the lower, right side of the bearing housing (**Figure 67**). Record the two numbers found on the edge of the driven pinion gear (**Figure 68**). If there is only one number, check the front of the gear for the second number.

2. Remove all sealant from the gasket surfaces. Avoid gouging or scratching the surfaces.

3. Clean the crankcase halves with solvent. Flush all bearings last, using clean solvent.

4. Dry the crankcase halves with compressed air. Blow through the oil passages.

WARNING

When drying the bearings with compressed air, do not allow them to spin. Because the bearings are not lubricated, damage could occur.

5. Inspect the bearings as follows:

a. Oil the engine bearings before inspecting their condition.

b. Check each bearing for roughness, pitting, galling and play. If rust is evident on the bearing, the engine oil has likely been contami-

nated with water. Replace any bearing that is not in good condition, or is a loose fit in the crankcase bore. Always replace the opposing bearing at the same time.

6. Inspect the crankcase for fractures around all mounting and bearing bosses, stiffening ribs and threaded holes. Refer repair to a dealership or machine shop.
7. Check all threaded holes for damage or sealant buildup. Clean threads with the correct size metric tap. Lubricate the tap with oil or tap fluid.

CRANKCASE SEAL REPLACEMENT

Input Shaft Oil Seal

The input shaft seal (**Figure 69**) is the only seal in the crankcase housings. The seal is removed from the outside of the case.

1. Remove the collar from the seal.
2. Pry out the seal. Place a block of wood on the case to improve leverage and protect the case from damage. If desired, warm the seal with a heat gun to ease removal.

CAUTION

When prying, do not allow the end of the tool to touch the seal bore. Scratches in the bore will cause leakage and heavy-handed prying can break the casting.

3. If a new bearing will be installed, replace the bearing before installing the new seal.
4. Clean the oil seal bore.
5. Apply grease to the lip and side of the new seal.
6. Place the seal over the bore, with the closed side of the seal facing out. The seal must be square to the bore.
7. Press the seal evenly until it is flush with the bore. If necessary, use a driver that fits at the perimeter of the seal to seat it in the bore.
8. Install the collar with the beveled edge facing in.

5

CRANKCASE BEARING REPLACEMENT

When replacing crankcase bearings, note the following:

1. Refer to Chapter One for general removal and installation techniques.
2. Where used, remove the bearing retainer (**Figure 70**) before bearing removal. When installing retainers, clean the bolt threads and install the bolts using threadlocking compound. Tighten the bolts to 10 N•m (89 in.-lb.).
3. Identify each bearing before removing it. Note any number identification.
4. Record the orientation of each bearing in its bore.

Removal and Installation

All crankcase bearings shown in **Figure 71** and **Figure 72** can be removed with a press or a blind bearing puller. Special tools are not required. Always use a press for bearings that are accessible from both sides of the housing. The crankcase must be disassembled to access all bearings. Remove and install bearings using the following steps. Read the entire procedure before replacing any bearing.

1. Remove the seal and/or retainer from the bearing, if applicable.
2. Heat the crankcase as described in Chapter One.
3. For a bearing that will be pressed out, support the heated crankcase on wooden blocks, allowing space for the bearing to fall from the bore.
4. Remove the damaged bearing from the bore, using a press or bearing puller.
5. Clean and inspect the bore. Check that all oil holes (where applicable) are clean.
6. Place the new bearing in a freezer and chill it for at least one hour.
7. When the bearing is chilled, reheat the crankcase.
8. Support the heated crankcase on wooden blocks. Make sure the crankcase is supported directly below the bearing.
9. Lubricate the mating surface of the bore and bearing. Place the bearing squarely over the bore and check that it is properly oriented.
10. Press the bearing into place using a driver that fits on the outer bearing race.
11. Install the bearing retainer and/or seal (if applicable).

ENGINE BALANCER

Inspection

The engine uses a rotating balancer to dampen vibration that is inherent to a single-cylinder engine. The balancer weight is synchronized with the crankshaft, and is driven by a gear located on the left end of the crankshaft.

1. Inspect the balancer.
   a. Install the balancer into its crankcase bearings and check for play between the parts.
   b. Inspect the bearing surfaces (A, **Figure 73**), keyway (B) and threads (C) for damage.
   c. Inspect the fit of the gear, key and nut on the balancer shaft.
2. Refer to *Crankcase* in this chapter to install the balancer.

OIL PUMP

The oil pump is chain-driven by the balancer shaft. The oil pump shaft not only operates the rotors in the oil pump, but also drives the water pump. The tang at the exposed end of the oil pump shaft engages with the back of the water pump.

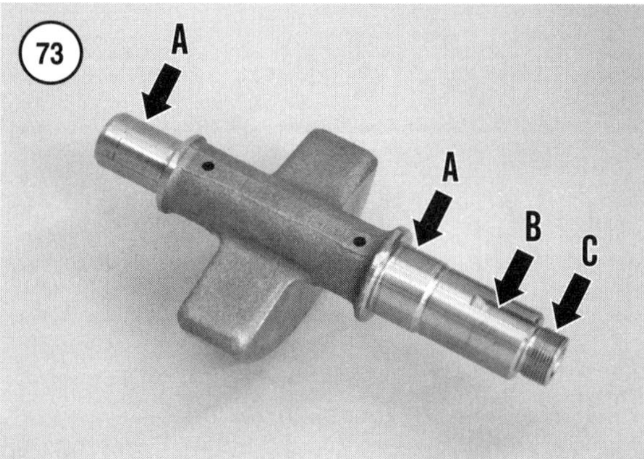

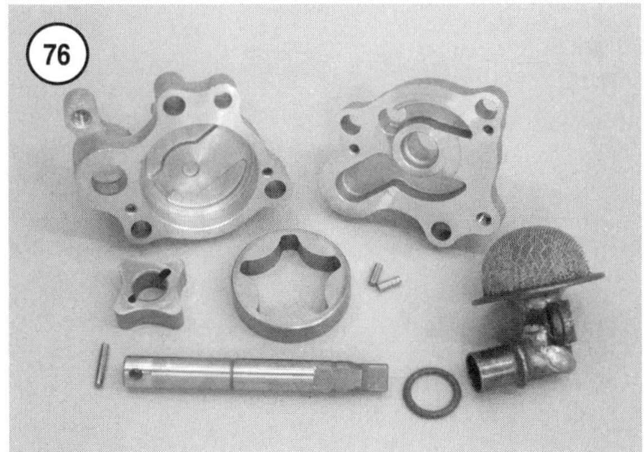
76

77

78

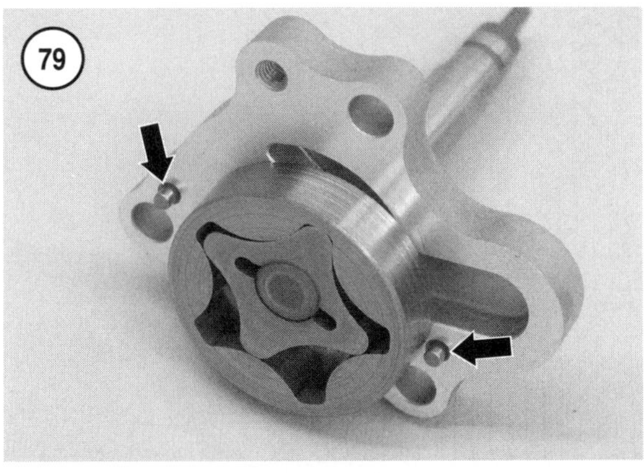
79

Disassembly and Assembly

1. Remove the strainer and O-ring (**Figure 74**).
2. Remove the rotor cover screw (**Figure 75**). Then disassemble the pump (**Figure 76**).
3. Disassemble the oil pump relief valve (**Figure 77**). Remove the snap ring, washer, spring and plunger from the valve.
4. Inspect the parts as described in this section.
5. Assemble the oil pump relief valve (**Figure 77**) as follows:
   a. Insert the plunger into the spring. Then insert both parts into the valve body. The wide side of the plunger must enter the valve body first. The spring must stay engaged with the plunger.
   b. Place the washer against the spring.
   c. Install the snap ring against the washer. The sharp edge of the snap ring should face out.
   d. Lightly press on the washer to ensure there is spring pressure on the plunger.
   e. Install a new, lubricated O-ring on the valve body.
6. Assemble the pump as follows:
   a. Lubricate the parts with engine oil.
   b. Insert the shaft through the housing. Then install the inner rotor and pin on the shaft (**Figure 78**). Pull the shaft back and engage the pin with the inner rotor.
   c. Install the outer rotor and locating pins (**Figure 79**).
   d. Install the rotor cover (**Figure 75**). Apply threadlocking compound to the screw threads. Then tighten the screw securely.
   e. Install the strainer (**Figure 74**). Install a new lubricated O-ring on the strainer. Apply threadlocking compound to the bolt threads and tighten it to 10 N•m (89 in.-lb.).
7. Refer to *Crankcase* in this chapter to install the relief valve and oil pump.

Inspection

1. Clean the parts in solvent.
2. Use compressed air to blow the strainer clean. After cleaning, pour a small amount of engine oil into the strainer and allow it to drain any stray particles.
3. Inspect the rotor set and rotor cover for wear and scoring in the areas shown (**Figure 80**).
4. Insert the rotors into the body and make the following checks:
   a. Align the tips of the rotors and measure the clearance between the tips (A, **Figure 81**). Refer to **Table 2** for specifications.

5

   b. Measure the clearance between the outer rotor and the cover (B, **Figure 81**). Refer to **Table 2** for specifications.
5. Inspect the pin and shaft.
   a. The pin should fit into the shaft hole with minimal side play.
   b. The pump shaft should fit in the pump body with minimal perceptible play.
6. Inspect the oil pump relief valve (**Figure 77**). The parts should show no signs of wear.

CRANKSHAFT

The crankshaft and crankpin are a press-fit. The assembly is supported at each end by a ball bearing.

Unless obviously damaged, the crankshaft does not have to be removed for most inspection procedures. To install the crankshaft, a crankshaft installer tool is required to pull the crankshaft into the crankcase.

Removal

1. Attach a crankcase separating tool (Yamaha part No. YU-01135-A), or similar puller as shown in **Figure 82**. Thread the bolts into the crankcase, keeping the center bolt squarely positioned on the end of the crankshaft. Lubricate the tool threads and contact point on the crankshaft.
2. If available, use a heat gun to heat the area around the bearing.
3. Working on a stable surface, turn the center bolt and pull the crankcase from the crankshaft.
4. Inspect the crankshaft as described in this section.

Tools

To install the crankshaft, a crankshaft installation set is required (**Figure 83**). The parts include: crankshaft installation kit (pot, bolt, nut and spacer) (Yamaha part No. YU-90050), pot spacer (part No. YM-91044), spacer (not shown) (part No. 90890-01309) and male/female threaded adapter.

Installation

1. Place the left crankcase on wooden blocks, with the open side of the housing facing down. Allow plenty of space below the crankcase for handling the crankshaft.
2. Use a heat gun to heat the area around the bearing bore. This will slightly expand the bore and aid in bearing installation.
3. Thread the adapter into the end of the crankshaft. Lubricate the surface of the adapter after it is seated.

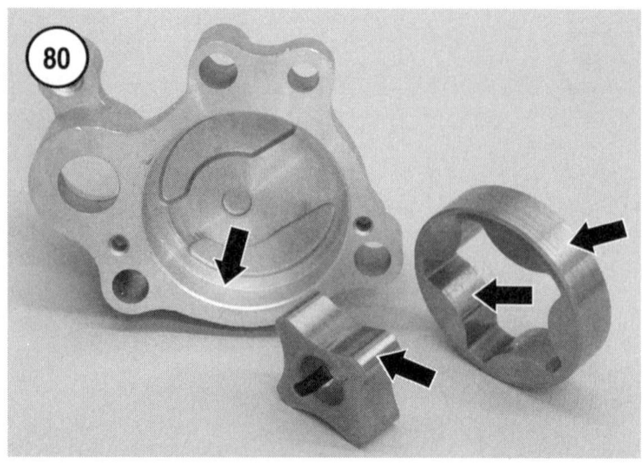

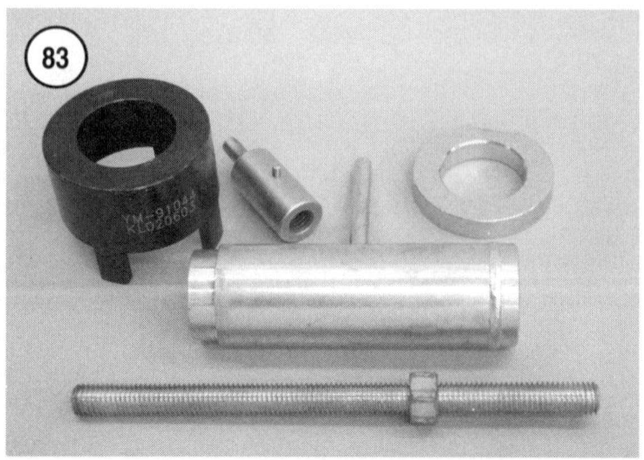

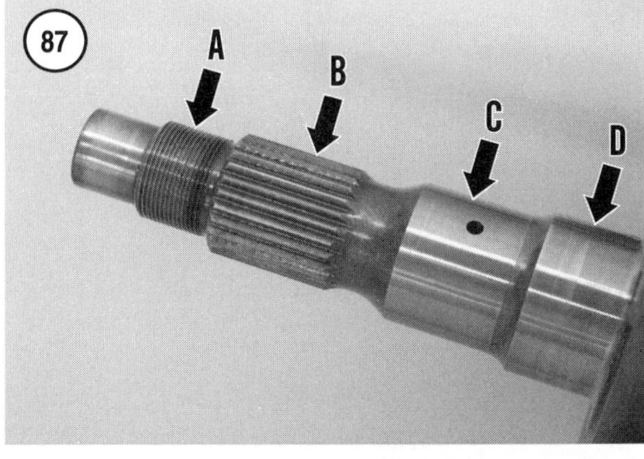

4. Lubricate the interior of the installer pot (**Figure 84**).
5. Assemble and align the parts over the crankcase bore (**Figure 85**).
6. Hold the crankshaft under the housing and thread the bolt completely into the adapter.
7. Hold the assembly stable and turn the nut to draw the crankshaft bearing toward the bore. As the adapter nears the pot, make sure the pin on the adapter enters the groove in the pot.
8. Check that all parts are properly aligned. Then turn the nut and fully seat the bearing into the crankcase.
9. Remove the tool and support the left crankcase so the open side is facing up.

Inspection

Handle the crankshaft assembly carefully during inspection. Do not place the crankshaft where it could accidentally roll off the workbench. The crankshaft is an assembly-type, with its two halves joined by a crankpin. The crankpin is pressed into the flywheels and aligned, both vertically and horizontally, with calibrated equipment. If any part of the crankshaft assembly is worn or damaged, have a dealership evaluate all the parts to determine the practicality of repair.

CAUTION

*Do not remove the buffer boss (***Figure 86***). The boss is an interference fit on the crankshaft. If the boss or bearing is damaged, have the parts replaced by a machine shop.*

1. Clean the crankshaft with solvent and dry with compressed air. Lubricate the rod bearing and shaft bearing with engine oil.
2. Inspect both ends of the crankshaft.
   a. Inspect the shaft threads (A, **Figure 87**). Minor damage can be corrected with a thread file.
   b. Inspect the splines (B, **Figure 87** and A, **Figure 88**) for damage.
   c. Inspect the oil passage (C, **Figure 87**) for cleanliness.
   d. Inspect the keyway (B, **Figure 88**) and seating surface (C) for the rotor and starter clutch. Burnishing can be removed with 320-grit Carborundum cloth.
   e. Inspect the bearing surface (D, **Figure 87**) for scoring, heat discoloration or other damage. Minor imperfections can be removed with 320-grit emery cloth.
3. Inspect the bearing for heat discoloration, roughness, pitting, galling and play. If rust is evident on the

bearing, the engine oil has likely been contaminated with water. If bearing replacement is necessary, have the bearing and buffer boss replaced by a machine shop.

4. Inspect the connecting rod.
   a. Inspect the rod small end (**Figure 89**) for scoring, galling or heat damage. Refer to Chapter Four for rod bore, piston pin and piston inspection.
   b. Inspect the connecting rod for radial clearance (**Figure 90**). Mount the crankshaft in a set of V-blocks and accurately measure play. Refer to **Table 1** for specifications. If the tools are not available, grasp the rod and feel for radial play in all directions. There should be no perceptible play.
   c. Measure the connecting rod side clearance (**Figure 91**). Fully seat the feeler gauge against the crankpin to make the measurement. Refer to **Table 1** for specifications.

CAUTION

If the connecting rod must be replaced, the crankshaft and crankpin oil passages must be realigned with a maximum tolerance of 1 mm (0.040 in.) or less.

5. Measure the flywheel width (**Figure 92**). If the runout exceeds the specification in **Table 1**, have a dealership evaluate and possibly true the crankshaft.
6. Support the crankshaft as shown in **Figure 93**. Use a dial indicator and measure runout at the two points shown. If the runout exceeds the specification in **Table 1**, have a dealership evaluate and possibly true the crankshaft.
7. If the engine exhibited abnormal vibration, or if crankshaft damage is suspected, check the crankshaft alignment before assembling the engine.

MIDDLE GEAR ASSEMBLY

CAUTION

*Before cleaning or removing parts in the right crankcase, record any middle gear assembly specifications that are marked on the parts. These numbers are required when shimming the middle gear assembly. Some numbers are permanently engraved on the parts while other numbers are only indicated with a marking pen. Often, these numbers are faint and may be completely removed when cleaning. Record the number at the lower, right side of the bearing housing (**Figure 94**). Record the two numbers found on the edge of the driv-*

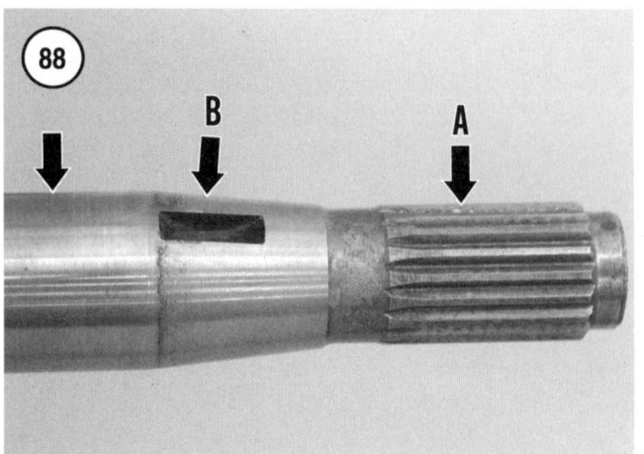

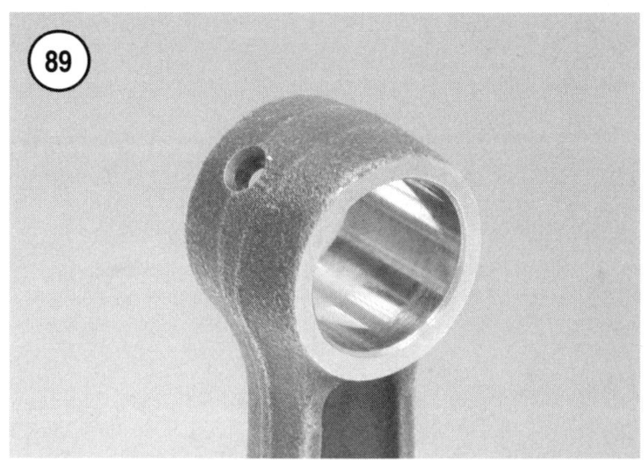

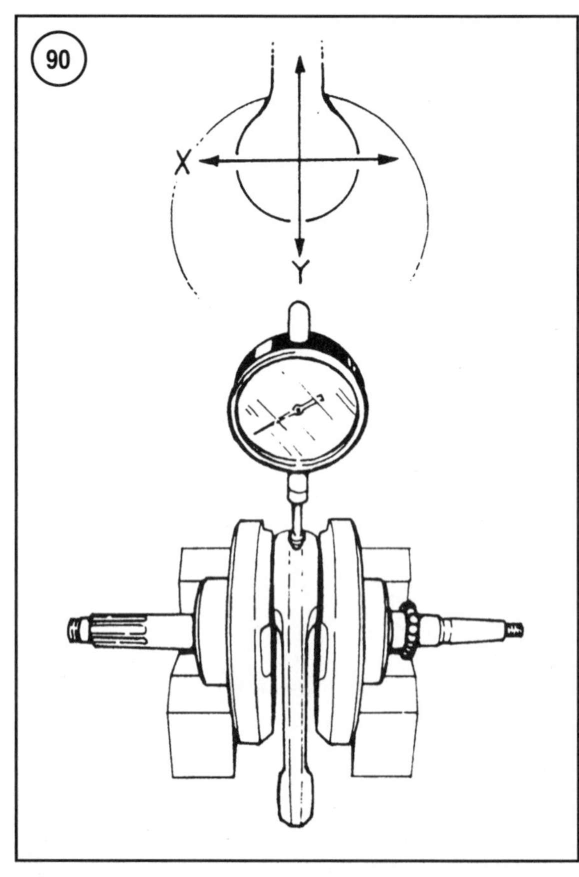

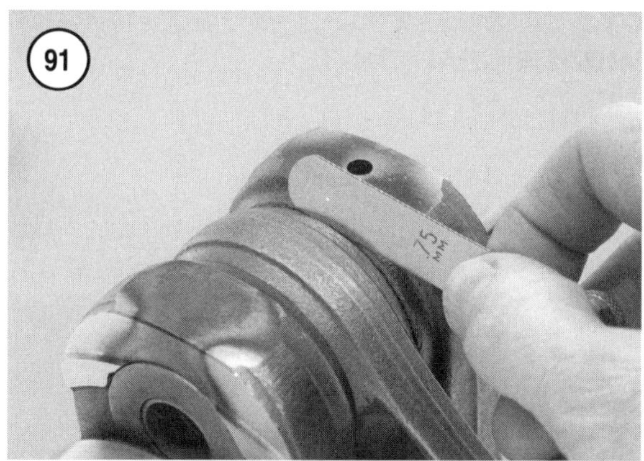

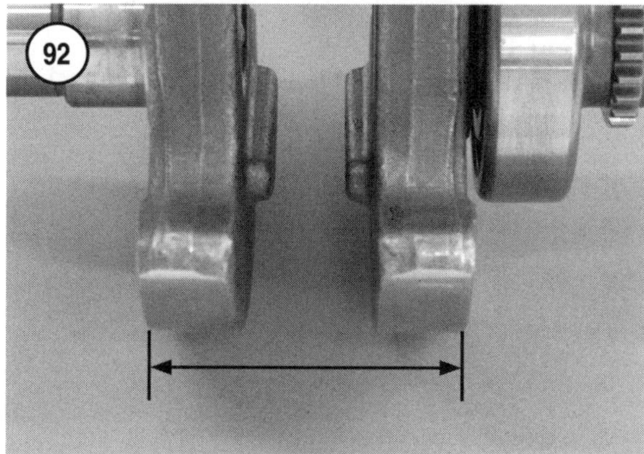

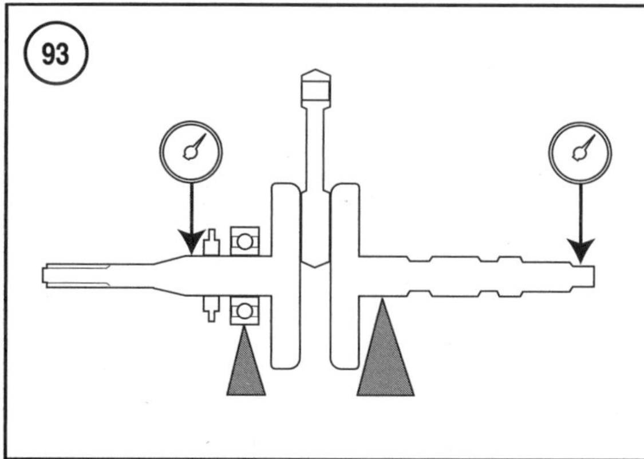

*en pinion gear (**Figure 95**). If there is only one number, check the front of the gear for the second number.*

5

Right Crankcase Middle Gear Unit Inspection, Disassembly and Assembly

Refer to **Figure 96**.

1. Inspect the middle gear unit for wear and damage. Bearings are located at each end of the housing (**Figure 97**) to support the shaft and driven pinion gear. Unless the bearings or other visible parts are damaged, do not disassemble the unit.
   a. Make sure the splines are uniform and symmetrical.
   b. Check gear teeth for damage and pitting.
   c. Check the bearing housing for cracks.
   d. Inspect the bearings. The shaft should turn smoothly with no binding or play. If bearing damage is evident, disassemble the housing to determine which bearing(s) and other parts are damaged.
   e. If necessary, perform the following steps to disassemble and replace parts in the housing.
2. For 2002 models, separate the U-joint yokes at the front of the shaft as follows:
   a. Remove the circlip (**Figure 98**) from each of the four bearings.
   b. Drive or press one of the U-joint arms toward the opposite bearing, driving the bearing out of the yoke. Drive the U-joint in the opposite direction, removing the remaining bearing on that axis. Repeat this step to remove the remaining bearings and U-joint.
   c. Reverse this procedure to assemble the U-joint. Pack the bearings with molybdenum disulfide grease. Then press the bearings into the yokes with a driver that fits on the outer edge of the bearing.
3. Remove the U-joint yoke/coupling (**Figure 99**) from the front shaft as follows:

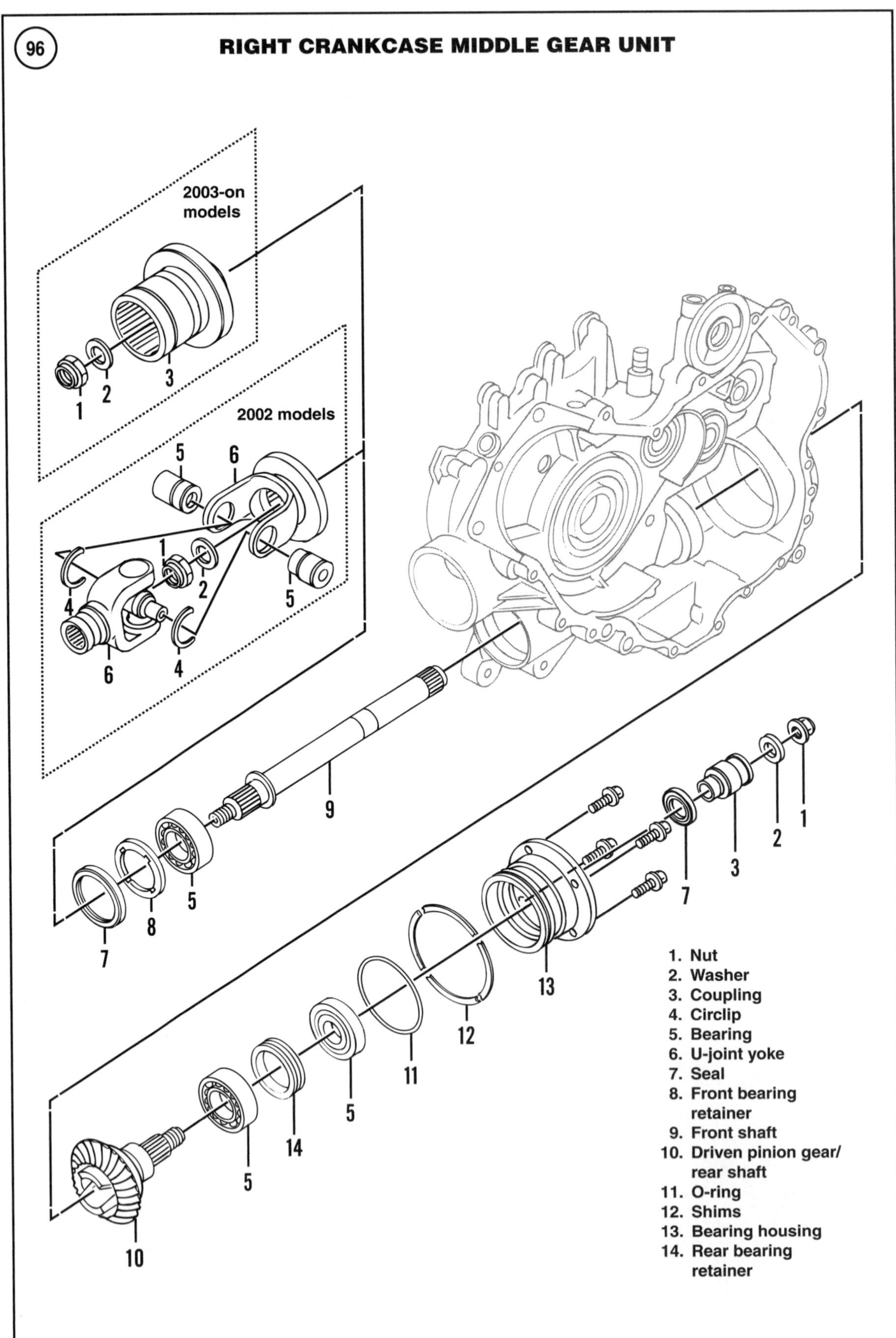
96
RIGHT CRANKCASE MIDDLE GEAR UNIT
2003-on models
2002 models
1. Nut
2. Washer
3. Coupling
4. Circlip
5. Bearing
6. U-joint yoke
7. Seal
8. Front bearing retainer
9. Front shaft
10. Driven pinion gear/ rear shaft
11. O-ring
12. Shims
13. Bearing housing
14. Rear bearing retainer

97

98

99

100

101

a. For 2002 models, hold the U-joint yoke in a vise with soft jaws so the nut can be removed. A universal joint holder (Yamaha part No. YM-04062) is another option available for holding the yoke. Remove the nut, washer and yoke.

b. On 2003-on models, hold the coupling in a vise with soft jaws so the nut can be removed. A coupling gear holder (Yamaha part No. YM-01486) is another option available for holding the coupling. Remove the nut, washer and coupling.

4. Remove the coupling (**Figure 100**) from the rear shaft as follows:

a. Hold the coupling in a vise with soft jaws so the nut can be removed. A coupling gear/middle shaft holder (Yamaha part No. YM-01230) is another option available for holding the coupling.

b. Remove the nut, washer and coupling.

5. Remove the bearing housing assembly (**Figure 101**).

6. Remove the seal and bearing retainer at the front of the shaft. Remove the front bearing retainer with a ring nut wrench (Yamaha part No. YM-38404), or a similar tool.

CAUTION

The bearing retainer has left-hand threads. Turn the wrench clockwise to loosen the retainer.

7. Remove the shaft and front bearing as follows:

a. At the rear of the shaft, protect the shaft threads by temporarily installing the nut onto the shaft threads. Thread the nut on until it is nearly flush with the end of the shaft.

b. Place a driver against the nut. Then tap the shaft and bearing forward until they can be removed.

8. Inspect the removed parts for wear and damage.

9. Inspect the front shaft bearing. Lubricate the bearing with engine oil and rotate the shaft. The shaft

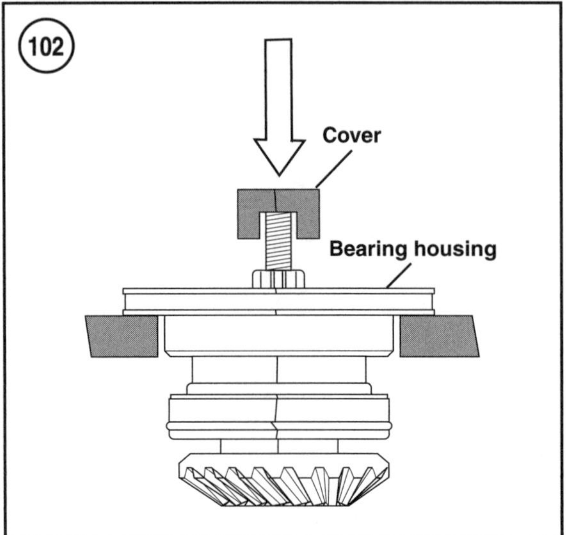

should turn smoothly with no axial or radial play. If bearing damage is evident, remove the bearing from the shaft. Use a socket or driver that fits onto the inner bearing race to seat the new bearing onto the shaft.

10. Inspect the bearings in the bearing housing. Lubricate the bearings with engine oil and rotate the shaft. The shaft should turn smoothly with no axial or radial play. If bearing damage is evident, disassemble and replace the bearing(s) in the housing as follows:

a. Remove the oil seal.
b. Support the bearing in a press so the driven pinion gear can be pressed out of the housing (**Figure 102**). Cover the shaft threads with an appropriate size socket. Then press the gear out of the housing.
c. Mount a pilot bearing puller onto the exposed bearing. Then pull the bearing from the bore (**Figure 103**) of the housing.
d. Lock the bearing housing in a vise with soft jaws and remove the rear bearing retainer. Remove the rear bearing retainer with the bearing retainer wrench (Yamaha part No. YM-04128), or a similar tool.

CAUTION

The bearing retainer has left-hand threads. Turn the wrench clockwise to loosen the retainer.

e. Remove the other bearing from the housing. If necessary, press the bearing from the housing.
f. Lubricate the new bearings and install them into the housing. Press the bearings into place using a driver that fits onto the outer bearing race.
g. Apply threadlocking compound to the rear bearing retainer. Then tighten the rear retainer to 110 N•m (81 ft.-lb.).

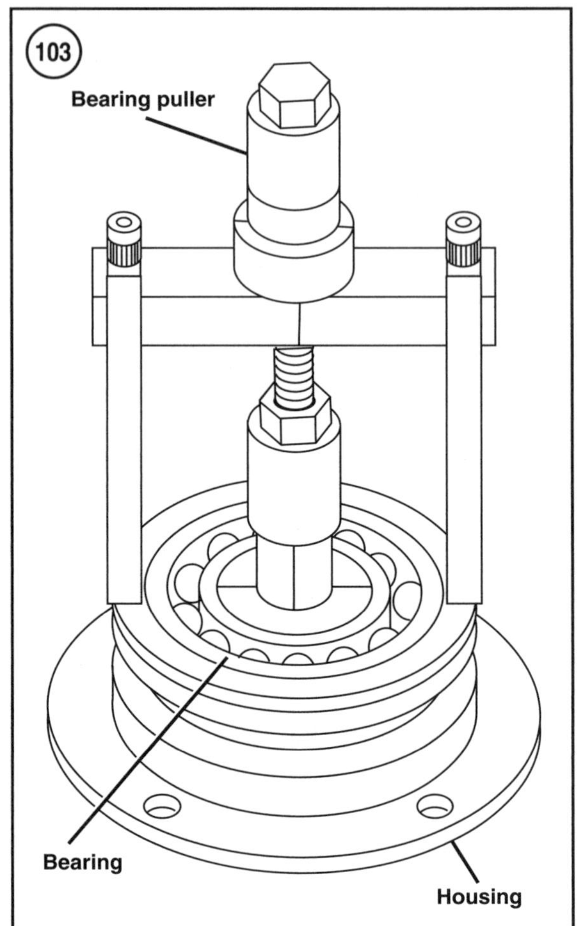

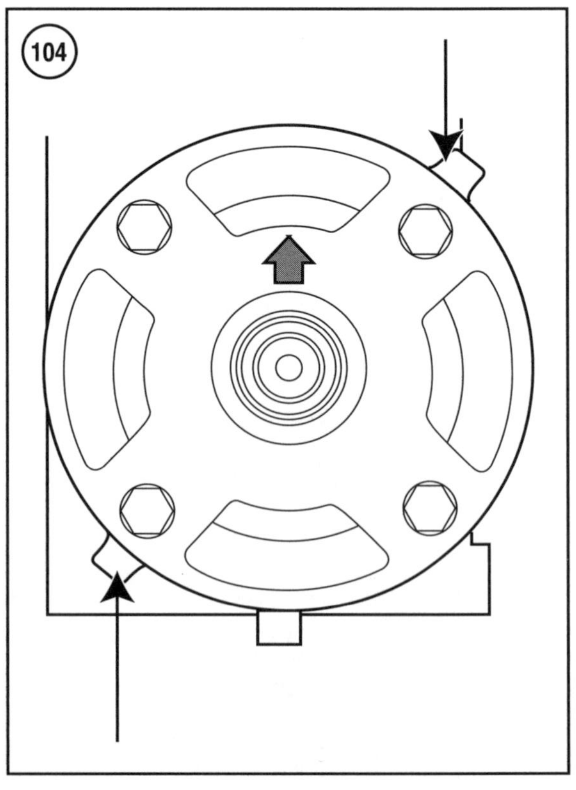

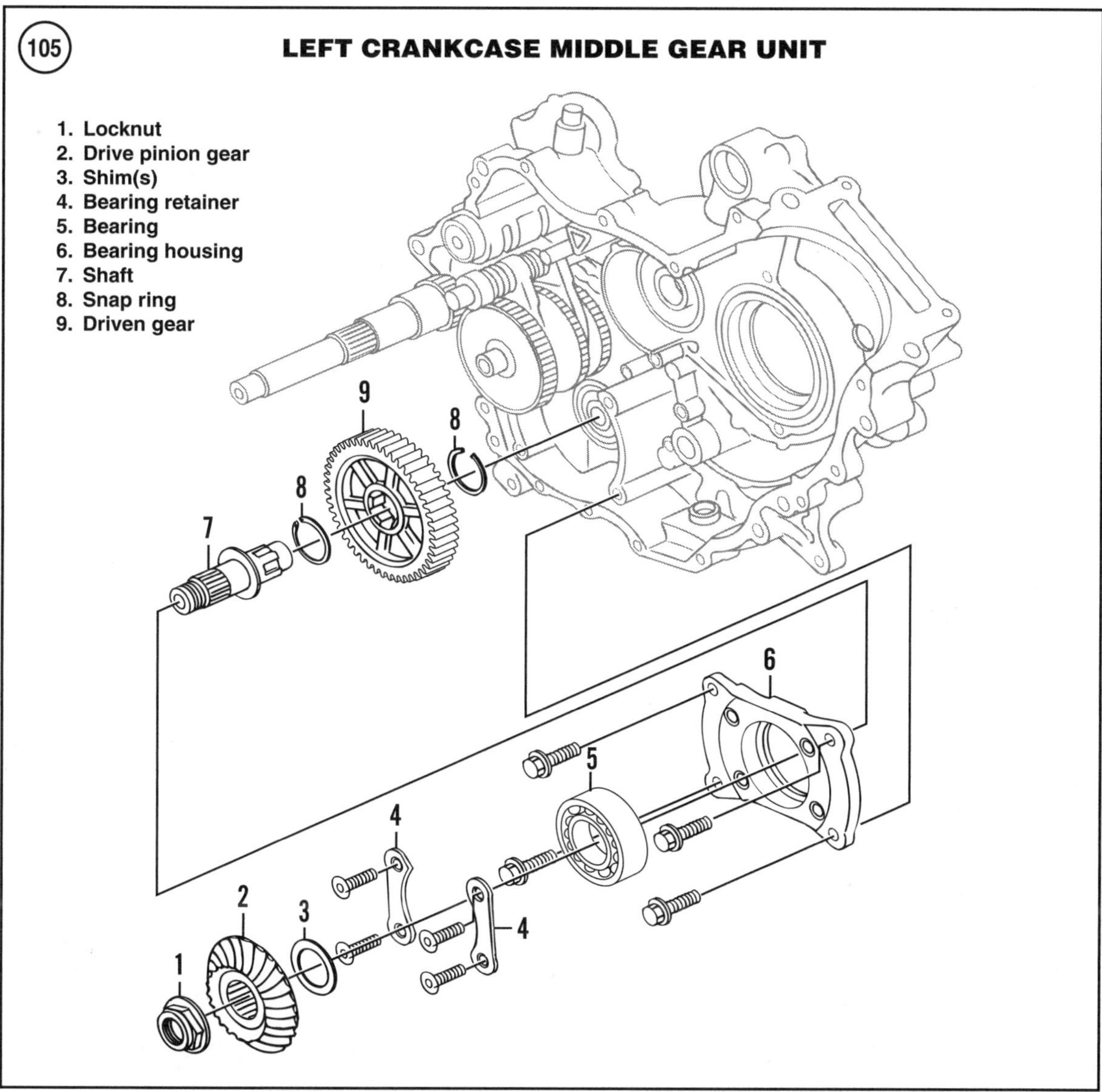

5

h. Lubricate the driven pinion gear and seat it into the bearings.

i. Apply grease to the lips and sides of a new seal. Place the seal over the bore, with the closed side of the seal facing out. Evenly press the seal into the bore by hand.

11. Reverse this procedure to assemble and install the middle gear unit. Note the following:

a. Refer to *Middle Gear Assembly Shim and Lash Adjustment* in this chapter.

b. Lubricate the parts with engine oil.

c. When installing the front shaft, seat the shaft bearing into its bore with a socket or driver that fits onto the outer bearing race.

d. Apply threadlocking compound to the front bearing retainer. Then tighten the front retainer to 80 N•m (59 ft.-lb.).

e. Install a new, lubricated O-ring on the bearing housing.

f. Install the bearing housing so the housing arrow and shim tabs are in the positions shown in **Figure 104**.

g. Tighten the bearing housing bolts to 25 N•m (18 ft.-lb.).

h. Tighten the U-joint yoke/coupling nut to 97 N•m (72 ft.-lb.).

Left Crankcase Middle Gear Unit Inspection, Disassembly and Assembly

Refer to **Figure 105**.

1. Inspect the middle gear unit (**Figure 106**) for wear and damage. Do not disassemble the unit if it is in good condition.

a. Check that splines are uniform and symmetrical.
b. Check gear teeth for damage and pitting.
c. Check the bearing housing for cracks.
d. Check for loose bearing retainers.

2. Inspect the bearing. Lubricate the bearing with engine oil and rotate the shaft. The shaft should turn smoothly with no axial or radial play. If bearing damage is evident, disassemble and replace the bearing in the housing as follows:

a. Remove the outer snap ring, driven gear and inner snap ring (**Figure 107**).
b. Lock the shaft in a vise with soft jaws and straighten the punched area on the locknut (**Figure 108**).
c. Remove the locknut, drive pinion gear and shim(s).
d. Remove the shaft from the vise.
e. Lock the bearing housing in a vise with soft jaws and remove the bearing retainers.
f. Remove the bearing from the housing. If necessary, press the bearing from the housing.
g. Lubricate and install the new bearing, seating it into the housing. If necessary, seat the bearing with a driver that fits onto the outer bearing race.
h. Apply threadlocking compound to the bearing retainer screws. Then install the bearing retainers and tighten the screws to 29 N•m (21 ft.-lb.).
i. Refer to *Middle Gear Assembly Shim and Lash Adjustment* in this chapter.
j. Install the shaft, shim(s), drive pinion gear and a new locknut. Use a punch to lock the nut to the shaft (**Figure 108**).
k. Install the inner snap ring, driven gear and outer snap ring (**Figure 107**). Install the snap rings so the sharp edge faces away from the gear.

MIDDLE GEAR ASSEMBLY SHIM AND LASH ADJUSTMENT

If the crankcase, bearing housing or drive pinion gear were replaced in the left crankcase, the unit must be properly shimmed to create the correct clearances between the parts. Likewise, if the crankcase, bearing housing or driven pinion gear were replaced in the right crankcase, the unit must be shimmed to create the correct clearances between the parts. Also check clearance whenever wear is evident on original parts that are being reused.

Drive Pinion Gear Shim Selection

The drive pinion gear is in the left crankcase half. The drive pinion gear is correctly positioned by shimming the gear either away or toward the driven pinion gear, located in the right crankcase. Refer to **Figure 105**.

1. Determine the shim size with the formula: A = a + b – 17.0 – 55.0.
2. Note the number (shown as a decimal) on the drive gear bearing housing (**Figure 109**). In the example, the number is +0.02. This number is added to 7.5. Negative numbers are subtracted from 7.5. The result is the *a* variable of the shim formula.
3. Note the lower number (shown as a decimal) on the right crankcase (b, **Figure 110**). In the example,

106

107

108

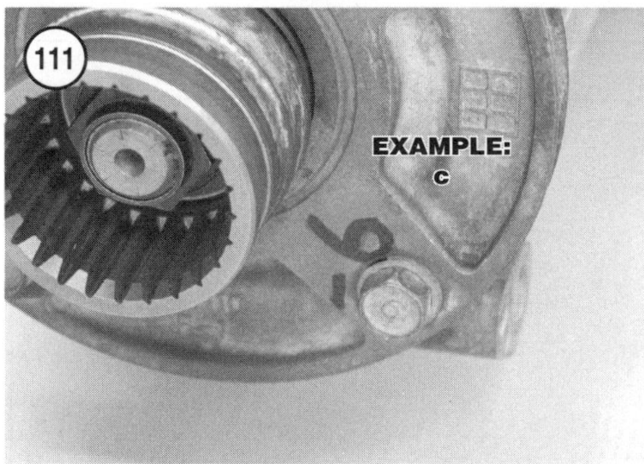

the number is 65.00. This is the *b* variable of the shim formula.

4. The example equation is now: A = 7.52 + 65.00 – 17.0 – 55.0. The result is: A = 0.52. Round the numeral in the hundredths position as follows:
   a. Round 0-2 to 0.
   b. Round 3-7 to 5.
   c. Round 8 and 9 to 10.
5. After rounding the result, the correct shim size is 0.50 mm thick. Drive pinion gear shims are available in 0.10, 0.15, 0.20, 0.30, 0.40, and 0.50 mm thick.
6. Install the shim(s) onto the shaft of the drive pinion gear assembly.

Driven Pinion Gear Shim Selection

The driven pinion gear is in the right crankcase. The driven pinion gear is positioned by shimming the bearing housing either away or toward the drive pinion gear, located in the left crankcase. Refer to **Figure 96**.

1. Determine the shim size with the formula: B = c – d + e – f + g – 0.05.
2. Note the number shown (c, **Figure 111**) on the driven gear bearing housing. It indicates a decimal value displayed in hundredths. The number in this example is –0.06. Subtract negative numbers from 76; add positive numbers to 76. The result here is the *c* variable of the shim formula, or 75.94.
3. Note the number shown (d, **Figure 112**) on the driven pinion gear. It indicates a decimal value displayed in hundredths. This number may also appear on the back of the gear. The number in this example is –0.02. Subtract negative numbers from 60; add positive numbers to 60. The result here is the *d* variable of the shim formula, or 59.98.
4. Note the number shown (e, **Figure 112**) on the pinion drive gear. It indicates a decimal value displayed in hundredths. In this example, the number indicates –0.14. Subtract negative numbers from 80.5; add positive numbers to 80.5. The result here is the *e* variable of the shim formula, or 80.36.
5. Note the number (shown as a decimal) on the left crankcase (**Figure 113**). In the example, the number is 97.25. This is the *f* variable of the shim formula.
6. Note the upper number (shown as a decimal) on the right crankcase (**Figure 110**). In the example, the number is 1.61. This is the *g* variable of the shim formula.
7. The example equation is now: B = 75.94 – 59.98 + 80.36 – 97.25 + 1.61 – 0.05. The result is: B = 0.63. Round the numeral in the hundredths position as follows:
   a. Round 0-2 to 0.
   b. Round 3-7 to 5.
   c. Round 8 and 9 to 10.

8. After rounding the result, the correct shim size is 0.65 mm thick. Driven pinion gear shims are available in 0.10, 0.15, 0.20, 0.30, 0.40, and 0.50 mm thicknesses.
9. Install the shim(s) on the bearing housing of the driven pinion gear assembly.

Shim and Lash Adjustment

After the middle gear assembly is installed in both crankcase housings, check gear lash to verify the shim selection. Gear lash is measured with a gear lash measurement tool (Yamaha part No. YM-01467, **Figure 114**), or its equivalent, and a dial indicator.

1. Temporarily assemble the two crankcase halves so the lash measurement can be made. It is not necessary to install all assemblies into the crankcase. Install several bolts to hold the crankcase together.
2. In the left crankcase, lock the driven gear into position. Wrap a screwdriver with a shop cloth and insert the tool through the speed sensor hole on the outside of the housing. Work the tool into the gear so it cannot move when measuring lash.
3. Clamp the gear lash measurement tool onto the driven pinion gear shaft (**Figure 115**). Position the tool so the arm can contact the dial indicator.
4. Position a dial indicator in contact with the measurement tool and 46 mm (1.8 in.) from the center of the shaft. Make sure the dial indicator is stable and set to read gear lash in both directions.
5. Gently rotate the driven pinion gear shaft clockwise until lash between the parts is eliminated. Note the dial indicator reading.
6. Gently rotate the driven pinion gear shaft in the opposite direction until lash between the parts is eliminated. Note the dial indicator reading.
7. Calculate the total side to side gear lash.
8. Remove the screwdriver from the driven gear and rotate the shaft 90°. Lock the gear into place. Continue checking the gear lash each 90° until the driven pinion gear shaft has turned one full turn.
9. Determine the average reading of the four checks. Final middle gear lash should be 0.1-0.3 mm (0.004-0.012 in.). If necessary, adjust the shim size for either or both the drive pinion gear and the driven pinion gear bearing housing.
10. After installation of the replacement shim(s), repeat the gear lash adjustment procedure to verify gear lash is within specification.

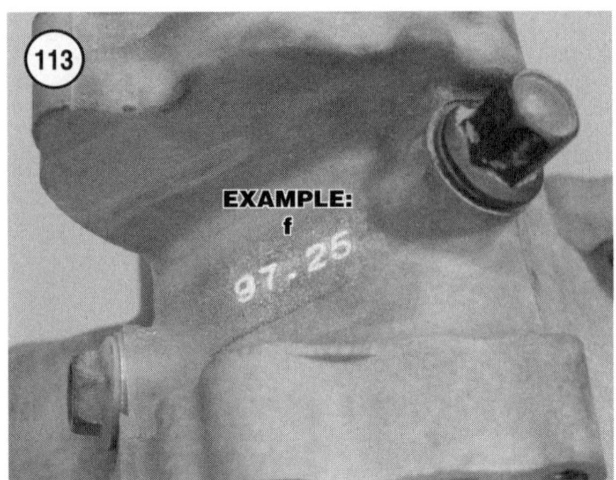

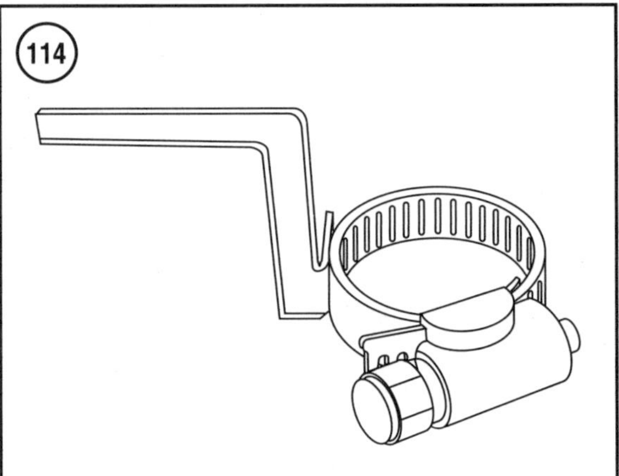

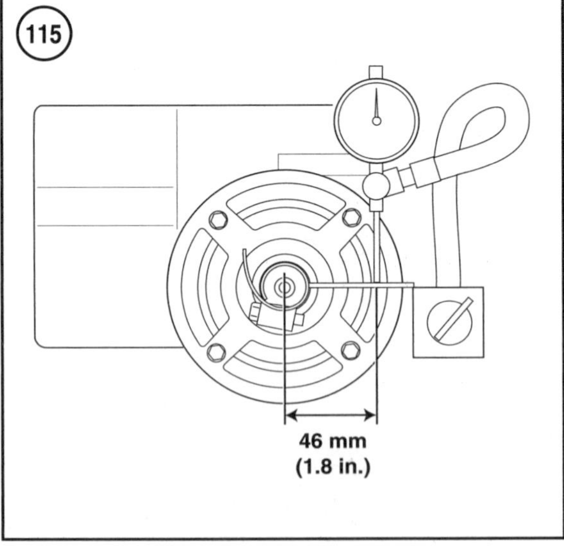

Table 1 ENGINE LOWER END SPECIFICATIONS

	New mm (in.)	Service limit mm (in.)
Connecting rod		
Big end side clearance	0.35-0.65 (0.0138-0.0256)	1.0 (0.0394)
Big end radial clearance	0.010-0.025 (0.0004-0.0010)	–
Crankshaft		
Flywheel width	74.95-75.0 (2.9508-2.9528)	
Runout	–	0.03 (0.0012)
Middle gear lash	0.1-0.3 (0.004 - 0.012)	–

Table 2 OIL PUMP SPECIFICATIONS

	New mm (in.)	Service limit mm (in.)
Oil pump		
Inner rotor tip clearance	0.03-0.10 (0.0012-0.0039)	0.15 (0.006)
Outer rotor to cover (side) clearance	0.03-0.10 (0.0012-0.0039)	0.17 (0.007)
Oil pressure at 1500 rpm	65 kPa (9.4 psi)	–
Bypass valve set pressure	441-637 kPa (64-92 psi)	–

Table 3 ENGINE LOWER END TORQUE SPECIFICATIONS

	N•m	in.-lb.	ft.-lb.
Balancer driven gear locknut	110	–	81
Crankcase bearing retainer bolts	10	89	–
Crankcase bolts	10	89	–
Crankcase oil drain plug	30	–	22
Engine mounting bolts			
Front engine mounting bolts (large)	33	–	24
Front engine mounting bolts (small)	10	89	–
Rear engine mounting throughbolt (large)	56	–	41
Rear engine mounting bolts (small)	10	89	–
Rubber damper to frame nut	42	–	31
Middle drive gear assembly (left crankcase)			
Bearing housing bolts	32	–	24
Bearing retainer screws	29	–	21
Drive pinion nut	145	–	107
Middle driven gear assembly (right crankcase)			
Bearing housing bolts	25	–	18
Bearing retainer (front)	80	–	59
Bearing retainer (rear)	110	–	81
Driven pinion gear nut	150	–	111
Front shaft U-joint yoke/coupling nut	97	–	72
Oil filter fitting	63	–	46
Oil pipe banjo bolts			
Delivery pipe (to transmission)	18	–	13
Lower pipe (to crankshaft and top end)	35	–	26
Oil pump mounting bolts	10	89	–
Oil pump relief valve retainer bolts	10	89	–
Rear cam chain guide bolts	8	71	–
Recoil starter housing bolts	14	–	10
Reverse switch	20	–	15
Shift drum stopper bolt	18	–	13
Starter pulley bolt	55	–	41

CHAPTER SIX

CLUTCH AND SHEAVES

This chapter covers the drive belt cover, outer bearing housing, drive-belt, primary and secondary sheaves, right crankcase cover and clutch. Refer to **Tables 1-3** at the end of the chapter for specifications.

DRIVE BELT COVER

Removal, Inspection and Installation

1. Remove the front fender, rear fender, right footrest panel and air duct (Chapter Sixteen).
2. Remove the bolts from the perimeter and center of the drive belt cover (**Figure 1**).
3. Remove the cover and gasket. If the cover jams against the brake pedal, remove the pedal at the pivot.
4. Clean the cover, gasket and plug (**Figure 2**). Then inspect the parts for damage. It is not abnormal for the interior of the cover to have an accumulation of debris.
5. Reverse these steps to install the drive belt cover. Note the following:
   a. Fit the gasket onto the cover before installing.
   b. Tighten the cover bolts to 10 N•m (89 in.-lb.).

OUTER BEARING HOUSING

The outer bearing housing (**Figure 3**) fits over the primary sheave. A bearing inside the housing supports the outer end of the clutch housing shaft. The clutch housing is located behind the primary sheave.

Removal, Inspection and Installation

1. Remove the drive belt cover as described in this chapter.
2. Remove the bolts from the outer bearing housing (**Figure 3**).
3. Remove the housing and account for the two dowels (**Figure 4**).
4. Inspect the housing for cracks and damage.
5. Inspect the housing bearing and seal. If the bearing does not operate smoothly, replace the bearing and seal as follows:
   a. Remove the retaining bolt (A, **Figure 5**), cover (B) and seal (C).
   b. Remove the bearing (D, **Figure 5**) with a bearing puller.
   c. Lubricate the new parts with waterproof grease.
   d. Drive the new bearing into place with a driver that fits onto the outside perimeter of the bearing.

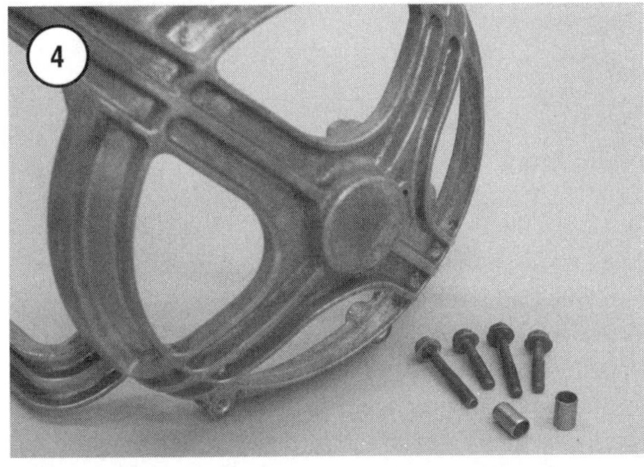

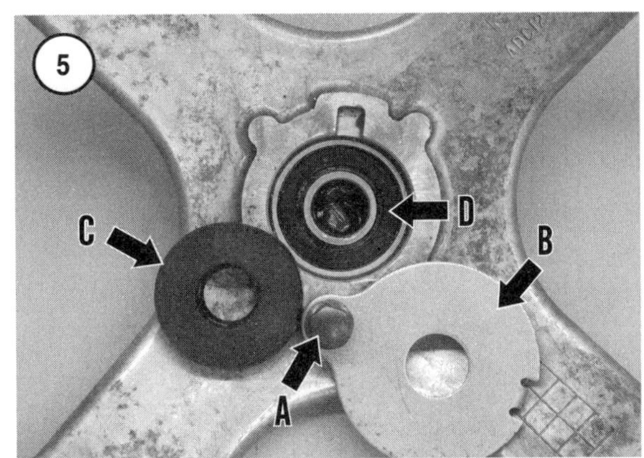

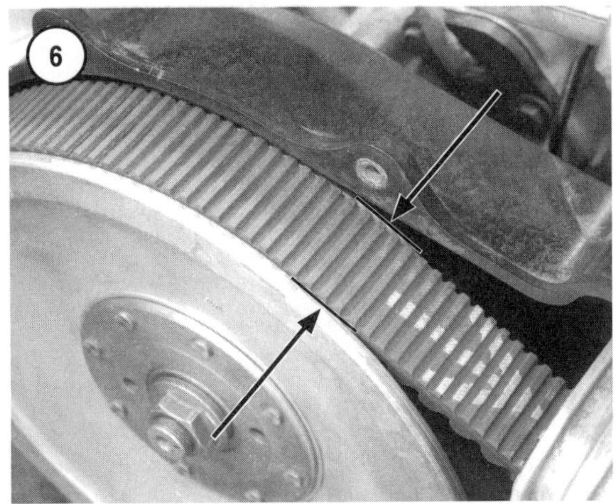

e. Install the seal. The bearing cover can be used to evenly press the seal into place.

f. Wipe all excess grease from the housing.

6. Reverse these steps to install the outer bearing housing. Note the following:

a. Make sure the dowels are installed.

b. Tighten the outer bearing housing bolts to 10 N•m (89 in.-lb.).

DRIVE BELT INSPECTION AND REPLACEMENT

Anytime the drive belt cover is removed, inspect the condition of the drive belt. If planning on removing both sheaves, do not use the drive belt replacement procedure in this section. Refer to *Primary and Secondary Sheaves* in this chapter.

Inspection

1. Remove the drive belt cover as described in this chapter.

2. Inspect the drive belt.

a. Measure the width of the belt (**Figure 6**). Refer to **Table 2** for specifications.

b. Inspect the drive belt for wear, cracks, contamination and damaged teeth.
c. If necessary, refer to the belt replacement procedure in this section.

Replacement

1. Remove the outer bearing housing as described in this chapter.
2. Spread the secondary sheave by installing two 6–1.0 × 45-mm bolts into the sheave hub (**Figure 7**). Alternately tighten the bolts until the sheave is fully spread and the drive belt is loose.
3. Remove the drive belt.
4. Locate the arrow on the new drive belt. Then install the drive belt with the arrow pointing forward, when the arrow is at the top of the sheaves (**Figure 8**).
5. Remove the bolts from the secondary sheave hub. Alternately loosen the bolts until the sheave is tight. While loosening the bolts, it is helpful to rotate the secondary sheave counterclockwise to help the belt in rising to the top of the sheave.
6. Install the outer bearing housing and drive belt cover as described in this chapter.

PRIMARY AND SECONDARY SHEAVES

Refer to *Drive Belt Inspection and Replacement* in this chapter for inspection.

Removal

1. Remove the drive belt cover and outer bearing housing as described in this chapter.
2. Rotate the sheaves counterclockwise and locate the direction arrow on the drive belt. If the arrow is not visible, mark the drive belt with an arrow pointing forward (**Figure 8**).
3. Hold the outside of the primary sheave (A, **Figure 9**) with a sheave holder (Yamaha part No. YU-01880), or a clutch holding tool. Use care when gripping the housing.
4. Remove the outside secondary sheave nut (B, **Figure 9**).
5. *Loosen* the primary sheave locknut (C, **Figure 9**). While applying inward pressure to the pulley cam (D, **Figure 9**), remove the nut and washer. Hold the pulley cam in place and remove the primary sheave from the shaft. Place the sheave with the pulley cam facing up. If the pulley cam is not kept pushed in, there is a chance that the internal weights will fall out of position. If this occurs, the sheave will have to be disassembled and the weights repositioned.
6. Remove the shaft collar, drive belt, primary fixed sheave and secondary sheave.

7. Disassemble and inspect the parts as described in this section.

Installation

1. Clean the clutch housing shaft (A, **Figure 10**) and transmission input shaft (B). Then lightly lubricate the shafts and splines with waterproof grease.
2. Install the primary fixed sheave onto the clutch housing shaft.
3. Install the secondary sheave onto the transmission input shaft. Then spread the secondary sheave by

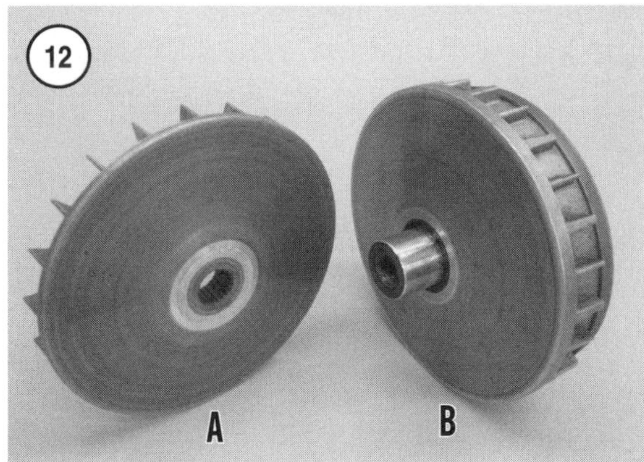

installing two 6–1.0 × 45-mm bolts into the sheave hub (**Figure 11**). Alternately tighten the bolts until the sheave is fully spread.

4. Locate the arrow on the drive belt. Then install the drive belt with the arrow pointing forward, when the arrow is at the top of the sheaves (**Figure 8**). The drive belt is manufactured to run in one direction.
5. Install the shaft collar and primary sheave, keeping pressure on the pulley cam (D, **Figure 9**). If the pulley cam is not resting evenly in the sheave, a weight(s) has moved out of position. Disassemble and reposition the weight(s) as described in this section.
6. Install the primary sheave washer and finger-tighten the locknut (C, **Figure 9**).
7. Hold the primary sheave (A, **Figure 9**) with a sheave holder or clutch holding tool. Use care when gripping the housing. Tighten the primary sheave locknut to 120 N•m (89 ft.-lb.). Do not pinch the belt when tightening the nut.
8. Install and finger-tighten the secondary sheave nut (B, **Figure 9**). Then remove the bolts from the secondary sheave hub. Alternately loosen the bolts until the sheave is tight. While loosening the bolts, it is helpful to rotate the secondary sheave counterclockwise to raise the belt to the top of the sheave. The belt must be taut between the primary and secondary sheaves so the secondary sheave nut can be tightened.
9. Again, hold the primary sheave (A, **Figure 9**) with a sheave holder or clutch holding tool. Use care when gripping the housing.
10. Tighten the outside secondary sheave nut (B, **Figure 9**) to 100 N•m (74 ft.-lb.).
11. Install the outer bearing housing and drive belt cover as described in this chapter.

6

Disassembly, Inspection and Assembly

Primary sheave

The primary sheave is mounted on the clutch housing shaft and consists of two major pieces. The fixed sheave (A, **Figure 12**) is a single plate that remains in one position on the shaft, while the sliding sheave (B) can move toward or away from the fixed sheave, depending on shaft speed. As shaft speed increases, centrifugal weights inside the sliding sheave push it toward the fixed sheave. This forces the drive belt higher in the sheave assembly. As shaft speed decreases, the weights apply less force and the belt moves lower in the sheave assembly. This raising and lowering of the belt works in conjunction with the secondary sheave to provide variable gear ratios.

1. Disassemble the sliding sheave as follows:
   a. Remove the shaft collar from the sheave.
   b. Remove the screws from the cap (**Figure 13**). Then evenly pry the cap off the sheave.

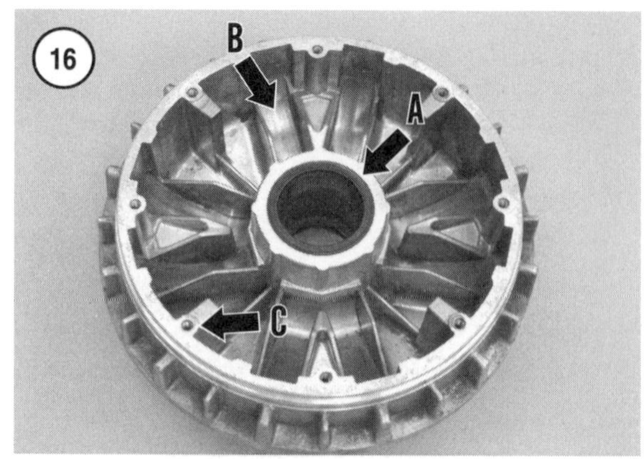

Resistance from the O-ring (**Figure 14**) at the perimeter of the sheave will be felt during removal.

c. Remove the pulley cam (A, **Figure 15**) and weights (B) from the sheave.

2. Clean the parts in solvent and dry with compressed air.
3. Inspect the primary sheave as follows:
   a. Inspect the interior of the sliding sheave. Replace the seals (A, **Figure 16**) if the bore was scored or there was water or debris in the bore during disassembly. The weight ramps (B, **Figure 16**) should appear polished, but not scored or worn. If operating the machine in extremely dusty conditions, heavy accumulations of dirt can pack in the sheave, causing the weights to drag and operate erratically. Inspect the splines (C, **Figure 16**) that engage with the pulley cam sliders. The splines should be smooth with no cracks or damage.
   b. Inspect and measure the weights (**Figure 17**). Refer to **Table 2** for specifications. If the covers on the weights are heat distorted, this may indicate that the weights were jammed in one position. Inspect for debris buildup in the sheave.
   c. Inspect the pulley cam. Inspect the splines (A, **Figure 18**) for wear. Inspect the weight ramps

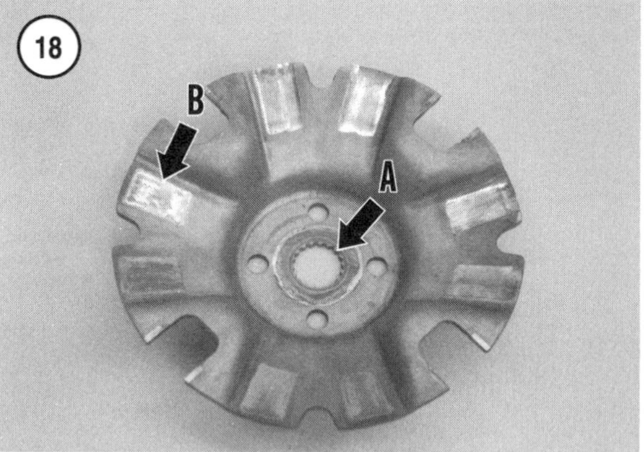

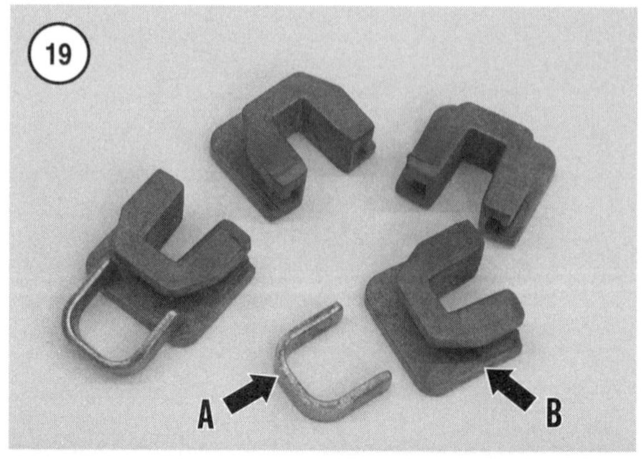

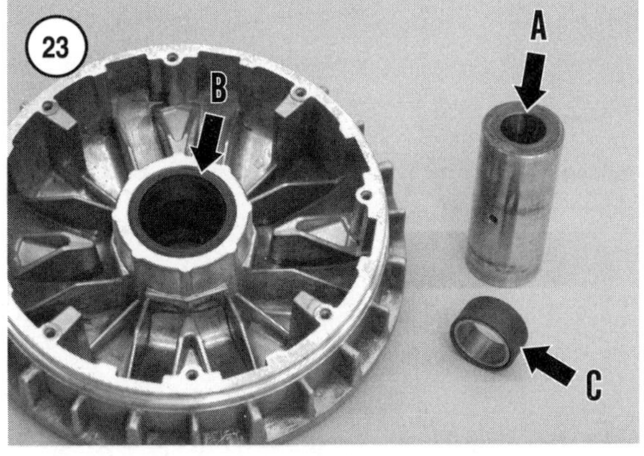

(B, **Figure 18**) for uneven wear and scoring. If the ramps appear unequally worn, the weights are not uniformly engaging or applying even pressure on the sliding sheave.

d. Inspect the spacers (A, **Figure 19**) and sliders (B) for wear. Replace the sliders if the inner face is worn or distorted. The sliders must be in good condition so the sliding sheave does not drag or jam against the pulley cam.

e. Inspect the fixed sheave and shaft collar (**Figure 20**). Inspect the sheave for cracks and broken fins. Check the collar for scoring.

f. Inspect the cap and mounting hardware (**Figure 21**) for damage. Replace the O-ring.

4. Assemble the sliding sheave as follows:
   a. Insert the spacers into the sliders. Then install the parts on the pulley cam (**Figure 22**).
   b. Apply waterproof grease to the *inside* of the shaft collar (A, **Figure 23**), sliding sheave bore and seals (B). Also apply the grease to the outer surface of the weights (C, **Figure 23**).
   c. Insert the weights into the sheave. Then place the pulley cam over the weights (**Figure 15**).
   d. Install a new, lubricated O-ring onto the sheave. Then press the cap into place (**Figure 13**).
   e. Tighten the sheave cap screws to 3 N•m (27 in.-lb.).
   f. Store the sliding sheave with the pulley cam facing up. When handling the sheave, keep pressure on the pulley cam. If the pulley cam does not remain pushed in, the weights may fall out of position.

Secondary sheave

The secondary sheave is mounted on the transmission input shaft and is driven by the primary sheave. The secondary sheave consists of two sheave halves and a spring. The fixed sheave (A, **Figure 24**) remains in one position on the shaft, while the spring-loaded sliding sheave (B) can move away from or toward the

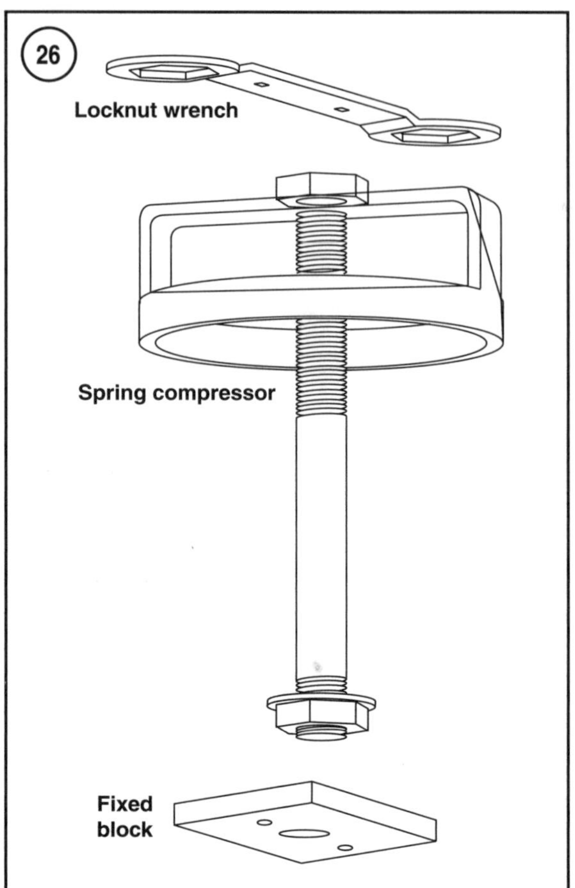

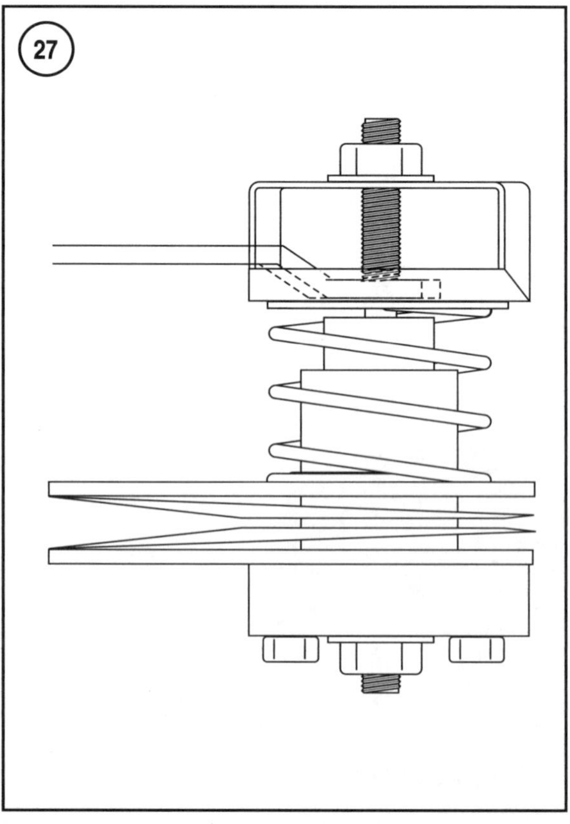

toward the fixed sheave. At low sheave speed, the sheave halves are pressed close together by the spring and the drive belt is seated near the outer edge of the assembly. As sheave speed increases, the drive belt is driven downward, pushing the sliding sheave outward and compressing the spring. As sheave speed decreases, the spring forces the sliding sheave back toward the fixed sheave, forcing the drive belt back toward the outer edge of the assembly. This raising and lowering of the belt works in conjunction with the primary sheave to provide variable gear ratios.

1. Inspect the secondary sheave as follows:
   a. Inspect the spring (A, **Figure 25**). The spring must be undamaged and tight against the spring seats.
   b. Inspect the shaft (B, **Figure 25**) for corrosion, scoring and other damage. If corrosion or water is evident at the seal, the seals are leaking.
   c. Inspect the faces (C, **Figure 25**) of the secondary sheaves for corrosion and damage. If corrosion is evident on the sheave faces or shaft, this might mean the sheaves are jammed. This can be caused by damaged guide pins, excessive corrosion and debris.
   d. Inspect the splines and bore (D, **Figure 25**) for corrosion and damage.
2. If necessary, disassemble the secondary sheave as follows. Use the sheave spring compressor (Yamaha part No. YM-04134), sheave fixed block (part No. YM-04135) and locknut wrench (part No. 90890-01348) (**Figure 26**). Refer to **Figure 27** and **Figure 28**.
   a. Bolt the block to the fixed sheave. Use the two bolt holes near the sheave bore.
   b. Mount the spring compressor squarely on top of the spring seat. Insert the wrench into the compressor access hole, then pass the drawbolt through the compressor, wrench, sheave and block. The end of the bolt with the most

28 SECONDARY SHEAVE

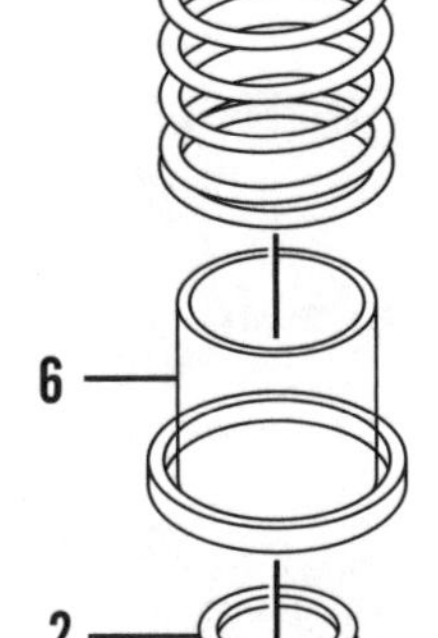

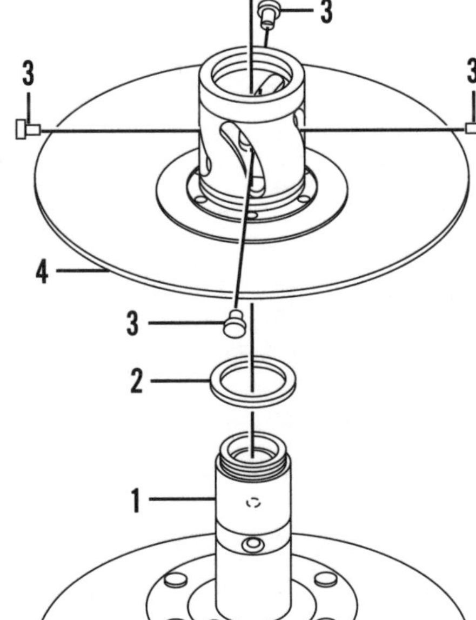

1. Fixed sheave
2. Seal
3. Guide pin
4. Sliding sheave
5. O-ring
6. Spring seat
7. Spring
8. Nut

29

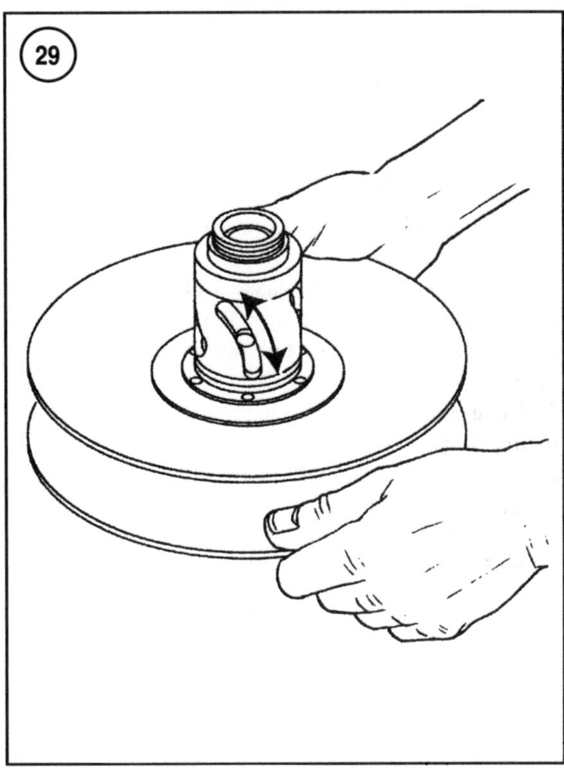

threads must be at the top. Install and finger-tighten the nuts to stabilize the assembly.

c. Lock the fixed block in a vise and tighten the compressor nut until the spring is compressed enough to access the sheave nut.
d. Remove the inside secondary sheave nut. Then slowly relieve the pressure on the compressor.
e. Replace all O-rings and seals.
f. Lubricate the O-rings, seals, guide pins and sheave bores with Bel-Ray assembly lubricant or an equivalent.
g. Repeat this procedure to install the sheave nut after repairing and assembling the parts.
h. Tighten the inside secondary sheave nut to 90 N•m (66 ft.-lbs.) using the torque adapter function of the locknut wrench.

3. Inspect the sheave (**Figure 28**) and note the following:

a. Clean the parts in solvent and dry with compressed air.
b. Measure the spring free length. Refer to **Table 2** for specifications.
c. Assemble the sheaves and inspect the action of the guide pins and cam grooves (**Figure 29**). The two sheaves should operate smoothly. Replace the guide pins if wear is evident. Replace both sheaves if the cam grooves are excessively worn or the parts are excessively loose.

RIGHT CRANKCASE COVER

Removal and Installation

1. Remove the primary and secondary sheaves as described in this chapter.
2. Remove the bolts from the center and perimeter of the crankcase cover (**Figure 30**).
3. Remove the cover and gaskets.
4. Clean the cover and gaskets (**Figure 31**). Then inspect the parts for damage. It is not abnormal for the interior of the cover to have an accumulation of debris.
5. Clean the clutch and transmission shaft compartments (**Figure 32**).
6. Reverse these steps to install the right crankcase cover. Note the following:
   a. Fit the gaskets onto the cover before installing.
   b. Tighten the cover bolts to 10 N•m (89 in.-lb.).

30

31

CLUTCH

The centrifugal clutch assembly is located in a housing (**Figure 33**) at the end of the crankshaft and transmits power to the primary sheave. The clutch consists of a clutch housing and a centrifugal shoe assembly that is locked to the crankshaft. As engine speed is raised, the shoe assembly centrifugally expands, engaging with the clutch housing. As engine speed is lowered, the shoe assembly contracts and disengages from the clutch housing.

The clutch is also equipped with a one-way clutch, located between the clutch housing and shoe assembly. The one-way clutch provides engine braking when the shoe assembly is disengaged from the clutch housing, as when descending a hill at idle speed.

32

Removal and Installation

1. Remove the right crankcase cover as described in this chapter.
2. Check the general condition of the one-way clutch before removing the clutch from the engine. Check the one-way clutch as follows:
   a. Turn the clutch housing shaft counterclockwise. The shaft should turn freely.
   b. Turn the clutch housing shaft clockwise. The shaft should lock.
   c. If the one-way clutch fails either test, remove and inspect the one-way clutch.
3. Drain the oil from the engine as described in Chapter Three.
4. Loosen the bolts on the bearing housing. Make several passes and loosen each bolt one-fourth turn until all bolts are loose. Remove the clutch housing assembly and account for the dowels (**Figure 34**).

33

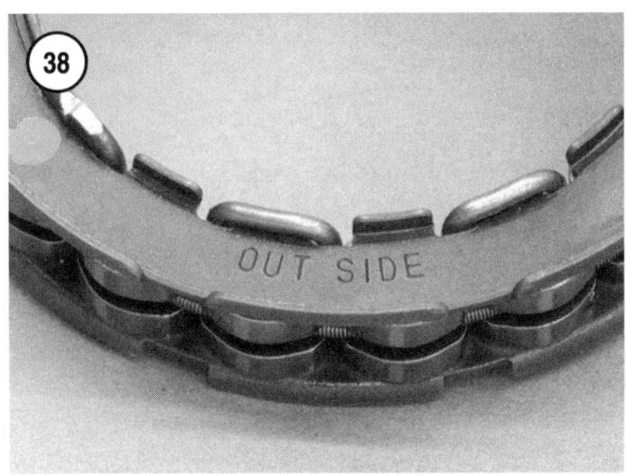

5. Straighten the punched area on the clutch locknut (**Figure 35**).
6. Hold the shoe assembly with a clutch holding tool (**Figure 36**). Then remove the locknut.
7. Inspect and repair the parts (**Figure 37**) as described in this section.
8. Reverse these steps to install the parts. Note the following:
   a. Lubricate the clutch shoe pivots and clutch housing bearings with engine oil.
   b. Install a new clutch locknut. Tighten the nut to 160 N•m (118 ft.-lb.).
   c. Lock the nut to the shaft threads with a punch (**Figure 35**).
   d. Lubricate the one-way clutch with molybdenum disulfide grease.
   e. Install the one-way clutch with the arrow and/or the word OUTSIDE (**Figure 38**) facing the clutch housing.
   f. Install a new bearing housing gasket.
   g. Tighten the bearing housing bolts, working in a crossing pattern. Tighten the bolts to 10 N•m (89 in.-lb.).
   h. Check the engine oil level.
9. Check the one-way clutch for proper operation.
   a. Turn the clutch housing shaft counterclockwise. The shaft should turn freely.
   b. Turn the clutch housing shaft clockwise. The shaft should lock.
   c. If the one-way clutch fails either test, remove and inspect the one-way clutch.

6

Inspection and Repair

1. Clean the parts in solvent and dry with compressed air.
2. Inspect the one-way clutch. If the one-way clutch is damaged, replace the one-way clutch and clutch housing as a set.
   a. Inspect the clutch sprags (A, **Figure 39**) for scoring, wear and heat damage. Make sure the

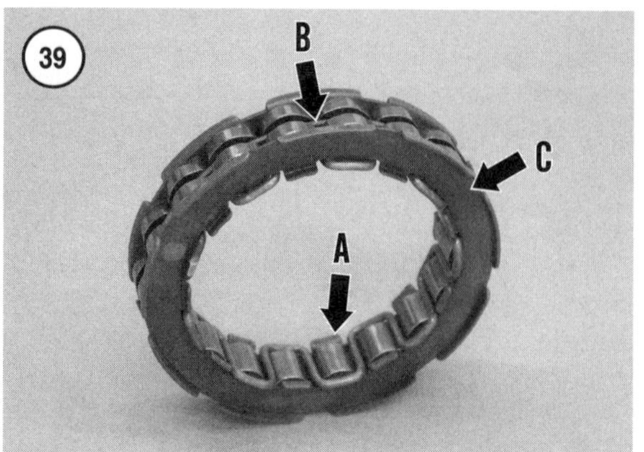

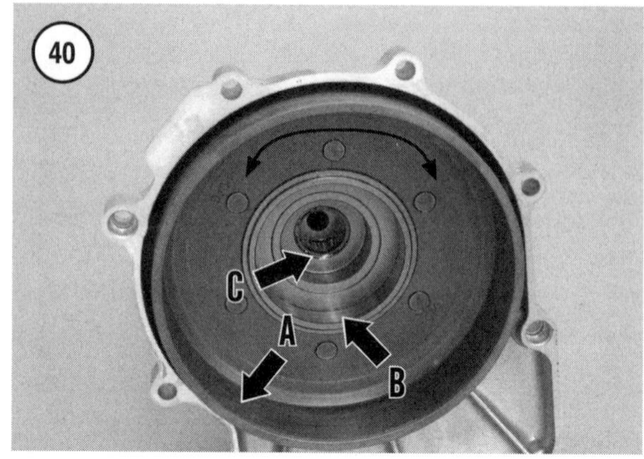

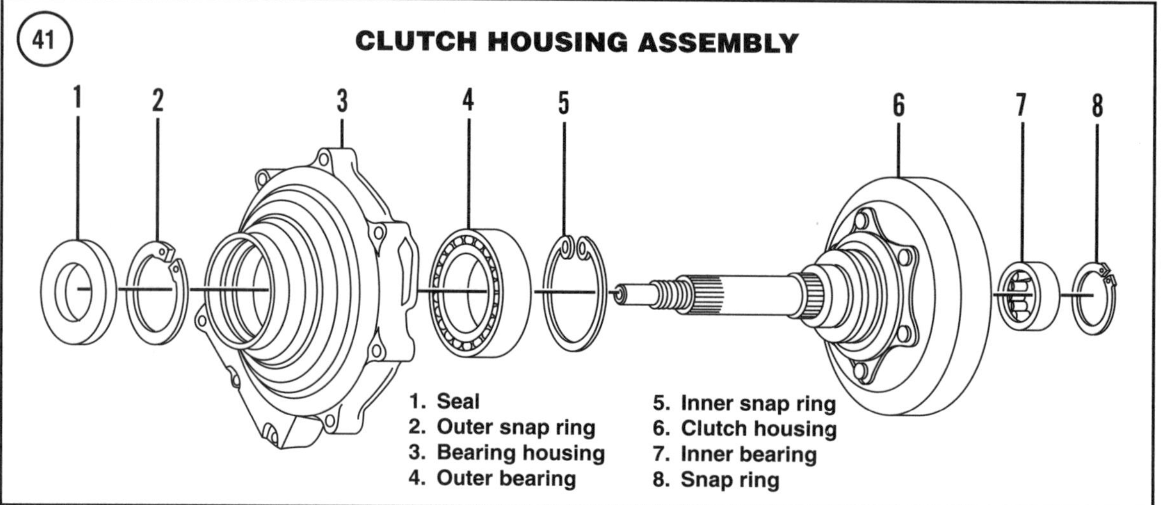

retainer spring (B, **Figure 39**) firmly holds the sprags in place.

b. Make sure each sprag is free to pivot and that all sprags are resting in the same position.
c. Inspect the clutch cage (C, **Figure 39**) for cracks and damage.
d. Test the one-way clutch. Install the one-way clutch with the arrow and/or the word OUTSIDE (**Figure 38**) facing the clutch housing. Insert the clutch shoe assembly into the clutch housing. Hold the clutch shoe assembly and rotate the housing shaft. When turning the housing shaft clockwise, the shaft should lock. When turning the housing shaft counterclockwise, the shaft should turn freely.

3. Inspect the clutch housing and bearing housing.
   a. Inspect the clutch shoe contact area (A, **Figure 40**) for scoring, wear and heat damage.
   b. Inspect the one-way clutch contact area (B, **Figure 40**) for scoring, wear and heat damage. If the clutch housing is damaged, replace the one-way clutch and clutch housing as a set.
   c. Inspect the inner bearing (C, **Figure 40**) for corrosion, pitting and other damage. Lubricate the rollers with engine oil and rotate the bearing. Make sure the rollers operate smoothly. If the bearing is damaged, remove the snap ring and remove the bearing with a bearing puller. Install the new bearing with a driver that fits the outside diameter of the bearing.
   d. Inspect the outer bearing in the bearing housing (**Figure 41**). Rotate the clutch housing shaft and check for smooth operation. If damaged, replace the bearing. Remove the seal and outer snap ring. Slide the clutch housing out of the bearing, and then remove the inner snap ring securing the bearing. Drive the bearing out of its bore in the bearing housing. Then, install a new bearing and the inner snap ring. Slide the clutch housing through the new bearing, and install the outer snap ring. Install a new seal anytime the clutch housing is removed from the bearing housing.
   e. Inspect the clutch housing shaft (A, **Figure 42**) and seal (B). Inspect the shaft for damaged splines (C, **Figure 42**) and threads (D). Remove corrosion with emery cloth. Replace the seal if oil leaks are evident.

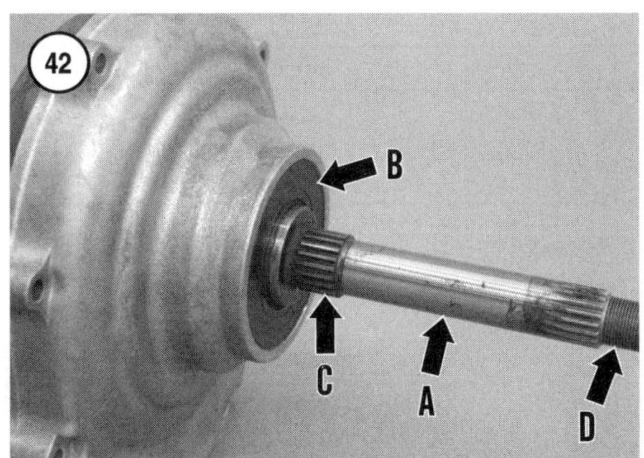

6

4. Inspect the clutch shoe assembly.
   a. Inspect the splines, guides and one-way clutch contact area. Inspect the splines for damage (A, **Figure 43**). If pitting or corrosion is evident, the engine oil has likely been contaminated with water. Check that all shoe guides (B, **Figure 43**) are tight and not worn. Inspect the one-way clutch contact area (C, **Figure 43**) for scoring, wear and heat damage. Discoloration where the shoe plate and boss join is normal.
   b. Inspect the springs, levers (A, **Figure 44**), pivots and retainer clips. Look for broken or weak springs (B, **Figure 44**). The springs are available as a replacement part. Always replace springs as a set. Inspect the pivots (C, **Figure 44**) for tightness and broken or missing clips (D). Make sure all shoes are equally seated. If not, check for worn or jammed levers, pivots and springs.
   c. Inspect the shoes for wear, heat damage and contamination. Measure the shoe thickness (**Figure 45**). Refer to **Table 1** for specifications. If shoe thickness varies, check for damaged pivots and springs.
5. Clean and inspect the crankshaft. Inspect the splines (A, **Figure 46**) and bearing surface (B) for damage. If pitting or corrosion is evident, check the engine oil for water contamination.
6. Install the clutch as described in this section.

Tables 1-3 are on the following page.

Table 1 CLUTCH SPECIFICATIONS

	New mm (in.)	Service limit mm (in.)
Clutch shoe thickness (six plates)	1.5 (0.06)	1.0 (0.04)
Clutch in revolutions	1900-2300 rpm	–
Clutch stall revolutions	3350-3850 rpm	–

Table 2 SHEAVE AND DRIVE BELT SPECIFICATIONS

	New mm (in.)	Service limit mm (in.)
Drive belt width	33.2 (1.31)	29.9 (1.18)
Primary sheave weight outside diameter	30.0 (1.18)	29.5 (1.16)
Secondary sheave spring free length	124.2 (4.89)	121.2 (4.77)

Table 3 CLUTCH AND SHEAVE TORQUE SPECIFICATIONS

	N•m	in.-lb.	ft.-lb.
Bearing housing bolts	10	89	–
Clutch locknut	160	–	118
Drive belt cover bolts	10	89	–
Primary pulley sheave cap screws	3	27	–
Primary sheave locknut	120	–	89
Right crankcase cover bolts	10	89	–
Secondary sheave nut (inside)	90	–	66
Secondary sheave nut (outside)	100	–	74

CHAPTER SEVEN

TRANSMISSION AND SHIFT MECHANISMS

7

This chapter covers the transmission and shift mechanisms. This includes the select lever assembly, external shift mechanism and transmission. To access the transmission, engine removal and crankcase separation is necessary.

Refer to **Table 1** and **Table 2** at the end of the chapter for specifications.

SELECT LEVER ASSEMBLY

NOTE
If poor shifting is occurring, check the select lever shift rod for proper adjustment (Chapter Three) before removing the select lever components.

Removal and Installation

1. Park the machine on level ground.
2. Remove the front fender assembly (Chapter Sixteen).
3. Shift the select lever into neutral. Then disconnect the cable (A, **Figure 1**) and spring (B) at the front brake master cylinder.
4. Remove the shift arm (**Figure 2**).
5. Remove the bolts securing the select lever unit to the frame (**Figure 3**).
6. Reverse this procedure to install the parts. Note the following:
   a. Tighten the shift arm pivot bolt to 14 N•m (10 ft.-lb.).
   b. Tighten the select lever mounting bolts to 25 N•m (18 ft.-lb.).
   c. Adjust the select lever cable (Chapter Three).
   d. Check the adjustment of the select lever shift rod (Chapter Three).

SELECT LEVER CABLE REPLACEMENT

1. Park the machine on level ground.
2. Remove the front fender assembly (Chapter Sixteen).
3. Shift the select lever into neutral. Then disconnect the cable (A, **Figure 1**) and spring (B) at the front brake master cylinder.
4. Disconnect the cable at the select lever unit (**Figure 4**).
5. Reverse this procedure to install the parts. Note the following:
   a. Lubricate the new cable with an aerosol cable lubricant.
   b. Adjust the select lever cable (Chapter Three).
   c. Check the adjustment of the select lever shift rod (Chapter Three).

EXTERNAL SHIFT MECHANISM

The external shift mechanism links the action of the select lever to the transmission. When the select lever is shifted, the external shift mechanism rotates the transmission shift drum to the appropriate gear position. If poor shifting is occurring, check the select lever shift rod for proper adjustment (Chapter Three) before removing the shift mechanism components.

Removal and Installation

1. Park the machine on level ground.
2. Remove the seat, left fuel tank side panel and engine side cover (Chapter Sixteen).
3. Shift the select lever into neutral.
4. Remove the shift arm (**Figure 2**).
5. Remove the bolts (A, **Figure 5**) and ground cable (B) from the shift lever cover. Remove the cover and gasket.
6. Remove the dowel (A, **Figure 6**) and upper shift lever (B).
7. Remove the lower shift lever assembly (**Figure 7**).
8. Inspect the parts for wear or damage (**Figure 8**). It is not necessary to disassemble the lower shift lever. If the cover seal is leaking, replace it.

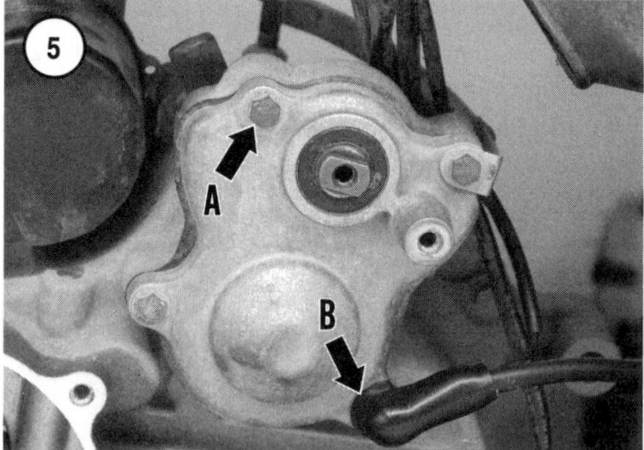

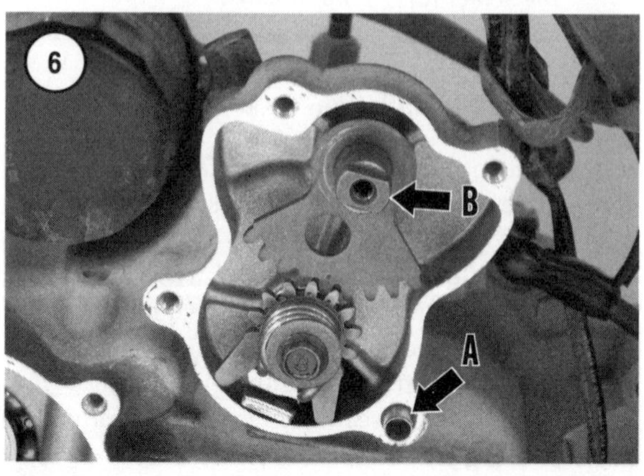

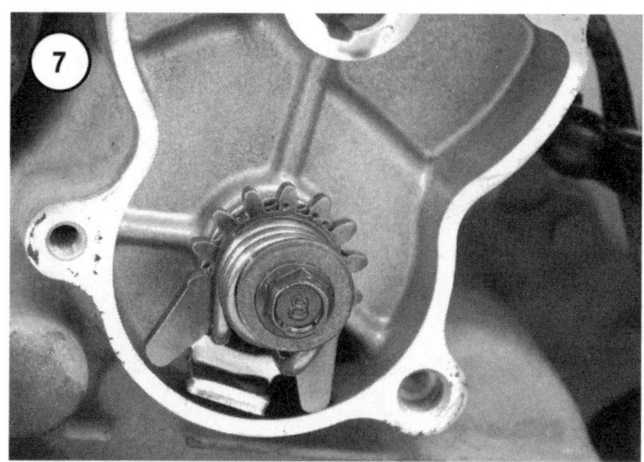

7

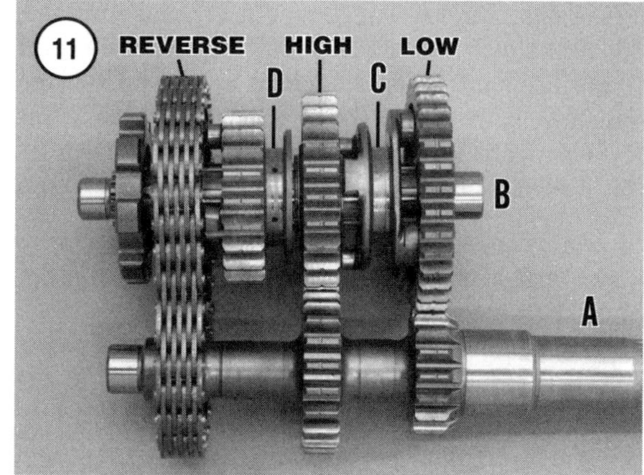

11

8

9

10

9. Reverse this procedure to install the parts. Note the following:
   a. Make sure the select lever is in neutral.
   b. When installing the upper shift lever, install the lever so the punch mark is between the two punch marks on the lower lever (**Figure 9**).
   c. Tighten the lower shift lever bolt to 14 N•m (10 ft.-lb.).
   d. Tighten the shift lever cover bolts to 10 N•m (89 in.-lb.).
   e. Tighten the shift pivot arm bolt to 14 N•m (10 ft.-lb.).
   f. Check for proper shifting. If necessary, adjust the select lever cable and rod (Chapter Three).

7

TRANSMISSION

Operation

The machine is equipped with a dual-range, constant-mesh transmission, plus a chain-driven reverse gear. The transmission shafts, shift forks and shift drum are located in the left crankcase housing (**Figure 10**).

The gears on the input shaft (A, **Figure 11**) are fixed in position, and are meshed with their free-wheeling, high or low-range gear on the output shaft (B). Similarly, the reverse gear sprocket on the input shaft is fixed, while the output shaft sprocket free-wheels. To make the high/low gear ranges active, the dog clutch (C, **Figure 11**) slides laterally and locks itself against the selected gear. Since the dog clutch is splined to the output shaft, the selected gear range becomes active and the output shaft turns.

Reverse gear is activated by the dogs on the side of the drive gear (D, **Figure 11**). The splined drive gear not only engages and disengages reverse, but transfers all power from the output shaft (forward and reverse) to the middle drive gear unit, located below the transmission.

To engage and disengage the gears and sprocket, the dog clutch and drive gear are moved by shift forks. The shift forks are guided by the shift drum, which is controlled by the select lever. As the select lever is operated, the shift drum rotates and guides the forks to engage or disengage the sprocket and gears on the output shaft.

Service

The engine crankcase must be separated to remove the transmission and shift assemblies. Refer to *Crankcase* in Chapter Five.

After the transmission is removed from the crankcase, disassembly, inspection and assembly can be performed. Careful inspection of the parts is required, as well as keeping the parts oriented so they can be properly reassembled. If necessary, slide the parts onto a long dowel or screwdriver after removing each part, or make a permanent mark on each part to indicate position and orientation.

Always install new snap rings. Snap rings fatigue and distort after removing them. Do not reuse them, even though they appear to be in good condition. To install a new snap ring without distorting it, hold the closed side of the snap ring with a pair of pliers while spreading the open side with snap ring pliers (**Figure 12**). While holding the spread ring with both tools, slide it over the shaft and into position. Only spread the snap ring just far enough to install it.

Usually, snap rings have one rounded edge, while the other side has a sharp edge (**Figure 13**). The inner sharp edge prevents the snap ring from lifting out of the shaft groove when lateral pressure is applied to the snap ring. Always look at the inner and outer edges of the snap ring. Some snap rings are manufactured with the inner and outer sharp edge on opposite sides. If a snap ring has no identifiable sharp edge, the snap ring can be installed in either direction. When a snap ring is installed on a splined shaft, position the snap ring gap over a groove (**Figure 14**) in the shaft splines.

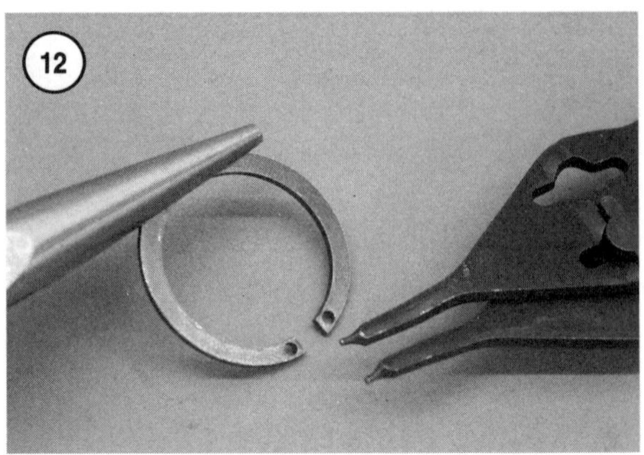

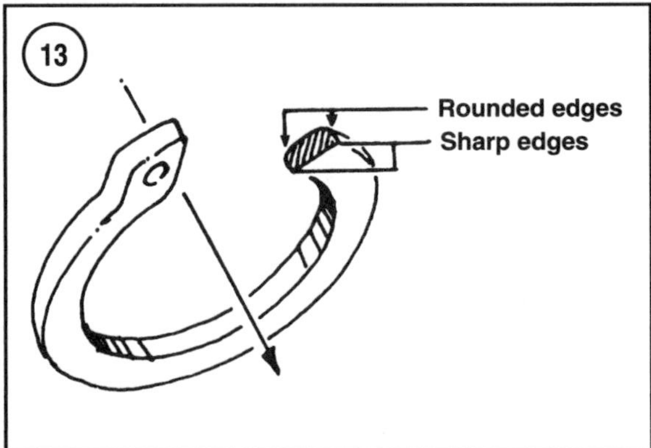

Input Shaft

Removal and inspection

Refer to **Figure 15**. Replace any worn or damaged parts.

1. Disengage the input shaft (**Figure 16**) from the reverse chain.
2. Inspect the shaft for the following:
   a. Broken or damaged gear teeth (**Figure 17**).
   b. Worn or damaged splines (A, **Figure 18**).
   c. Damaged threads (B, **Figure 18**). Mildly damaged threads can be trued with a die.
   d. Wear, galling or other damage on the bearing (C, **Figure 18**) or bushing (D) surfaces. A blue discoloration on any surface indicates excessive heat.
3. Inspect the reverse sprocket and chain for the following:
   a. Broken or worn sprocket teeth (A, **Figure 19**).
   b. Chain binding. The chain links (B, **Figure 19**) should be uniformly firm and flexible.
4. Lubricate, wrap and store the input shaft until it is ready to install into the crankcase. Install the complete transmission assembly as described in Chapter Five.

15

TRANSMISSION

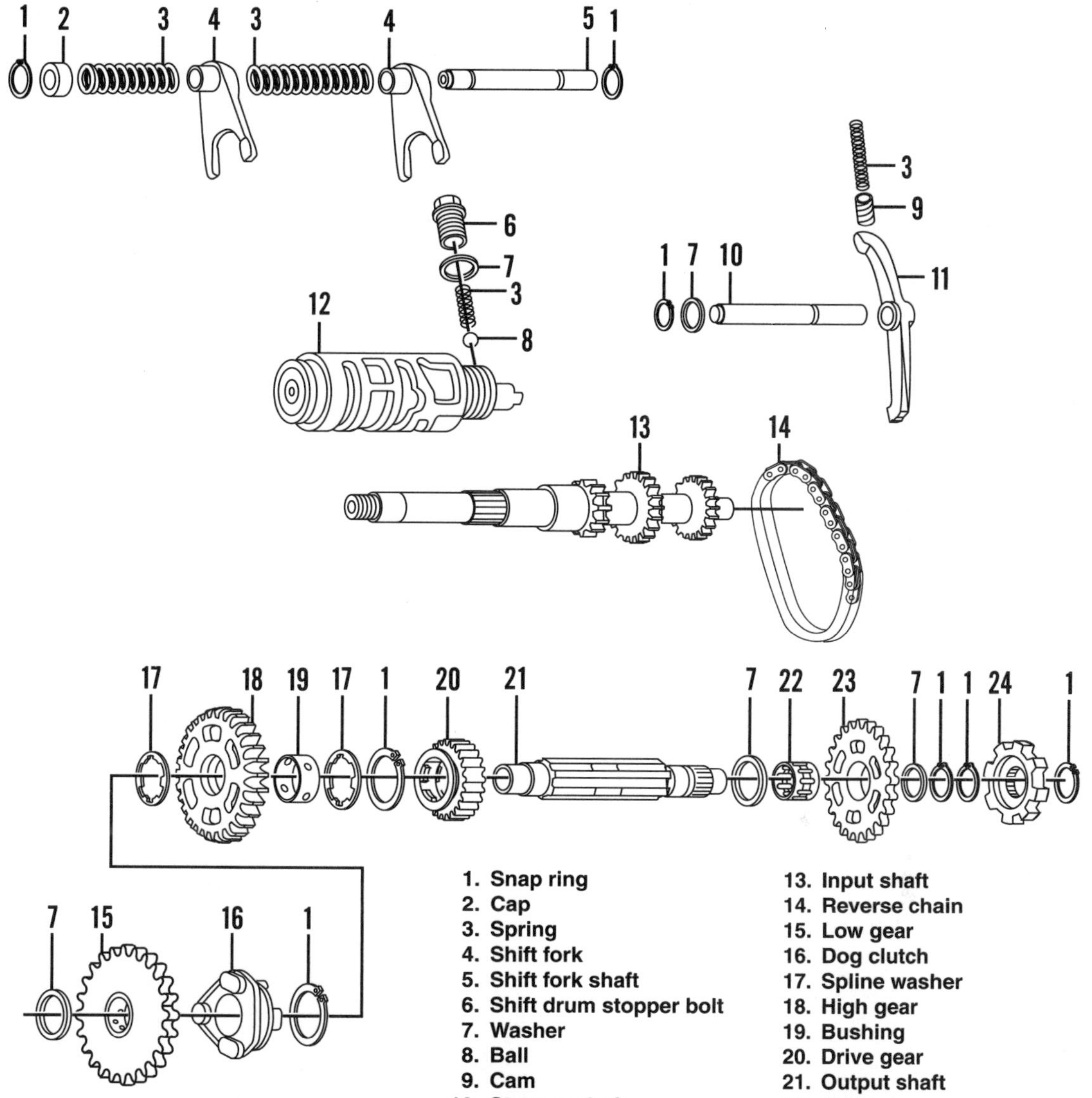

1. Snap ring
2. Cap
3. Spring
4. Shift fork
5. Shift fork shaft
6. Shift drum stopper bolt
7. Washer
8. Ball
9. Cam
10. Stopper shaft
11. Stopper lever
12. Shift drum
13. Input shaft
14. Reverse chain
15. Low gear
16. Dog clutch
17. Spline washer
18. High gear
19. Bushing
20. Drive gear
21. Output shaft
22. Bearing
23. Reverse sprocket
24. Stopper wheel

16

17

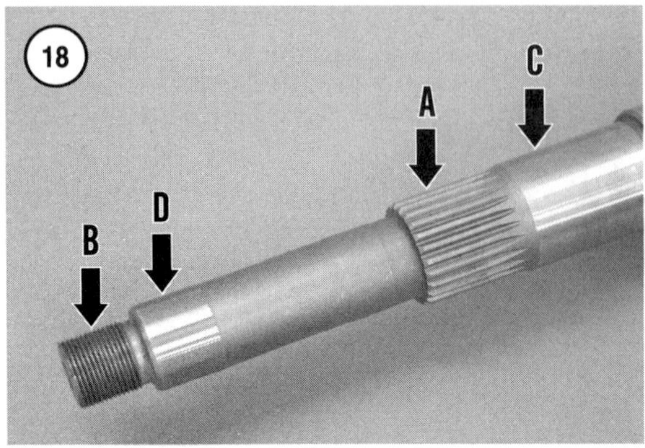

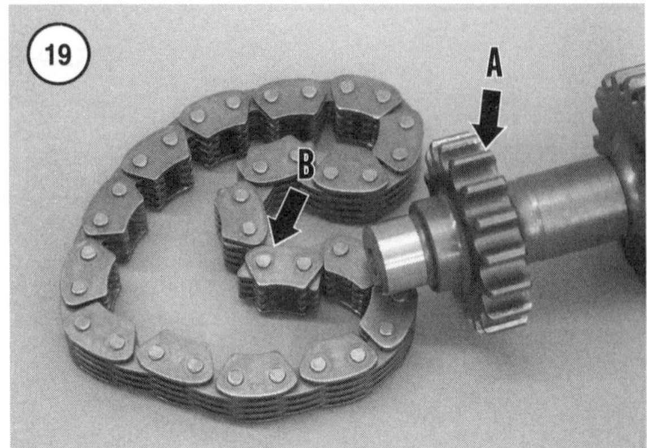

Output Shaft

Refer to **Figure 15**. Replace any worn or damaged parts.

Disassembly

1. Disassemble the right end of the output shaft in the following order:
   a. Washer.
   b. Low gear.
   c. Dog clutch.
   d. Snap ring.
   e. Spline washer.
   f. High gear.
   g. Bushing.
   h. Spline washer.
   i. Snap ring.
   j. Drive gear.
2. Disassemble the left end of the output shaft in the following order:
   a. Snap ring.
   b. Stopper wheel.
   c. Snap ring.
   d. Snap ring.
   e. Washer.
   f. Reverse sprocket.
   g. Bearing.
   h. Washer.
3. Inspect each part as described in this section, then return it to its place until assembly.

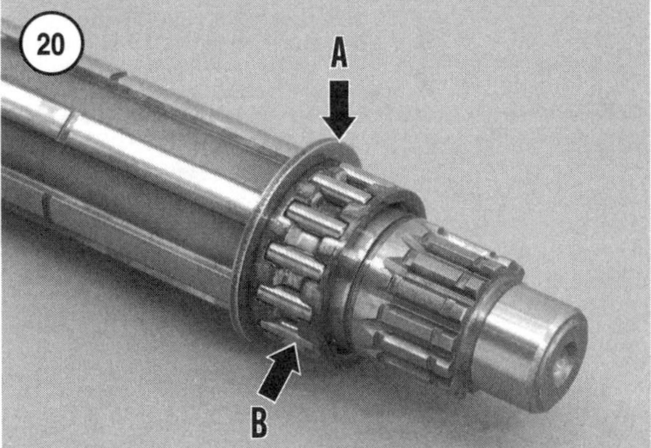

Assembly

Before beginning assembly, have new snap rings on hand. Throughout the procedure, the orientation of the parts is made in relation to the end of the output shaft on which the parts are being installed. Refer to **Figure 15**.

1. Clean and dry all parts before assembly. Lubricate all parts with engine oil.
2. Assemble the left end of the output shaft as follows:

a. Install the washer (A, **Figure 20**) and bearing (B).

b. Install the reverse sprocket (**Figure 21**). The flat side of the sprocket must face *out* (toward shaft end).

c. Install the washer (A, **Figure 22**) and two snap rings. Install the inner snap ring (B, **Figure 22**) with the sharp edge facing *out* (toward shaft end). Install the outer snap ring (C, **Figure 22**) with the sharp edge facing *in* (away from shaft end). Position the outer snap ring gap over a groove in the shaft (**Figure 14**).

d. Install the stopper wheel (A, **Figure 23**) and snap ring (B). The flat side of the stopper wheel must face *out* (toward shaft end). Install the snap ring with the sharp edge facing *out* (toward shaft end). Position the snap ring gap over a groove (**Figure 14**) in the shaft splines.

3. Assemble the right end of the output shaft as follows:

a. Install the drive gear (**Figure 24**). The drive gear shift fork groove must face *out* (toward shaft end).

b. Install the snap ring (A, **Figure 25**), spline washer (B) and bushing (C). Install the snap ring with the sharp edge facing *in* (away from shaft end). Position the snap ring gap over a groove in the shaft splines (**Figure 14**).

c. Install high gear (**Figure 26**). The gear recesses must face *out* (toward shaft end).

d. Install the spline washer (A, **Figure 27**) and snap ring (B). Install the snap ring with the sharp edge facing *out* (toward shaft end). Position the snap ring gap over a groove in the shaft (**Figure 14**).

e. Install the dog clutch (**Figure 28**). The large gear dogs must face *out* (toward shaft end).

f. Install low gear (A, **Figure 29**) and the washer (B). The flat side of the gear must face *out* (toward shaft end).

4. Make sure the shaft assembly appears as in **Figure 30**. Make sure the parts spin, slide and en-

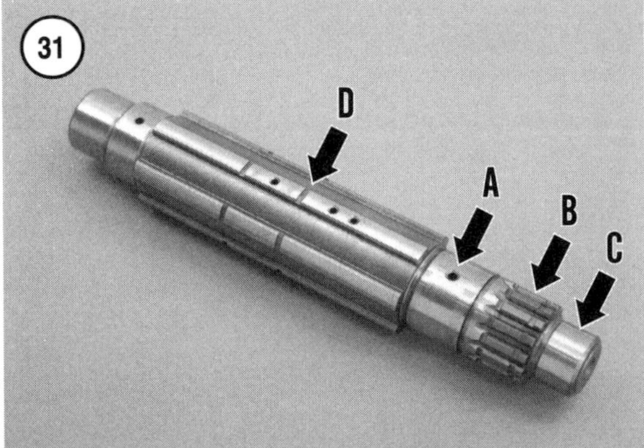

gage as required. Wrap and store the assembly until it is ready to install into the crankcase. Install the complete transmission assembly as described in Chapter Five.

Inspection

1. Inspect the output shaft for the following:
   a. Clean oil holes (A, **Figure 31**).
   b. Worn or damaged splines (B, **Figure 31**).
   c. Rounded or damaged snap ring grooves.
   d. Wear, galling or other damage on the bearing/bushing surfaces (C, **Figure 31**). A blue discoloration on any surface indicates excessive heat.
   e. Unusual wear, damage or discoloration on the gear sliding surfaces (D, **Figure 31**).
   f. Shaft runout. With the output shaft mounted in a centering jig, use a dial indicator to measure runout. Measure on a smooth surface. Then refer to **Table 1** for the specification.
2. Inspect the gears for the following:
   a. Broken or damaged teeth (A, **Figure 32**).
   b. Scored, galled or fractured bore (B, **Figure 32**). The bushing oil pockets should not be worn away. A blue discoloration indicates excessive heat. Discoloration and galling are commonly caused by diluted oil or oil starvation.

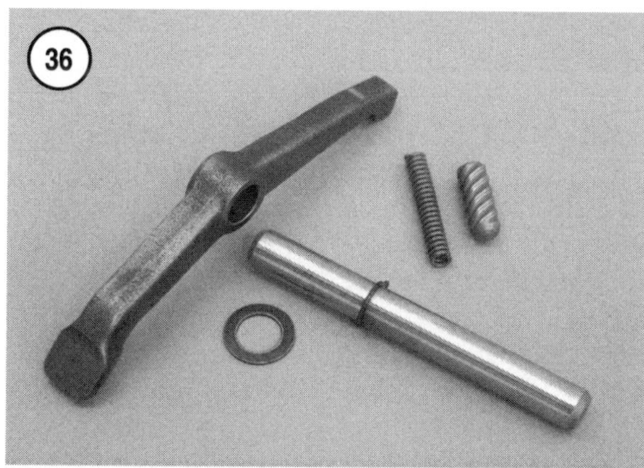

c. Worn or damaged splines (C, **Figure 32**).

d. Smooth gear operation on the shaft. Make sure the gears fit firmly on the output shaft and spin smoothly and freely.

e. Worn, damaged or rounded gear recesses (A, **Figure 33**) and engagement dogs (B). Any wear on the dogs and mating recesses should be uniform. If the dogs are not worn evenly, the remaining dogs will be over stressed and possibly fail. Check the engagement of the dogs by placing the parts at their appropriate positions on the output shaft, then twisting the parts together. Check for positive engagement in both directions. If damage is evident, also check the condition of the shift forks as described in this chapter.

NOTE

The side of the dogs and recesses that carries the engine load will wear and eventually become rounded. The unloaded side of the parts will remain unworn. Rounded dogs and recesses will cause the transmission to jump out of gear.

3. Inspect the shift fork grooves in the dog clutch and drive gear for the following:

a. Clean oil holes (A, **Figure 34**).

b. Wear, scoring or other damage in the shift fork grooves (B, **Figure 34**).

c. Shift fork fit. Inspect the fit of each fork in its mating groove and check for binding, uniform contact and clearance.

4. Inspect the reverse sprocket and bearing for the following:

a. Sprocket bore (A, **Figure 35**) and bearing (B) damage. Inspect the parts for damage and fit. Make sure the parts fit together with minimal play and spin freely on the output shaft.

b. Broken or worn sprocket teeth (C, **Figure 35**).

c. Worn, damaged or rounded sprocket recesses (D, **Figure 35**) and drive gear engagement dogs. Any wear on the dogs and mating recesses should be uniform. If the dogs are not worn evenly, the remaining dogs will be over stressed and possibly fail. Check the engagement of the dogs by placing the parts at their appropriate positions on the output shaft, then twisting the parts together. Check for positive engagement in both directions. If damage is evident, also check the condition of the shift forks, as described in this chapter.

5. Inspect the stopper shaft and lever assembly (**Figure 36**). The parts should show no wear or damage. Make sure the small end of the lever locks into the stopper wheel (**Figure 37**).

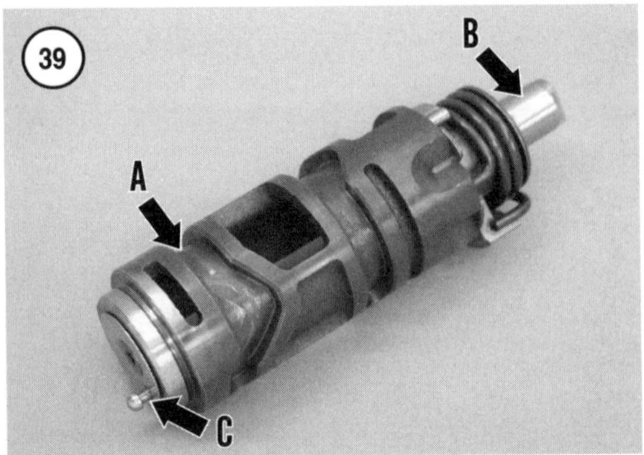

6. Inspect the bushing and washers (**Figure 38**). The parts should show no wear or damage. Make sure the bushing fits in the high gear bore with minimal play and spins freely on the output shaft.
7. Install the parts onto the output shaft as described in this section.

SHIFT DRUM AND FORKS

When the transmission is shifted, the shift drum and fork assembly engage and disengage the gears and sprocket on the transmission output shaft. Gear shifting is done by the shift forks, which are guided by cam grooves in the shift drum.

It is important that the shift drum grooves, shift forks and mating shift fork grooves be in good condition. Excessive wear between the parts causes unreliable and poor engagement of the gears. This can lead to premature wear of the engagement dogs and other parts. Refer to **Figure 15**. Replace worn or damaged parts.

Inspection and Repair

1. Clean all parts in solvent and dry with compressed air.
2. Inspect the shift drum for the following:
   a. Worn shift drum grooves (A, **Figure 39**). Worn grooves can prevent complete gear engagement, which can cause wear on the engagement dogs and recesses.
   b. Worn or damaged load-bearing surfaces (B, **Figure 39**). Fit the shift drum into each crankcase half and check for play or binding. Make sure the guide pin (C, **Figure 39**) is not damaged or broken.
   c. Broken spring (A, **Figure 40**) and shift drum stopper assembly. Make sure the spring is tight to the shift drum. Inspect the stopper ball and spring for damage. Make sure the area between the depressions (B, **Figure 40**) in the shift drum is not worn.

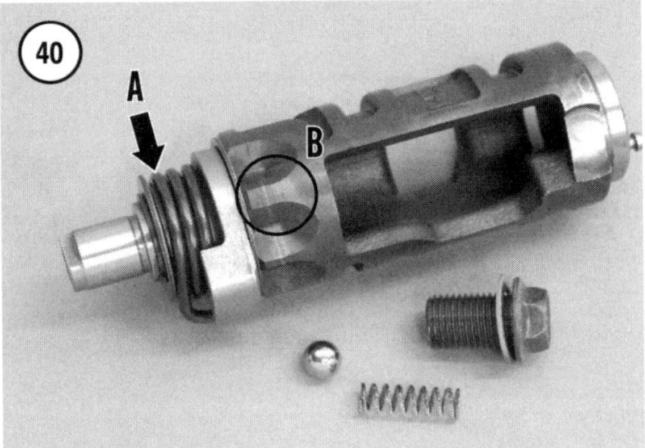

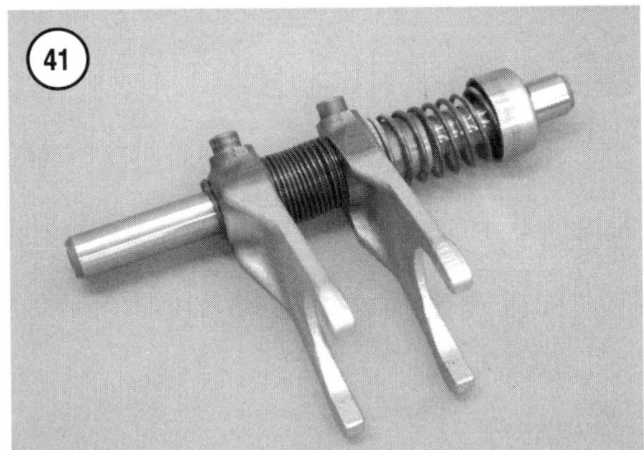

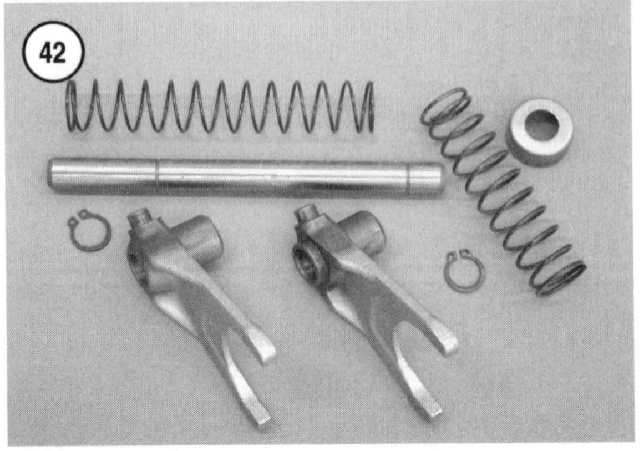

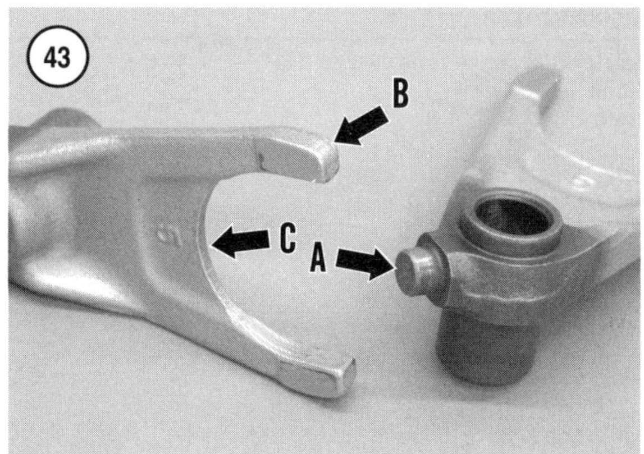

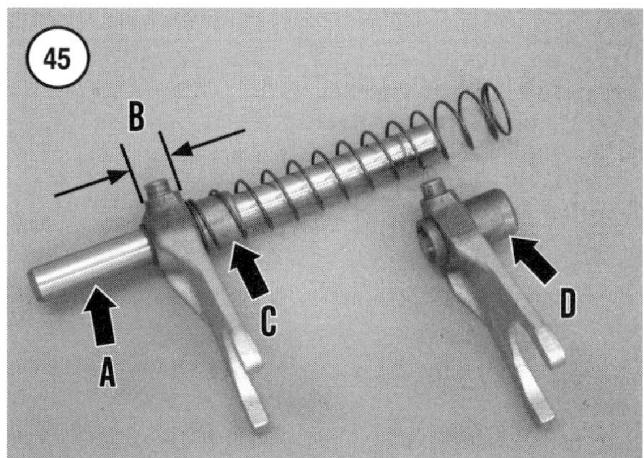

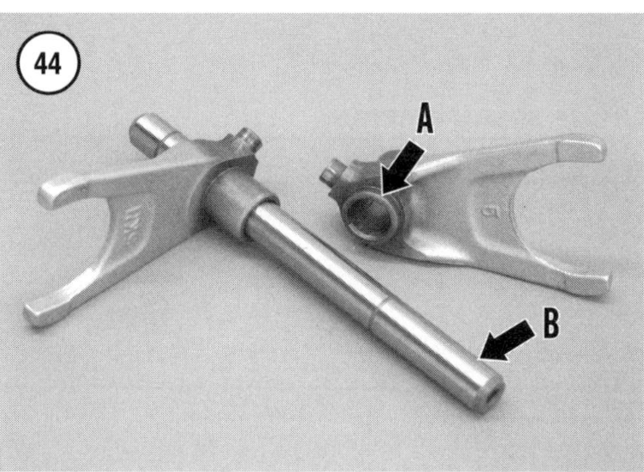

3. If the shift fork assembly (**Figure 41**) is in good condition, it is not necessary to disassemble the parts. If parts are worn, or if the cause of poor shifting is unknown, remove the snap rings and disassemble the parts (**Figure 42**). Inspect and assemble the parts in the following steps.
4. Inspect the shift forks for the following:
   a. Guide pin (A, **Figure 43**). Make sure the pin is symmetrical and not flat on the side. Make sure the pin passes through its mating groove on the shift drum without binding or excessive looseness.
   b. Shift fork claw (B, **Figure 43**). Make sure the claw is not worn. A polished appearance at the contact points is normal.
   c. Shift fork radius (C, **Figure 43**). Make sure the radius and sides are not worn. If wear is evident, the fork is binding in the shift fork groove. This could be caused by a worn or damaged fork bore, fork shaft, shift drum or gear.
5. Inspect the shift fork bore (A, **Figure 44**) and shaft (B). Make sure the bore is smooth and the fork slides and pivots smoothly on the shaft. There should be no excessive play or tightness. Make sure the shaft rolls freely on a flat surface and the shaft surface is free of galling, scoring or pitting.
6. Inspect the springs and shaft cap for damage.
7. Assemble the shift fork assembly. Install new snap rings. In substep c, all remaining parts are installed, compressed and locked onto the shaft. Have the parts and snap ring oriented before doing substep c.
   a. Install a new snap ring at the left end of the shaft. This end has the greatest distance from the snap ring groove to the end of the shaft (A, **Figure 45**). Install the snap ring with the sharp edge facing the end of the shaft.
   b. Install shift fork 2 and the longer spring onto the shaft. Shift fork 2 is wider near the guide pin than shift fork 1 (B, **Figure 45**). Make sure the spring fits over the shift fork boss (C, **Figure 45**).
   c. Install shift fork 1, the shorter spring (marked with white paint), cap and snap ring. Make sure the spring fits over the shift fork boss (D, **Figure 45**). Install the snap ring with the sharp edge facing the end of the shaft.
   d. Make sure the assembly appears as in **Figure 46** and **Figure 41**.
8. Install the parts as described in Chapter Five.

Table 1 and Table 2 are on the following page.

Table 1 TRANSMISSION SPECIFICATIONS

Type	V-belt automatic with reverse
Primary reduction system	V-belt
Secondary reduction system	Shaft drive
Secondary reduction ratio	
2002 and 2003	7.944 (39/24 × 24/18 × 33/9)
2004-on	9.544 (41/21 × 24/18 × 33/9)
Subtransmission ratio	
2002 and 2003	
Low	2.466 (37/15)
High	1.474 (28/19)
2004-on	
Low	2.059 (35/17)
High	1.238 (26/21)
Reverse gear ratio	1.471 (25/17)
Output shaft runout	0.03 mm (0.001 in.)

Table 2 TRANSMISSION TORQUE SPECIFICATIONS

	N•m	in.-lb.	ft.-lb.
Lower shift lever bolt	14	–	10
Select lever shift rod locknut	15	–	11
Select lever unit mounting bolts	25	–	18
Shift arm pivot bolt	14	–	10
Shift drum stopper bolt	14	–	10
Shift lever cover bolts	10	89	–

CHAPTER EIGHT

FUEL SYSTEM

This chapter covers the fuel system.

Refer to Chapter Three for air filter service, throttle cable adjustment and cable lubrication.

Refer to **Table 1** at the end of the chapter for carburetor specifications. When working on the fuel system, observe the safety practices described in Chapter One.

CARBURETOR

Operation

The Mikuni BSR is a vacuum-controlled, or constant velocity, carburetor. It uses both a throttle valve and diaphragm-operated slide to regulate fuel to the engine. The throttle valve (**Figure 1**) is on the output side of the carburetor and is connected to the throttle cable. It is not connected to any fuel-regulating device. The slide and diaphragm assembly, located at the center of the carburetor (A, **Figure 2**), regulates fuel by a jet needle at the bottom of the slide. The diaphragm is sealed at the top of the carburetor by the vacuum chamber cover (B, **Figure 2**). The diaphragm divides and seals the large chamber into a lower and upper chamber.

During operation, when the throttle valve is opened, air demand and speed through the carburetor is increased. As air passes under the slide, air pressure drops in that area. This low air pressure is vented to the upper diaphragm chamber. The lower diaphragm chamber is vented to atmospheric pressure. This difference in pressure causes the slide and jet needle to rise, allowing fuel to pass into the carburetor throat. When the throttle valve is closed, the pressure differential lowers, allowing the slide and jet needle to lower.

System Functions

Common factors that affect carburetor performance are altitude, temperature and engine load. Before disassembling the carburetor, understand the function of the pilot, needle and main jet systems. If the engine is not running or performing up to expectations, check the following before adjusting or replacing the components in the carburetor:

1. Throttle cable. Make sure the cable is not dragging and is correctly adjusted.
2. Choke. Make sure the choke fully opens and closes.
3. Fuel flow. Make sure fuel is adequately flowing from the fuel tank to the carburetor.
4. Air filter. Make sure the filter is clean.
5. Ignition timing. Check that timing is correct.
6. Muffler. Make sure the muffler is not restricting flow.
7. Brakes. Make sure the brake pads are not dragging on the discs.

Pilot jet

The pilot system controls the air/fuel mixture from closed throttle to about one-fourth throttle. By one-fourth throttle, its effectiveness is diminished and the jet needle system becomes the primary source for the air/fuel mixture. The pilot system consists of the pilot air jet, pilot jet and pilot mixture screw. Air enters the pilot system through the pilot air jet (A, **Figure 3**). The pilot jet (A, **Figure 4**) draws fuel from the float chamber and mixes it with the air from the pilot air jet. The atomized air/fuel mixture passes to the pilot mixture screw (B, **Figure 4**), where it is regulated and discharged into the carburetor throat. Turning the pilot mixture screw in *leans* the air/fuel mixture entering the engine, and turning the screw out *richens* the mixture.

Jet needle

The jet needle (**Figure 5**) is connected to the slide and controls the mixture from approximately one-fourth to three-fourths throttle. Air enters the main air jet (B, **Figure 3**), where it passes to the needle jet holder (C, **Figure 4**). The needle jet holder mixes fuel from the float chamber with the air from the main air jet. The atomized air/fuel mixture passes to the needle jet, where it is regulated by the jet needle into the throat of the carburetor. As the throttle is opened, the needle rises and fuel is regulated by the needle taper. The vertical position of the needle in the slide is adjustable to increase (richen) or decrease (lean) fuel flow from the needle jet (**Figure 6**).

Main jet

The main jet (D, **Figure 4**) is located at the end of the needle jet holder. From approximately three-fourths to full throttle, the main jet becomes effective and controls the air/fuel mixture.

Choke

The choke system or starter bypass consists of a plunger assembly (**Figure 7**) and a starter jet (E, **Figure 4**). The jet passes fuel to an orifice that can be opened and closed by the plunger needle. When the choke is operated, the plunger needle is withdrawn from the fuel orifice and also opens an air passage. As the engine is cranked, a rich air/fuel mixture is drawn into the carburetor throat. When closed, the choke plunger blocks the air and fuel passages.

This type of choke is most effective if the throttle remains closed during startup to maintain high vacuum at the air and fuel passages.

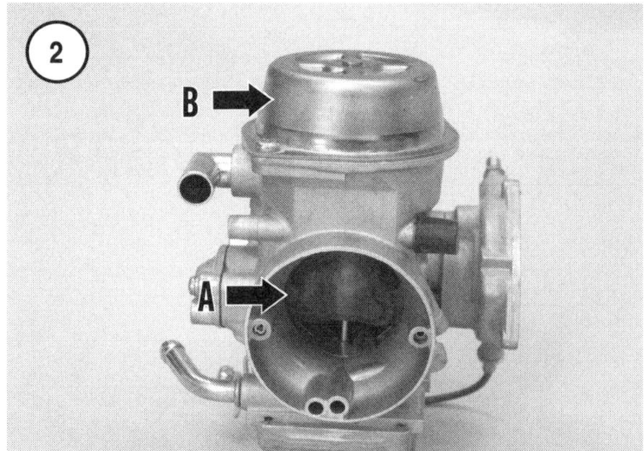

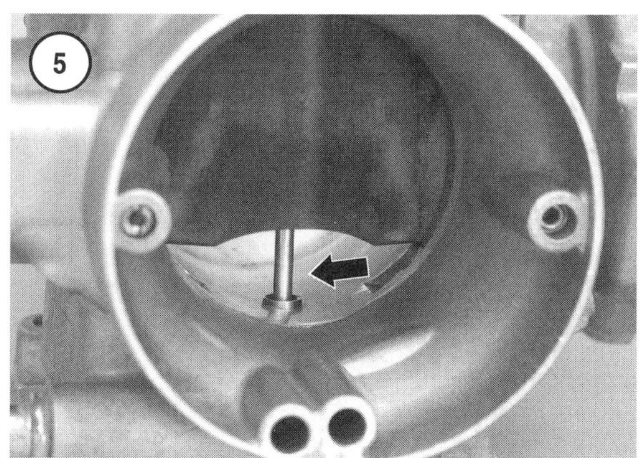

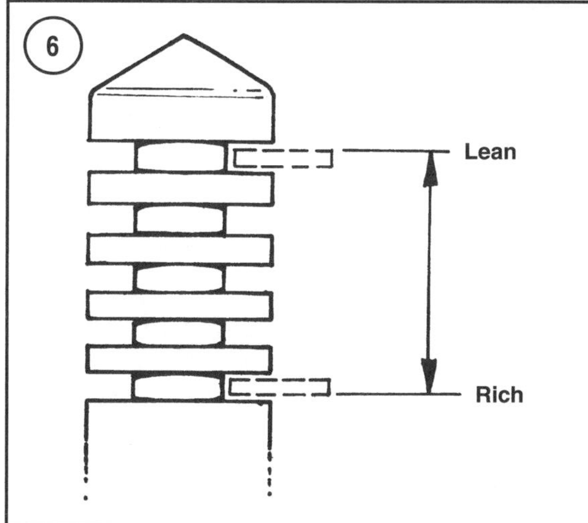

Air cutoff valve

The function of the air cutoff valve (**Figure 8**) is to richen the pilot jet system air/fuel mixture during compression braking, such as descending steep grades, when the engine speed is high, but the throttle is closed. Without this valve, the engine will develop a lean air/fuel mixture in the pilot system, which will cause backfiring and possibly engine damage. The air cutoff valve consists of a diaphragm, spring and cover. The function of the assembly is to open and close an air passage in the diaphragm chamber. The passage is linked to the pilot system.

During acceleration and steady running speeds, the diaphragm plunger keeps the passage open. During deceleration, when the throttle valve is closed, engine vacuum vents to the air cutoff valve cover. The vacuum pulls the diaphragm out, closing the passage in the chamber. This reduces the amount of air going to the pilot jet system, and a rich fuel mixture is discharged into the throat of the carburetor.

When acceleration resumes, the vacuum holding the diaphragm out is reduced, and the spring pushes the diaphragm down, again creating a normal fuel mixture in the pilot jet system.

8

Removal and Installation

1. Park the machine on level ground.
2. Remove the seat, fuel tank side panels, fuel tank and pan (Chapter Sixteen).
3. Remove the carburetor vent hose and the drain hose.
4. Loosen the clamps and position the carburetor so the choke and throttle cables can be disconnected conveniently.
5. At the left side of the carburetor, remove the choke plunger (**Figure 9**). If necessary, remove and inspect the plunger as described in this chapter.
6. At the right side of the carburetor, remove the throttle cable as follows:
   a. Remove the throttle valve cover (**Figure 10**).
   b. At the handlebar, loosen the cable locknut (A, **Figure 11**) and turn the adjuster (B) in to create slack in the cable.
   c. Turn the throttle valve clockwise and lock it in place to ease removal of the cable holder. A small bolt (A, **Figure 12**) works well to hold the throttle valve in position.
   d. Twist and pull the cable holder (B, **Figure 12**) from the cable end.

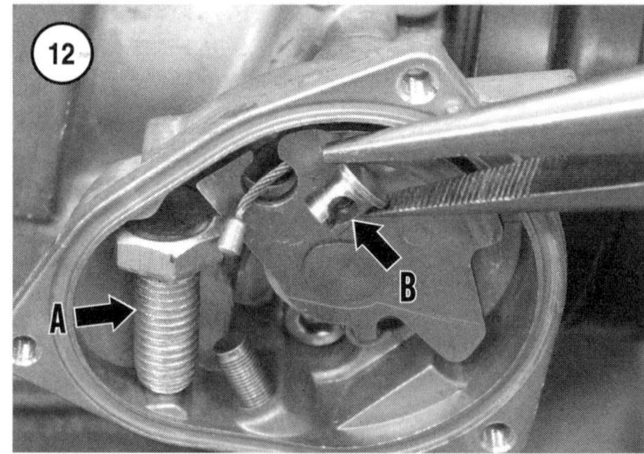

e. Loosen the locknut (A, **Figure 13**) and remove the cable adjuster (B) from the carburetor.

7. Loosen the clamps from the air filter housing duct and intake duct.

8. Remove the carburetor.

9. Reverse this procedure to install the carburetor. Note the following:

a. If necessary, set the pilot mixture screw to its initial setting.

b. Clean and lightly lubricate the inside edges of the ducts so the carburetor will easily seat. The intake tube is notched to mate with the intake manifold and carburetor (**Figure 14**). Check that all parts mate correctly.

c. Check that the notch in each clamp is correctly engaged with its rubber mount.

d. Check the fuel, vent and drain hose routing.

e. Inspect and adjust the throttle cable (Chapter Three).

f. Check the carburetor for leaks.

g. If necessary, adjust the idle speed and pilot mixture screw settings (Chapter Three).

Disassembly and Assembly

During disassembly, keep all parts identified and organized. Refer to **Figure 15**.

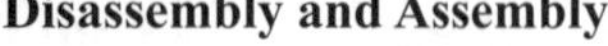

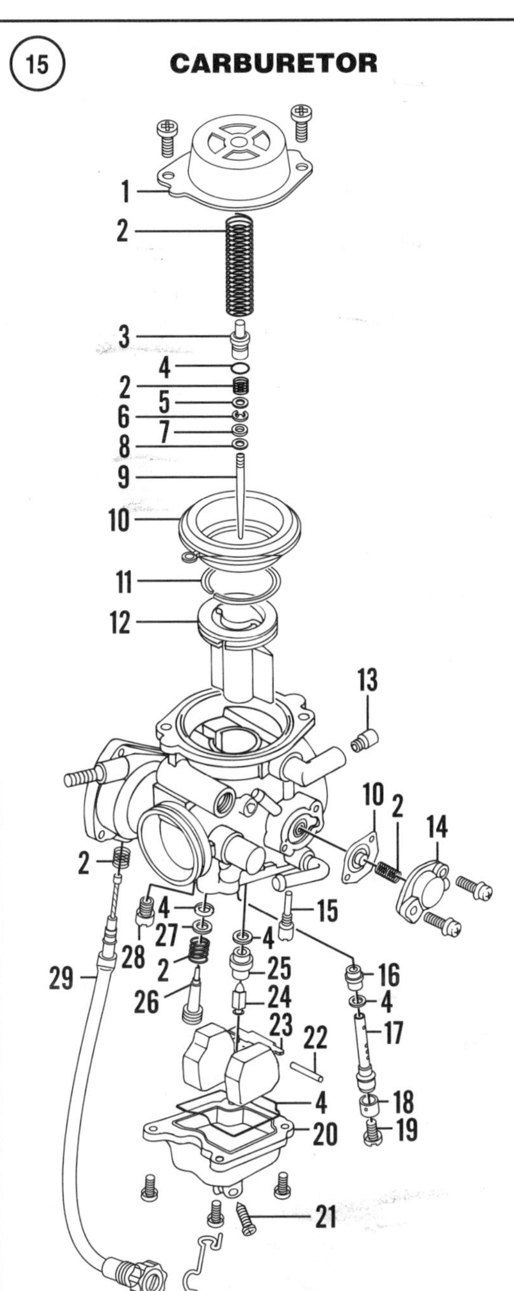

1. Vacuum chamber cover
2. Spring
3. Jet needle stopper
4. O-ring
5. Washer (thick)
6. E-clip
7. Spacer
8. Washer (thin)
9. Jet needle
10. Diaphragm
11. Ring
12. Slide
13. Pilot air jet
14. Air cutoff valve cover
15. Pilot jet
16. Needle jet
17. Needle jet holder
18. Main jet baffle
19. Main jet
20. Float chamber
21. Drain screw
22. Pin
23. Float
24. Float valve
25. Float valve seat
26. Pilot mixture screw
27. Washer
28. Starter (choke) jet
29. Throttle stop screw

1. Remove the carburetor as described in this section.
2. Remove the diaphragm cover and slide assembly as follows:
   a. Remove the cover (**Figure 16**). The cover is under slight spring pressure. Hold the cover in place while removing the screws. Then lift off the cover.
   b. Remove the spring (**Figure 17**).
   c. From the intake side, push up on the slide and lift it from the carburetor (**Figure 18**).

CAUTION

Do not lift or hold the slide by the diaphragm. Do not allow the jet needle to

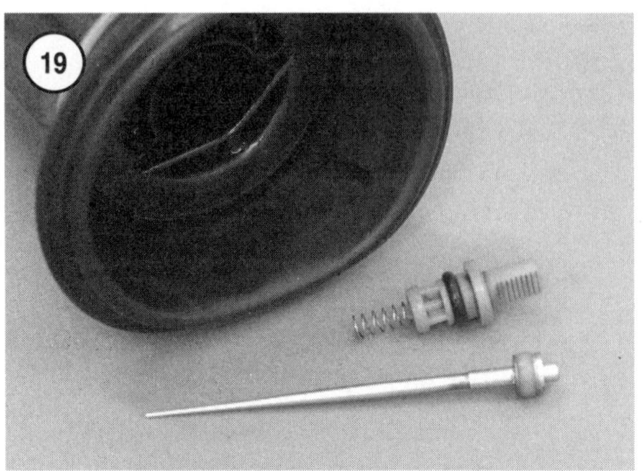

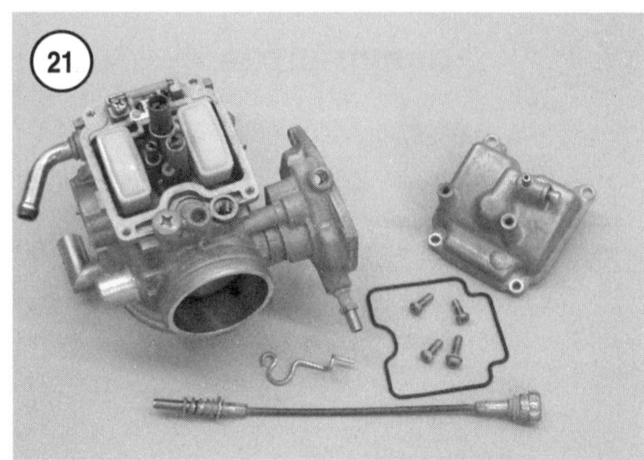

get damaged as it is raised and handled.

d. Remove the jet needle stopper from the slide. Then remove the jet needle assembly (**Figure 19**). Note the position of the clip on the jet needle. Removing the clip is not necessary; however, if a new needle is required, the clip should be installed in its original position.

3. Remove the air cutoff valve cover, spring and diaphragm (**Figure 20**). The cover is under spring pressure. Hold the cover in place while removing the screws.

4. Remove the throttle stop screw, holder and float chamber (**Figure 21**). Remove the drain screw and O-ring from the chamber.

5. Remove and disassemble the float assembly as follows:

   a. Remove the pin retaining screw (**Figure 22**).
   b. Carefully lift out the float, pin and float valve (**Figure 23**).
   c. Slide the clip and float valve off the float tab.

6. Remove the float valve seat as follows:

   a. Remove the retaining screw (**Figure 24**).
   b. Twist and remove the float seat (**Figure 25**). Do not grip the seat inside the bore. Scratches in the seat will cause leaks past the float valve.

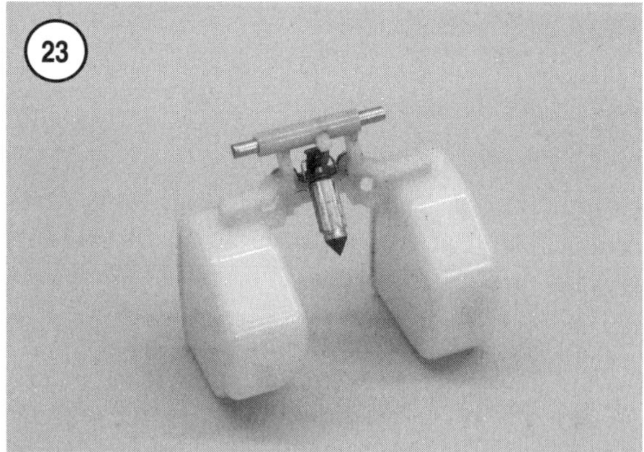

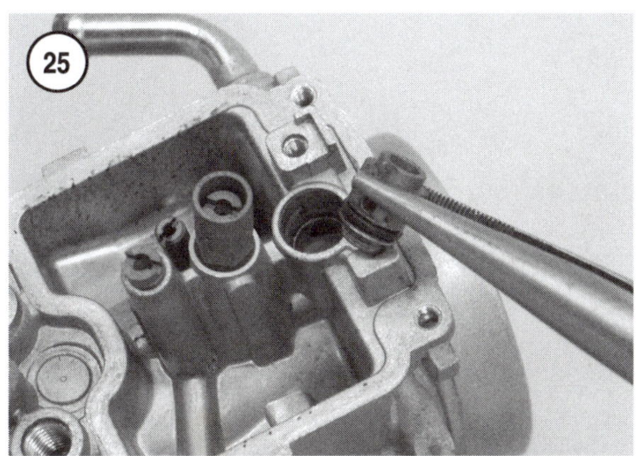

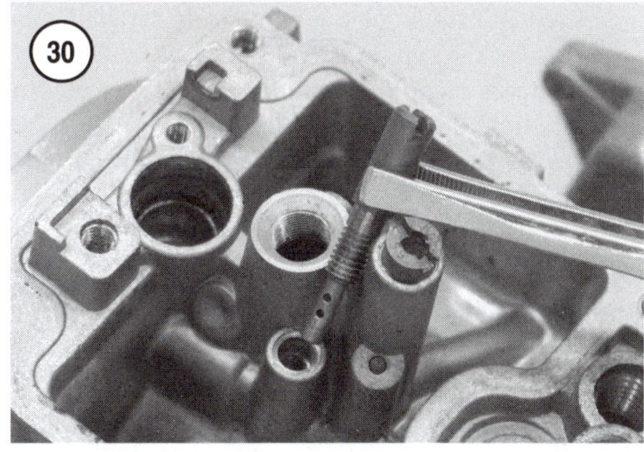

7. Remove the pilot mixture screw (**Figure 26**) as follows:
   a. If a plug is installed over the screw, remove the plug by drilling through it with a *small* drill bit. Do not use a bit larger than 1/8 in. A large drill bit might damage the pilot mixture screw and the internal threads. When drilling, use a light touch and mark the bit 1/4 in. from the end to indicate when to stop drilling. Thread a sheet metal screw into the hole. Then pull the plug from the bore.
   b. Make a scratch on the edge of the bore, in line with the slot in the screw. Use this scratch as a reference point when installing the screw.
   c. Turn the screw clockwise and accurately count the number of turns it takes to seat the screw into the carburetor.
   d. Record the number of turns.
   e. Remove the pilot mixture screw, spring, washer and O-ring.
8. Remove the main jet assembly as follows:
   a. Remove the main jet and baffle (**Figure 27**).
   b. Remove the needle jet holder (**Figure 28**).
   c. Remove the needle jet (**Figure 29**). Unseat the jet by hand. If necessary, use a wood or plastic dowel to help unseat the jet. Do not use tools that could scratch the inner surface of the jet.
9. Remove the pilot jet (**Figure 30**).

10. Remove the starter (choke) jet (**Figure 31**).
11. Remove the pilot air jet (**Figure 32**).
12. Clean and inspect the parts as described in this chapter.
13. Refer to *Carburetor, System Functions* in this chapter for the function of the jets and their affect on performance.
14. Reverse this procedure to assemble the carburetor. Note the following:
    a. Install new, lubricated O-rings.
    b. Do not confuse the starter jet and main jet. They are similar in appearance and fit in either location. The main jet has a *large* hole in its center.
    c. When installing the pilot mixture screw, lightly seat the screw. Then turn it out the number of turns recorded during disassembly. Refer to the reference mark on the carburetor for the original setting. If the number of turns is not known, refer to **Table 1** for the initial setting. Adjust the pilot mixture screw setting as described in *Engine Tune-Up* (Chapter Three).
    d. Attach the float valve and clip to the float before installing the parts.
    e. Check and adjust the float height. Refer to *Float Adjustment* in this chapter.
    f. Install the slide assembly and diaphragm cover last. When installing the slide assembly, the small O-ring tab on the diaphragm (**Figure 33**) must be seated in the edge of the carburetor before installing the cover.
    g. Install the carburetor as described in this chapter.

Cleaning and Inspection

Use a cleaner specifically for carburetors. Do not use a cleaner on rubber and plastic parts that will damage them. Follow the manufacturer's instructions when using the cleaner.

CAUTION
Do not clean the jet orifices or seats with wire or drill bits. These items can scratch the surfaces and alter the air/fuel mixture, or cause leaks.

1. Clean the carburetor. Use compressed air to clean all passages, orifices and vents in the carburetor body.
2. Inspect the main jet (A, **Figure 34**), needle jet assembly (B), pilot air jet (C), starter (choke) jet (D) and pilot jet (E). Check that all holes are clean and undamaged.
3. Inspect the pilot mixture screw assembly and choke plunger (**Figure 35**).

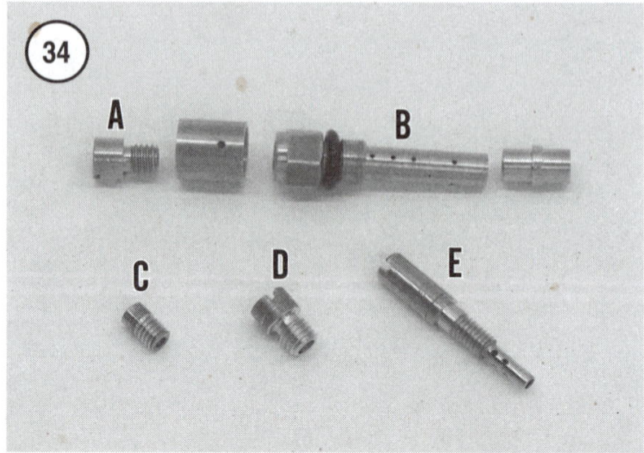

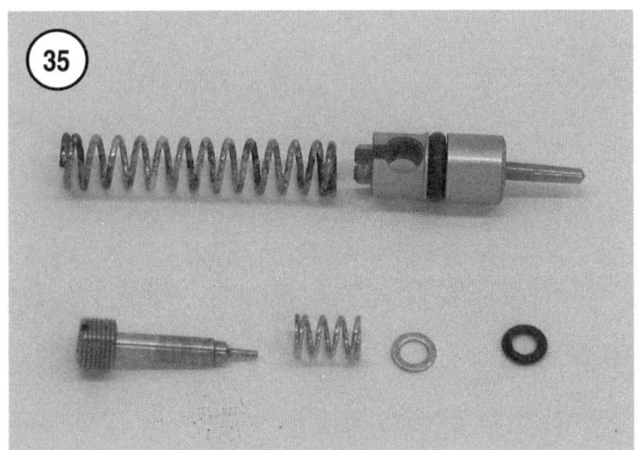
35

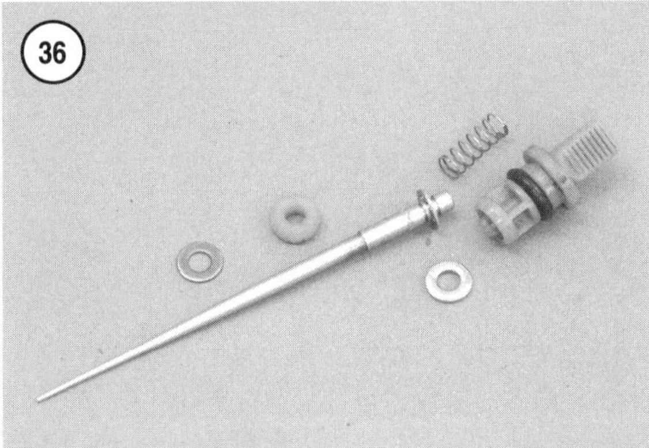
36

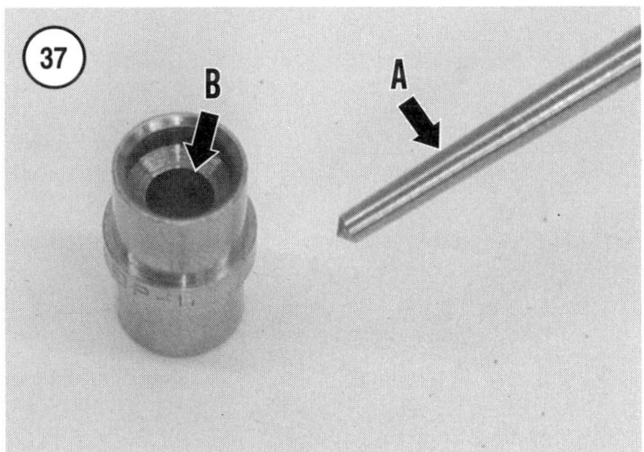

37

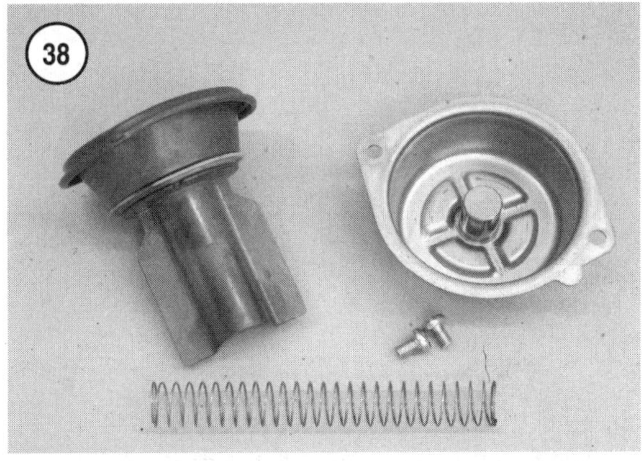
38

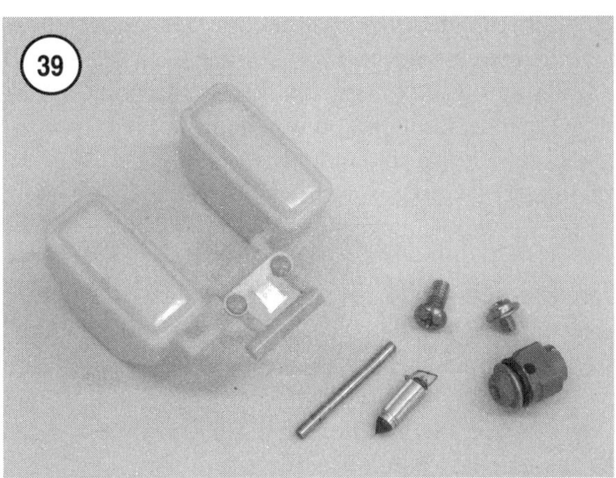
39

a. Inspect the screw and plunger tips for dents or wear.
b. Make sure the spring coils are resilient and not crushed.

4. Inspect the jet needle assembly (**Figure 36**). Make sure the jet needle is smooth, straight and evenly tapered. If the needle (A, **Figure 37**) or needle jet (B) is stepped, dented, worn or bent, replace the parts.

5. Inspect the diaphragm, slide, vacuum chamber cover and spring (**Figure 38**).

a. Inspect the slide for wear and scratches. Fit the slide into the carburetor body and check for smooth vertical operation. Make sure the slide has minimal front-to-back play.
b. Inspect the diaphragm for dryness, tears and holes. The diaphragm *must* be undamaged in order to isolate the pressure differences that are above and below the diaphragm. A leaking diaphragm will prevent the slide from reaching/maintaining its normal level, for any throttle position off idle. Engine performance will be noticeably diminished.
c. The vacuum chamber cover *must* be undamaged in order to maintain low pressure in the upper chamber of the carburetor. A bent sealing area or loose cover will affect engine performance similarly to a damaged diaphragm.

6. Inspect the float and float valve assembly (**Figure 39**).

a. Inspect the rubber tip of the float valve (A, **Figure 40**). If it is stepped or dented, replace the float valve.
b. Lightly press on the spring-loaded pin (B, **Figure 40**) in the float valve. Make sure the pin easily moves in and out of the valve. If it is varnished with fuel residue, replace the float valve.
c. Inspect the float valve seat. Make sure the seat is clean and scratch-free. If it is not, the float valve will not seat properly and the carburetor will overflow.

   d. Inspect the float and pin. Submerge the float in water and check for leaks. Replace the float if water or fuel is evident inside the float. Check that the float pin is straight and smooth. It must be a slip-fit in the float.
7. Inspect the float chamber assembly (**Figure 41**).
   a. Make sure all residue is removed from the interior of the bowl.
   b. Inspect screw threads for damage.
   c. Inspect the tip of the drain screw. If damaged, the drain screw will allow fuel to pass out the drain.
   d. Inspect the overflow tube for cleanliness.
8. Inspect the air cutoff valve assembly.
   a. The diaphragm (**Figure 42**) must be free of damage in order to operate properly.
   b. Make sure the pin on the back of the diaphragm is not worn.
   c. Make sure the air passages are clean.
9. Inspect the air cutoff valve chamber.
   a. Inspect the vent holes (A, **Figure 43**) and ball valve (B) for cleanliness.
   b. Make sure the ball valve moves freely. Apply light pressure to unseat the ball. Then release pressure. The spring-loaded ball should seat itself against the hole.

10. Inspect the throttle valve assembly. Make sure the spring (A, **Figure 44**) is clean and the cable holder is tight on the shaft (B). Make sure the throttle valve plate fully opens and closes and is tightly screwed to the shaft.

11. Inspect the throttle stop screw and cover assembly.
   a. Inspect the throttle stop screw (A, **Figure 45**) for straightness and thread damage. Make sure the spring coils (B, **Figure 45**) are resilient and not crushed.
   b. If damaged, replace the O-ring (C, **Figure 45**) on the cover.

Float Adjustment

The float (**Figure 39**) and float valve (**Figure 40**) maintain a constant fuel level in the float chamber. As fuel is used, the float lowers and allows more fuel past the valve. As the fuel level rises, the float closes the valve when the required fuel level is reached. If the float is out of adjustment, the fuel level will be too high or low. A low fuel level causes the engine to run too lean. A high fuel level causes the engine to run too rich. It may also cause fuel overflow.

1. Remove the carburetor as described in this section.
2. Remove the float chamber.
3. Lightly touch the float to ensure the float valve is seated.

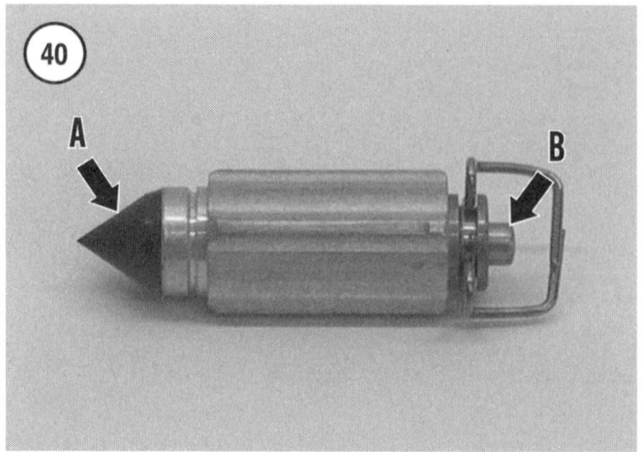

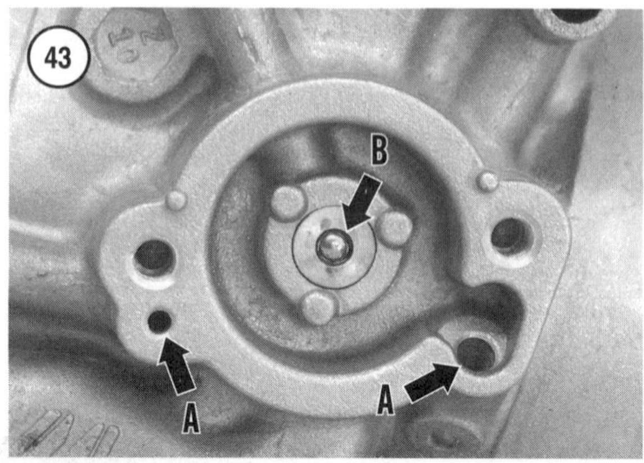

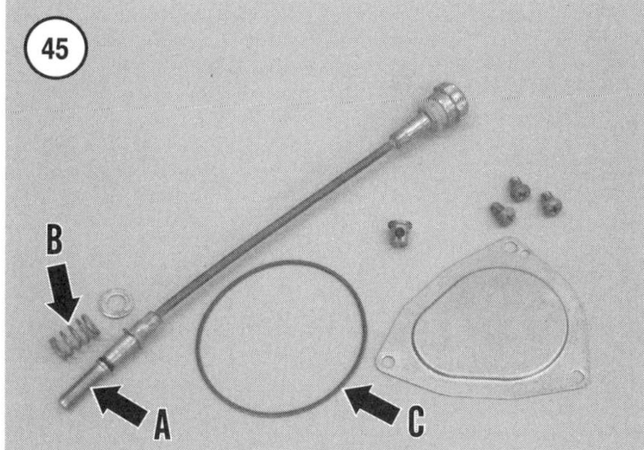

4. Lay the carburetor on its side so the float valve hangs freely. Tilt the carburetor until the tab on the float lightly *touches* the spring-loaded pin in the valve (**Figure 46**). The tab must not compress the pin.
5. Measure the distance from the carburetor gasket surface to the highest point on the float (**Figure 47**). Refer to **Table 1** for the float height.
6. If necessary, reset float height as follows:
   a. Remove the float assembly from the carburetor.
   b. Remove the float valve and clip.
   c. Bend the float tab in the appropriate direction to raise or lower the float. Use care when bending the tab to prevent breaking the plastic lugs or float.
   d. Assemble the float and recheck the height. Adjust, if necessary.
7. Install the float chamber.

FUEL VALVE

Removal, Inspection and Installation

1. Remove the seat, fuel tank side panels and fuel tank (Chapter Sixteen).
2. Drain the fuel from the tank.
3. Remove the screws securing the fuel valve to the tank, then pull the valve straight out of the tank.
4. If installed, remove the screw securing the fuel valve knob to the valve assembly (**Figure 48**).
5. Remove the screws from the cover plate (**Figure 49**).
6. Remove the plastic washer and outer valve (**Figure 50**). Note that the stem on the outer valve has an arrow that points forward.
7. Remove the wave washer and inner valve (**Figure 51**). Note that the inner valve has an arrow that points forward.
8. Remove the O-rings from the inner valve (A, **Figure 52**) and fuel valve body (B).
9. Clean and inspect the parts (**Figure 53**).

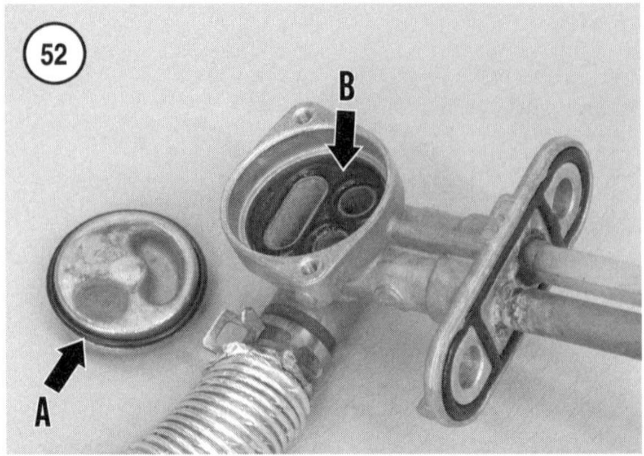

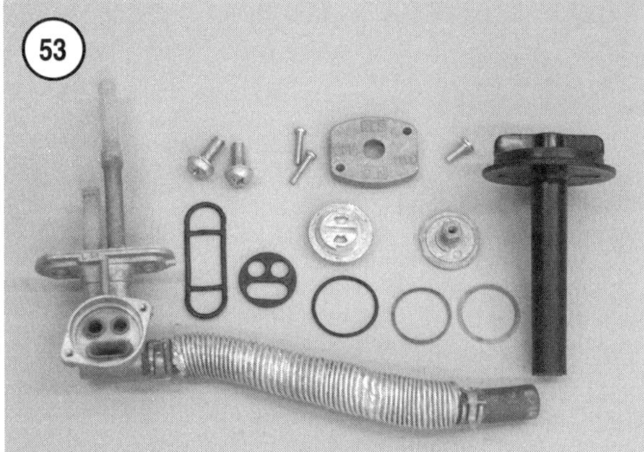

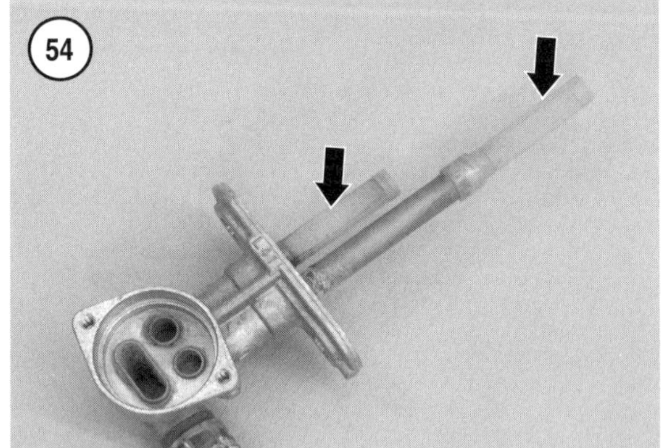

a. Look for buildup in the screen filters (**Figure 54**). If buildup is evident, lightly scrub the screens with a nylon brush and solvent. Carefully blow compressed air through the screen, from the inside to the outside.
b. Inspect and clean buildup from the valve passages.
c. Replace all O-rings.
d. The wave washer must be capable of applying pressure to the outer valve. If resistance is not felt when tightening the cover plate screws, the washer is fatigued and needs to be replaced.
e. Inspect the remaining parts for damage.

10. Assemble the valve. Note the following:

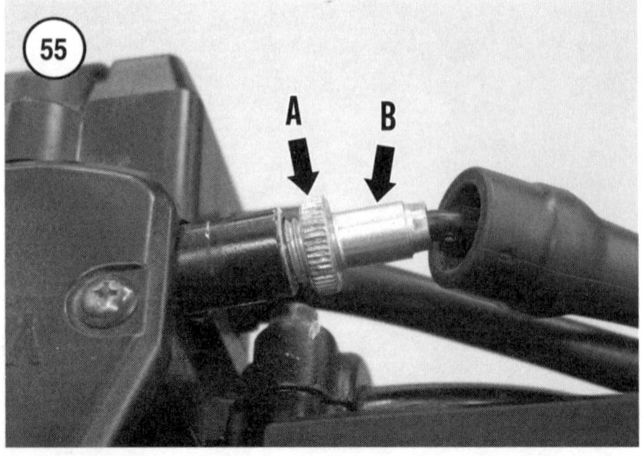

56

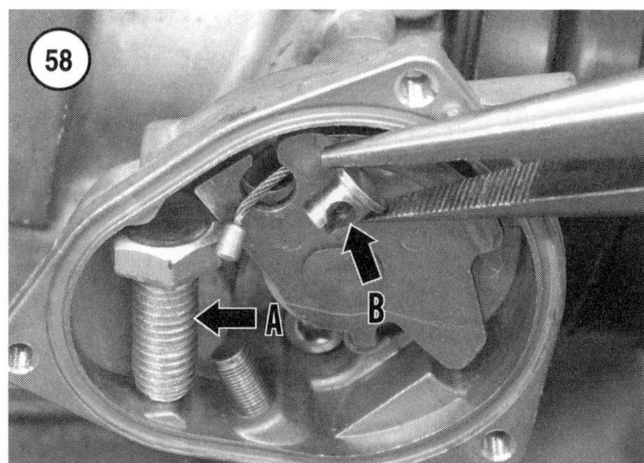

58

57

59

a. Lightly lubricate the O-rings.
b. Assemble the inner and outer valves so the arrows on the parts point forward.
c. Install the fuel valve into the fuel tank and equally tighten the screws.
d. Install the fuel valve knob and screw after the fuel tank is mounted onto the frame.

11. Install the bodywork (Chapter Sixteen).
12. When filling the tank, start with a small amount of fuel and check for leaks. Operate the fuel valve and check for leak-free operation.

THROTTLE CABLE REPLACEMENT

1. Park the machine on level ground.
2. Remove the seat, fuel tank side panels, fuel tank and pan (Chapter Sixteen).
3. At the handlebar, remove the cable as follows:
   a. Loosen the cable locknut (A, **Figure 55**) and turn the adjuster (B) in to create slack in the cable.
   b. Remove the throttle housing cover. Then remove the cable from the throttle lever (**Figure 56**).
   c. Turn the cable adjuster out and remove the cable from the handlebar.
4. At the carburetor, remove the throttle cable as follows:
   a. Loosen the clamps and position the carburetor so the throttle cable can be disconnected.
   b. Remove the throttle valve cover (**Figure 57**).
   c. Turn the throttle valve clockwise and lock it in place to ease removal of the cable holder. A small bolt (A, **Figure 58**) works well to hold the throttle valve in position.
   d. Twist and pull the cable holder (B, **Figure 58**) from the cable end (**Figure 58**).
   e. Loosen the locknut (A, **Figure 59**) and remove the cable adjuster (B) from the carburetor.
   f. Remove the cable from the carburetor.
5. Note how the cable is routed. Then pull the cable from the frame.
6. Reverse this procedure to install the new cable. Note the following:
   a. Clean the housings and levers before assembly.
   b. Follow the routing of the original cable.
   c. Lubricate the cable with aerosol cable lubricant. Lubricate the cable ends, lever and throttle valve guide with grease.
   d. Adjust the cable (Chapter Three).
   e. Install the bodywork after verifying proper adjustment and operation.

Table 1 is on the following page.

Table 1 CARBURETOR SPECIFICATIONS

Type	Mikuni BSR constant velocity
Bore diameter	42 mm
Fuel level	4.5 mm (0.18 in.) above float chamber gasket surface
Float height	13 mm (0.51 in.) above float chamber gasket surface (gasket removed)
Idle speed	1450-1550 rpm
Intake vacuum	30.7-33.3 kPa (9.07-9.83 in. Hg)
Jet needle	
Clip groove position	2
Number	6JP9-53-2
Main jet number	153.8
Needle jet number	O-0M
Pilot jet number	40
Pilot mixture screw	2 1/2 turns out (initial setting)
Starter jet number	55
Throttle valve number	105

CHAPTER NINE

ELECTRICAL SYSTEM

This chapter covers the electrical system:

Refer to **Table 1** and **Table 2** at the end of this chapter for specifications. Refer to Chapter One for electrical fundamentals. Refer to Chapter Two for general electrical testing.

ELECTRICAL COMPONENT REPLACEMENT

Most motorcycle dealerships and parts suppliers will not accept the return of any electrical part. If you cannot determine the exact cause of any electrical system malfunction, have a dealership retest that specific system to verify your test results. If you purchase a new electrical component(s) and then find that the system still does not work properly with the new part(s) installed, you will probably be unable to return the unit for a refund.

Consider any test results carefully before replacing a component that tests just *slightly* out of specification, especially for resistance. A number of variables can affect test results dramatically. These include: the testing meter's internal circuitry, ambient temperature and conditions under which the machine has been operated. All instructions and specifications have been checked for accuracy; however, successful test results depend to a great degree upon individual accuracy.

IGNITION AND CHARGING SYSTEM OPERATION

A permanent magnet alternator is located on the left end of the crankshaft, and is the source of energy used for charging the battery. The capacitor discharge ignition (CDI) system is powered by the battery. When the engine is cranking or running, current from the battery goes to the CDI unit and is stored in a capacitor. When the alternator rotor is in the correct position for ignition, the ignition pickup coil signals the CDI unit to release the stored charge to the coil. The charge of current into the coil primary windings induces a much higher voltage in the secondary windings, which fires the spark plug.

When the engine is running, the current produced by the alternator is sent to the regulator/rectifier. The power is converted to direct current and regulated to the battery by the regulator/rectifier.

ALTERNATOR COVER

Removal and Installation

The stator and pickup coil are mounted on the inside of the alternator cover.

1. Remove the seat, left fuel tank side panel, engine side cover and left footrest panel (Chapter Sixteen).
2. Drain the engine oil (Chapter Three).
3. Drain the coolant (Chapter Three).
4. Remove the water pump (Chapter Ten).
5. Remove the recoil starter (**Figure 1**) as described in Chapter Five.
6. Remove the starter pulley (**Figure 2**) as described in Chapter Five.
7. Disconnect the stator and pickup coil leads (A, **Figure 3**). Then remove the bolts (B, **Figure 3**) from the perimeter of the cover.
8. Pull the alternator cover away from the engine. Magnetic resistance will be felt as the cover is unseated.

WARNING

Keep your fingers away from the edge of the cover to avoid pinching them.

9. Remove the cover gasket and account for the two cover dowels (**Figure 4**).
10. Remove and/or test the stator and pickup coil as described in this chapter.
11. Reverse this procedure to install the stator and alternator cover. Note the following:
    a. Lubricate the gears, shafts and bearings with engine oil.
    b. Install a new cover gasket.
    c. Apply sealant to the electrical lead grommet. Then seat the lead into the cover.
    d. Make sure all wires are routed correctly and secured.
    e. Clean the electrical connections. Then apply dielectric grease to the connectors when assembling the cover.
    f. Working in a crossing pattern, tighten the alternator cover bolts to 10 N•m (89 in.-lb.).

STATOR AND PICKUP COIL

Removal and Installation

The stator and pickup coil are mounted on the inside of the alternator cover. The stator and pickup coil can be tested without removing them from the cover. Refer to *Charging System* and *Ignition System* in this chapter.

1. Remove the alternator cover as described in this chapter.
2. Remove the three screws from the stator (**Figure 5**).

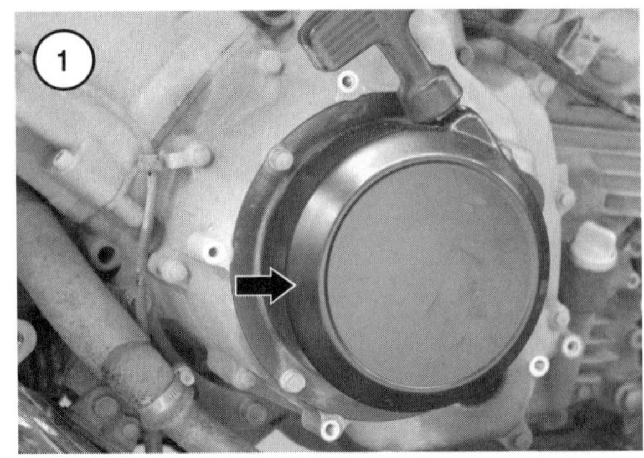

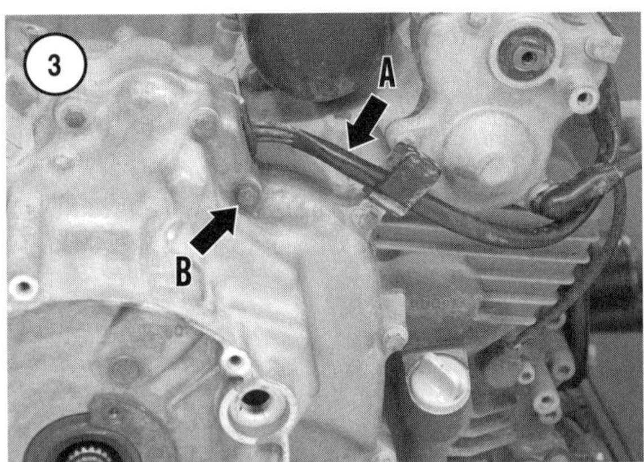

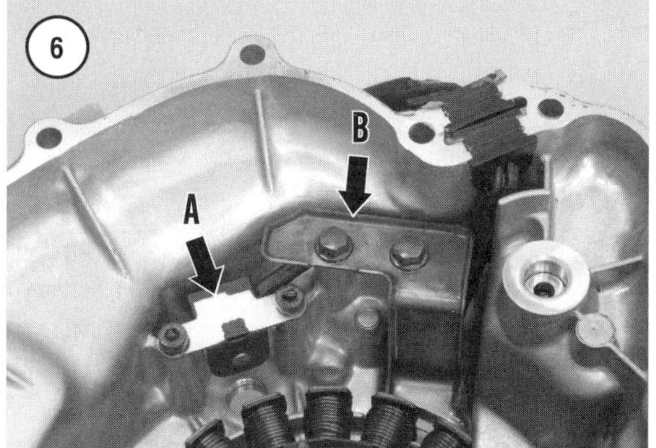

3. Remove the two bolts from the pickup coil (A, **Figure 6**).
4. Remove the wiring harness clamp (B, **Figure 6**) from the cover.
5. Remove the wire grommet from the cover. Then remove the parts.
6. Reverse this procedure to install the stator and pickup coil. Note the following:
   a. Apply threadlocking compound to the bolt and screw threads.
   b. Tighten the stator, clamp and pickup coil fasteners to 10 N•m (89 in.-lb.).

9

ROTOR, STARTER CLUTCH AND STARTER GEARS

The starter clutch is mounted on the back of the rotor. The clutch is engaged with the starter gear during engine cranking, then disengages when the engine starts. The rotor must be removed to access the starter clutch, starter gear and starter idle gear.

The starter clutch can be checked for freewheel and lockup without removing the rotor. To check the clutch, turn the starter gear *clockwise* (**Figure 7**). The gear should turn freely and smoothly in that direction. Try to turn the gear *counterclockwise*. The gear should not turn when the rotor is held stationary. If the gear turns in both directions or is always locked up, disassemble and inspect the clutch assembly.

Removal and Installation

A rotor puller (Yamaha part No. YM-01404) (**Figure 8**), or three-leg puller, is required to remove the rotor assembly from the crankshaft. The two-part puller is threaded onto the rotor (**Figure 9**). Then the drawbolt is tightened to remove the rotor. If a three-leg puller (**Figure 10**) is used, the three bolts are equally threaded into holes in the rotor. After the puller is squarely mounted, the drawbolt is tightened to remove the rotor.

10

11

1. Remove the alternator cover as described in this chapter.
2. Remove the rotor as follows:
   a. To help removal, spray penetrating lubricant into the rotor bore and Woodruff key area. Apply grease to the end and threads of the rotor puller.
   b. Thread the outer part of the puller onto the rotor threads. Then thread the drawbolt into the puller. Seat the drawbolt against the end of the crankshaft (**Figure 9**).
   c. Hold the puller with a wrench and tighten the drawbolt to loosen the rotor (**Figure 11**). Use wrenches that provide high leverage. Jam the holding wrench against the footboard mounts for easier handling of the removal wrench.
   d. Remove the rotor.
3. Remove the Woodruff key (**Figure 12**) and starter gear.
4. Remove the washer (**Figure 13**) from the crankshaft.
5. Remove the starter idle gear, bearing and shaft (**Figure 14**).
6. Inspect and lubricate the parts (**Figure 15**) as described in this section.
7. Reverse this procedure to install the rotor, starter clutch and starter gears. Note the following:
   a. Make sure the starter gear is installed with the clutch contact area facing out.
   b. The rotor must be lightly seated on the crankshaft before installing the alternator cover. If the rotor is not seated, it will slide to the end of the crankshaft and magnetize itself to the stator as the alternator cover is being installed. To prevent this, temporarily install the starter pulley and tighten it against the rotor. Remove the starter pulley after the rotor is adequately seated.

12

13

Inspection

1. Inspect the clutch for proper operation as follows:

14

15

16

17

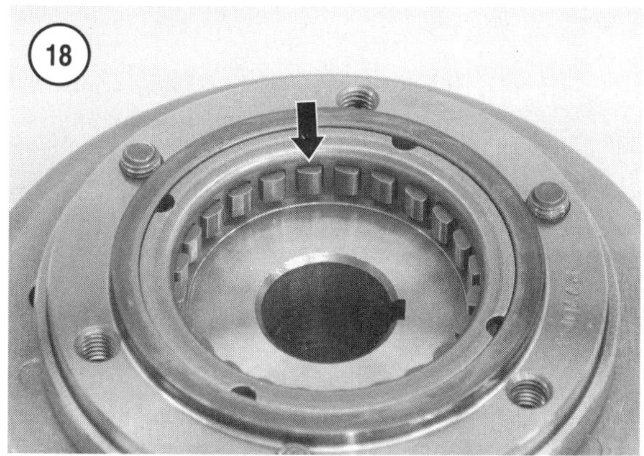
18

19

a. With the starter gear facing up, turn the gear *counterclockwise*. The gear should turn freely and smoothly in that direction (**Figure 16**).

b. Try to turn the gear *clockwise*. The gear should lock.

c. If the gear turns in both directions or is always locked up, disassemble and inspect the clutch assembly.

2. Remove the starter gear from the rotor. Turn the gear counterclockwise and twist it squarely away from the rotor.

3. Clean and inspect the starter gear, clutch and idle gear assembly.

a. Inspect the starter gear teeth (A, **Figure 17**), bushing (B) and sprag contact area for wear or damage.

b. Inspect the clutch sprags (**Figure 18**). Make sure they are clean, undamaged and operate smoothly. If the clutch is damaged, replace the clutch as described in Step 4.

CAUTION

The starter clutch sprags can potentially be damaged if the engine kicks back, particularly at engine startup. Crankshaft reversal puts a high load on the sprags. To minimize potential damage to the sprags, keep the starter button engaged until the engine is definitely started.

c. Inspect the starter idle gear (A, **Figure 19**), bearing (B) and shaft (C). Fit the bearing and shaft into the gear and check for play or roughness.

4. If the clutch is damaged, remove the clutch from the rotor as follows:

a. Remove the starter clutch mounting bolts (**Figure 20**). Then remove the clutch assembly from the rotor.

b. Install the new clutch assembly. Install the clutch so the arrow is visible and facing away from the rotor. The arrow will point clockwise.

c. Apply threadlocking compound to the bolts. Then tighten the starter clutch mounting bolts equally in several passes to 30 N•m (22 ft.-lb.).

5. Inspect the rotor.

a. Inspect the magnetic wall (A, **Figure 21**) of the rotor for cracks and damage.

WARNING

Replace the rotor if it is damaged. The rotor material can shatter at high crankshaft speeds and cause injury and/or engine damage.

b. Inspect the bore (B, **Figure 21**), keyway and threads for damage.

c. Inspect the interior and exterior of the rotor for debris and damage . The strip on the outside of the rotor (C, **Figure 21**) must not be damaged.

d. Inspect the Woodruff key and washer for damage.

NOTE

If the Woodruff key is bent or sheared, the rotor will not be properly aligned on the crankshaft, causing the engine to be out of time.

6. Inspect the crankshaft. Inspect the splines (A, **Figure 22**), keyway (B) and taper (C) for damage.
7. Lubricate the bearing, shaft, gears and clutch sprags with engine oil.
8. Install the parts as described in this section.

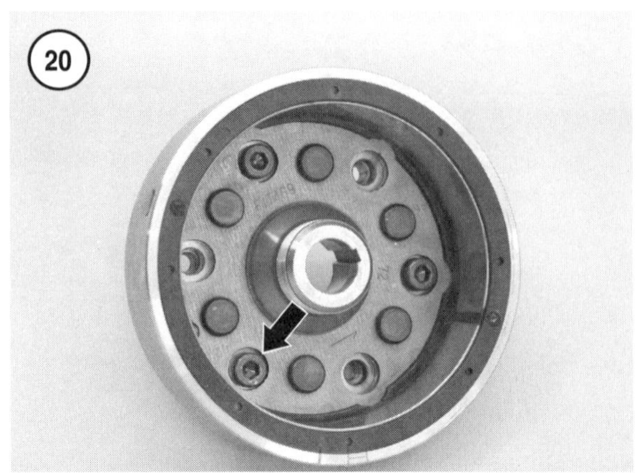

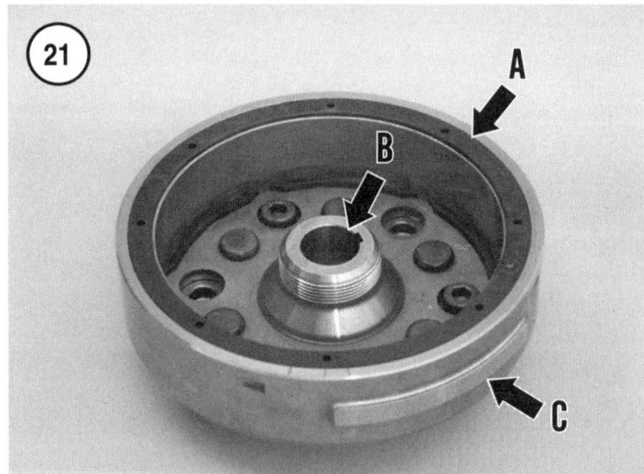

STARTER

Removal and Installation

Refer to **Figure 23**.

1. Remove the seat and fuel tank side panels (Chapter Sixteen).
2. Disconnect the negative cable from the battery.
3. Disconnect the positive cable from the starter (A, **Figure 24**).
4. Remove the mounting bolts (B, **Figure 24**). Using a length of wood, tap the starter out of the crankcase. Do not directly strike the starter. The starter is sealed to the cover by an O-ring, which will cause resistance during removal.
5. Disassemble, inspect and test the starter as described in this section.
6. Reverse this procedure to install the starter. Note the following:

a. Lubricate the O-ring on the starter end cover before inserting it into the crankcase.

b. Make sure the fiber washers on the cable post are in good condition. The washers must insulate the cable from the starter housing.

c. Clean all cable connections. Then apply dielectric grease to fittings and connectors before tightening.

d. Tighten the starter mounting bolts to 8 N•m (71 in.-lb.).

Disassembly and Assembly

Refer to **Figure 23**.

1. Note the alignment marks on the housing and end covers (**Figure 25**). Then remove the two hous-

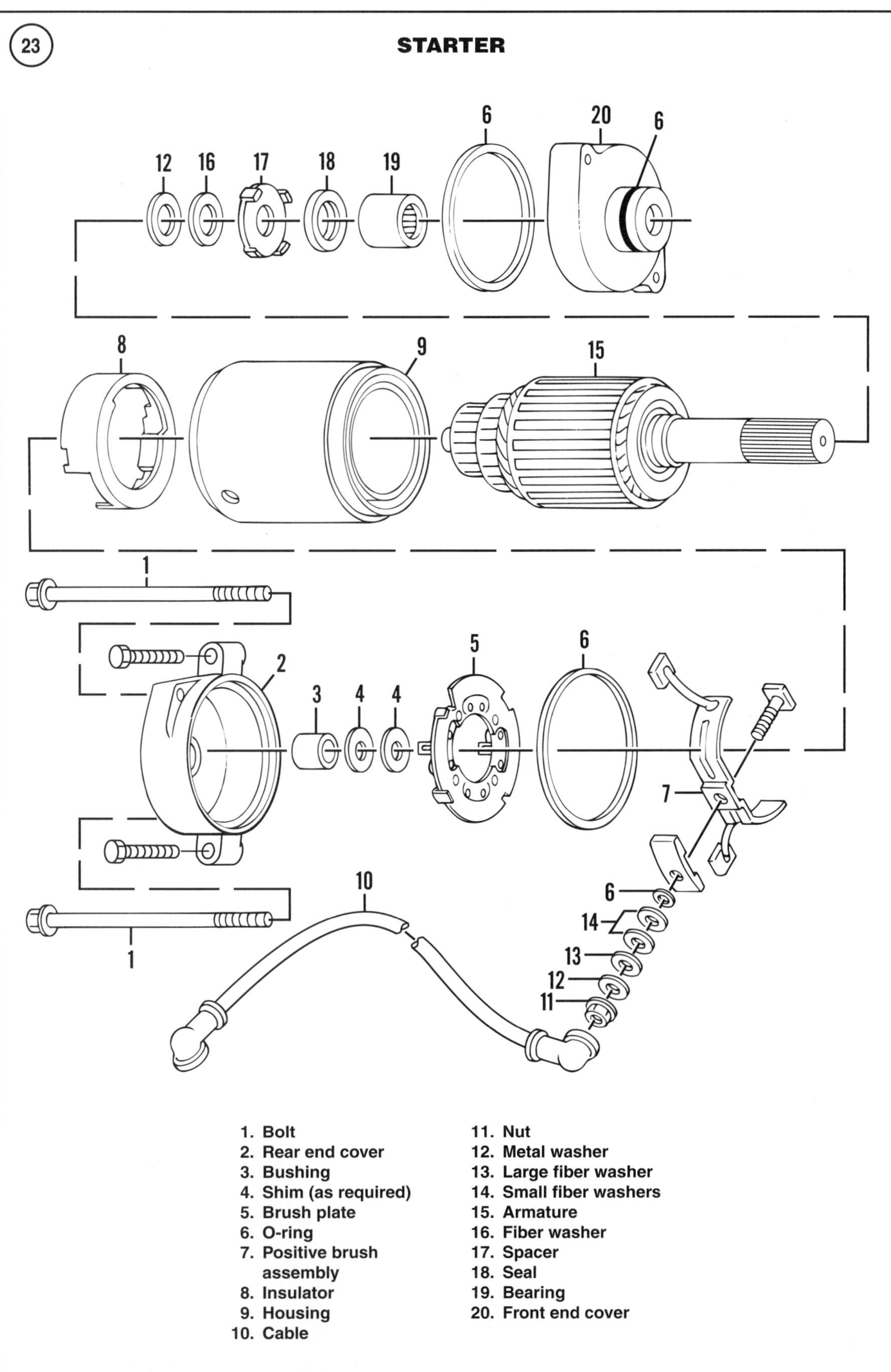
23
STARTER
1. Bolt
2. Rear end cover
3. Bushing
4. Shim (as required)
5. Brush plate
6. O-ring
7. Positive brush assembly
8. Insulator
9. Housing
10. Cable
11. Nut
12. Metal washer
13. Large fiber washer
14. Small fiber washers
15. Armature
16. Fiber washer
17. Spacer
18. Seal
19. Bearing
20. Front end cover

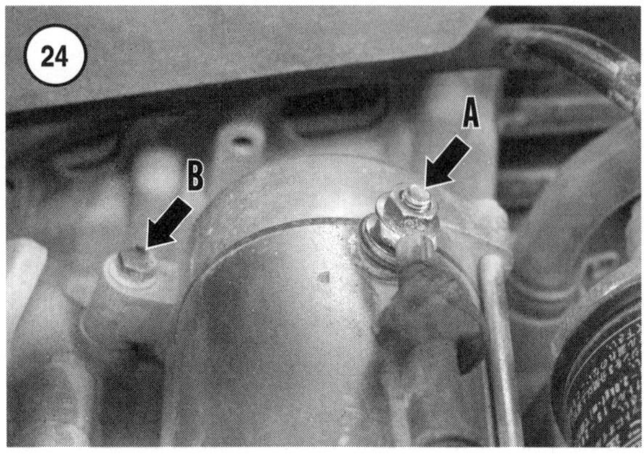

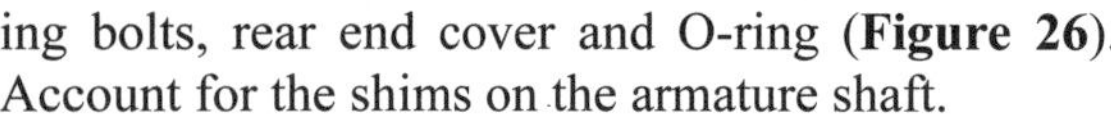

ing bolts, rear end cover and O-ring (**Figure 26**). Account for the shims on the armature shaft.

NOTE
If disassembling the starter to check just the brush condition, remove only the rear end cover. The brushes can be inspected and the cover reinstalled if further disassembly is not required.

2. Remove the front end cover and O-ring (**Figure 27**). Account for the spacer and washers on the armature shaft.
3. Remove the armature, brush plate assembly and insulator from the starter housing.
4. Note the small projection (A, **Figure 28**) on the positive brush assembly. Then make a reference mark on the brush plate (B, **Figure 28**). If removing the positive brushes from the brush plate, reinstall the terminal on this side of the plate. The projection should point toward the mark. Installing the brush plate is not possible if these marks are not correctly oriented.
5. Inspect and test the starter components as described in this section.
6. Assemble the starter as follows:
   a. Align and install the insulator (**Figure 29**).
   b. Check the orientation of the small projection (A, **Figure 28**) on the insulator, and the brush plate reference mark (B), then install the parts. The brush plate must seat in the housing (A, **Figure 30**) and the insulation on the positive brushes (B) must pass through the plate and into the insulator.
   c. Install the O-ring, washers and nut onto the terminal. The O-ring must fit between the terminal and housing to prevent shorting.
   d. To allow the armature to be installed, the brushes must be held back so the commutator can pass between the brushes. Use small plastic ties, positioned near the upper edge of each brush holder, to retain the brushes and springs (**Figure 31**).

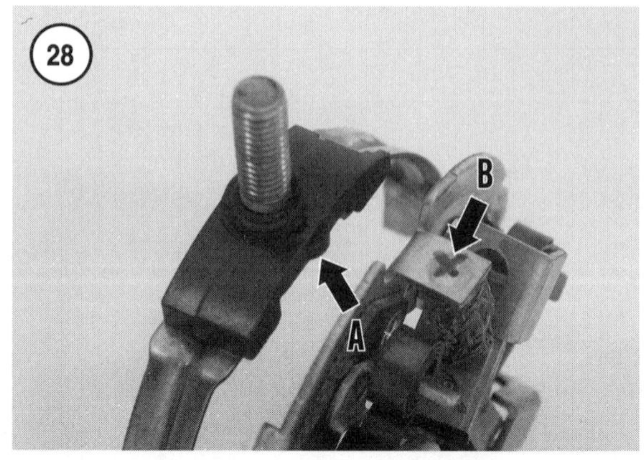

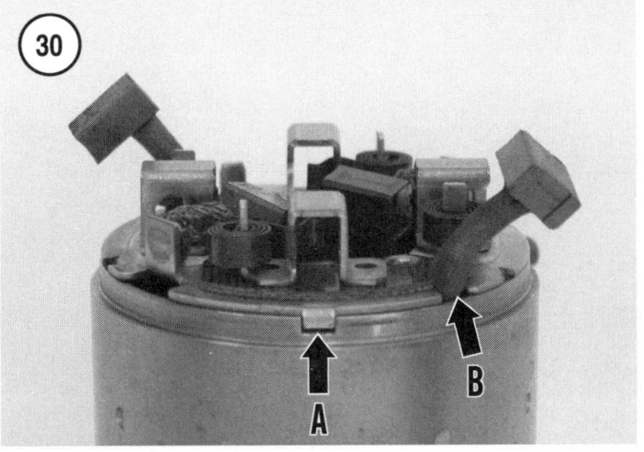

e. Hold the brush plate in position and install the armature. Remove the plastic ties as the commutator passes between the brushes. The assembly should appear as shown in **Figure 32**.

f. Install the O-ring and shims at the rear of the starter. Then install the rear end cover. Insert the tab on the brush plate into the notch on the cover (**Figure 33**).

g. Install the O-ring spacer and washers at the front of the starter. Then install the front end cover. Check that the marks on the covers and housing are aligned (**Figure 25**).

h. Install and tighten the housing bolts.

i. Install a new, lubricated O-ring onto the front end cap (**Figure 34**).

j. Perform the *Operational Test* described in this section.

k. Install the starter as described in this section.

Inspection and Testing

Refer to **Figure 23**.

1. Clean the parts as required. Use a solvent specifically for electric motors to remove buildup and contamination, particularly between the commutator bars.

2. Inspect the condition of the housing and end covers.
   a. The armature should fit into the covers with little or no play.
   b. Inspect the condition of the bushing (A, **Figure 35**), bearing (B) and seal (C). Lubricate the parts with waterproof grease. Remove excess grease that could migrate to the armature, commutator or brush assembly.
3. Inspect and test the commutator.
   a. Measure the outside diameter (**Figure 36**). Refer to **Table 1** for specifications.
   b. Inspect the bar height. The commutator bars should be taller than the insulation between the bars (**Figure 37**). Refer to **Table 1** for the undercut specification.
   c. Inspect the bars for discoloration. If a pair of bars is discolored, this indicates grounded armature coils.
   d. Inspect the bars for scoring. Mild scoring can be repaired with fine emery cloth.
   e. Check for continuity across all adjacent pairs of commutator bars (**Figure 38**). There should be continuity across all pairs of bars.
   f. Check for continuity between each commutator bar and the armature shaft (**Figure 39**). There should be no continuity.
4. Inspect the brush plate assembly.
   a. Inspect the condition of the brush springs. If rusted or broken, replace the brush plate.
   b. Measure the length of each brush (**Figure 40**). Refer to **Table 1** for specifications.
5. Inspect the armature shaft and splines (**Figure 41**). If the splines are worn, check the condition of the starter gear and idle gear, located in the alternator cover.
6. Inspect the spacer, shims, washers and insulator for damage.
7. Assemble the starter as described in this section.

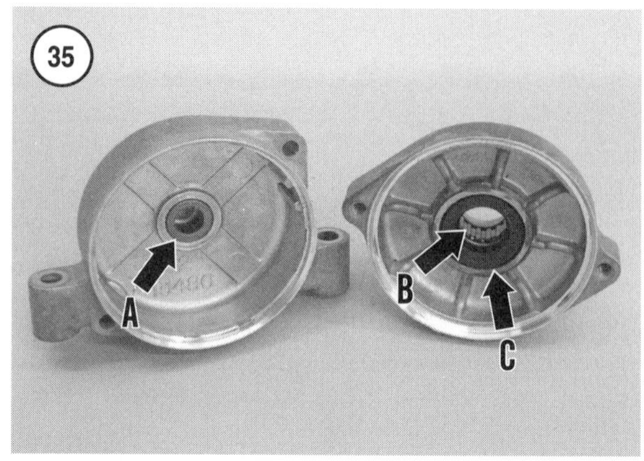

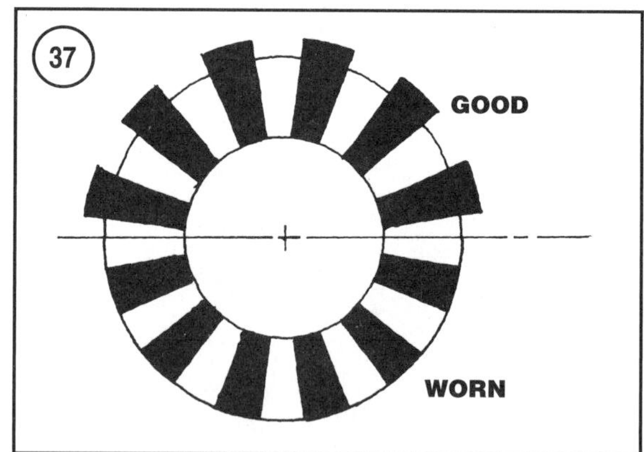

Operational Test

The starter can be tested while installed.

WARNING
When connecting a battery to the starter, use jumper cables to make the connections. Light gauge wire will burn. Since sparks will likely occur when the test connection is made, perform the test away from all flammable sources.

1. Place the select lever in park if the starter is installed.
2. Disconnect the positive cable from the starter (A, **Figure 24**).

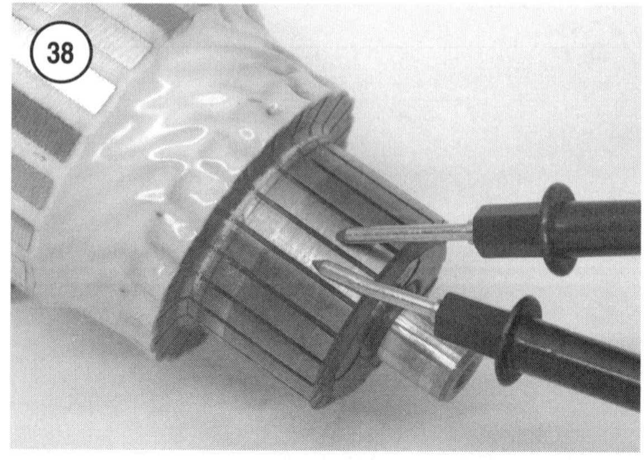

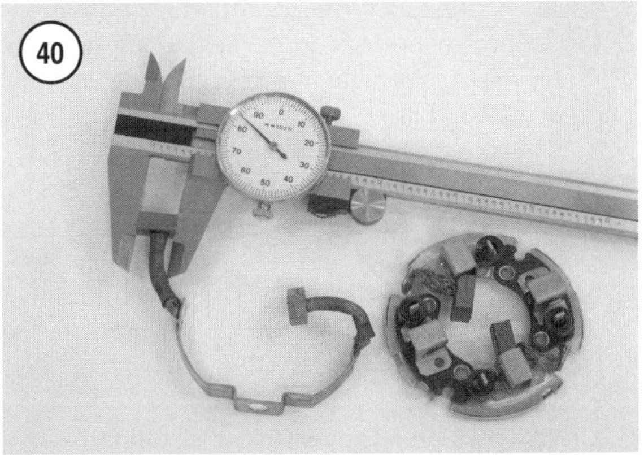

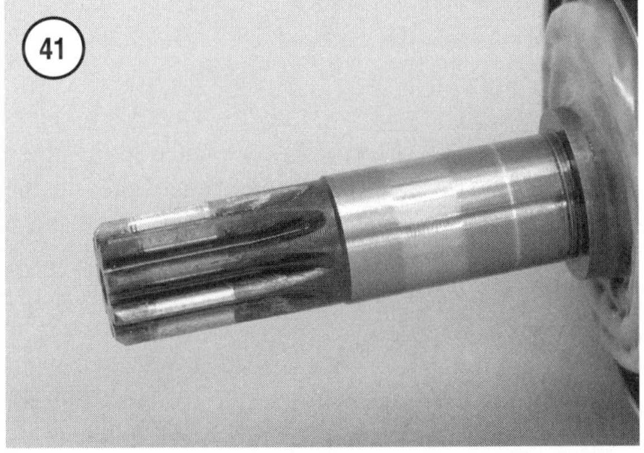

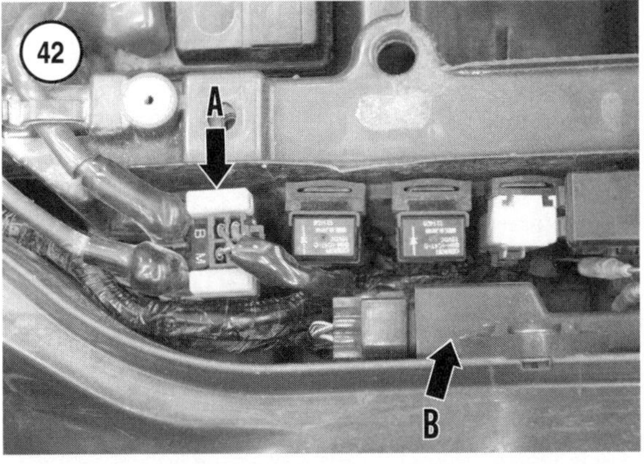

3. Connect the negative cable from a 12-volt battery to the starter.
4. Quickly touch and remove the positive battery cable to the positive starter terminal.
   a. If the starter turns, it is in good condition. Check the starter relay and cables for damage.
   b. If the starter does not turn, and the starter is not installed, the starter is faulty.
   c. If the starter does not turn, and it is installed, remove the starter and repeat the test. If the starter works after removing it, check for possible jamming of the starter idle gear or starter gear.

STARTING SYSTEM SWITCHES

The starting system switches include the starter relay, diode, ignition switch, engine stop switch, starter button, gear position switch and rear brake switch.

Starter Relay Test

The starter relay (A, **Figure 42**) is located under the seat. The starter relay connects the battery to the starter. The relay is designed to temporarily carry the high electrical load between the parts during start-up. The relay is activated when the starter button is pressed.

1. Disconnect the negative battery cable and then the positive cable.
2. Remove the starter relay.
3. Connect an ohmmeter to the cable terminals on the relay.
4. Connect a 12-volt battery to the relay. Connect the positive battery lead to the blue/white wire terminal.
5. Observe the meter. Then momentarily touch the negative battery lead to the blue/black wire terminal.
   a. If the meter reads no resistance, the relay is in good condition. Check the starter and cables for damage.
   b. If the meter indicates resistance in the relay, the relay is faulty.

Diode Tests

The diode is located in the compartment under the front fender hood. The diode allows current to flow in one direction. Use an ohmmeter to test the diode for directional continuity.

1. Disconnect the diode.
2. Test the diode as follows:
   a. Connect the negative meter probe to the black/yellow wire terminal and the positive meter probe to the blue/red wire terminal There should be continuity.

b. Reverse the meter probe connections. There should be no continuity.
3. Replace the diode if it fails either of these tests.

IGNITION SYSTEM

Precautions and Inspections

Note the following:

1. Never disconnect electrical connections while the engine is running or cranking.
2. Turn the ignition switch off before disconnecting or connecting electrical components.
3. Handle parts with care.
4. Before testing components, make sure the battery, fuse and spark plug are in good condition, and are not the cause of poor performance. Refer to Chapter Three for battery replacement and charging procedures.
5. Make sure the switches operate correctly.
6. Check wiring for poor connections, corrosion and shorts before replacing components connected to the wiring.
7. Work slowly and methodically and use test equipment that is in good condition. Record all measurements.

Main Ignition Fuse Inspection

The ignition fuse holder is located on top of the starter relay, under the seat (A, **Figure 42**). Use an ohmmeter to check the fuse for continuity. Even though a fuse may appear to be in good condition, a fine break in the fuse element is not always visible. A fine break in the element can also indicate continuity when tested cold, then break continuity when it is hot.

CDI Unit

The CDI unit is located under the seat (B, **Figure 42**). No specifications are provided by the manufacturer for CDI unit testing. If the components in the following tests pass inspection, replace the CDI unit after eliminating all other possibilities. Refer to *Electrical Component Replacement* in this chapter.

Ignition Coil and Spark Plug Cap Test

The ignition coil is located behind the air duct, at the front of the machine. Check the coil for resistance in the primary and secondary coils. Refer to **Table 1** for specifications.

1. Remove the spark plug cap from the plug.
2. Disconnect the orange wire from the coil.

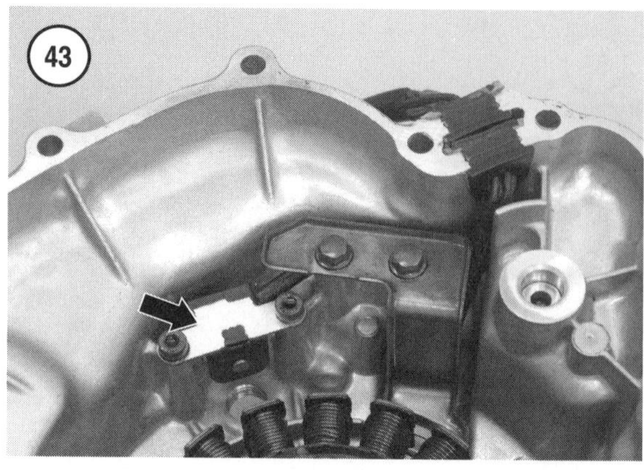

3. Check ignition coil primary resistance as follows:
   a. Connect one meter probe to the coil terminal for the orange wire and the other meter probe to the coil base.
   b. Measure the resistance.
4. Check ignition coil secondary resistance as follows:
   a. Remove the spark plug cap from the spark plug lead.
   b. Connect one meter probe to the coil terminal for the orange wire and the other meter probe to the spark plug lead.
   c. Measure the resistance.
5. Check spark plug cap resistance as follows:
   a. Connect the meter probes to each side of the cap.
   b. Measure the resistance.

Pickup Coil Test

The pickup coil (**Figure 43**) is located in the alternator cover. The pickup coil can be checked at the wire connector, located above the starter.

1. Separate the connector.
2. Identify the half of the connector that leads to the pickup coil.
3. Measure the coil resistance as follows:
   a. Connect one meter probe to the white/red wire and the other probe to the white/green wire. Refer to **Table 1** for specifications.
   b. If the pickup coil is not within specification, check the wiring harness for damage and shorting.
   c. If necessary, remove the alternator cover and recheck the wiring harness and coil. Flex the harness as the check is being made to detect erratic continuity. If the coil fails the check, replace the pickup coil/stator assembly.
4. Measure the resistance between the pickup coil and ground. Ground one of the meter probes to the engine (or the alternator cover, if removed). Touch the other probe to the white/red wire, then to the white/green wire. There should be no continuity. Any other reading indicates a short. Check for a pinched

wire under the pickup coil or damage that would short it out. If no damage can be detected, replace the pickup coil/stator assembly.

Rotor Rotation Direction Sensing Coil Test

The rotor rotation direction sensing coil is located in the alternator cover and is part of the stator and pickup coil assembly. The sensing coil connector is located above the starter.

1. Separate the connector.
2. Identify the half of the connector that leads to the coil.
3. Measure the coil resistance as follows:
   a. Connect one meter probe to the red wire and the other probe to the white/blue wire. Refer to **Table 1** for specifications.
   b. If the coil is not within specification, check the wiring harness for damage and shorting.
   c. If necessary, remove the alternator cover and recheck the wiring harness and coil. Flex the harness as the check is being made to detect erratic continuity. If the coil fails the check, replace the pickup coil/stator assembly.
4. Measure the resistance between the coil and ground. Ground one of the meter probes to the engine (or the alternator cover, if removed). Touch the other probe to the white/blue wire, then to the red wire. There should be no continuity. Any other reading indicates a short requiring pickup coil/stator assembly replacement.

Ignition Timing Inspection

The ignition timing is not adjustable. Check the timing to verify CDI unit and pickup coil operation.

1. Warm up the engine to operating temperature.
2. Remove the recoil starter (Chapter Five).
3. Remove the plug from the timing hole (**Figure 44**).
4. Connect a timing light following the manufacturer's instructions.
5. Start the engine and allow it to idle at 1450-1550 rpm.
6. Direct the timing light into the timing hole and observe the timing mark. The index mark should be aligned between the vertical marks (**Figure 45**) in the timing hole. If the timing is incorrect:
   a. Test the pickup coil. If the pickup coil is in good condition, replace the CDI unit with a known good unit and compare the results. Specifications for testing the CDI unit are not available.
   b. If the CDI unit passes all checks, inspect the Woodruff key securing the rotor to the crankshaft. If the key is bent or sheared, the rotor-to-crankshaft alignment will be off, causing the engine to be out of time.
7. Turn off the engine and disconnect the test equipment.
8. Lubricate the O-ring on the plug. Then screw the plug into the timing hole.
9. Install the recoil starter.

CHARGING SYSTEM

Refer to Chapter Three for battery replacement and charging procedures.

Precautions and Inspections

Note the following:

1. Never disconnect electrical connections while the engine is running or cranking.
2. Turn off the ignition switch before disconnecting or connecting electrical components.
3. Handle parts with care.
4. Check wiring for poor connections, corrosion and shorts before replacing components connected to the wiring.
5. Before testing components, make sure the battery is in good condition, and is not the cause of poor performance.

6. Work slowly, methodically and use test equipment that is in good condition. Record all measurements.

Battery

Voltage test (unloaded)

Perform an unloaded voltage test to determine the basic state of battery charge.

1. Disconnect the battery cables and allow the battery to remain undisturbed for at least 4 hours.
2. Connect a voltmeter to the negative and positive terminals (**Figure 46**).
3. Measure the voltage.
   a. A fully charged battery will have a minimum of 12.8 volts.
   b. A battery that is approximately 75 percent charged will have a minimum of 12.5 volts.
   c. A battery that is approximately 50 percent charged will have a minimum of 12.0 volts.
4. If battery charging or replacement is required, refer to the procedures in Chapter Three.

Voltage test (loaded)

1. Connect a voltmeter to the negative and positive battery terminals, while the cables are still attached.
2. Turn on the headlights to high beam.
3. Measure the loaded voltage.
   a. A battery in good condition will have a minimum of 11.5 volts.
   b. If battery charging or replacement is required, refer to the procedures in Chapter Three.

Current draw test

If the battery is in good condition, but it discharges at a rapid rate when the machine is not used, check the electrical system for a current draw. A short in a wire or component in the electrical system can allow the battery to discharge to ground. Accumulations of dirt and moisture can also create a path to ground. It is normal for accessories, such as clocks, to draw current when the machine is turned off.

1. Remove the front fender hood, seat, fuel tank and fuel tank side panels so the electrical connectors and components can be accessed.
2. Turn the ignition switch off.
3. Disconnect the negative battery cable.
4. Make sure the battery is fully charged.

CAUTION
Before connecting the ammeter in the next step, set the range selector to its highest setting. If there is an excessive amount of current flow, the meter may be damaged.

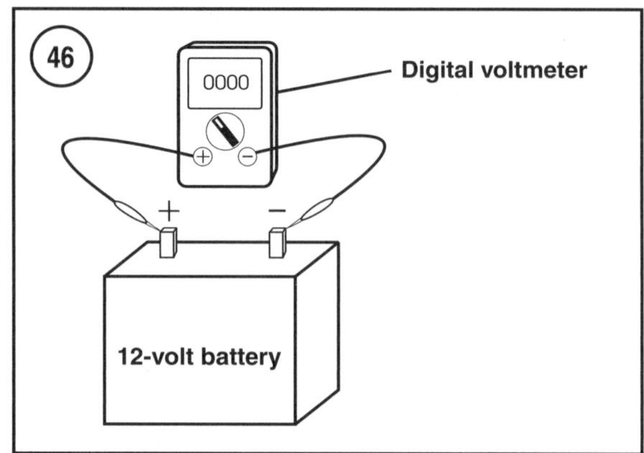

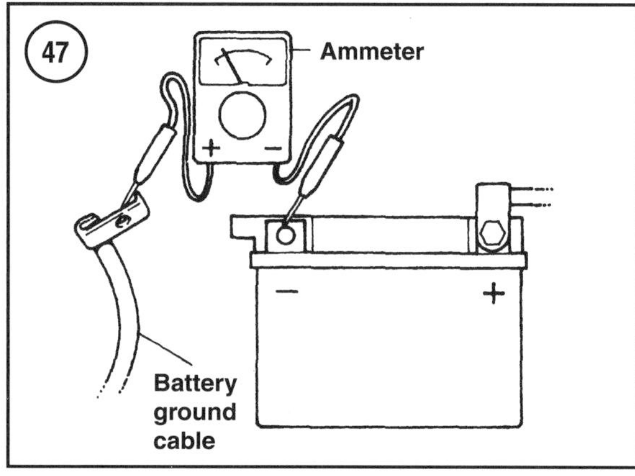

5. Connect the ammeter to the negative battery cable and terminal as shown in **Figure 47**.
6. Check the connectors.
   a. Refer to the appropriate wiring diagram at the end of the manual for circuits and part identifications.
   b. Disconnect those parts that are known to draw current when the ignition switch is off. If the meter then indicates no current draw, one of the parts is drawing excessive current. Inspect the specific part(s) and connectors for shorts and damage.
   c. If necessary, continue to separate the connectors of additional parts. Working with one connector at a time, disconnect and connect the connectors until the meter indicates no current draw. When this occurs, the shorted circuit has been isolated.

Regulator/Rectifier Output Voltage Test

The regulator/rectifier is located in front of the left rear shock absorber and behind the air duct. The reg-

48

49

ulator/rectifier converts the alternating current produced by the alternator into direct current to charge the battery and power the electrical system. The unit also regulates the charging voltage to the battery.

1. Make sure the battery is in good condition and charged.
2. Start the engine and allow it to reach operating temperature. Then turn off the engine.
3. Check the regulator/rectifier output voltage as follows:
   a. Connect a voltmeter to the negative and positive battery terminals (**Figure 46**).
   b. Start the engine and momentarily raise the engine speed to 3000 rpm.
   c. The meter should indicate 14.1-14.9 volts (unloaded) as the engine speed is raised.
   d. If the output voltage is significantly higher than 15 volts, the regulator/rectifier may not be adequately grounded, or is faulty. If the output voltage does not rise with engine speed, the regulator/rectifier or stator coils are faulty. Before replacing parts, check the condition of the stator charging coils, wiring harness and battery.

Stator Charging Coils Test

The stator coils are located in the alternator cover (**Figure 48**). The stator coils can be checked at the wire connector, located above the starter. Check the charging coils for resistance and continuity.

1. Separate the connector.
2. Identify the half of the connector that leads to the stator.
3. Measure the coil resistance as follows:
   a. Connect the meter probes to the white wires. Check all three combinations of the white wires. Refer to **Table 1** for specifications. The resistance between all pairs of white wires should be within the specifications.
   b. If the charging coils are not within specifications, check the wiring harness for damage and shorting.
   c. If necessary, remove the alternator cover and recheck the wiring harness and coils. Individually check the full length of the harness wires for continuity. There should be near zero resistance in all wires. Flex the harness as the check is being made to detect erratic continuity.
   d. If the harness is not shorted, check the coils at the white wire connections on the stator. If the coils fail the check, replace the pickup coil/stator assembly.
4. Measure the resistance between the coils and ground. Ground one of the meter probes to the engine (or the alternator cover, if removed). Touch the other probe to the white wires. There should be no continuity. Any other reading indicates a short. Check for a pinched wire or damage that would short it out. If no damage is evident, replace the pickup coil/stator assembly.

FAN SYSTEM

An electric radiator fan turns on to increase airflow through the radiator if the coolant temperature reaches 75° C (167° F). The fan circuit consists of the fan, sending unit and circuit breaker. The fan is turned on and off by the sending unit, located at the bottom of the radiator (**Figure 49**). The sending unit is thermally sensitive and controls power to the fan. When the engine coolant is cold, the sending unit has an open circuit and the fan is inoperative. If the coolant temperature exceeds the normal operating temperature, the sending unit circuit closes. The fan turns on and runs until the coolant temperature falls, causing the sending unit circuit to open.

When testing or troubleshooting the fan system, it is important that all connections are clean and tight. During assembly, apply dielectric grease to connections to prevent corrosion.

Fan Test

1. Separate the fan connector.

2. Identify the half of the connector that leads to the fan.
3. Connect a 12-volt battery to the motor leads. Connect the positive battery lead to the blue wire and the negative battery lead to the black wire.
 a. If the fan does not turn on, replace the fan.
 b. If the fan turns on, test the fan circuit breaker.

Fan Circuit Breaker Test

The fan circuit breaker is located under the seat and to the rear of the CDI unit. The circuit breaker is encased in a small vinyl pack.

1. Disconnect the circuit breaker leads.
2. Measure the resistance in the circuit breaker as follows:
 a. Connect the meter probes to the circuit breaker leads.
 b. If the resistance is anything other than zero, replace the circuit breaker.

Fan Sending Unit Test

1. Drain the cooling system (Chapter Three).
2. Remove the connector from the sending unit (**Figure 49**). Then remove the sending unit from the radiator.
3. Clean and inspect the sending unit for damage.
4. Test the sending unit at ambient temperature as follows:
 a. Connect an ohmmeter to the sending unit terminals. Note the meter reading.
 b. If the reading indicates continuity, the sending unit is faulty. Low resistance in the part could cause the fan to come on too soon and/or not turn off.
5. Test the sending unit at operating temperature as follows:
 a. Connect an ohmmeter to the sending unit terminals.
 b. Suspend the part (A, **Figure 50**) and thermometer (B) in a container of water. The temperature sensor and threads must be submerged. Do not allow the parts to touch the bottom or side of the container.
 c. Slowly heat the water and observe the thermometer and ohmmeter readings. Do not excessively overheat the switch.
 d. As the sending unit is heated, there should be continuity at approximately 75° C (167° F).
 e. As the sending unit is cooled, there should be *no* continuity at approximately 68° C (154° F).
 f. Replace the sending unit if it does not operate within the specifications.

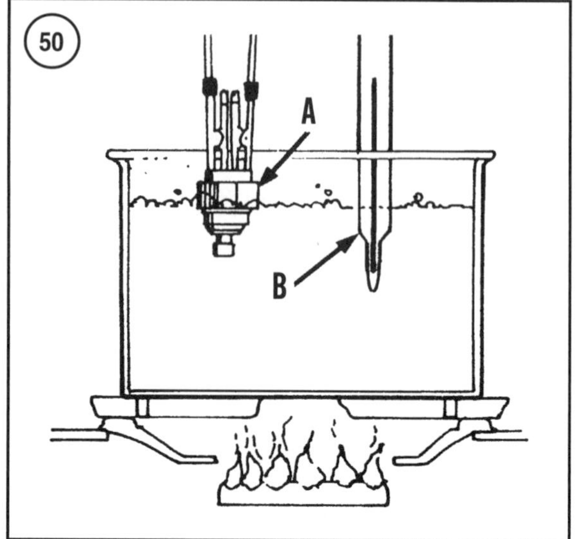

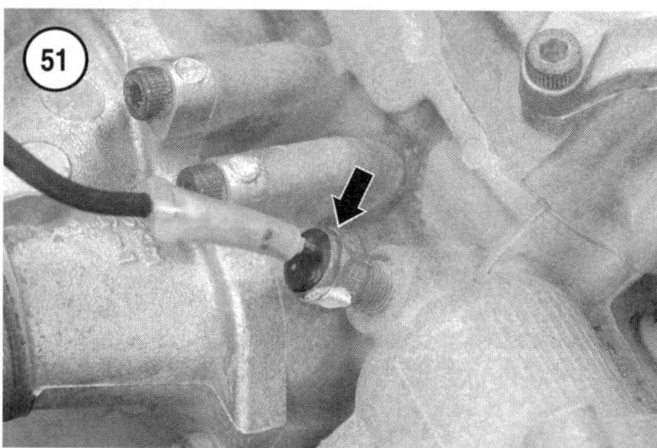

6. Apply sealant to the sending unit threads. Then install it into the radiator. Tighten the sending unit to 28 N•m (21 ft.-lb.).
7. Fill and bleed the cooling system (Chapter Three).

COOLANT TEMPERATURE WARNING SYSTEM

The coolant temperature warning light is turned on and off by the sending unit, located on the cylinder head (**Figure 51**). At normal coolant operating temperatures, the sending unit has no continuity and the coolant temperature light remains off. If the coolant temperature rises beyond normal operating temperatures, the sending unit circuit closes and the coolant temperature light indicates overheating. The light remains on until the coolant temperature falls, causing the sending unit circuit to open.

Coolant Temperature Sending Unit Test

If the warning light is on all the time, or comes on soon after engine startup, perform the following

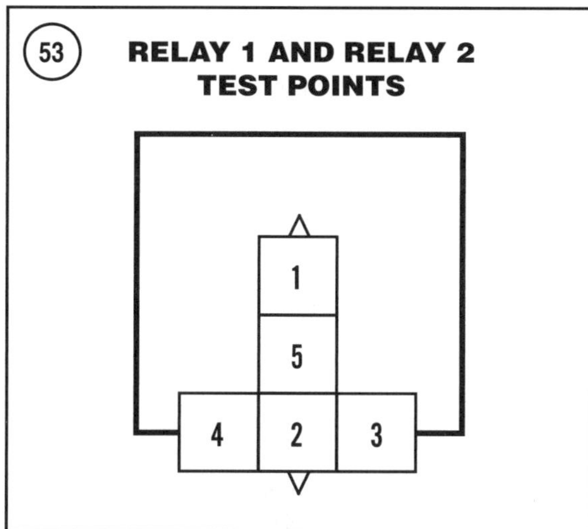

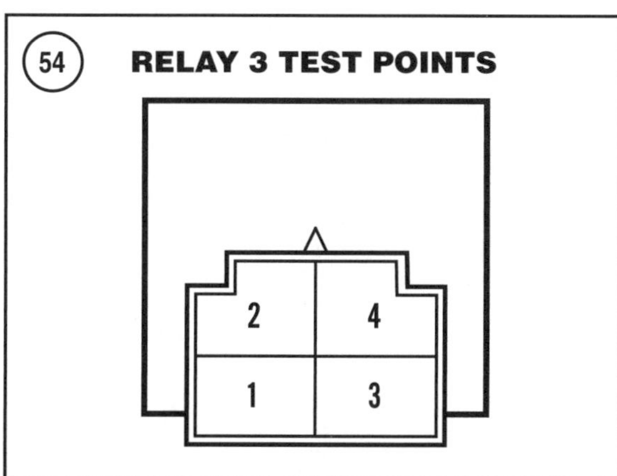

sending unit test. The test checks for continuity when the switch is at ambient to normal operating temperature. Normally, the switch should *not* have continuity in this temperature range.

If the warning light does not turn on, and all other possible causes of failure have been checked, replace the sending unit. Since the sending unit normally closes (allows continuity) at approximately 117° C (243° F) to 123° C (253° F) to turn on the warning light, it is not practical or safe to heat and test the switch.

1. Remove the connector from the sending unit (**Figure 51**).
2. Clean and inspect the unit for corrosion or damage.
3. Test the sending unit at ambient temperature as follows:
   a. Connect an ohmmeter to the sending unit terminal and to ground. Note the meter reading.
   b. If the reading indicates continuity, the sending unit is faulty. Low resistance in the part can cause the light to come on too soon and/or not turn off.
   c. Replace the sending unit (Chapter Ten).
4. Test the sending unit at operating temperature as follows:
   a. Connect an ohmmeter to the sending unit terminal and ground.
   b. Start the engine and observe the meter as the engine coolant is brought to operating temperature.
   c. If the meter indicates continuity at any time during engine warmup, the sending unit is faulty.
   d. Replace the sending unit (Chapter Ten).

FOUR-WHEEL DRIVE RELAYS AND GEAR MOTOR

Relay Tests

The four-wheel drive relays (**Figure 52**) are located under the seat. The relays are part of the gear motor control system. Before testing the relays, make sure the main switch, battery, four-wheel drive circuit fuse and wiring connections are in good condition, and not the cause of inoperation. Remove the relays and test them at the workbench. An ohmmeter and a 12-volt battery in good condition are required to test the relays.

1. Relay 1 and Relay 2 are identical. Test the relays as follows:
   a. Refer to **Figure 53** for the connection and test points on the bottom of each relay.
   b. Connect the ohmmeter to positions 1 and 2. The meter should indicate continuity.
   c. Connect the ohmmeter to positions 1 and 5.
   d. Connect the 12-volt battery to the relay. Connect the positive battery lead to position 3. Observe the meter. Then momentarily touch the negative battery lead to position 4. The meter should indicate continuity.
   e. If the meter does not indicate continuity for both tests, the relay is faulty.
2. Test relay 3 as follows:
   a. Refer to **Figure 54** for the connection and test points on the bottom of the relay.

b. Connect the ohmmeter to positions 1 and 2.
c. Connect the 12-volt battery to the relay. Connect the positive battery lead to position 3. Observe the meter. Then momentarily touch the negative battery lead to position 4. The meter should indicate continuity. If the meter does not indicate continuity, the relay is faulty.

Gear Motor Test

Test the gear motor for shaft rotation in both directions. To perform the test, assemble two C-size batteries and leads as shown in **Figure 55**. The batteries must be joined in series to create 3 volts. Note how the position of the battery leads are reversed to change the motor rotation. Perform both tests at the 5-pin connector (**Figure 56**) on the motor.

1. Connect the battery leads to the gear motor terminals as shown in **Figure 55**. The motor shaft should turn in the directions indicated for each test. If the motor fails either test, replace the motor.
2. If the motor is in good condition, make sure the paint marks on the motor and pinion gear are aligned (**Figure 57**). The marks must be aligned in order to correctly synchronize the motor with the shift fork sliding gear during installation of the motor into the differential. If necessary, operate the motor to align the marks.

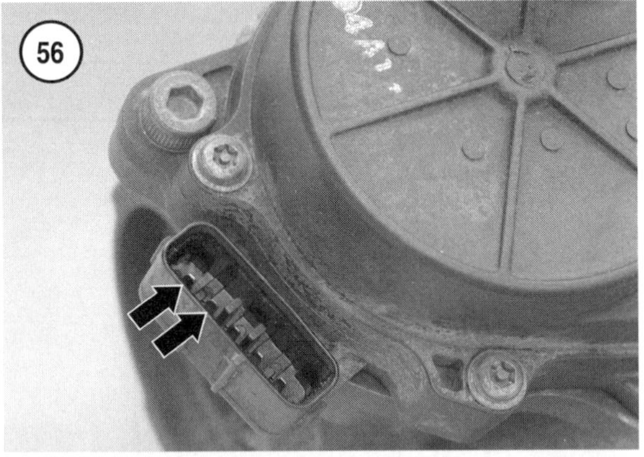

INDICATOR CIRCUITS

Check the indicator circuits in the meter assembly for continuity using an ohmmeter. Test the LEDs and switches by connecting the meter to the appropriate color-coded wires in the connector plug, or to the part itself. Simulate the conditions when the part should activate and make the check. Refer to *Switches* in this chapter and the appropriate wiring diagram at the end of the manual.

SWITCHES

Continuity Test

Test the switches for continuity using an ohmmeter or a self-powered test light (Chapter Two). Operate the switch in each of its operating positions and compare the results with the switch continuity diagrams included in the wiring diagrams at the end of the manual. For example, **Figure 58** shows the continuity diagram for a typical switch. The line joining the two terminals shows continuity. When the switch button is pressed, there should be continuity between the green and black terminals. An ohmmeter connected between these two terminals should indicate

58 **SWITCH**

Color / Position	Green	Black
FREE		
PUSH	●	●

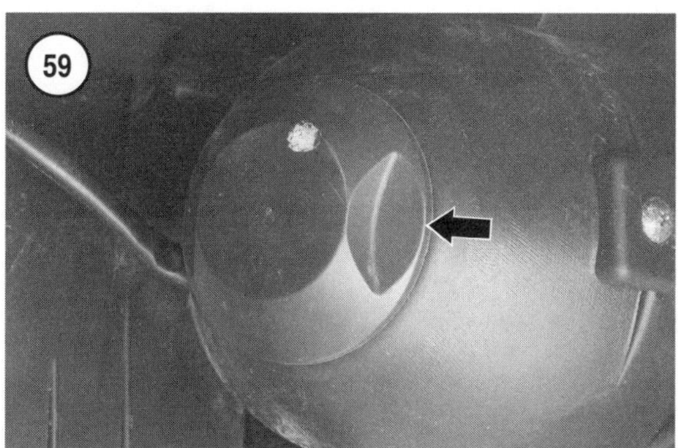

59

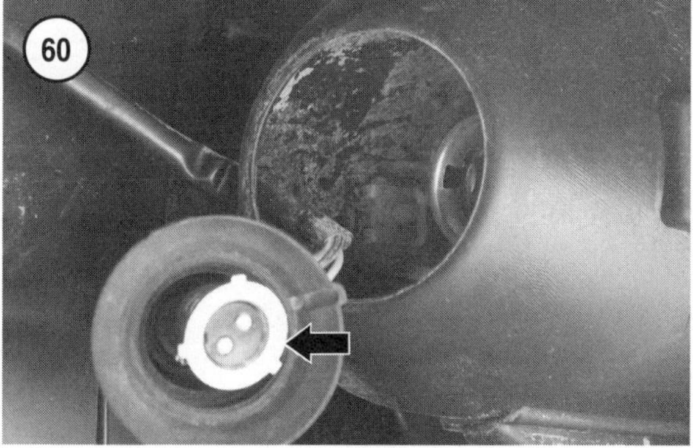

60

continuity, or a test light should illuminate. When the button is free or released, there should be no continuity between the same terminals.

HEADLIGHTS

Bulb Replacement

1. Remove the cover at the rear of the headlight assembly (**Figure 59**).
2. Remove the cover from the bulb holder.
3. Push in on the bulb holder (**Figure 60**), turn the holder counterclockwise, and remove the holder.
4. Remove the bulb.

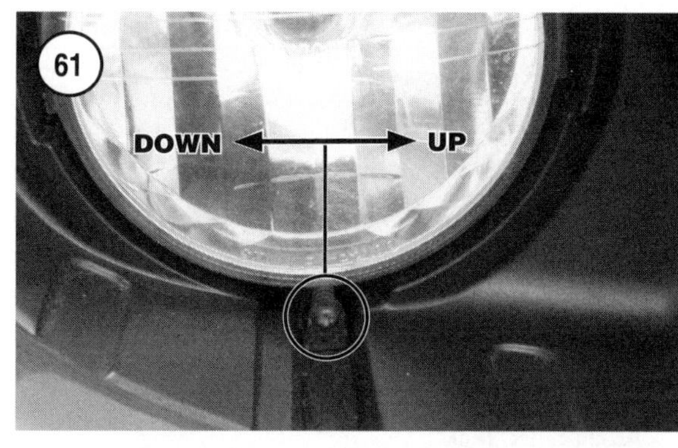

61

62

CAUTION

When handling the new bulb, do not touch the glass with bare hands. Handle the bulb with a clean cloth. Bulbs are sensitive to oil or other contaminants on their surface. Contaminants prevent heat dissipation from the bulb, which can cause shortened bulb life.

5. Seat the new bulb into the socket.
6. Install the bulb holder and covers.

Headlight Adjustment

To raise the headlight beam, turn the adjuster screw (**Figure 61**) clockwise. To lower the headlight beam, turn the adjuster screw counterclockwise.

TAILLIGHT

Bulb Replacement

1. Remove the seat, rear carrier, bracket and fender panel (Chapter Sixteen) to access the taillight bulb.
2. Turn the bulb holder (**Figure 62**) counterclockwise and remove the holder.
3. Remove the bulb.
4. Seat the new bulb into the socket.
5. Install the bulb holder and bodywork.

Table 1 and Table 2 are on the following page.

Table 1 ELECTRICAL SYSTEM SPECIFICATIONS

Alternator	
Type	Three-phase AC
Output	14 volts/21 amps at 5000 rpm
Battery	
Type	YTX20L-BS
Capacity	12 volt, 18 amp-hour
Cooling temperature sending unit	
Continuity	Approx. 117-123° C (243-253° F)
Fan sending unit	
Continuity	Approx. 75° C (167° F)
No continuity	Approx. 68° C (154° F)
Fuses	
Auxilary DC jack	10 amp
Backup (for odometer)	10 amp
Four-wheel drive	3 amp
Headlight	15 amp
Ignition	10 amp
Main	30 amp
Signal system	10 amp
Ignition coil resistance	
Primary coil	0.18-0.28 ohm
Secondary coil (spark plug lead cap removed)	6.32-9.48K ohms
Ignition spark gap (minimum gap with spark plug cap installed)	6 mm (0.24 in.)
Ignition system type	DC CDI unit
Ignition timing*	12° BTDC at 1500 rpm
Light bulbs	
Headlights (krypton bulbs)	12 volt, 30W/30W each bulb
Taillight/brake light	12 volt, 5W/21W
Indicators	LED
Pickup coil resistance (white/red to white/green wires)	459-561 ohms
Rectifier no-load output voltage	14.1-14.9 volts
Rotor rotation direction sensing coil resistance (red to white/blue wires)	
2002	0.104-0.127 ohm
2003-on	0.063-0.077 ohm
Spark plug	
Type	NGK DPR8EA-9
Gap	0.8-0.9 mm (0.031-0.035 in.)
Spark plug cap resistance	10K ohms
Stator coil resistance (white to white wires)	0.32-0.43 ohm
Starter	
Armature coil resistance	0.025-0.035 ohm
Brush length	12.5 mm (0.49 in.)
Service limit	5 mm (0.20 in.)
Commutator outside diameter	28 mm (1.10 in.)
Service limit	27 mm (1.06 in.)
Mica undercut	0.7 mm (0.03 in.)
Starter relay coil resistance	4.18-4.62 ohms

*Not adjustable.

Table 2 ELECTRICAL SYSTEM TORQUE SPECIFICATIONS

	N•m	in.-lb.	ft.-lb.
Alternator cover bolts	10	89	–
Coolant temperature sending unit	8	71	–
Fan sending unit	28	–	21
Pickup coil bolts	10	89	–
Starter clutch bolts	30	–	22
Starter pulley bolt	55	–	41
Starter mounting bolts	8	71	–
Stator bolts	10	89	–
Wire harness (stator) clamp bolts	10	89	–

CHAPTER TEN

COOLING SYSTEM

This chapter covers the radiator, fan, fan sending unit, coolant temperature sending unit, thermostat and water pump.

Refer to **Table 1** and **Table 2** at the end of this chapter for specifications.

Refer to Chapter Three for cooling system maintenance. Refer to Chapter Nine for electrical testing procedures.

COOLING SYSTEM SAFETY

WARNING

Do not remove the radiator cap immediately after or during engine operation. The liquid in the cooling system is hot and under pressure. Wait for the engine to cool and then place a shop cloth over the cap. Slowly turn the cap to relieve any pressure. Turn the cap to the safety stop and check that all pressure is relieved. To remove the cap from the radiator, press the cap down past the safety stop and twist it free.

RADIATOR AND FAN

During engine operation, hot coolant from the engine returns to the radiator by the upper hose. The coolant loses heat as it circulates to the bottom of the radiator. The coolant then returns to the engine by the lower hose. If the coolant returning to the engine is still too hot, the fan sending unit, located at the bottom of the radiator, turns on the fan. Refer to *Fan Sending Unit* in this chapter.

Removal and Installation

1. Drain the cooling system (Chapter Three).
2. Disconnect the coolant reservoir hose and fan connector.
3. Disconnect the upper radiator hose (**Figure 1**).
4. Disconnect the lower radiator hose (A, **Figure 2**) and fan sending unit (B).
5. Remove the mounting bolts and collars from the bottom of the radiator.
6. Remove the radiator and fan assembly.
   a. If fan removal is necessary, remove the bolts securing the fan to the radiator.
   b. If necessary, refer to Chapter Nine to test the fan.
7. Inspect the radiator as described in this section.
8. Reverse this procedure to install the radiator and fan. Note the following:
   a. Install the radiator mounting bolts and collars. Tighten bolts to 7 N•m (62 in.-lb.).
   b. Replace hoses that are hard, cracked or deteriorating both internally and externally. Hold each hose and flex it in several directions to check for damage. For a hose that is difficult to install on a fitting, dip the hose end in hot water until the rubber has softened. Then install the hose.

c. Install clamps in their original positions.
d. Fill the cooling system (Chapter Three). Check for leaks.

Radiator Inspection

1. Clean the exterior of the radiator with a low-pressure water spray. Allow the radiator to dry.
2. Check for damaged cooling fins. Straighten bent fins with a screwdriver. If more than 20 percent of the cooling area is damaged, replace the radiator.
3. Check the seams and other soldered connections for corrosion (green residue). If corrosion is evident, there could be a leak in that spot. Perform a cooling system pressure check as described in Chapter Three. If the equipment is not available, take the radiator to a radiator repair shop to have it flushed and pressure checked.
4. Fill the radiator with water and check the flow rate out of the radiator. If the flow rate is slow, or if corrosion or other buildup is visible, take the radiator to a radiator repair shop to have it flushed and pressure checked.

FAN SENDING UNIT

The fan sending unit (B, **Figure 2**) is mounted next to the lower radiator hose (A). When coolant temperature at the radiator outlet is approximately 75° C (167° F), the sending unit circuit closes and turns on the fan. When coolant temperature drops below 68° C (154° F) The sending unit circuit opens, and the fan shuts off.

Removal and Installation

1. Drain the cooling system (Chapter Three).
2. Remove the wire connector from the sending unit.
3. Remove the sending unit from the radiator.
4. Clean the sending unit and the threads in the radiator.
5. Test the sending unit as described in Chapter Nine.
6. Reverse these steps to install the sending unit. Note the following:
   a. Apply sealant to the sending unit threads.
   b. Tighten the sending unit to 28 N•m (21 ft.-lb.).
   c. Fill the cooling system (Chapter Three).

COOLANT TEMPERATURE SENDING UNIT

The coolant temperature sending unit is mounted on the cylinder head (**Figure 3**). When coolant temperature is too high, the sending unit circuit closes and turns on the coolant temperature warning light. At low and normal coolant temperature, the sending unit circuit is open and the light remains off.

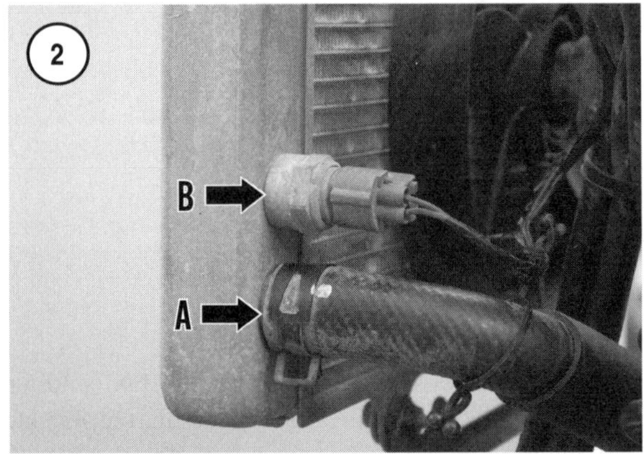

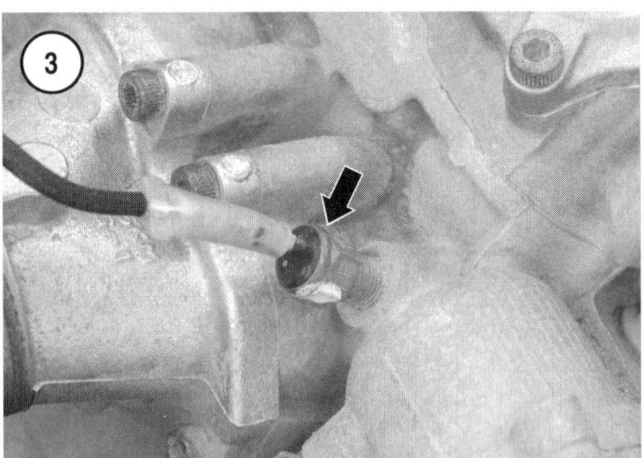

Removal and Installation

1. Drain the cooling system (Chapter Three).
2. Remove the wire connector from the sending unit.
3. Remove the sending unit from the cylinder head.
4. Clean the sending unit and the threads in the cylinder head.

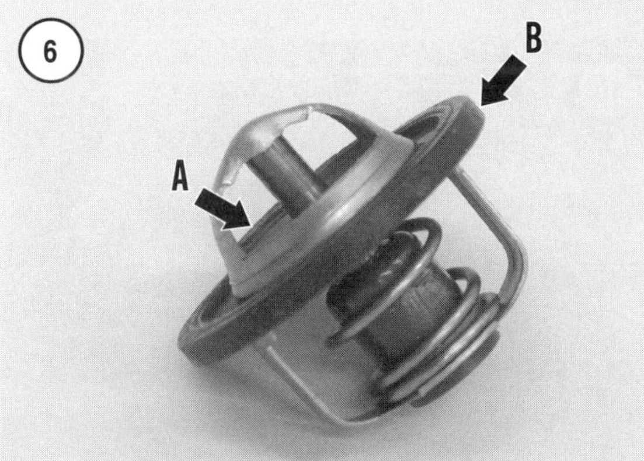

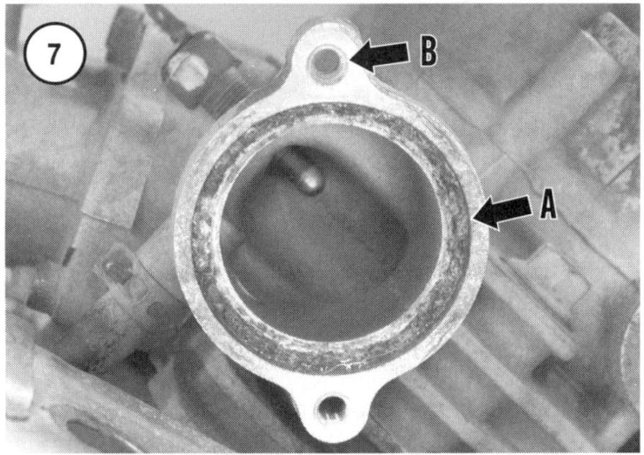

5. Test the sending unit as described in Chapter Nine.
6. Reverse these steps to install the sending unit. Note the following:
   a. Apply sealant to the sending unit threads.
   b. Tighten the sending unit to 8 N•m (71 in.-lb.).
   c. Fill the cooling system (Chapter Three).

THERMOSTAT

The engine thermostat is located in a housing on the right side of the engine (**Figure 4**). The thermostat is a temperature-sensitive valve that opens and closes, depending on the coolant temperature in the cylinder head. At startup, the thermostat is closed to retain coolant in the water jackets around the engine. When the cylinder head coolant temperature begins to exceed the ideal operating temperature, the thermostat opens, and the coolant passes from the engine to the radiator, where it is cooled. Since the temperature of the incoming coolant is low, the thermostat closes and reduces the flow to the radiator. As the temperature of the coolant rises again, the cycle is repeated.

Removal, Inspection and Installation

1. Drain the cooling system (Chapter Three).
2. Remove the bolts securing the thermostat cover to the housing. Then remove the cover and thermostat (**Figure 5**).
3. Inspect and clean the thermostat.
   a. Visually inspect the valve (A, **Figure 6**) in the thermostat. The valve should be closed when the thermostat is cold. If the valve is cold and open, replace the thermostat.
   b. Wash the thermostat in cool water. If necessary, use a soft brush to scrub any accumulation of debris off the thermostat. If an accumulation of rubber particles is evident, inspect the radiator hoses for internal deterioration.
   c. Inspect the condition of the rubber seal (B, **Figure 6**).
   d. If desired, open the drain bolt at the water pump and flush the cylinder head, cylinder and water pump with clean water.
   e. Clean the bolts, thermostat housing (A, **Figure 7**) and threaded holes (B). Remove residue from all surfaces.
4. To test the thermostat:
   a Suspend it and an accurate thermometer in a container of water (**Figure 8**). Do not allow the parts to touch the bottom or side of the container. Slowly heat the water and observe the thermostat valve. When the thermostat begins to open, observe the temperature on the ther-

mometer. The thermostat should open between 50-54° C (122-129° F).

b. Continue to raise the temperature to 70° C (158° F). At this temperature, the thermostat valve should be fully open, which is about 8 mm (0.31 in.).

c. Replace the thermostat if it does not meet the conditions of the tests.

5. Install the thermostat with the air bleed hole (**Figure 9**) at the top of the opening.

6. Lubricate the rubber seal with coolant. Then install the thermostat into the housing cover. Bolt the cover into place. Tighten the cover bolts to 10 N•m (89 in.-lb.).

7. Fill the cooling system (Chapter Three). Check for leaks.

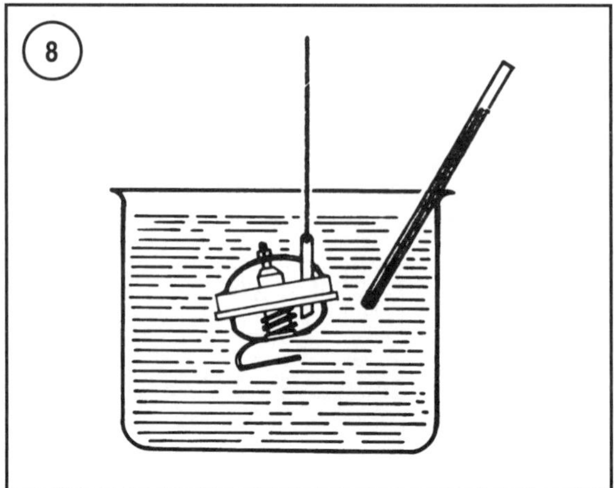

WATER PUMP

There is an inspection hose (A, **Figure 10**) for the water pump located at the front edge of the housing. If a coolant leak is evident from this hose, the pump mechanical seal is leaking. If an oil leak is evident, the oil seal is leaking.

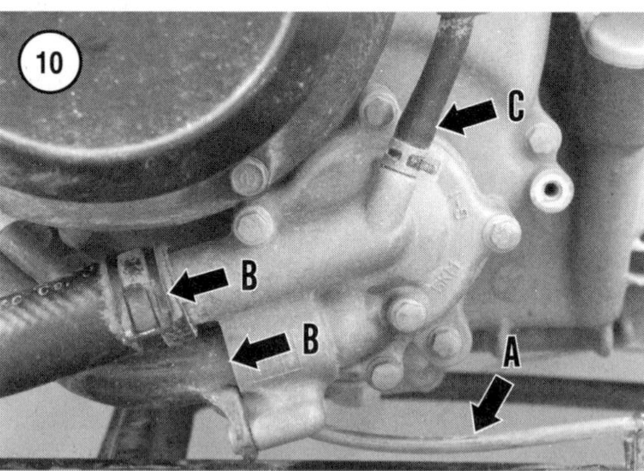

Removal, Inspection and Installation

Refer to **Figure 11**.

1. Remove the left footrest panel after removing the required bodywork to drain the cooling system.
2. Drain the cooling system (Chapter Three).
3. Drain the engine oil (Chapter Three).
4. Remove the hoses (B, **Figure 10**) and outlet pipe (C) from the water pump. Account for the O-ring on the outlet pipe.
5. Remove the two bolts securing the water pump to the engine (**Figure 12**).
   a. If necessary, lightly tap the pump to loosen it from the crankcase.
   b. Pull the pump straight out. Account for the O-ring on the back of the pump.
6. Remove the cover bolts, cover (A, **Figure 13**) and gasket (B).
7. At the back of the pump, remove the snap ring (**Figure 14**). Then pull the impeller from the housing.
8. Inspect the parts.
   a. Inspect the impeller and shaft for damage (**Figure 15**).
   b. Inspect the cover for damage and cleanliness (**Figure 16**).
   c. Inspect the face of the mechanical seal on the impeller (A, **Figure 17**) and in the housing (B). In order to seal properly, both faces must be smooth and free of scoring or damage. When installed, the impeller seal should fit firmly against the seal in the housing. Since the seal in the housing is spring loaded, it maintains pressure on the seals and compensates for wear. If necessary, replace the mechanical seal and oil seal as described in this section.
   d. Inspect the bearing in the housing (**Figure 18**). The bearing should turn smoothly with no play. If necessary, replace the bearing as described in this section.
   e. Inspect and clean the bolt holes (A, **Figure 19**) and impeller shaft drive tang (B) in the engine.

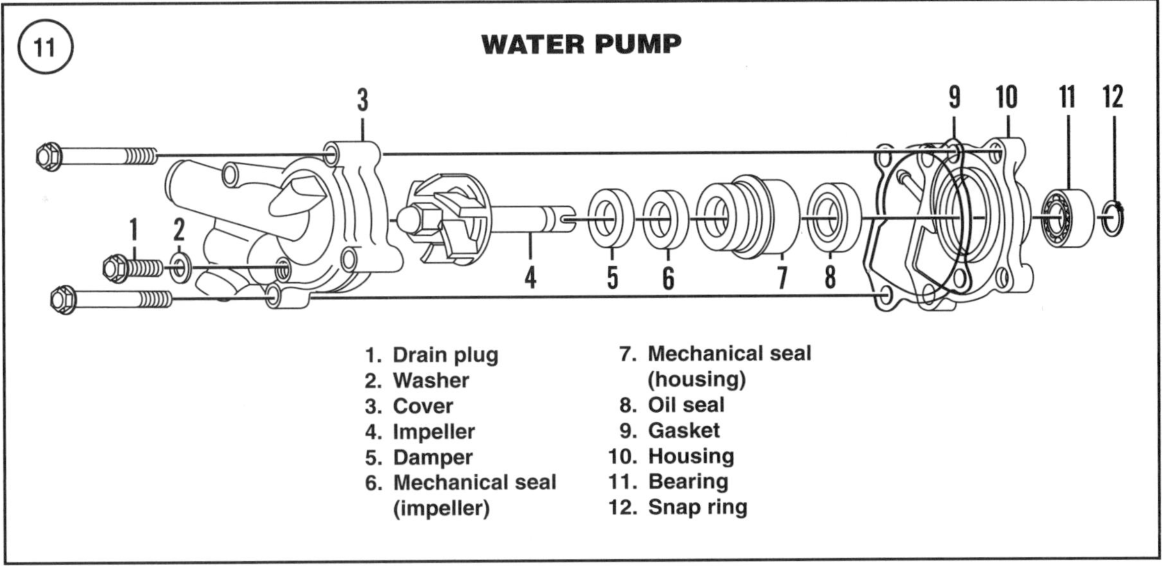

1. Drain plug
2. Washer
3. Cover
4. Impeller
5. Damper
6. Mechanical seal (impeller)
7. Mechanical seal (housing)
8. Oil seal
9. Gasket
10. Housing
11. Bearing
12. Snap ring

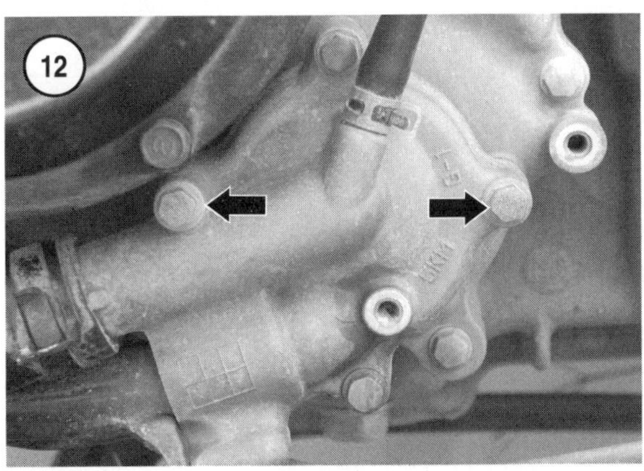

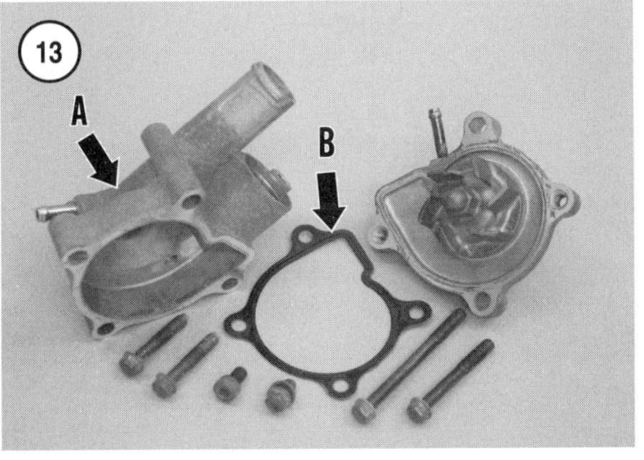

9. Reverse these steps to assemble and install the water pump. Note the following:
   a. Lubricate both faces of the mechanical seal with coolant.
   b. Install a new snap ring (**Figure 14**) on the impeller with the sharp edge facing out.
   c. Install new, lubricated O-rings on the pump housing and outlet pipe.
   d. Install a new cover gasket (B, **Figure 13**).
   e. Lubricate the bearing with engine oil.
   f. Carefully engage the water pump with the drive tang in the engine.
   g. Tighten all bolts to 10 N•m (89 in.-lb.).
   h. Fill the cooling system (Chapter Three).
   i. Fill the engine with oil (Chapter Three).

10

16

18

17

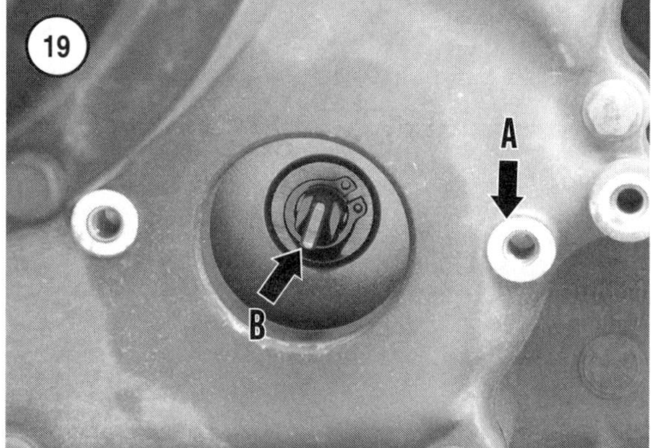

19

Bearing and Seal Replacement

Refer to **Figure 11**. The water pump has a two-piece mechanical oil seal. The mechanical seal prevents coolant in the pump chamber from passing toward the crankcase, while the oil seal prevents oil in the crankcase from passing toward the pump chamber. A drain and hose located between the seals allow leaking coolant or oil to drain to the outside of the engine. Whenever a leak is evident at the drain hose, replace the seals.

1. Replace the mechanical seal in the impeller as follows:
   a. Lift the seal and damper from the impeller. Clean the seal bore.
   b. Check the shaft for tilt (**Figure 20**). Maximum allowable tilt is 0.15 mm (0.006 in.). If tilt is excessive, the two halves of the mechanical seal will not make full contact, and leaks will be possible. If necessary, replace the impeller.
   c. Lubricate the new damper with coolant.
   d. Seat the new parts into the impeller by hand.
2. In the water pump housing, replace the remaining half of the mechanical seal and the oil seal. This procedure also includes removing the bearing. If available, use a heat gun to warm the mechanical seal and bearing before removal.

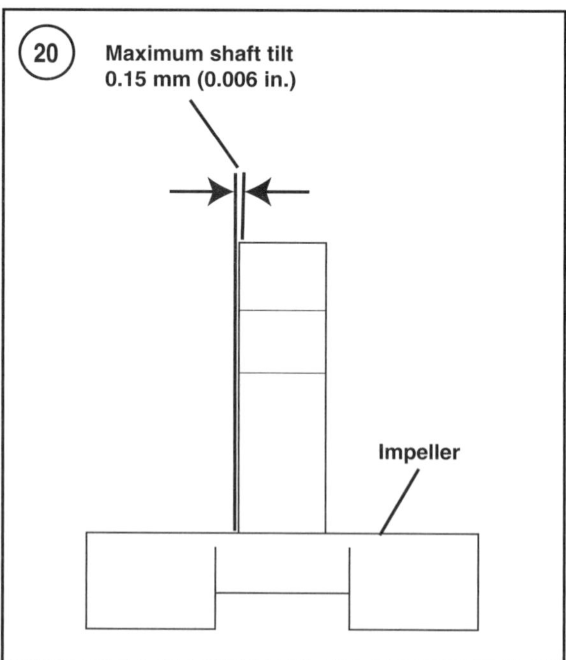

20

   a. Place a narrow drift against the back of the mechanical seal (**Figure 21**). Work around the seal and drive it from the bore. Avoid any contact with the surface of the bore. Do not pry the seal from the front side of the housing.

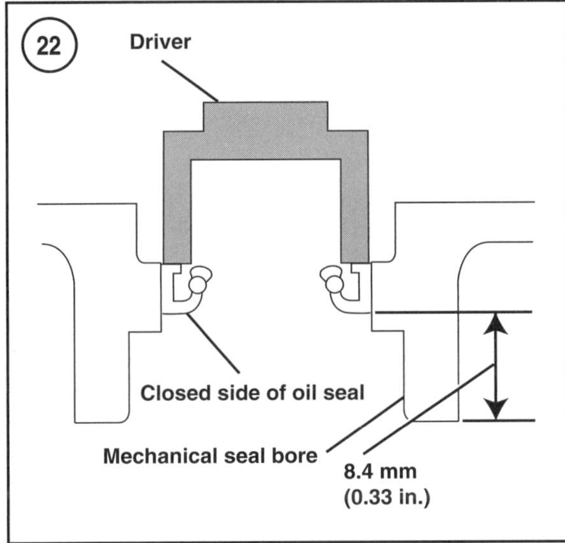

b. Support the housing with the bearing side down. Provide clearance for the bearing and seal to fall from the bore. Place a driver on the outside edge of the oil seal and drive it and the bearing from the bore.
c. Clean and inspect the housing.
d. Lubricate the oil seal with coolant.

e. Working from the bearing side of the housing, place the oil seal over the bore, with the closed side of the seal facing down (**Figure 22**). Note the required clearance for the drain hole. Press the seal into the bore using a driver or socket that fits onto the outer edge of the seal. Check the drain hole clearance.
f. Apply engine oil to the outer surface of the bearing. Then place the bearing over the housing bore with the manufacturer's marks facing down. Drive the bearing until it is fully seated. Use a driver that fits on the outer race of the bearing (**Figure 23**).
g. Support the housing with the bearing side down. Apply coolant to the outer surface of the mechanical seal. Then place the seal over the housing bore. Drive the seal using a driver or socket that fits onto the outer edge of the seal (**Figure 24**). If a thin-wall driver is not available, use a length of tubing or the mechanical seal installer (Yamaha part No. YM-33221). Make sure the driver fits onto the outer edge of the mechanical seal and does not contact the seal material.
h. Blow through the drain fitting (**Figure 25**) and make sure the drain is open.

Table 1 and Table 2 are on the following page.

Table 1 COOLING SYSTEM SPECIFICATIONS

Antifreeze type	Ethylene glycol containing anticorrosion inhibitors for aluminum engines
Coolant mixture	50:50 (antifreeze/distilled water)
Cooling system	
Capacity (including engine passages)	1.8 liters (1.9 U.S. qt.)
Radiator capacity	0.78 liter (0.82 U.S. qt.)
Reservoir capacity	0.3 liter (0.32 U.S. qt.)
Fan operating speed	2880 rpm
Radiator cap relief pressure	93.3-122.7 kPa (13.5-17.8 psi)
Thermostat	
Valve opening temperature	50-54° C (122-129° F)
Full open temperature	70° C (158° F)
Full open valve lift	8 mm (0.31 in.)
Water pump impeller shaft tilt	0.15 mm (0.006 in.) maximum

Table 2 COOLING SYSTEM TORQUE SPECIFICATIONS

	N•m	in.-lb.	ft.-lb.
Coolant temperature sending unit	8	71	–
Fan sending unit	28	–	21
Radiator mounting bolts	7	62	–
Thermostat housing bolts	10	89	–
Water pump mounting bolts	10	89	–
Water pump drain bolt	10	89	–
Water pump outlet hose bolt	10	89	–

CHAPTER ELEVEN

FRONT SUSPENSION AND STEERING

This chapter covers the front wheel, hub, suspension and steering components and tires. Refer to the tables at the end of this chapter for specifications.

FRONT WHEEL

Removal and Installation

1. Park the machine on level ground.
2. Loosen the lug nuts (**Figure 1**).
3. Raise and support the machine so the front wheels are off the ground.
4. Remove the lug nuts from the studs. Then remove the wheel from the hub. If removing more than one wheel, mark each wheel to install it in its original position.
5. If tire repair is required, make the repair as described in this chapter.
6. Clean the lug nuts and studs. If any studs are broken or damaged, replace the studs.
7. If vibration or tire wear is abnormal, check the wheel for excessive runout, as described in this chapter.
8. Check that the center cap is seated.
   a. On 2002 models, the cap fits in the wheel.
   b. On 2003-on models, the cap fits on the hub nut.

WARNING

If more than one wheel has been removed, make sure the direction arrow (on the tire sidewall, if applicable) is pointing forward when each wheel is mounted. The arrow must point forward to prevent possible tire failure.

9. Install the wheel onto the studs, with the valve stem facing out.
10. Install the lug nuts with the tapered side facing in (**Figure 2**). Then moderately tighten the nuts in a crossing pattern.
11. Lower the machine to the ground. Then equally tighten the lug nuts to 55 N•m (41 ft.-lb.).

FRONT HUB

Removal and Installation

1. Remove the front wheel as described in this chapter.

2A. On 2002 models, remove the cotter pin, hub nut and washer from the axle.
   a. If necessary, lock the front brakes and use a heat gun and penetrating oil to help loosen the nut.
   b. If the brakes do not prevent the hub from turning when loosening the nut, install two of the lug nuts backwards and against the hub (**Figure 3**). Place a long pry bar between the nuts and against the hub. The pry bar must reach the ground in order to lock the hub in place.

2B. On 2003-on models, remove the hub nut as follows:
   a. Remove the center cap from the hub nut (**Figure 4**).

b. Straighten the stake on the hub nut (**Figure 5**).
c. If necessary, lock the front brakes and use a heat gun and penetrating oil to help loosen the nut.
d. If the brakes do not prevent the hub from turning when loosening the nut, install two of the lug nuts backwards and against the hub (**Figure 3**). Place a long pry bar between the nuts and against the hub. The pry bar must reach the ground in order to lock the hub in place.

3. Remove the brake caliper mounting bolts (**Figure 6**). Then remove the caliper from the disc.
   a. Avoid kinking the brake hose.
   b. Suspend the caliper with a length of wire. Do not let the caliper hang by the brake hose.
   c. Insert a small wooden block between the brake pads. This will prevent the caliper piston from extending out of the caliper if the brake lever is operated.
4. Pull the hub from the axle splines. If removing the opposite hub, mark the hubs to reinstall them in their original positions.

NOTE

If the hub is seized to the splines, apply penetrating oil and lightly tap the back of the hub, near the center. If light tapping does not loosen the hub, use a puller to remove the hub from the axle.

5. Clean and inspect the hub for cracks (A, **Figure 7**), damaged splines (B) and broken studs (C).
6. Clean and inspect the axle splines (A, **Figure 8**) and threads (B). Use a wire brush to remove surface corrosion from the axle. On 2002 models, also check the O-ring, seated in the steering knuckle recess.
7. If necessary, remove the brake disc from the hub as described in Chapter Fifteen.
8. Reverse this procedure to install the hub. Note the following:
   a. Apply waterproof grease to the hub and axle splines. Wipe all excess grease from the hub and axle after installation. This prevents grease

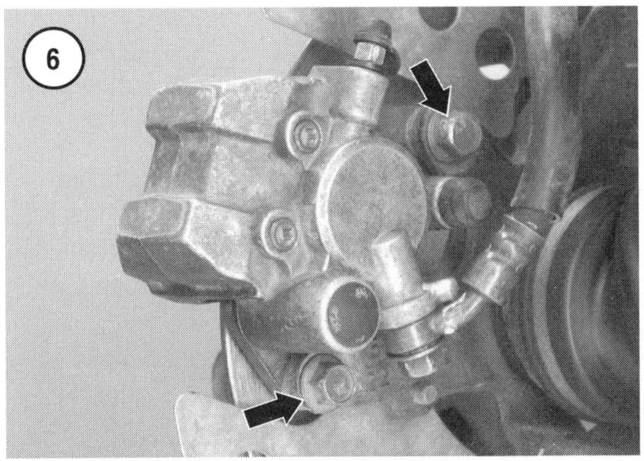

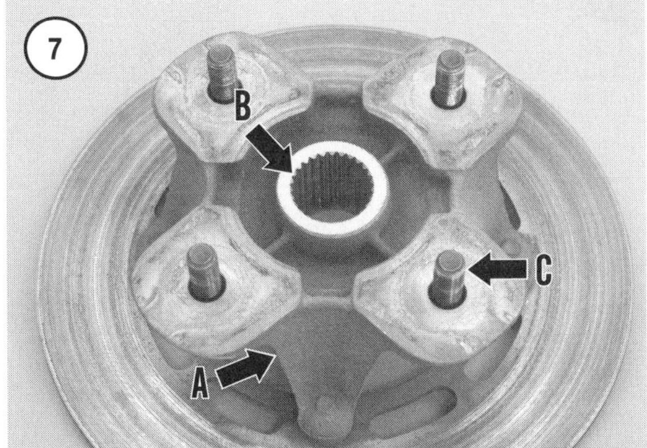

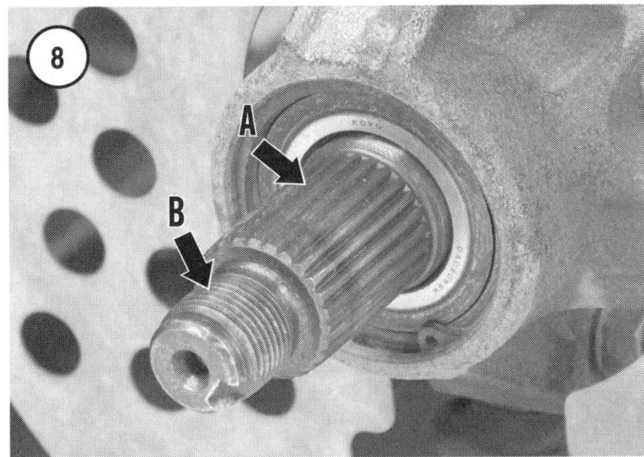

from being thrown onto the brake disc during machine operation.

b. Tighten the caliper mounting bolts to 30 N•m (22 ft.-lb.).

c. On 2002 models, tighten the hub nut to 200 N•m (148 ft.-lb.). Then install a new cotter pin.

d. On 2003-on models, install a new hub nut and tighten to 260 N•m (192 ft.-lb.). Then stake the nut into place.

e. Operate the brake lever several times to seat the pads.

TIE RODS

To improve access to suspension and steering components, remove the front fender assembly and skid plate (Chapter Sixteen).

Removal and Installation

1. Before removing the tie rods, make the following inspections for play and wear.

a. Park the machine on level ground with the wheels pointing straight ahead.

b. Lightly turn the handlebar toward the left, then toward the right while observing the tie rod ends. It is not necessary to actually turn the wheels. If the tie rod ends move vertically (removing play) as pressure is applied, they are worn or damaged.

c. Repeat the check with the wheels fully locked to the left, then the right. If there is vertical play in this position, the tie rod ends are worn.

2. Remove the front hub(s) as described in this chapter.

3. Remove the brake disc guard (**Figure 9**).

4. Remove the cotter pin (A, **Figure 10**) and nut (B) from the tie rod end at the steering knuckle. Apply penetrating oil to help separate the parts. Remove the tie rod end by one of the following methods:

a. If a ball joint remover is available (**Figure 11**), it can be used to separate the parts. If reusing the tie rod end, there is a risk of tearing the rubber boot when using this tool. To minimize the risk of damage, apply moderate pressure with the tool and allow it to sit. Often, the joint will separate after several seconds. If necessary, apply additional pressure and repeat the process.

b. If a ball joint remover is not available, a common puller can be used (**Figure 12**). The puller can be mounted as shown in **Figure 13**, and the tie rod end can be driven out of the bore. Install the tie rod nut at the end of the threads to protect them and to keep the puller centered.

5. Repeat Step 4 to remove the tie rod end (**Figure 14**) from the steering shaft. Mark the tie rod to install it in its original position.
6. Reverse these steps to install the tie rods. Note the following:
   a. Install the tie rods so the tie rod wrench flats (**Figure 15**) are closest to the wheel.
   b. Tighten both tie rod end nuts to 25 N•m (18 ft.-lb.).
   c. Install new cotter pins.
7. Check the toe-in adjustment as described in this section.

11

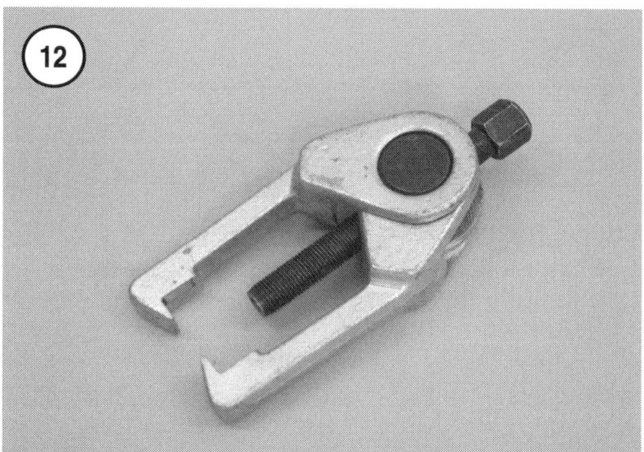
12

13

14

Inspection

CAUTION

The tie rod ends are sealed. Do not immerse the tie rod ends in solvent or any other liquid that could penetrate the boots. Wipe the ends with a shop cloth prior to inspection.

1. Inspect the tie rod for straightness. Replace the rod if it is bent.
2. Inspect the boot for tears and any entry of moisture or dirt into the joint.
3. Grasp the ball joint and swivel it in all directions, as well as vertically (**Figure 16**). Check for roughness, dryness and play. Replace the tie rod end if wear is evident.

Tie Rod Ends Disassembly and Assembly

1. Before removing the tie rod ends, measure the length of the exposed threads at each end of the tie rod (A, **Figure 17**). The measurements should be identical. If the measurements are different, determine the average of the two measurements. Refer to the measurement when installing the new tie rod ends. The tie rod lengths will be reasonably close, before actual toe-in adjustment is performed.
2. Hold the tie rod with a wrench locked on the tie rod flats (**Figure 15**).

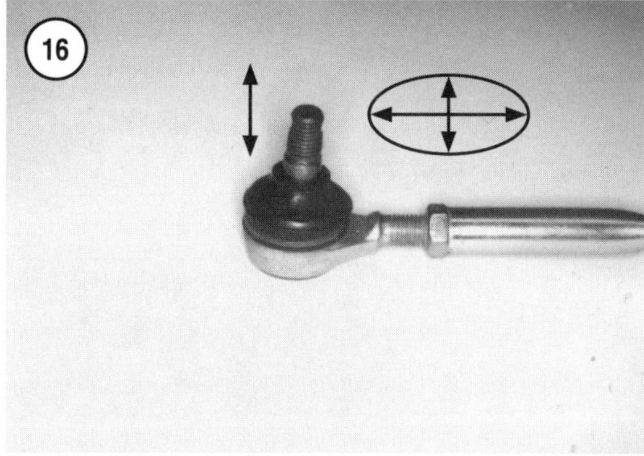

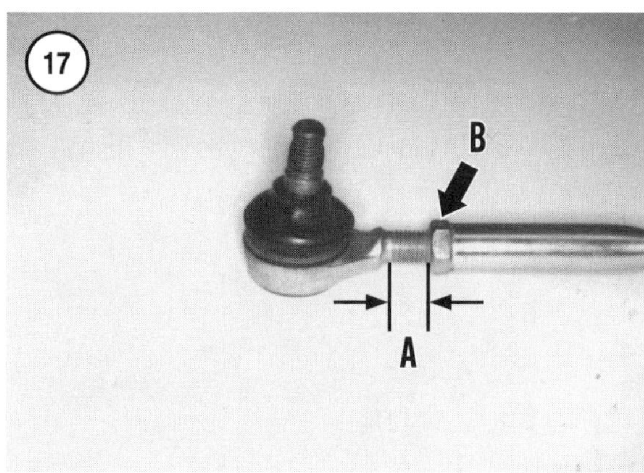

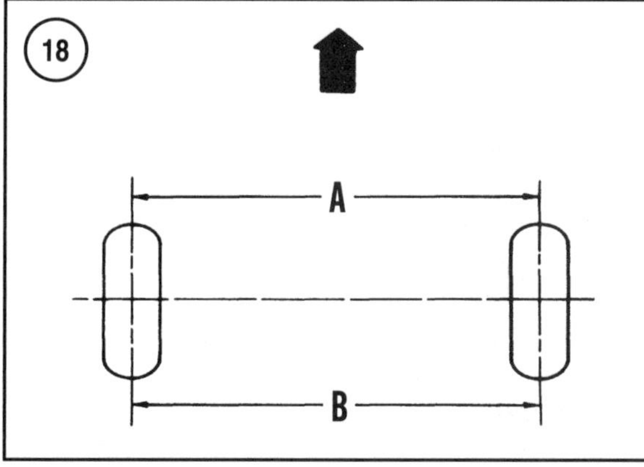

CAUTION

The outer tie rod end and locknut use a left-hand thread. The inner tie rod end and locknut use a right-hand thread. When loosening and tightening, note which direction each set of parts must be turned.

3. Loosen the tie rod adjusting sleeve locknut (B, **Figure 17**) and remove the tie rod end.
4. Clean the tie rod threads.
5. Thread the correct tie rod end into the tie rod.
6. Repeat the procedure for the remaining tie rod end.
7. Adjust the length of each tie rod as follows:
   a. Equally adjust the tie rod ends to achieve the initial measurement made in Step 1. The length of the exposed threads at each end must be identical.
   b. When the adjustments are achieved, finger-tighten the locknuts to hold the positions. Tighten the locknuts after the tie rods have been installed and the toe-in adjustment has been made.
   c. Check the toe-in adjustment as described in this section.

Toe-In Adjustment

If the toe-in is correct, the front of the tires will point *in* slightly, and the rear of the tires will point *out*.

Proper toe-in adjustment cannot be achieved if the tie rods, ball joints or steering knuckle bearings are worn. Replace worn parts before adjusting toe-in.

1. Inflate all tires to the recommended pressure (**Table 2**).
2. Park the machine on level ground. Allow space behind the machine so it can be rolled backward.
3. Point the handlebar straight ahead.
4. On both front tires, make a chalk mark at the center of the tread. The mark should be level with the centerline of the axle and at the front of the tire.
5. Measure distance A between the tires as shown in **Figure 18**. Record the measurement.
6. Roll the machine backwards until the marks are at the back of the tire and level with the axle.
7. Measure distance B between the tires as shown in **Figure 18**. Record the measurement.
8. Subtract measurement A from measurement B.
   a. If the difference is 0-10 mm (0-0.4 in.), toe-in is correct.
   b. If toe-in is not correct, perform Step 9.

NOTE

If the tie rods are not adjusted identically, handlebar alignment will not be centered with the wheels.

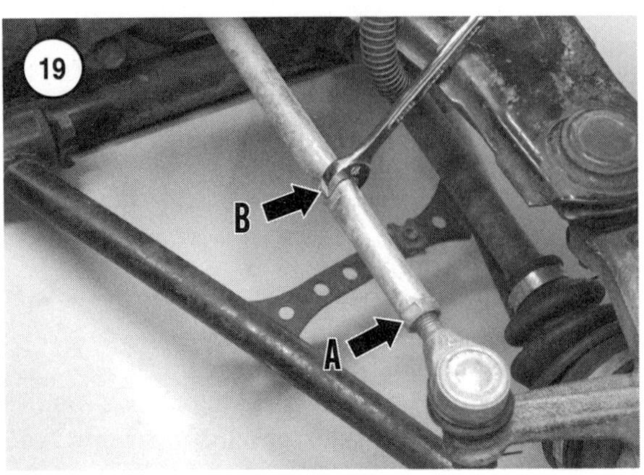

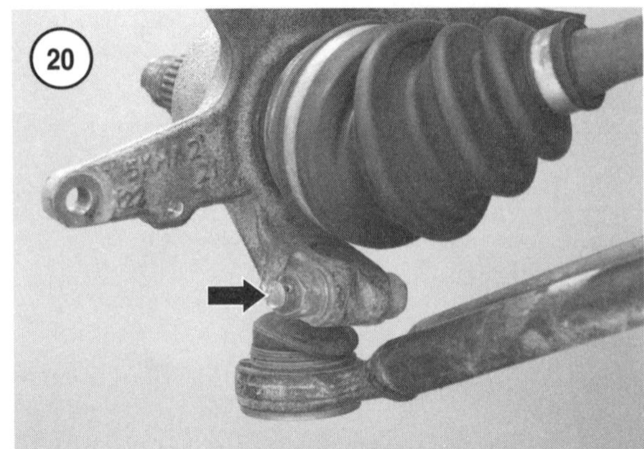

9. Adjust *both* tie rods equally as follows:
   a. Make a small reference mark on the top of each tie rod. Use the marks to verify that both tie rods are turned equal amounts.

CAUTION
The outer tie rod end and locknut use a left-hand thread. The inner tie rod end and locknut use a right-hand thread. Note which direction each set of parts must be turned when loosening and tightening the parts.

   b. Loosen the tie rod adjusting sleeve locknut (A, **Figure 19**) on both tie rod ends.
   c. Equally turn each tie rod with a wrench fitted to the flats on the rod sleeve (B, **Figure 19**).
   d. Recheck the measurements.
   e. When toe-in is correct, tighten the tie rod adjusting sleeve locknuts to 25 N•m (18 ft.-lb.).
   f. Turn the handlebar from side to side and make sure all ball joints pivot properly.
   g. Test ride the machine slowly to ensure that all adjustments are correct.

STEERING KNUCKLE

Removal and Installation

1. Remove the front hub as described in this chapter.
2. Remove the outer tie rod end as described in this chapter.
3. Remove the axle protector and brake hose holder bolt.
4. Remove the lower control arm ball joint as follows:
   a. Remove the pinch bolt assembly (**Figure 20**).
   b. Spread the split in the knuckle (**Figure 21**) with a narrow chisel, then lightly tap the lower control arm out of the knuckle. Use care when separating the parts.
5. Remove the upper control arm as follows:
   a. Remove the cotter pin and nut (**Figure 22**)

24

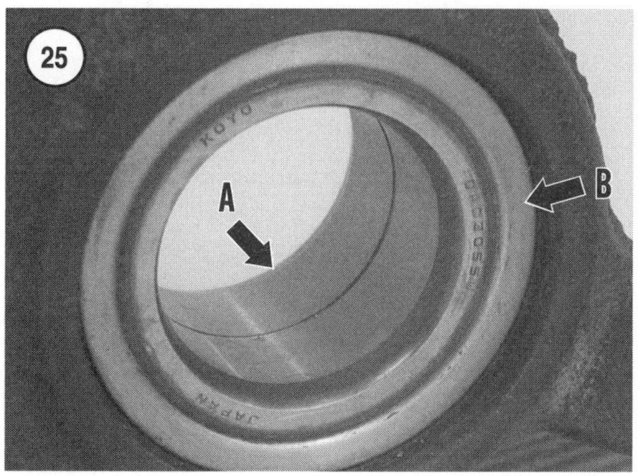

25

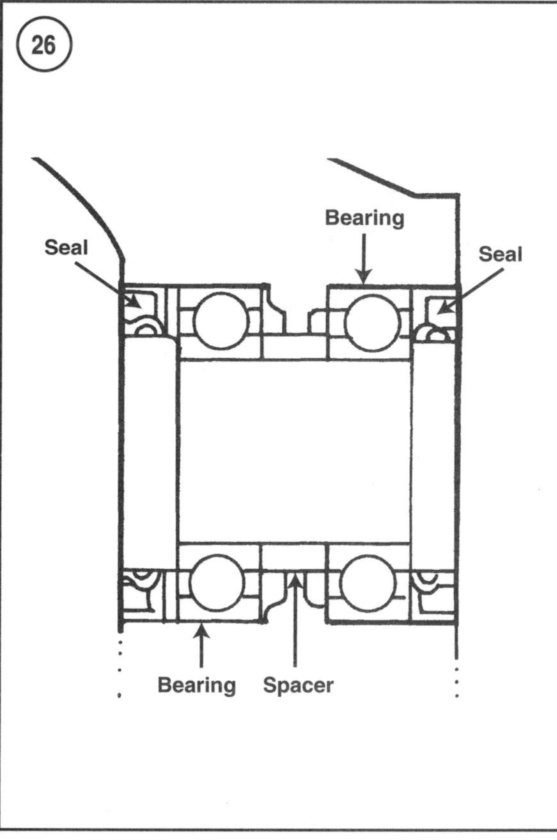

26

from the upper control arm. Apply penetrating oil to help separate the ball joint from the steering knuckle. If the ball joint or control arm become damaged, they are only available as a single part number.

b. Use a ball joint remover to separate the parts (**Figure 23**). If the control arm will be reused, use the tool carefully to prevent damaging the rubber boot. To minimize the risk of damage, apply moderate pressure with the tool and allow it to sit. Often, the joint will separate after several seconds. If necessary, apply additional pressure and repeat the process.

c. Pull the knuckle away from the axle.

6. Inspect the steering knuckle as described in this section.

7. Reverse these steps to install the steering knuckle. Note the following:

a. Lubricate the bearings, seals and O-ring (if used) with waterproof grease.

b. Finger-tighten the nuts and bolts until all parts are assembled.

c. Tighten the steering knuckle pinch bolt to 48 N•m (35 ft.-lb.).

d. Tighten the upper control arm ball joint nut to 25 N•m (18 ft.-lb.).

e. Install new cotter pins.

Inspection

1. On 2002 models, remove the O-ring from the outer bore.

2. Wipe the steering knuckle clean. Do not submerge the bearings and seals in solvent.

3. Inspect the tapered bores and mounting arms for cracks and other damage. If damage is evident, replace the steering knuckle (**Figure 24**).

4. Inspect the bearings (A, **Figure 25**) and seals (B).

a. Check each bearing for play and roughness. If rust, dirt or moisture is evident, the seals are leaking.

b. On 2002 models, inspect the rubber seals for tears and leaks.

c. On 2003-on models, inspect the metal seals for damage and leaks.

d. If necessary, replace the bearings and seals as described in this section.

Bearing and Seal Replacement

2002 models

For 2002 models, the steering knuckle uses two seals, two bearings and a spacer. Use a press to install the bearings. Refer to **Figure 26**.

1. Pry the seals from their bores.

2. Wedge the spacer to one side, then drive out the inner bearing. Use a drift to work around the perimeter of the inner race. Support the steering knuckle so the bearing can fall from the bore. Do not wedge or cock the bearing in the bore.
3. Remove the spacer and drive out the remaining bearing.
4. Clean the steering knuckle and spacer.
5. Apply waterproof grease to the bearings, seals and spacer.
6. Place the outer bearing squarely over its bore, then press it into place. Use a driver that fits onto the outside edge of the bearing.
7. Install the spacer and then press the inside bearing into place.
8. Install the seals. Use a driver that fits onto the outside edge of the seals.

2003-on models

On 2003-on models, the steering knuckle has a single bearing that has double-ball races. The bearing is also permanently sealed on both sides. Use a press to remove and install the bearing. Refer to **Figure 27**.
1. Remove the snap ring from the outer bore.
2. Turn the steering knuckle over and press the bearing out of the bore. Support the steering knuckle so the bearing can fall from the bore. Do not wedge or cock the bearing in the bore.
3. Clean the steering knuckle.
4. Apply waterproof grease to the bearing.
5. Place the bearing squarely over the outer bore, then press it into place. Use a driver that fits onto the outside edge of the bearing.
6. Install a new snap ring with the sharp edge facing out.

CONTROL ARMS

To improve access to suspension and steering components, removing the front fender assembly may help.

Removal and Installation

1. Remove the front wheel as described in this chapter.
2. Remove the skid plate and axle protectors. Remove the air duct if disassembling the left control arms.
3. Completely remove the steering knuckle as described in this chapter, or remove just the control arms from the steering knuckle as described in *Steering Knuckle* in this chapter. It is not necessary to remove the front hub or disconnect the tie rods.

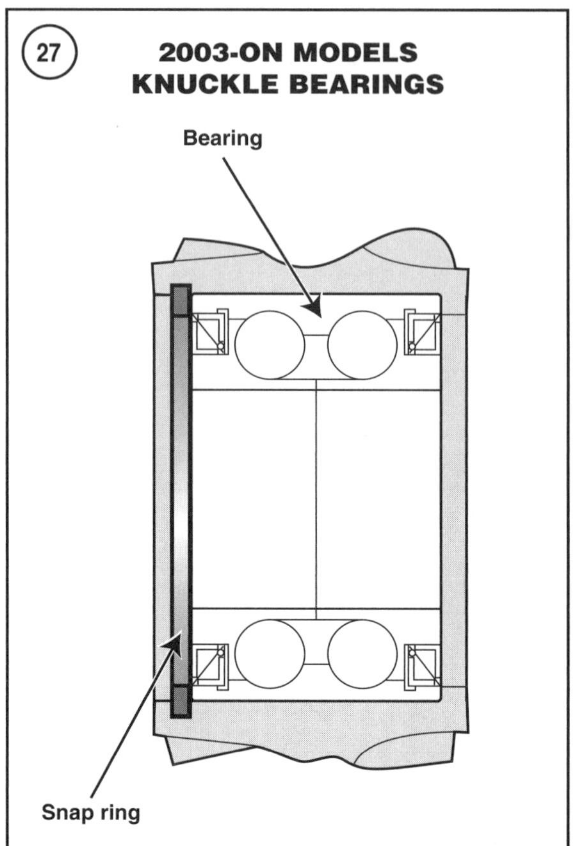

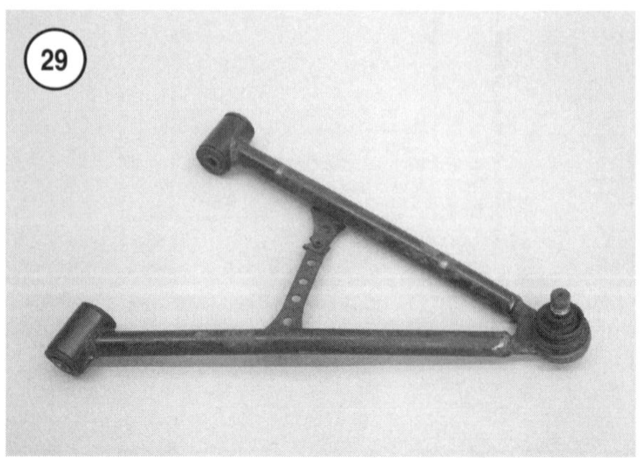

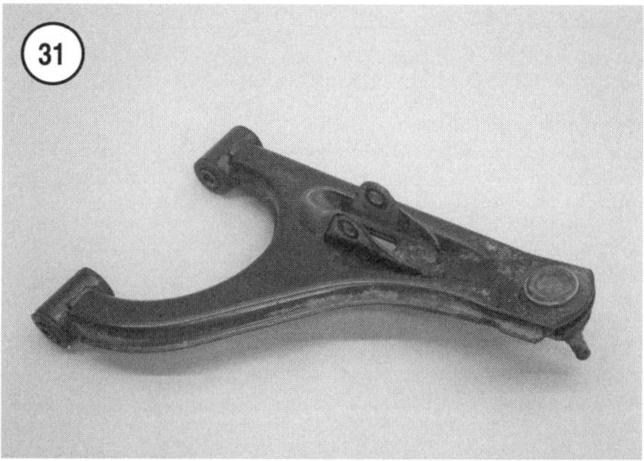

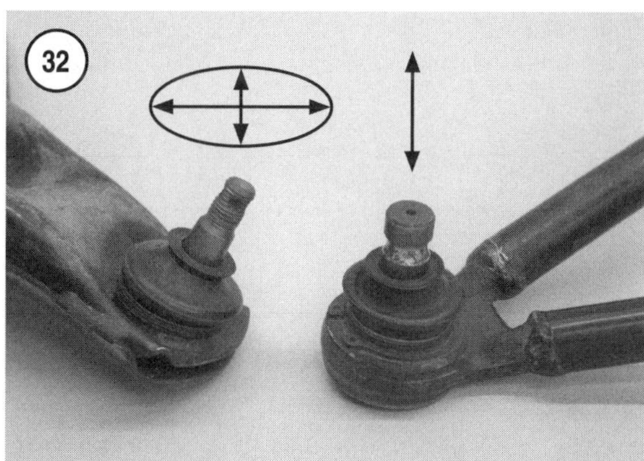

4. Before removing the control arms, grasp each arm and lever it from side to side. If play is noticeable, check the bushings for wear.
5. Remove the bolts (**Figure 28**) from the lower control arm. Then remove the control arm (**Figure 29**).
6. Remove the bottom bolt on the shock absorber. Pivot and secure the shock absorber out of the way.
7. Remove the bolts (**Figure 30**) from the upper control arm. Then remove the control arm (**Figure 31**).
8. Inspect the control arms as described in this section.
9. Reverse these steps to install the control arms. Note the following:
   a. If both pairs of control arms have been removed, verify that they are being installed on the correct side of the machine.
   b. Lubricate the bushings and pivot bolts with waterproof grease. Avoid lubricating the bolt threads.
   c. Install the control arm bolts so the heads face forward.
   d. Finger-tighten the nuts and bolts until all parts are attached to the steering knuckle.
   e. Tighten the shock absorber and control arm fasteners to 45 N•m (33 ft.-lb.).

Inspection

CAUTION

The ball joints are sealed. Do not immerse the ball joints in solvent or any other liquid that could penetrate the boots. Wipe the ball joints clean with a shop cloth prior to inspection.

1. Clean the control arms.
2. Inspect all welded joints on the control arms. Check for fractures, bending or other damage. If damage is evident, replace the control arm, or have a dealership or machine shop weld the damaged section and test the strength of the control arm.
3. Inspect the ball joint boots for tears and any entry of moisture or dirt into the joint.
4. Grasp each ball joint (**Figure 32**) and swivel it in all directions, including vertically. Check for roughness, dryness and play. For the upper control arm, the ball joint is integral to the control arm and the complete assembly must be replaced if the ball joint is damaged. Replacement ball joints are available for the lower control arm. If necessary, replace the ball joint in the lower control arm as described in this section.
5. Inspect the control arm pivot bushings (**Figure 33**). Inspect each bushing for play and damage. If necessary, replace damaged bushings by pressing them out of the control arm.

6. Inspect the shock absorber mounts in the upper control arm for damage and elongated bolt holes.
7. Inspect all pivot bolts and nuts for any damage.

Ball Joint Replacement

1. Remove the retainer (A, **Figure 34**), boot (B) and snap ring (C) from the top of the ball joint.
2. Note which side is the top of the control arm.
3. Secure the control arm in a press so the perimeter of the bore is supported. Allow space under the joint so it may pass out of the control arm.
4. Squarely press the ball joint from the control arm.
5. Clean the bore. Then turn over the control arm. Insert the new ball joint through the bottom of the control arm with the stud (D, **Figure 34**) facing the proper direction.
6. Again, secure the control arm in the press with the perimeter of the bore supported. Then press the new ball joint into place.
7. Install a new snap ring with the sharp edge facing out.

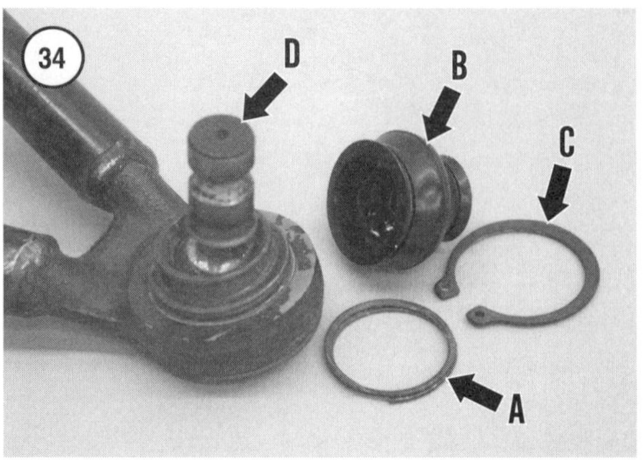

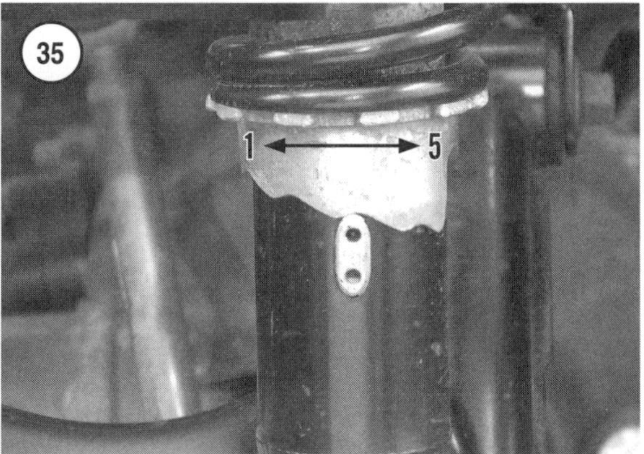

SHOCK ABSORBERS

The front shock absorbers are equipped with five spring-preload positions. Set both front shock absorbers to the same position by using a shock absorber spanner to rotate the cam at the bottom of the spring (**Figure 35**). The least amount of spring preload is in the first position, while the most preload is in the fifth position. The standard setting is the second position.

Removal and Installation

1. Park the machine on level ground.
2. Raise and support the machine so the front wheels are slightly touching the ground. The mounting bolts are easier to remove if there is minimal load on the shock absorber.
3. Set the shock absorber to the first position (softest).
4. Remove the lower mounting bolt (**Figure 36**).
5. Remove the upper mounting bolt (**Figure 37**).
6. Remove the shock absorber and inspect it as described in this section.
7. Reverse these procedures to install the shock absorbers. Note the following:
   a. Apply waterproof grease to the bushings and mounting bolts. Avoid lubricating the bolt threads.
   b. Tighten the shock absorber fasteners to 45 N•m (33 ft.-lb.).
   c. Set the shock absorber to the desired position. Refer to **Table 3** for settings.

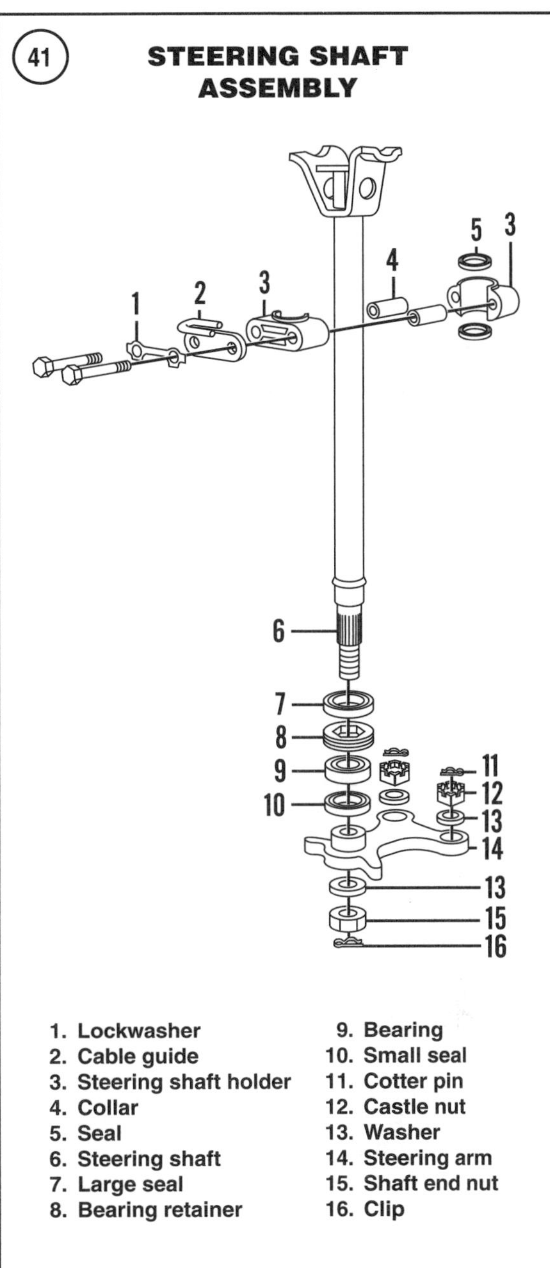

Inspection

If the shock absorber (**Figure 38**) is damaged or worn, replace it as a complete unit. The shock absorber is not rebuildable. Always replace both shock absorbers if either unit is damaged.

1. Inspect and clean the lower bushing, pivot and mounting bolt. Fit each part into its mating part and check for wear and play.
2. Inspect the preload adjuster (**Figure 39**) and notches for damage.
3. Inspect the shock body for severe dents that can affect operation.
4. Inspect the shock for oil leaking from the rod seal.
5. Inspect the spring for damage or looseness. Measure the spring free length. Refer to **Table 1** for the required length.
6. Inspect and clean the upper bushing (A, **Figure 40**) and mounting bolt (B). Fit the bolt into the bushing and check for wear or play.

STEERING SHAFT

Removal and Installation

Refer to **Figure 41**.

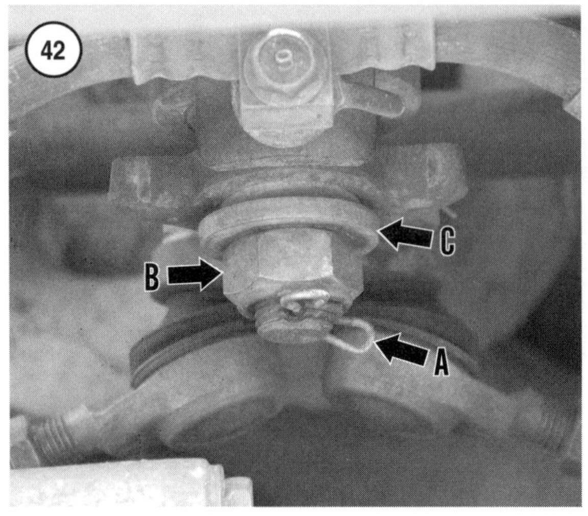

1. Remove the front fender assembly (Chapter Sixteen).
2. Remove the handlebar as described in this chapter. Reposition and secure the handlebar out of the way. Avoid kinking the cables and brake hose. Keep the brake fluid reservoir upright.
3. Remove the pin (A, **Figure 42**), nut (B) and washer (C) from the end of the steering shaft.
4. If the steering arm or steering shaft bearing and seals are damaged, remove the tie rod ends from the steering arm as described in this chapter. The tie rods do not have to be removed in order to remove the steering shaft or to replace the bearing and seals.
5. Bend the lockwasher tabs away from the bolts. Then remove the two bolts securing the steering shaft holders, cable guide, collars and seals (**Figure 43**).
6. Lift and remove the steering shaft from the lower bearing (**Figure 44**). If necessary, use a soft mallet to unseat the shaft from the steering arm.
7. Inspect the steering shaft assembly as described in this section.
8. Reverse these steps to install the steering shaft. Note the following:
   a. Install the steering shaft with the paint mark at the top of the shaft (A, **Figure 45**), pointing forward.
   b. Apply waterproof grease to the shaft, seals, bearing and steering shaft holders.
   c. Finger-tighten all bolts and verify correct alignment of the parts before tightening any bolts.
   d. Install a new lockwasher onto the steering shaft holder bolts. Then tighten the bolts to 23 N•m (17 ft.-lb.). Bend the lockwasher tabs against the bolt heads.
   e. Tighten the steering shaft end nut to 180 N•m (133 ft.-lb.).
   f. Install new cotter pins, where removed.
   g. Check toe-in as described in this chapter.

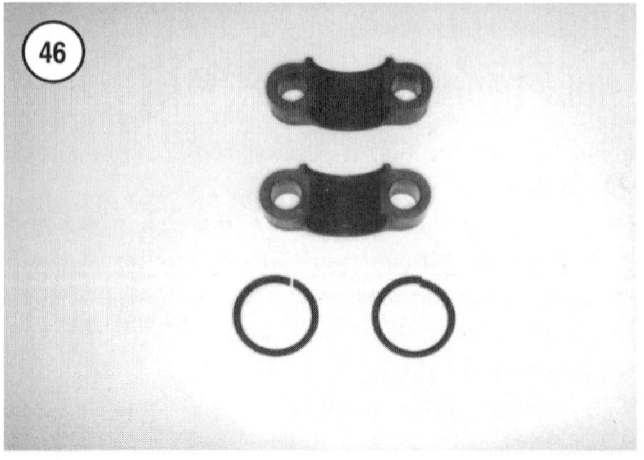

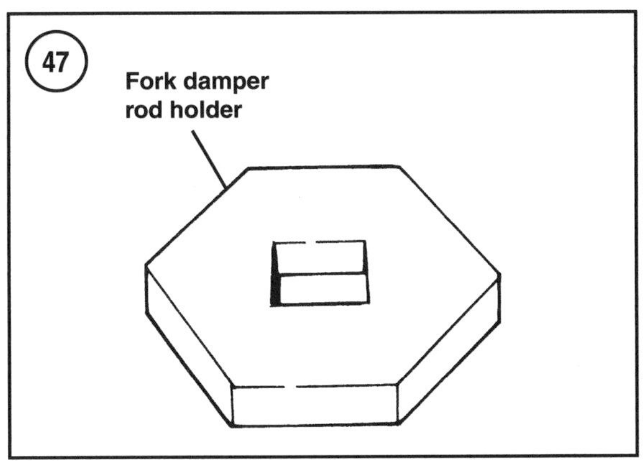

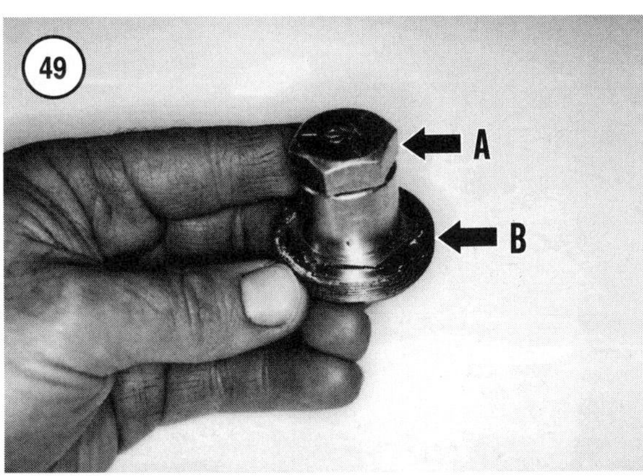

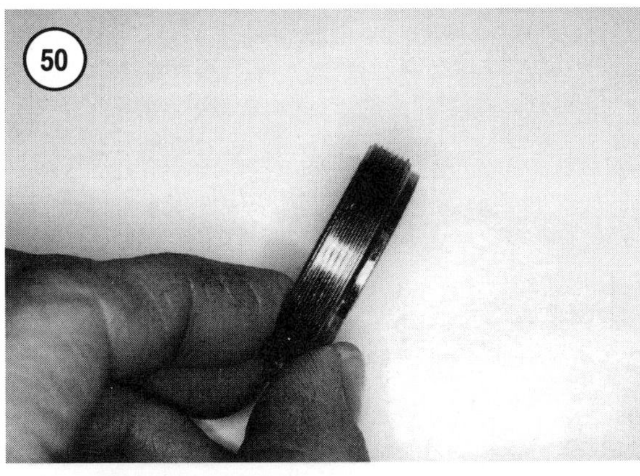

Inspection

Refer to **Figure 41**.

1. Wipe the steering shaft clean.
2. Inspect the steering shaft for the following:
   a. Distortion or damage along the length of the shaft.
   b. Wear at the steering shaft holder mount.
   c. Cracked or damaged handlebar mounting plate.
   d. Damaged threads, splines or cotter pin hole.
   e. If removed, inspect the steering arm for enlarged tie rod holes. If the arm is installed, make sure the tie rod ends are tight in the holes.
3. Inspect the steering shaft holder assembly and seals for wear or damage (**Figure 46**). The steering shaft holder halves should fit together with no binding.
4. Inspect the steering shaft seals and bearing (**Figure 44**).
   a. Inspect the seals for wear and deterioration.
   b. Inspect the bearing by turning its inner race. The bearing should turn smoothly without play.
   c. If necessary, replace the bearing and seals as described in this section.

Steering Shaft Bearing and Seals Replacement

11

To remove the bearing retainer, a 30-mm damper rod holder (Yamaha part No. YM-01327), or an equivalent tool (**Figure 47**), is required. An effective tool can also be made with a 30-mm hex nut, spacer and bolt (**Figure 48**). Note how the tool (A, **Figure 49**) engages with the bearing retainer (B). Refer to **Figure 41**.

1. Pry the upper and lower seals from the bearing holder.
2. Remove the bearing retainer from the top of the bearing holder.
3. Remove the bearing.
4. Clean the retainer and bearing holder bore.
5. Apply waterproof grease to the new bearing and seals.
6. Insert the bearing into the bearing holder. Install the bearing so the manufacturer's marks face up.
7. Install the bearing retainer with the shouldered side facing down (**Figure 50**). Tighten the bearing retainer to 65 N•m (48 ft.-lb.).
8. Install the seals.
   a. Note that the upper seal is larger than the lower seal.
   b. Use a drawbolt (**Figure 51**) to install the seals.

c. Install both seals with their closed side facing out. Drive each seal until it is flush with the edge of the holder.

HANDLEBAR

Adjustment

If the handlebar needs to be repositioned, adjustment can be made by loosening the *rear* bolts securing the upper holders (B, **Figure 45**). Tilt the handlebar to the desired position. Then tighten the front holder bolts, followed by the rear. Tighten the bolts to 20 N•m (15 ft.-lb.).

Removal and Installation

1. If replacing the handlebar, remove the following components:
   a. Fuel tank breather hose and handlebar cover. Pull straight up to unclip the cover.
   b. Security bands.
   c. Four-wheel drive switch (A, **Figure 52**).
   d. Front brake master cylinder (B, **Figure 52**) and throttle assembly (C). Secure the master cylinder so it remains upright.
   e. Rear hand brake and switch assembly (A, **Figure 53**). Use a small tool to release the barb that secures the switch to the brake lever.
   f. Left handlebar switch (B, **Figure 53**).
   g. Handlebar grips. Spray lubricant under the grip to soften the adhesive. Compressed air can also be used to lift and free the grips.
   h. Handlebar holder bolts and holders.
2. If reusing the handlebar, inspect the handlebar as described in this section.
3. Reverse these steps to install the handlebar. Note the following:
   a. The punch marks (**Figure 54**) on the upper holders must face forward. Tighten the front holder bolts, followed by the rear. Tighten all bolts to 20 N•m (15 ft.-lb.).
   b. If installing new grips, clean the handlebar grip surface with solvent, such as electrical contact cleaner. Apply hand grip cement by following the manufacturer's instructions carefully.
   c. Tighten the front brake master cylinder mounting bolts to 7 N•m (62 in.-lb.).
   d. On 2002-2003 models, position the rear hand brake and switch assemblies so they are spaced 66 mm (2.6 in.) from side to side (**Figure 55**).
   e. On 2004-on models, position the rear hand brake and switch assemblies so they are spaced 74.5 mm (2.9 in.) from side to side (**Figure 55**).

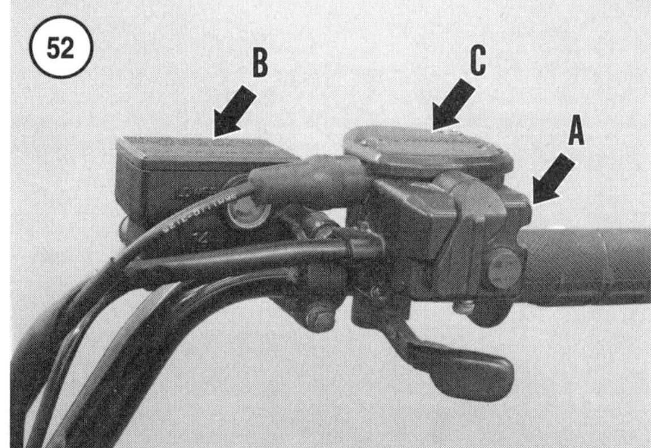

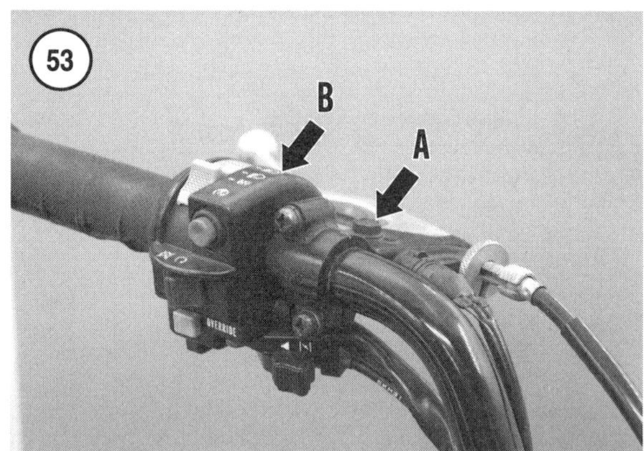

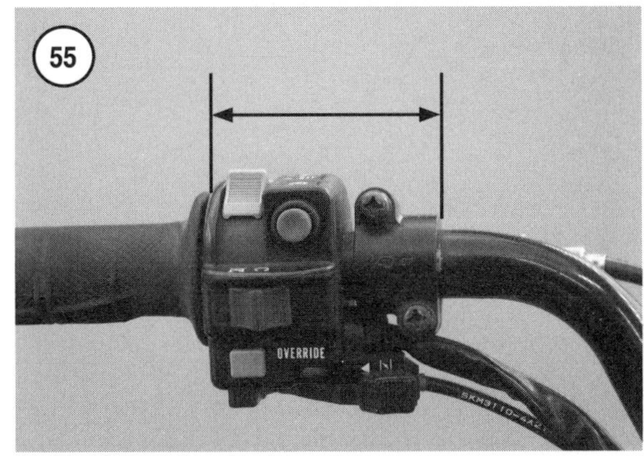

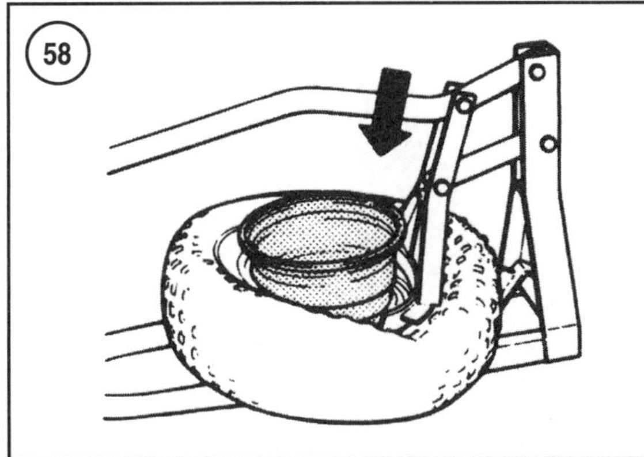

f. Check the riding position and adjust the handlebar, if necessary. Turn the handlebar side to side and check for cable binding.

Inspection

WARNING
Never attempt to straighten, weld or heat a damaged handlebar. The metal can weaken and possibly break when riding the machine.

1. Inspect the handlebar for cracks, bends or other damage. If the handlebar is made of aluminum, check closely where the handlebar is clamped to the holders and at the brake lever. If cracks, scores or other damage is evident, replace the handlebar. Damage in these areas can cause the handlebar to break.
2. Inspect the threads on the mounting bolts and in the holders. Clean all residue from the threads. Replace bolts that are damaged or stressed.
3. Clean the handlebar holders and handlebar with solvent or electrical contact cleaner.

TIRES

The tubeless, low-pressure tires used are designed for off-road use. Rapid wear will occur if the machine is ridden on paved surfaces. If a puncture occurs, a tire plug may be used temporarily. A tire plug is not suitable as a permanent repair. Patch the tire as soon as possible.

11

Tire Changing

The tire-to-rim seal on ATV tires is very tight and requires using a bead breaker tool (**Figure 56**). After the bead is broken, tire irons and rim protectors are required to remove and install the tire.

1. Remove the valve stem core and deflate the tire.
2. Lubricate the tire bead and rim flanges with a rubber lubricant. Press the sidewalls down to allow the lubricant to penetrate the bead. Also lubricate the sidewall where the bead breaker will make contact.
3. Position the wheel under the bead breaker tool (**Figure 57**).
4. With the tool seated against the rim, press down on the lever to break the tire bead from the rim. Work around the rim, using the bead breaker and hand pressure to break the tire free (**Figure 58**).
5. Turn the wheel over and repeat Steps 2-4.
6. Lubricate the tire beads and rim flanges to prepare for using the tire irons.

7. Place rim protectors or other padding (split rubber hose works well) on the rim edge. Position the protectors where the tire irons will be inserted.

CAUTION
Failure to use rim protectors could damage the wheel. This could cause an air leak at the bead.

8. Insert the tire irons between the rim and tire (**Figure 59**). Pry the tire bead over the rim. If removal is difficult, move the tire irons closer together and free smaller sections of the bead at a time.
9. When the upper sidewall is completely free, lift the lower sidewall up so it can be removed as described in Steps 6-8.
10. Clean and inspect the rim sealing surfaces (**Figure 60**). The surfaces must be straight, clean and smooth in order to seal properly.
11. Replace the valve stem as follows:
  a. Remove the valve stem by pulling it out, from inside the rim.
  b. Lubricate the new valve stem with rubber lubricant.
  c. Insert the new valve stem through the rim hole, then pull it out until it seats into place (**Figure 61**).
12. Inspect the tire bead and rim for cleanliness.
13. Check the tire sidewall for the direction arrow or the *This Side Out* marking.
14. Place the tire with the sidewall markings facing up. Then wet the tire bead with water.
15. Insert the wheel (valve stem facing up) into the tire (**Figure 62**). Hand-fit as much of the wheel into the tire as possible.
16. Use the rim protectors and tire irons to finish installing the bead. Push the rim to the opposite side of the tire so the second bead can be installed.
17. Turn the assembly over and hand-fit as much of the wheel into the tire as possible (**Figure 63**).
18. Use the rim protectors and tire irons to finish installing the bead.
19. Install the valve stem core.

WARNING
*Do not inflate the tire past the recommended pressure. Tire explosion and injury is possible. The pressure shown in **Table 2** is for original equipment tires. Check the sidewall if installing aftermarket tires.*

20. Apply water to the rim beads. Then inflate the tire to the bead seating pressure indicated on the sidewall.
21. If the tire beads do not seat because of air leaks, place a tight strap around the perimeter of the tread.

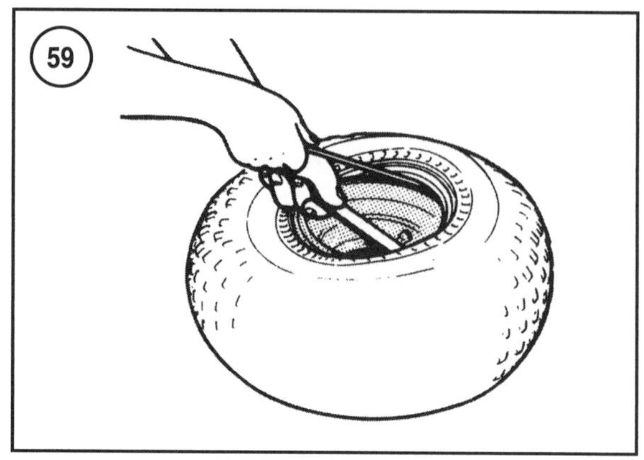

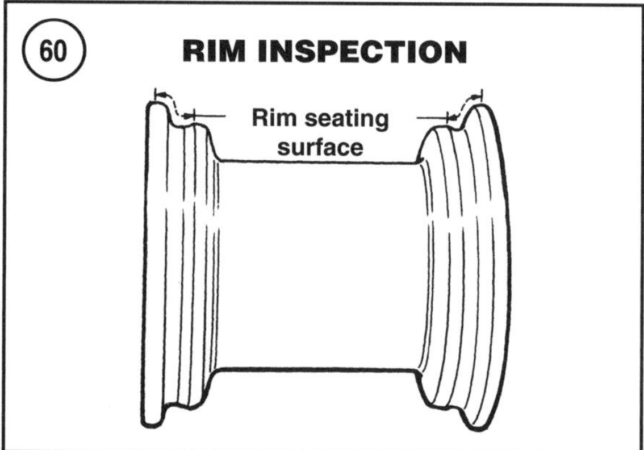

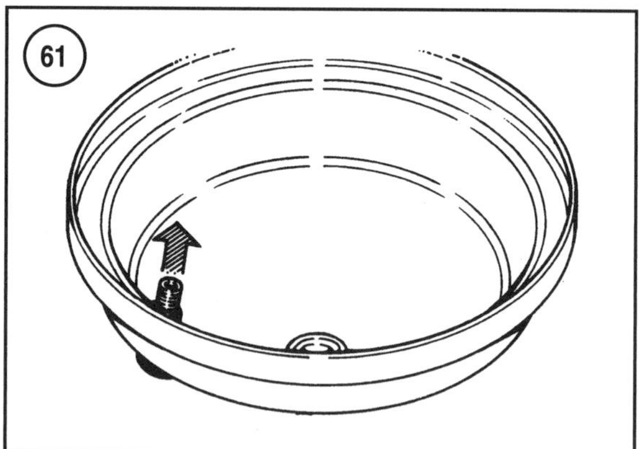

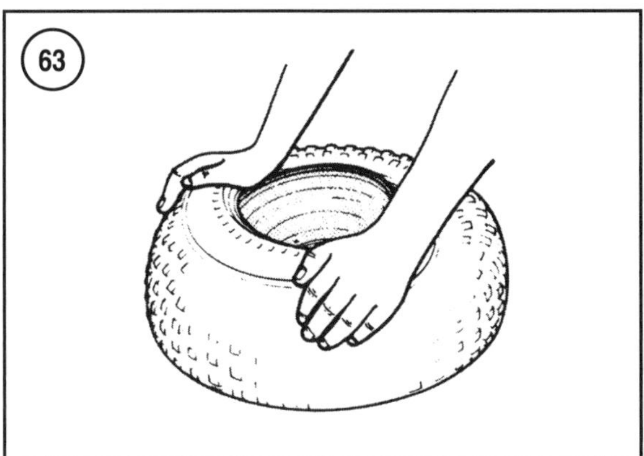

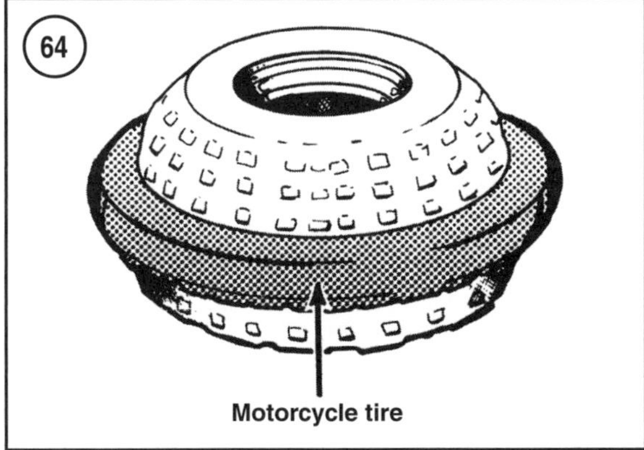

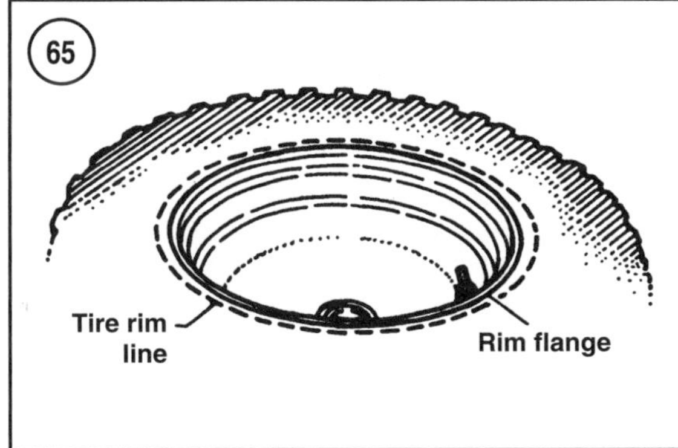

If correctly sized, a motorcycle tire will also work (**Figure 64**).

22. After inflation, check the rim lines on both sides of the tire to ensure the beads are seated. If the beads are seated correctly, the rim lines will be parallel with the rim flanges as shown in **Figure 65**. If the beads are not seated correctly, deflate the tire and break the bead. Apply additional water to the tire bead. Reinflate the tire and check the bead alignment.

23. When the tire is properly seated, do the following:
   a. Remove the valve core to deflate the tire.
   b. Wait 1 hour to let the tire adjust on the rim.
   c. Install the valve core and inflate the tire to the operating pressure in **Table 2**.

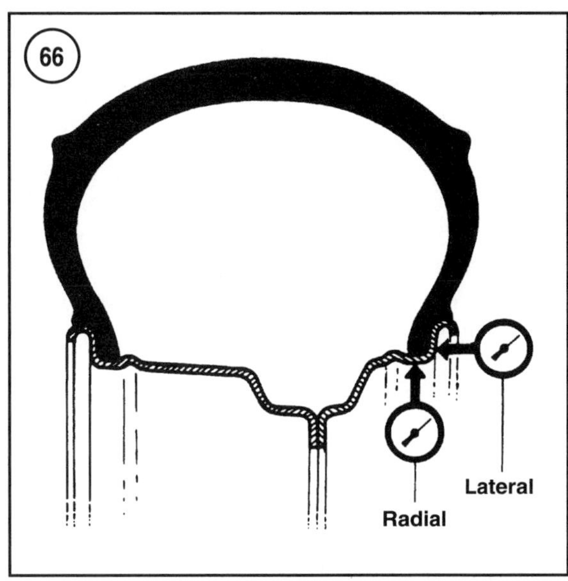

   d. Apply water to the beads and valve stem and check for leaks.

Patching

Follow the manufacturer's instructions when using a patch repair kit. If instructions are not available, use the following procedure.

1. Remove the tire as described in this section.
2. Mark the puncture location. Then remove the object puncturing the tire.
3. Working from inside the tire, roughen the area around the puncture. The roughened area should be larger than the patch to be applied. If the repair kit does not provide a tool to roughen the area, use coarse sandpaper or any object that will lightly scrape and roughen the surface.
4. Clean the roughened area with a non-oily solvent.
5. Apply a small amount of the adhesive to the roughened area. Allow the adhesive to dry for about 30 seconds to become tacky.
6. Remove the backing from the patch. Do not touch the newly exposed surface of the patch.
7. Center the patch over the puncture. Then press the patch into place. Do not raise or slide the patch once it contacts the adhesive.
8. If a roller is available, press the patch into place and make sure that the edges are tightly sealed. If a roller is not available, use a smooth, hard object.
9. Install the tire on the wheel as described in this section.

WHEEL RUNOUT

If vibration or tire wear is abnormal, check the axle/steering knuckle bearings for wear and play.

Replace damaged bearings to get an accurate runout reading. If the bearings are in good condition, check the wheel for excessive radial and lateral runout (**Figure 66**).

1. Park the machine on a level surface. Then raise the front and rear of the machine so all wheels are off the ground. If checking the front wheels, secure the handlebar tightly so the wheels cannot move laterally.
2. Clean the perimeter of the wheel where it will contact the dial indicator.
3. Mount a dial indicator on a stable surface and in contact with the wheel. Either type of runout can be measured first. Zero the gauge so it can measure runout in both directions as the wheel is turned.
4. Turn the wheel and watch the amount of runout measured on the gauge. If possible, have an assistant turn one of the other wheels, so the wheel being checked is not handled. Since the machine is four-wheel drive, all wheels will turn together.
5. Maximum runout is 2 mm (0.08 in.) in either direction. Replace the wheel if it is out of specification.

Table 1 FRONT SUSPENSION AND STEERING SPECIFICATIONS

Front shock absorber	
Type	Coil spring/oil damper
Travel	86 mm (3.39 in.)
Spring free length	295 mm (11.61 in.)
Spring rate	20 N/mm (114 lb./in.)
Front suspension	Double wishbone
Front wheel travel	170 mm (6.7 in.)
Steering	
Camber angle	0°
Caster angle	5°
Kingpin angle	11°
Kingpin offset	0 mm (0 in.)
Toe-in	0-10 mm (0-0.4 in.)
Trail	26 mm (1.02 in.)

Table 2 TIRE AND WHEEL SPECIFICATIONS

Tires	
Type	Tubeless radial
Sizes	
Front	AT25 × 8-12 Dunlop KT131
Rear	AT25 × 10-12 Dunlop KT135
Inflation pressure (cold)	
Front	
Standard	35 kPa (5.1 psi)
Minimum	32 kPa (4.6 psi)
Maximum	38 kPa (5.5 psi)
Rear	
Standard	30 kPa (4.4 psi)
Minimum	27 kPa (3.9 psi)
Maximum	33 kPa (4.8 psi)
Bead seating pressure	250 kPa (36.3 psi) maximum
Tire wear limit	3 mm (0.12 in.)
Wheels	
Size	
Front	12 × 6.0 AT
Rear	12 × 7.5 AT
Runout (radial and lateral)	2 mm (0.08 in.)

Table 3 FRONT SHOCK ABSORBER SETTING

	Standard	Minimum (soft)	Maximum (hard)
Spring preload	2	1	5

Table 4 FRONT SUSPENSION AND STEERING TORQUE SPECIFICATIONS

	N•m	in.-lb.	ft.-lb.
Control arm-to-frame fasteners	45	–	33
Front brake caliper mounting bolts	30	–	22
Front brake master cylinder mounting bolts	7	62	–
Front wheel hub nut			
2002	200	–	148
2003-on	260	–	192
Front wheel lug nuts	55	–	41
Handlebar holder bolts	20	–	15
Shock absorber mounting fasteners	45	–	33
Steering knuckle pinch bolt	48	–	35
Steering shaft bearing retainer	65	–	48
Steering shaft end nut	180	–	133
Steering shaft holder bolts	23	–	17
Tie rod adjusting sleeve locknut	25	–	18
Tie rod end nuts	25	–	18
Upper control arm ball joint nut	25	–	18

CHAPTER TWELVE

FRONT AXLES AND DIFFERENTIAL

This chapter covers the front axles, differential and front drive shaft. Refer to the tables at the end of this chapter for specifications.

FRONT AXLES

Removal and Installation

Refer to **Figure 1**.

1. If desired, remove the front fender assembly and skid plate (Chapter Sixteen) to improve access.
2. Drain the lubricant from the differential (Chapter Three).
3. Remove the steering knuckle (Chapter Eleven).
4. Grasp the axle and quickly pull it straight out of the differential (**Figure 2**). The circlip at the inboard end of the axle will cause slight resistance when disengaging the axle.
5. Inspect the axle (**Figure 3**) as described in this section.
6. Reverse this procedure to install the axle(s). Note the following:
   a. Lubricate the seals on the differential with molybdenum disulfide grease.
   b. Install a new circlip at the inboard end of the axle (**Figure 4**).
   c. After installation, lightly pull on the axle to make sure it is locked in place.
   d. Fill the differential with lubricant (Chapter Three).

Inspection

1. Clean the axle and splines. Do not submerge the axle boots in solvent. The CV joints (under the boots) are packed with grease.
2. At the ends of the axle, inspect the following:
   a. Hub nut threads (A, **Figure 5**). Inspect for stripped or damaged threads.
   b. Splines (B, **Figure 5**). Check for worn, distorted and broken splines. At the outboard end of the axle, install the respective hub and feel for play. At the inboard splines, if corrosion is evident, water has entered the differential.
   c. Bearing and seal surfaces (C, **Figure 5**). Check for scoring, galling, corrosion and other damage. If damage is evident, inspect the matching bearing in the differential or steering knuckle.
   d. Boots and clamps (D, **Figure 5**). The boots must not be torn or cracked. The clamps should tightly grip the boot and axle. A loose or torn boot will allow dirt and moisture to

1

FRONT AXLE

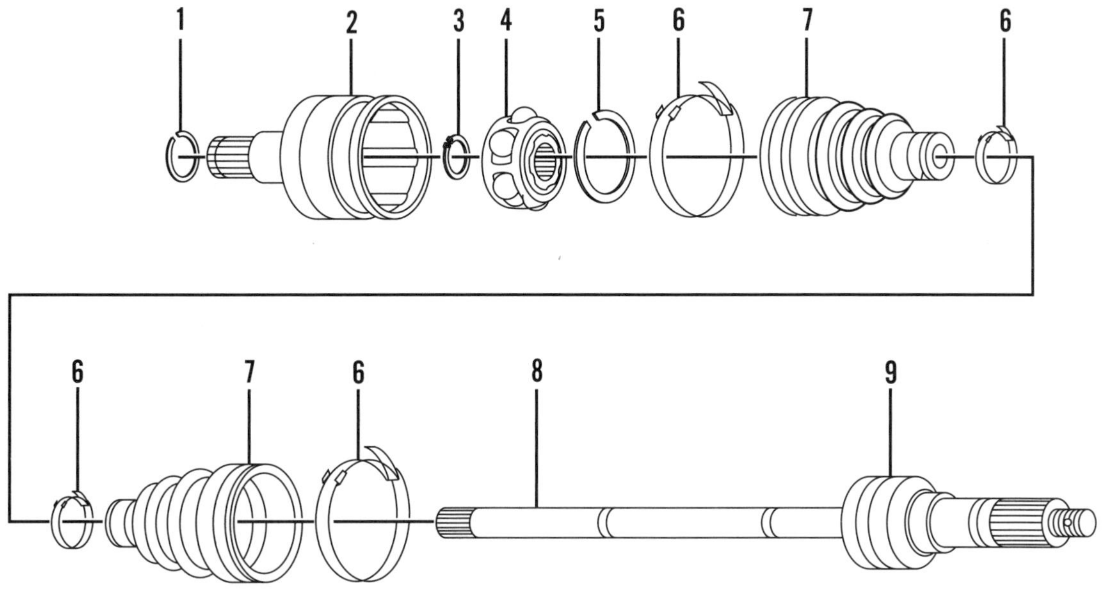

1. Circlip
2. Inboard CV joint
3. Snap ring
4. Bearing
5. Retaining ring
6. Clamp
7. Boot
8. Axle shaft
9. Outboard CV joint

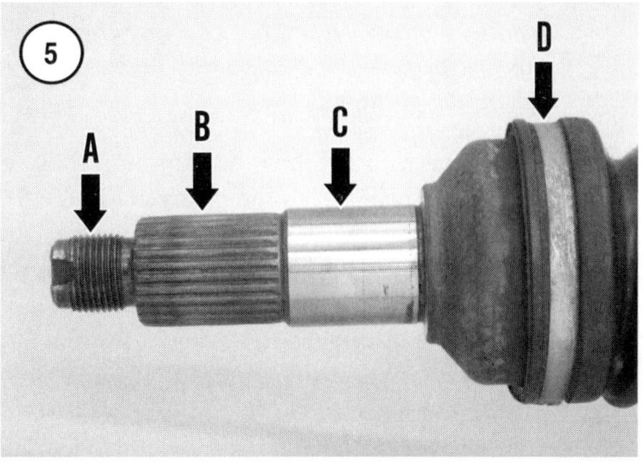

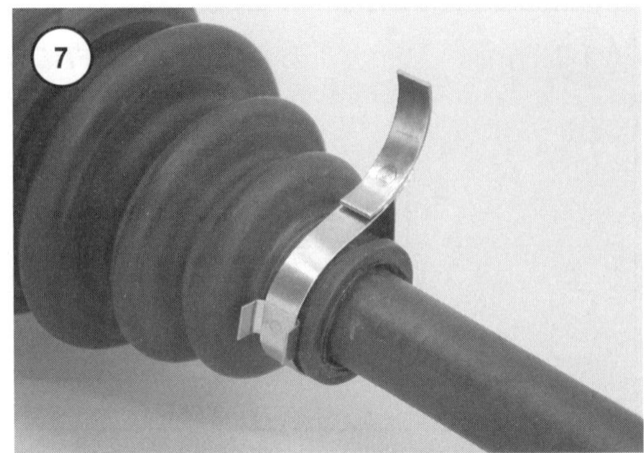

enter the CV joint, possibly causing excessive damage. If necessary, refer to *CV Joint Boot Replacement* in this section.

e. CV joints. Pivot the end of the axle and check for roughness and play in the joint. If roughness is evident, disassemble and inspect the parts as described in *CV Joint Boot Replacement* procedure in this section. If roughness or play remains after cleaning and lubrication, replace the worn parts.

3. Visually check the axle for straightness. Replace the axle if it is bent. A bent axle can damage the bearings in the steering knuckle and differential.

CV Joint Boot Replacement

The boots are removed by disassembling the inboard CV joint. For clarity, the CV joint is shown with clean parts. Normally, the parts are packed with molybdenum disulfide grease. Refer to **Figure 1**.

1. Remove the clamps from both boots as follows:
   a. Pry open the locking tabs on the clamps (**Figure 6**).
   b. Bend the clamps open (**Figure 7**) and slide the inboard boot to the center of the axle.

NOTE
The boots and large clamps are not identical in size. Keep the clamps with their respective boots and note the boot locations on the axle.

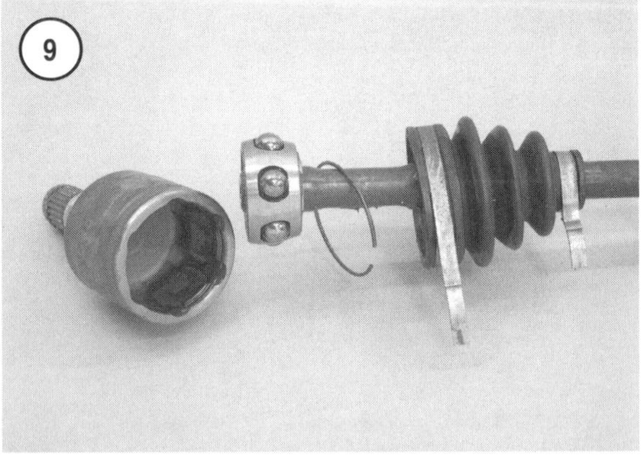

2. Wipe the inner edge of the inboard joint. Then remove the retaining ring from the groove (**Figure 8**).
3. Disassemble the CV joint (**Figure 9**). Use care when handling and wiping the parts. The balls in the bearing can fall from the race.
4. Remove the snap ring from the shaft (**Figure 10**). Then remove the bearing assembly. If necessary, lightly tap the shaft out of the bearing.
5. Remove the boots and clamps from the axle.

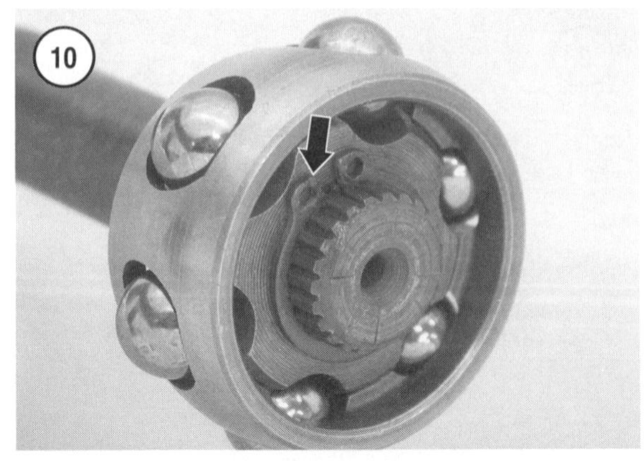

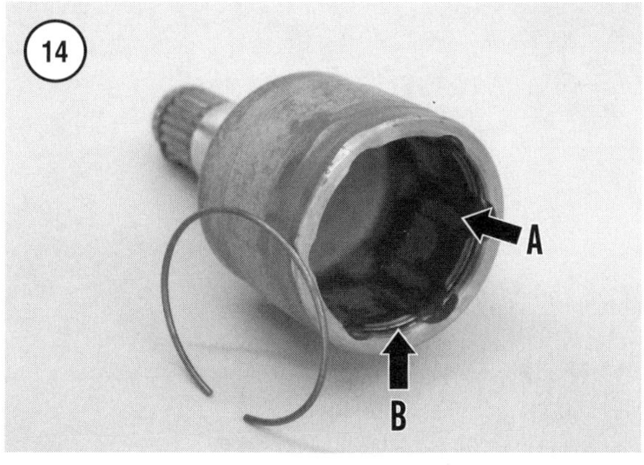

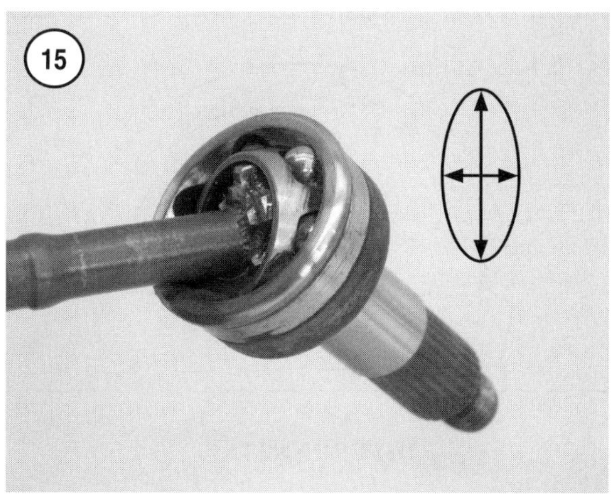

6. Clean the axle assembly in solvent and inspect both joint assemblies.

7. Inspect the following parts of the inboard CV joint:

   a. Bearing assembly (**Figure 11**). Check parts for scoring, galling, pitting, corrosion and other damage.
   b. Bearing and shaft splines (**Figure 12**). Check the splines for wear and corrosion. If corrosion is evident, water has entered past the boot. Check the boot and clamps for damage.
   c. Engagement shaft. Inspect the bearing surface (A, **Figure 13**), splines (B) and circlip groove (C). Check for wear and corrosion. If corrosion is evident, water has entered the differential.
   d. CV joint and retainer ring. Inspect the ball guides (A, **Figure 14**) and retainer ring groove (B) in the joint. Check the parts for wear and corrosion. The guides should be smooth and not scored.

8. Inspect the outboard CV joint (**Figure 15**). Pivot the end of the axle and check for roughness and play in the joint. If roughness or play is evident, replace the axle. The axle and outer CV joint are not available separately.

9. Reverse this procedure to assemble the axle. Note the following:

   a. The outboard boot and large clamp are larger in diameter than the inboard boot and large clamp.
   b. Install the ball and race assembly onto the shaft with the wide side facing out (**Figure 10**).
   c. Install a new snap ring (**Figure 10**) with the sharp edge facing in.
   d. Install a new retaining ring. Install the retaining ring with the ends positioned as shown in **Figure 16**.
   e. Pack the CV joints with molybdenum disulfide grease.

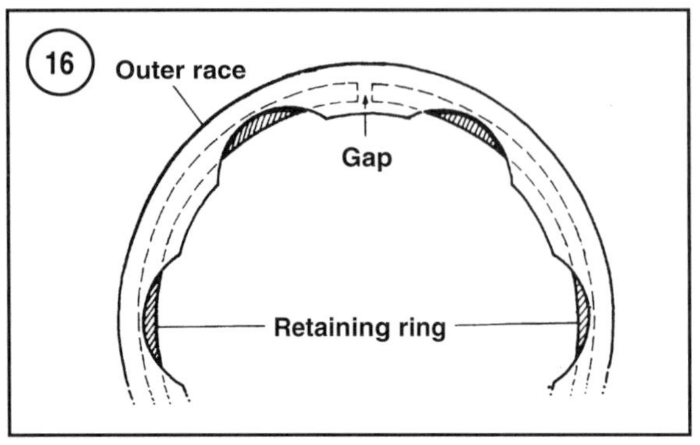

DIFFERENTIAL

Removal and Installation

1. Shift the differential into two-wheel drive. This will index the gear motor with the sliding gear in the differential.
2. Drain lubricant from the differential (Chapter Three).
3. Remove the front fender assembly and skid plate (Chapter Sixteen).
4. Remove the right lower control arm as described in Chapter Eleven.
5. Remove the right front axle as described in this chapter.
6. Remove the vent hose and disconnect the gear motor electrical connectors (**Figure 17**).
7. On 2002 models, slide the boot away from the end of the drive shaft.

NOTE

In the following steps, the differential is removed without removing components from the left side of the machine. With assistance, the differential can be disengaged from the left axle during removal of the differential. This method eliminates disassembling the left side of the machine.

8. Remove the differential mounting bolts (**Figure 18**).
9. With assistance, raise and tilt the differential (**Figure 19**) so the left axle can be disengaged.
10. Use a mallet to tap the case away from the left axle (**Figure 20**). Do not use excessive force to separate the parts.
11. Remove the differential from the drive shaft and away from the frame (**Figure 21**).
12. Remove the drive shaft from the rear coupler. Inspect the drive shaft assembly as described in this chapter.
13. Inspect the differential as described in this section.
14. Reverse this procedure to install the differential. Note the following:

21

22

23

24

a. Lubricate the coupler and drive shaft splines with waterproof grease.
b. For 2002 models, check that the boot, washer and spring (**Figure 22**) are mounted at the front coupler of the drive shaft.
c. For 2003-on models, check that the spring (**Figure 23**) is mounted in the rear coupler of the drive shaft.
d. Insert the drive shaft into the engine and differential. Then position and align the differential with the left axle. Check that the axle is aligned in the differential. Then use a mallet to seat the differential onto the axle.
e. Tighten the differential mounting bolts to 55 N•m (41 ft.-lb.).
f. Operate the motor from the four-wheel drive switch and check that the gear motor engages and disengages the front axles. Perform this check before installing the suspension and steering components.
g. Fill the differential with lubricant (Chapter Three).

Preliminary Inspection

If the differential is in good condition, use the following procedure to inspect the parts. If the differential is damaged internally, disassemble the differential as described in this section.

1. Clean the differential with solvent and wipe the parts clean. Do not immerse the differential in solvent.
2. Inspect the drive unit housing for cracks or other damage.
3. Turn the pinion gear shaft (**Figure 24**) and inspect the internal bearings that support the shaft and differential gear unit. While turning the shaft, check for roughness, noise, play and binding. The bearings should turn smoothly and quietly. If damage or excessive play is evident, disassemble the gear case as described in this section to isolate the damaged part(s).
4. Inspect the axle seals and pinion gear shaft seal for leaks or damage. If necessary, replace the seals as described in this section.

Disassembly

Refer to **Figure 25**.

1. Remove the gear motor and O-ring (**Figure 26**).
   a. The bottom mounting bolt is a Torx-type security bolt. If necessary, use locking pliers to remove the bolt. Then replace the bolt with a common socket head bolt.

25

DIFFERENTIAL

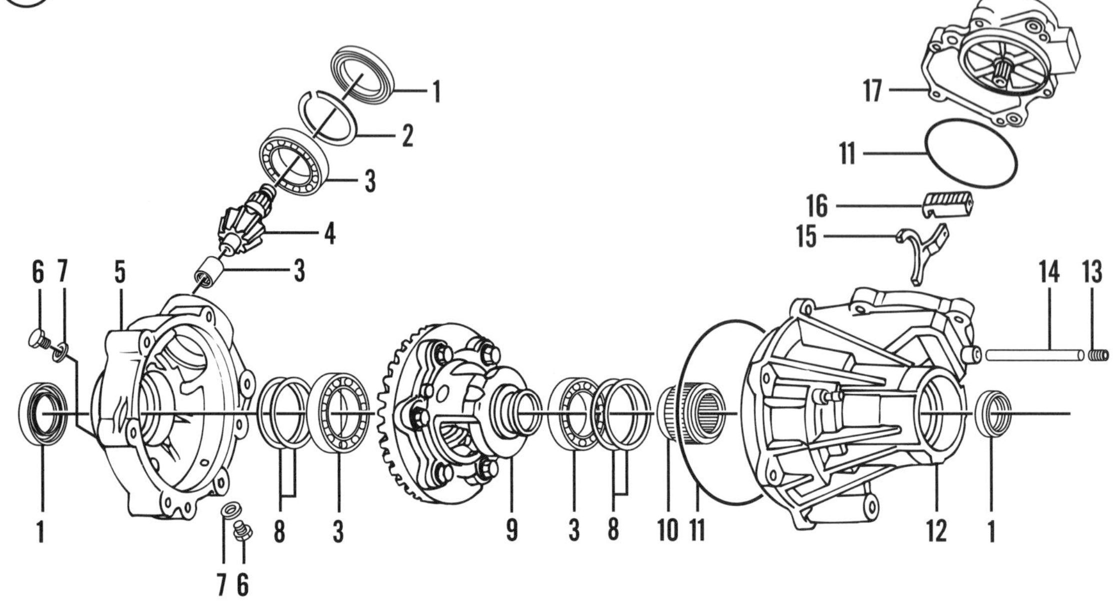

1. Seal
2. Snap ring
3. Bearing
4. Pinion gear shaft
5. Right differential housing
6. Plug
7. Washer
8. Shim(s)
9. Differential gear unit
10. Clutch
11. O-ring
12. Left differential housing
13. Setscrew
14. Shifter shaft
15. Shift fork
16. Shift fork sliding gear
17. Gear motor

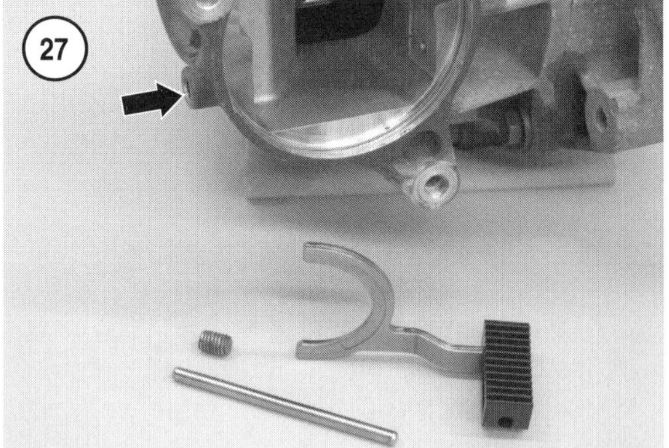

b. Carefully pry equally around the perimeter of the motor. An O-ring increases resistance to removal.

2. Remove the setscrew, shifter shaft, shift fork and shift fork sliding gear (**Figure 27**). It is not necessary to remove the sliding gear from the shift fork.

3. Work in a crossing pattern and loosen the bolts at the perimeter of the differential housing. Loosen each bolt one-fourth turn before removing all of the bolts.

4. With the left housing facing up, pry around the housing equally at the pry points. Separate the housings (**Figure 28**).

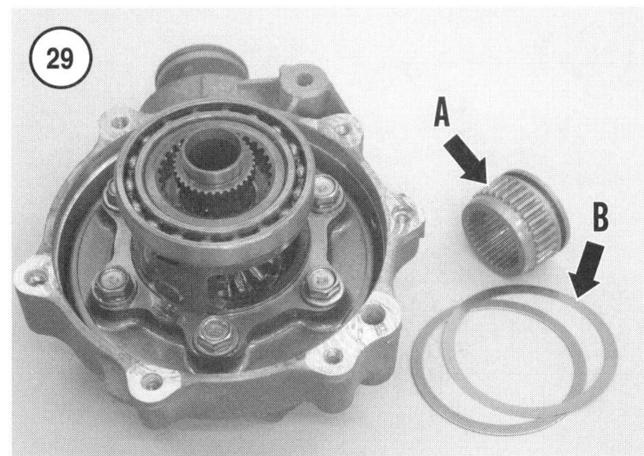

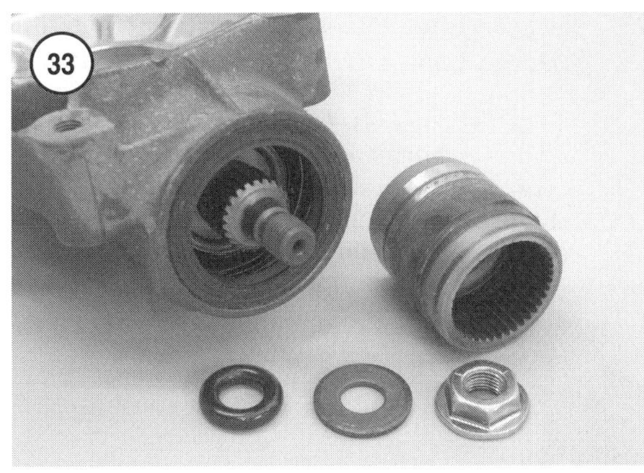

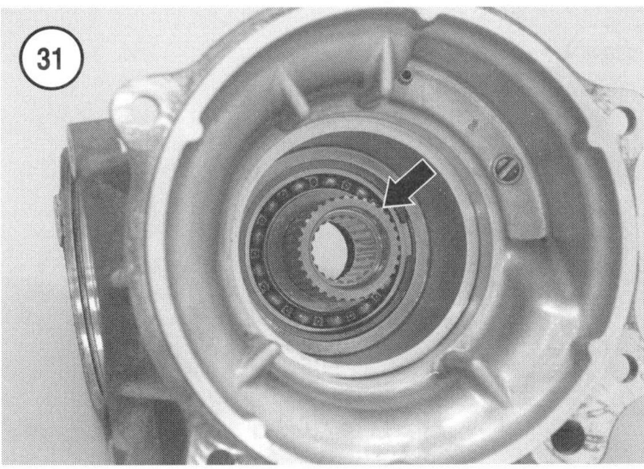

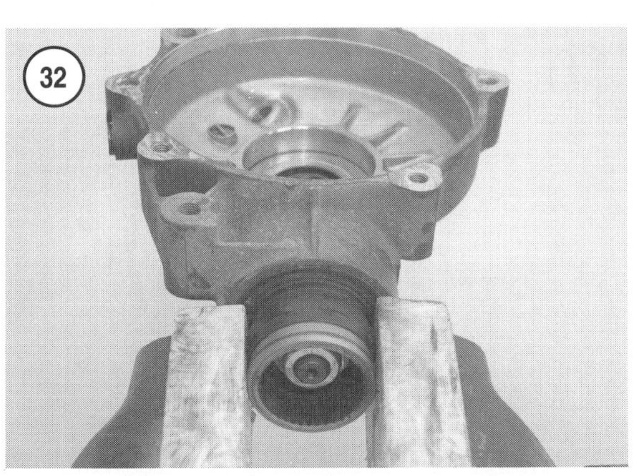

5. Remove the clutch (A, **Figure 29**) and shim(s) (B) from the right housing. Mark the shim(s) to install it into its original position.
6. Remove the differential gear unit (A, **Figure 30**) and shim(s) (B) from the right housing. Mark the shim(s) to install it into its original position.
7. Do not remove the clutch adapter (**Figure 31**) from the left housing unless the bearing or adapter is damaged. If removal is necessary, tap or press the adapter out of the bearing.
8. If the pinion gear shaft, seal or bearings are obviously damaged, disassemble the parts using the following substeps.

CAUTION
Removing the shaft assembly is usually not required or recommended since bearing damage often occurs during removal and assembly.

a. On 2002 models, disassemble the drive shaft U-joint, as described in this chapter. Do not damage the gasket surface on the housing.
b. Hold the U-joint yoke/coupling (**Figure 32**) in a vise with soft jaws so the nut can be removed. On 2002 models, use the universal joint holder (Yamaha part No. YM-04062) to hold the yoke. On 2003-on models, use the coupling gear holding tool (Yamaha part No. YM-01486) to hold the coupling.
c. Remove the U-joint yoke/coupling nut, the washer and the O-ring (**Figure 33**).
d. Pry the seal from its bore.
e. Remove the snap ring.
f. To ease removal, heat the exterior of the shaft bore with a heat gun. Then tap the end of the pinion gear shaft (**Figure 34**) to drive the shaft and ball bearing out of the housing. Use a soft drift when tapping the shaft.
g. Use a blind bearing puller to remove the needle bearing.

9. Clean and inspect the parts. If necessary, refer to *Axle Bearing and Seal Replacement* in this section.

CAUTION
*Do not remove the paint marks on the gear motor housing and pinion gear (**Figure 35**). Use the marks to synchronize the motor with the shift fork sliding gear during assembly. Also, do not disassemble the gear motor or remove the gear from the motor.*

Inspection

Refer to **Figure 25**.

1. Inspect the differential gear unit as follows:
   a. Inspect the ring gear teeth (A, **Figure 36**). If damage or uneven wear is evident, also inspect the pinion gear teeth. If the ring gear is damaged, replace the complete differential gear unit. The gear is not available separately.
   b. Inspect the differential bearings (B, **Figure 36** and A, **Figure 37**). Lubricate the bearings with gear oil. Then turn each bearing and check for roughness, noise, play and binding. The bearings should turn smoothly and quietly. If damage or excessive play is evident, replace the bearings as described in this section.
   c. Inspect the differential gear cluster (B, **Figure 37**). If damage or uneven wear is evident, replace the differential unit. Do not attempt to disassemble the unit. Replacement parts are not available.
   d. Inspect the splines (C, **Figure 37**). Slide the clutch onto the splines and check the parts. The splines in both parts should be straight and the parts should slide together easily.
   e. Inspect the bolts and bosses (D, **Figure 37**) for looseness or cracks.
2. Inspect the left differential housing as follows:
   a. Inspect the housing for cracks and damage.
   b. Inspect the splines (A, **Figure 38**) on the clutch adapter. Slide the clutch onto the adapter and check the parts. The splines in both parts should be straight and the parts should slide together easily.
   c. Inspect the bearing (B, **Figure 38**). Lubricate the bearing with gear oil. Then turn the bearing and check for roughness, noise, play and binding. The bearing should turn smoothly and quietly. If damage or excessive play is evident, replace the bearing as described in this section.
   d. Inspect the seal for damage or leaks. If necessary, replace the seal as described in this section.

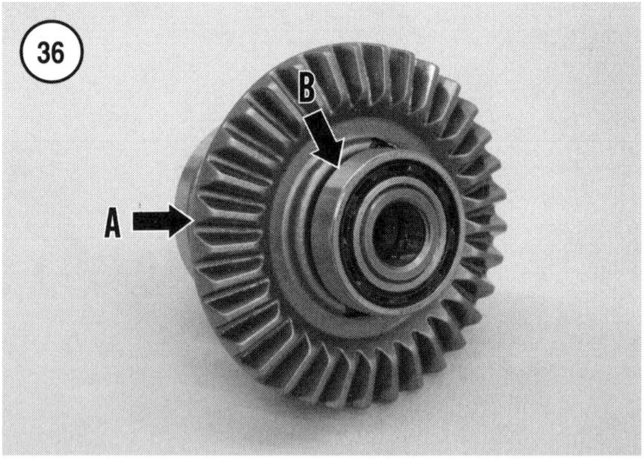

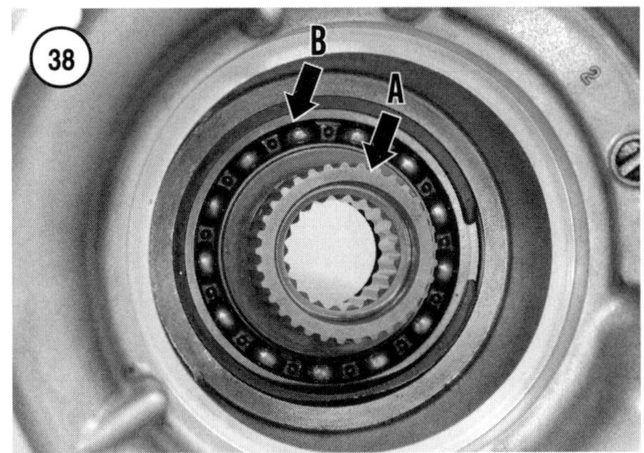

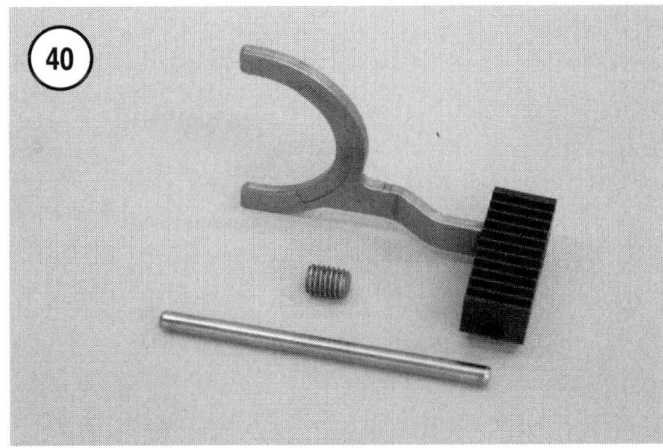

3. Inspect the right differential housing and pinion gear shaft (**Figure 39**) as follows:

a. Inspect the housing for cracks and damage.

b. Inspect the pinion gear shaft and bearings. Inspect the gear teeth for damage. Lubricate the bearings with gear oil. Then turn the shaft and check the bearings for roughness, noise, play and binding. The bearings should turn smoothly and quietly. If damage or excessive play is evident, replace the bearings, seal and snap ring as described in this section.

c. Inspect the seal for damage or leaks. If necessary, replace the seal as described in this section.

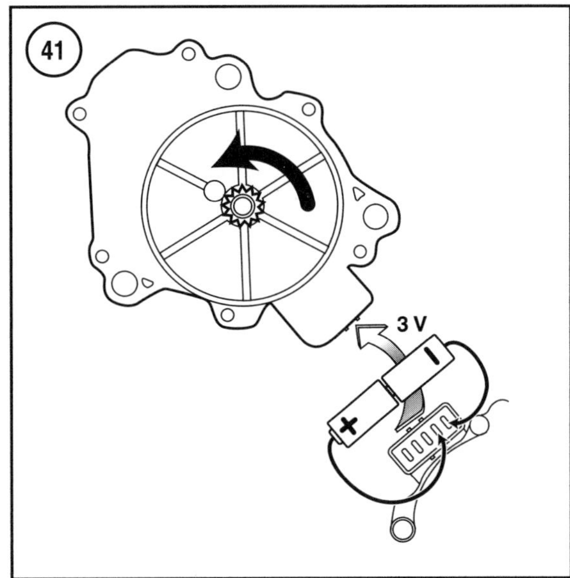

4. Inspect the shift fork, shift fork sliding gear and shaft (**Figure 40**) for wear or damage. If the gear teeth are damaged, inspect the drive pinion on the gear motor. Replace any parts that are damaged or bent.

5. Inspect the gear motor for damage to the pinion gear, case and electrical connectors. If necessary, test the gear motor for proper operation (Chapter Nine). If the motor is in good condition, make sure the paint marks on the motor and pinion gear are aligned (**Figure 35**). The marks must be aligned in order to synchronize the motor with the shift fork sliding gear during assembly. If necessary, align the marks as follows:

a. Assemble two C-size batteries and leads as shown in **Figure 41**. The batteries must be joined in series to create 3 volts.

b. Connect the battery leads to the 5-pin gear motor terminals as shown in **Figure 41**. The motor gear should turn *counterclockwise*. Allow the motor to run until the paint mark on the gear is aligned with the paint mark on the motor housing.

12

Assembly

During assembly, apply molybdenum disulfide grease to all splines and seals. Apply gear oil to the bearings and gear unit components. Refer to **Figure 25**.

1. If the pinion gear shaft was removed, install new bearings, a new snap ring, seal and O-ring. Note the following:

a. Lubricate the parts before assembly.

b. Seat each bearing with a driver that fits onto the outside diameter of the bearing. If necessary, heat the exterior of the bore with a heat gun, to ease installation of the bearings.

c. Install the snap ring with the sharp edge facing out.
d. Do not install the U-joint yoke/coupling at this time. The differential unit must be properly shimmed before the parts can be installed.

2. Install the shim(s) and differential gear unit into the right housing (**Figure 30**).
3. With the right housing facing up, install the shim(s) and clutch (**Figure 29**). The groove in the clutch must face up.
4. Install a new, lubricated O-ring onto the left housing. Then squarely seat the housing against the right housing. Make sure the clutch and clutch adapter engage as the housings are joined.
5. Install and tighten the housing bolts, working in a crossing pattern. Tighten the bolts to 25 N•m (18 ft.-lb.).
6. If required, shim the differential unit.

CAUTION

If replacing the pinion gear shaft, differential gear unit or housings, the differential must be shimmed to create the specified clearances between the parts. Also check the clearance whenever wear is evident on original parts that are reused. Refer to ***Gear Lash Inspection/Adjustment*** *in this section.*

7. If removed, install the U-joint yoke/coupling. Note the following:

a. Install a new, lubricated O-ring under the washer.
b. Hold the yoke/coupling in a vise with soft jaws so the nut can be installed (**Figure 32**). On 2002 models, use the universal joint holder (Yamaha part No. YM-04062) to hold the yoke. On 2003-on models, use the coupling gear holding tool (Yamaha part No. YM-01486) to hold the coupling.
c. Apply threadlocking compound to the U-joint yoke/coupling nut. Tighten the nut to 62 N•m (46 ft.-lb.).
d. On 2002 models, assemble the drive shaft U-joint. Refer to *Front Drive Shaft* in this chapter.

8. Install the shift fork, shift fork sliding gear, shifter shaft and setscrew (**Figure 27**). Make sure the shift fork is seated in the clutch groove. Apply threadlocking compound to the setscrew.
9. Install the gear motor as follows:

a. Make sure the paint marks on the motor and pinion gear are aligned (**Figure 35**). If necessary, align the pinion gear as described in *Inspection* in this section.

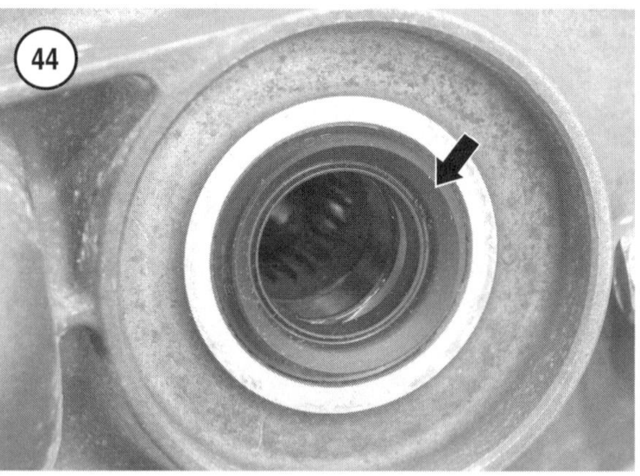

b. Install a new, lubricated O-ring onto the gear motor.
c. Slide the shift fork sliding gear and shift fork completely to the left (**Figure 42**). In this position, the differential is in two-wheel drive.

CAUTION

The motor gear and the shift fork sliding gear must remain in their set positions until the parts are engaged. If the parts are not aligned properly, the indicator light at the handlebar and the actual differential mode may differ.

45

46

47

d. To ensure the shift fork sliding gear does not move when installing the motor, use long 8-mm bolts to squarely guide the motor into the housing (**Figure 43**). When the motor is seated, remove the guide bolts and install the mounting bolts. Tighten the bolts to 13 N•m (10 ft.-lb.).

10. Install the differential as described in this section.

Axle Bearing and Seal Replacement

If only seal replacement is required, the seals can be removed from the outside of the differential. Removal and disassembly of the differential is not required. The removal of the axles is required. To replace axle bearings the differential must be removed and disassembled. Refer to **Figure 25**.

1. Remove and install the axle seals as follows:
   a. Remove the front axles as described in this chapter.
   b. Pry or pull the seal (**Figure 44**) from its bore. To ease removal, heat the seal with a heat gun.
   c. Clean the bore and pack the seal with molybdenum disulfide grease.
   d. Hand-fit the seal so it is squarely in the bore.
   e. Place a driver over the seal. The driver should seat against the outside diameter of the seal.
   f. Drive the seal into place.
   g. Install the front axles as described in this chapter.
2. Remove the axle bearings as follows:
   a. Remove the differential from the machine as described in this section.
   b. Disassemble the differential as described in this section.
   c. Determine which bearing(s) (**Figure 38** and **Figure 45**) must be replaced.
   d. To remove the bearings on the differential gear unit (**Figure 45**), support the bearing in a press so the gear unit points down. Hold the gear unit and press on the axle holder (**Figure 46**) until the bearing is removed. Do not drop or damage the gear unit.
   e. If the bearing in the left differential housing (**Figure 38**) is damaged, remove the seal, clutch adapter and snap ring. It may be necessary to tap or press the adapter out of the bearing. Press the bearing out of the bore. To ease removal, heat the housing around the bearing bore with a heat gun.
3. Install the axle bearing(s) as follows:
   a. If replacing the bearing(s) on the differential gear unit, support the gear unit in a press, under the ring gear. Support the gear unit as close to the center as possible. Make sure the manufacturer's marks on the bearing are facing up (**Figure 47**). Lubricate the bearing and axle holder with gear oil, then squarely press the bearing onto the axle holder. Use a driver that fits onto the perimeter of the *inside* bearing race.
   b. If replacing the bearing in the left differential housing, lubricate the bearing and bore with gear oil. Make sure the manufacturer's marks on the bearing are facing up (**Figure 47**). Heat the housing around the bearing bore. Then

squarely press the bearing into place. Use a driver that fits onto the *outside* diameter of the bearing. Install the snap ring with the sharp edge facing up. Then install the clutch adapter. Install a new seal.

4. Assemble and install the differential as described in this section.

Gear Lash Inspection/Adjustment

Gear lash inspection is necessary if replacing the pinion gear shaft, ring gear, differential gear unit or housings. Also, check clearance whenever reusing worn original parts after disassembly of differential.

Measure gear lash with a gear lash measurement tool (Yamaha part No. YM-01467) or equivalent (**Figure 48**), and a dial indicator.

1. Lock the differential case in a vise or to a stable surface. Secure the case so the drain hole is facing up.
2. Lock the ring gear into place with a 10–1.25 × 80-mm bolt (**Figure 49**). Finger-tighten the bolt into the drain hole just enough to keep the ring gear from moving.
3. Clamp the gear lash measurement tool onto the pinion gear shaft (**Figure 50**). Position the tool so the arm can contact the dial indicator.
4. Position a dial indicator in contact with the measurement tool and 21 mm (0.83 in.) from the center of the pinion gear shaft (**Figure 50**). The dial indicator must be stable and set to read gear lash in both directions.
5. Gently rotate the pinion gear shaft clockwise until lash between the parts is eliminated. Note the dial indicator reading.
6. Gently rotate the pinion gear shaft in the opposite direction until lash between the parts is eliminated. Note the dial indicator reading.
7. Calculate the total side-to-side gear lash.
8. Loosen the lock bolt and rotate the pinion gear shaft 90°. Finger-tighten the bolt, readjust the gear lash measurement tool, and repeat the check. Continue checking the gear lash until the shaft has rotated one full turn.
9. Determine the average reading of the four checks. Final gear lash should be 0.05-0.25 mm (0.002-0.0098 in.). If adjustment is necessary, refer to *Disassembly* in this section to disassemble the differential housings. Adjust the differential gear unit as follows:
   a. If gear lash is too low, increase the right shim thickness. If the shim adjustment needed is 0.1 mm (0.004 in.) or greater, decrease the left shim thickness by an equal amount.
   b. If gear lash is too high, increase the left shim thickness. If the shim adjustment needed is 0.1 mm (0.004 in.) or greater, decrease the right shim thickness by an equal amount.

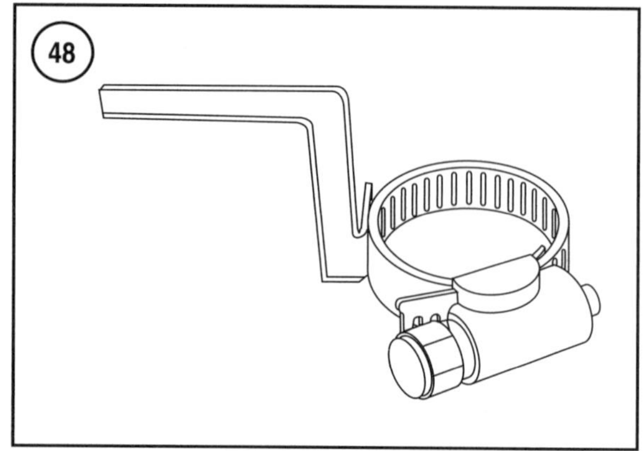

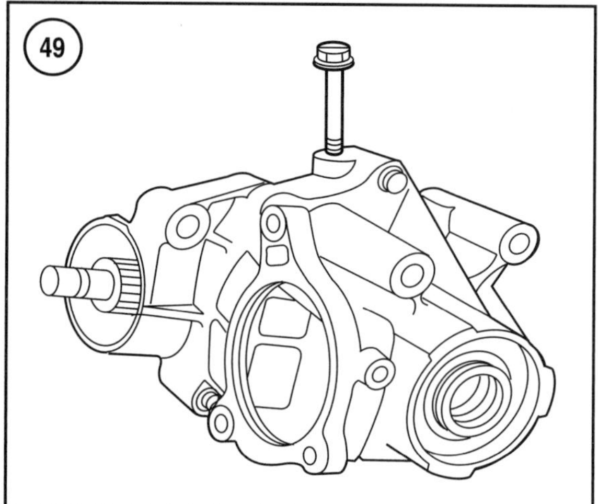

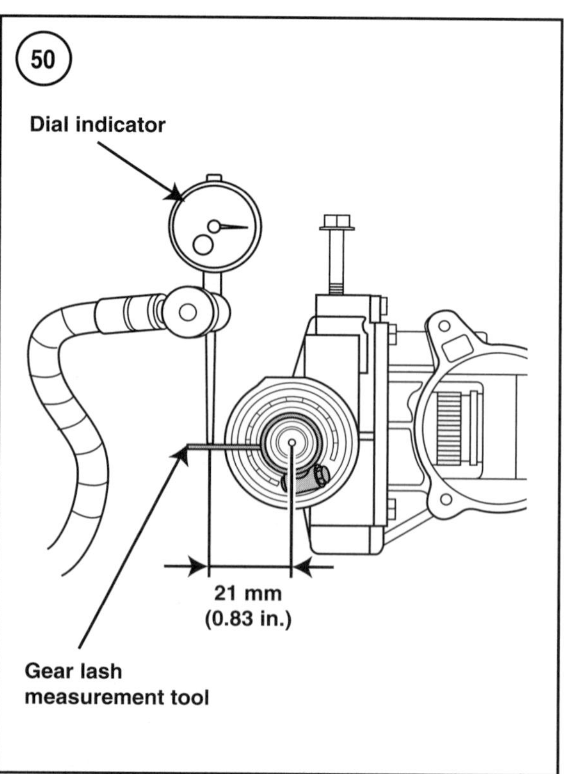

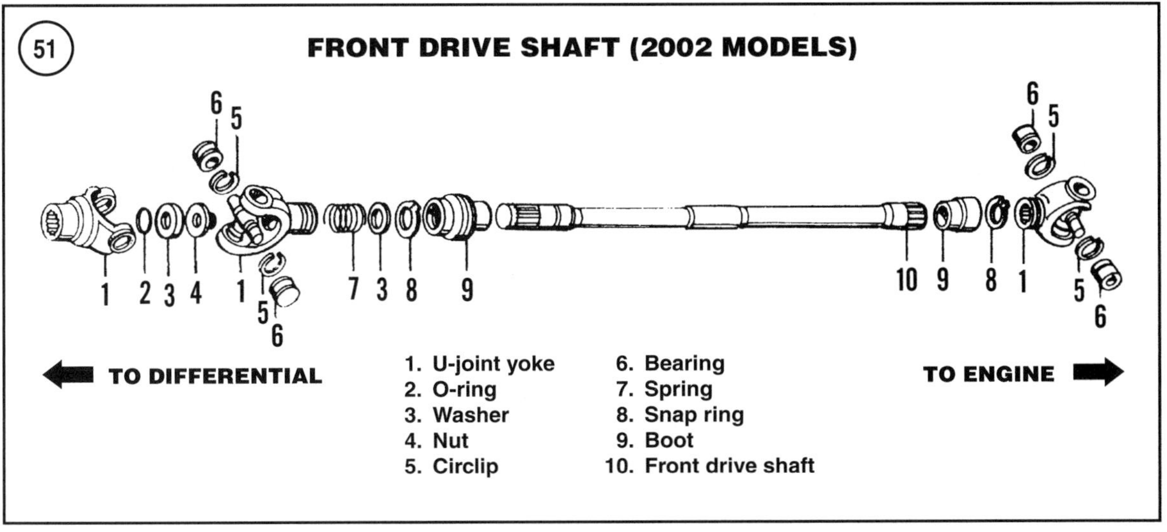

c. Gear unit shims are available in 0.1 mm increments from 0.1-0.5 mm thick. Shims are also available in 0.5 mm increments from 1.0-2.5 mm thick.

10. After installing the replacement shim(s), assemble the differential housings. Repeat the gear lash adjustment procedure to verify gear lash is within specifications.

11. Refer to *Assembly* in this section to install the drive shaft U-joint/coupling, shift fork, shift fork sliding gear, shifter shaft, setscrew and gear motor.

FRONT DRIVE SHAFT

Removal and Installation

Remove and install the drive shaft as described in *Differential, Removal and Installation* in this chapter.

Inspection

On 2002 models, the drive shaft is splined to U-joints, connected to the engine and differential (**Figure 51**). The drive shaft and U-joints are replaceable individually. On 2003-on models, a flexible joint is attached at each end of the drive shaft (**Figure 52**) and is splined to a coupler, connected to the engine and differential (**Figure 53**). This type of drive shaft is only replaceable as a complete unit.

1. On 2002 models:
   a. Inspect the splines (A, **Figure 54**), washer (B) and snap ring (C) for damage. The snap rings must be tight on the shaft. If the snap rings are replaced, install the snap rings with the sharp edge facing in. Splined parts should fit together with minimal or no play.
   b. Inspect the drive shaft for straightness. Replace the drive shaft if it is bent. A bent drive shaft can damage bearings and cause excessive vibration.
   c. Inspect the spring (**Figure 55**). The spring must compress slightly when the drive shaft is installed within the U-joint yoke.
   d. Inspect the boots (**Figure 56**). The boots must not be torn or damaged and should firmly grip the U-joint couplers.

12

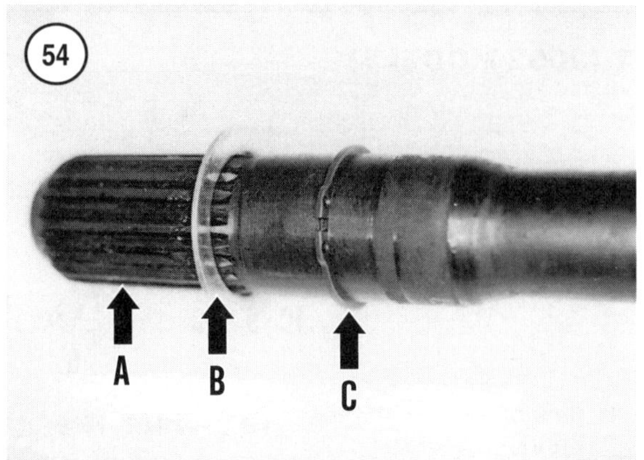

e. Inspect the U-joints for bearing damage. The bearings should operate smoothly with no play. If necessary, replace the U-joint bearings as described in this section.

2. On 2003-on models:
   a. Inspect the splines (A, **Figure 57**), clamps (B) and boots (C) for damage. Splined parts should fit together with minimal or no play. The boots should in good condition, with no evidence of water and debris entering the coupling. The boots are not available separately.
   b. Inspect the drive shaft for straightness. Replace the drive shaft if it is bent. A bent drive shaft can damage bearings and cause excessive vibration.
   c. Inspect the spring and covers (**Figure 58**). The spring must compress slightly when the drive shaft is installed. If damaged, the covers are available separately.
   d. Inspect the joints at each end of the drive shaft. The joints should pivot smoothly in all directions with no play. If damage is evident, replace the drive shaft assembly.

U-Joint Replacement (2002 Models Only)

Refer to **Figure 51**.

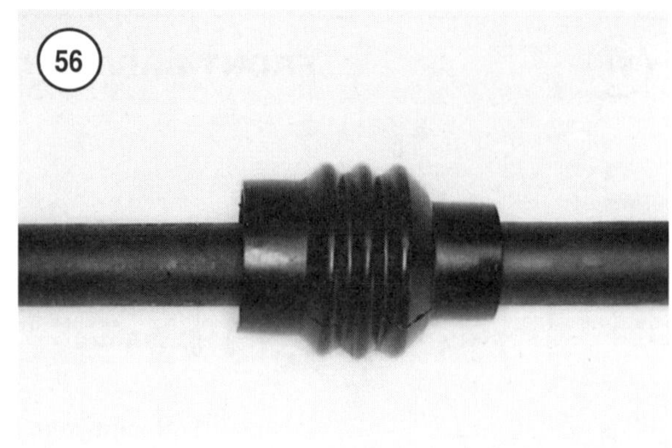

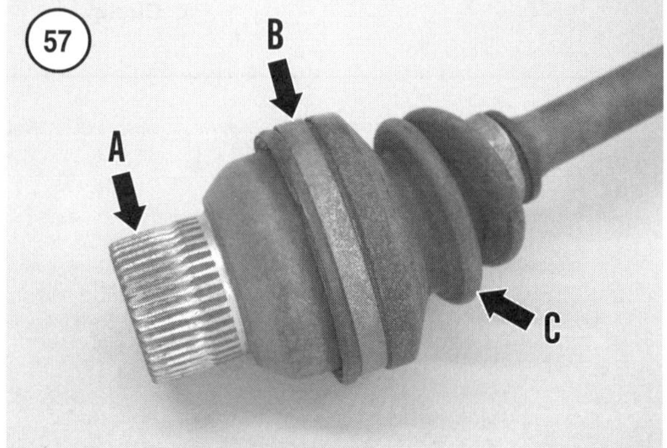

1. Remove the differential as described in this chapter.
2. Remove the drive shaft from the front and rear U-joint couplers.
3. Inspect the drive shaft assembly as described in this section.
4. Replace worn U-joints as follows:
   a. Remove the circlip (**Figure 59**) from each of the four bearings.
   b. Drive or press one of the U-joint arms toward the opposite bearing, driving the bearing out of the yoke. Drive the U-joint in the opposite direction, removing the remaining bearing on that axis. Repeat this step to remove the remaining bearings and U-joint.
   c. Pack the new bearings with molybdenum disulfide grease. Install the U-joint. Then press the bearings into the yokes with a driver that fits onto the outer edge of the bearing. Drive the bearings in until the circlip grooves are visible.
   d. Install the circlips.
   e. Lubricate the U-joints, coupler and drive shaft splines with waterproof grease.
5. Install the drive shaft and differential as described in this chapter.

Table 1 FRONT AXLE AND DIFFERENTIAL SPECIFICATIONS

Differential gear lash	0.05-0.25 mm (0.002-0.0098 in.)

Table 2 FRONT AXLE AND DIFFERENTIAL TORQUE SPECIFICATIONS

	N•m	in.-lb.	ft.-lb.
Control arm-to-frame nuts	45	–	33
Differential housing bolts	25	–	18
Differential mounting bolts	55	–	41
Differential oil drain plug	10	89	–
Differential oil fill plug	23	–	17
Gear motor mounting bolts	13	–	10
U-joint yoke/coupling nut	62	–	46

CHAPTER THIRTEEN

REAR SUSPENSION

This chapter covers the rear wheel, hub and suspension components. Refer to the tables at the end of this chapter for specifications.

REAR WHEEL

Removal and Installation

1. Park the machine on level ground.
2. Loosen the lug nuts (**Figure 1**).
3. Raise and support the machine. The rear wheels must be off the ground.
4. Remove the lug nuts from the studs. Then remove the wheel from the hub. If removing more than one wheel, mark each wheel to install it in its original position.
5. If tire repair is required, refer to Chapter Eleven.
6. Clean the lug nuts and studs. If any studs are broken or damaged, replace the studs.
7. If vibration or tire wear is abnormal, check the wheel for excessive runout (Chapter Eleven).

WARNING

If more than one wheel was removed, make sure the direction arrow (on the tire sidewall, if applicable) is pointing forward when each wheel is mounted. The arrow must point forward to prevent possible tire failure.

8. Install the wheel onto the studs, with the valve stem facing out.
9. Install the lug nuts with the tapered side facing in (**Figure 2**). Then moderately tighten the nuts in a crossing pattern.
10. Lower the machine to the ground. Then equally tighten the lug nuts to 55 N•m (41 ft.-lb.).

REAR HUB

Removal and Installation

1. Remove the rear wheel as described in this chapter.

2A. On 2002 models, remove the cotter pin, hub nut and washer from the axle.

   a. If necessary, lock the brakes and use a heat gun and penetrating oil to help loosen the nut.
   b. If the brakes do not prevent the hub from turning when loosening the nut, install two of the lug nuts backwards and against the hub (**Figure 3**). Place a long pry bar between the nuts and against the hub. The pry bar must reach the ground in order to lock the hub in place.

2B. On 2003-on models, remove the hub nut as follows:

   a. Remove the center cap from the hub nut (**Figure 4**).

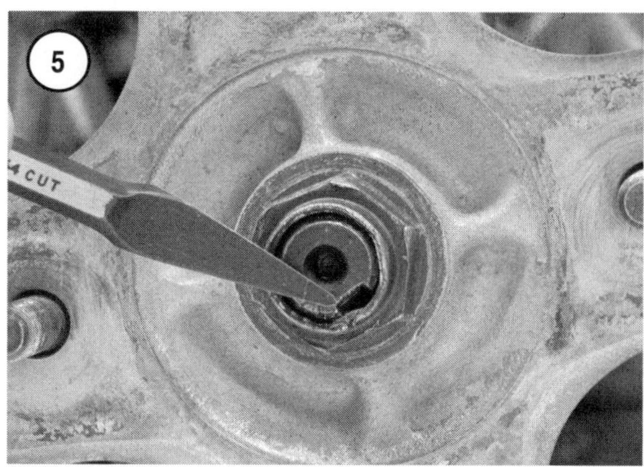

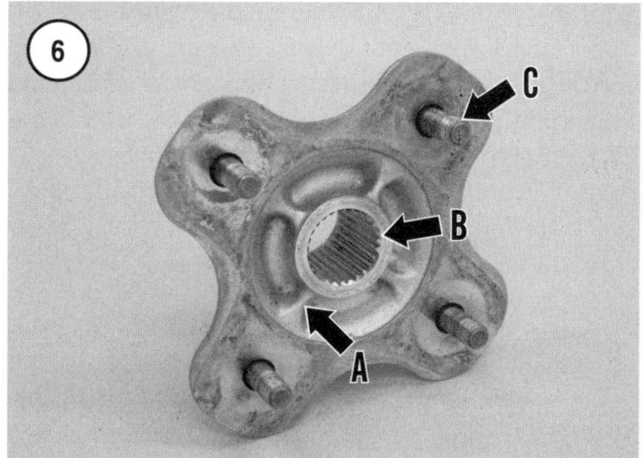

b. Straighten the stake on the hub nut (**Figure 5**).

c. If necessary, lock the brakes and use a heat gun and penetrating oil to help loosen the nut.

d. If the brakes do not prevent the hub from turning when loosening the nut, install two of the lug nuts backwards and against the hub (**Figure 3**). Place a long pry bar between the nuts and against the hub. The pry bar must reach the ground in order to lock the hub in place.

3. Pull the hub from the axle splines. If removing the opposite hub, mark the hubs to reinstall them in their original positions.

NOTE

If the hub is seized to the splines, apply penetrating oil and lightly tap the back of the hub, near the center. If light tapping does not loosen the hub, use a puller to remove the hub.

4. Clean and inspect the hub for cracks (A, **Figure 6**), damaged splines (B) and broken studs (C).

5. Clean and inspect the axle splines (A, **Figure 7**) and threads (B). Use a wire brush to remove surface corrosion from the axle. On 2002 models, also check the O-ring, seated in the knuckle recess.

6. Reverse this procedure to install the hub. Note the following:

13

a. Apply waterproof grease to the hub and axle splines.
b. On 2002 models, tighten the hub nut to 200 N•m (148 ft.-lb.). Then install a new cotter pin.
c. On 2003-on models, install and tighten a new hub nut to 260 N•m (192 ft.-lb.). Then stake the nut into place.

REAR KNUCKLE

Removal and Installation

1. Remove the rear hub as described in this chapter.
2. Remove the bolts securing the knuckle to the upper and lower control arms (**Figure 8**). Account for the covers (A, **Figure 9**) and pivots (B) in the knuckle.
3. Inspect the knuckle as described in this section.
4. Reverse these steps to install the knuckle. Note the following:
   a. Lubricate the bearings, seals and O-ring (if used) with waterproof grease.
   b. Install the knuckle with the grease fittings facing out (A, **Figure 10**).
   c. Install the knuckle so the arrow and UPSIDE (B, **Figure 10**) are pointing up.
   d. Finger-tighten the nuts and bolts until all parts are assembled.
   e. Tighten the knuckle mounting bolts to 45 N•m (33 ft.-lb.).

Inspection

1. On 2002 models, remove the O-ring from the outer bore.
2. Wipe the knuckle clean. Do not submerge the bearings and seals in solvent.
3. Inspect the knuckle (A, **Figure 11**) and grease fittings (B) for damage. Replace the knuckle if it is cracked or bent. Replace damaged grease fittings.
4. Inspect the bushings and pivots (**Figure 12**) for wear and corrosion. The pivots should rotate smoothly and fit firmly in the bushings.
5. Inspect the covers (A, **Figure 13**) and seals (B) for damage. The seals must fit tightly on the knuckle to prevent the entry of water and debris.
6. Inspect the bearings and seals.
   a. Check each bearing (**Figure 14**) for play and roughness. If rust, dirt or moisture is evident, the seals are leaking.
   b. On 2002 models, inspect the rubber seals for tears and leaks.
   c. On 2003-on models, inspect the metal seals for damage and leaks.

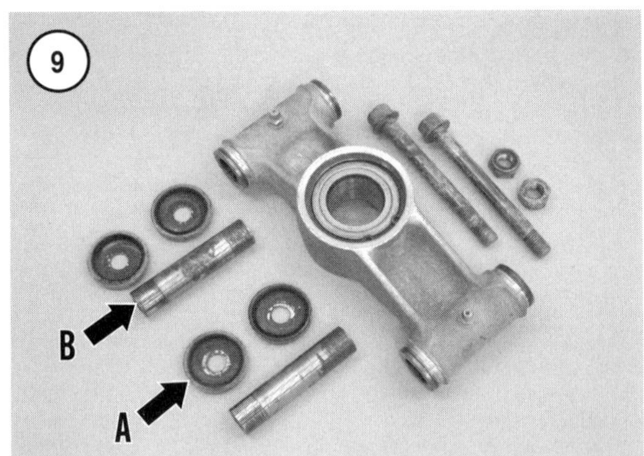

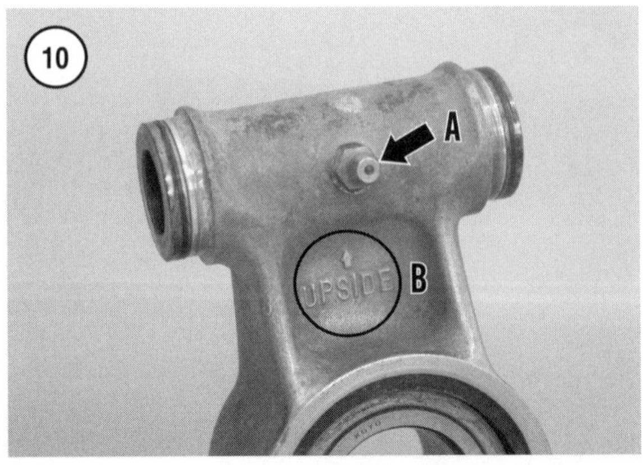

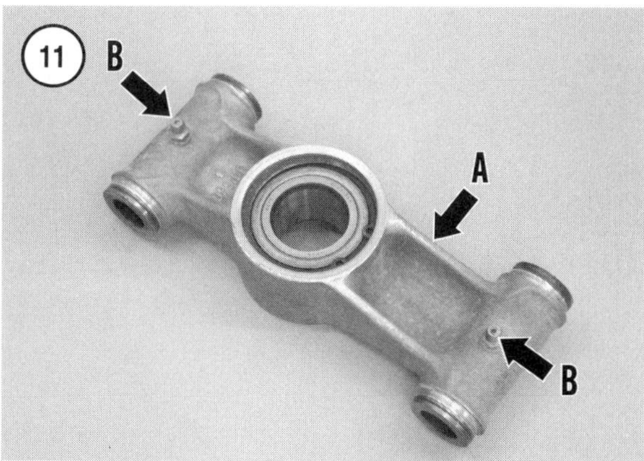

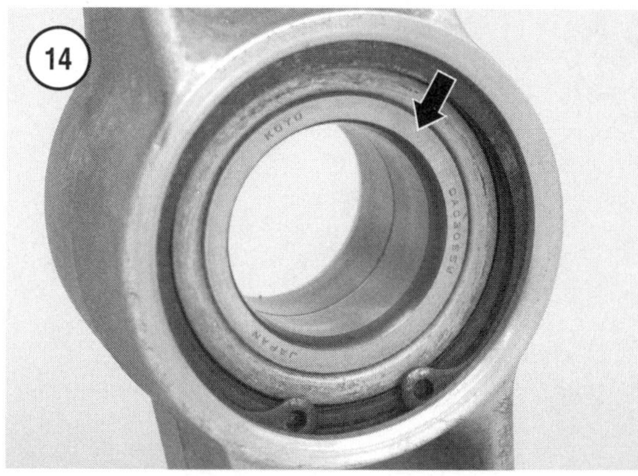

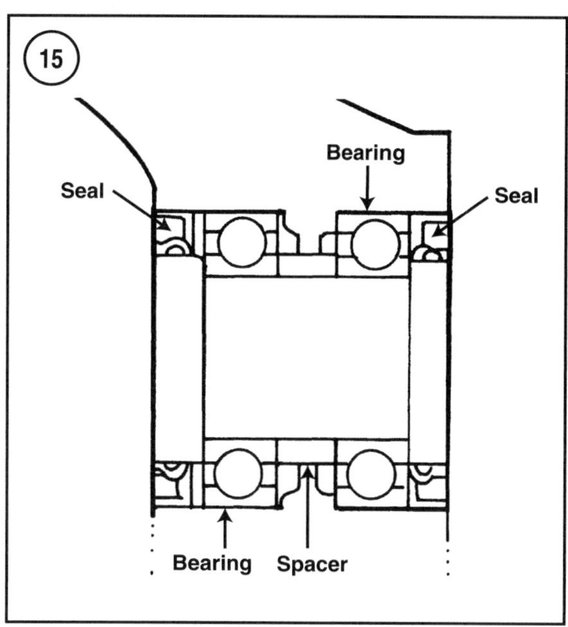

d. If necessary, replace the bearings and seals as described in this section.

Bearing and Seal Replacement

2002 models

On 2002 models, the knuckle uses two seals, two bearings and a spacer. Use a press to install the bearings. Refer to **Figure 15**.

1. Pry the seals from their bores.
2. Wedge the spacer to one side. Then drive out the inner bearing. Use a drift to work around the perimeter of the inner race. Support the knuckle so the bearing can fall from the bore. Do not wedge or cock the bearing in the bore.
3. Remove the spacer and drive out the remaining bearing.
4. Clean the knuckle and spacer.
5. Apply waterproof grease to the bearings, seals and spacer.
6. Place the outer bearing squarely over its bore. Then press it into place. Use a driver that fits onto the outside edge of the bearing.
7. Install the spacer and then press the inside bearing into place.
8. Install the seals. Use a driver that fits onto the outside edge of the seals.

2003-on models

On 2003-on models, the knuckle uses a single bearing that has double-ball races. The bearing is also permanently sealed on both sides. Use a press to remove and install the bearing. Refer to **Figure 16**.

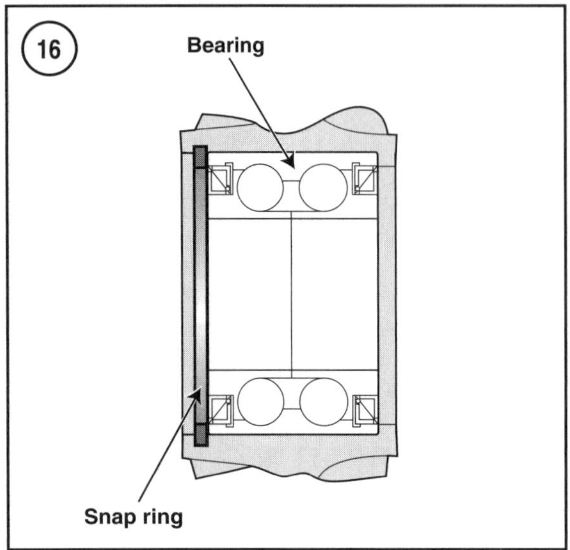

1. Remove the snap ring from the outer bore.
2. Turn the knuckle over and press the old bearing out of the bore. Support the knuckle so the bearing can fall from the bore. Do not wedge or cock the bearing in the bore.
3. Clean the knuckle.
4. Apply waterproof grease to the bearing.
5. Place the new bearing squarely over the outer bore. Then press it into place. Use a driver that fits onto the outside edge of the bearing.
6. Install a new snap ring, with the sharp edge facing out.

STABILIZER

Removal, Inspection and Installation

1. Remove the rear wheels as described in this chapter.
2. Remove the stabilizer joint from both lower control arms (**Figure 17**). Use a 14-mm wrench to hold the joint so the nut can be loosened (**Figure 18**).
3. Remove the bolts securing the stabilizer holders (**Figure 19**).
4. Inspect the stabilizer for bends, cracks and other damage.
5. Inspect the stabilizer joints (**Figure 20**). Pivot the joint in all directions, as well as vertically. Replace the joints if wear or looseness is evident.
6. Reverse these steps to install the stabilizer. Note the following:
   a. Finger-tighten the nuts and bolts until all parts are assembled.
   b. Tighten the stabilizer joint nuts (**Figure 17**) to 48 N•m (35 ft.-lb.).
   c. Tighten the stabilizer holder bolts (**Figure 19**) to 30 N•m (22 ft.-lb.).

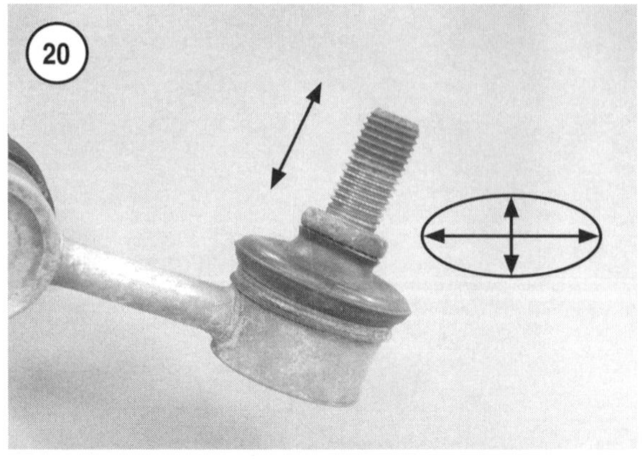

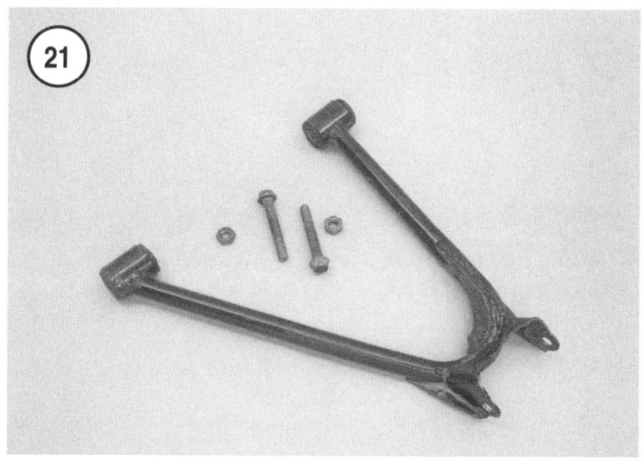

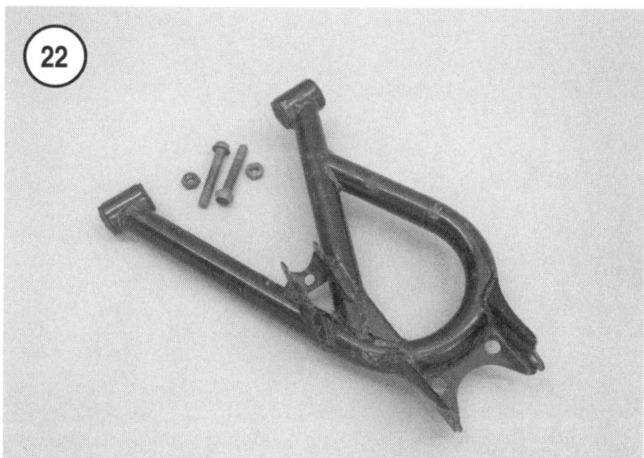

CONTROL ARMS

Removal and Installation

The following procedure describes the removal of the upper control arm (**Figure 21**) and lower control arm (**Figure 22**). Each control arm can be removed independently of the other.

1. Remove the rear wheel as described in this chapter.
2. Remove the upper arm as follows:
   a. Remove the upper bolt in the knuckle (A, **Figure 23**). It is not necessary to remove the rear hub. The hub is removed for clarity only.
   b. Before removing the arm, grasp the arm and leverage it side to side. If play is noticeable, check the bushings for wear.
   c. Remove the bolts from the upper arm (**Figure 24**), then remove the arm. Note that the bolt heads are to the outside of the arm. On 2002 models, account for the covers at the outside of each bushing. If both upper arms are removed, mark the arms for installation into their original positions.
3. Remove the lower arm as follows:
   a. Remove the rear protector.
   b. Remove the lower bolt in the knuckle (B, **Figure 23**). It is not necessary to remove the rear hub. The hub is removed for clarity only.
   c. Remove the lower shock absorber bolt (A, **Figure 25**) and stabilizer joint nut (B). Use a 14-mm wrench to hold the joint so the nut can be loosened (**Figure 18**).
   d. Before removing the arm, grasp the arm and leverage it side to side. If play is noticeable, check the bushings for wear.
   e. Remove the bolts securing the stabilizer holders and move the stabilizer aside for clearance. Then remove the bolts from the lower control arm (**Figure 26**).
4. Inspect the arms as described in this section.
5. Reverse these steps to install the arms. Note the following:

a. If both pairs of arms have been removed, verify that they are being installed on the correct side of the machine.
b. Lubricate the bushings and pivot bolts with waterproof grease. Avoid lubricating the bolt threads.
c. On 2002 models, install the bushing covers on the outside of each bushing.
d. For the upper arm, the open side of the knuckle mounting bracket must face down.
e. For the lower arm, the open side of the knuckle mounting bracket must face up.
f. Install the control arm bolts so the heads face out.
g. Finger-tighten the nuts and bolts until all parts are assembled.
h. Tighten the rear knuckle mounting bolts to 45 N•m (33 ft.-lb.).
i. Tighten the shock absorber and control arm-to-frame bolts to 45 N•m (33 ft.-lb.).
j. Tighten the stabilizer joint nuts to 48 N•m (35 ft.-lb.).
k. Tighten the stabilizer holder bolts to 30 N•m (22 ft.-lb.).

Inspection

1. Clean the arms.
2. Inspect all welded joints on the arms. Check for fractures, bending or other damage. If damage is evident, replace the control arm.
3. Inspect the pivot bushings (**Figure 27**). Inspect each bushing for play and damage. If necessary, replace damaged bushings by pressing them out of the control arm.
4. Inspect the shock absorber and stabilizer joint mounts (**Figure 28**) for damage and elongated bolt holes.
5. Inspect all pivot bolts and nuts for wear, bends or damaged threads.

31

33

32

34

SHOCK ABSORBERS

The rear shock absorbers are equipped with five spring-preload positions. Set both shock absorbers to the same position by using a shock absorber spanner to rotate the cam at the bottom of the spring (**Figure 29**). The least amount of spring preload is in the first position, while the most preload is in the fifth position. The standard setting is the second position.

Removal and Installation

1. Park the machine on level ground.
2. Raise and support the machine. The rear wheels must be slightly off the ground.
3. Set the shock absorber to the first position (softest).
4. Remove the lower mounting bolt (**Figure 30**).
5. Remove the upper mounting bolt (**Figure 31**).
6. Remove the shock absorber and inspect it as described in this section.
7. Reverse these procedures to install the shock absorbers. Note the following:
   a. Apply waterproof grease to the bushings and mounting bolts. Avoid lubricating the bolt threads.
   b. Tighten the shock absorber mounting bolts to 45 N•m (33 ft.-lb.).
   c. Set the shock absorber to the desired position. Refer to **Table 3** for settings.

Inspection

If the shock absorber (**Figure 32**) is damaged or worn, replace it as a complete unit. The shock absorber is not rebuildable. Always replace both shock absorbers if either unit is damaged.

1. Inspect and clean the lower bushing, pivot and mounting bolt. Fit each part into its mating part and check for wear and play.
2. Inspect the preload adjuster and notches (**Figure 33**) for damage.
3. Inspect the shock body for severe dents that can affect shock operation.
4. Inspect the shock for oil leaking from the rod seal.
5. Inspect the spring for damage or looseness. Measure the spring free length (**Figure 33**). Refer to **Table 1** for the required length.
6. Inspect and clean the upper bushing (A, **Figure 34**) and mounting bolt (B). Fit the bolt into the bushing and check for wear and play.

Tables 1-4 are on the following page.

13

Table 1 REAR SUSPENSION SPECIFICATIONS

Rear shock absorber	
Type	Coil spring/oil damper
Travel	95 mm (3.74 in.)
Spring free length	277 mm (10.91 in.)
Spring rate	36.4 N/mm (204 lb./in.)
Rear suspension	Double wishbone
Rear wheel travel	225 mm (8.85 in.)

Table 2 TIRE AND WHEEL SPECIFICATIONS

Tires	
Type	Tubeless radial
Sizes	
Front	AT25 × 8-12 Dunlop KT131
Rear	AT25 × 10-12 Dunlop KT135
Tire pressure (cold)	
Front	
Standard	35 kPa (5.1 psi)
Minimum	32 kPa (4.6 psi)
Maximum	38 kPa (5.5 psi)
Rear	
Standard	30 kPa (4.4 psi)
Minimum	27 kPa (3.9 psi)
Maximum	33 kPa (4.8 psi)
Bead seating pressure	250 kPa (36.3 psi) maximum
Tire wear limit	3 mm (0.12 in.)
Wheels	
Size	
Front	12 × 6.0 AT
Rear	12 × 7.5 AT
Runout (radial and lateral)	2 mm (0.08 in.)

Table 3 REAR SHOCK ABSORBER SETTING

	Standard	Minimum (soft)	Maximum (hard)
Spring preload	2	1	5

Table 4 REAR SUSPENSION TORQUE SPECIFICATIONS

	N•m	in.-lb.	ft.-lb.
Lower and upper control arm-to-frame bolts	45	–	33
Rear knuckle mounting bolts	45	–	33
Rear wheel hub nut			
2002 models	200	–	148
2003-on models	260	–	192
Rear wheel lug nuts	55	–	41
Shock absorber mounting bolts	45	–	33
Stabilizer holder bolts	30	–	22
Stabilizer joint nuts	48	–	35

CHAPTER FOURTEEN

REAR AXLES AND FINAL DRIVE

This chapter covers the rear axles, rear drive shaft and final drive unit. Refer to the tables at the end of this chapter for specifications.

REAR AXLES

Removal and Installation

Refer to **Figure 1**.

1. Remove the rear knuckle (Chapter Thirteen).
2. Drain the final drive unit (Chapter Three).
3. Grasp the axle and quickly pull it straight out of the differential (**Figure 2**). The circlip at the inboard end of the axle will cause a slight resistance when disengaging the axle.
4. Inspect the axle as described in this section.
5. Reverse this procedure to install the axle(s). Note the following:
   a. Lubricate the seals on the final drive unit with molybdenum disulfide grease.
   b. Install a new circlip at the inboard end of the axle (**Figure 3**).
   c. After installation, lightly pull on the axle to make sure it is locked in place.
   d. Fill the final drive unit with lubricant (Chapter Three).

Preliminary Inspection

1. Clean the axle and splines. Do not submerge the axle boots in solvent. The CV joints (under the boots) are packed with grease.
2. At the ends of the axle, inspect the following:
   a. Hub nut threads (A, **Figure 4**). Look for stripped or damaged threads.
   b. Splines (B, **Figure 4**). Check for worn, distorted and broken splines. At the outboard end of the axle, install the respective hub and feel for play. At the inboard splines, if corrosion is evident, water has entered the final drive unit.
   c. Bearing and seal surfaces (C, **Figure 4**). Check for scoring, galling, corrosion and other damage. If damage is evident, inspect the matching bearing in the final drive unit or rear knuckle.
   d. Boots and clamps (D, **Figure 4**). The boots must not be torn or cracked. The clamps should tightly grip the boot and axle. A loose or torn boot allows dirt and moisture to enter the CV joint, possibly causing damage. If necessary, refer to *CV Joint Boot Replacement* procedure in this section.
   e. CV joints. Pivot the end of the axle and check for roughness and play in the joint. If roughness is evident, disassemble and inspect the parts as

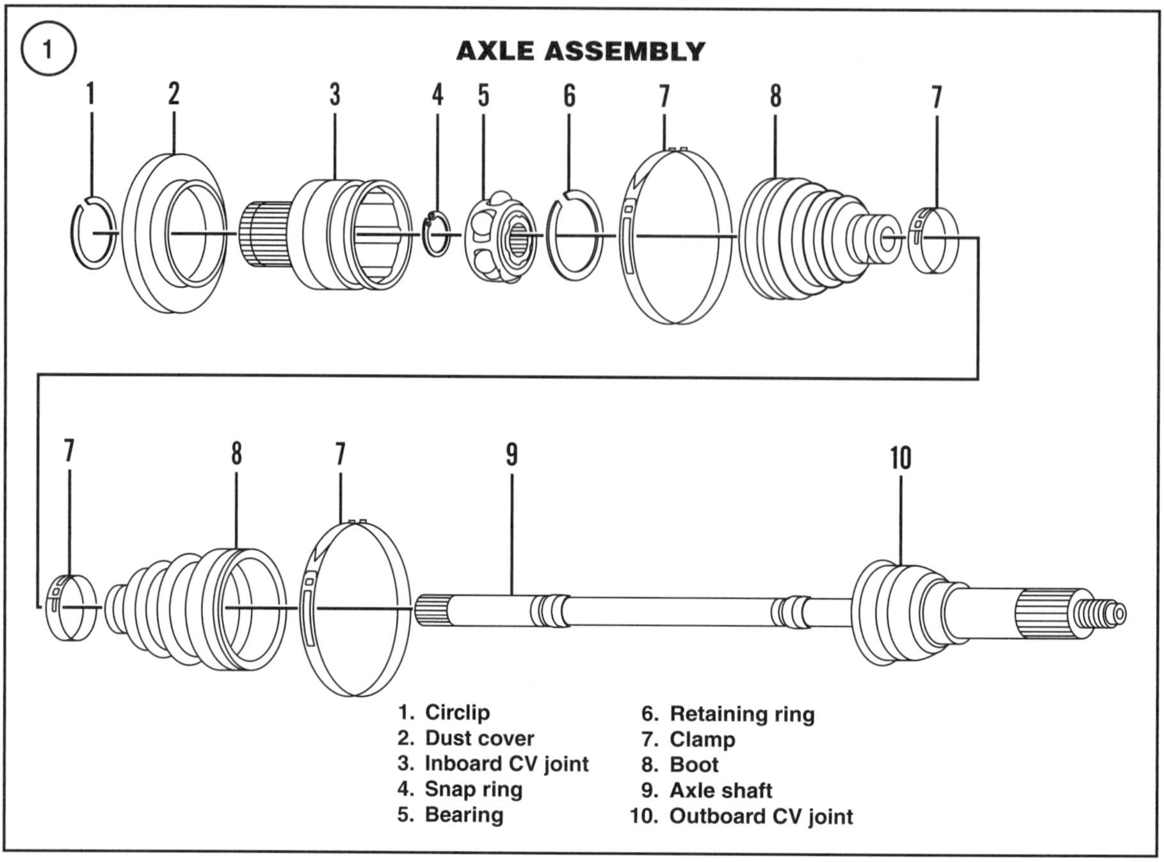

1

AXLE ASSEMBLY

1. Circlip
2. Dust cover
3. Inboard CV joint
4. Snap ring
5. Bearing
6. Retaining ring
7. Clamp
8. Boot
9. Axle shaft
10. Outboard CV joint

described in *CV Joint Boot Replacement* in this section. If roughness or play remains after cleaning and lubrication, replace the worn parts.

3. Visually check the axle for straightness. Replace the axle if it is bent. A bent axle can damage the bearings in the rear knuckle and final drive unit.

CV Joint Boot Replacement

The boots are removed by disassembling the inboard CV joint. For clarity, the CV joint is shown with clean parts. Normally, the parts are packed with molybdenum disulfide grease. Refer to **Figure 1**.

1. Remove the clamps from both boots as follows:
   a. Pry open the locking tabs (**Figure 5**) on the clamps.
   b. Bend the clamps open (**Figure 6**) and slide the inboard boot to the center of the axle.
2. Wipe the inner edge of the inboard joint. Then remove the retaining ring from the groove (**Figure 7**).
3. Disassemble the CV joint (**Figure 8**). Use care when handling the parts. The balls in the bearing can fall from the race.
4. Remove the snap ring from the shaft (**Figure 9**). Then remove the bearing assembly. If necessary, lightly tap the shaft out of the bearing.
5. Remove the boots and clamps from the axle.

2

3

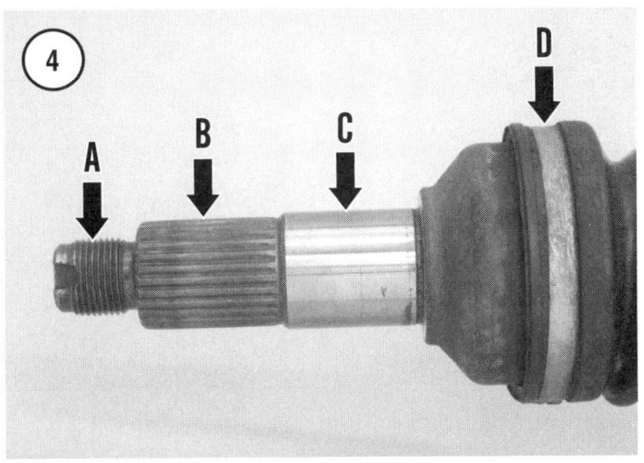

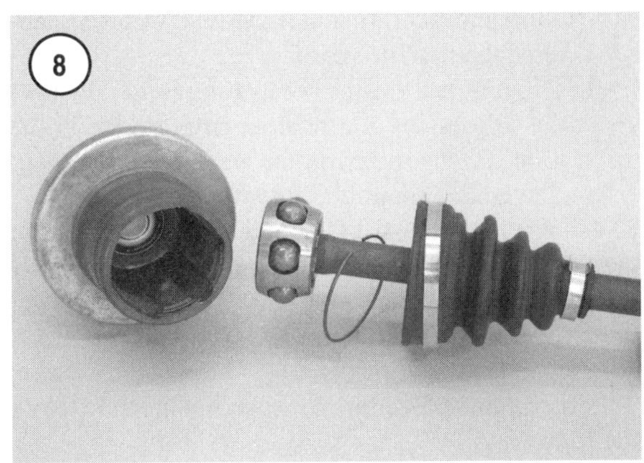

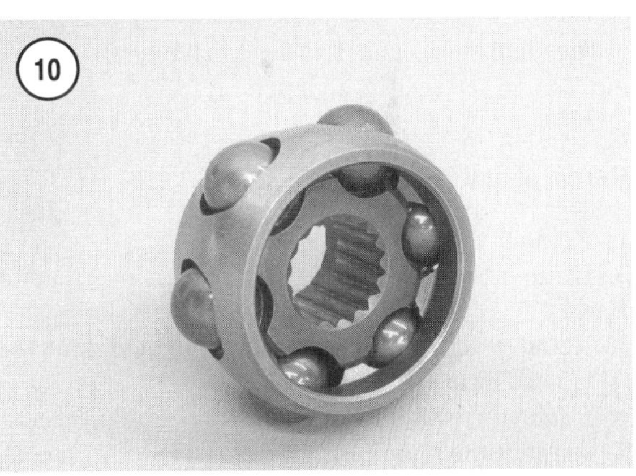

6. Clean the axle assembly in solvent and inspect both joint assemblies.
7. Inspect the following parts of the inboard CV joint:
   a. Bearing assembly (**Figure 10**). Check each part for scoring, galling, pitting, corrosion and other damage.
   b. Bearing and shaft splines (**Figure 11**). Check the splines for wear and corrosion. If corrosion is evident, water has entered past the boot. Check the boot and clamps for damage.
   c. Engagement shaft (**Figure 3**). Inspect the splines and circlip groove. Check for wear and

corrosion. If corrosion is evident, water has entered the final drive unit.

d. CV joint and retainer ring (**Figure 12**). Inspect the ball guides and retainer ring groove in the joint. Check the parts for wear and corrosion. The guides should be smooth and not scored.

8. Inspect the outboard CV joint (**Figure 13**). Pivot the end of the axle and check for roughness and play in the joint. If roughness or play is evident, replace the axle. The axle and outer CV joint are not available separately.

9. Reverse this procedure to assemble the axle. Note the following:

a. The outboard CV boot and large clamp are smaller in diameter than the inboard CV boot and large clamp.

b. Install the ball and race assembly onto the shaft (**Figure 9**) with the wider side facing outward.

c. Install a new snap ring (**Figure 9**) with the sharp edge facing in.

d. Install a new retaining ring. Install the retaining ring so the ends are seated in the groove and positioned between the ball guides.

e. Pack the CV joints with molybdenum disulfide grease.

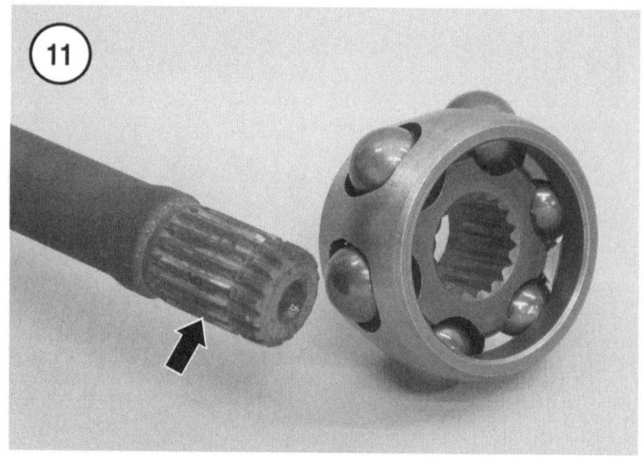

FINAL DRIVE UNIT

The final drive unit and rear drive shaft are removed and serviced as an assembly.

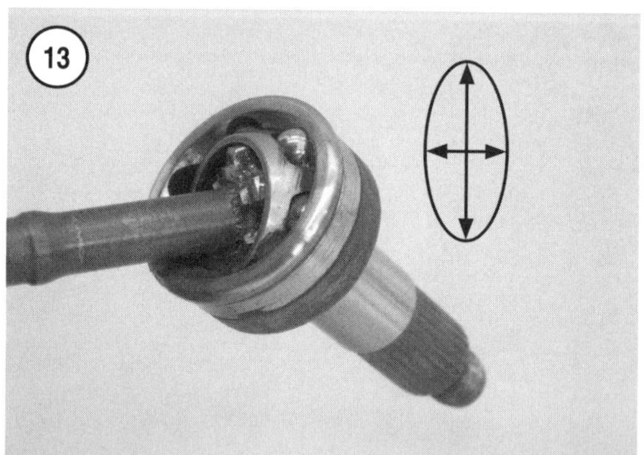

Removal and Installation

1. Remove the skid plate.
2. Drain lubricant from the final drive unit (Chapter Three).
3. Remove the left rear wheel, hub and knuckle (Chapter Thirteen).
4. Remove the air duct and left lower arm protector.
5. Remove the rear brake caliper (Chapter Fifteen).
6. Remove the left axle as described in this chapter.
7. Disconnect the stabilizer joint and stabilizer holder from the left lower arm (Chapter Thirteen).
8. Remove the vent hose from the final drive unit.
9. Remove the bolts from the lower arm. Then pivot the arm away to make clearance for removing the final drive unit bolts.

NOTE

In the following steps, the final drive unit is removed, without removing components from the right side of the machine. With assistance, the final drive unit can be disengaged from the right axle during removal of the final drive

15

16

17

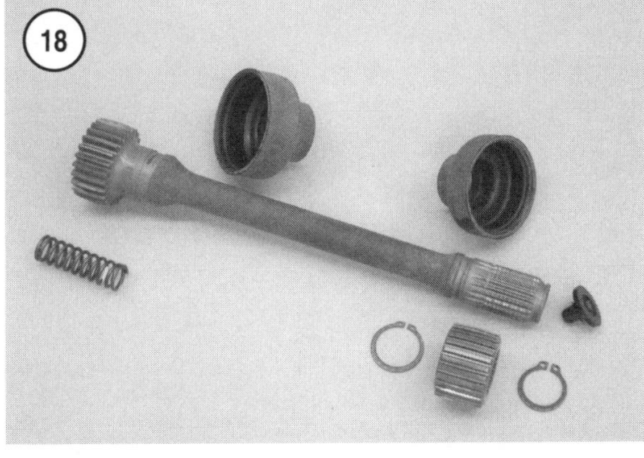
18

unit. This method eliminates disassembling the right side of the machine.

10. Loosen the bolts securing the final drive unit to the frame.
11. Support the final drive unit. Then remove the mounting bolts (**Figure 14**).
12. With assistance, pull the final drive unit and drive shaft back and away from the mounting brackets (**Figure 15**).
13. Raise and tilt the final drive unit to the left, so the right axle can be disengaged.
14. Use a mallet to tap the case away from the right axle (**Figure 16**). Do not use excessive force to separate the parts.
15. Remove the final drive unit and drive shaft out the back of the frame (**Figure 17**). Account for the spring at the front of the drive shaft.
16. Inspect the final drive unit and drive shaft as described in this section.
17. Reverse this procedure to install the drive shaft and final drive unit. Note the following:
    a. Lubricate the coupling and drive shaft splines with waterproof grease.
    b. Insert the drive shaft into the engine and final drive unit. Then position and align the final drive unit with the right axle. Make sure the axle is aligned in the final drive unit. Then use a mallet to seat the unit onto the axle.
    c. Tighten the final drive mounting bolts to 55 N•m (41 ft.-lb.).
    d. Fill the final drive unit with lubricant (Chapter Three).

Preliminary Inspection

If the final drive unit and drive shaft are in good condition, use the following procedure to clean and inspect the parts. If the final drive unit is damaged internally, disassemble, inspect and service the unit as described in this section.

1. Clean the drive shaft with solvent and disassemble the parts (**Figure 18**). Wipe the final drive unit clean. Do not immerse the final drive unit in solvent.
2. Inspect the final drive unit case for cracks or other damage.
3. Inspect the drive shaft as follows:
    a. Inspect the splines on the drive shaft (A, **Figure 19**) and coupling (B and C) for wear or damage. The coupling and shaft should fit together with minimal or no play.
    b. Inspect the snap ring grooves (D, **Figure 19**) for damage. The snap rings must be tight on the shaft.
    c. Inspect the splines and spring (**Figure 20**) at the front of the shaft for wear or damage.

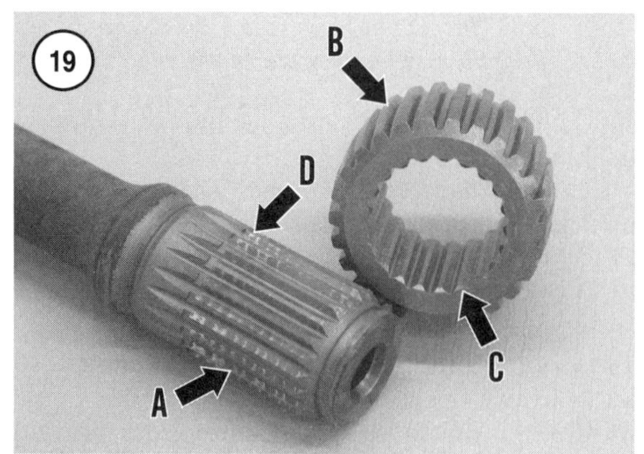
19
B
D
C
A

23

20

24

21

25

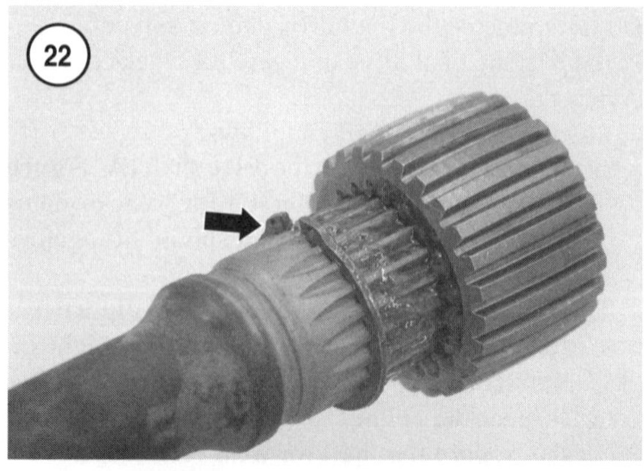
22

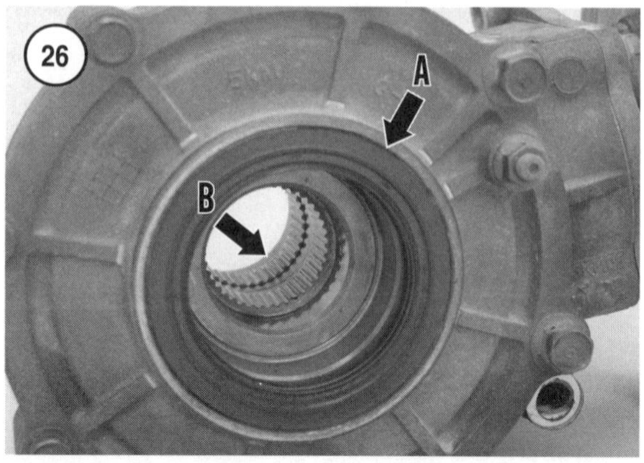
26
A
B

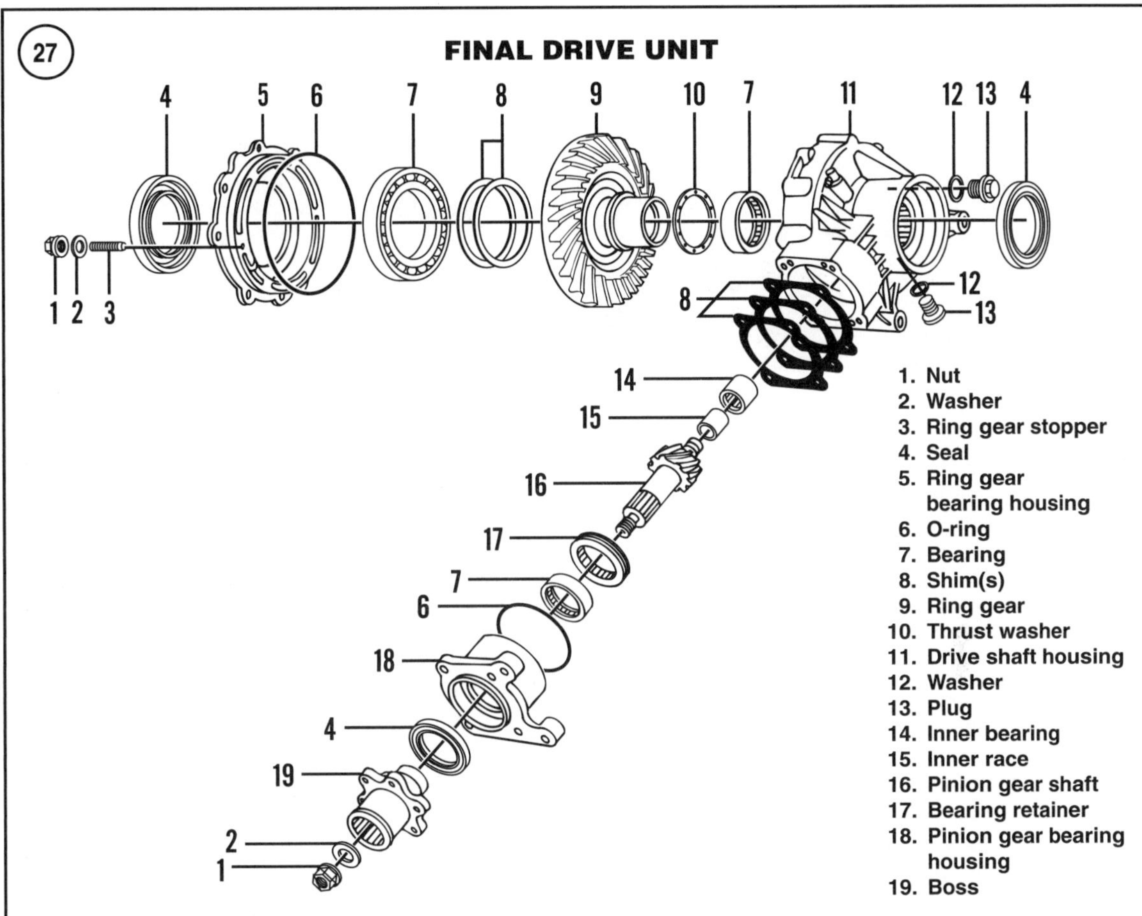

   d. Inspect the drive shaft for straightness.
   e. Inspect the boots and damper (**Figure 21**). The boots must be in good condition to prevent the entry of water and debris into the splined parts.
4. Assemble the drive shaft as follows:
   a. Lubricate the boots with waterproof grease, then slide the boots to the center of the drive shaft. The large boot goes to the front of the shaft.
   b. At the rear of the shaft, install a new snap ring with the sharp edge facing in (**Figure 22**).
   c. Apply waterproof grease to the shaft splines, then install the coupling.
   d. Install a new snap ring with the sharp edge facing out (**Figure 23**). Apply waterproof grease to the coupling. Then install the boot and damper.
   e. Apply waterproof grease to the splines at the front of the shaft. Then install the boot and spring (**Figure 24**). Use grease to hold the spring in place.
5. Inspect the boss and seal on the pinion gear shaft.
   a. Inspect the splines (**Figure 25**) for wear or damage. The drive shaft should fit into the boss with minimal or no play.
   b. Inspect the shaft seal for leaks. If oil is leaking past the seal, replace the seal as described in this section.
6. Inspect the axle seals (A, **Figure 26**) and internal splines (B) for wear or damage. Inspect the seals for tears, distortion or other damage. If rust, dirt or moisture is evident in the housing, the vent hose or seals are leaking. If necessary, replace the seals as described in this section. If internal damage is evident, disassemble the final drive unit as described in this section.
7. Turn the pinion gear shaft and inspect the internal bearings that support the shaft and ring gear. While turning the shaft, check for roughness, noise, play and binding. The bearings should turn smoothly and quietly. If damage or excessive play is evident, disassemble the final drive unit as described in this section to identify the damaged part(s).

Disassembly and Assembly

Refer to **Figure 27**.

1. Work in a crossing pattern and loosen the bolts at the perimeter of the ring gear bearing housing (**Figure 28**). Loosen each bolt one-quarter turn be-

fore removing the bolts. Do not remove the ring gear stopper and nut.

2. Remove the bearing housing and shim(s) (**Figure 29**). To unseat the bearing housing, pry around the housing equally at the pry points.

3. Remove the ring gear and thrust washer (**Figure 30**).

CAUTION

*Note the number (**Figure 31**) marked on the ring gear. Record this number, and indicate if it is positive or negative. This number is required when shimming the final drive unit. The number may be faint and often is removed completely when the parts are cleaned. After cleaning the ring gear, make sure to mark it again with the same number.*

4. If the pinion gear shaft, bearings, housing or seal is obviously damaged, remove the boss, brake disc and pinion gear bearing housing assembly using the following substeps. If damaged, the pinion gear shaft and ring gear are only available as a set.

NOTE

Removing the pinion gear shaft assembly is usually not required or recommended, since bearing damage can occur during removal and assembly. Disassemble the parts only when damage is evident.

a. Lock the brake disc in a vise with soft jaws so the pinion gear shaft nut can be removed (**Figure 32**). Use care in handling and securing the parts.
b. Remove the nut and washer from the end of the pinion gear shaft. Then remove the boss and brake disc (**Figure 33**). If just the seal is damaged, replace it as described in *Bearing and Seal Replacement* in this section. Removing the pinion gear bearing housing is not required.
c. Remove the four bolts securing the pinion gear housing to the final drive unit assembly.

33

34

35

36

d. Twist and remove the pinion gear housing and shim(s) (**Figure 34**). Avoid damaging the inner needle bearing race, which may come out with the pinion gear shaft (**Figure 35**). If the race or inner bearing is damaged, replace both parts.

NOTE
*If the parts are seized, apply penetrating lubricant to all joints. Then use a narrow drift to tap the shaft and pinion gear housing free. An access hole is provided in the drive shaft housing (**Figure 36**).*

e. Replace the bearings as described in *Bearing and Seal Replacement* in this section.

5. Inspect the parts as described in this section.
6. Reverse this procedure to assemble the final drive unit. Note the following:

CAUTION
*If replacing the pinion gear shaft, ring gear, drive shaft housing or bearing housing, check the final drive unit gear lash. Also check clearance whenever reusing worn original parts. Refer to **Gear Lash Inspection/Adjustment** in this section.*

a. Install new O-rings.
b. Apply molybdenum disulfide grease to all O-rings, bearings and seals.
c. Tighten the ring gear bearing housing bolts in a crossing pattern.
d. Tighten the 8-mm ring gear and pinion drive bearing housing bolts to 23 N•m (17 ft.-lb.).
e. Tighten the 10-mm ring gear bearing housing bolts to 40 N•m (30 ft.-lb.).
f. Tighten the pinion gear shaft nut to 70 N•m (52 ft.-lb.).

14

Inspection

In addition to the *Preliminary Inspection* procedure, make the following checks after the final drive unit has been disassembled.

1. Inspect the teeth on the ring gear and pinion gear (**Figure 37** and **Figure 38**). If damage or uneven wear is evident on either part, replace the ring gear and pinion gear shaft as a set. These parts are not available separately. If necessary, refer to the disassembly procedure in this section to remove the pinion gear bearing housing and pinion gear shaft from the final drive unit.
2. Inspect the bearings that support the ring gear (**Figure 39** and **Figure 40**). Lubricate the bearings with gear oil. Then insert the ring gear into each bear-

ing. Turn the bearing and check for roughness, noise, play and binding. The bearings should turn smoothly and quietly. If damage or excessive play is evident, replace the bearings as described in this section.

Bearing and Seal Replacement

Refer to **Figure 27** when replacing bearings and seals in the final drive unit. Refer to *Disassembly and Assembly* in this section to access the parts.

Left ring gear bearing and seal

The left ring gear bearing (A, **Figure 41**) and seal (B) are located in the drive shaft housing. A press is recommended for removing and installing the parts. If only seal replacement is required, removing or disassembling the final drive unit is not necessary. The seal can be removed from the outside of the final drive unit, after the axle is removed.

1. Remove the final drive unit as described in this section.
2. Remove the bearing housing and ring gear assemblies as described in this section.
3. Pry the seal from its recess. Place a shop cloth under the tool to prevent damage to the drive unit. To ease removal, heat the seal with a heat gun.
4. Support the housing in a press with the seal bore facing up.
5. Place a driver against the back edge of the roller bearing. Then drive the bearing from the bore.
6. Clean and dry the bore.
7. Before installing the new bearing and seal, note the following:
   a. Install the new bearing and seal with the manufacturer's marks facing up.
   b. Apply molybdenum disulfide grease to the bearing and seal. Pack grease into the bearing cavities and into the back of the seal.
8. Install the bearing as follows:
   a. Support the housing with the bearing bore facing up.
   b. Place the bearing *squarely* over the bearing bore. To ease installation, heat the bearing bore with a heat gun.
   c. Place a driver over the bearing. The driver should seat against the outside diameter of the bearing.
   d. Drive the bearing into place (**Figure 39**).
9. Install the seal as follows:
   a. Support the housing with the seal bore facing up.
   b. Hand-fit the seal so it is squarely in the bore.
   c. Place a driver over the seal. The driver should seat against the outside diameter of the seal.

   d. Drive the seal into place.
10. Install the ring gear and bearing housing assemblies as described in this section.
11. Install the final drive unit as described in this section.

Right ring gear bearing and seal

The right ring gear bearing and seal are located in the bearing housing (**Figure 40**). A press is recommended for removing and installing the parts. If replacing just the seal, removal or disassembly of the

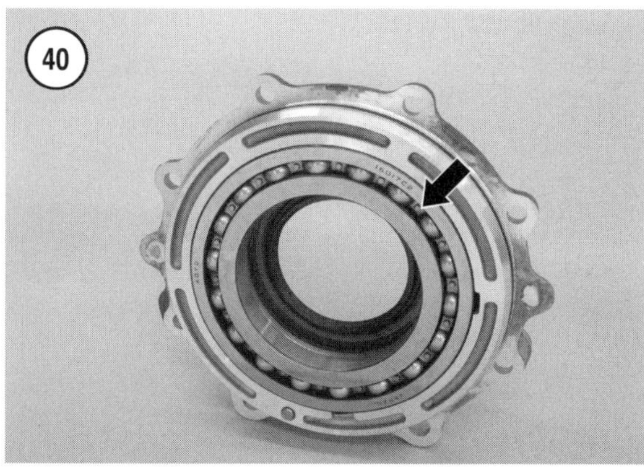

final drive unit is not necessary. The seal can be removed from the outside of the final drive unit after the axle is removed.

1. Remove the final drive unit as described in this section.
2. Remove the bearing housing as described in this section.
3. Pry the seal (**Figure 42**) from its recess. Place a shop cloth under the tool to prevent damage to the housing. To ease removal, heat the seal with a heat gun.
4. Support the housing in a press with the seal bore facing up.
5. Place a driver against the back edge of the ball bearing. Then drive the bearing from the bore.
6. Clean and dry the bore.
7. Before installing the new bearing and seal, note the following:
   a. Install the new bearing and seal with the manufacturer's marks facing up.
   b. Apply molybdenum disulfide grease to the bearing and seal. Pack grease into the bearing cavities and into the back of the seal.
8. Install the bearing as follows:
   a. Support the housing with the bearing bore facing up.
   b. Place the bearing *squarely* over the bearing bore. To ease installation, heat the bearing bore with a heat gun.
   c. Place a driver over the bearing. The driver should seat against the outside diameter of the bearing.
   d. Drive the bearing into place.
9. Install the seal as follows:
   a. Support the housing with the seal bore facing up.
   b. Hand-fit the seal so it is squarely in the bore.
   c. Place a driver over the seal. The driver should seat against the outside diameter of the seal.
   d. Drive the seal into place.
10. Install the bearing housing as described in this section.
11. Install the final drive unit as described in this section.

Pinion gear bearings and seal

The pinion gear shaft is supported and sealed at the outer end by a ball bearing and seal, located in the pinion gear bearing housing (**Figure 43**). The shaft is supported at the inner end by a roller bearing, seated in the drive shaft housing (**Figure 44**). The inner bearing is removable with hand tools, while a press is recommended for all other steps. If replacing just the seal, removal of the final drive unit is necessary, but disassembly of the unit is not required. The seal can be removed from the outside of the final drive unit once the boss and brake disc are removed from the pinion gear shaft.

1. Remove the final drive unit as described in this section.
2. Remove the bearing housing, ring gear assembly and pinion gear bearing housing as described in this section.
3. Replace the outer bearing in the pinion gear bearing housing as follows:
   a. Support the housing in a press so the pinion gear points down.
   b. Place a driver onto the perimeter of the shaft (**Figure 45**). Then drive the shaft out of the housing. Avoid damaging the shaft threads or splines.
   c. Pry the seal from its recess. Place a shop cloth under the tool to prevent damage to the housing. To ease removal, heat the seal with a heat gun.
   d. Remove the bearing retainer with a ring nut wrench.
   e. Support the housing in a press so the bearing points down. Then drive the bearing out of the housing.
4. Clean and dry the bore.
5. Before installing the new outer bearing and seal, note the following:
   a. Install the new bearing and seal with the manufacturer's marks facing up.
   b. Apply molybdenum disulfide grease to the bearing and seal. Pack grease into the bearing cavities and into the back of the seal.
6. Install the outer bearing as follows:
   a. Support the housing with the bearing bore facing up.
   b. Place the bearing *squarely* over the bearing bore. To ease installation, heat the bearing bore with a heat gun.
   c. Place a driver over the bearing. The driver should seat against the outside diameter of the bearing.
   d. Drive the bearing into place.
   e. Apply threadlocking compound to the bearing retainer. Then tighten the retainer to 170 N•m (125 ft.-lb.).
7. Install the seal as follows:
   a. Support the housing with the seal bore facing up.
   b. Hand-fit the seal so it is squarely in the bore.
   c. Place a driver over the seal. The driver should seat against the outside diameter of the seal.
   d. Drive the seal into place.
   e. Inspect the boss contact area (**Figure 46**) for nicks or burrs that may cause the seal to leak. Polish minor damage with emery cloth until the surface is smooth.

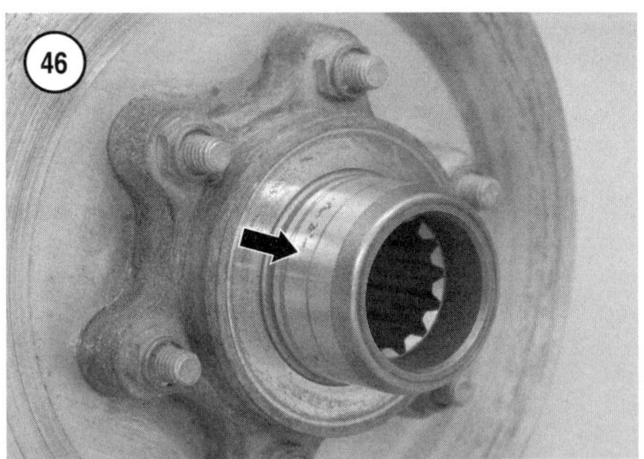

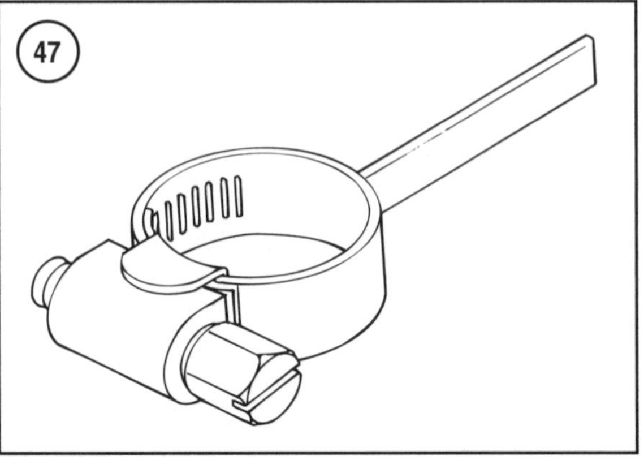

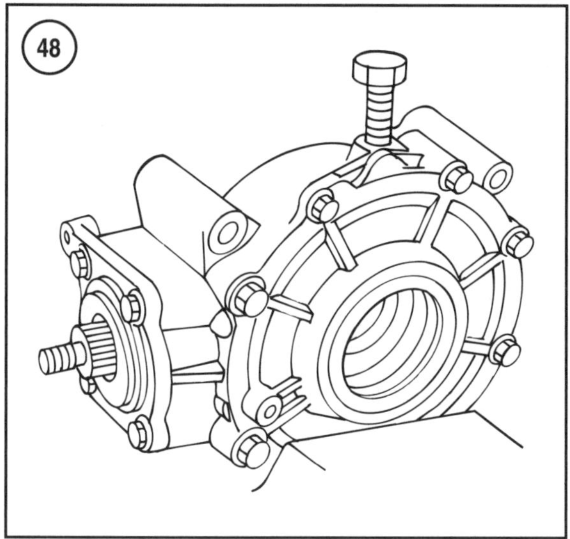

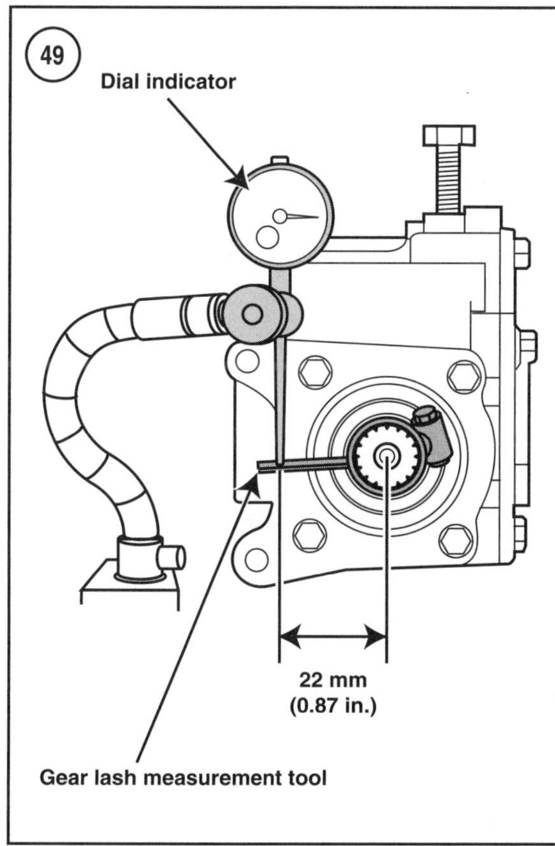

8. Replace the inner bearing as follows:
   a. Pass a narrow drift through the access hole (**Figure 44**), placing the drift against the bearing.
   b. Drive the bearing from the bore.
   c. Pack grease into the new bearing.
   d. Place the new bearing *squarely* over the bearing bore. To ease installation, heat the bearing bore with a heat gun.
   e. Place a driver over the bearing. The driver should seat against the outside diameter of the bearing.
   f. Drive the bearing into place.
   g. Remove the old inner bearing race from the end of the pinion gear shaft (**Figure 35**).
   h. Lightly tap the new inner bearing race onto the end of the shaft. Use a driver that fits on the entire end of the race. Do not directly strike the race.

Gear Lash Inspection/Adjustment

If replacing the pinion gear shaft, ring gear or drive shaft housing, inspect and adjust the final drive unit gear lash to obtain the correct clearances between the parts. Also check clearance whenever using worn original parts. Refer to **Figure 27** when adjusting the final drive unit gear lash.

After the final drive unit is assembled, check the gear lash to verify that shim selection is correct. Measure lash with a gear lash measurement tool (Yamaha part No. YM-01231), or equivalent (**Figure 47**), and a dial indicator.

NOTE

Use the following procedure only after the final drive unit has been disassembled and inspected as described in this section.

1. Lock the final drive unit in a vise or to a stable surface. Secure the case so the drain hole is facing up.
2. Lock the ring gear in place with a 14–1.50 × 40-mm bolt (**Figure 48**). Finger-tighten the bolt into the drain plug hole just enough to keep the ring gear from moving.
3. Clamp the gear lash measurement tool onto the pinion gear shaft (**Figure 49**). Position the tool so the arm can contact the dial indicator.
4. Position a dial indicator in contact with the measurement tool and 22 mm (0.87 in.) from the center of the pinion gear (**Figure 49**). The dial indicator must be stable and set to read gear lash in both directions.
5. Gently rotate the pinion gear clockwise until lash between the parts is eliminated. Note the dial indicator reading.
6. Gently rotate the pinion gear in the opposite direction until lash between the parts is eliminated. Note the dial indicator reading.
7. Calculate the total side-to-side gear lash.
8. Loosen the lock bolt and rotate the pinion gear 90°. Finger-tighten the bolt, readjust the gear lash measurement tool, and repeat the check. Continue

14

checking the gear lash until the pinion gear has rotated one full turn.

9. Determine the average reading of the four checks. Final drive gear lash should be 0.1-0.2 mm (0.004-0.008 in.). If necessary, adjust the ring gear in or out as follows:

a. If gear lash is too low, decrease the ring gear shim thickness. If the shim adjustment needed is 0.2 mm (0.008 in.) or greater, increase the thrust washer thickness by an equal amount.
b. If gear lash is too high, increase the ring gear shim thickness. If the shim adjustment needed is 0.2 mm (0.008 in.) or greater, decrease the thrust washer thickness by an equal amount.
c. Ring gear shims are available in 0.05 mm increments from 0.25-0.50 mm thick.
d. Ring gear thrust washers are available in 0.1 mm increments from 1.2-2.1 mm thick.
e. After installing the replacement shim(s) or washer, recheck the gear lash.

CAUTION
Determine the shim/washer requirements in the order presented in this procedure. While determining each shim size, assemble the shim(s) and related components so the next shim can be calculated.

Pinion gear shim

Use the following procedure to determine the shim size(s) for the pinion gear assembly (**Figure 50**).

1. Determine the shim size with the formula: **A = a + (c – b) – d**.
2. The fixed value of *a* in the shim formula is 92.5.
3. Note the number shown (*b*, **Figure 51**) on the pinion gear bearing housing for the *b* measurement. It indicates a decimal value. Use the number closest to the corner of the housing. The number in this example is +0.90. Add this number to 34 to get the *b* variable of the shim formula, or 34.90 here.
4. Note the *other* number shown (**c**, **Figure 51**) on the pinion gear bearing housing for the *c* measurement. It indicates a decimal value. The number in this example is +0.34. Add this number to 55 to get the *c* variable of the shim formula, or 55.34 here.
5. Note the *smaller* number shown (*d*, **Figure 52**) on the drive shaft housing for the *d* measurement. It indicates a decimal value. The number in this example is + 0.05. Add this number to 112 to get the *d* variable of the shim formula, or 112.05 here.
6. The example is now: A = 92.5 + (55.34 – 34.90) – 112.05. The result is: A = 0.89. Round the hundredths numeral as follows:

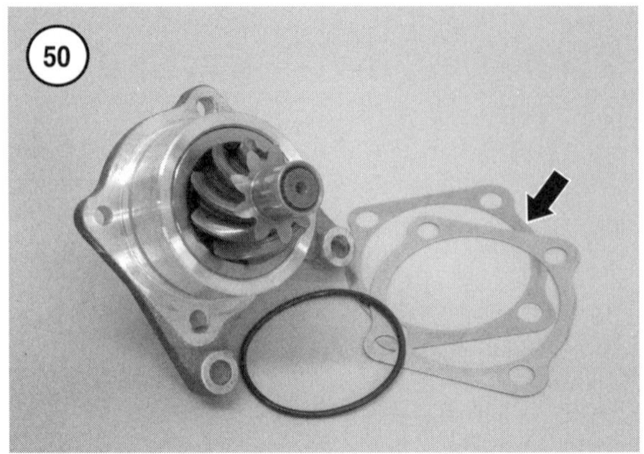
50

51

52

53

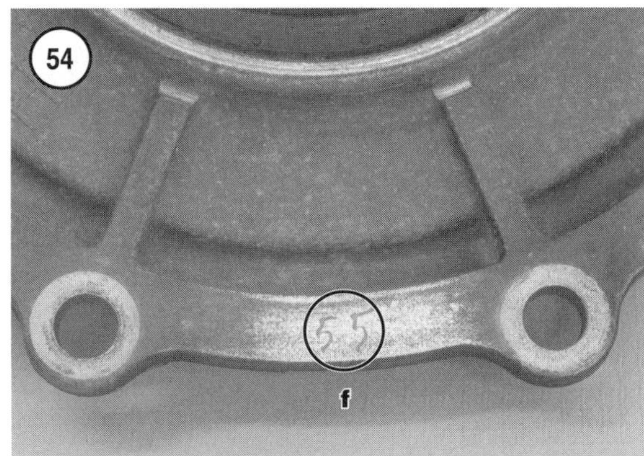

a. Round 0-2 to 0.
b. Round 3-7 to 5.
c. Round 8 and 9 to 10.

7. After rounding the result, the correct shim size (A) for the example is 0.90 mm thick. Pinion gear shims are available in 0.15, 0.30, 0.40, 0.45, 0.50 and 0.60 mm thick.
8. Install the shim(s) and the pinion gear assembly.

Ring gear shim

Use the following procedure to determine the shim(s) size for the ring gear (**Figure 53**).

1. Determine the shim size with the formula: **B = e – f – (g + h)**.
2. Note the *larger* number shown (*e*, **Figure 52**) on the drive shaft housing for the *e* measurement. It indicates a decimal value. The number in this example is 0.98. Add this number to 50 to get the *e* variable of the shim formula, or 50.98 here.
3. Note the number shown (*f*, **Figure 54**) on the ring gear bearing housing for the *f* measurement. It indicates a decimal value. The number in this example is 0.55. Add this number to 1 to get the *f* variable of the shim formula, or 1.55 here.
4. Note the number shown (*g*, **Figure 55**) on the ring gear for the *g* measurement. It indicates a decimal value displayed in hundredths. The number in this example is –0.03. Some ring gears may display a positive number. Add this number to 35 to get the *g* variable of the shim formula. The result for the example here is 34.97.
5. The fixed value of *h* (the bearing thickness) in the shim formula is 14.0.
6. The example is now: B = 50.98 – 1.55 – (34.97 + 14.0). When calculated, B = 49.43 – 48.97. The result is: B = 0.46. Round the hundredths numeral as follows:

a. Round 0-2 to 0.
b. Round 3-7 to 5.
c. Round 8 and 9 to 10.

7. After rounding the result, the correct shim size (B) for the example is 0.45 mm thick. Ring gear shims are available in 0.05 mm increments from 0.25-0.50 mm thick.
8. Install the shim(s) on the ring gear.

Ring gear thrust washer

Use the following procedure and Plastigage to determine the thrust washer size for the ring gear (**Figure 56**).

1. Place four strips of Plastigage on the ring gear hub (**Figure 57**). Equally space the strips around the

hub. Then place the original thrust washer over the strips.

NOTE
In the following step, do not rotate the pinion gear or ring gear while measuring the clearance.

2. Install the ring gear assembly, shim(s) and bearing housing into the drive shaft housing. Tighten the bearing housing bolts in a crossing pattern.
   a. Tighten the 8-mm bearing housing bolts to 23 N•m (17 ft.-lb.).
   b. Tighten the 10-mm bearing housing bolts to 40 N•m (30 ft.-lb.).
3. Disassemble the bearing housing and ring gear. Then measure the Plastigage (**Figure 58**).
   a. Correct ring gear thrust clearance is 0.1-0.2 mm (0.004-0.008 in.).
   b. If necessary, resize the washer and repeat the procedure so clearance is within specification. Ring gear thrust washers are available in 0.1 mm increments from 1.2-2.1 mm thick.
4. Install the washer onto the ring gear.

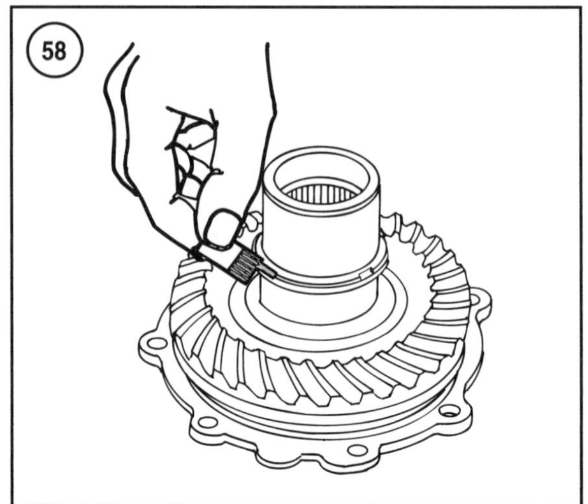

Ring gear stopper shim

Use the following procedure to adjust the ring gear stopper clearance (**Figure 59**).
1. Install the shim(s) onto the ring gear.
2. Seat the bearing housing onto the ring gear. Then measure the gap between the ring gear and ring gear stopper. Correct ring gear stopper clearance (A, **Figure 59**) is 0.30-0.60 mm (0.012-0.024 in.). If necessary, loosen the locknut (B, **Figure 59**) and adjust the ring gear stopper so clearance is within specification. Apply threadlocking compound to the locknut threads. Then tighten the locknut to 16 N•m (12 ft.-lb.).

Table 1 REAR AXLE AND FINAL DRIVE SPECIFICATIONS

Final drive gear lash	0.1-0.2 mm (0.004-0.008 in.)
Ring gear stopper clearance	0.3-0.6 mm (0.012-0.024 in.)
Ring gear thrust clearance	0.1-0.2 mm (0.004-0.008 in.)

Table 2 REAR AXLE AND FINAL DRIVE TORQUE SPECIFICATIONS

	N•m	ft.-lb.
Bearing housing		
8-mm bolts	23	17
10-mm bolts	40	30
Bearing retainer	170	125
Final drive mounting bolts	55	41
Final drive oil drain plug	23	17
Final drive oil fill plugs	23	17
Pinion gear shaft nut	70	52
Ring gear stopper locknut	16	12

CHAPTER FIFTEEN

BRAKES

This chapter covers the brake system. This includes brake pads, master cylinders, calipers, discs and left hand brake cable. Refer to the tables at the end of this chapter for specifications.

Refer to Chapter Three for brake fluid level inspection, brake pad/disc inspection, and the adjustment of the brake levers, brake pedal and rear brake light switch.

BRAKE OPERATION

The front and rear brake calipers are hydraulically actuated by master cylinders. The master cylinders are connected to a pedal and/or hand lever, which applies and controls pressure in the brake line.

The front brake calipers *float* on pins and automatically remain centered over the disc. When pressure is applied, the caliper piston and inner brake pad move toward the brake disc. As pad pressure against the disc rises, the caliper slides and pulls the outer brake pad into contact with the disc. When pressure is relieved, the piston, inner pad and caliper assembly slightly retract from the disc, allowing the disc to spin freely. As the pads wear, the piston in the caliper extends, automatically keeping the pads adjusted and centered around the disc. It is important not only to ensure that the piston can extend and retract, but that the caliper is free to move on its mounting bracket.

The rear brake caliper is bolted into a stationary position and uses two caliper pistons on both sides of the brake disc. When pressure is applied, the pistons and pads extend to contact the disc. When pressure is relieved, both piston and pad sets slightly retract from the disc, allowing the wheel to spin freely. As the pads wear, the pistons in the caliper extend, automatically keeping the pads adjusted and centered around the disc.

BRAKE SERVICE

Observe the following when working on a brake system:

1. Keep brake fluid off painted surfaces, plastic and decals. The fluid will damage these surfaces. If fluid does contact these surfaces, quickly flush the surface thoroughly with clean water.
2. Keep the fluid reservoirs closed except when changing the fluid.
3. Replace brake fluid frequently. The fluid absorbs moisture from the air and will cause internal corrosion of the brake system. Fresh fluid is clear to slightly yellow. If the fluid is obviously colored, it is contaminated.
4. Do not reuse brake fluid or use new fluid that has been in a partially used container for any length of time.
5. When rebuilding brake system components, lubricate new parts with fresh DOT 4 fluid before assembly. Do not use petroleum-based solvents. These can swell and damage rubber components.
6. Bleed the brake system whenever the system has been opened for service, such as loosening a brake

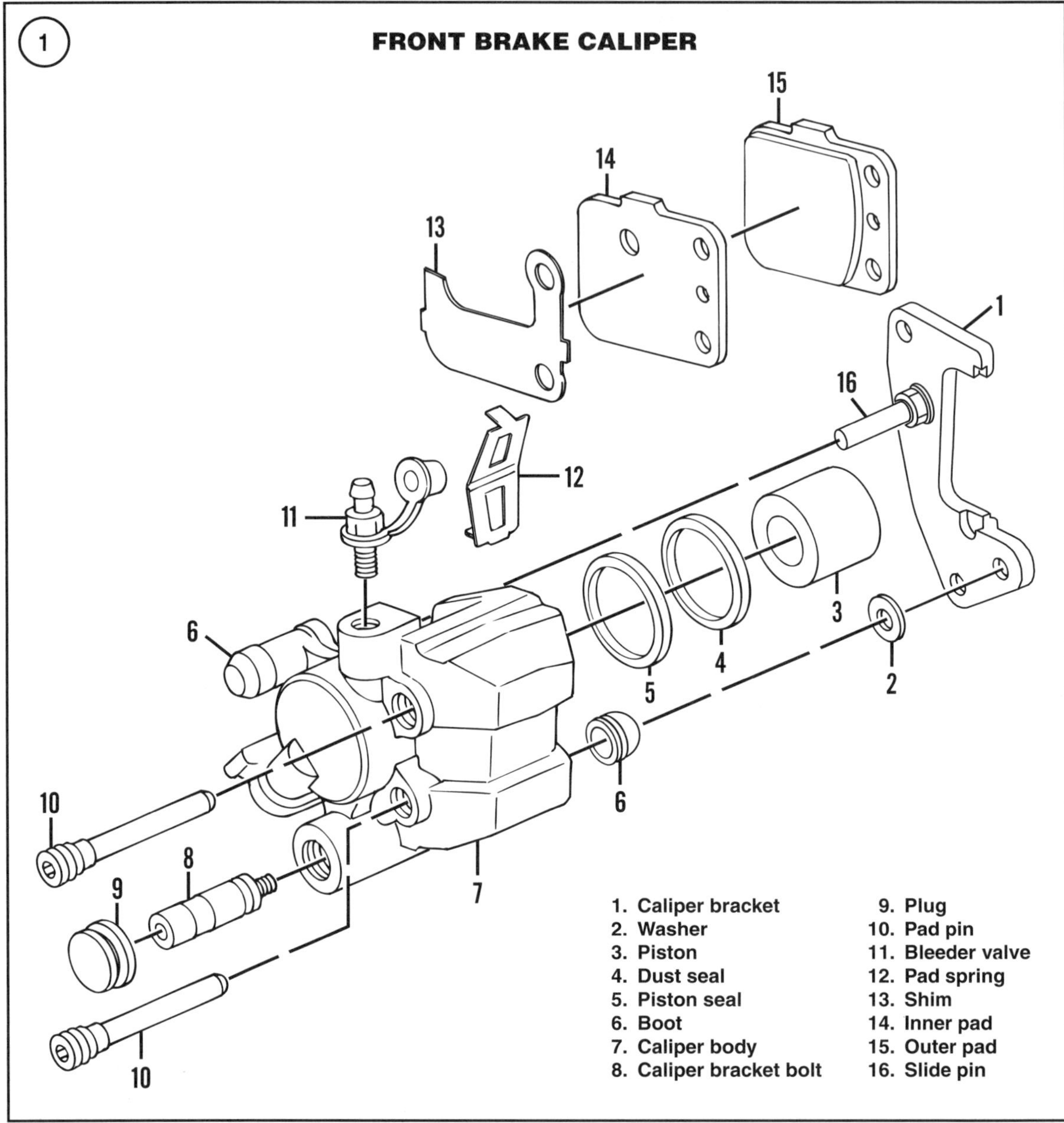

hose banjo bolt or other brake line connector. Air in the system will make the brake action spongy.

FRONT BRAKE PADS

Brake pad wear depends on riding habits, conditions and pad material. Replace the pads when they are worn to within 1 mm (0.040 in.) of the backing plate, or have been contaminated with oil or other chemicals.

Replacement

The brake pads can only be replaced by removing the caliper from the steering knuckle. The brake hose does not have to be removed from the caliper. Support the caliper and do not allow it to hang by the brake hose. When replacing brake pads, replace both sets of pads in the front calipers.

Refer to **Figure 1**.

1. Place the machine in two-wheel drive.
2. Remove the front wheel (Chapter Eleven).
3. Loosen the pad pins (A, **Figure 2**).
4. Remove the caliper mounting bolts (B, **Figure 2**). Then remove the caliper from the disc. Avoid kinking the brake hose.
5. Press down on the pads to relieve the pressure on the pad pins. Then remove the pins.
6. Remove the pads and shim.

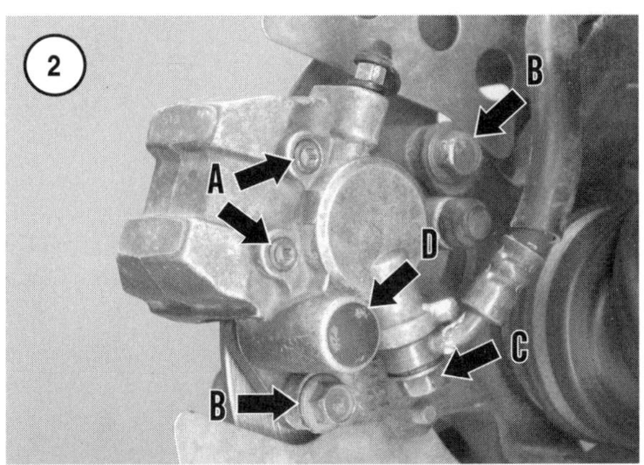

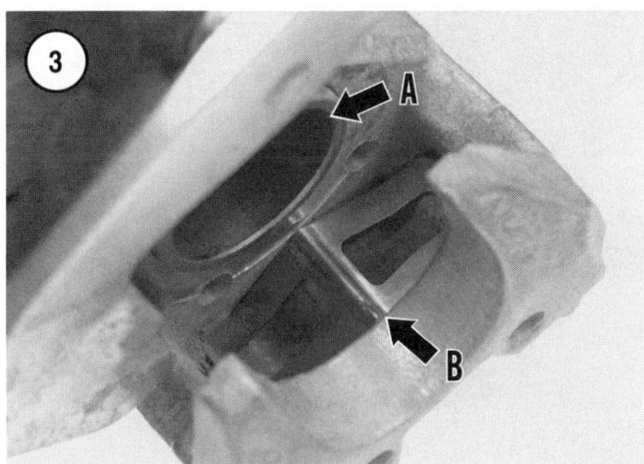

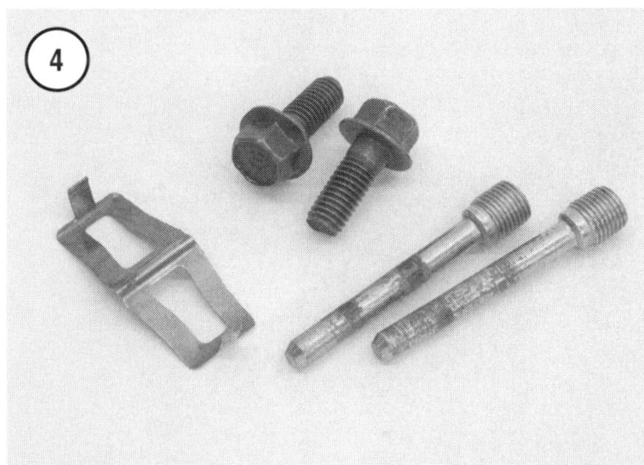

CAUTION

Do not operate the brake lever with the pads removed. The caliper piston can come out of the bore.

7. Clean and inspect the visible portion of the piston. Remove light corrosion with fine emery cloth. If the piston surface is heavily corroded and cannot be cleaned, remove and repair the caliper as described in this chapter. A corroded or pitted piston can leak when it is pressed back through the seals.

CAUTION

In the following step, monitor the level of fluid in the master cylinder reservoir. Brake fluid will flow back into the reservoir when the caliper piston is pressed into the bore, possibly causing the reservoir to overflow.

8. Grasp the caliper and press the caliper piston (A, **Figure 3**) down into the bore, creating room for the new pads.
9. Remove the pad spring (B, **Figure 3**).
10. Clean the interior of the caliper and inspect for the following:
   a. Leaks or damage around the piston, bleeder valve and hose connection.
   b. Damaged or missing boots.
   c. Excessive drag of the caliper bracket when it is moved in and out of the caliper. If corrosion or water is evident around the rubber boots, clean and lubricate the parts with silicone brake grease.
11. Inspect the pad pins, pad spring and mounting bolts (**Figure 4**). The pins and spring must be in good condition to allow the inner pad to move slightly when installed.
12. Inspect the pads and the shim (**Figure 5**) on the back of inner pad for wear and damage.
   a. Replace the pads when they are worn to within 1 mm (0.040 in.) of the backing plate. This is indicated on some pads by a wear indica-

tor (**Figure 6**) at the edge of the pads. Always replace pads that have been contaminated with oil or other chemicals. Always replace the shim when installing new brake pads.

b. If the pads are worn unevenly, the caliper is probably not sliding correctly on the caliper bracket. The caliper must be free to *float* on the slide pins. Buildup or corrosion on parts can hold the caliper in one position, causing brake drag and excessive pad wear.

13. Install the pad spring with the small tabs pointing out.
14. Install the inner pad and shim, seating the pad against the piston.
15. Install the outer pad.
16. Press down on the pads. Then align and install the pad pins. Tighten the pins after installing the caliper.
17. Spread the pads so there is clearance to fit the caliper over the brake disc (**Figure 7**).
18. Position the caliper over the brake disc and hub assembly. Then slide the caliper into place.
19. Install and tighten the caliper mounting bolts to 30 N•m (22 ft.-lb.).
20. Tighten the pad pins to 18 N•m (13 ft.-lb.).
21. Operate the brake lever several times to seat the pads.
22. Check the brake fluid reservoir and adjust the fluid level as necessary.
23. With the wheels raised, make sure the hub spins freely and the brake operates properly.
24. Install the front wheel (Chapter Eleven).

FRONT BRAKE CALIPER

Removal and Installation

1. Place the machine in two-wheel drive.
2. Remove the front wheel (Chapter Eleven).
3. If the caliper will be disassembled, perform the following:
   a. Drain the brake system as described in this chapter.
   b. Loosen the pad pins (A, **Figure 2**) and the caliper bracket bolt (D) located under the rubber plug while the caliper is secured.
   c. Loosen the brake hose banjo bolt (C, **Figure 2**). Leave the bolt finger-tight. It will be removed in a later step.
4. Remove the caliper mounting bolts (B, **Figure 2**), then slide the caliper away from the disc. Avoid kinking the brake hose.

5A. If the caliper will be left attached to the brake hose, but not disassembled and serviced:
   a. Suspend the caliper with a length of wire. Do not let the caliper hang by the brake hose.

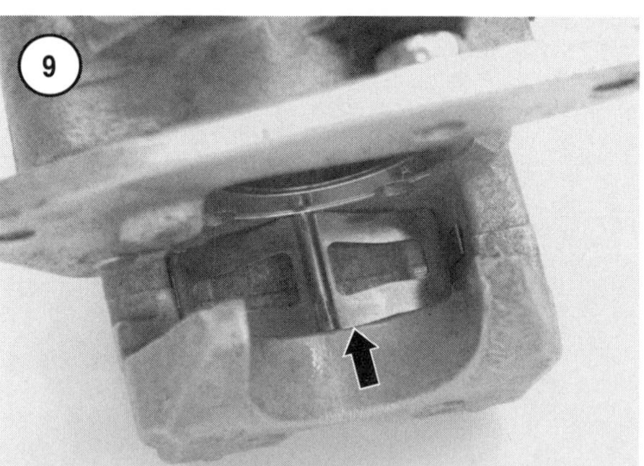

   b. Insert a small wooden block between the brake pads. This will prevent the caliper piston from being pushed out of the caliper if the brake lever is operated.

5B. If the caliper will be disassembled, perform the following:
   a. Remove the banjo bolt and washers from the brake hose. Have a shop cloth ready to absorb any excess brake fluid that leaks from the hose.
   b. Wrap the hose end to prevent brake fluid from damaging other surfaces.
   c. Drain excess brake fluid from the caliper.
   d. Inspect the caliper as described in this section.

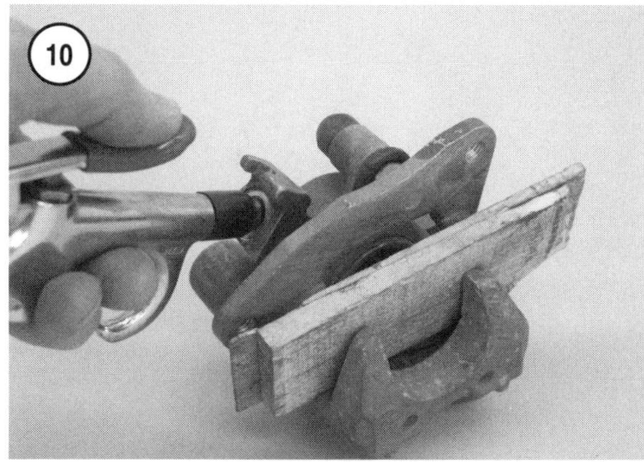

6. Reverse this procedure to install the caliper. Note the following:
   a. Install and tighten the caliper mounting bolts to 30 N•m (22 ft.-lb.).
   b. Install new washers onto the banjo bolt. Position the brake hose against the guide on the caliper. Then tighten the brake hose banjo bolt to 27 N•m (20 ft.-lb.).
7. If the caliper was rebuilt, or the brake hose disconnected from the caliper, fill and bleed the brake system as described in this chapter.
8. Operate the brake lever several times to seat the pads.
9. Check the brake fluid reservoir and adjust the fluid level as necessary.
10. With the wheels raised, check that the hub spins freely and the brake operates properly.
11. Install the front wheel (Chapter Eleven).

Inspection

Refer to **Figure 1**.

1. Remove the caliper as described in this section.
2. Remove the pad pins (**Figure 8**). Press down on the pads to relieve the pressure on the pad pins while removing them.
3. Remove the brake pads and pad spring (**Figure 9**). If necessary, press the caliper piston into the bore so the spring can be removed.
4. Remove the piston from the caliper bore using compressed air (**Figure 10**). Do not attempt to pry the piston out of the caliper.
   a. Place the caliper on a padded work surface.
   b. Close the bleeder valve on the caliper so air cannot escape.
   c. Place a strip of wood, or similar pad, in the caliper. The pad will cushion the piston when it comes out of the caliper.

WARNING

Wear eye protection when using compressed air to remove the piston. Keep fingers away from the piston discharge area.

   d. Lay the caliper so the piston will discharge downward.
   e. Insert an air nozzle into the brake hose fitting. If the nozzle does not have a rubber tip, wrap the nozzle with tape. This will allow the nozzle to seal tightly and prevent thread damage.
   f. Place a shop cloth over the entire caliper to catch any spray that may discharge from the caliper.
   g. Apply pressure and listen for the piston to *pop* from the caliper.
5. Remove the caliper bracket bolt and boot (A, **Figure 11**). Remove the boot from the bolt before pulling it out of the caliper.
6. Remove the caliper bracket and washer (B, **Figure 11**).
7. Remove the slide pin boot (C, **Figure 11**).
8. Remove the bleeder valve and cap (D, **Figure 11**).
9. Remove the dust seal (**Figure 12**) and piston seal.
10. Inspect the caliper assembly as follows:
   a. Clean all passages with compressed air.
   b. Clean all parts that will be reused with fresh DOT 4 brake fluid or isopropyl (rubbing) alcohol. Use a wood or plastic-tipped tool to clean

the seal and boot grooves. Use clean brake fluid to aid in cleaning the piston, bore and seal grooves.

c. Inspect the caliper bore for wear, pitting or corrosion.
d. Measure the inside diameter of the front caliper bore (**Figure 13**). Refer to **Table 1** for specifications.
e. Inspect the piston. Remove light corrosion with fine emery cloth. If the piston surface (**Figure 14**) is heavily corroded and cannot be adequately cleaned, replace the piston. A corroded or pitted piston can leak when it is pressed back through the seals.
f. Inspect the pad pins, pad spring and mounting bolts (**Figure 4**). The pins and spring must be in good condition to allow the inner pad to move slightly when installed. Make sure both small tabs on the spring are not corroded or missing.
g. Inspect the caliper bracket and slide pin for wear, pitting or corrosion.
h. Inspect the boots for deterioration.
i. Inspect the bleeder valve for clogging and damage.
j. Inspect the shim on the back of the inner brake pad (**Figure 5**). Replace the shim if corroded or damaged. Always replace the shim when installing new brake pads.
k. Inspect the brake pads. Replace the pads when they are worn to within 1.0 mm (0.040 in.) of the backing plate. This is indicated on some pads by a wear indicator (**Figure 6**) at the edge of the pads. Always replace pads that have been contaminated with oil or other chemicals. If the pads are worn unevenly, the caliper is probably not sliding correctly on the caliper bracket. The caliper must be free to *float* on the slide pin and retainer bolt. Buildup or corrosion on the parts can hold the caliper in one position, causing brake drag and excessive pad wear.

11. Install a new piston seal (A, **Figure 15**) and dust seal (B) as follows:
    a. Soak the new seals in fresh brake fluid for 15 minutes.
    b. Coat the caliper bore and piston with brake fluid.
    c. Seat the piston seal and then the dust seal (**Figure 16**) into the caliper grooves. The piston seal goes in the back groove.
    d. Install the piston, with the open side facing out (A, **Figure 17**). Gently twist the piston past the seals. Then press the piston to the bottom of the bore.
12. Install the boots and caliper bracket bolt as follows:

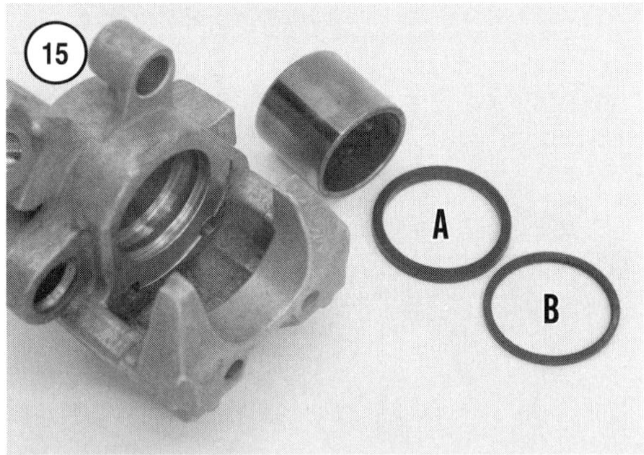

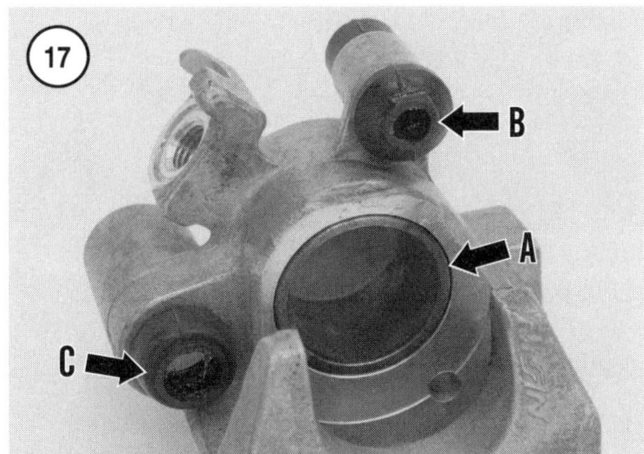

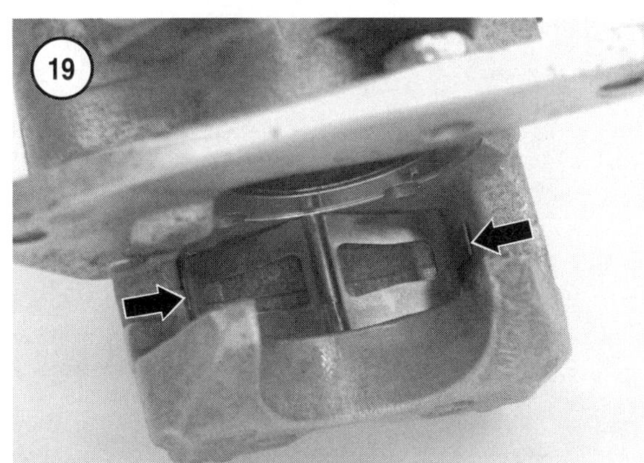

   a. Apply silicone brake grease to the interior of the boots and to the bracket bolt.
   b. Install the slide pin boot into the caliper (B, **Figure 17**). If necessary, apply a light coat of grease to the exterior of the large boot to help pass it through the caliper.
   c. Pass the bracket bolt through the caliper. Then install the boot over the end of the bolt (C, **Figure 17**).

13. Install the caliper bracket as follows:
   a. Lubricate the slide pin on the bracket. Then install it onto the caliper.
   b. Align the bracket with the caliper bracket bolt. Place the washer over the bolt. Then tighten the bracket bolt (**Figure 18**) to 23 N•m (17 ft.-lb.).
   c. Install the rubber plug.

14. Install the bleeder valve and cap.

15. Install the pad spring with the small tabs pointing out (**Figure 19**).

16. Install the inner pad and shim, seating the pad against the piston.

17. Install the outer pad.

18. Press down on the pads. Then align and install the pad pins. Tighten the pins to 18 N•m (13 ft.-lb.).

19. Spread the pads (**Figure 20**) so there is clearance to fit the caliper over the brake disc.

20. Install the caliper as described in this section.

FRONT MASTER CYLINDER

Removal and Installation

1. Cover and protect the bodywork and area surrounding the master cylinder.

CAUTION

Do not allow brake fluid to splash from the reservoir or hose. Brake fluid can damage painted and plastic surfaces. Clean up any spills immediately by flooding the area with water.

2. Drain the brake system as described in this chapter.

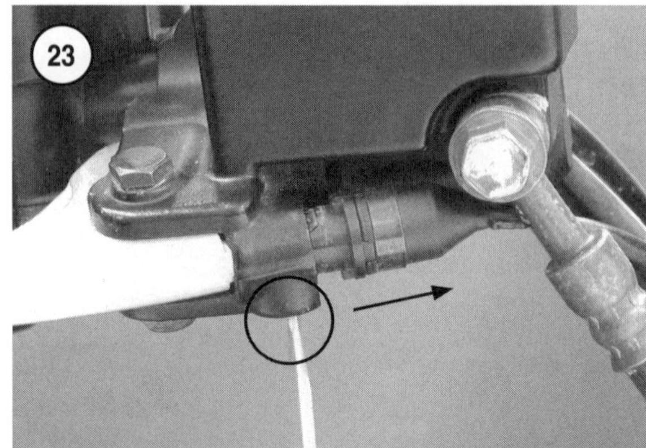

3. Remove the four-wheel drive switch (**Figure 21**).
4. Remove the cap and diaphragm. Verify that the master cylinder (**Figure 22**) is empty. Wipe the interior of the reservoir to absorb all remaining fluid.
5. Remove the brake switch from the master cylinder. Use a small tool to press on the barb (**Figure 23**) that locks the switch to the master cylinder.
6. If rebuilding the master cylinder, loosen the brake lever pivot bolt (A, **Figure 24**) while the master cylinder remains secured.
7. Remove the brake hose banjo bolt (B, **Figure 24**) from the master cylinder as follows:
   a. Remove the banjo bolt and washers from the brake hose. Have a shop cloth ready to absorb any excess brake fluid that leaks from the hose.
   b. Wrap the hose end to prevent brake fluid from damaging other surfaces.
8. Remove the bolts (A, **Figure 25**) and clamp (B) securing the master cylinder to the handlebar. Then remove the master cylinder.
9. Inspect the master cylinder as described in this section.
10. Reverse this procedure to install the master cylinder. Note the following:
    a. The mounting clamp must be installed so *UP* and the arrow (C, **Figure 25**) are facing up. Tighten the upper bolt first, then the bottom bolt. Tighten the master cylinder mounting bolts to 7 N•m (62 in.-lb.).
    b. Position the brake hose fitting (B, **Figure 24**) so it is parallel to the handlebar and passes into the handlebar cover.
    c. Install new washers onto the brake hose banjo bolt. Tighten the bolt to 27 N•m (20 ft.-lb.).
11. Fill the brake fluid reservoir and bleed the brake system as described in this chapter.

NOTE

Brake lever adjustment is not required. If properly bled, the brake lever will automatically adjust.

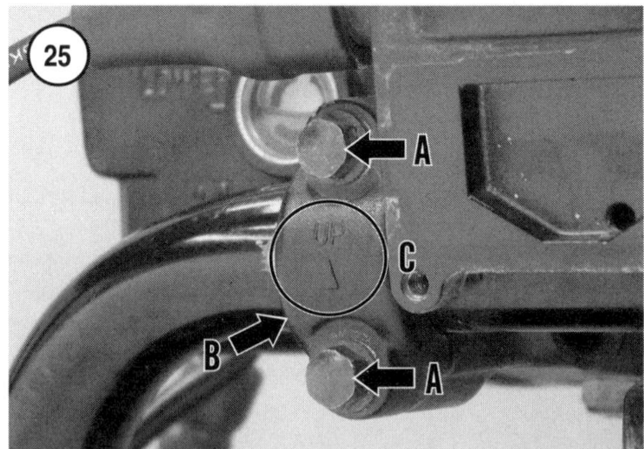

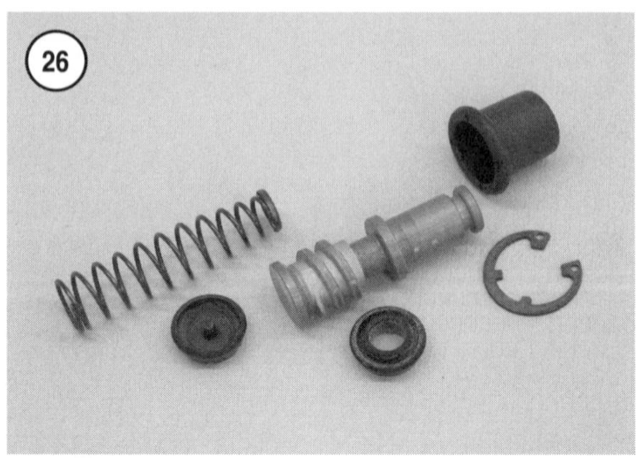

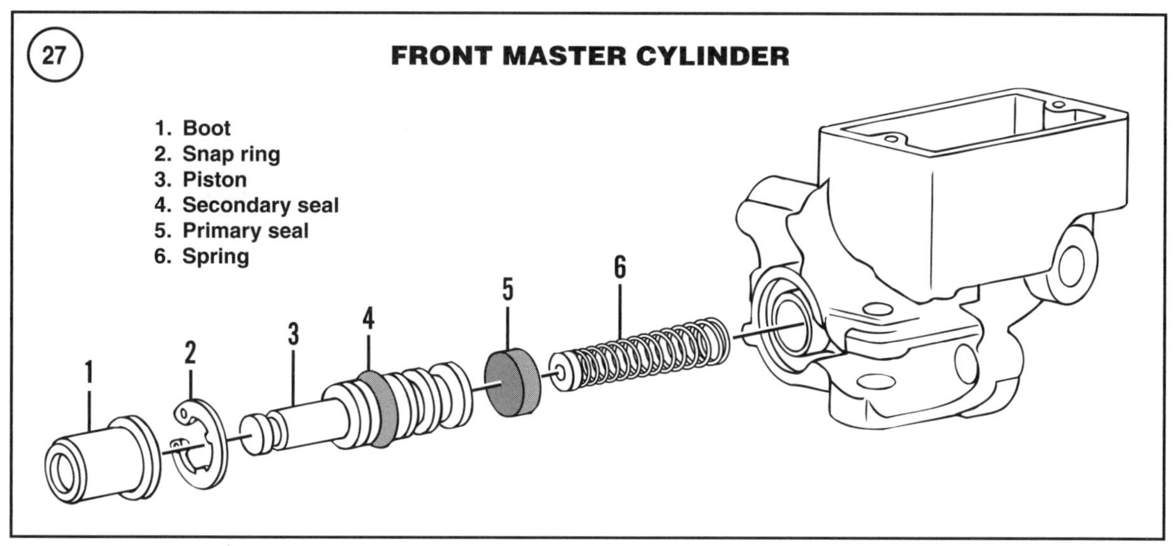

15

Inspection

The boot, snap ring, piston, seals and spring (**Figure 26**) are available as a replacement kit. Refer to **Figure 27**.

1. Remove the master cylinder as described in this section.
2. Remove the brake lever pivot bolt and lever (**Figure 28**).
3. Remove the boot from the piston (**Figure 29**).
4. Remove the snap ring from the master cylinder (**Figure 30**) as follows:
   a. Press down on the piston to relieve pressure on the snap ring. Then remove the snap ring.
   b. Slowly relieve the pressure on the piston.
5. Remove the piston and spring assembly from the bore (**Figure 31**).
6. Remove the plastic strainer (**Figure 32**) from the reservoir. Work around the strainer, raising it equally and in several passes.

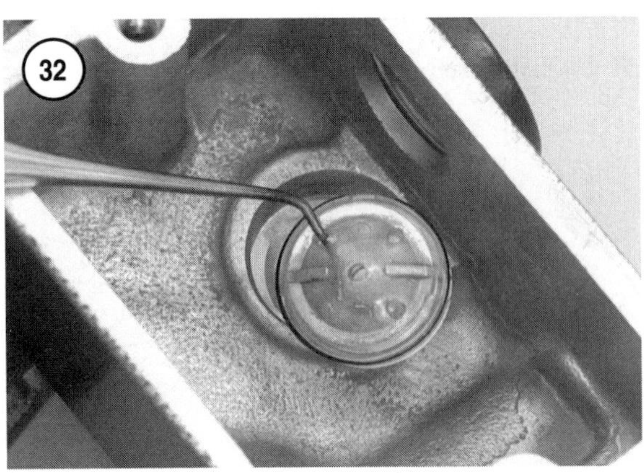

7. Inspect the master cylinder assembly.
   a. Clean all parts that will be reused with fresh DOT 4 brake fluid or isopropyl (rubbing) alcohol.
   b. Inspect the cylinder bore for wear, pitting or corrosion.
   c. Measure the inside diameter of the master cylinder bore (**Figure 33**). Refer to **Table 1** for specifications.
   d. Inspect and clean the threads and orifices in the reservoir (**Figure 34**). Clean with compressed air.
   e. Inspect the brake lever bores and pivot bolt for wear (**Figure 35**).
   f. Inspect the diaphragm and reservoir cap for damage (**Figure 36**).
   g. Inspect the mounting hardware and banjo bolt for corrosion and damage (**Figure 37**). Install new washers onto the banjo bolt.

8. Install and seat the strainer. Apply fresh brake fluid to the O-ring. Then press the strainer into place. Use a nut driver with a socket that fits the outside edge of the strainer to apply equal pressure (**Figure 38**).

9. Assemble the spring, piston and seals (**Figure 39**) as follows:
   a. Soak the seals in fresh DOT 4 brake fluid for 15 minutes. This will soften and lubricate the seals. Apply brake fluid to the piston so the secondary seal can slide over the end.
   b. Mount the primary seal (A, **Figure 40**) onto the small end of the spring.
   c. Mount the secondary seal (B, **Figure 40**) onto the piston. Identify the wide (open) side of the seal. When installed, the wide side of the seal *must* face in the direction of the arrow (**Figure 40**).

10. Install the spring assembly, piston assembly and snap ring into the master cylinder as follows:
    a. Lock the master cylinder in a vise with soft jaws. Do not overtighten the vise or damage could occur.
    b. Lubricate the master cylinder bore and piston assembly with fresh brake fluid.

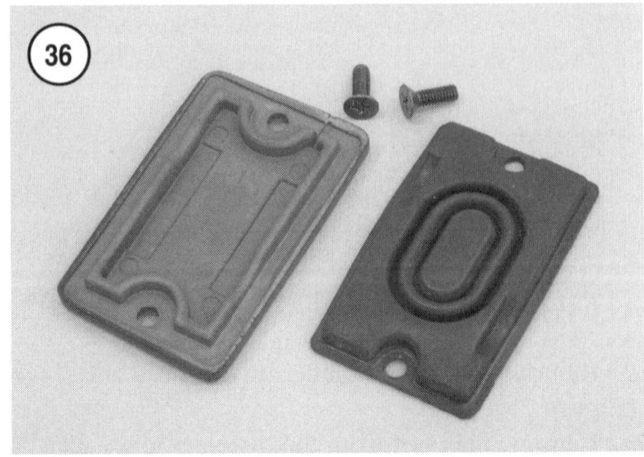

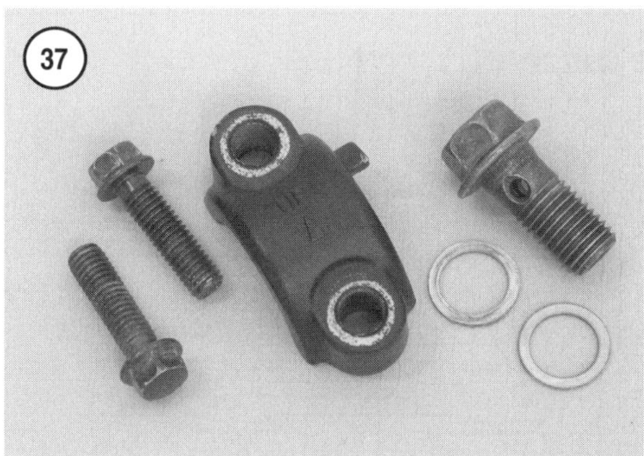

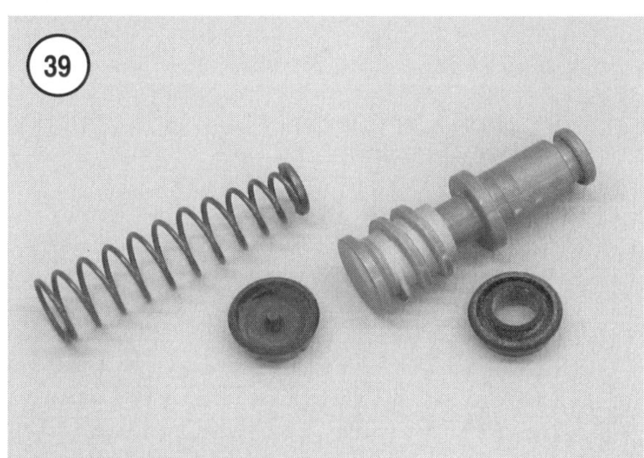

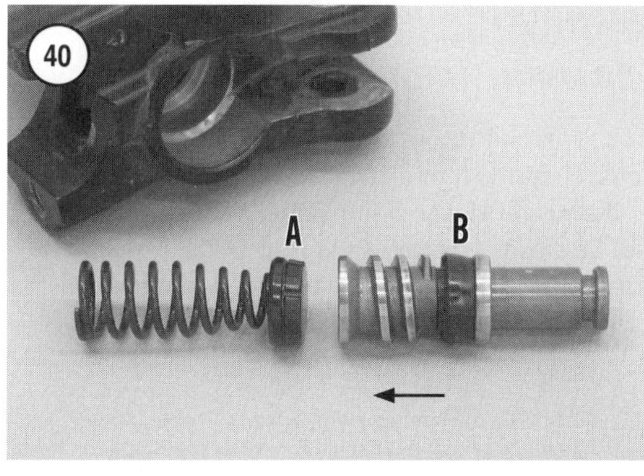

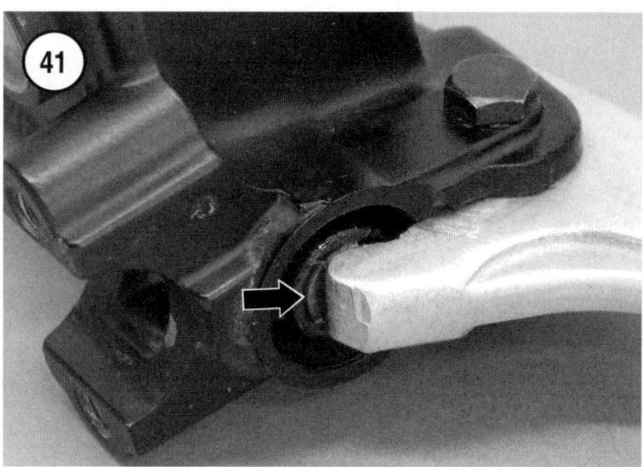

c. Insert the spring and piston assemblies into the master cylinder bore.
d. Place the snap ring over the end of the piston, resting it on the edge of the bore. The sharp edge of the snap ring must face out.
e. Place a screwdriver over the end of the piston. Then compress the snap ring with snap ring pliers.

CAUTION
In the following step, do not allow the piston to pop out of the bore and possibly damage the seals.

f. Press the piston into the master cylinder with the screwdriver while guiding the snap ring into place. Keep the screwdriver in position until the snap ring seats.

11. Apply silicone brake grease to the inside of the boot. Seat the boot in the cylinder bore and around the piston.
12. Install the lever and pivot bolt. Apply waterproof grease to the pivot bolt and lever contact point (**Figure 41**) at the piston.
13. Loosely screw the diaphragm and cap onto the reservoir. Note that the cap is not rectangular. Install the cap so the printing on the cap is readable from the rider's position.
14. Install the master cylinder as described in this section.

REAR BRAKE PADS

Brake pad wear depends on riding habits, conditions and the pad material. Replace the pads when they are worn to within 1 mm (0.040 in.) of the backing plate, or have been contaminated with oil or other chemicals.

Replacement

Refer to **Figure 42**.

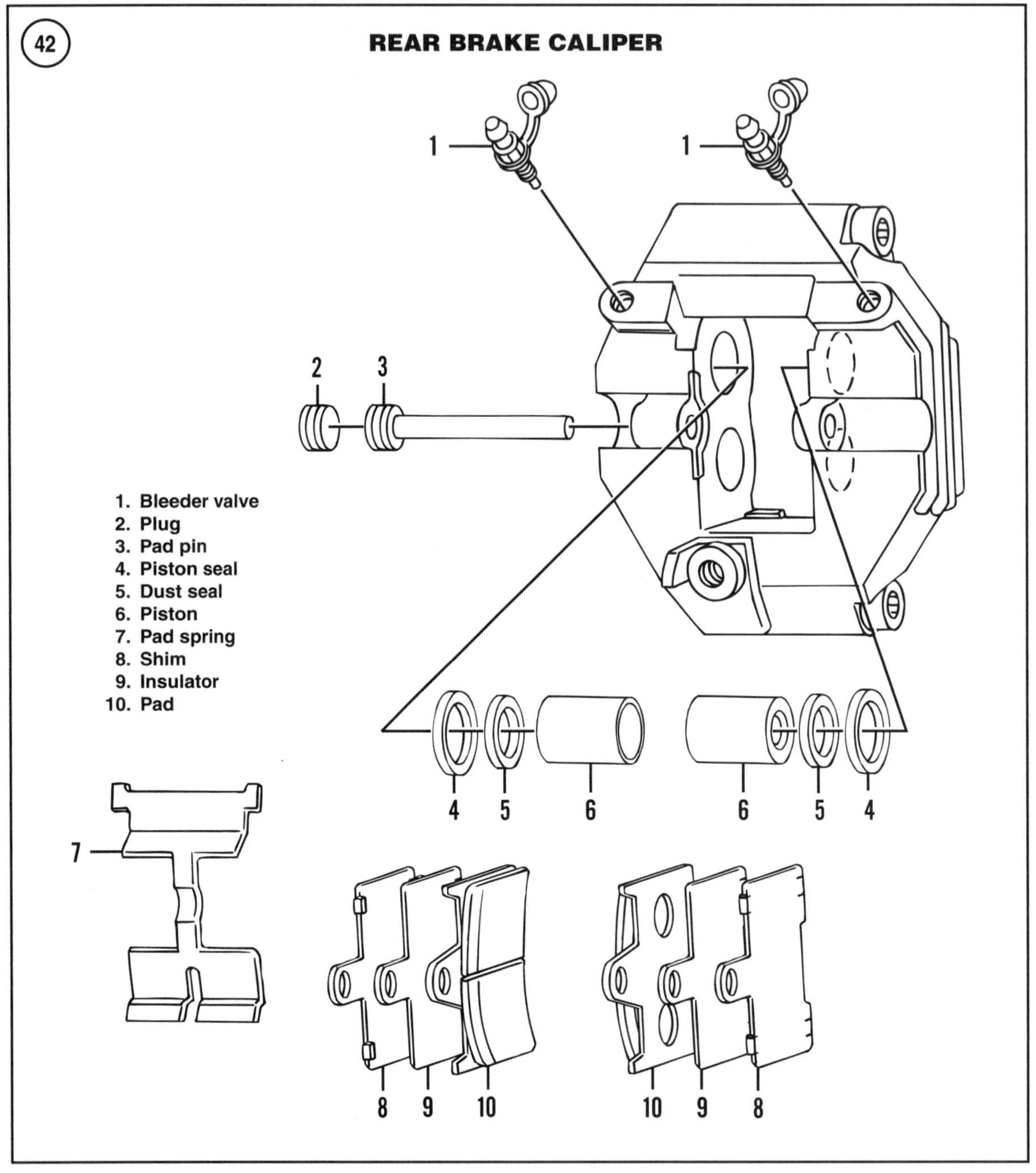

1. Place the machine in two-wheel drive and set the select lever to neutral. Secure the machine so it cannot roll.
2. Remove the left rear wheel (Chapter Thirteen).
3. Remove the plug and loosen the pad pin (**Figure 43**).
4. Press down on the pad spring to relieve the pressure on the pad pin. Then remove the pin and pad spring.
5. Remove the pads (**Figure 44**).

CAUTION

Do not operate the brake pedal or rear brake lever with the pads removed. The caliper pistons can come out of the bores.

6. Clean and inspect the visible portion of the pistons. Remove light corrosion with fine emery cloth. If the piston surfaces are heavily corroded and cannot be cleaned, remove and inspect the caliper as described in this chapter. A corroded or pitted piston can leak when it is pressed back through the seals.

CAUTION

In the following step, monitor the level of fluid in the master cylinder reser-

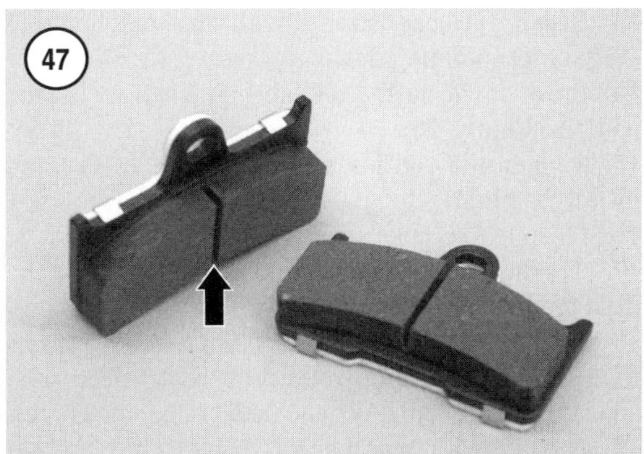

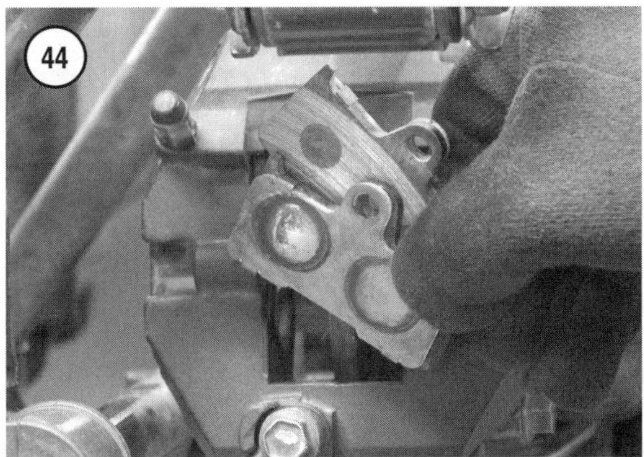

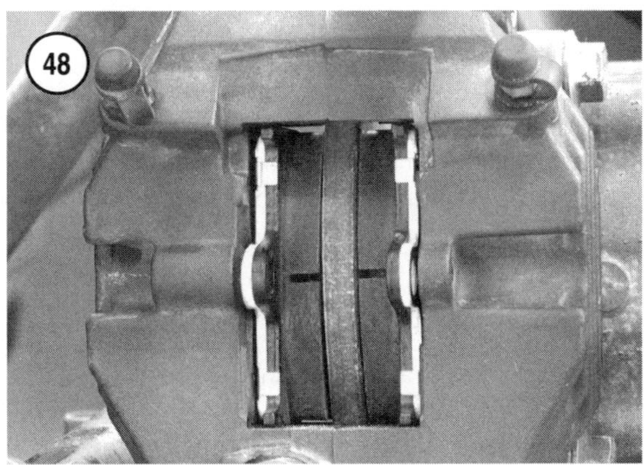

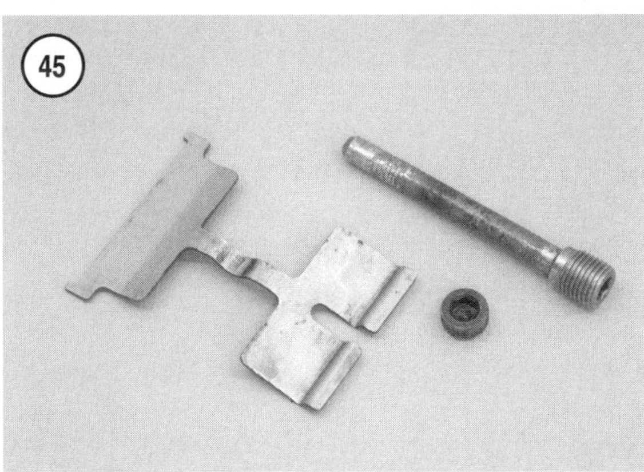

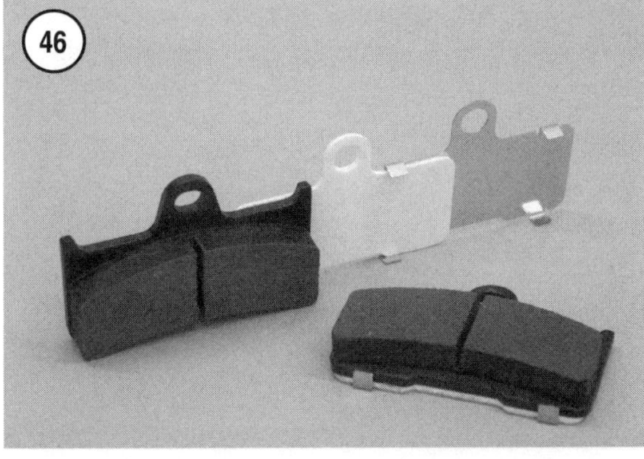

voir. Brake fluid will flow back into the reservoir when the caliper pistons are pressed into the bore, possibly causing the reservoir to overflow.

7. Grasp the caliper and press the caliper pistons back into the bores, creating room for the new pads.
8. Clean the interior of the caliper and inspect for any leaks or damage around the pistons, bleeder valves and hose connection.
9. Inspect the plug, pad pin and pad spring (**Figure 45**). The pin and spring must be in good condition to allow the pads to slightly move when installed. Make sure all tabs on the spring are not corroded or missing.
10. Inspect the pads, insulators and shims (**Figure 46**) for wear and damage. Replace the pads when they are worn to within 1.0 mm (0.040 in.) of the backing plate, as shown by the wear indicator groove (**Figure 47**) in the face of each pad. Always replace pads that have been contaminated with oil or other chemicals. Replace the insulators and shims if corroded or damaged. Always replace the insulators and shims when installing new brake pads.
11. Assemble the pad, insulator and shim sets as shown in **Figure 46**.
12. Seat the pad sets into the caliper and against the pistons (**Figure 48**).

13. Install the pad spring with the notched tab (**Figure 49**) pointing down.
14. Press down on the pad spring. Then insert the pad pin (**Figure 50**).
15. Tighten the pad pin to 18 N•m (13 ft.-lb.) and install the plug.
16. Operate the brake several times to seat the pads.
17. Check the brake fluid reservoir and adjust the fluid level as necessary.
18. With the wheels raised, check that the disc spins freely and the brake operates properly. If necessary, adjust the rear brake lever and pedal (Chapter Three).
19. Install the left rear wheel (Chapter Thirteen).

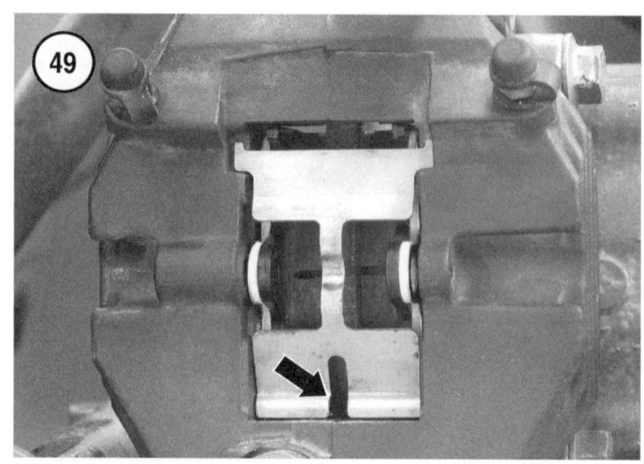

REAR BRAKE CALIPER

Removal and Installation

1. Place the machine in two-wheel drive and set the select lever to neutral. Secure the machine so it cannot roll.
2. Remove the left rear wheel (Chapter Thirteen).
3. If disassembling the caliper, perform the following:
   a. Drain the brake system as described in this chapter.
   b. Remove the plug and loosen the pad pin (A, **Figure 51**), while the caliper is secured.
   c. Loosen the brake hose banjo bolt (A, **Figure 52**). Leave the bolt finger-tight. It will be removed in a later step. If the brake hose must be removed from the machine, also remove the hose clamp (B, **Figure 52**) from the stabilizer holder bolt.
4. Remove the caliper mounting bolts (B, **Figure 51**). Remove the caliper from the disc. Avoid kinking the brake hose.

5A. If the caliper will be left attached to the brake hose, but not disassembled and serviced:
   a. Suspend the caliper with a length of wire. Do not let the caliper hang by the brake hose.
   b. Insert a small wooden block between the brake pads. This will prevent the caliper pistons from being pushed out of the caliper if the rear brake lever or pedal is operated.

5B. If disassembling the caliper, perform the following:
   a. Remove the banjo bolt and washers from the brake hose. Have a shop cloth ready to absorb excess brake fluid that leaks from the hose.
   b. Wrap the hose end to prevent brake fluid from damaging other surfaces.
   c. Drain excess brake fluid from the caliper.
   d. Inspect the caliper as described in this section.

6. Reverse this procedure to install the caliper. Note the following:

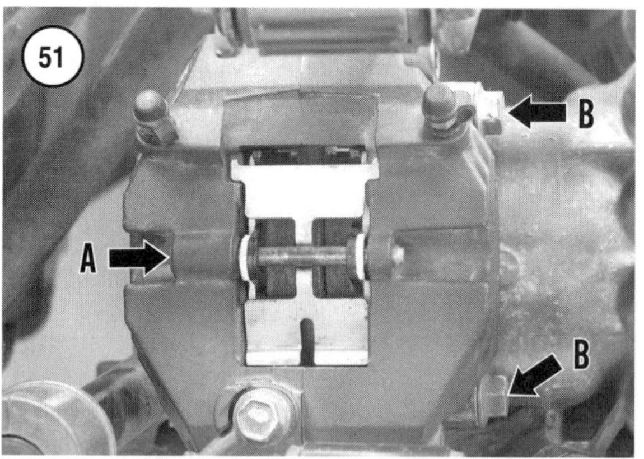

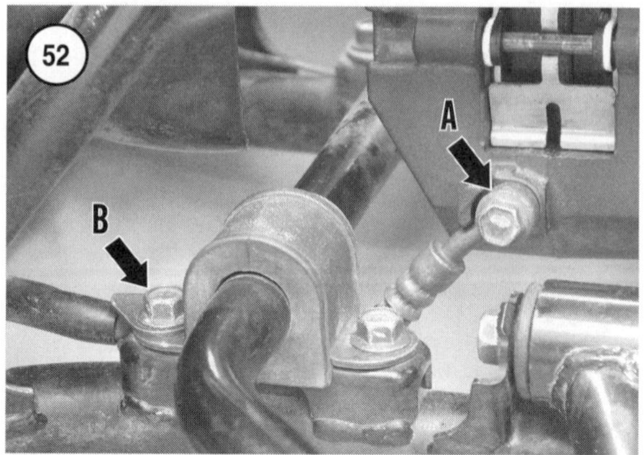

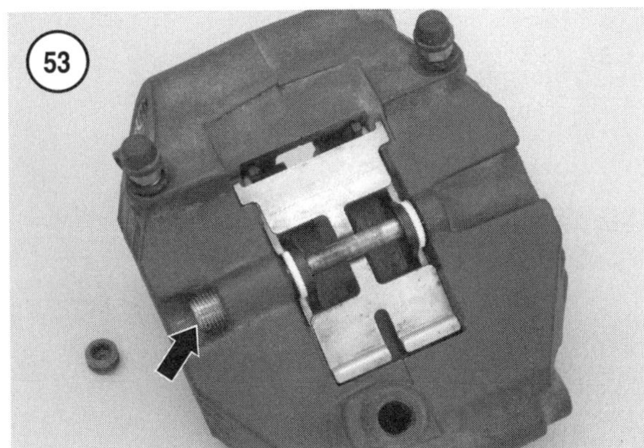

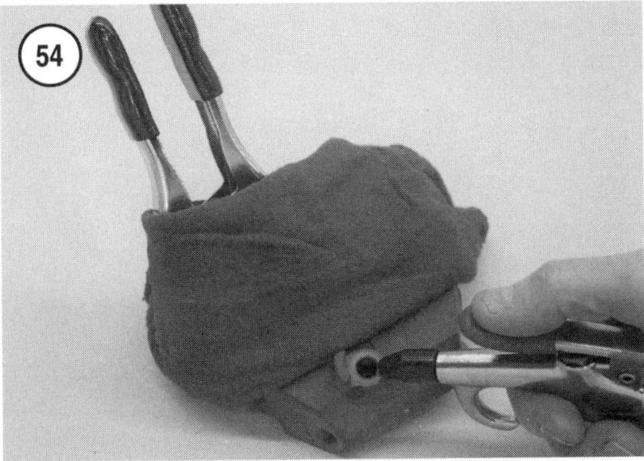

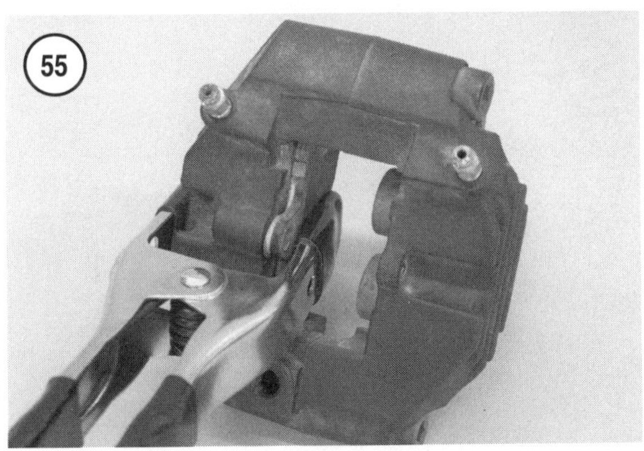

a. Install and tighten the caliper mounting bolts to 40 N•m (30 ft.-lb.).
b. If removed, install new washers onto the brake hose banjo bolt. Seat the brake hose against the guide on the caliper (A, **Figure 52**). Then tighten the banjo bolt to 30 N•m (22 ft.-lb.). If removed, tighten the bolt (B, **Figure 52**) securing the hose clamp to 30 N•m (22 ft.-lb.).
c. If the caliper was rebuilt, or the brake hose disconnected from the caliper, fill and bleed the brake system as described in this chapter.

7. Operate the brake several times to seat the pads.
8. Check the brake fluid reservoir and adjust the fluid level as necessary.
9. Check the adjustment of the rear brake lever, pedal and select lever (Chapter Three).
10. With the wheels raised, make sure the disc spins freely and the brake operates properly.
11. Install the left rear wheel (Chapter Thirteen).

Inspection

Refer to **Figure 42**.

1. Remove the caliper as described in this section.
2. Remove the plug. Then loosen the pad pin (**Figure 53**).
3. Press down on the pad spring to relieve the pressure on the pad pin. Then remove the pin and pad spring.
4. Remove the pads.
5. Clean the interior of the caliper.
6. Remove the piston pairs from the caliper bores using compressed air (**Figure 54**) as follows:
   a. Place the caliper onto a padded work surface.
   b. Close the bleeder valves on the caliper so air cannot escape.
   c. On one side of the caliper, press the pistons back into their bores. Clamp a block of wood, or a brake pad assembly over the pistons (**Figure 55**). The pistons must be held securely.

WARNING

Wear eye protection when using compressed air to remove the pistons. Keep fingers away from the piston discharge area.

   d. Wrap a shop cloth through the discharge area and over the caliper to catch any spray that may occur.
   e. Insert an air nozzle into the brake hose fitting (**Figure 54**). If the nozzle does not have a rubber tip, wrap the nozzle with tape. This will allow the nozzle to seal tightly and prevent thread damage.
   f. Progressively apply pressure and ease the pistons out of the bores until they can be removed by hand (**Figure 56**). If a piston ejects from the caliper before the other piston is loose, partially insert and block the free piston until the remaining piston ejects.
7. Remove the bleeder valves and caps.
8. Remove the dust seals and piston seals from the bores.

CAUTION

Do not separate the caliper halves.

9. Inspect the caliper assembly as follows:
   a. Use compressed air to clean all passages.

56

57

b. Clean the pistons and bores with fresh brake fluid or isopropyl (rubbing) alcohol. Use a wood or plastic-tipped tool to clean the seal grooves.
c. Inspect the caliper bores for wear, pitting or corrosion.
d. Measure the inside diameter of the rear caliper bores. Refer to **Table 1** for specifications.
e. Inspect the pistons. Remove light corrosion with fine emery cloth. If the piston surfaces (**Figure 57**) are heavily corroded and cannot be adequately cleaned, replace the pistons. A corroded or pitted piston can leak when it is pressed back through the seals.
f. Clean and inspect the pad pin, spring, bleeder valves and mounting hardware (**Figure 58**). The pin and spring must be in good condition to allow the pads to slightly move when installed. Make sure all tabs on the spring are not corroded or missing.
g. Inspect the pads, insulators and shims (**Figure 46**) for wear and damage. Replace the pads when they are worn to within 1.0 mm (0.040 in.) of the backing plate, as shown by the wear indicator groove (**Figure 47**) in the face of each pad. Always replace pads that have been contaminated with oil or other chemicals. Replace the insulators and shims if corroded or damaged. Always replace the insulators and shims when installing new brake pads.

10. Install new piston seals (A, **Figure 59**) and dust seals (B) as follows:
a. Soak the new seals in fresh brake fluid for 15 minutes.
b. Coat the caliper bores and pistons with brake fluid.
c. Seat a piston seal and then a dust seal into each caliper bore. The piston seal goes into the back groove.
d. Install the pistons with the open side facing out. Gently twist each piston past the seals. Then press the piston to the bottom of the bore.

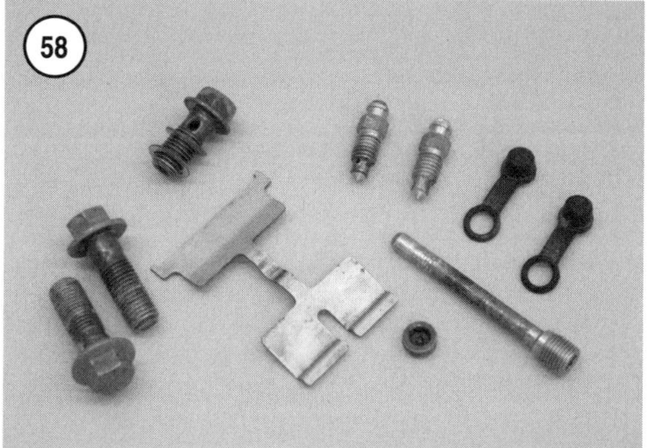
58

59

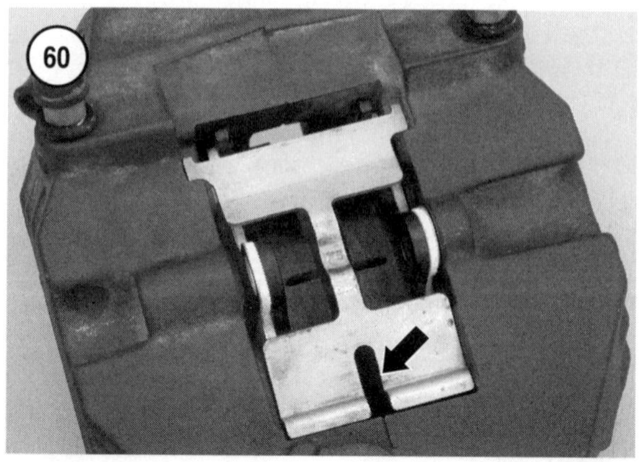
60

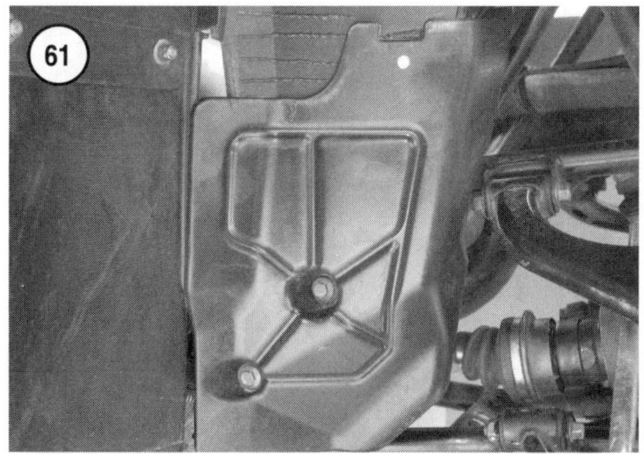

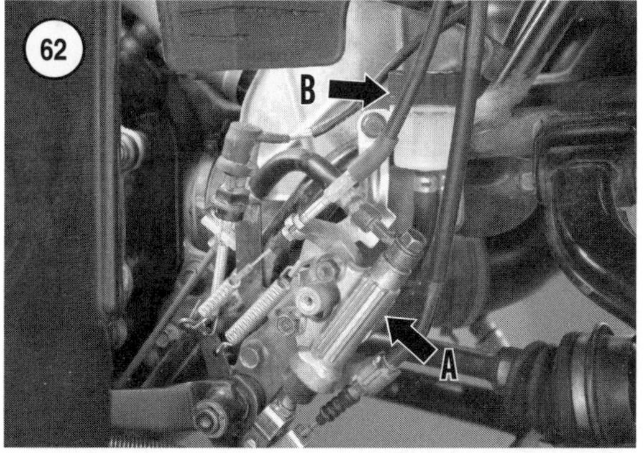

11. Install the bleeder valves and caps.
12. Assemble the pad, insulator and shim sets as shown in **Figure 46**.
13. Seat the pad sets into the caliper and against the pistons.
14. Install the pad spring with the notched tab (**Figure 60**) pointing down.
15. Press down on the pad spring. Then insert the pad pin (**Figure 53**).
16. Tighten the pad pin to 18 N•m (13 ft.-lb.) and install the plug.
17. Spread the pads so there is clearance to fit the caliper over the brake disc.
18. Install the caliper as described in this section.

REAR MASTER CYLINDER

Removal and Installation

1. Remove the right front wheel (Chapter Eleven).
2. Remove the master cylinder cover (**Figure 61**) to access the master cylinder assembly (A, **Figure 62**) and reservoir (B). If additional access is desired, also remove the right footrest panel (Chapter Sixteen).
3. Drain the brake system as described in this chapter.
4. Disconnect the master cylinder reservoir as follows:
   a. Remove the reservoir cap, diaphragm holder and diaphragm and verify that the reservoir is empty. Wipe the interior of the reservoir dry. Then install the cap assembly to prevent any leaks during removal.
   b. Remove the bolt (**Figure 63**) securing the reservoir.
5. Remove the banjo bolt (**Figure 64**) and washers from the brake hose. Have a shop cloth ready to absorb excess brake fluid that leaks from the hose. Wrap the hose end to prevent brake fluid from damaging other surfaces.
6. Remove the master cylinder mounting bolts (**Figure 65**).

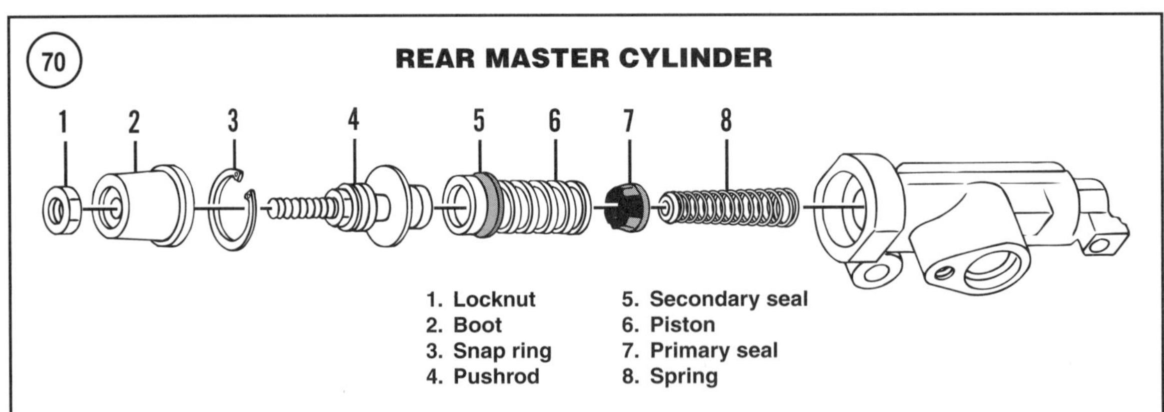

7. Remove the master cylinder using one of the following methods:
   a. Position the master cylinder so access to the pushrod adjuster (A, **Figure 66**) and locknut (B) is available. Loosen the locknut and turn the adjuster until it separates from the clevis.
   b. Remove the E-clip and washers (**Figure 67**) from the brake pedal pivot. Slide the pedal outward to create the necessary clearance to remove the clevis pin. If desired, remove the right footrest panel to improve access.
8. Inspect the master cylinder as described in this section.
9. Reverse this procedure to install the master cylinder and reservoir. Note the following:
   a. If the clevis assembly was separated from the pushrod during master cylinder removal, start the threads of the pushrod into the clevis nut before installing the master cylinder mounting bolts.
   b. Tighten the master cylinder mounting bolts to 23 N•m (17 ft.-lb.).
   c. Install new washers onto the brake hose banjo bolt. Position the upper washer so the stop is against the rear master cylinder. Tighten the banjo bolt to 30 N•m (22 ft.-lb.).

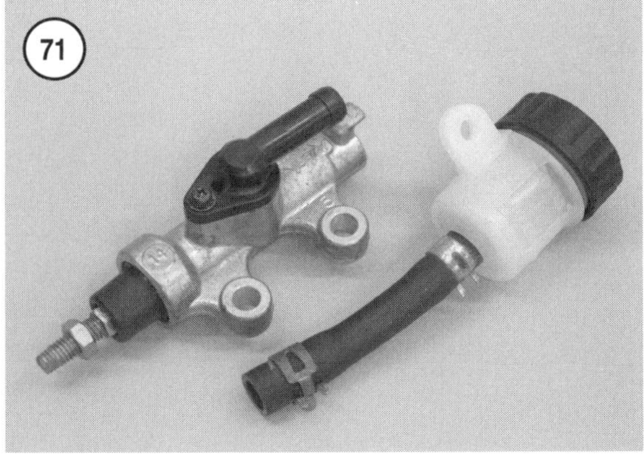
71

72

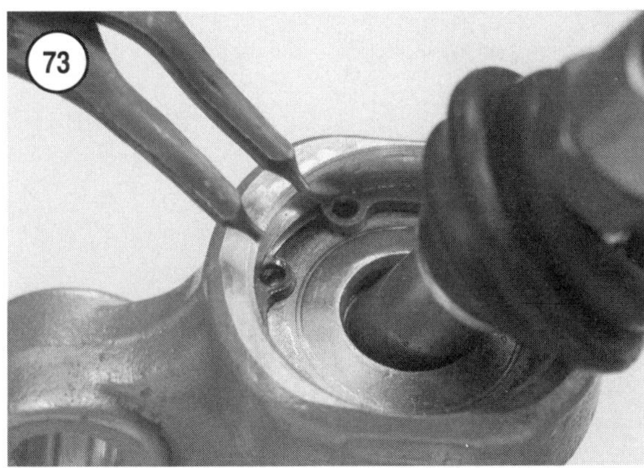
73

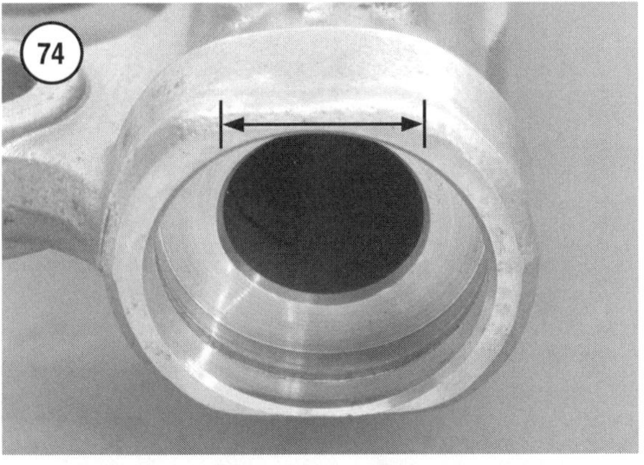
74

d. If removed, install a new cotter pin onto the clevis pin.

10. Set the initial clearance (**Figure 68**) between the adjuster and locknut to 5-6 mm (0.20-0.24 in.). If necessary, loosen the locknut and turn the adjuster until the clearance is achieved. Tighten the locknut.

11. Fill the brake fluid reservoir and bleed the brake system as described in this chapter. Check the adjustment of the rear brake lever, pedal and select lever (Chapter Three).

12. Install the right front wheel (Chapter Eleven) and right footrest panel (Chapter Sixteen), if removed.

Inspection

The piston and pushrod assemblies (**Figure 69**) are available as a replacement kit. The pushrod clevis and locknut are not part of the kit. Refer to **Figure 70**.

1. Remove the master cylinder and reservoir as described in this section.
2. Remove the reservoir and hose from the fitting (**Figure 71**).
3. Remove the screw that secures the hose fitting to the master cylinder. Then remove the fitting and internal O-ring (**Figure 72**).
4. Remove the snap ring (**Figure 73**) from the master cylinder as follows:
   a. Unseat the boot from the cylinder bore and fold it away from the snap ring.
   b. If desired, lock the cylinder into a vise with soft jaws.
   c. Press and tilt the pushrod to relieve pressure on the snap ring. Then remove the snap ring with snap ring pliers.
   d. Slowly relieve the pressure on the piston.
5. Remove the pushrod, piston and spring assemblies from the bore.
6. Inspect the master cylinder assembly.
   a. Clean all parts with fresh DOT 4 brake fluid or isopropyl (rubbing) alcohol.
   b. Inspect the cylinder bore for wear, pitting or corrosion.
   c. Measure the inside diameter of the rear master cylinder bore (**Figure 74**). Refer to **Table 1** for specifications.
   d. Inspect and clean the threads and orifices in the master cylinder (**Figure 75**). Clean with compressed air.
   e. Inspect the mounting hardware and banjo bolt (**Figure 76**) for wear or damage. Replace the washers.
   f. Inspect the reservoir assembly (**Figure 77**) for damage.

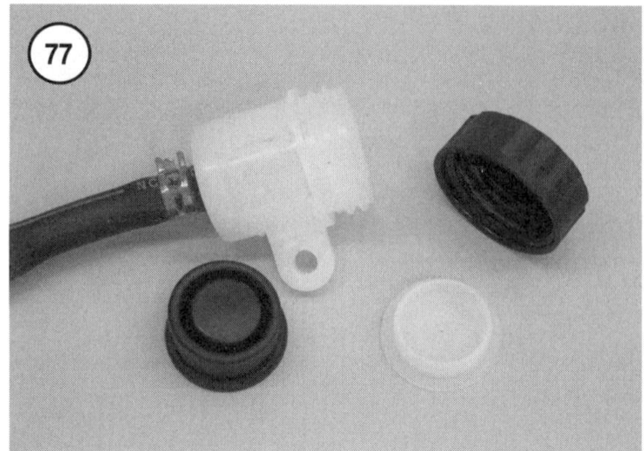

7. Install the boot, snap ring and locknut (**Figure 78**) on the pushrod. The sharp edge of the snap ring must face out.
8. Assemble the piston, seals and spring (**Figure 79**) as follows:
   a. Soak the seals in fresh DOT 4 brake fluid for 15 minutes. This will soften and lubricate the seals.
   b. Apply brake fluid to the piston so the secondary seal can slide over the end.
   c. Mount the primary seal onto the spring and the secondary seal onto the piston. Identify the wide (open) side of the secondary seal. When installed, the wide side of the seal *must* face in the direction of the arrow (**Figure 79**).
9. Install the spring, piston and pushrod assemblies into the master cylinder as follows:
   a. If desired, lock the cylinder in a vise with soft jaws. Do not overtighten the vise or damage could occur.
   b. Lubricate the master cylinder bore, seals and piston with fresh brake fluid.
   c. Apply a small amount of silicone brake grease to the contact area of the pushrod.
   d. Insert the spring and piston assemblies into the cylinder bore.
   e. Compress the snap ring with snap ring pliers.

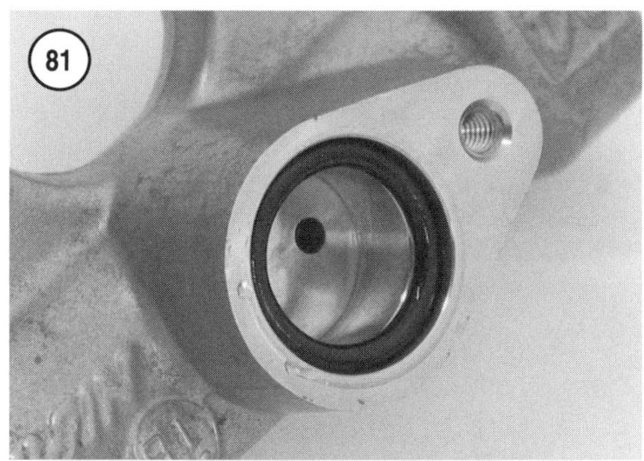

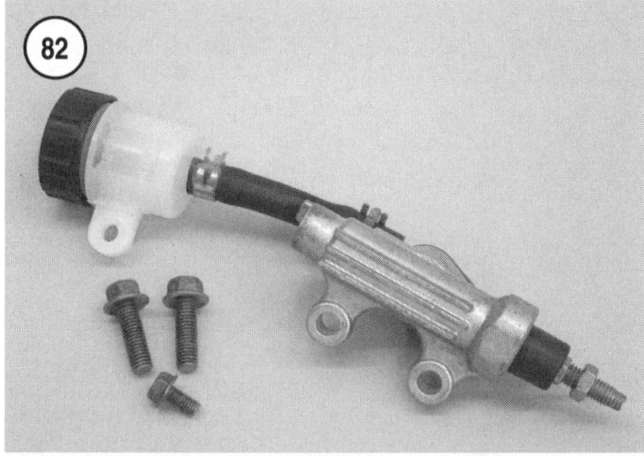

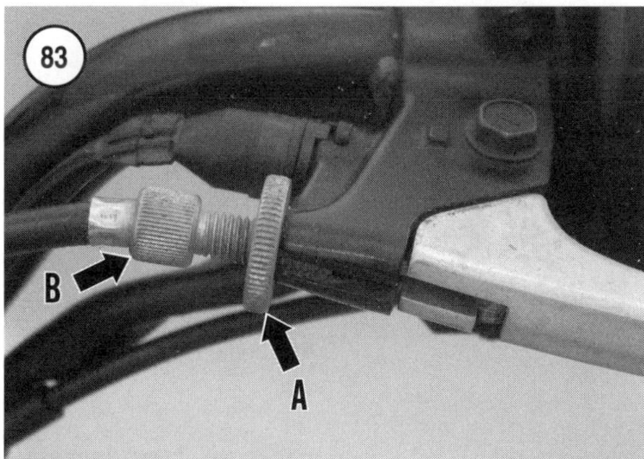

CAUTION

In the following step, do not allow the piston to pop out of the bore and possibly damage the seals.

f. Press and tilt the pushrod in the master cylinder while guiding the snap ring into place. If the snap ring does not easily seat, release the snap ring and use the tip of the pliers to press it into the groove. Keep the pushrod compressed until the snap ring seats.

10. Apply silicone brake grease to the inside of the boot. Seat the boot into the cylinder bore and around the pushrod (**Figure 80**).

11. Install a new, lubricated O-ring into the master cylinder (**Figure 81**). Then lock the hose fitting into the O-ring. Install the retaining screw.

12. Install the diaphragm, diaphragm holder and cap onto the reservoir.

13. Install and clamp the reservoir assembly to the master cylinder (**Figure 82**).

14. Install the master cylinder as described in this section.

LEFT HAND BRAKE CABLE REPLACEMENT

1. At the handlebar, loosen the brake cable locknut (A, **Figure 83**). Then turn the adjuster (B, **Figure 83**) in until the cable can be removed from the lever and adjuster assembly.
2. At the rear brake master cylinder, remove the cotter pin, washer and clevis pin (A, **Figure 84**).
3. Remove the adjuster nut (B, **Figure 84**) and remove the cable from the holder.
4. Note the routing of the cable while removing it from the machine.
5. Clean the lever and clevis pin. Then lubricate them with lithium grease.
6. Lubricate the new cable with an aerosol cable lubricant. Lubricate the cable ends and clevis with lithium grease.
7. Route the cable from the master cylinder to the handlebar lever.
8. Attach the clevis to the master cylinder and install a new cotter pin.
9. Fit the cable adjuster and nuts into the cable holder. Finger-tighten the nuts.
10. At the handlebar, attach the cable to the lever and thread the adjuster to the center of its travel.
11. Adjust the left hand brake cable (Chapter Three).

BRAKE SYSTEM DRAINING

To drain the brake fluid from the system, use an 8-mm wrench, a tip-resistant container and a length of clear tubing that fits firmly onto the bleeder valve. Use the following procedure to drain either the front or rear brakes.

CAUTION
Brake fluid can damage painted and finished surfaces. Use water to immediately wash any surface contaminated with brake fluid.

1. Attach one end of the tubing to the bleeder valve and place the other end into the container (**Figure 85**). For the rear brake, attach a tube to each bleeder valve (**Figure 86**).
2. Loosen the master cylinder cap. Then open the bleeder valve(s) so fluid can pass into the tubing.
3. Pump the brake lever/pedal to force the fluid from the system.
4. When the system no longer drips fluid, close the bleeder valve(s).
5. Make sure the master cylinder is empty. Wipe the interior of the reservoir to absorb all remaining fluid.
6. Dispose of the brake fluid in an environmentally safe manner.

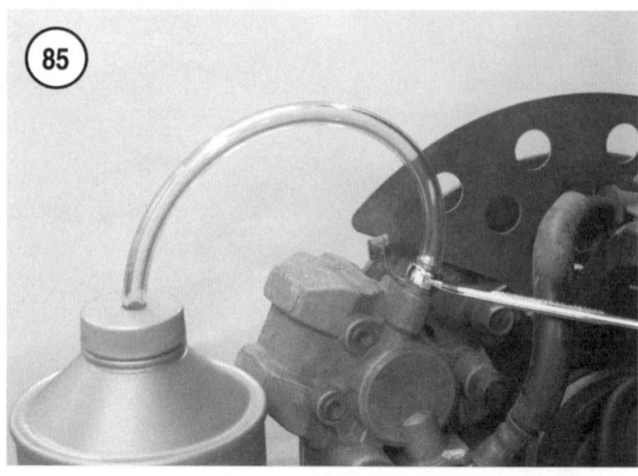
85

86

87

BRAKE SYSTEM BLEEDING

Whenever the brake fluid is replaced, or if the brake lever or pedal feels spongy, bleed the brakes to purge all air from the system. Before bleeding the brakes, check all brake components for leaks and fittings and hoses for deterioration, damage or looseness. The brake system can be bled manually or by using a vacuum pump. Both methods are described in this section.

Brake Fluid Reservoirs

The reservoirs must not be over or under filled. Note the following when working with each reservoir.

1. Front brake reservoir:
   a. Remove the reservoir cap and diaphragm.
   b. Keep the reservoir filled between the top of the sight glass and the lower mark on the reservoir (**Figure 87**) during the bleeding procedure.
   c. After bleeding, replenish the reservoir to the upper mark. Then install the diaphragm and cap.
2. Rear brake reservoir:
   a. Remove the master cylinder cover (**Figure 88**), located behind the right front wheel.
   b. Remove the cap, diaphragm holder and diaphragm.
   c. During the bleeding procedure, keep the reservoir filled between the lower and upper marks as indicated on the reservoir (**Figure 89**).
   d. After bleeding, replenish the reservoir to the upper mark. Then install the diaphragm, diaphragm holder and cap.

Manual Bleeding

To manually bleed the brake system, use an 8-mm wrench, a tip-resistant container and a length of clear tubing that fits firmly onto the brake bleeder.

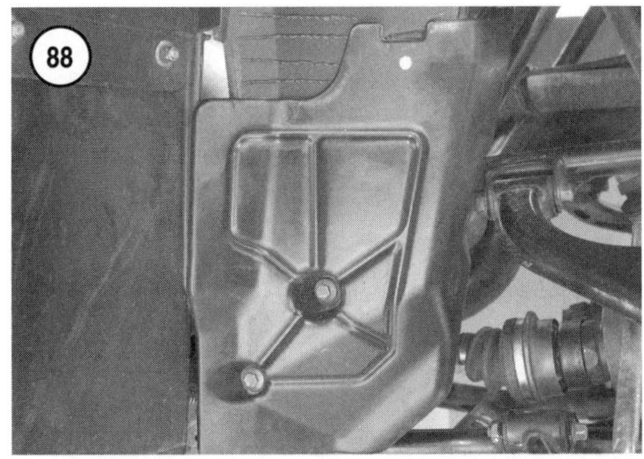
88

89

Bleeding the system is much easier if two people perform the procedure. One person can open and close the bleeder valve while the other person operates the brake lever or pedal. Use the following procedure to bleed either the front or rear brake.

CAUTION
Brake fluid can damage painted and finished surfaces. Use water and immediately wash any surface that becomes contaminated with brake fluid.

1. Attach one end of the tubing to the bleeder valve and place the other end into the container (**Figure 85**). If bleeding the rear brake, bleed the two valves individually.
2. Fill the reservoir to the upper level with fresh DOT 4 brake fluid.
3. Apply pressure (do not pump) to the brake lever or pedal. Then open the bleeder valve. As the fluid is forced from the system, the lever/pedal will travel its full length of operation. When the lever/pedal can move no farther, hold the lever/pedal in the *down* position and close the bleeder valve. Do not allow the lever or pedal to return to its *up* position before the bleeder valve is closed. Air will be drawn back into the system.

CAUTION
In the following step, release the lever/pedal slowly. This minimizes the chance of fluid splashing out of the reservoir as excess fluid in the brake line is returning to the reservoir.

4. When the bleeder valve is closed, release the lever/pedal so it returns to its resting position. Check the fluid level in the reservoir and replenish, if necessary.

NOTE
During the bleeding process, the reservoir must contain fluid during the entire procedure. If the reservoir becomes empty, air will enter the system and the bleeding process will have to be repeated.

5. Repeat Step 3 and Step 4 until clear fluid (minimal air bubbles) is seen passing from the bleeder valve. When bleeding the rear caliper, recheck the first valve for air pockets after bleeding the second valve.

NOTE
If small bubbles (foam) remain in the system after several bleeding attempts, close the reservoir and allow the system to stand undisturbed for a few hours. The system will stabilize and the air can be purged as large bubbles.

6. The bleeding procedure is completed when the feel of the lever/pedal is firm.
7. Check the brake fluid reservoir and fill the reservoir to the upper level, if necessary.
8. Tighten the bleeder valve to 6 N•m (53 in.-lb.).
9. Dispose of used brake fluid in an environmentally safe manner.

Vacuum Bleeding

To vacuum-bleed the brake system, use an 8-mm wrench and a vacuum pump with a bleeder attachment (**Figure 90**). Use the following procedure to bleed either the front or rear brake.

CAUTION
Brake fluid can damage painted and finished surfaces. Use water and immediately wash any surface that becomes contaminated with brake fluid.

1. Check that the banjo bolts are tight at the master cylinder and caliper.
2. Attach the vacuum pump to the bleeder valve. Suspend the tool with wire. This allows the tool to be released when the fluid reservoir needs to be refilled.

3. Fill the reservoir to the upper level with fresh DOT 4 brake fluid.

NOTE
During the bleeding process, the reservoir must contain fluid during the entire procedure. If the reservoir becomes empty, air will enter the system and the bleeding process will have to be repeated.

4. Pump the handle on the brake bleeder to create a vacuum.
5. Open the bleeder valve and draw the air and fluid from the system. Close the valve *before* the fluid stops moving or the vacuum pump gauge reads zero. Replenish the fluid level in the reservoir.
6. Repeat Step 4 and Step 5 until clear fluid (minimal air bubbles) is seen passing from the bleeder. The bleeding procedure is completed when the feel of the lever/pedal is firm. When bleeding the rear caliper, recheck the first valve for air pockets after bleeding the second valve.
7. Check the brake fluid reservoir and fill the reservoir to the upper level, if necessary.
8. Tighten the bleeder valve to 6 N•m (53 in.-lb.).
9. Dispose of used brake fluid in an environmentally safe manner.

BRAKE DISC

The condition of the brake discs and pads are often a reflection of one another. If disc scoring is evident, inspect the pads and disc as soon as possible. Disc scoring is often caused by excessively worn brake pads. When the soft pad material is completely worn away, the steel backing plate (**Figure 91**) scores the disc. If damage is evident, perform the inspection described in this section.

Maintain the discs by keeping them clean and corrosion-free. Use solvent that is not oil-based to wipe off grit that accumulates on the discs and at the edge of the pads.

Replace worn or damaged discs. The discs cannot be machined.

Inspection

1. Measure the thickness of each disc at several locations around its perimeter (**Figure 92**). Refer to **Table 1** for specifications. Replace the disc if it is out of specification.
2. Measure disc runout as follows:
   a. Mount a dial indicator (**Figure 93**) on a stable surface and in contact with the disc.
   b. Zero the gauge.

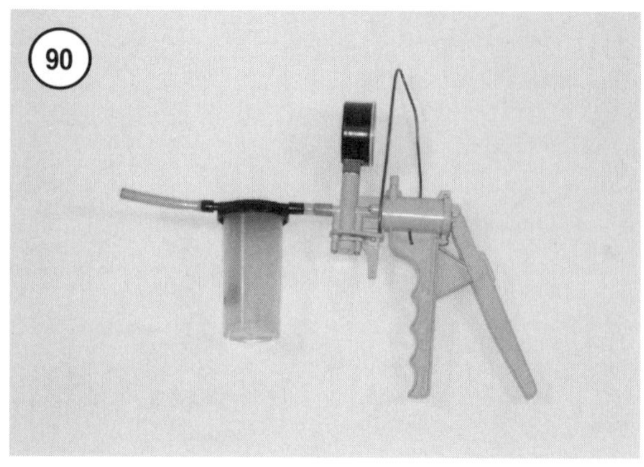
90

91

92

   c. Turn the hub and note the amount of runout measured on the gauge.
   d. Refer to **Table 1** for the runout service limit. Replace the disc if it is out of specification.

NOTE
If disc runout is out of specification, check the condition of the disc mounts and bolts. Also check the condition of the axle bearings (front discs) and final drive unit bearings (rear disc) before replacing the disc. If the mounts or bearings are not in good condition, the

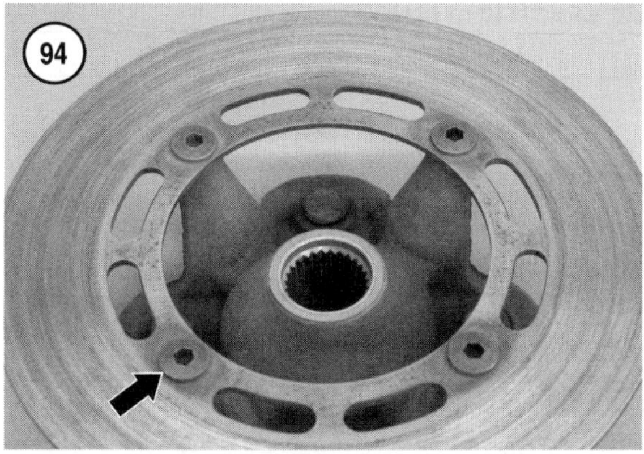

damaged parts should be replaced before disc runout is determined.

Removal and Installation

Front discs

The discs are mounted to the wheel hubs with bolts. Remove and install the discs as follows:

1. Remove the wheel hub and disc from the axle (Chapter Eleven).
2. Remove the bolts (**Figure 94**) that secure the disc to the hub.
3. Clean the bolts and mounting holes.
4. Reverse this procedure to install the disc. Note the following:
   a. Apply nonpermanent threadlocking compound to the bolt threads.
   b. Tighten the bolts in several passes and in a crossing pattern.
   c. Tighten the disc bolts to 30 N•m (22 ft.-lb.).
   d. Check the disc for runout as described in this section.

Rear disc

The disc is bolted to the flange on the final drive unit. Remove and install the disc as follows:

1. Remove the final drive unit (Chapter Fourteen).
2. Remove the bolts (**Figure 95**) that secure the disc to the flange.
3. Clean the bolts and mounting holes.
4. Reverse this procedure to install the disc. Note the following:
   a. Apply nonpermanent threadlocking compound to the bolt threads.
   b. Tighten the bolts in several passes and in a crossing pattern.
   c. Tighten the disc bolts to 10 N•m (89 in.-lb.).
   d. Check the disc for runout as described in this section.

Table 1 BRAKE SPECIFICATIONS

	New mm (in.)	Service limit mm (in.)
Brake disc runout		
Front	–	0.15 (0.006)
Rear	–	0.10 (0.004)
Brake disc thickness		
Front	3.5 (0.14)	3.0 (0.12)
Rear	8.5 (0.34)	8.0 (0.32)

(continued)

Table 1 BRAKE SPECIFICATIONS (continued)

	New mm (in.)	Service limit mm (in.)
Brake pad thickness		
Front	4.2 (0.17)	1.0 (0.04)
Rear	7.0 (0.28)	1.0 (0.04)
Caliper bore inside diameter		
Front	32.0 (1.26)	–
Rear	22.65 (0.89)	–
Master cylinder bore inside diameter		
Front	14.0 (0.55)	–
Rear	14.0 (0.55)	–

Table 2 BRAKE TORQUE SPECIFICATIONS

	N•m	in.-lb.	ft.-lb.
Bleeder valve	6	53	–
Brake hose banjo bolts			
Front	27	–	20
Rear	30	–	22
Caliper mounting bolts			
Front	30	–	22
Rear	40	–	30
Disc bolts			
Front	30	–	22
Rear	10	89	–
Front caliper bracket bolts	23	–	17
Master cylinder mounting bolts			
Front	7	62	–
Rear	23	–	17
Pad pins	18	–	13
Stabilizer holder bolt	30	–	22

CHAPTER SIXTEEN

BODY

This chapter covers the body panels.

BODY PANEL FASTENERS

The body panels are secured with a variety of fasteners. Refer to the following:

1. Plastic rivets (**Figure 1**). When aligning holes in adjoining panels, insert the rivet through both parts. Twist the center lock one-quarter turn *clockwise* to expand the rivet and lock the parts together. To remove the rivet, twist the center lock one-quarter turn *counterclockwise*, which allows the rivet to contract. The center lock is not threaded and should not be turned more than one-quarter turn to install or remove the rivet. The center lock is part of the rivet and should not removed.
2. Prong and grommet (**Figure 2**). This type of fastener uses a flared prong that fits into a rubber grommet. This friction-fit fastener is often used on small access panels, or on panels that are not stressed. To ensure the grommet remains pliable, apply a rubber protectant. The parts will also engage and disengage easier.
3. Tabs (**Figure 3**). Tabs are commonly used where panels overlap. The tab is typically on the upper panel and is inserted into a slot in the lower panel. Tabs can also be hooked. After the hooked tab is in the slot, light pressure on the panel will lock and pull the panels togethers, creating a uniform joint.
4. Bolts, nuts and screws. These fasteners are used where maximum strength is required to hold a panel in place. Whenever these fasteners are removed, clean the threads and apply anti-seize compound before installation. Loosely install all bolts and screws. Make sure the panel is properly aligned and seated. Then tighten the fasteners. Refer to **Table 6** in Chapter One for torque recommendations on fasteners without a specification.

SEAT

Removal and Installation

Refer to **Figure 4**.

1. Pull up on the seat release, located at the rear of the seat (**Figure 5**). Then raise the rear of the seat.
2. Pull back on the seat to disengage the prongs from the front mount.
3. To install the seat, align and lock the prongs around the front mount.
4. Slide the seat forward and lock the rear of the seat into place.
5. Lightly lift the rear of the seat to ensure it is locked.

FUEL TANK SIDE PANELS

Removal and Installation

Refer to **Figure 4**.

1. Remove the seat as described in this chapter.
2. To remove the panel, do the following:
   a. Disengage the tabs and prong at the top of the panel.
   b. Pull the panel back and upward to disengage the tabs.

3. To install the panel do the following:
   a. Install the tabs at the front of the panel.
   b. Install the tabs at the lower rear of the panel.
   c. Install the tabs and prong at the top of the panel.
   d. Press on the prong to seat it into the grommet.
4. Install the seat.

FUEL TANK COVER AND FUEL TANK

Removal and Installation

Refer to **Figure 6**.

1. Turn the fuel valve off (**Figure 7**).
2. Remove the seat and fuel tank side panels as described in this chapter.
3. Remove the handlebar cover.
4. Remove the plastic rivets from the front of the cover and the bolts from the rear of the cover.
5. Remove the fuel cap. Then remove the fuel tank cover. Install the fuel cap after removing the cover.
6. At the fuel tank:
   a. Disconnect the fuel sending unit lead.
   b. Disconnect and plug the fuel line.
   c. Remove the screw from the fuel valve knob. Then remove the knob.
   d. Remove the bolts and collars from the corners of the fuel tank.

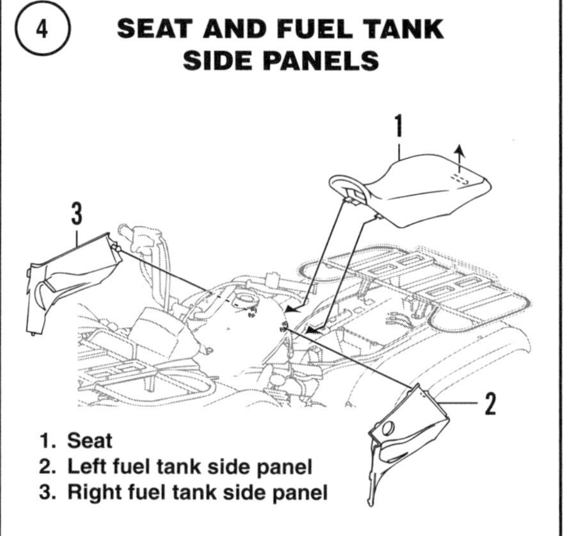

1. Seat
2. Left fuel tank side panel
3. Right fuel tank side panel

   e. Check that the fuel cap is tight. Then lift the fuel tank from the machine.
7. If necessary, remove the fuel tank pan as follows:
   a. Carefully remove and mark the breather hoses and their locations in the pan.
   b. Remove the plastic rivets and bands that secure the pan.

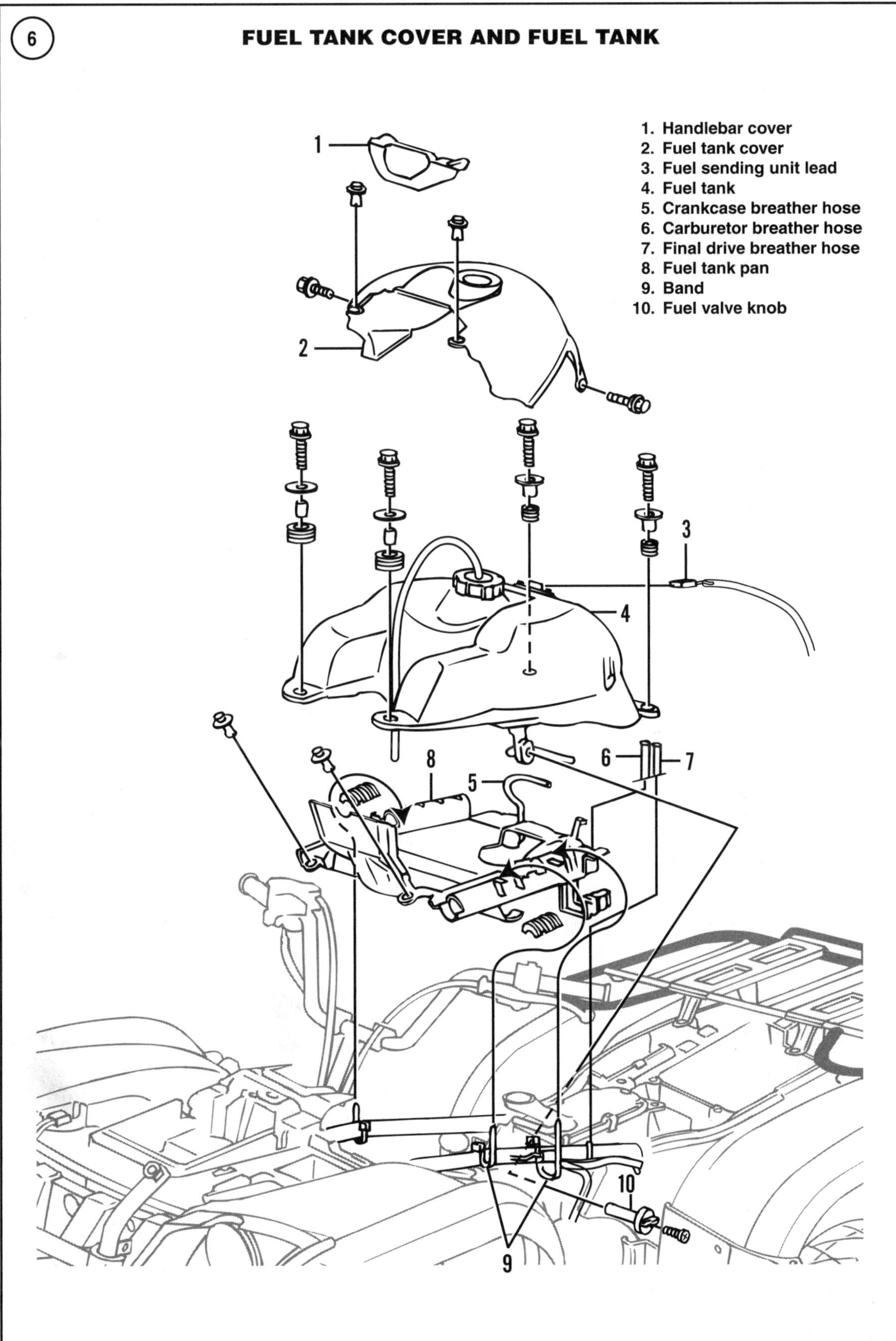
6
FUEL TANK COVER AND FUEL TANK
1. Handlebar cover
2. Fuel tank cover
3. Fuel sending unit lead
4. Fuel tank
5. Crankcase breather hose
6. Carburetor breather hose
7. Final drive breather hose
8. Fuel tank pan
9. Band
10. Fuel valve knob
1
2
3
4
5
6
7
8
9
10

c. Remove the pan from the frame.
8. Reverse this procedure to install the pan, fuel tank and fuel tank cover. Note the following:
  a. Tighten all fasteners securely.
  b. Check that the fuel tank breather hose is routed through the handlebar cover.
  c. Turn on the fuel valve and check for leaks.

ENGINE SIDE COVER AND SIDE PANEL

The engine side cover and side panel are on the left side of the engine. The side panel has three prongs that lock into the engine side cover.

Removal and Installation

1. Remove and install the side panel as follows:
  a. Remove the side panel by pulling out at the front indentions (A, **Figure 8**), then releasing the prong and grommet from the rear indention. It is normal for the rear grommet to remain on the prong.
  b. Install the side panel by sliding the rear grommet into the engine side cover notch. Then pivot and press the front prongs into the engine side cover.
2. Remove and install the engine side cover as follows:
  a. Remove the bolts at the perimeter of the engine side cover (B, **Figure 8**). Then remove the engine side cover from the engine.
  b. Install the engine side cover. Then loosely install all bolts. Make sure the engine side cover is seated. Then tighten the bolts securely.

FRONT CARRIER

Removal and Installation

Refer to **Figure 9**.
1. Remove the covers from the front fender hood.
2. Remove the bolts below the covers.
3. Remove the bolts securing the carrier to the front bumper.
4. Remove the bolts in the wheel wells that secure the fenders to the carrier.
5. Remove the carrier.
6. Reverse this procedure to install the carrier. Tighten all carrier bolts (except those in the wheel wells) to 33 N•m (24 ft.-lb.). Tighten the wheel well bolts securely.

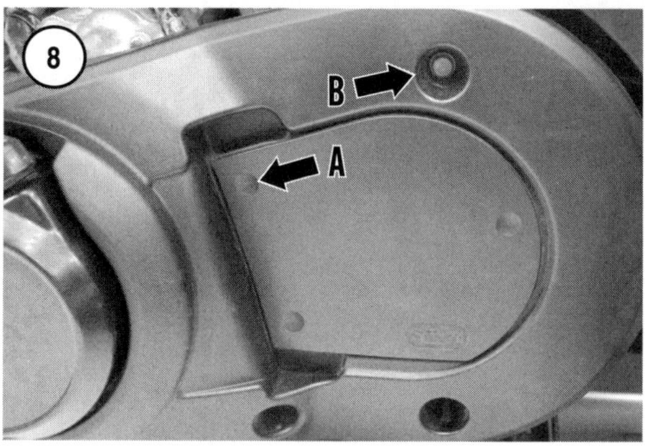

FRONT FENDER HOOD

Removal and Installation

Refer to **Figure 9**.
1. Remove the front carrier assembly as described in this chapter.
2. Remove the plastic rivets from the rear corners of the hood.
3. Remove the hood.
4. Reverse this procedure to install the hood.

FRONT BUMPER AND SKID PLATE

Removal and Installation

Refer to **Figure 9**.
1. Remove the skid plate.
2. Remove the bolts securing the carrier to the top of the bumper.
3. Remove the bolts securing the bumper to the frame.
4. Remove the bumper.
5. Reverse this procedure to install the bumper and note the following:
  a. Tighten the bumper-to-frame bolts to 33 N•m (24 ft.-lb.).
  b. Tighten the skid plate bolts to 9 N•m (80 in.-lb.).

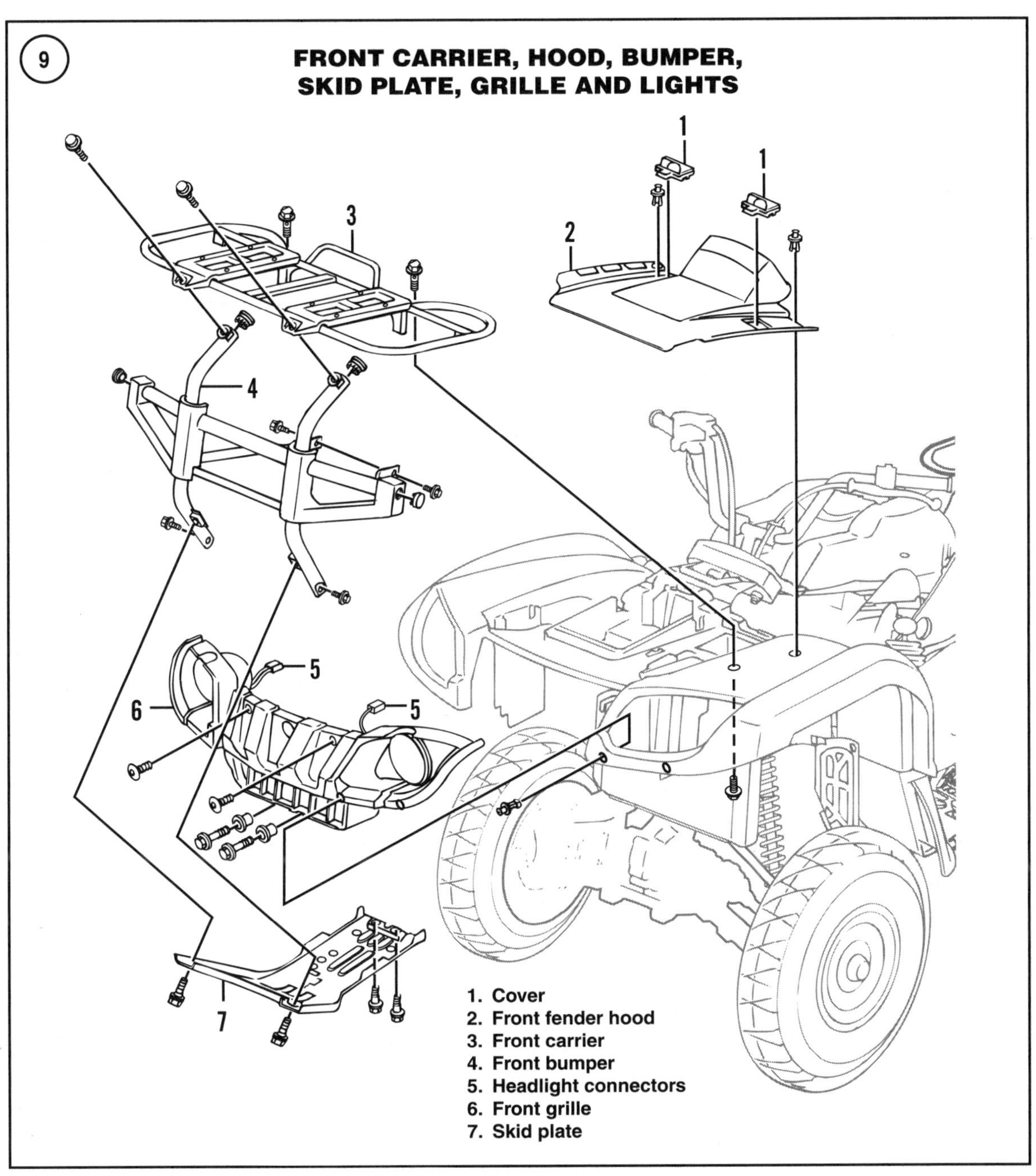

FRONT GRILLE AND LIGHTS

Removal and Installation

Refer to **Figure 9**.

1. Remove the front bumper and skid plate as described in this chapter.
2. Disconnect the headlight wiring.
3. Remove the plastic rivets from the grille.
4. Remove the screws at the top of the grille.
5. Remove the bolts and collars at the bottom of the grille.
6. Remove the grille and lights.
7. Reverse this procedure to install the grille assembly. Apply threadlocking compound to the screws and tighten securely.

FRONT FENDER ASSEMBLY

Removal and Installation

Refer to **Figure 10**.

1. Remove the seat and fuel tank side panels as described in this chapter.
2. Remove the fuel tank cover as described in this chapter.

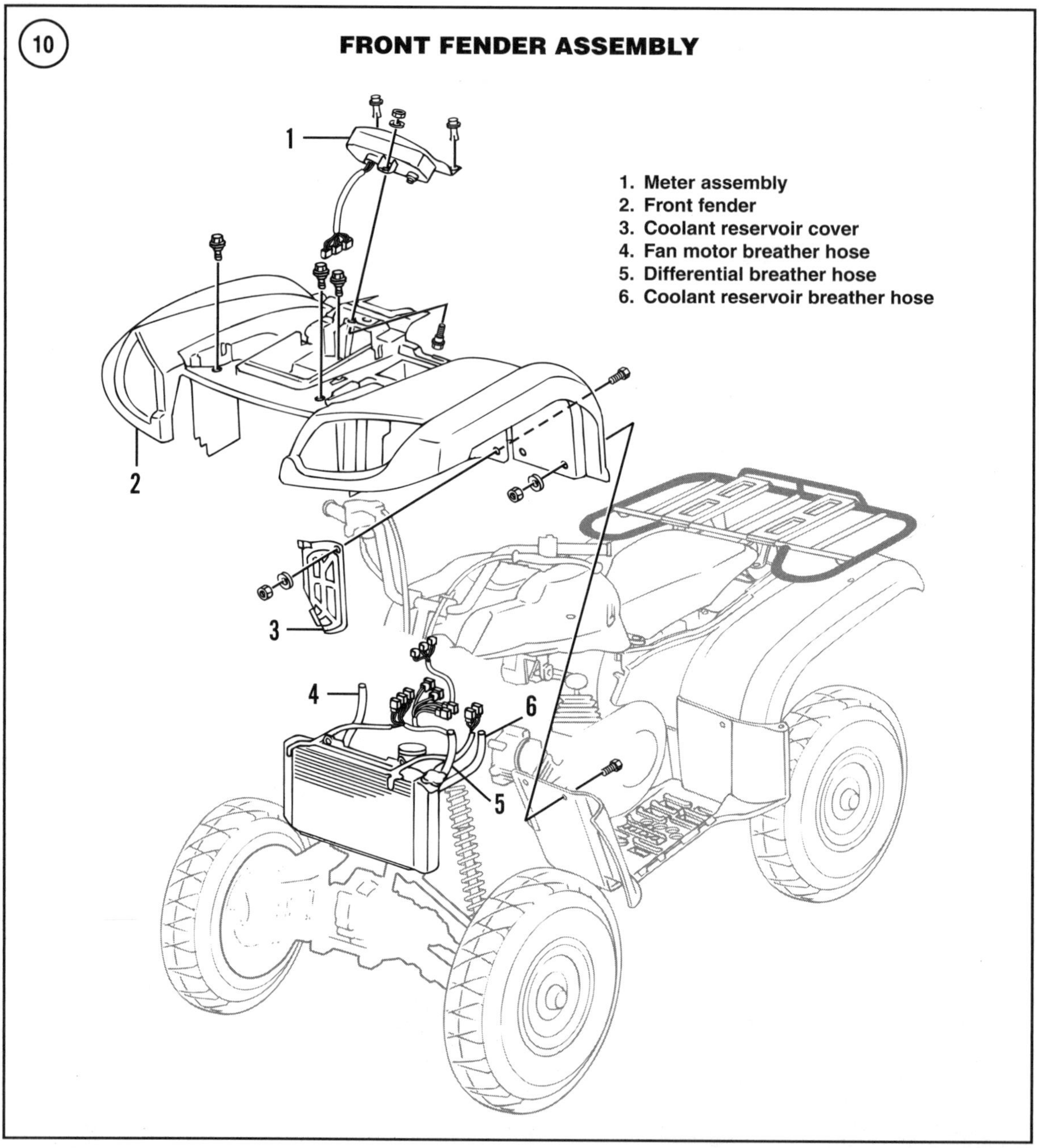

(10)

FRONT FENDER ASSEMBLY

1. Meter assembly
2. Front fender
3. Coolant reservoir cover
4. Fan motor breather hose
5. Differential breather hose
6. Coolant reservoir breather hose

3. Remove the front carrier assembly as described in this chapter.
4. Remove the front fender hood as described in this chapter.
5. Remove the front bumper and skid plate as described in this chapter.
6. Remove the front grille and lights as described in this chapter.
7. Disconnect and remove the meter assembly.
8. Disconnect the wiring connectors that pass through the fender. Label each connector (**Figure 11**) for reassembly.
9. Remove the breather hoses that pass through the fender. Accurately mark their locations in the fender.

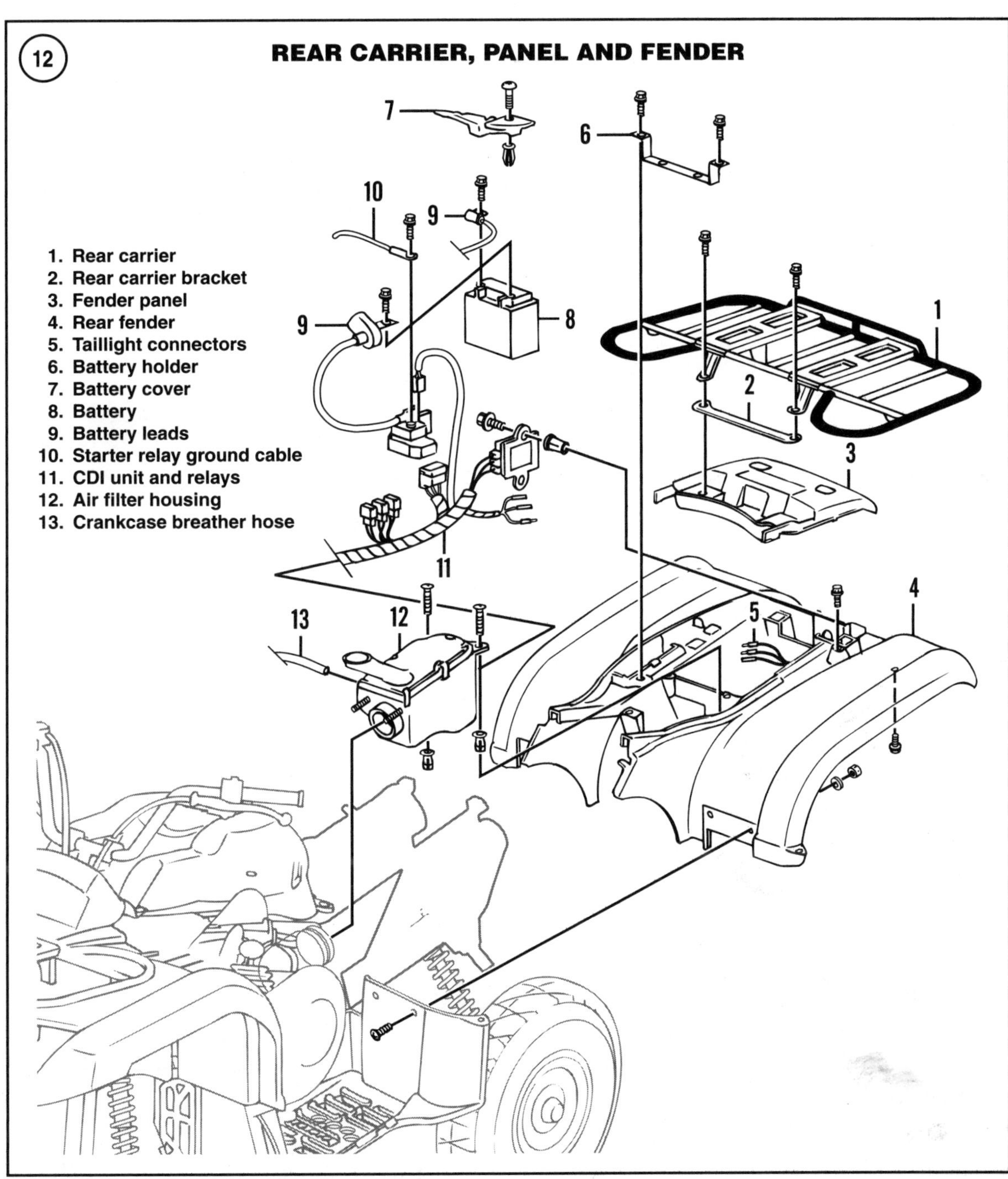

10. Remove the coolant reservoir cover, located in the left fender well.

11. Remove the bolts securing the fender to the top of the frame.

12. Make sure all wiring is clear of the fender. Then raise and move the fender forward and away from the machine.

13. Reverse these steps to install the fender. Note the following:

   a. Tighten all fasteners securely.
   b. Make sure all wiring is routed so it is not pinched or stressed.
   c. Clean all electrical connectors with contact cleaner.
   d. Apply dielectric grease to the wiring connectors before assembling.

REAR CARRIER AND FENDER PANEL

Removal and Installation

Refer to **Figure 12**.

1. Remove the seat as described in this chapter.

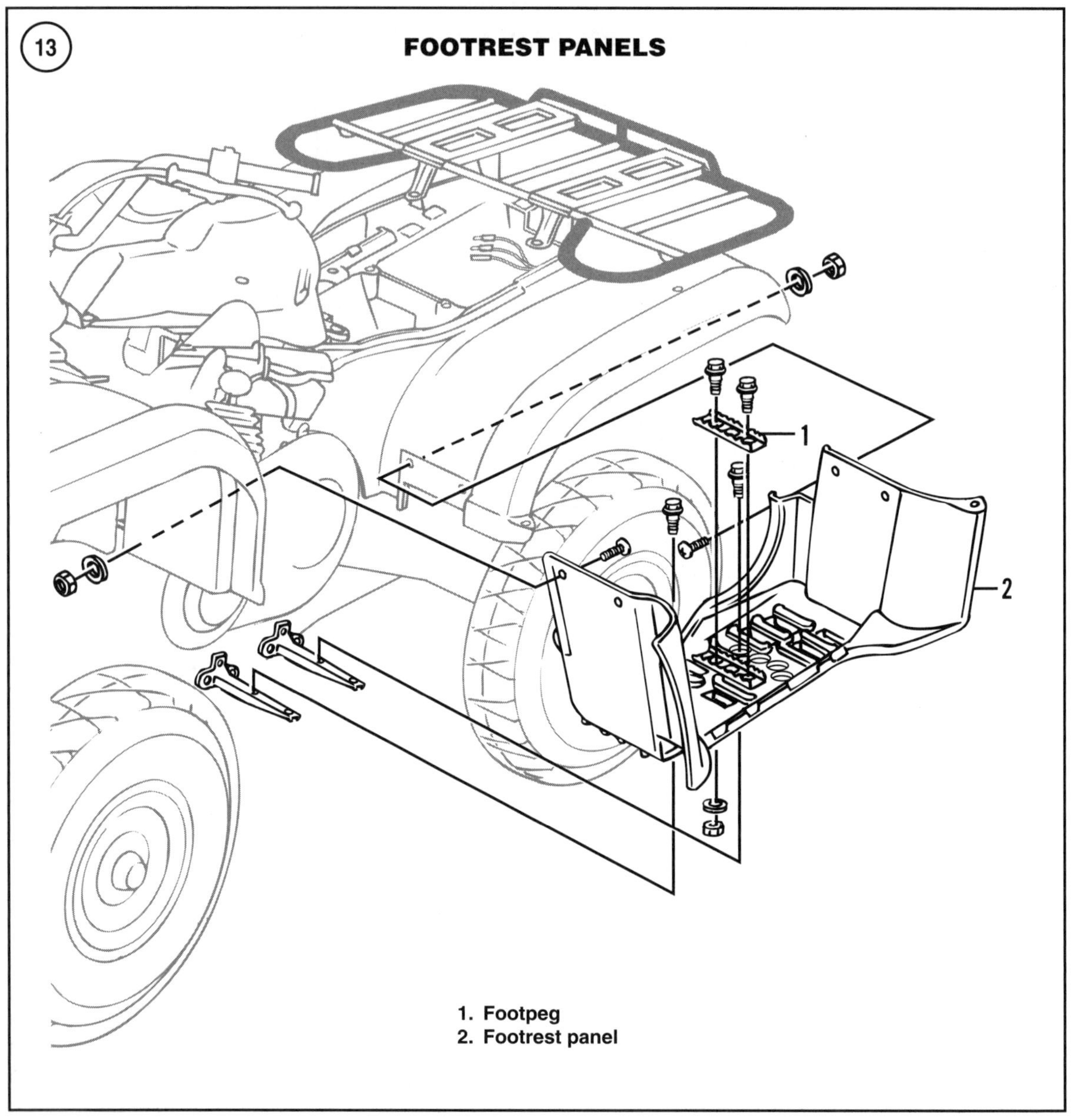

2. Remove the bolts securing the carrier to the frame.
3. Remove the bolts in the wheel wells that secure the fenders to the carrier.
4. Remove the carrier.
5. Remove the rear carrier bracket.
6. Remove the fender panel.
7. Reverse this procedure to install the fender panel and carrier. Tighten all fasteners securely.

REAR FENDER

Removal and Installation

Refer to **Figure 12**.

1. Remove the seat and fuel tank side panels as described in this chapter.
2. Remove the rear carrier as described in this chapter.
3. Disconnect and remove the battery.
4. Disconnect the taillight.
5. In the left side of the rear fender compartment, disconnect the starter relay ground cable.
6. Remove the CDI unit and relay harness from the fender. The parts can remain connected to the harness.
7. Remove the air filter housing and crankcase breather hose.
8. Make sure all wiring is clear of the fender. Then raise and move the fender back and away from the machine.
9. Reverse these steps to install the fender.
10. Tighten all fasteners securely.

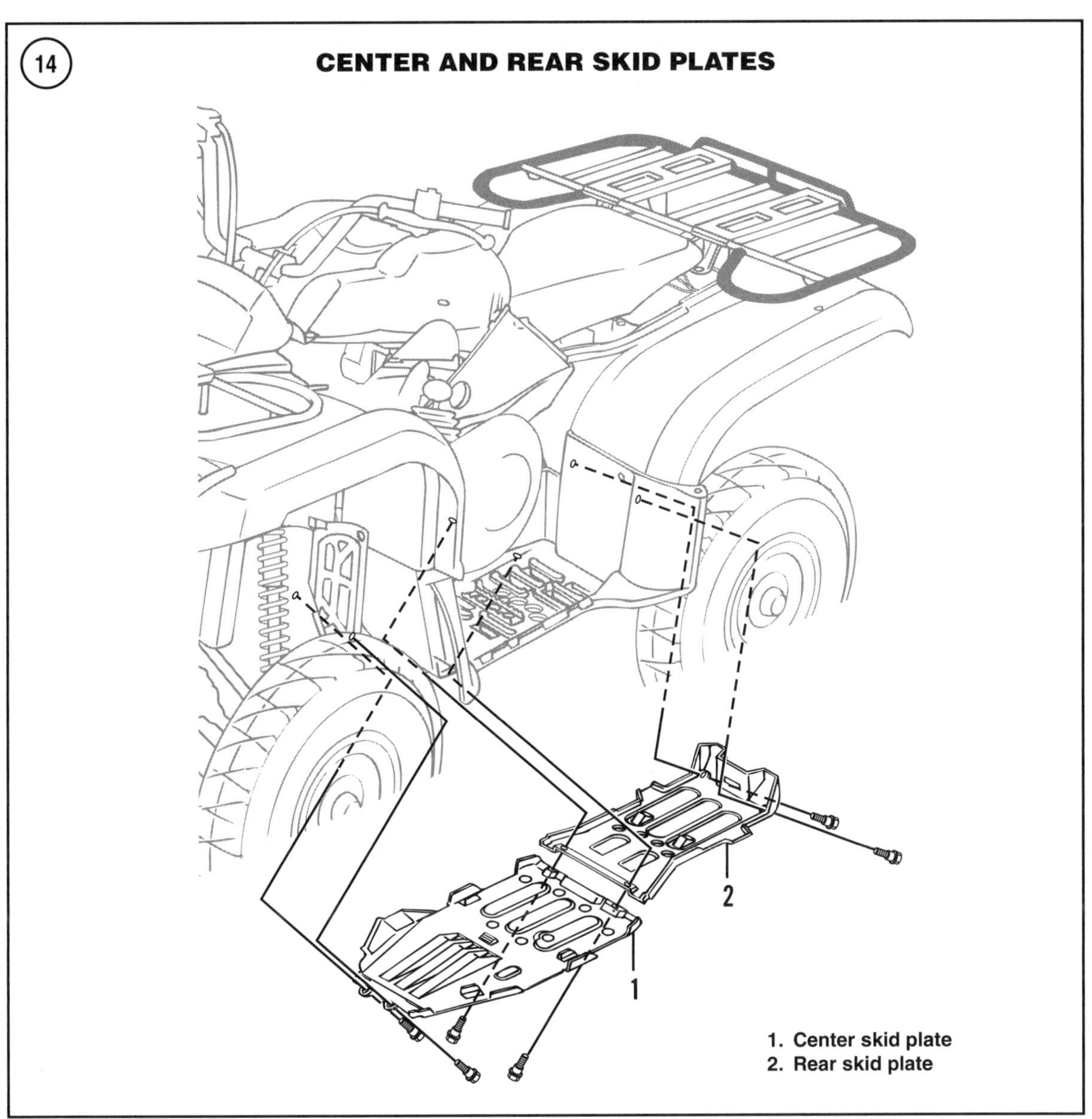

FOOTREST PANELS

Removal and Installation

Refer to **Figure 13**.

1. Remove the fuel tank side panels as described in this chapter.
2. Remove the footpeg and bolts from the top of the footrest panel.
3. Remove the screws, washers and nuts securing the front and rear of the footrest panel.
4. Remove the footrest panel.
5. Reverse this procedure to install the footrest panel.
6. Tighten all fasteners securely.

CENTER AND REAR SKID PLATES

Removal and Installation

Refer to **Figure 14**.

1. Remove the bolts securing the skid plates.
2. Install the skid plates as follows:
   a. Loosely install the rear bolts into the rear skid plate.
   b. Loosely install the front bolts into the center skid plate. Check that the center skid plate overlaps the rear skid plate.
   c. Raise and align both skid plates where they overlap. Then install the center bolts.
   d. Tighten all bolts securely when the skid plates are aligned and seated.

Table 1 is on the following page.

Table 1 BODY TORQUE SPECIFICATIONS

	N•m	in.-lb.	ft.-lb.
Front carrier bolts (not in wheel wells)	33	–	24
Front skid plate bolts	9	80	–
Bumper-to-frame bolts	33	–	24

INDEX

A

Air filter . . . 47-48
  housing drain . . . 49
Alternator cover . . . 166
Axles
  boot inspection . . . 49
  front . . . 212-215
    front drive shaft . . . 225-227
    specifications . . . 227
    torque specifications . . . 227
  rear . . . 237-240
    specifications . . . 252
    torque specifications . . . 252
  troubleshooting . . . 38

B

Balancer and oil pump gears . . . 101-103
Battery . . . 42-43, 178
Body
  carrier
    front . . . 282
    rear . . . 285-286
  engine side cover and panel . . . 282
  fender
    front
      assembly . . . 283-285
      hood . . . 282
  fender
    rear . . . 286
      panel . . . 285-286
  footrest panels . . . 287
  front bumper . . . 282
  fuel tank
    and cover . . . 280-282
    side panels . . . 279-280
  grille . . . 283
  lights . . . 283
  panel fasteners . . . 279
  seat . . . 279
  skid plate
    center and rear . . . 287
    front . . . 282
  torque specifications . . . 288
Brakes . . . 55-58
  adjustments . . . 55
  bleeding . . . 274-276
  caliper
    front . . . 256-259
    rear . . . 266-269
  disc . . . 276-277
  draining . . . 273-274
  left hand brake cable replacement . . . 273
  master cylinder
    front . . . 259-263
    rear . . . 269-273
  operation . . . 253
  pads
    front . . . 254-256
    rear . . . 263-266
  service . . . 253-254
  specifications . . . 277-278
  torque specifications . . . 278
  troubleshooting . . . 39
Bumper . . . 282

17

C

Cable
  adjustment . . . 53-55
  lubrication . . . 48
Cam chain and rear guide . . . 103-104
Camshaft and cam chain tensioner . . . 72-75
Carburetor . . . 151-161
  adjustment . . . 60
  float drain . . . 53
  specifications . . . 164
Carrier
  front . . . 282
  rear and fender panel . . . 285-286
CDI unit . . . 176
Charging system . . . 177-179
  operation . . . 165
Choke cable adjustment . . . 54-55
Clutch . . . 134-137
  drive belt
    cover . . . 126
    inspection and replacement . . . 127-128
  outer bearing housing . . . 126-127
  right crankcase cover . . . 134
  specifications . . . 138
  torque specifications . . . 138
Compression test . . . 60-61
Control arms
  front . . . 200-202
  rear . . . 233-234
Conversion formulas . . . 24-25
Coolant temperature
  sending unit . . . 186-187
  warning system . . . 180-181
Cooling system . . . 50-52
  coolant temperature sending unit . . . 186-187
  fan . . . 185-186
    sending unit . . . 186
  radiator . . . 185-186
  safety . . . 185
  specifications . . . 192
  thermostat . . . 187-188
  torque specifications . . . 192
  water pump . . . 188-191
Crankcase . . . 104-111
  bearing replacement . . . 111-112
  right cover . . . 134
  seal replacement . . . 111
Crankshaft . . . 114-116
Cylinder . . . 83-86
  head . . . 76-78
    cover . . . 68-72

D

Differential . . . 216-225
  front drive shaft . . . 225-227
  front . . . 45-47
  specifications . . . 227
  torque specifications . . . 227
  troubleshooting . . . 38
Diode . . . 175-176
Drain inspection . . . 49-50
Drive belt
  case drain . . . 49
  cover . . . 126
  inspection . . . 53
    and replacement . . . 127-128
  specifications . . . 138
Drive shaft
  lubrication . . . 48
  troubleshooting . . . 38

E

Electrical system
  alternator cover . . . 166
  CDI unit . . . 176
  charging coils . . . 179
  charging system . . . 165, 177-179
  component replacement . . . 165
  coolant temperature warning system . . . 180-181
  fan system . . . 179-180
  four-wheel drive relays . . . 181-182
  fundamentals . . . 16
  fuse (main) . . . 176
  gear motor . . . 181-182
  headlights . . . 183
  ignition coil . . . 176
  ignition system . . . 165, 176-177
  indicator circuits . . . 182
  pickup coil . . . 166-167, 176
  regulator/rectifier . . . 178-179
  rotor . . . 167-170, 177
  specifications . . . 184
  starter . . . 170-175
    clutch and gears . . . 167-170
  starting system switches . . . 175-176
  stator . . . 166-167
  switches . . . 182-183
  taillight . . . 183
  testing . . . 30-34
  torque specifications . . . 184
  troubleshooting . . . 30-34
  wiring diagrams . . . 295-299
Engine . . . 95-96
  balancer . . . 112
  break-in . . . 41
  lower end . . . 95-96
    balancer . . . 101-103, 112
    cam chain and rear guide . . . 103-104
    crankcase . . . 104-111
      bearing replacement . . . 111-112

seal replacement . . . 111
crankshaft . . . 114-116
middle gear assembly . . . 116-122
shim and lash adjustment . . . 122-124
oil pump . . . 112-114
gears . . . 101-103
specifications . . . 125
recoil starter . . . 97-101
specifications . . . 125
torque specifications . . . 125
oil and filter . . . 43-44
side cover and panel . . . 282
specifications . . . 92
top end
camshaft and cam chain tensioner . . . 72-75
cylinder . . . 83-86
head and cover . . . 68-78, 76-78
exhaust system . . . 67-68
piston and rings . . . 86-92
specifications . . . 92-93
torque specifications . . . 93-94
valves . . . 79-83
troubleshooting
noise . . . 36-37
performance . . . 34-36
spark test . . . 30
starting system . . . 29-30, 34
Exhaust system . . . 53, 67-68

F

Fan
and radiator . . . 185-186
sending unit . . . 186
system . . . 179-180
Fasteners . . . 3-6
inspection . . . 48-49
Fender
front
assembly . . . 283-285
hood . . . 282
rear . . . 286
panel . . . 285-286
Final drive . . . 44-45, 240-252
specifications . . . 252
torque specifications . . . 252
troubleshooting . . . 38
Footrest panels . . . 287
Four-wheel drive relays and gear motor . . 181-182
Frame noise
troubleshooting . . . 37
Fuel system . . . 53
carburetor . . . 151-161
specifications . . . 164
throttle cable replacement . . . 163
valve . . . 161-163
Fuel tank
and cover . . . 280-282
side panels . . . 279-280
Fuse (main) . . . 176

G

Gear motor . . . 181-182
Grille . . . 283

H

Handlebar . . . 206-207
Handling . . . 39
Headlights . . . 183
Hub
front . . . 193-195
rear . . . 228-230

I

Ignition system . . . 176-177
operation . . . 165
timing . . . 60
Indicator circuits . . . 182

L

Leakdown test . . . 37
Lights . . . 283
Lubrication
control cable . . . 48
front drive shaft . . . 48
oil and filter . . . 43-44
rear suspension pivot . . . 48
recommended lubricants,
fluids and capacities . . . 65
schedule . . . 64-65

M

Maintenance
See also Lubrication
air filter . . . 47-48
axle boot inspection . . . 49
battery . . . 42-43, 178
brake system . . . 55-58
carburetor adjustment . . . 60
control cable adjustment . . . 53-55
cooling system . . . 50-52
drain inspection . . . 49-50
drive belt inspection . . . 53
engine oil change . . . 43-44
exhaust system . . . 53
fastener inspection . . . 48-49
final drive . . . 44-45
front differential . . . 45-47
fuel system . . . 53

17

Maintenance (continued)
pre-ride inspection 41
schedule 64-65
specifications 66
speed limiter adjustment. 49
tire inspection 59
torque specifications 66
Metric, decimal and fractional equivalents 26
Metric, tap and drill sizes 26
Middle gear assembly 116-122
shim and lash adjustment 122-124
troubleshooting 38
Muffler 53, 67-68

O

Oil
and filter 43-44
change/check 43-47
pump 112-114
gears 101-103
specifications 125
Outer bearing housing 126-127

P

Pickup coil and stator 166-167
Piston and rings 86-92
Pre-ride inspection 41

R

Radiator and fan 185-186
Rear knuckle 230-232
Rear suspension pivot lubrication 48
Rear wheel 228
Recoil starter 97-101
Rotor, starter clutch and starter gears 167-170

S

Seat 279
Select lever
adjustment 55
assembly 139
cable replacement 139
drain 49
Serial numbers 3
Sheaves
crankcase cover 134
drive belt
cover 126
inspection and replacement 127-128
outer bearing housing 126-127
primary and secondary 128-133
specifications 138
torque specifications 138
Shift mechanism
external 140-141
shift drum and forks 148-149
Shock absorbers
front 202-203
setting 210
rear 235
setting 236
Shop supplies 6-8
Skid plate
center and rear 287
front 282
Spark plug 61-64
Specifications
axle
front 227
rear 252
body 288
brakes 277-278
carburetor 164
clutch 138
cooling system 192
differential 227
dimensions 24
drive belt 138
electrical system 184
engine 92
lower end 125
top end 92-94
final drive 252
lubrication schedule 64-65
maintenance 66
schedule 64-65
oil pump 125
recommended lubricants,
fluids and capacities 65
sheave 138
shock absorber setting
front 210
rear 236
steering 210-211
suspension
front 210-211
rear 236
tire 210, 236
torque specifications
axle
front 227
rear 252
body 288
brakes 278
clutch 138
cooling system 192
differential 227
electrical system 184
engine
lower end 125
top end 93-94

final drive 252
maintenance 66
sheave 138
steering 211
suspension
front 211
rear 236
transmission 150
transmission 150
tune-up 66
weight 24
wheel 210, 236
Speed limiter adjustment 49
Stabilizer 232
Starter 170-175
clutch, gears and rotor 167-170
relay 175
Starting system switches 175-176
Stator and pickup coil 166-167
Steering
control arms 200-202
handlebar 206-207
knuckle 198-200
shaft 203-206
specifications 210
torque specifications 211
troubleshooting 39
Storage 23-24
Suspension
front
control arms 200-202
hub 193-195
shock absorbers 202-203
specifications 210
tie rods 195-198
tires 207-209
torque specifications 211
wheel 193
runout 209-210
rear
control arms 233-234
hub 228-230
knuckle 230-232
shock absorbers 235
rear setting 236
specifications 236
stabilizer 232
tire 236
torque specifications 236
wheel 228, 236
Switches 182-183

T

Taillight 183
Technical abbreviations 25-26
Thermostat 187-188
Throttle cable
adjustment 53-54
replacement 163
Tie rods 195-198
Tires 207-209
front
specifications 210
inspection 59
Tools 8-13
measuring 13-16
Torque
recommendations 27
specifications
axles
front 227
rear 252
body 288
brakes 278
clutch 138
cooling system 192
differential 227
electrical system 184
engine
lower end 125
top end 93-94
final drive 252
maintenance 66
sheaves 138
steering 211
suspension
front 211
rear 236
transmission 150
Transmission 141-148
select lever
assembly 139
cable replacement 139
specifications 150
torque specifications 150
troubleshooting 37-38
Troubleshooting
axles 38
brake system 39
differential 38
drive shafts 38
engine
noise 36-37
performance 34-36
spark test 30
starting system 29-30, 34
final drive unit 38
frame noise 37
leakdown test 37
middle gear unit 38
steering and handling 39

Troubleshooting (continued)
testing 30-34
transmission 37-38
water damage 28
Tune-up 59
compression test 60-61
ignition timing 60
spark plug 61-64
specifications 66
valve clearance 59-60

V

Valves 79-83
clearance 59-60

W

Water damage 28
Water pump 188-191
Weight 24
Wheel
front 193
specifications 210
rear 228
runout 209-210
Wiring diagrams 295-299

WIRING DIAGRAMS

18

2002-2003 GRIZZLY YFM660FP 2WD AND 4WD

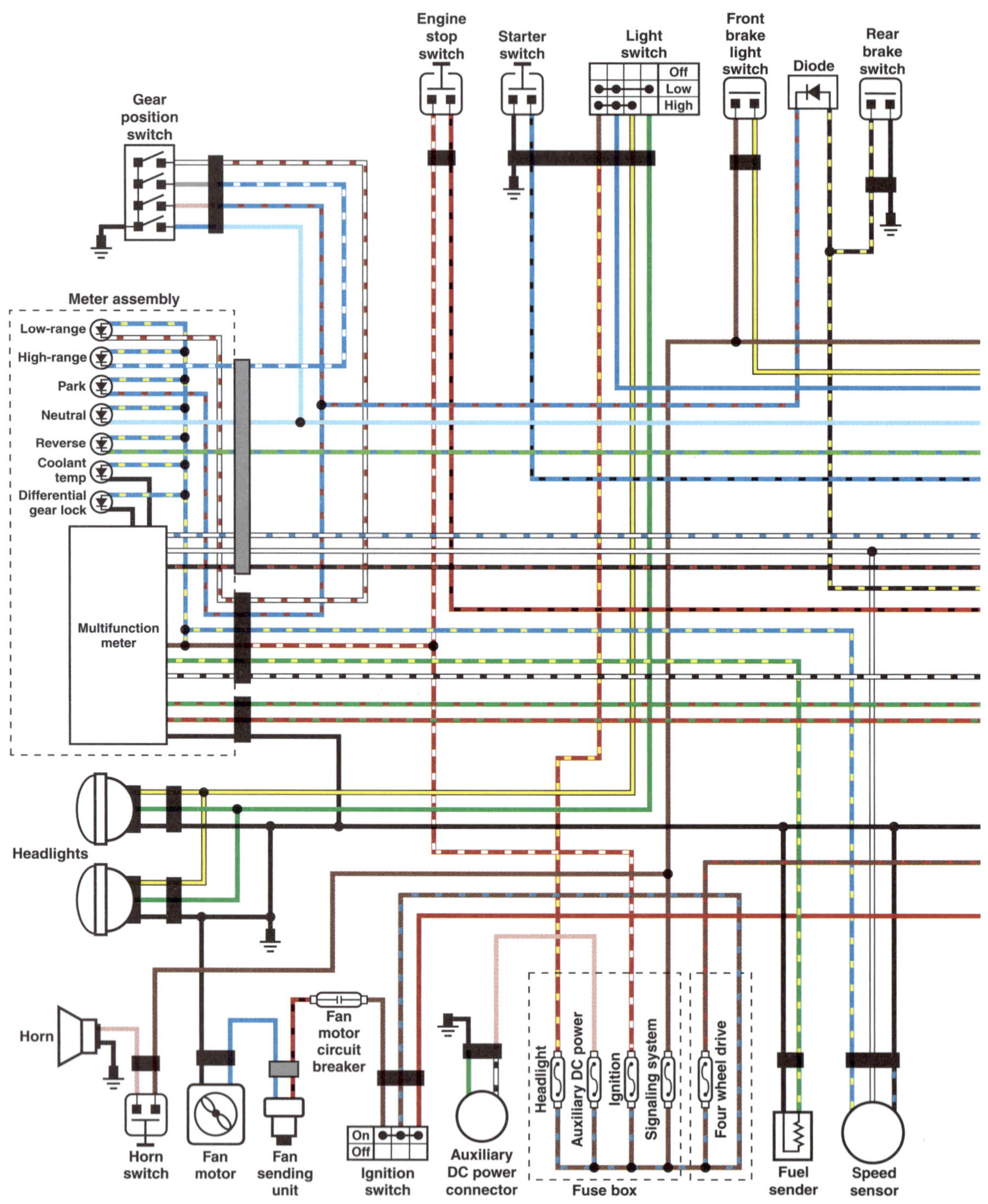

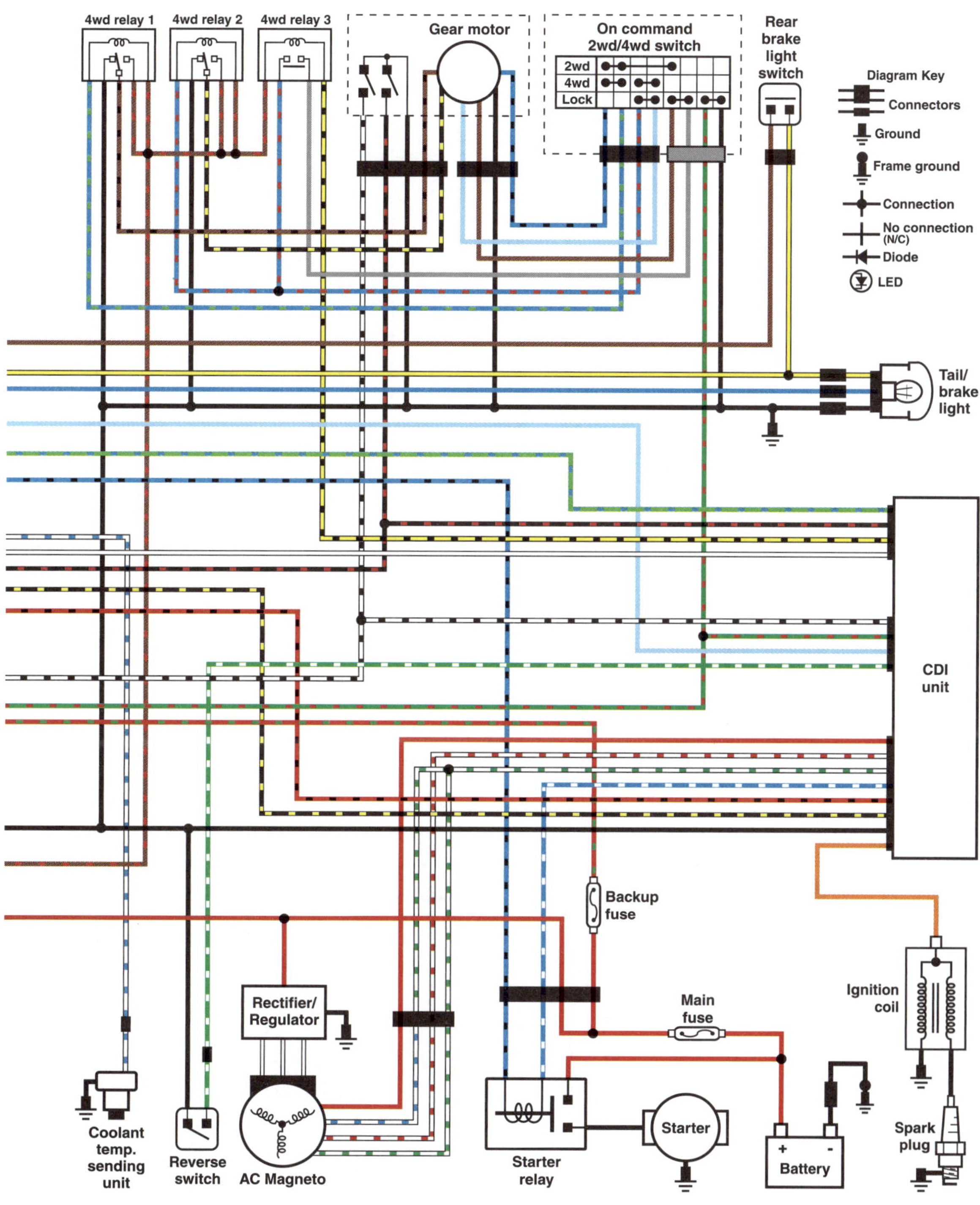
4wd relay 1
4wd relay 2
4wd relay 3
Gear motor
On command
2wd/4wd switch
2wd
4wd
Lock
Rear
brake
light
switch
Diagram Key
Connectors
Ground
Frame ground
Connection
No connection
(N/C)
Diode
LED
Tail/
brake
light
CDI
unit
Backup
fuse
Ignition
coil
Main
fuse
Rectifier/
Regulator
Coolant
temp.
sending
unit
Reverse
switch
AC Magneto
Starter
relay
Starter
Battery
Spark
plug

2004-ON GRIZZLY YFM660FS 2WD AND 4WD

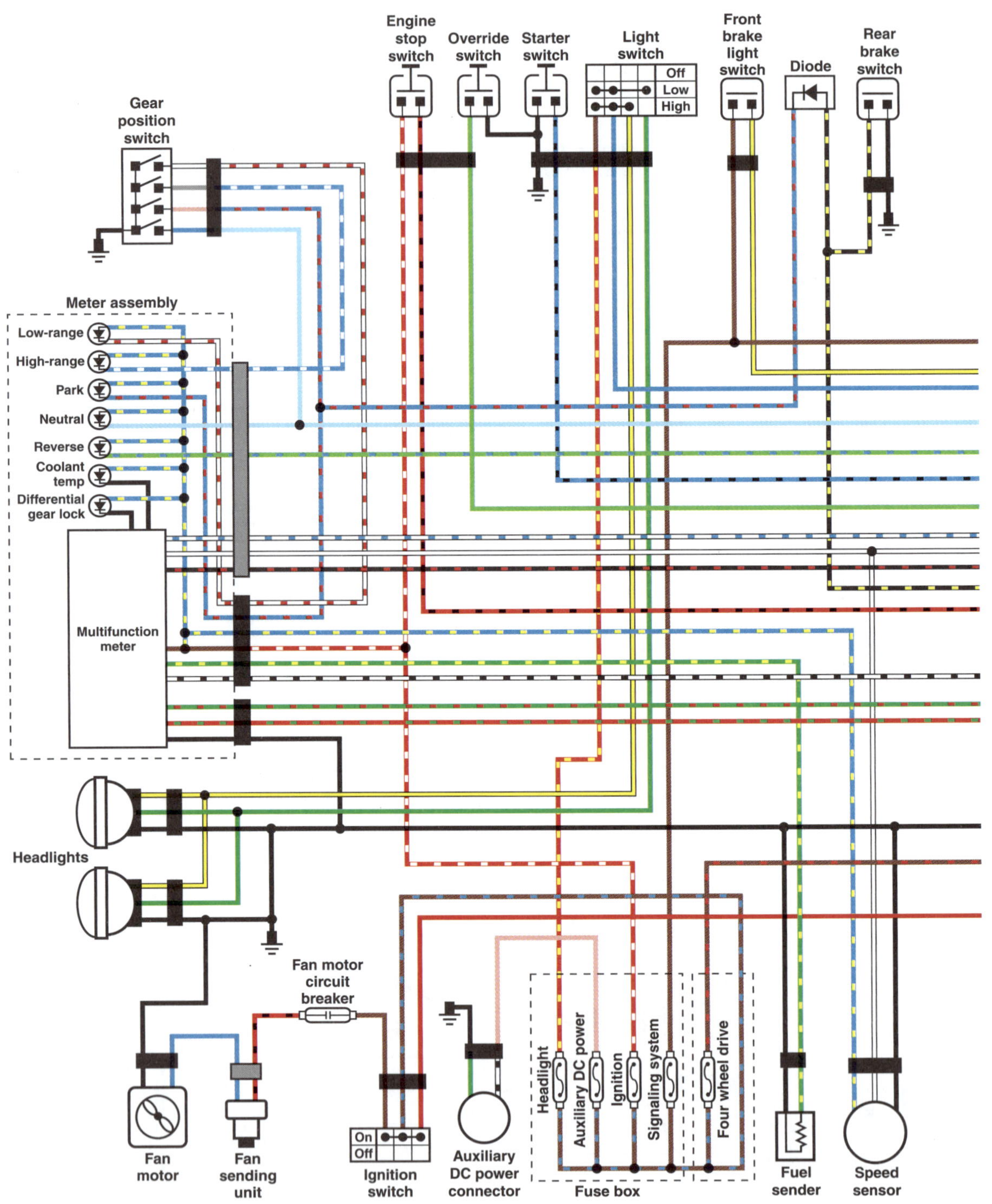

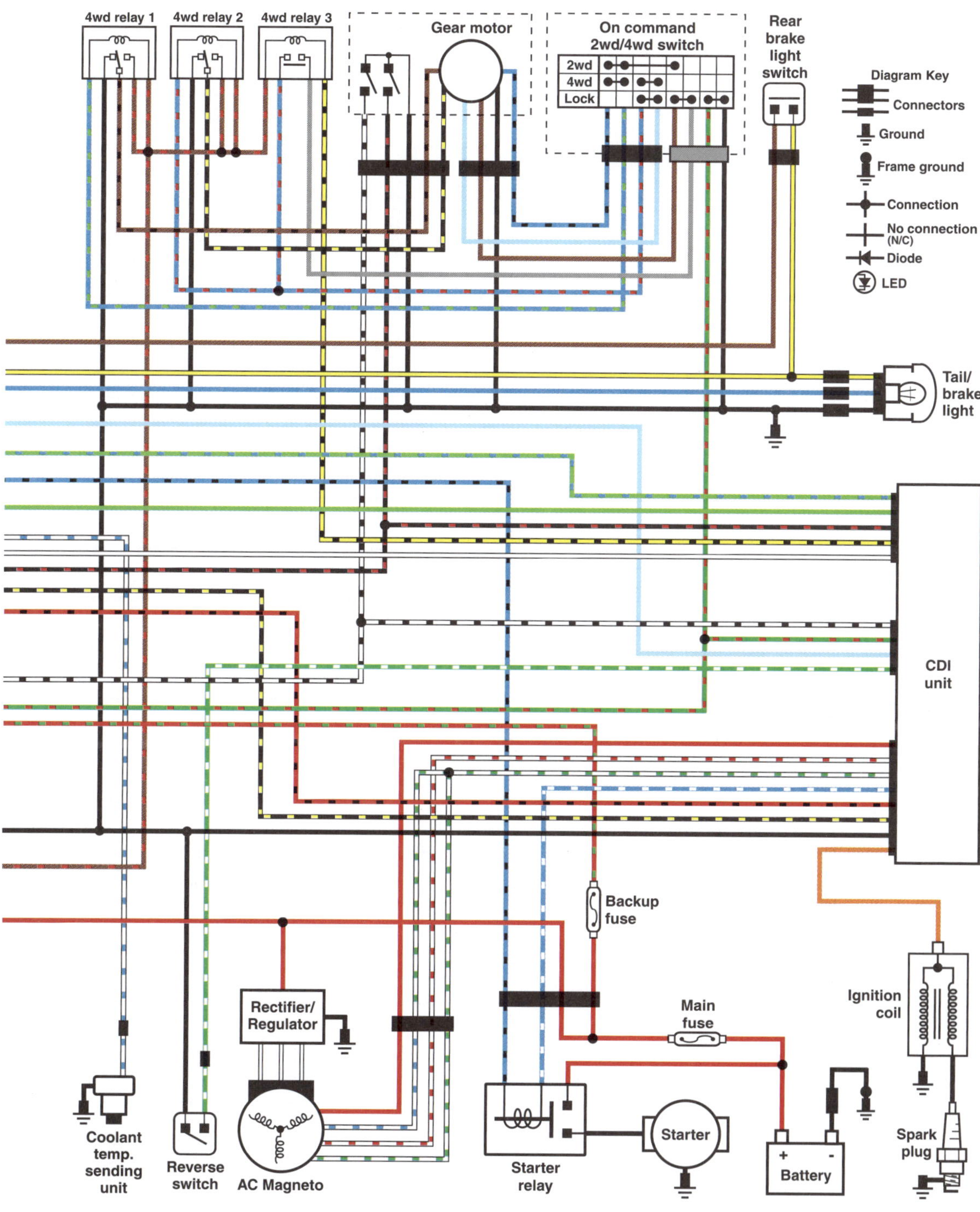
4wd relay 1
4wd relay 2
4wd relay 3
Gear motor
On command
2wd/4wd switch
2wd
4wd
Lock
Rear
brake
light
switch
Diagram Key
Connectors
Ground
Frame ground
Connection
No connection
(N/C)
Diode
LED
Tail/
brake
light
CDI
unit
Backup
fuse
Rectifier/
Regulator
Main
fuse
Ignition
coil
Coolant
temp.
sending
unit
Reverse
switch
AC Magneto
Starter
relay
Starter
Battery
Spark
plug

MAINTENANCE LOG

Date	Hours	Type of Service